Competitive
Economic
Systems

GEORGE P. ADAMS, Jr.

Professor of Economics and
Chairman of the Department of Economics
Cornell University

THOMAS Y. CROWELL COMPANY

New York · 1955

MANUFACTURED IN THE UNITED STATES OF AMERICA
BY THE VAIL-BALLOU PRESS, INC., BINGHAMTON, N. Y.

Preface

On the day before this preface was written the United States Information Agency announced the publication of a book (*Soviet World Oulook—A Handbook of Communist Statements,* Washington, 1954) purporting, among other things, to demonstrate Russian scepticism about the ability of the capitalist and communist worlds to co-exist. That scepticism, which is not confined to the far side of the iron curtain, is itself a demonstration that different economic, social, and political systems are in competition with each other today.

For competition to take place, however, the competing entities must have something in common as well as something in opposition. Contemporary capitalism, communism, socialism and the perhaps dormant but not dead roots of fascism, competing as they do for the allegiance of living men, have in common the industrialism that resulted from the great technological revolution of the last two centuries and that underlies the power centers of the world of today. It will be argued, particularly in the last chapter of this book, that, *economically,* contemporary systems have more in common than in opposition and that the very real opposition that does exist among them rests upon major differences in their *political* and *social* structures. That opposition expresses itself fundamentally in the different normative orientations of these contemporary systems: individual welfare, for example, or national power.

The author's indebtedness to his colleagues is profound and deep. Those colleagues, nevertheless, shall be nameless here. Definition excludes as well as includes, and the author does not wish inadvertently to exclude from mention any of the many people who have contributed by their learning, their patience, their wit—and sometimes even their irritation—to whatever merit this book may have. Nor does the author wish even indirectly to impute to anyone but himself responsibility for any errors or misjudgments that may be found.

Other obligations, however, must be spelled out. The staff of the Cornell University Library, as is their wont, were tireless in according bibliographical assistance, and they have my thanks. Gratitude is also due the staff of the British Information Services in New York, who went out of their way to track down obscure quotations and who were most helpful in securing permission to quote from official British documents. Acknowledgment is made, too, for the permission to quote so graciously extended by the many publishers to whom specific reference is made in footnotes.

Finally, but by no means least, mention must be made of the author's severest but most helpful critic. That critic considers economics to be a most dismal science, but nevertheless made the observation, after a sampling of the manuscript: It does not grip like Trollope, but it can be read.

GEORGE P. ADAMS, JR.

September, 1954

Contents

PART THREE

The Socialist and Marxist Dissent

PART FOUR

Competing Systems as Going Concerns

PART ONE

Economic Systems in General

The Appraisal and Comparison

of Economic Systems

W HEN a housewife is praised for being economical she has the right to conclude that she uses her money to buy the kinds of things her family wishes or needs to have, and in quantities that are properly balanced. She does on a small scale exactly what a nation does on a large, but neither she nor the nation could satisfy the needs that economic activity purports to satisfy without some kind of system. An economic system is the name given to the set of institutions, existing within and among nations, by which needs are satisfied.

The satisfaction of needs is a far more complicated matter than perhaps it sounds. Needs are plural, and plural needs frequently compete with one another. They may compete in three different ways: (1) present and future needs are often in competition, (2) mutually inconsistent needs are always in competition, and (3) needs that cannot all be satisfied because there are insufficient resources to satisfy all of them are inevitably in competition. Let us illustrate.

(1) A student living away from home on a slim allowance does not have to be told how the beginning and the end of each month compete for priority

in expenditure.   That is competition between the present and the future, and it exists for the nation as well as for the individual.   Americans, for example, do not always find it easy to make up their minds whether it is better to import oil today in order to safeguard our petroleum reserves for posterity, or to use our own oil today in the hope that new reserves, or even new fuels, may be found tomorrow.

(2) A student sometimes has difficulty deciding whether to go to the movies or to study economics; that is competition between mutually inconsistent needs, and that form of competition exists, also, for a nation.   Americans, for example, cannot simultaneously have prices low enough to please all consumers and high enough to satisfy all producers.   The controversy in the United States over governmental support of agricultural prices reflects exactly that kind of competition.

(3) A student occasionally must choose between buying a ticket to a football game or buying a badly needed shirt; that is competition between needs competing for the same, scarce resources, and a nation, too, confronts the same kind of choice.   In perhaps most parts of the world today, improvement of the standard of living and improvement of the means of national defense are in competition, simply because there are too few resources to improve both at once.

Such forms of competition create complications that can become anxieties; they involve choices that are difficult for the individual to make, as we can see in the people about us who have come to grief through lack of foresight or through bad planning.   Nations, too, must choose, and nations, too, can err; many, although of course not all, of the problems confronting the contemporary world are the fruits of such error.

DIFFERENCES AMONG ECONOMIC SYSTEMS

One of the functions of economics is the search for reasons why problems of choice arise and how those problems can be solved.   Although not everybody pays attention to economics, nevertheless everybody lives in an economy and under some economic system.   We take that for granted when conditions are easy and tranquil, because, for most of us, an economic system is nothing more than the established way of getting the business of life done.   Simply because we are so used to that way, we do not have to recognize it as a system; we do not even have to understand it.   If, how-ever, we should suddenly be thrust into a different economic system, as ordinary Russians were after the Bolshevik Revolution; or if we should suddenly become aware of different systems that seem to threaten ours, our alertness together with our need for understanding would be likely to be aroused.   That alertness is being aroused today.   Communism, socialism, and some forms of fascism exist, today, alongside American capitalism, and their supporters compete, not only among themselves, but also with Amer-icans to establish some "best" way of getting the ordinary business of life done.

At this point, a reflective American might ask a pointed question: Why should there be different economic systems if men, generally, have the same needs and if the *technological* means of satisfying those needs are the same, everywhere, and if the principles of wise choice among competing needs have any validity?

Different systems, nevertheless, do exist, and they do so for two im-portant reasons.   First, there really are different ways of accomplishing the same thing.   We can, for instance, rely upon either wisdom or strength to accomplish certain purposes.   Suppose we wish to distribute pennies among small boys: we may either plan some way of distribution that seems fair, and then pass out our pennies according to our plan, or we may simply fling our pennies among the boys and watch the scramble.   In either case, the pennies get distributed.

Second, different men, or nations, have different orders of priority among even the same needs, and different priorities sometimes involve different systems.   If, for example, we rank initiative and adventuresomeness higher than material security, we shall allow the venturesome considerable leeway, even though his activities imperil the security of more passive men.   If, however, our priority is the other way about, we will repress the adventurer in order not to disturb those who are complacent in some established, time-hallowed routine.

Different economic systems do exist alongside each other today, and be-cause their co-existence involves friction and sometimes strife, we seek under-standing of what the issue is all about.   To get understanding, we need a standard of comparison, and to secure that standard we shall start with an attempt to identify the fundamental orientation of our American system—that is, the values and ends that we think our system should foster and con-serve.   Next, we shall consider certain alternative orientations, other values that either pertain to other systems, or that, on occasion, have been thrust upon Americans by such forces as war. Finally, we shall try to suggest certain tests that may be used to appraise the actual performance of any system upon which we may happen to fix our eyes.

THE AMERICAN SYSTEM AS A STANDARD OF COMPARISON

The Idealized Orientation

Americans, like most other peoples, are concerned today with the preservation of their way of life. Among Americans there is no universal agreement on what their way of life, in all its details, is; but disagreement, distasteful as it may be to idealists as well as to ants, has itself been very much a part of the American past. It has in fact been so much a part of that past that perhaps a fifth freedom, the freedom to disagree, might be added to the four freedoms enunciated by Franklin Roosevelt. Despite their disagreements, however, Americans have given their loyalty to at least the concept of freedom as a precious ingredient of their way of life. The road between the concept and its realization is one of sharp curves, narrow bridges, and steep ascents which recurrently engender doubts whether the brakes and steering mechanisms of the vehicles which may traverse that road are secure against the strains which the road will impose upon them. Certain vehicles, indeed, have been summarily ruled off the road and certain subsidiary routes have been closed to traffic; and, of course, the irresponsible operation of all vehicles on all highways, including our symbolic road, is disallowed. While all this still occasions some grumbling and sometimes evasion, it has little to do with contemporary anxiety about the American way of life, for few Americans really wish to retrace their steps. Their concern is with their future course.

Where does the road go and how shall the unmapped hazards it may offer be surmounted? It is characteristic of the road to freedom that it is constructed only as it is traveled, and the territory through which it must pass appears precipitous and formidable. Should the car turn to the Right or to the Left? Or should it perchance be stopped where it is and all further progress, in the name of security, be eschewed? If the car is to continue, how fast should it be driven? Who is to decide its course? Is it safe to permit passengers to distract the driver by constant and shrill exhortations to alter his course and change his speed? Above all, what heed should be given to demands that the vehicle itself be redesigned?

Freedom from want. Among the four freedoms is freedom from want. It became such, at least to those to whom freedom from want is desirable as an object of deliberate national policy, largely because want persists despite the astonishing economic progress of the Western World during the past two centuries. We must be clear, however, what we mean. We all want, but it is not all wants from which we are to be freed. It is, specifically, the want of employment, of assured daily bread, of security against the grinding material anxiety which men increasingly feel to be both unnecessary and intolerable. The determination of the minimum standard of living or decency beneath which no one should be permitted to sink is difficult, but need not concern us now. A greater difficulty which must concern us arises when we seek to assure that minimum, once it is defined, to everyone. How can this best be done, and what will be the by-products of the venture? One answer, the orthodox one to many mature Americans, asserts that only by letting the economic system substantially alone can *achievable* freedom from want, without deleterious consequences, be assured. Other Americans answer that various forms of governmental intervention in economic processes appear to promise either greater success or faster accomplishment, or both. Confronted by the charge that governmental intervention is inefficient because it stifles initiative or breeds a parasitic bureaucracy, or by the charge that although intervention might assure some freedom from want but only at the cost of lost economic or even political freedom or by the cessation of further economic progress, interventionists are driven to give careful thought to what they mean by intervention and to what their kind of intervention might bring in its wake. When this happens, people find themselves arguing about different kinds of economic systems. In the contemporary United States, capitalism, socialism, fascism, and communism are types of systems about whose merits and demerits opinion widely differs.

The argument would be complicated enough if freedom from want were its only focus, but of course it is not. During wartime national survival takes such precedence over all other goals that material welfare must sometimes be deliberately sacrificed to it. Because war, prospective or actual, still looms upon the horizon, a continual balancing of the claims of defense and of opulence is forced upon those who, even indirectly, attempt to reach a conclusion as to what some economic system is for. The argument about systems, accordingly, may turn upon both ends and means: What purposes should an economic system serve, and by what system can the selected purposes best be achieved?

Welfare. Henceforward it will be assumed that Americans expect their economy normally to be oriented toward welfare. That is to say, they expect of it the assurance of decent living standards, without necessarily being precise as to what they mean by the phrase; and in time they expect, or hope, that living standards will rise. This issue is nothing new. At the beginning of the modern era, to go back no further, Francis Bacon speculated upon the turning of natural forces "to the occasions and uses of life" and the "relief of man's estate."

This formulation is still too simple for our purposes and we must make the following interpretive qualifications. *First,* although welfare and defense frequently compete with each other for scarce resources, as the expression *guns or butter* symbolizes, in a deeper sense they are mutually consistent: guns today are sometimes unhappily necessary if we are to have butter tomorrow, and yet, men must have some butter today if they are to produce guns at all. We still need both, and our problem becomes that of determining how much of each we can or should have. The apportionment of resources between these two ends is an exceedingly difficult problem whose solution cannot be attempted here. We assume, simply, that Americans want both welfare and whatever measure of defense seems necessary, given the state of the world at any moment of time.

Second, the American interpretation of the basic issue is individualistic in at least two senses germane to our inquiry. Americans wish to have a say in the making of decisions affecting them, and they wish to determine for themselves the ingredients of their own welfare. They wish, at the very least, to be heard with respect when they make suggestions about such things as the hours and conditions of their work, and they prefer free markets in which to make their purchases to a rationing system under which they are simply issued what someone else thinks they should have. Their choice, in other words, is for a free rather than an authoritarian system, but to a very considerable extent their perplexity and concern turn on the compatibility of freedom from dictation and freedom from want.

Third, men create political as well as economic systems, and this introduces yet another complication. We can classify an economic system as capitalist, communist, socialist, or fascist, but we can also refer quite meaningfully to the American variety of capitalism, the Russian form of communism, the trend toward a peculiarly British form of socialism, and the extreme form which fascism took in Germany. Put another way, while there is much in common between American and Canadian capitalism, or between the policies advocated by the Labour Parties of Great Britain and of New Zealand, or between Russian and Yugoslav communism, or between German and Italian fascism, there are also significant differences. How bewildering, but also how exciting it is to attempt to thread one's way among the forms and structures of different economic systems when these are embodied in the flesh and blood of different political and national systems as well! Our focus here must be the debate by Americans upon the economic system best adapted to American needs within the context of the free political institutions which comprise American political democracy.

Finally, both economic and political systems may appear either as ideals or as actualities, and both are very different from country to country and from century to century. Consider capitalism. Just as there are differences between American and Canadian capitalism today, so are there differences between the American capitalism of the 1850's and that of the 1950's. Similarly, the capitalism of the economic textbooks does not stand in one-to-one correspondence with the capitalism of the market place. This is still too simple, for the "capitalism" of Adam Smith [1] is very different from that of John Maynard Keynes. At this point, it should hardly be necessary to adduce the different pictures of capitalism held by its defenders and its opponents. Wall Street and the Kremlin have, indeed, little in common.

Amidst all this confusion we, like Archimedes, clearly need a place to stand. Let us accordingly take it for granted that an economy of abundance is desirable, that the economic freedom ascribed to capitalism by its supporters together with the political freedom of democracy is also desirable, and with this perspective proceed to examine more systematically the clash of systems which is so marked a characteristic of the age in which we live. Other peoples living under other systems are also caught up in this clash, but since their perspectives appear frequently strange and sometimes repugnant to Americans, the American perspective—or, to be more exact, the perspective which we can perhaps best assume to be American—will be the point from which we start.

---

[1] The word is set in quotes because it did not exist in Adam Smith's day. Ironically enough, it was Karl Marx who gave the word its currency as the name of an economic system.

The Actual Orientation of the American Economic System

We must recognize that the point from which we start is an idealized one, idealized in the sense that it is a picture of how we think our system *would* work if all went well, without difficulties, or interruptions, or frustrations. In actual fact, of course, there have been many frustrations and interruptions. Our American system developed as part of world capitalism, and the shape of capitalism was formed by the great Industrial Revolution that began toward the end of the eighteenth century. In the wake of that industrialization have appeared three great sources of disturbance: (1) despite increased economic interdependence among the nations of the world for such things as raw materials, skills, and markets, the imminence and the impact of war have anything but diminished; (2) despite the tremendous increase in both productive capacity and the volume of production, the vulnerability of ordinary men to either unemployment or to the loss through inflation of the purchasing power of their incomes has increased; and (3) the emergence of alternative forms of economic organization and control has today placed capitalism, where it survives, on the defensive.

(1) The fact and prospect of war have thrust into the foreground a desire for economic self-sufficiency as insurance against the economic hazards of war. For example, although the United States has been unable to produce watch movements as cheaply as Switzerland, watch movements are still produced in this country, under tariff protection, in order to develop, then conserve, domestic skills important to national defense; and the consumer is expected to pay. Again, the contemporary British effort to reduce imports of even cheap foreign food arises largely out of the loss of British means of payment—a condition for which past wars are largely responsible. Measures such as these run counter to the fundamental rationale of capitalism: the argument that capitalism is of all systems the one best suited to provide consumers with the most welfare at minimum cost. Such measures, also, abridge the division of labor upon which, as Adam Smith realized, an exchange economy must rest; they infringe the economic freedom of importers, although economic freedom has been trumpeted as one of the cornerstones of capitalism, and they violate the consumer's right to purchase—although controlled markets are anathema, or ought to be, to the sturdiest defenders of capitalism.[2]

---

[2] This also is over-simplified. The capitalistic United States has been protectionist for other reasons than either national defense or deficient foreign exchange, and this despite the almost unanimous preference of economists for free trade.

(2) The second source of disturbance, the increased vulnerability to unemployment at one extreme or to inflationary dwindling of the value of income and savings at the other, is perhaps more immediately obvious to the man in the street. Past or prospective war may increase the taxes he must pay, but he pays taxes anyway and he seldom inquires into the use made of his taxes. Also, he rarely realizes that national defense may cause him to pay more for a watch than he otherwise would. The loss of his job, however, or the fear of losing it, or the fact that he cannot buy as much with his money as he once could—those facts come home to him at once. Any man, however, who was not himself unemployed at some time during the 'thirties was afraid of becoming so, and he wanted something done about it. That same man knew, during the early 'fifties, that his dollars had lost value, and he wanted something done about that too. In either case, the government appeared to be the authority of ultimate recourse, even though, under capitalism, the government is supposed to be economically inactive. The economic freedom that has been presumed to be part of the American way of life has, accordingly, been somehow fenced in, even in the name of economic welfare. American capitalism has been put somewhat on the defensive because the one-time rugged individualists within it have begun to run to government for help.

(3) The third source of disturbance is in part the resultant of the first two. At home there has been continuing examination and modification of the economic forces and institutions generated by capitalism, and abroad there has been deliberate and planned experimentation with alternative forms of economic organization. This simultaneous existence of free private enterprise, of planned economies with varying degrees of private enterprise, and of totalitarian systems has meant that the deficiencies, and still more the failures, of any going system under which men live have inevitably been contrasted in mens' minds with the potential, or alleged, advantages of other systems. During the 'thirties, for example, unemployed Americans were importuned to consider the allegations of full employment in the Soviet Union, while distraught capitalists were regaled with visions of industrial peace in the fascist countries.

From within and without, then, capitalist society has been subjected to pressure—pressure at least to modify capitalism, and at most to abandon it. We must take care not to misinterpret that pressure. Before we consider that our own system is in jeopardy, we must be certain that the elements against which pressure is exerted are essential, rather than incidental or transitory, elements. We must also inquire whether the standards accepted by opponents of our system are standards acceptable to us.   Frequently they are not, because the standards held by critics of capitalism are based upon other orientations of economic activity than the orientation we have tried to set for ourselves.

Other Orientations

Earlier in this chapter we referred to an economic system as the set of institutions by which our material wants are satisfied.   Let us now give a more precise definition: an economic system is the set of institutions by which a society provides itself with goods and services, apportions resources among different uses, and distributes incomes among people.   *All* economic systems must perform those same services, but that fact and the fact that all systems produce, to some extent, the same kinds of goods, should not be permitted to obscure the very real differences in purpose and actuality that can be found among different systems.   Specifically, we should take care not to *assume* that other peoples seek *exactly* the same goals as we ourselves, for a society inevitably decides for itself and according to its own standards the kinds of goods it shall produce and the purposes which production shall serve.   Thus, in the seventh and sixth centuries before Christ the Spartan city-state devoted itself almost exclusively to the production of the means and arts of war,[3] exactly as Nazi Germany devoted itself in the 1930's.

Or, an economic system may be designed primarily, as Adam Smith put it, "to provide a plentiful revenue or subsistence for the people," and secondarily to provide the state "with a revenue sufficient for the public services." [4]   What Smith wrote suggests not only that the production of material wealth should be the function of an economic system but also that this wealth should be preponderantly devoted to the support of the general standard of living through providing people in general with "a plentiful revenue."

Yet, one may conceive an economic system designed for the production, although not for the general distribution, of wealth.   Systems approximating this principle have existed.   Heckscher asserts that the economic writers known as mercantilists who dominated the seventeenth century reached this general principle: "Wealth for the nation but wealth from which the majority of the people must be excluded." [5]

[3] J. B. Bury, *A History of Greece,* London, 1927; p. 131.
[4] Adam Smith, *Wealth of Nations,* Cannan edition, London, 1904; Vol. I, p. 395.
[5] Eli Heckscher, *Mercantilism,* London, 1935; Vol. II, p. 166.

As a final illustration of these diversities in orientation consider the Jesuit theocracy which existed in Paraguay between 1609 and 1761. Landauer writes,

Although the Jesuits made great and successful efforts to promote the welfare of the natives and created an island of humanitarian policy among the horrors of early colonial administration, it was not their only purpose to provide the Indians with the necessities of life. To them the establishment of a church organization, amply supplied with all the material requisites of cult and power, was a goal of superior importance.[6]

Here we have yet another system, one oriented to the production of wealth, to be sure, but only in conformity with some principle deemed higher than mere production in and for itself.

THE COMPARISON OF ECONOMIC SYSTEMS

Different economic systems have thus served, or been thought to serve, different purposes. Reduced to their simplest terms, a military economy characteristically produces armaments, a welfare economy consumers' goods, a prestige economy luxuries for its favored classes, and a church economy or theocracy the means of subsistence for "use" rather than "profit." Nevertheless, production, distribution, and allocation remain the functions of all economic systems although these may be and frequently are oriented to different ends. The differences, of course, are not mutually exclusive. No military economy can afford to neglect the health and morale of its subjects; a welfare economy may so define welfare as to prohibit as illicit the distribution of things deemed immoral or unhealthy by its rulers in spite of the desire of many of its subjects to possess and consume just those products,[7] while Adam Smith's famous remark that defense is of more importance than opulence can be held applicable to any kind of system, simply because in a world that is always in internal competition and sometimes in overt strife, undefended welfare is in peril.

Yet differences in orientation are always real and sometimes portentous.

[6] Carl Landauer, *Theory of National Economic Planning,* 1st. edition, University of California Press, Berkeley, 1944; pp. 111–112.

[7] As good an example as any is the unhappy attempt to prohibit the sale of alcoholic liquors in the United States.

It is a real difference between the thirteenth and twentieth centuries that the economic surplus of the former went largely into the erection of cathedrals, while that of the latter, at least in the United States, is largely utilized in the production of automobiles and television sets. It was a difference portentous for the world that Nazi Germany directed its surplus into armaments while the surplus of such democracies as Denmark was absorbed in welfare. It is at just this point that a principle in the political sphere may be coming into cautious international recognition: the activities of a society remain its own affair only so long as they do not constitute a threat to other societies. But what does constituting a threat mean? Long before the autumn of 1939 everyone knew that Nazi Germany constituted a threat, although, unhappily, recognition of that threat brought only paralysis to most of Germany's threatened neighbors. But suppose for the sake of argument that in the course of the next century people in the Soviet Union should attain a standard of living higher than that enjoyed by the average American. That attainment would constitute a threat to the American system to the extent that Americans became sympathetic to proposals that their form of economic organization be replaced by the Russian. Here, however, the ground has shifted, for what would then be compared would be the relative efficiencies of the two systems in attaining an end common to each, and not a comparison of the purposes and ends of the two systems. Russian superiority in building pyramids would scarcely be interpreted as a threat to the American system unless Americans should somehow come to regard pyramid building as a competitive activity.

If economic systems, then, are oriented to different basic ends, the standards accepted in any one system may be invalid as tests of the performance of any other. Are there any standards at all that might be used to *compare* systems? Efficiency comes at once to mind, because efficiency is a recognizable concept regardless of the nature of the performance whose efficiency is in question. The fact that someone may dislike eggs need not debar him from acknowledging the efficiency with which an omelet is cooked.

Superficially, efficiency seems an admirable test, particularly for the economic systems that are currently in competition. All are animated by the forces of modern industrial technology, all seek a high volume of production and pay at least lip service to the ideals of prosperity and full employment, and all respond more or less in the same way to the economic threat presented by the occurrence of war. Since both national strength and productivity, in this modern age, depend upon the utilization of the productive techniques released by the Industrial Revolution, the efficiency with which these techniques are used constitutes one basis for the evaluation of economic systems.   Here, also, caution must be exercised lest the mere volume of production, or character of production, or even capacity to produce be interpreted superficially.

For example, the volume of American production during the depression was decisively below the minimum level needed to insure the efficient utilization and full employment of American resources, and this has frequently been interpreted as a reflection upon the efficiency of the American system. On the other hand, the prodigious increase in production which began in 1940 and which enabled the United States really to fill its role as the "arsenal of democracy" revealed a strength which was one of the decisive factors in winning the Second World War.   Before, therefore, the under-utilization of capacity characteristic of depression is adduced as final evidence of the exhaustion and stagnation of the American economy, a further question must be answered: Is susceptibility to really serious depression a fundamental and incurable characteristic of a capitalist system, or can that susceptibility be eliminated by a full-employment policy to supplement, without abandoning, the elements of free private enterprise?

Again, at the conclusion of the Second World War the well-known hunger of Russian soldiers in Germany and Austria for such things as watches and cameras clinched, in many minds, the conclusion that the Soviet economic system was unable to produce consumers' goods on a scale adequate to satisfy the wants of the Russian people.   Acceptance of that conclusion, likewise, should rest upon proper evaluation of the impact of the war upon the Russian economy, of the relative newness of modern industrial technology in Russia, and more significantly, of the Soviet concentration upon the production of capital equipment rather than of consumers' goods.

Finally, when the end of the war brought to many Englishmen a deep concern over the relative technical backwardness of such important British industries as textiles and coal-mining, that concern became manifest in the results of the British general election of 1945 which turned largely on the issue of whether or not to nationalize key industries.[8]   That election revealed that most Englishmen then believed that private capitalism in England had outlived its usefulness.   Nevertheless, the questions have still to

---

[8] Of course, technical backwardness *per se* was not a significant factor in that election.   It is still true, however, that in 1945 the majority of Englishmen demonstrated their loss of faith in both the efficiency and the social justice of the traditional British economic system.

be raised whether or not British technical backwardness in some industries was an inevitable ultimate concomitant of the British system, or whether or not the fact of British industrial pre-eminence throughout most of the nineteenth century had induced a degree of complacency among British industrialists which might yet be overcome by renewed energy, investment, and industrial research within the framework of the old system.

It is apparent that very precise standards of evaluation must be found before one economic system can properly be compared with another. These standards, for contemporary purposes, must clearly be oriented about the concept of efficiency; but that concept is meaningless unless we are aware of both the purposes and the possible costs of efficiency. In what follows, the general functions of any economic system will be discussed together with relevant questions concerning alternative means of carrying out these functions; and at the end of the chapter an attempt will be made to formulate essential criteria by which one system can meaningfully be compared with another.

The Basic Problem of Allocation

The essential task confronting any economic system is that of apportioning the resources at its disposal among competing alternative uses. This is so both because resources are nowhere so abundant as to satisfy all wants, and because the utilization of resources in any manner involves costs in the form of labor expended, capital used up, and alternative uses foregone. The fundamental economic problem, hence, is that of deciding which wants should be given priority in their satisfaction. Guns or butter, in this sense, are genuine alternatives regardless of the form of economic society within which the question is posed.

The existence of commodity surpluses from time to time should not obscure this fundamental fact. The surpluses of cotton and wheat in depression America were surpluses only in the sense that sufficiently remunerative markets could not be found for them, but not at all in the sense that all wants for food and clothing had been satisfied. The surpluses which have existed, therefore, indicate some sort of breakdown of the economic machinery but are no evidence that the basic economic problem, the distribution of the products of scarce resources, has been solved. We are still far from that sort of economy of abundance.

Mistakes in the character of production should not be permitted to obscure our failure so far, to solve the problem of scarcity. An economic system might produce such quantities of aspirin that their disposal might create more headaches than the aspirin itself could cure, but all we could legitimately conclude from this would be that the problem of producing aspirin had been solved. As long as other wants remained unsatisfied the economy would be well advised to transfer some of the men, materials, and equipment hitherto directed to the production of aspirin to other types of service.

This is not to deny that societies have existed in which the economic problem, as it has been defined here, has been of insignificant proportions but only because those societies have been oriented to other purposes than ours. Customary wants in certain primitive communities, for example, are so few that they can be satisfied with a minimum of exertion. An amusing illustration can be found in the reports of German traders in Africa before the First World War complaining of the accursed lack of wants (*Verdammte Bedürfnislosigkeit*) of the natives, which made the introduction of the wage system and a market economy more difficult than it would otherwise have been. This, however, means simply that wants have been scaled down to the capacity of whatever economic mechanism exists, and compels us to recognize that the relationship between wants and the capacity of the prevailing economic organization is partly a matter of cultural context, but it is very far from meaning that societies into which modern industrial techniques have penetrated have solved the basic economic problem. It will be a long time before any modern society can avoid having to decide which wants to disregard for the sake of satisfying more urgent ones, although it is probably also true that the wealthier modern economies can tolerate a larger margin of waste, irrespective of their particular form of organization, than poorer ones.

We must not interpret our need to ration our resources mechanistically. The possession of leisure, for example, is as legitimate a want as the possession of an automobile although it may not always appear to be an economic want because, unlike automobiles, leisure is not a commodity which is advertised for sale. But the progressive shortening of the working day in the course of the last century can be interpreted just as truly as an express recognition of this want as it can be by the suspicion that the productive capacity of the modern economy has been tending to outstrip the modern capacity to consume.

Thus modern economies, like ancient, must husband their resources.

This involves some sort of rationing system which can be based either upon custom;[9] or upon some automatic mechanism, such as the free market, in which the price system is depended upon to indicate the collective preferences of consumers; or upon the basis of deliberate governmental decisions, as has been the case in the Soviet Union.   Under modern conditions in which new processes, new commodities, and even new tastes are continually appearing, custom plays a relatively minor role in determining the particular uses to which resources shall be put, although it is by no means wholly absent.   The fact, for example, that Germans habitually drink beer, Frenchmen wine, and Americans, shall we say, soft drinks, is largely a matter of custom which guides, within these limits, the allocation of resources.   In an economy such as our own in which consumers may purchase almost anything they wish and can afford and where no central direction of production exists, manufacturers allocate resources to the production of whatever they think they can sell and rely upon the market to prove them right or wrong. The fact that producers can influence the market through salesmanship or advertising does not invalidate the conclusion that consumers' collective market decisions can be decisive in determining the ways in which resources are to be utilized not immediately, because decisions take time to become effective, but in the long run.   An illustration is afforded in the fate which befalls the manufacturers of women's clothing who guess wrongly what next season's styles are going to be.

But even in the United States the hand of government must be added to the behavior of consumers in shaping the character of production.   Narcotic drugs may not be freely offered upon the market regardless of the wants of individual consumers, and—again regardless of the wants of individual consumers—a modicum of education must be "consumed."   Taxation, the tariff, and public works are other examples of the ways in which the allocation of resources is influenced by government even in free enterprise economies.   Taxation influences allocation because the individual's free impact on the structure of production and sale is reduced, and even distorted, by the amount of his tax; the tariff, because foreign resources whose cheapness might appeal to the consumer lose that advantage by the extent to which the tariff increases their cost; and public works, partly because sooner or later they are financed out of the individual's pocket and partly because

[9] The allocation by American manufacturers of men's clothing of labor, capital, and equipment for the production of vests is customary in this sense, since it is questionable whether the wearing of vests is really essential to the comfort, decency, or convenience of the American male.

the steel, concrete, and labor used by government in their construction might have been employed otherwise, had they been available, by independent individual producers.   As an extreme case, the experience of war brings into sharp relief the manner and extent of the deliberate rationing of resources which even free enterprise economies are sometimes called upon to undertake.   Priorities, price control, requisitioning, conscription, and rationing itself are among the means employed to achieve this purpose.

In the end, the government itself may assume complete responsibility for apportioning resources among competing uses.   In its extreme form this would mean not only that it would decide how much steel and cotton, for example, were to be distributed respectively to various steel-using and cotton-using industries, but also that it would assign individual workers to employment in particular steel, cotton, and subsidiary enterprises.   In a more liberal form, the allocation of physical resources could still be held in complete control while individual workers would remain free to seek whatever employment they could find.   From the viewpoint of the laborer this would not differ perceptibly from the situation in freer economies, except that the satisfaction of his wants as a consumer might, although not necessarily, be more restricted; and, of course, the individual's opportunity to establish his own business within the limits of his capital and skill would be severely limited, if it existed at all.

Any economic system, then, has the responsibility to reach decisions as to the manner in which the resources at its disposal are to be utilized and to provide machinery for executing these decisions.   As part of this responsibility, any economic system must make arrangements for providing its individual members with their respective shares of the goods and services it produces; this is simply one aspect of the basic economic problem of allocating resources.   As above, the alternative means of carrying out this function range between the theoretical extreme, in a free enterprise economy of leaving the individual free to select whatever occupation he may choose within the limits of his own capacities and to spend his earnings according to his own tastes, and the other theoretical extreme in a planned economy, of assigning employment and issuing each member of society whatever supplies and services the responsible authorities consider it proper and reasonable that he should have.[10]   In the former case, the allocative

---

[10] There is a third variant, the ideal of pure communism: "In parallel to social cooperative production, goes on social enjoyment of the fruits obtained.   There are no rapacity and extortion, no superior claims of owners, no lion's shares arrogated to idlers.   After the necessary deductions have been made for the maintenance of

responsibility is entrusted to the market, in the latter it is borne by a planner.

In practice, contemporary systems of economic organization combine elements of each procedure.   In our own society, individuals earn their incomes as best they can and have considerable freedom to spend them as they choose.   Yet minimum wage laws, unemployment relief, and old age pensions are examples of governmental intervention to assure the individual of at least the minimum means of support, even though in many cases it may be an insignificant minimum.   Similarly the construction and maintenance of highways, the establishment of a public health system, the enforcement of compulsory primary education, and the maintenance of public police and fire departments reveal that there are certain forms of resource allocation which society believes ought to be provided, but which individuals cannot or will not provide for themselves; hence the state assumes the responsibility.   A forteriori, in wartime, even in free private enterprise economies, the intervention of the state in the distribution of incomes, and particularly in the ways these may be spent, is especially apparent.

In the Soviet Union, on the other hand, the distribution of individual incomes is far more a matter of deliberate policy decisions.   The state decides what things shall be produced and in what quantities; resources are then allocated in accordance with the basic plan, and wages and salaries are fixed to conform with the comparative urgencies of different occupations and types of production and distribution.   Yet even under these circumstances, some freedom of individual decision may remain.   The Soviet state goes much further than the American in determining aptitudes and guiding young men and women in their choice of careers.   But, apart from the extensive and grim forced labor system, Soviet citizens in good standing do possess some formal freedom to choose their own careers from among those which the state has decided to encourage or permit; and, although rationing has been in existence throughout most of the history of the Soviet Union, there is still an area within which individuals may distribute their purchases according to their own choice from the still narrow limits of available consumer goods and services.

---

public institutions and social enterprises, the wealth is enjoyed by all the members of society; and not according to their contributions, but in harmony with higher principles.   The narrow bourgeois notion of right is banished, and society inscribes on its flag: 'From each according to his capabilities; to each according to his needs.' " *Cf.* M. M. Bober, *Karl Marx's Interpretation of History,* Harvard University Press, Cambridge, 1927; p. 259.   This, however, like Heaven, has never been described at first hand, and perhaps it is just as well.

In summary, then, any economic system must orient itself toward some selected end or ends. In theory these ends are many, and not always mutually consistent. But in practice each contemporary system which has any significance in the world today attempts to achieve two goals in varying proportions and degrees. The liberal systems tend to emphasize the welfare of their members as manifested in the standard of living; the totalitarian systems give greater weight to the security of the state in the form of an industrial structure relatively immune to disturbances emanating from abroad, capable in the last resort of resisting at any moment overt assault, and one to which the interests of the individual are decisively subordinated. Given its own purposive emphasis, any economic system must mobilize its resources in some manner consistent with its basic purpose, since until that far-off day comes when all wants can be met, only those deemed important can be acknowledged. In other words, means for directing resources toward selected ends must be found; and as a very important part of this latter task machinery must be devised for assigning human resources their appropriate roles in the economy and for providing individuals their proportionate and appropriate shares of the total output of the system. This immediately suggests certain significant tests which can be applied to an economic system.

Criteria of Economic Efficiency

The volume of production is perhaps the most obvious test of economic efficiency. Everyone knows that this is greater in the United States than in China, and to a degree this indicates that the American system is more highly developed and functions more effectively than the Chinese. But the mere volume of production tells us little: Luxembourg, for example, produces less steel than the United States, but its *per capita* production of steel is sometimes greater. Clearly, the volume of production must be fitted to the size and resources of the country. Possibly the extent to which a country's production is adequate to meet its own needs might be considered. Yet the Chinese economy functions, and so does the Abyssinian; and some people appear to doubt whether, in the absence of war, the American economy does or can. Nevertheless, production (along with exchange and distribution) is the function of an economic system, and together with other tests, the volume of production can properly be used to evaluate a system.

The economy of production, examined with discrimination, is another criterion. Productivity per man-hour in important industries has sometimes been used as a standard by which to compare different economic systems. When the information can be obtained, and the industries being considered are really comparable, a comparison in these terms can be genuinely fruitful. But care should be taken not to read too much into the results. A sudden intensification of effort, for example, like that which accompanies a wartime emergency, may be followed by an increase in productivity, but increases attributable to this cause are unlikely to be permanently maintained [11] and should not, therefore, be taken as norms. In any case, man-hour productivity in general is far less susceptible to measurement than productivity in specific industries, and the question under consideration here is the comparison of economic systems as a whole.

One way out might be to consider how far up the scale the satisfaction of wants goes. Before the outbreak of the Second World War the German people had to sacrifice butter for guns: the American, at least until the war was well advanced, had both. Of course the Germans could have had both, too, if they had been satisfied to rearm less intensively. Later, even the Americans had to begin giving things up. But comparisons of this sort come perilously close to judging one system by the standards of another. This is perfectly legitimate if done deliberately and in full awareness of the implications; it is not legitimate if comparisons of this nature are utilized in efforts to persuade others to accept conclusions based upon principles they do not accept. In any event, all this simply reinforces the point already made, that none of these tests should be applied individually; it is their combination and joint context that should be considered significant.

Disparity in the quantity and variety of resources at the disposal of different areas under different systems need not invalidate comparisons based on productivity. Switzerland has fewer resources than either the United States or Germany, but, by concentrating upon what they can produce effectively and by exchanging the surplus for other things, the Swiss have been able to attain and maintain a comfortable standard of living and a smoothly functioning economy. The real test, in other words, of the efficiency of an economic system is the use it makes of the resources at its disposal.

The stability of production is a third, and important, test. An economic system which maintains a steady productive pace is utilizing its resources more effectively than one which may, in the long run, maintain the same average pace but only by fluctuating between periods of intense productivity and periods of deep depression. The extent to which productive resources,

[11] *Cf.* A. C. Pigou, *The Political Economy of War,* New York, 1941; Ch. III.

especially labor, are employed and kept employed constitutes a very real, and probably generally acceptable, test of an economic system. Here, also, however, caution is necessary. A progressive economy in which men constantly seek new processes, new products, and even new wants necessarily undergoes certain slack periods in which some resources must await re-employment. Progress entails obsolescence, change means displacement, and both obsolescence and displacement have unpleasant overtones. The reconciliation of change and stability is intricate and difficult—so much so that deliberate judgment rather than the mechanical apportionment of weights in a formula must be used in determining the *significance,* to say nothing of the measurement, of the unemployment attributable to progress.

The volume, efficiency, and stability of production, then, are tests which with due care may be applied to the important economic systems of the modern world. These alone, however, would still give an incomplete picture, for an economic system is something more than a congeries of institutions to transform and allocate resources; it is a form of organization worked by *people* whom, in the long run, it must satisfy. It is in this sphere that the effective comparison of economic systems is likely to be made in coming years.

The position of the individual within a system is a fourth, and possibly the most important test—at least to Americans who accept individualism as a principle desirable in itself. It is involved in all the other tests, most immediately, perhaps, in the third, the stability of production. Individual security and satisfaction, however, comprise more than merely freedom from want and fear, although these are important. They include freedom to do things, to resist things, to think and say things—even to make a fool of oneself.

The easiest way to provide the negative security of an assured job and a guaranteed minimum standard of living would be to assign each individual his role in society, provide him with his stipend, and then simply operate him like a mechanical rabbit on a race track. It is conceivable that an economic system might be organized on this principle, and that the individuals so organized might become so convinced of the superiority of their system that any alternative would seem distasteful. This could very easily be the case if the negative security of freedom *from* things should come to seem more important than the positive security of freedom *for* things, and if men should come to believe that the only means of achieving the former were the complete regimentation of the economy. Most of us, however, will probably agree that the future would be dark indeed, if the only alternatives confronting modern man were economic security without freedom, or freedom with no security at all.

It is for this reason that the position of the individual within different forms of economic organization is so important. His present role and function, his prospects in the future, and the potential development of the economic system to which he belongs—all these bear, first, upon his well-being and therefore upon his efficiency, and ultimately upon the performance and efficiency of the system to which he belongs.

———————————————————————2

How Economic Systems May Change

THE WORLD has seen not only many different proposals for organizing economic activity, but different actual types of economic systems as well. Some of these, like Christianity and purely competitive capitalism, have "never been tried"; others are going concerns today, while still others have played their role on the stage of history and then vanished. The impermanence of some systems suggests that among the things to be considered by those interested in the forms of economic organization is the prospect of the eventual dissolution of any one of them.

TYPES OF CHANGE

Dissolution which is rapid, comprehensive, and violent is comparatively easy both to identify and to describe, and violent dissolution can occur; the Bolshevik Revolution in Russia leaps to mind. An economic system in imminent danger of violent overthrow is unstable, not only because it may at any moment go under in blood and fire, but also because perception of that danger may result in such drastic transformation, undertaken to avert the danger, that the system evolves into something quite unlike its original form.   Many of the defensive measures taken by capitalist countries, particularly after the Second World War, are of exactly that nature, so that one of the reasons, for example, why the American economy of the 1950's seems so different from that of the 1890's is to be found in the American reaction to activities and forces feared as subversive.   Unhappily, the American resistance to subversion has sometimes tempted Americans to imitate the methods of subversion, and thereby to endanger freedom in the name of freedom.   Freedom from fear is indeed a buttress to the stability of a system.

An economic system, however, may be subject to the dynamic forces of change without necessarily being exposed to the danger of dissolution.   Dissatisfied elements within it may press for reform, and to the extent that their demands are extreme and their efforts successful, the very warp and woof of the system upon which they operate may be transformed.   The economic changes undergone by postwar England are of this nature, and if capitalism is indeed subject to internal tensions which will eventually transform it into socialism we are entitled to say that capitalism is unstable and impermanent. As we shall see, socialists assert that capitalism is in fact exposed to just such tensions.

More difficult to analyze is the inexorable change arising neither from hostile assault nor from reformist pressure, but from dynamic forces inherent in the very body of a system.   Capitalism has been perhaps the most dynamic of all systems, and part of its dynamism consists in its extraordinary adaptability and its readiness to exploit economic opportunity.   Capitalism has been unstable, unstable in the sense that its carriers have always been willing and sometimes eager to forswear old ways for new, to develop the undeveloped, and even to break the old bottles if they will not hold the new wine.   Its wake is littered with broken bottles, and sometimes the breakage has seemed insupportable so that, in capitalism, reformist pressure culminating in some men in downright hatred has perversely joined hands with capitalism's inherent dynamism to mold, to transform, to change, even to destroy.   The transformation of any system as dynamic as capitalism has been is, therefore, the resultant of a complex of forces, and its form at any moment depends upon the particular balance prevailing among the forces of dissolution, of reform, and of development.

We have observed that the first two of these forces are, in principle, comparatively easy to identify and to keep distinct, complicated though they be in fact.   The line between a drastic reformer and a mild revolutionist, if such there be, is sometimes very finely drawn, with the dividing point between them a matter for perhaps arbitrary definition. Nevertheless, the presence or absence of pressure for violent expropriation, or of comprehensive as against gradual or piecemeal reform, may still serve as differentiating characteristics. Russian communism and British socialism are really different things.

The developmental forces pressing within a dynamic system like capitalism are intricate. For our purposes they may be resolved into two great groups: (1) those which are concerned with seizing discerned or suspected opportunities, and (2) those concerned with dissolving or smashing the obstacles to their own full expansion. Both groups are akin and both are to some extent different aspects of the same process—the striving toward the most effective exploitation of available natural and human resources. The two groups working together within the matrix of developing capitalism made possible the stupendous economic development which has been named the Industrial Revolution. When these forces are powerful and clamant, as they have been under capitalism, the system which engenders and nurtures them undergoes constant change, sometimes pulsing and vigorous, sometimes slow and even imperceptible, operating, so to speak, beneath the surface, sometimes even quiescent or dormant. Changing technology, the discovery of new processes and products, the opening of new markets, the development of virgin lands, the pulsations of the business cycle—all are among the manifestations of this dynamic process. One of its important concomitant results has been the emergence of great organized groups each seeking its own ends as it conceives and interprets them, and all forming alliances or coming into conflict with each other according as the discerned interests of any one group are felt to accord or to clash with the interests of any other. Organized capital in a sense begot organized labor, and the two together, in the same sense, brought into being organized government to curb their excesses and to hold the two in harness. In the United States, just as organized industry has on the whole sought to protect itself, by tariff, against the sale of the products of its foreign competitors within what it considers its private preserve, so has organized labor allied itself with other groups to control and restrict the tide of foreign immigrants seeking entry to *its* private preserve. In this great process of organization, alliance, and counter-alliance, interests become vested and powerful; but as even vested interests may be, or feel themselves to be, intermittently threatened, the massive flow of capitalist development has been uneven, sometimes accelerated, sometimes retarded. That flow, moreover, has always been shaped and sometimes deflected by the interplay among themselves of opposing and allied interests and by the interplay among interests already vested and those seeking to become so.

Balancing Change—Equilibrium

Here we may discern the deeper meaning of the economist's use of *equilibrium* as a tool of analysis. The equilibrium among supply, demand, price, and output, so familiar and yet so bewildering to so many generations of students, is a reflection on a very small scale of that great equilibrium among massive but ever-changing forces—economic, social, political, and technological—which any system, no matter how dynamic it may be, must maintain if it is to survive. In a dynamic system that equilibrium need not be stable; in fact, it will not be. Under capitalism, each state of equilibrium in this larger sense has almost invariably been succeeded by another, and often rapidly so, but each state is nonetheless the resultant of all the forces which have been operating up to that moment within and upon the economy. A snowball, increasing in speed and size as it rolls down a hillside, is where it is at each moment and has its direction determined for the next moment because of all the forces operating upon it up to that moment in exactly the same sense. That the forces themselves change is shown by the fact that the course of the snowball is erratic, and by the fact that no two descending snowballs are likely to follow the same course, maintain the same speeds, or attain the same sizes. It is just so with dynamic economies. The course of each is erratic, and no two have exactly the same history.

Many students have been disturbed by the unreal quality of equilibrium analysis in the narrower sense. It is unreal. It is particularly unreal in its simpler forms simply because it is oversimplified and because it conceals both the sensitivity and vulnerability to change and the tendency to change which "really" characterizes a dynamic economy. To acknowledge this need be no more than to acknowledge that reality is too vast and too complicated to be grasped all at once. To say, however, that equilibrium is unreal because it seems static whereas economic life is dynamic, is like denying the reality of motion pictures because a film strip is nothing but a succession of stills.

Let us, then, look more closely at the processes of change—first those more spectacular ones which threaten or culminate either in the dissolution or in some abrupt and fundamental change in an economic system, and

then those which manifest themselves in economic transformation through a
never-ending succession of different states of equilibrium.

Dissolution

Most defenders of an established order tend to believe in its permanence
unless it is seriously threatened or actually overturned, and then their defense shifts to the normative principle that it "ought" to be permanent.
Thus, the defenders of capitalism deny the existence of any really serious
instability in the system, but acknowledge with trepidation the existence
of enemies, both within and without; likewise the communists, convinced as
they are of the internal strength, moral superiority, and fundamental cor-
rectness of the Soviet system, still manifest deep concern toward the threat
from capitalist states that seem to encircle them.

The most serious and sometimes the most immediately obvious source of
instability with respect to any particular economic system, then, is the
danger of violent overturn, either from without or within.   But assault from
without seems more significant as the subject of fear than as something that
really happens.   It is true that military defeat—to say nothing of victory!
—in the twentieth century has occasioned profound economic changes.
But it would be naive to assume that the overthrow of what is considered a
hostile *economic* system was the only, or even the primary, purpose of recent
military assaults.   During the Second World War Prime Minister Chamberlain of Great Britain publicly denied that the war was an ideological war,
and it is certainly true that profoundly different economic systems were
aligned against the Axis powers; and while many people looked upon the
fascist and Nazi economic systems with abhorrence, the war arose even more
as the result of age-old political antagonisms and national rivalries.   While
most people disapprove, and may even fear, alien forms of economic organization, the right of any people to organize their own economic life according to their own preferred pattern is still conceded.   The time may
come when alternative economic systems become so charged with moral and
emotional content that, like the religious systems of the sixteenth century,
the world becomes conceived as too small to contain more than one; and an
indication that that day has dawned will be the change from mere distrust or
fear of foreign ways to a general determination to embark upon crusades to
extirpate them.

The world, however, has seen recent examples of economic systems being overturned, not by outsiders, but by their own dissatisfied members—the Bolshevik Revolution in Russia being probably the most conspicuous case. This is true at least in the sense that that revolution designedly and admittedly was directed toward the destruction of the old system.   On the other hand, the Fascist Revolution in Italy, the Nazi seizure of power in Germany, and General Franco's revolt in Spain received support from many people who believed that these movements were designed to protect the old systems from revolution from the left.   Be that as it may, overturn from within may properly be charged to whatever really dissatisfied, organized groups exist within a system, and which are determined to achieve change and are convinced that change by gradual and peaceful means is either impossible or too slow.

Violent overturn thus occurs either when an economy is successfully assailed from without, as capitalist Czechoslovakia was engulfed by the Soviet octopus, or when internal dissatisfaction or despair march hand in hand to destroy a system from within.

Reformist Change

Violent dissolution may occur when dissatisfied elements threaten an economy internally and are too powerful to be resisted, whilst the threatened system is too inflexible to make the adjustments which might modify or disarm the opposition.   On the other hand, when violence is forsworn by an opposition and when there exist alternative means by which the objectives of an opposition may be ultimately, if gradually, attained, we have the type of change we have named reformist.   The nationalization of some industries and the extension of social services in postwar Britain are of this order, and so, on a larger canvas, is the movement toward the welfare state in more than one contemporary economy—including our own.   Such changes may even be brought about by conservatives who initiate them in order to forestall more drastic changes demanded by an opposition.   The expression *Tory reform* is familiar in England, where exactly this process has occurred more than once.   More familiar to Americans is the process within a democratic society whereby a liberal, or leftist, opposition may be voted into office in order to bring about quite sweeping changes without abruptly or entirely transforming the old order.   The New Deal can perhaps be taken as an illustration.

The distinction among the various kinds and colors of reformists, from the palest of pinks to the most sanguinary reds, is extremely difficult to draw. In the United States the line is formally drawn at the point where force and violence are advocated or accepted as the means of change. This line, however, is not as distinct as it may formally appear because of general unwillingness to accept at face value all disavowals of propensities toward violence. Communists nearly always make such disavowals, but because few non-communists today believe that communists mean what they say there is a tendency, at least in contemporary America, to prohibit activities which are, sometimes rashly or hysterically, interpreted as communist.

The really important distinctions, however, are more than matters of degree. There is first a non-reformist distinction between stubborn refusal to accept any change whatever and acceptance, however reluctant, of change legally brought about. Next, there is the distinction between impatient insistence that Utopia be achieved today at whatever cost, and the patience to be satisfied today with what can be accomplished today and to wait until tomorrow for what must be deferred until then in the wisdom that haste must sometimes be made slowly. Finally, there is the distinction between a system so rigid that change must be cataclysmic to occur at all, and one sufficiently flexible to make provision for change when the forces working toward it are powerful enough to accomplish it by accepted means.

Bearing these important distinctions in mind, we must now turn to the forces themselves which work toward the immediate dissolution or toward the eventual fundamental reform of an economic system.

FORCES WORKING TOWARD CHANGE

Dispossessed Classes

Dispossessed classes within a society, or what Toynbee has called an "internal proletariat," constitute probably the most important focus of instability and potential threat to an established order. This need not necessarily mean groups entirely destitute of property; dispossession in this context may imply simply a sense that its bearers are the victims of economic discrimination, or have feelings of frustration in that the avenues of advancement appear to be closed to them. It is important to notice that this sort of disposition may lead either to violent or to peaceful change, depending upon the peaceful structure and balance of the system in which dispossession exists.   It is also important to notice that dispossession may ignite a powder trail leading either to the left or to the right.   It will turn leftward if dispossessed classes believe that it is an aristocracy resting upon wealth or hereditary privilege that thwarts their ambitions.   Dispossession, however, may just as easily turn to the right if a ruling class wishes to forestall a revolt. Some of the more extreme apprehensions about the preservation of some national "way of life" arise from fear lest "radical" activities literally dispossess the carriers of some established culture.   Two illustrations, one historical, one contemporary, may be offered.   In 1796 the Vicomte de Bonald, a French aristocrat in exile because of the French Revolution, wrote a book to challenge the principles of political liberty and of freedom of thought.   He believed that it was those principles that animated the revolutionaries who were seeking to destroy the aristocracy to which he belonged and which, he really believed, represented French civilization.

The contemporary illustration is less extremist.   British conservatives look back wistfully to the yesterday when they could afford to live in those gracious, stately mansions with which our own Mount Vernon may be compared.   Like Mount Vernon itself, those homes are being turned into museums, and there are many people who feel that their disappearance, as homes, represents the loss of something more valuable than anything an equalitarian age can provide in their place.

Nevertheless, even though conservative sentiment exists and is sometimes powerful, there is considerable feeling that most historical changes have resulted in freeing rather than freezing the "progressive" elements of a system, the elements that, at least after a change, are conceded to have been working toward desirable reform.   That feeling that historical change has been "progressive" reflects partly the afterglow of nineteenth-century confidence in the Idea of Progress, the belief that historical movements proceed onward and upward.   It reflects, also, a sometimes curious refraction of historical perspective arising, in its turn, from complacent assurance that whatever is, is somehow right.   Revolutions, and even reforms, are dreadful things to those who are broken, impoverished, or embittered by them, but their very success tends to confine the embitterment to a generation or so at the most:

> Treason doth never prosper; what's the reason?
> If it doth prosper, none dare call it Treason.

Acceptance of Idea of Progress

Anyway, to most people perhaps, progress appears more respectable than reaction. Americans, particularly, like to think of themselves as up to date and they like to think of both their community and their country as growing. Except in periods of trouble, men who dislike progress and who argue against it are accorded comparatively less attention than "sound" progressives. When there is trouble, however, reaction may acquire merit through its connotation of stability, and when there is organized violence, counter-revolution may acquire respectability. In some rough measure, indeed, counter-reform and counter-revolution emerge in a degree proportionate to that in which pressure for reform exists. The reason is simple. The possessors of vested rights and interests become fearful of expropriation whenever the possibility of expropriation comes to be apprehended. Accordingly, the right is provoked into a reactionary policy at just those times when the left is becoming embittered by a sense of economic discrimination without apparent prospect of relief.

Tension Between Progress and Reaction

A society in this unhappy condition becomes torn by dissension between a relatively small upper class in possession of most of the material perquisites of a comfortable existence and receiving the lion's share of the output of goods and services, and a larger lower class performing the routine and manual labor of the society, living in at least relative austerity, and obsessed by feelings of insecurity, frustration, and resentment. The contrast is not inevitably one between unproductive possessors of undeserved wealth and an exploited but essentially productive proletariat (although for propaganda purposes the contrast is often put in that form), but between a class that believes itself to be and may genuinely be, the very carrier of civilization and progress which could not be maintained without the education, leisure, and wealth which appertain to it, and a class that has become increasingly conscious of exclusion from, and antagonism toward the body politic. Revolutions do not occur because propagandists persuade people who had not hitherto thought of rebellion, to revolt, nor are they carried out to realize the plausible and rosy dreams of reformers. It is hard to conceive a society entirely without malcontents, but malcontents are not particularly dangerous until they begin really to multiply, and their multiplication is less the product

of golden tongues or poison pens than it is the spontaneous development of
sensations of frustration and repression which eventually become intolerable.
Intolerability, in turn, has too frequently and freely been attributed to an
unequal division of wealth and income.   In the United States, in fact, that
inequality has traditionally been defended as an element of strength in the
American system in that it constitutes the only effective incentive for the
typical American.   Inequality becomes indefensible only when it is associated with a rigid caste system, because then a man's incentive to better his
condition becomes *in*effective.   If the system should ever break down so that
many men could scarcely earn a decent living and more men feared that the
same fate might befall themselves, continued great inequality of wealth and
income could easily assume menacing hues.   What is really intolerable is
the progressive disorganization of a system with all its stultifying effects
upon the prospects and ambitions of the masses of people.   Dispossession,
in other words, is something which men who undergo it feel coming upon
them, and it must come upon a great many men and be protracted over a
considerable period of time and must be considered irremediable, except
through violent action, before it comes to be significant as a revolutionary
force.   Its symptoms are general—enduring poverty existing side by side
with wealth and conspicuous consumption that mock the pretensions to
efficiency and justice which the beneficiaries of such a system tend to reiterate
with increasing shrillness.

For a revolution or a really radical reformist movement to succeed, members of the dispossessed classes (in the sense in which the term has here
been used) require and must obtain a program comprising both a critique of
the old order and a general outline of the new.   Such movements are based
as much, if not more, upon a yearning *toward* something as they are upon a
revolt *against* something, and the fact that no such movement follows the
precise pattern drawn up for it by its planners does not weaken the appeal
inherent in the picture of many an idealized society.   That appeal may, but
need not, present as radical a contrast with the existing order as Plato's ideal
republic, for example, contrasted with fourth-century Athens, or as the classless and stateless society of pure communism set against twentieth-century
Russia.   On the other hand, it may, like the ideal capitalism of the Manchester liberal, be no more than a picture of the existent system purged
of its imperfections and abuses.   But if these imperfections and abuses appear irremovable except through some very drastic purge, or if the ideal
society seems unattainable by slow, gradual, and continuous reform, and if

the idealized picture presents an appeal sufficiently powerful to elicit the attempt to realize it, a necessary though not yet sufficient condition for revolution exists.

Role of Intellectuals — Provide illumination (Both Sides)

This critique of the existing order and the portrayal of the order which is in principle to succeed it is the function of men who, for want of a better term, may be called the intellectuals of the movement. This is not to say that intellectuals are necessarily radicals. Both conservatism and reaction have their intellectuals. The Nazi Alfred Rosenberg's *Myth of the Twentieth Century,* full of bad history, philosophy, and sociology as it is, provided the German National Socialist movement with the rationalization that convinced it that it was riding the "wave of the future." An intellectual in this sense need not be "right," or even logical in his thinking; all that is necessary is to find someone, here called the intellectual, who can provide a revolutionary movement with a philosophy, a rationale, and sometimes a program, which can capture the imaginations of men who need the particular variety of philosophy offered. Rosenberg is an example of an intellectual in our sense, who deliberately aligned himself with an extremist right-wing movement. Sometimes a movement can find intellectuals whose work can be turned to purposes their authors might have disavowed. Mussolini's designation of Georges Sorel as one of the creators of fascism is a case in point. Sorel's *Réflexions sur la Violence* (1908) was a defense of the creative power (violence) of the proletariat set against the technical economic power (force) of the bourgeoisie, which presumably was to lead to a new epoch in history in which a new "élite" would attain power. Actually, the élite characteristic of fascism was of a different order from that envisioned by Sorel.

Right-wing movements thus have their intellectuals, but to the extent that these movements are successful the *status quo* is perpetuated—albeit sometimes to an exaggerated degree. Change in any fundamental sense does not occur, and there is nothing for one concerned with change to write about. For our purposes, here, the real significance of the intellectual—to the extent that he and his work are relevant—lies in paving the way toward some new conception of society. This statement, of course, applies only to societies which are ripe for change or overturn. Many, possibly most, intellectuals who can be named in this connection would be aghast at being called revolutionaries and would recoil from some of the consequences of their activities could they live to see them.[1]   A few, like Marx or Lenin, may deliberately organize and identify themselves with revolutionary groups, and some, like Proudhon,[2] may themselves be members of dispossessed classes who put their imaginations and intellects into the service of economic and social reform.   But most intellectuals whose work has actual or potential significance for revolution or drastic reform have performed their work either for its own sake in following the bent of their own interests, or in some lonely hope of *persuading* others into a desired course of action—despite the fact that a revolutionary situation is precisely one in which force rather than persuasion appears to offer the only release.

By their familiarity with information and theories of which others are unaware, intellectuals are often able to see the economic order in which they live in a wider and different context from the conventional one; its shortcomings, injustices, and irrationalities come to stand out in bolder relief, and a frequent result is that they attempt to portray a society in which these are absent.   Plato, Sir Thomas More, and Austin Tappan Wright in our own age [3] are random examples of intellectuals whose gentle criticism of the social order characteristic of their own day took the form of an implicit contrast with one more ideal.   None of these men were revolutionaries or even reformers in the looser sense; yet Plato's hero, Socrates, and Sir Thomas More himself, were executed for what was called treason, but what was really a refusal to conform to elements in the existing order which they considered wrong; and Wright's hero ultimately abandoned American civilization in favor of Islandian.   The connection of this sort of work with

---

[1] E.g.: "As convinced believers in the power of reason to bring about progress, the *philosophes* (French intellectuals of the eighteenth century) one and all, strongly condemned popular uprisings. . . . Violent revolution, as a method of progress, was something that the *philosophes* could not even imagine, and nothing would have so horrified them as to hear their names invoked during the violent scenes of the French Revolution."   J. Salwyn Schapiro, *Condorcet and the Rise of Liberalism,* Harcourt, Brace & Co., New York, 1934; p. 58.

[2] Pierre-Joseph Proudhon was an early nineteenth-century socialist with leanings toward anarchism, who wrote voluminously and usually obscurely, and who is probably best remembered for his aphorism, *Property is theft.*   He was born into extreme poverty but managed to educate himself, largely by the indiscriminate reading of the books that came into the shop where he was employed as a printer's compositor during his youth.

[3] Wright's *Islandia* (New York, 1942) is a fascinating modern Utopia in which there are political disagreements but no class struggle, a high standard of living but no machinery, a social democracy without demagoguery, a high and widely diffused culture without artificiality or aridity, and private property without exploitation.

specific programs of reform is usually diffused and remote, but to the extent that Utopias are read, criticism of the established order is indirectly disseminated.

Direct proposals for economic and social reform constitute a more immediate channel through which intellectuals may animate and reinforce popular demands for changes in the *status quo*. A classical example is the role played by French intellectuals during the eighteenth century. Toward the end of the *ancien régime* both Church and State were moribund, and the middle classes, who were becoming increasingly literate, and who thus constituted a public for the intellectuals, felt themselves dispossessed in the sense that discerned opportunities for advancement were blocked. All that was needed now for a serious uprising was an ideal and a program, and exactly these were furnished by the French intellectuals of the enlightenment.

There are two things to be noticed. *First,* it is not always the ragged and the destitute who are the only source of trouble. It is true that the ragged and the destitute were carried along by the French Revolution and did much to carry it as well,[4] but the meaning of the French Revolution is not proletarian. What that Revolution did, both in industry and agriculture, was to set the scene for the development in France of bourgeois capitalism.

Second, the French Revolution brings out the important distinction between a revolutionary overturn of an entire social order, and an uprising directed against specific abuses. The German Peasants' Revolt of 1524 was sparked in part by the intellectuals of the German Reformation, but the peasants' fundamental grievances arose out of the institution of serfdom, the denial of fishing and hunting rights, and their lack of influence in the appointment of village priests.[5] Anyone can formulate his own grievances and even revolt against them if he be so inclined, but the high emotional tension of a revolution directed against a system rather than against specific abuses or specific individuals requires some sort of philosophic formulation which can then be put in terms capable of influencing the imaginations of the common carriers of the revolution.

These Frenchmen of whom we have been writing were not personally revolutionaries; many of them were on good personal terms with the French

[4] *Sans-culottes,* the popular symbol of the Revolution, means literally, without trousers.

[5] *Cf.* L. Cristiani, "The Reformation on the Continent," in Edward Eyre, *European Civilization, Its Origin and Development,* Oxford, 1936; Vol. IV, p. 78.

court, and most of them believed that the reforms they advocated could be achieved without revolution.[6] They relied upon reason, they trusted in progress, their writing for the most part was dispassionate and detached, they condemned popular uprisings—but they paved the way for the French Revolution.

It is here that the role of the intellectual in breaking the ground for social change is most impressive. Few Utopias get written; gentle satire, oblique criticism, and symbolic withdrawal from the world kindle passions but rarely; and overt revolutionists—whether revolutionary by word or by deed—are hard to come upon within the ranks of intellectuals, although occasionally they do exist. But intellectuals by their very nature are critical, and sometimes perfectionist; they seek the logic of events and the implications of institutions before these become generally manifest, and in their role as critics they may accelerate the emergence of tensions whose embryonic existence they have already discerned. That is why authoritarian states maintain Thought Police, and why even democratic states sometimes make apprehensive attempts to contain the activities of the intellectual. For in any society men whose concern is with the maintenance of the *status quo* are unable to alleviate the tensions which may arise; all they can do is to sugar them over, as the Fascist *Dopolavoro* or the Nazi *Kraft durch Freude* attempted to provide workers with other satisfactions than that of organized defense of their own interests; or to deflect them against scapegoats, as middle class German resentment against impoverishment was diverted against the Jews; or, as a last resort, to prohibit outright their public recognition or expression.

Dispossessed classes, then, are the carriers, and intellectuals are the illuminators of whatever tensions a social-economic system may develop. The significance of these tensions, together with their consequences, depends on whether they are rooted in the very structure of the system or arise from more superficial abuses, and on whether the system itself permits of orderly, designed change or must be violently broken in order to bring about that

---

[6] "Without demanding revolution, probably without even wishing to imply it, the *encyclopédistes* contributed to the self-consciousness of the bourgeois class, which was destined to accomplish it. The practical reforms which they proposed as potentially realizable within the framework of the *ancien régime*—definitions of the constitution, guaranty of individual liberty, state protection of science and industry, reform of the criminal law, limitation of privileges, improvement of administration and in particular of the fiscal system—became the program of the Constituent Assembly of 1789." Article "Encyclopédistes," *Encyclopedia of the Social Sciences,* The Macmillan Co., New York, 1937; Vol. V, p. 530. *Cf.,* also, Schapiro, *op. cit.,* Ch. III.

change. A fundamental tension developed out of the economic shock caused by the First World War. A symptom of that tension was the world-wide withdrawal from foreign trade which took place after that war, a withdrawal that was greatly intensified during the depression of the 'thirties. The American Pure Food Act of 1906 that was passed to protect consumers against adulterated or contaminated food, is an instance of a corrected abuse. The deliberate acceptance of socialism in England in 1945 illustrates the peaceful acceptance of a radical change, while the Russian Revolution of 1918 exemplifies the violent breaking of an old order.

SLOW AND CONTINUOUS REFORMIST CHANGE

The sources of instability within an economic system have so far been discussed in reference to drastic and fundamental changes which may occur either through deliberate though peaceful adaptation or through violent revolution, or—more rarely—through forceful imposition from without. But economic systems are susceptible not only to drastic reform,[7] whether by violence or not, but also to piecemeal reform and to a powerful evolutionary development.

The forces working for piecemeal reform are similar to those responsible for the more sweeping overturns; groups feel themselves frustrated or subject to discrimination and therefore, with or without the assistance of the intellectual, act to bring pressure against some point within the system rather than against the system itself. The labor movement is a conspicuous illustration; and any pressure group, whether seeking to redress a grievance or simply to improve its position, and whether officially recognized or working under cover,[8] plays this role. Any such group which has sufficient strength

[7] Any drastic social change becomes accepted as a reform after the event. For example, a large and influential women's organization in the United States proudly incorporates the term *Revolution* in its official title, although the social philosophy of its members often recalls that of the Tories who fled the new United States after 1783.

[8] Pressure groups are conspicuous in, but not confined to, democracies. The Guelphs and the Ghibellines in Renaissance Italy were pressure groups which took the form of warring factions; cliques of courtiers at despotic courts are pressure groups; and the factions which inevitably emerge even within contemporary totalitarian systems are also pressure groups. It is probable that Fritz Thyssen's fall from Nazi grace was less the result of any refusal to accept fascism than the consequence of the

and whose purposes and methods appear to be in conformity with, rather than alien to, the folkways of the society in which it operates, is continually bringing about changes. The American system, for example, has been a business system in the sense that business enterprise has been presumed to be the cornerstone of material welfare and the carrier of economic progress. The result has been that business pressures, as a rule, have been accepted as consistent with the logic of the American system, while upstream pressures resisted by business have met greater resistance. For a long time business could control output in order to protect prices without arousing nearly the clamor caused by labor unions seeking to protect wages by essentially the same device—the control of the supply of labor. If Professor Slichter is right in predicting that the American economy will become laboristic,[9] we may expect the pressures exerted by labor to become accepted while those opposed to labor will be shrugged off, if weak, and cried down, if powerful. This does not mean that no pressures running counter to the generally dominant ones ever succeed—witness the Anti-Trust Acts that were passed despite the power of business at the time they were passed, and such labor legislation as the Taft-Hartley Act that was passed, not when labor was weak, but when it was strong.

Exactly the same thing takes place in an authoritarian regime, although official repression of dissident elements forces dissidence underground, with the result that when it does break through, violence from one side or the other may erupt—witness the recurring purges in communist countries. Whatever the façade, there is really no such thing as a genuinely monolithic society in which all interests are in harmony and none in conflict. Some authoritarian societies, such as the Soviet Union, permit, and even encourage, a measure of carefully controlled internal criticism in order both to forestall this sort of development and to inhibit too great a degree of inertia, sloth or complacency on the part of the ruling elements.

---

fact that the pressure he was exerting was strong enough to irritate but not strong enough to overwhelm competing pressures.

[9] *Cf.* Sumner H. Slichter, *The American Economy, Its Problems and Prospects,* New York, 1949; pp. 7–13.

DYNAMIC EVOLUTION

Most societies undergo change which is reflected in the constant passage of legislation or the emission of decrees designed to modify, to improve, or to adapt particular institutions or processes to changing needs. There is, however, a deeper sense in which an economic system is subject to change, a change which includes and explains much of the legislation just mentioned, but which expresses itself in many other ways as well. Economic events have implications, economic groups have programs, economic forces provoke reactions, economic conflicts invite resolution, economic opportunities seek exploitation, and the result is that economic societies evolve.

Contemporary industrial society, for example, reveals contours far different from those marking the economies of the nineteenth century, to say nothing of earlier centuries. A very important element in the evolution undergone by contemporary society has been the ever-larger role played by the business corporation. The joint-stock companies about which Adam Smith wrote in 1776 (the famous East India Company is an example) were cumbrous and unwieldy institutions for which Smith saw little future, except in activities like supplying a city with water, where operations could be reduced to sheer routine. Contemporary corporations are both powerful and efficient, but they did not become so until the legal procedure for incorporation was made easy and, above all, until stockholders were accorded limited liability. These two important legal steps, taken early in the nineteenth century by both England and the United States, and later by other countries, were followed by other legislation extending greater and greater freedom to the corporation, particularly in the countries named. That legislation itself, however, was a reaction to deeper forces, such as the increasing need for capital by the efficient business unit. Those requirements, themselves, arose out of the Industrial Revolution and the political, social, and economic institutions which both generated it and followed from it. The development of the corporation, in turn, has culminated in the present day in the dominance of "big business," which, in its turn, is forcing changes in the responsibilities of government, in the organization and behavior of labor, and in the implications of economic individualism.

Every modern industrial society, however organized, is subject to evolutionary pressures arising out of changing technology, mounting social tensions, and developing governmental intervention.   Every such society is therefore "dynamic."   Whether or not this dynamic quality is a source of instability depends upon the adaptability of the system and upon its ability to assuage the tensions created by change itself.   The emergence of tensions is always characteristic of a dynamic system, even though the degree of exploitation may be far less than in a static society.   In a static society men are accustomed to their "place" and things go on as they apparently always have, with the result that the possibility of individual, let alone class, advancement by any means at all is remote and sometimes scarcely realized.[10] The stability of a dynamic system depends also upon its capacity to turn whatever forces may be present to the needs of the system: in other words, to master them.   A sketchy discussion of some of these forces may make this clear.

(1) The basic industries of the modern economy, whether capitalist, socialist, or communist, require expensive and intricate capital equipment; they need to be operated steadily and at a rate close to capacity if they are to be operated economically; and to a constantly increasing degree they require integration among themselves in order that each may be assured both an outlet for its products and a steady and dependable inflow of raw materials and component parts which will neither fall short of requirements nor clog the channels of distribution.   Each requires an elaborate hierarchy of directors, managers, and foremen who, in their individual and mutual relationships, resemble the civil service bureaucracy of the modern state.[11] Each of these industries, moreover, is responsible directly and indirectly for a significant proportion of the jobs upon which modern man depends for his living.   A collapse of any one of these industries has a threefold and cumulative effect upon the economy in which it operates: it throws its own workers out of employment, it narrows the market for the raw materials and parts it normally purchases and thereby creates unemployment "behind" it, and it deprives its customers of supplies and by so doing may create unem-

---

[10] Ancient Babylonia seems to have been static, at least to an amateur, yet the possibility of tension certainly was there: "The free labourers were in all probability in some ways the worst off of the population, for their pay rarely amounted to more than their daily food, and they were not entitled to the protection which the slave received from his master. . . . The Babylonians had a most modern idea of 'law and order,' and to this was no doubt due their commercial stability which survived all wars and conquests unimpaired."   (H. R. Hall, *The Ancient History of the Near East,* The Macmillan Co., New York, 1927; p. 204.)

[11] *Cf.* Kurt Wiedenfeld, *Kapitalismus und Beamtentum,* Berlin, 1932; *passim.*

ployment "in front of" it.   To be stable, every economy characterized by modern industrialism must keep its industries running.

(2) Again, modern industrialism implies a degree of interdependence which necessarily limits individual freedom to establish or abandon enterprises at will or to conduct them according to the whim of their operators. This has been reflected in the United States in severe governmental limitation upon the economic freedom of industries deemed to be "affected with a public interest" and in more and more sheer regulation of other industries. Suppose, now, this process of making explicit the necessity for fitting essential and "strategic" [12] industries into a common mold—one in which their mutual responsibilities and functions become socially defined—should arouse tensions.   Suppose those tensions arise among groups which see their independence threatened or which suspect that this process represents a turn away from the "right" or "natural" economic order.   We can then say that an element of instability has been introduced into the system.

(3) Furthermore, this very interdependence results in a heightened vulnerability to change itself.   The introduction of the railroad certainly injured both the canal and stagecoach "industries" in nineteenth-century America but the country was able to withstand this injury, partly because its effects were limited and partly because economic development itself was proceeding rapidly enough to absorb displaced resources relatively easily. But as the economy evolved, two things happened.   The amount of capital fixed in particular industries, which themselves were becoming tied increasingly tightly into a common mesh, increased to such an extent that the financial loss threatened by a technological development that might force the premature scrapping of equipment became steadily greater.   Also, as the country appeared to be "filled in" by past industrialization, some of the more obvious opportunities for re-employing resources which had been thrown out of employment by change appeared themselves to be exhausted.[13]

A point is reached, in other words, where the impact of change becomes more severe with respect to its financial cost, and employment of resources, and to its general, though surely short-run, effect upon the economy as a

[12] "A factor may be said to have strategic importance if it has real power to control other factors, and to determine the general character of the result; and it has peculiar strategic importance if, in addition, we have power to control it . . ."   Cf. J. M. Clark, *Strategic Factors in Business Cycles,* National Bureau of Economic Research, New York, 1934; pp. 6–7.
[13] Cf. Appendix, pp. 94–106, for a discussion of the thesis that the American economy is, or shortly may be, threatened by stagnation of this sort.

whole. If atomic energy should ever displace coal or if the light metals become generally used in place of steel, an economy which hitherto had been based upon coal and steel would face a more difficult transitional period than did the economy in which the automobile replaced the horse.

(4) Finally—as a fourth but by no means completing illustration—to the extent that automatic processes and subdivided operations become increasingly characteristic of machine-dominated industry, their impact upon the worker leads to a peculiar paradox. He becomes increasingly insignificant as an individual, yet his role in the machine process takes on added significance by virtue of the intensified sensitivity of the manufacturing process to any interruption in the smooth and carefully proportioned flow of materials and parts. The man with a monkey wrench is anonymous until he throws it into the machinery.

To the degree that this need for disciplined labor is imposed upon industry by the very structure and logic of industry, society has two choices. It may attempt to develop a class of worker so completely adapted to routine, repetitive and monotonous tasks that initiative, independence, and responsibility become bred out of him,[14] which in general was the pattern essayed by fascist states; or society must attempt such a broadening of democracy that workers assigned to routine operations both understand their functional importance in the economy which gives them employment, and have also opportunities outside their work for rounding out their lives according to patterns which they have had some hand in selecting. To do nothing exposes society to the danger of developing a frustrated and dissatisfied working class feeling increasingly apart and resentful of the society in which they live and thereby creating a tension which may ultimately imperil the structure of that society itself.

These are but instances of the kinds of problem which follow in the wake of developing industrialism. Their impact upon different forms of industrial organization will obviously vary, as will be seen when particular systems are discussed in greater detail. But any economic system is exposed to hazards, some of them inherited from the past, some appearing as the system moves into the future. A new system, whether established by bullet, ballot, or even by inertia, may slough off many of the tensions which the past has bequeathed to it, but like an infant industry or a kitten, it will find that birth has its own hazards which it may or may not survive. An established order,

[14] For a fictional picture of a society of this sort, cf. Aldous Huxley, *Brave New World,* Garden City, 1932.

unless completely paralyzed like the French before 1789 or the Russian before 1917, has survived the perils of birth and it may not be confronted with the risks of drastic improvization; but it has the future with its dangers before it, and it confronts these with both the strength of its tradition and whatever weaknesses its history may have generated. A static society is free from the risks of change, but also without its adventure and opportunity; and in any event, the few static societies that exist in today's world (the Arab states are an example) are primitive and backward. They may also be short-lived, because their static character renders them vulnerable to penetration, peaceful or otherwise, by states that have vital force precisely because they are dynamic.

In the last analysis, the stability of a dynamic society—and this is no contradiction in terms—depends upon its capacity for ordered and controlled adaptation, its ability to satisfy both the material and the moral needs of its members, and upon the courage, intelligence, and self-restraint of its dominant elements.

PART TWO

Capitalism and Industrialism

3

The Rationale of Capitalism

APITALISM, like other going economic systems, has been
subject to attack since its inception. In our own day
the attack upon capitalism has become so formidable
that some of its defenders have attempted appeasement rather than counter-
attack and that appeasement, in part, has taken the form of finding new and
more benign names for an old dog.   Not everyone has liked this process; in
1943 the President of the United States Chamber of Commerce had this to
say about it:

> I do not hesitate to say that the word upon which to fix the national mind
> at this time is simply, outrightly and frankly, *capitalism*. . . . We are too mealy-
> mouthed about the basic principle of our economic system.   We have been
> intimidated by all the tirades against "bloated capitalists" and "swollen profits."
> We fear that the word capitalism is unpopular.   So we take refuge in a nebulous
> phrase and talk about the "Free Enterprise System."   And we even run to cover
> in the folds of the flag and talk about the "American Way of Life." [1]

This argument about a word may have the justification that the word
itself appears to have been coined by enemies of the system for which the
word stands.[2]   The term "capitalism" is a label, and like all labels it carries

---

[1] Eric Johnston in the *Readers' Digest*, February, 1943, quoted by C. E. Ayres,
"Capitalism in Retrospect," *Southern Economic Journal*, April, 1943; p. 293.
[2] Both the *Oxford English Dictionary* and the *Encyclopedia of the Social Sciences*

connotations of which dictionaries are innocent.   As exercise is one thing
to a swimmer and another to a sybarite, so capitalism is what men make of
it.   Men make different things of it: to some it seems a setting within which
energy is released, initiative is stimulated, and the key to nature's treasures
released; to others capitalism is a prison to whose inmates the treadmill
is the only means of bare survival.   To earlier writers the clue to understanding could be found by piercing the veil of money; today, the veil of
interpretation must also be pierced.

That veil is thick but it can be pierced, and doing so reveals something
which purports to be a description of the actual and prevailing institutions
which comprise "capitalism" in any country at any specific time.   Because
a description is factual and facts can be verified, it is tempting at this point
to forget that description itself involves judgment and interpretation.
Which facts are significant?   In the American presidential election of 1952,
the domestic press emphasized the unprecedented number of votes cast, but
the Russian press was reported to have stressed the number of potential
voters who never appeared at the polls.   Both apathy and interest unquestionably existed, but the interpretation of their respective importance involves
judgment.   So with capitalism; what we do with the facts of high national
income, a depreciated dollar, an almost full volume of employment, an
enormous national debt, television in nearly every home that wants it, and assets yielding fixed incomes that seem with the passing of the years increasingly
insubstantial—what we make of these is largely determined by our presuppositions, and presuppositions are simply unconscious interpretations emerging
through the screen of our biases.   This is not peculiar to capitalism; the label
affixed to any economic system carries a purely specious appearance of
factual descriptiveness, but its connotation is the result of usually unconscious or unrealized screening.   Since screening is essentially a process of
separating, its significance lies in identifying what is separated from what:
whether the "bad" is abstracted from the "good" or the other way about.

What men think about an economic system, accordingly, depends upon
whether its essence, its rationale, emerges in their minds above or below
the mental screen through which the phenomena which seem to be characteristic of the system are sifted.   A screen is a pattern whose use consists

---

suggest that the word was given currency by socialists.   It is certainly true that until
less than a century ago the capitalist system was analyzed under the perhaps vain-
glorious title *Principles of Political Economy;* in 1867 Marx analyzed the system under
the title *Capital.*

either in cutting facts to its shape, or in measuring the conformity of facts to its design.   The rationale used to justify capitalism, or any other system, is a pattern regarded as something to which facts ought to be made to conform, or as something to which facts will of themselves increasingly conform, or—at worst—as something to which facts are regrettably ceasing to conform.   Just the opposite is true of the rationale used to condemn a system: facts should not conform to it, facts may regrettably be tending increasingly to conform, or they may happily be diverging from it more and more.

A rationale is therefore a sort of idealized picture of a society—idealized both because, like pure communism, the picture may have no counterpart in the real world, and because the picture may be regarded as something either toward which or away from which the world is moving; in any event the picture abstracts away from those elements in an existing society which appear unimportant, irrelevant, or imperfect.   The earlier idealized picture of a *laissez-faire* economy was forward-looking because the economic system of the time was regulatory and restrictive in a manner which reformers believed inhibited prosperity, both individual and national; the task, therefore, was to move *forward* into an era of greater freedom.   In this sense Turgot wrote:

What the State owes its citizens is the elimination of the restrictions which hamper their industry or which interfere with their use of the goods which their industry produces.   As long as these obstacles remain, whatever advantages they may still have will not reduce general poverty. . . . Even though men are mightily interested in whatever favors you may wish to secure for them, let them alone (*laissez-les faire*); there is the fundamental principle. . . . Men have sacred rights which are rooted in the very structure of society, rights which are derived from and are based upon the same laws which protect their property and their freedom.[3]

The contemporary idealized picture of capitalism tends somewhat to be backward-looking, because those holding it believe our society to have evolved *away from* the fundamental principles which assure well-being, affluence, and a thriving commerce.   For example,

 . . . let us consider the more general problem of the degeneration of competitive capitalism occasioned by the growth of *monopoly* and *interventionism* . . . this development is largely the result of the disintegration of the state and

[3] A. R. J. Turgot, article "Fondation," written about 1756 for the French *Encyclopedia; cf.* Turgot, *Oeuvres,* edited by M. Eugene Daire, Paris, 1844; Vol. I, pp. 305–306, 308.

of the exploitation of weak governments by sectional interests and pressure groups, for it has now become obvious that the working of competition presupposes a strong state which will with severity and impartiality provide the necessary legal and institutional framework of the competitive market.[4]

Let us now turn to that idealized picture of capitalism—there seems no real reason to avoid the term—which is used to justify the system; the opposing picture will be discussed in the chapter on socialism.

THE CAPITALISTIC REACTION AGAINST MERCANTILISM

The capitalistic system of free enterprise emerged in the late eighteenth and early nineteenth centuries because then intellectual criticisms of the old order reinforced and gave point to the pressure exerted by the rising commercial and industrial classes for a social and political environment in which their aptitudes, skills, and activities might have free play. That old order, now generally called mercantilism, had many of the elements of capitalism, but it did not have the very important one of individual freedom of enterprise. The mercantilists were avid for capital in the form of gold and silver; they sought a constantly expanding market, especially in international trade; they fostered manufacturing, primarily for the sake of exports; and they were intensely competitive, although the unit of competition was thought of as the state rather than the enterprise, and the enterprise rather than the individual. The intensity of the international competition for markets, for assured sources of raw materials, and for "treasure" compelled the state to bring under its control every factor and every force which might buttress its competitive position, exactly as today's competition between firms or industries compels the competitive unit to do its utmost to bring under its own control, to plan, even to absorb if need be, everything which may enable it to reduce costs, to retain or extend its market, or to assure it access to scarce and much sought resources. The essential difference between mercantilism and competitive capitalism was not the presence or absence of economic freedom *per se,* although that was a difference, and it counted. The really important difference, however, lay in the size and character of the economic

[4] *Cf.* Wilhelm Roepke, *International Economic Disintegration,* The Macmillan Co., New York, 1942; p. 5. Italics in the original. *Cf.,* also, the first chapter significantly entitled "The Abandoned Road," in F. A. Hayek, *The Road to Serfdom,* Chicago, 1944.

units which in *each* system were free to compete with one another, but which also in *each* system attempted to restrict the freedom of subordinate units. In mercantilism, that unit was the state itself; under capitalism, it came to be the firm.

The mercantilist era was also a warring era, and warfare, unless it is on so small a scale as to be waged from the *surplus* resources of an economy, as the colonial and peripheral wars of nineteenth-century Europe tended to be, is a most powerful ground for economic regimentation.

Competition itself is a form of warfare, although its severity and character depend upon the size and significance of the competing units and on the degree of their subordination to a more inclusive authority. The only real curb upon the conduct of war is expediency—international law to the contrary notwithstanding. When the competing and sometimes warring units are business corporations, the law of the land, whatever it may be, may impose some limitations upon "unfair" competitive methods, although even here inter-corporate competition sometimes is scarcely distinguishable from overt warfare. The early heyday of the Standard Oil Company is a sort of *locus classicus* for that form of aggressive competition:

> Nothing then remained but to drive out the small competitors. Rockefeller of Standard Oil had already adopted as his motto: "The coal-oil business belongs to us," evidently believing that some sort of divine right was involved. An extremely efficient and economical system was evolved. Information concerning the business of other concerns was obtained through railroad agents, stool pigeons, and bribery. Then every move of the competitor could be forestalled. Prices were cut below the cost of production in competing markets and the losses were recovered with interest elsewhere. Agents of the company were ordered to get control of the markets in their districts by any means they found most effective. Nearly every method was employed except arson, while accusations were made even on that score.[5]

The purpose of such competition is indistinguishable from the purpose of actual warfare: control, absorption, or elimination of the competitor. When the competing units are simply individuals the contest may be exactly as bitter, but its character is less violent, partly because the individual acting alone does not carry the weight, partly because the circumstances of individual trade compel him to compete by pleasing the customer rather than by monopolizing the market, and partly because the small individual operator is unable to influence price. Being small, that operator is incapable

---

[5] *Cf.* Fred A. Shannon, *Economic History of the People of the United States,* The Macmillan Co., New York, 1934; pp. 502–503.

of glutting his own market, with the result that for him competition means attempting to increase efficiency rather than to obliterate his competitor.

The mercantilist states were embedded in a matrix of existing or potential warfare, but the pressure of war then assumed a simpler form than that of today. Sixteenth- and seventeenth-century warfare was not mechanized, and consequently success depended less upon industrial production than upon the ability to pay an army. The result was that the accumulation of treasure—gold and silver at the disposal of the state—seemed crucial; and since few states had adequate indigenous resources of gold and silver, the only means of securing treasure appeared to be a state's competitive ability in foreign trade; and this, in turn, depended upon its capacity to develop as extensive a manufacturing industry as possible and one in which the spread between costs and prices should be maximized.

It was largely this issue upon which the struggle between mercantilism and economic freedom turned. Adam Smith, who systematized but did not completely originate the salient criticism of the old and the vindication of the emergent economic order, significantly entitled his great work, *An Inquiry into the Nature and Causes of the Wealth of Nations;* he maintained that the mercantilists were wrong, not because they wished to make the nation wealthy, but because they chose the wrong way to make it so and because they had too narrow a conception of what wealth is. By controlling economic activity and by imposing from above the pattern by which enterprise should operate, the mercantilists, Smith believed, inhibited the full release of nascent productive forces, simply because opportunity and initiative were confined. Merely to point this out, however, would have achieved nothing, since the great question revolved about the manner in which an economic system could show the fruits of organization if deliberate organization were abandoned. Competition being a form of warfare, would not unrestricted competition within a state come to resemble a war of each against all, with chaos, confusion, and mutual frustration the result? After all, the medieval economy out of which mercantilism emerged had controlled prices, imposed standards, determined the conditions of work, and restrained usury—all for the sake of an ethical principle of social organization; the mercantilist state had regulated the economy in the interests of its own power and prosperity. It is important to understand that the strong pull which *laissez-faire* still exerts upon many minds does so only because *laissez-faire* has been tried, and because *laissez-faire* accompanied, if it did not occasion, an amazing development of material production and welfare, and that it did so without tearing society apart.   Before that trial was made, no one could point to a society in which the economy had not been very tightly regulated, and consequently the task of proving that the absence of control need not spell anarchy was an uphill one.   Thus, before *laissez-faire* could become acceptable, it had to prove that economic freedom carried with it its own form of control; and its early defenders were not so naive as to deny the necessity of controlling unbridled self-interest.   Their answer lay in positing a social, political, and economic framework within which the expression of self-interest could be turned to social ends because the satisfaction of social ends was the only way in which self-interest, in a really competitive society, could be gratified.

ADAM SMITH'S DEFENSE OF LAISSEZ FAIRE

Here is how Adam Smith himself posed the question and then answered it:

The interests of the dealers . . . in any particular branch of trade or manufactures is always in some respects different from, and even opposite to, that of the public.   To widen the market and to narrow the competition, is always the interest of the dealers.   To widen the market may frequently be agreeable enough to the interest of the public; but to narrow the competition must always be against it, and can serve only to enable the dealers, by raising their profits above what they naturally would be, to levy, for their own benefit, an absurd tax upon the rest of their fellow citizens.   The proposal of any new law or regulation of commerce which comes from this order ought always to be listened to with great precaution, and ought never to be adopted till after having been long and carefully examined, not only with the most scrupulous, but with the most suspicious attention.   It comes from an order of men whose interest is never exactly the same with that of the public, who have generally an interest to deceive and even to oppress the public, and who accordingly have, upon many occasions, both deceived and oppressed it . . .

[However] Every individual is continually exerting himself to find out the most advantageous employment for whatever capital he can command.   It is his own advantage, indeed, and not that of the society which he has in view. But the study of his own advantage naturally, or rather necessarily, leads him to prefer that employment which is most advantageous to the society. . . . [As] every individual, therefore, endeavors as much as he can both to employ his capital in the support of domestic industry, and so to direct that industry that its produce may be of the greatest value; every individual necessarily labours to render the annual revenue of the society as great as he can.   He generally, indeed, neither intends to promote the public interest, nor knows how much he is promoting it. . . . He intends only his own security; and by directing that industry in such a manner as its produce may be of the greatest value, he intends only his own gain, and he is in this, as in many other cases, led by an invisible hand to promote an end which was no part of his intention. Nor is it always the worse for the society that it was no part of it. By pursuing his own interest he frequently promotes that of the society more effectively than when he really intends to promote it. . . .

All systems either of preference or of restraint, therefore, being thus completely taken away, the obvious and simple system of natural liberty establishes itself of its own accord. Every man, as long as he does not violate the laws of justice, is left perfectly free to pursue his own interest his own way, and to bring both his industry and capital into competition with those of any other man, or order of men. The sovereign is completely discharged from a duty, in the attempting to perform which he must always be exposed to innumerable delusions, and for the proper performance of which no human wisdom or knowledge could ever be sufficient; the duty of superintending the industry of private people, and of directing it towards the employments most suitable to the interests of the society. According to the system of natural liberty, the sovereign has only three duties to attend to: . . . first, the duty of protecting the society from the violence and invasion of other independent societies; secondly, the duty of protecting, as far as possible, every member of the society from the injustice or oppression of every other member of it, or the duty of establishing an exact administration of justice; and, thirdly, the duty of erecting and maintaining certain public institutions which it can never be for the interest of any individual, or small number of individuals, to erect and maintain; because the profit could never repay the expense to any individual or small number of individuals, though it may frequently do much more than repay it to a great society.[6]

The obvious and simple system that Smith suggested is not uncontrolled; it is very much controlled, only the control is exerted by no human will and enforced by no visible hand. Economic objectives are met simply by letting society itself reward with its patronage those who produce what society wishes, and punish by its neglect those who fail, while the responsibility of the state is limited to the performance of those things which individuals either cannot or will not do for themselves.

The system of natural liberty seems so obvious and so simple that one is tempted to wonder why its reign should have been so long delayed, and why, above all, societies which have tasted its simplicities should ever be induced to abandon them. In large part the answer lies in the dependence of capital-

[6] Adam Smith, *An Inquiry into the Nature and Causes of the Wealth of Nations,* G. P. Putnam's Sons, New York, 1904, Cannan edition; Vol. I, pp. 250, 419, 421; Vol. II, pp. 184–185.

ism upon certain preconditions without which it cannot operate with efficiency and to the full satisfaction of its members.   In the following discussion only the preconditions which are more or less peculiar to capitalism
will be considered.   Other factors, such as a system of law and the necessity of public order, which are essential to any system, will be taken for
granted.

PRECONDITIONS OF CAPITALISM

Private Property

Everyone knows that capitalism is based upon private property, but the
actual structure of this dependence may not be so obvious.   Consider,
for example, an individual who operates an enterprise upon leased land,
with borrowed capital and hired labor.   So far as that is so, the entrepreneur
clearly owns nothing but his own ability, and that could hold under any
system.   Moreover, for such an entrepreneur, his landlord, his creditors,
and his labor force—to say nothing of the tax collector—have a prior claim
to the greater part of his gross earnings.   There is nothing, in fact, in the
logic of the system to prevent individuals from behaving capitalistically even
though society collectively owned all land and capital equipment, provided
it were willing to lease these on standard terms to individual entrepreneurs.
Interestingly enough, something like this, although without involving complete collectivization of resources, has been suggested as a method to insure
full employment and economic justice without going all the way into socialism.   The suggestion consists in the proposal to provide a contrived *milieu*
in which plant managers would act *as if* they were full-blown capitalist entrepreneurs even though, without necessarily realizing it, they would be acting
in accordance with a central and designed plan.   The eighteenth-century
invisible hand has produced a twentieth-century shadow.   Adam Smith's
three functions of government would still be performed, but with the difference that the performance would no longer be neutral; the price mechanism
would be policed to *induce* individuals to pursue ends no part of their original
intentions.   The assertion is even made that such a system would have fewer
individual controls than the rigged capitalism under which Americans now
live.   Thus,

The business of the Ministry of Economic Planning is to establish the appropriate rules and to see that they are followed and that the price mechanism is kept in operation.   It is by promulgating and maintaining the general rules consciously directed toward the optimum operation of the whole economy that the *controlled economy* is distinguishable from the *uncontrolled economy* which does not so establish the general rules.   The uncontrolled economy will indeed generally show a more luxurious and complex growth of *particular* regulations. These naturally arise from attempts to correct particular failures resulting from the absence of any general plan for the economy as a whole.[7]

Paradoxically enough, the fact that private ownership of resources has happened to co-exist with capitalism may have obscured the real significance of private property in the system.   What is important is that the capitalist entrepreneur should have responsibility and command over the resources he uses, regardless of who owns them; and that he be rewarded in proportion to his skill in using those resources effectively and to ends revealed to him through the market.   The average owner (that is, the stockholder) frequently if not generally has little to say, and, indeed, shows little interest in how this responsibility shall be exercised, but that fact does not subtract from the capitalistic character of the enterprise in which he invests.   Capitalistic enterprise must have control over, but need not assume ownership of, the resources it utilizes.   The essence of capitalism lies in the assumption by the enterprise of the responsibility for determining both what it shall produce and how it shall do so.   Interferences like zoning ordinances or anti-pollution laws are thus really restrictions upon the raw forces of capitalism, and the fact that we are generally used to them and accept them and the fact that in themselves they are not serious restrictions should not prevent our recognizing these as the thin edge of a wedge the thick end of which is such things as priorities, compulsory delivery orders, and socially rigged markets which prevent entrepreneurs from making their own decisions.

The importance of private property for capitalism consists in the autonomy of its ownership.   Capitalism is individualistic in the sense, among others, that individuals are both permitted and expected to do as they please with their own.   They may hoard or consume, squander or invest, themselves employ or entrust to others to employ whatever it may be that they possess.   The textbooks define profit as the reward of ownership, and the fact that it can be so regarded reflects, quite simply, the belief that a system which induces rather than coerces individuals to make social use of their

---

[7] *Cf.* A. P. Lerner, *The Economics of Control,* The Macmillan Co., New York, 1944; pp. 64–65.   Italics in the original.

private property is a system in which private property will be socially utilized in the best interests of all.

Rationality

If the invisible hand is to guide the individual to promote an end which is no part of his intention, the individual must be capable of following that guidance; that is to say, he must be rational. He must be able to "smell out" a chance for profit; he must know, or be able to find out, where to lay his hands on necessary resources; he must be able to combine and utilize these to maximum effect; and he must be continually aware of what his competitors are doing, and continually sensitive to changes in the market. That is all obvious and simple and need not be belabored. What is, perhaps, not so obvious is the peculiar meaning rationality must take on if the system is to work. Rationality in this context means complete acceptance by society of differential profits as adequate guides to social needs as well as the individual's capacity to make the appropriate responses. Some social reformer might decide that society ought to consume vegetable cocktails in place of sherry, and by manufacturing them endeavor to bring about that reform. His enterprise could be managed with complete efficiency, but if society mulishly maintained a preference for sherry, neither the enterprise nor the reformer would be capitalistically rational. In other words, it is capitalistically irrational to believe that people do not generally know what is good for them or that they should not have what they think they want.

Again, rationality means acceptance of gain as the generally over-riding economic good—and in our society it usually is. Any withholding of resources, for example, is usually met by a would-be purchaser's raising his bid, even if it leads to a black market—than which nothing is more capitalistically rational—on the implicit assumption that no one will resist, or even ought to resist, a sufficiently high bid. If a sufficiently large number of resource-holders refused to make their resources available to entrepreneurs on the ground that to exploit them would make the countryside ugly, or because industrialism cuts off man's roots in God's earth, or because the factory system breeds slums, or for any other seemingly adequate reason, the system simply would break down. Such attitudes, also, are capitalistically irrational.

The rational individual, then, responds to the lure of gain as to a magnet and lets nothing else becloud his vision. His rationality selects his occupation and determines his procedure; and the rationality of the *system* lies in the purported coordination of independent individual decisions, taken in response to prices automatically generated in a free market, which the free price system brings about.

Mobility

Not only individuals but resources as well must be capable of responding to changes in taste or technique. This means, again simply and obviously, that labor can be drawn both to the occupations and to the places where economic exigencies may call it, and without the use of coercion; that capital can be withdrawn from unprofitable uses and placed in profitable employment; that entrepreneurs are alert to opportunities for producing new things or for producing old things in new and unfamiliar ways; that plants, in a word, can be "converted" whenever the need arises.

Mobility means still more than this: it means freedom. It means not only that men are free to move about from place to place without hindrance other than their own physical or financial limitations, but that men accept, despite their emotional or sentimental ties, the possibility of movement as something affecting *them*. One of the more astonishing manifestations of the vitality of early capitalism is the fact that, in the face of the traditions of stability and permanence in the pre-capitalist era and in spite of man's propensity to sink roots and form attachments and adhesions, so many deserted villages, abandoned farms, and ghost towns appeared as very present evidence of capitalist man's readiness to "cut the hauser and be away." This adaptability of early capitalism helped it to survive.

Mobility also means legal and social freedom to essay new tasks, to enter freely any occupation or industry for which men deem themselves fitted—in short, to do economically whatever men please without restraint, let, or hindrance. Mobility also means that men must abide by its consequences, must get out of unsuccessful enterprises rather than seek artificial protection of them, and must accept mobility for others as well as for themselves. Once in an industry, men must resist the temptation to deny admittance to potential competitors. In this sense, the tariff, the closed union or shop, and the passport are fundamentally inconsistent with the logic of the capitalist system, and one reason why capitalism is now faltering is the refusal of many of its beneficiaries to accept its full implications.

Internal Autonomy

In the ideally functioning capitalism of free enterprise we find that (1) the consumer is king, (2) competition is the goad, (3) profit is the goal, and (4) price is the guide.   In varying degrees the autonomy of all must remain intact if the system is to operate in harmony with its underlying principles.   By autonomy, we mean that the consumer is both free and able to exercise his uncoerced judgment, that competition is freely permitted within accepted standards of decency and fair play, and that both profit and price are spontaneously determined in the market rather than by the whim of a planner or by the pull of a fixer.

The consumer is king.   The consumer is king because only through the effective demand of consumers in the market can producers receive any clue to where profit lies and thus be guided to promote that social end which may be no part of their intention.   Much has recently been written to show that the consumer in fact is no king, that he buys by whim, so that whatever sovereignty he may have is exercised too capriciously for producers to be guided by it, that he is obedient to advertising and has accordingly abdicated sovereignty, that as the producer has extended his control over the market the consumer's demesne has become a limited monarchy indeed. This is not really fundamental, for tractable as the consumer may be, the purse strings remain within his or her power to close.   The fact that today's consumer prefers for his breakfast some kind of toasted, exploded, or otherwise tortured grain to oatmeal has inexorably been reflected in the kind of food which is produced and brought to market.   His essential sovereignty remains, no matter how many of its functions may be delegated, as long as goods are produced for a market in which the direction of expenditure is free.   The lady of the house does not *have* to buy a Fuller brush.

The scepter of this sovereignty is money, and sovereignty is impaired to the extent that the scepter is shortened through a shrinkage of income or its movement constricted by any roping off of the area in which it may wave. That is why, despite the criticism by physiocrats and liberals of overemphasis upon money and despite the sense that money is a means rather than an end, so much attention has been paid to it by economists.   The importance of money is not limited to capitalism, but money has nevertheless an importance in capitalism which is peculiar to that system: it is the means by which the most necessary and least invidious regulation of economic activity is exercised.   If, under capitalism, the monetary system breaks down or is abused, the least that can happen is its replacement by some spontaneous or informal substitute, like the cigarette-currency which appeared in Europe following the Second World War.   Unfortunately, all too often something more happens, usually because individuals feel themselves incapable of continuing to act with capitalistic rationality and seek some sort of very uncapitalistic protection or security.   When, for example, money loses too much of its value by reason of inflation, pressure arises to arrest the process artificially by the public control, or fixation, of prices.   Then, also, dissatisfaction with the size and purchasing power of incomes determined by the judgment of the capitalistic market of what a man's services are worth, leads to the application of pressure to adjust incomes by *other* than market processes—by such processes as legislative determination of minimum wages, or by executive definition of what farmers' incomes ought to be.

Under deflation, money acquires too much value—so much so that it becomes intolerably hard to acquire, and the same attempt sets in to bypass the economic system, or to keep it operating by repeated priming of its pump, simply because of disbelief that the system can continue to run by itself, or because of conviction that it does not run satisfactorily.   Demands then mount for protection through tariff, even though tariffs themselves are inconsistent with the capitalist precondition of mobility and impede the operation of competition—the essential regulatory force of capitalism. Others insist that production be undertaken for use rather than profit, as if really capitalistic production were undertaken for anything but use.   Boondoggling and pyramid-building are unlikely to be demanded by consumers in a healthy capitalism; if they were, their provision would, by definition, be for use.

Consumer sovereignty, in other words, cannot be exercised if money is unstable, simply because production is then undertaken for other reasons than the satisfaction of consumers' autonomous needs, and any other initiation of economic activity is essentially uncapitalistic.   It is for this reason that the one kind of thoroughgoing regulation by public authority that is perfectly consistent with capitalism, and indeed necessary for its survival, is the regulation of money and all that is commonly used for money.

Competition is the goad.   Competition is the goad in the capitalist system, because without it an entrepreneur could easily be tempted into what William Godwin happily called the "allurements of sloth."   Moreover, no other force than competition presumably exists to force the maintenance of minimum standards and—under favorable circumstances—to prevent the exploitation of insecure or exposed groups within the economy. In a strictly individualistic economy, competition among producers for resources and markets holds up the prices of the former and protects buyers in the latter, while competition among workers or among suppliers of capital and land, holds costs to a level which can be met by the normally efficient enterprise. Let it be recalled that to the early defenders of capitalism *laissez-faire* did not mean the absence of control; it meant that competition replaced the state as the primary agent of control. Any impairment of competition, therefore, meant a weakening of control, or, rather, the substitution of planned for automatic control.

Competition as a controlling force is necessarily competition among individuals so numerous that no one of them, and no likely combination among them, can dominate or influence the market; it is not competition among powerfully organized groups. If, for example, both industry and labor organize to restrict competition among their respective members, the labor market and the industry concerned are no longer subject to the autonomous controlling forces which presumably protects each, as well as society, from exploitation. Indeed, the organized bodies may themselves form a united front to bring under control other factors in the market in which they are jointly interested. The building trades in the United States are frequently cited for having done just that. This simply brings out the important point that, for competition as a regulatory device really to be effective, there must be no artificial or contrived inequalities among those who compete. Adam Smith himself stated quite explicitly that the exploitation of labor was largely due to the effective organization of "masters" in the face of ineffective, and repressed organization of labor. Here is another sphere where, under capitalism, the state has a recognized and proper function. If it does not intervene when competition is weakened or distorted, control will inevitably come to be exercised by private groups within the economy, and not necessarily to the public weal. The problem is old; the Romans asked, *Quis custodet ipsos custodes?,* and we use the same words when we ask, Who will police the police?

Profit is the goal. Profit is the goal, but what sort of activity is this goal supposed to elicit? Many contemporary economists refuse to consider profits as the return derived from routine entrepreneurial activities, maintaining, rather, that these are the "wages of management." Profit represents something over and above these. The wages of management constitute a sort of salary for the competent performance of a well-established, comparatively riskless task; profits are the return derived from the successful assumption of risk in projects to which imagination, daring, and energy have contributed.   That is really what the classical economists (the early nine-teenth-century Englishmen who established economics as a science) were speculating about when they wondered about the possibility of profits de-clining as society developed.   For example, one of those economists, David Ricardo, emphasized the consequences of ever-increasing population press-ing harder and harder upon the means of subsistence with the result that the cost of producing food might eventually absorb all profit.   Later econ-omists speculated upon what might happen were expansion and develop-ment to cease, were change to disappear, were society to produce what it needed by established and familiar techniques without the formation of new enterprises or the introduction of new commodities, and with the level of population stabilized and the structure of tastes frozen.   Economic systems of this kind have existed—ancient Egypt is an example—, but descriptions of such systems ring strange to modern ears.   Part of the contemporary criticism of socialism lies in the charge that a socialist state would be likely to assume that drab, unchanging hue, whereas capitalist profit, that dynamic element, provides the incentive to take chances that just might succeed. Profit represents the temptation to break through the fence across which the grass appears greener.

A return, however, over and above the wages of management, may be derived from another source than the successful assumption of risk or ven-ture into change.   A favorably situated enterprise may, and often does, receive profits through exerting some form of monopolistic power.   An enterprise sufficiently powerful may do so both by depressing the prices it pays for resources below the "competitive" level (which it can do in the absence of any competitive, alternative market for these), and by charging a higher than competitive price for its products (which it can do by refusing to produce as much as its customers could effectively demand and which it could technically produce).   This curtailment of supply is possible when firms exist that are powerful enough to dominate the market instead of simply adapting themselves to it.   The existence of that power illustrates the complicated character of such a system as capitalism, which is dynamic, which develops, but whose development in some respects violates the logic of its existence.   Private economic power frustrates the goading effect of competition and weakens the guiding force of price precisely because the guides come under restraint.

Prices are the guide. Prices are the guide. They do for free enterprise what the "Plan" does for a controlled economy. What society wants it will pay for, and what it will pay for it eventually will get.[8] If that guide is to operate effectively, two conditions must exist. *First,* society must be collectively able to make its demand effective: consumers must have incomes adequate to take aggregate supplies off the market, and to do *that* effectively their incomes must be determined in accordance with principles of distribution which assure the stability of the system. How that may be brought about will be discussed later. (See pages 67–68.)

Second, the guide must be really independent. A guide who follows the instructions of those he leads—to take that path rather than this—is no real guide. This means, essentially, that prices emerge *in* the market and that producers respond *to* them without exerting any conscious pressure *over* them. An "administered," controlled or artificially rigid price insulates its fixer from the very forces which are supposed to guide him to the desired end regardless of his original intention. Only autonomous prices can serve this purpose, and autonomous prices emerge only in markets where competition is "pure"—that is, "unalloyed with monopoly elements."[9] More precisely, prices can be autonomous only when no single individual or group of individuals is able to exert any perceptible influence upon the prices of things bought or sold, whether by deliberate action or as an incidental concomitant of ordinary business behavior. It also means that individuals act as individuals rather than in collusion to exert power beyond their individual strength. It is the insignificance of the individual rather than the purity of his motives that is crucial, for, as Adam Smith knew, few men can resist the temptation to monopolize when opportunity is present. By insignificance is meant no more than that the individual's contribution to supply or his augmentation of demand is so small that it passes unnoticed in the mass. Of course, sufficiently sensitive prices would respond proportionately to any change in demand or supply, exactly as a sufficiently sensitive gauge would

[8] "It is, after all, a very rare experience under capitalism to find that something you wish to buy cannot be had at any price." Barbara Wootton, *Plan or No Plan,* New York, 1935; p. 13. That has generally been true, even in times of the most severe material shortages. Black markets then become the capitalistic means of supplying such wants.

[9] Edward Chamberlin, *Theory of Monopolistic Competition,* Cambridge, 1936; p. 6.

measure the addition to the volume of water in a bath tub that can be made with an eye-dropper. But, perhaps fortunately, the price system is not so constructed; if it were, our economy might be even less stable than it now is.

All this is not to say that the much discussed decline of competition, or the existence of price control whether public or private, indicates collapse, for obviously neither does. In the *first* place, the ability to control prices which is enjoyed by many industries is not unlimited. A point is sooner or later reached beyond which further boosts become simply unprofitable; this is no more than the working out of consumers' sovereignty. For the consumer's purse is limited and his wants diversified, and his decision to spend his income this way rather than that is reflected, in the end, in the income statements of the firms which are available to him as sources of supply. What business price control does is to diffuse and distort the guiding force of price rather than to eliminate it. To the extent that an administered price is higher than the competitive, the consumer who pays it has less money to spend on the other things and his pattern of expenditure is correspondingly warped. On the other side, the recipient of the administered and higher price can cast a weighted vote on the market ballot in the degree to which his income is higher than it would otherwise be.

In the *second* place, the average consumer's pattern of expenditure is more or less fixed by custom, so that price manipulation tends to push the distortion to the periphery, leaving the basic structure relatively intact. In other words, in proportion as administered prices are higher than free, consumers will spend less on what to them are non-essentials, but they will endeavor to maintain their consumption of everyday items. In postwar England where the taxation of tobacco has reached extraordinary heights,[10] consumption of tobacco has scarcely diminished at all. This adjustment of purchases to price, however, will not hold for consumers at the extreme ends of the income scale. The very poor must postpone, or even abandon, essential purchases when prices pass beyond their means, while to the very rich price does not matter. The impact of price manipulation, then, depends upon the wealth of society and on the way that wealth is distributed.

In the *third* place, and finally, society itself sometimes finds it necessary to intervene in the process of price formation. The guiding function of free prices is a means rather than an end; it is a means not only of allocating

---

[10] In the spring of 1952 a package of twenty cigarettes, or an ounce of smoking tobacco, could scarcely be had for less than fifty cents; prices went up from there; and these prices were in terms of the dollar which was worth more after the depreciation of the pound.

resources in accordance with the collective desires of consumers expressed
through their effective demand, but also of rewarding individuals in proportion to their contribution to the economic process. If other ends should
supervene, such as the necessity of winning a war rather than pleasing consumers, other means clearly become appropriate. Sometimes even the
conventional means toward the traditional end become ineffective. We
have already seen how an unstable monetary system is inconsistent with the
preconditions of capitalism; we are now in a position to see how it may
render the guiding function of price completely ineffective. Under inflation, for example, people in the aggregate have more money than they can
spend at old prices, because the increase in the supply of money has outrun
any increase in the production of goods and services. Hence the only
people who get satisfied are those who reach the market first, or those who
can offer a premium to get scarce supplies. Individuals who are able to
offer, or match, that premium are rewarded, but the selection of those individuals is left to chance rather than to merit. Since not all prices or incomes change in the same proportion, as inflation progresses the price structure becomes distorted because it progressively fails to register the desires of
the generality of consumers. And since it becomes increasingly difficult,
and finally impossible, for production to keep pace with rising prices (because physical resources are exhaustible, while depreciating money is in-
exhaustible), the guiding function of prices becomes increasingly weak.
Under these conditions, particularly where political democracy prevails, the
free market becomes nugatory and is almost inevitably brought under control.

THE AUTOMATIC FUNCTIONING OF A CAPITALISTIC SYSTEM

The automatic functioning of the capitalistic system at its best can now be
briefly described. Consumers with incomes derived from their activities
as producers, lenders, workers, or sellers, purchase goods and services according to their means and their tastes. They act individually, but their
individual demands are collectively registered by the emptying of shelves
and the filling of cash boxes in the establishments they patronize. If some
goods remain unsold, they must be reduced in price if they are to sell at all,
and this price reduction, if permanent, serves first as a warning and finally
as a compulsion upon dealers to stock their shelves with other things.

Goods in great demand, on the other hand, must somehow be rationed, and rationing takes place by raising their prices, a process entirely consistent with the dealers' self-interest.

Dealers, in turn, adjust their orders with wholesalers, and wholesalers with manufacturers, to accord with the indicated preferences of their customers; in this way, consumers' preferences are reflected, through relative prices and profits, all the way back to the production of raw materials and the primary allocation of resources.

Consumers must have incomes in order to express these preferences. To acquire these, individuals are formally free to select whatever occupations best fit their tastes and aptitudes, but the occupations easiest to enter are those which conform to the pattern expressed in the market balloting of consumers. Most people seek employment in one form or another with the chosen few who operate productive enterprises, and having so decided they are dependent upon the enterprise which employs them unless or until they find better opportunities or the enterprise itself releases them. Others establish enterprises for themselves, and they benefit from them to the extent that they meet market demands without incurring losses. Their efficiency here is at stake, but efficiency consists in part in knowing or predicting what really is wanted. Employment and profits are high in enterprises for whose product there is brisk demand; but as demand or efficiency shifts, a cycle of birth and death of productive enterprises is constantly in process, with the owners of unsuccessful enterprises being relegated into less remunerative and less responsible roles. In this way, as enterprise meets the market demands of consumers it is correspondingly rewarded, and as in so doing it employs or purchases from other individuals, incomes are generated. The generation and expenditure of individual incomes is thus a circular flow which proceeds in the channels established by the demands of consumers and the attempts of producers to meet these demands.

Enterprise requires capital as well as labor and materials, capital which may be derived either from the savings of the enterprise itself or from the savings which others entrust to it, or from both. Savings consist of income which is not immediately spent, while capital comprises resources which are utilized to produce more things, or to produce things better. Upon the willingness both to save and to borrow depends the economy's ability to develop, to expand, and to become more efficient. The interest rate—which is a cost to the borrower and a lure to the saver—is just another of those prices, albeit a most important one, which serve to guide the otherwise unplanned economy.

Finally, workers compete with workers, producers with producers, savers with savers, borrowers with borrowers, and consumers with consumers. That competition is a sometimes decorous, sometimes bitter struggle for existence, in which the most efficient process and the most skilled individual receive the lion's share of the rewards, but in which, as long as the system remains flexible and resources mobile, any productive effort directed rationally toward revealed ends receives its appropriate recompense. Incomes are apportioned according to contributions made, exploitation is impossible because productivity under competition is the determinant of income, and society receives what it wants through processes as efficient as ability and resources permit. The system is individualistic, there is no "plan" and little need for deliberate control; but, like a magnet near individualistic iron filings, competition brings spontaneous order into an otherwise uncoordinated system.

4

Modern Industrialism

1. THE INCREASING RESPONSIBILITY OF THE STATE

THE OBVIOUS and simple system of natural liberty, in which free men compete for advantage upon equal terms and in so doing maximize their own well-being and make prosperous the nation under whose rubric their activities take place, ushered in the most stupendous increase in production the world had ever known. The system appeared to work, although even its successes did not stifle criticism. But the system also evolved, and in its evolution it underwent two major changes fraught with portent. The state, everywhere, was impelled to assume a constantly increasing measure of responsibility in business affairs, despite its intended confinement to protecting, policing, and providing what individuals could or would not provide for themselves; and the individual, everywhere, lost significance, independence, and responsibility, even though it was the independent and active individual upon whom the entire system presumably turned.

FORMS OF EARLY INTERVENTION

Protection of the Helpless

The first intervention of the liberal state in the affairs of businessmen and those dependent upon them appeared very early and could be defended as entirely consistent with the rationale of the system. The individual, be it remembered, was presumed to be rational, but women and children were special cases of individuals who possibly did not know their best interests and who, therefore, might perfectly properly be brought under the protection of the state.[1] Furthermore, even "rational," adult workers, unaided, proved unable to protect themselves against ill-ventilated mines, occupational diseases, exposed and dangerous machinery, and other similar hazards of employment; the state could, and in varying degrees did, intervene here; and soon it also began to provide some degree of security against indigent old age and protracted unemployment for which the individual victim could not be expected to assume sole responsibility.

Education

The extension of public education was another responsibility which the state was progressively compelled to assume and to a far greater degree than Adam Smith had ever envisaged. This was partly because an increasingly complex industrial society demanded a measure of literacy further and further down the industrial hierarchy; partly because the extension of political democracy, the framework within which industrial capitalism in England and the United States developed, required a literate electorate; and more fundamentally because a system founded on rationality required a mechanism by which rational behavior could be elicited. An illustration may make this clear.

The existence of poverty troubled men concerned to justify a rationally ordered *laissez-faire* world. Its very existence weakened the pretension that economic liberalism was the path to prosperity, but to attack it directly,

[1] *Cf.* W. C. Mitchell, "The Social Sciences and National Planning," in Findlay Mackenzie, *Planned Society, Yesterday, Today, and Tomorrow*, New York, 1937; p. 112.

and particularly by having the state assume responsibility for its alleviation, might undermine the very foundation of the *laissez-faire* system. For poverty, unlike the labor of women and children, was not peripheral; it was ever-present, extensive, and crucial. Under the influence of Malthus, the tendency of the poorer classes to multiply up to the limits of their possible subsistence was interpreted as "improvidence," a trait which education might expunge in a being capable of reason. Thus:

Almost everything that has been hitherto done for the poor has tended, as if with solicitous care, to throw a veil of obscurity over . . . the true cause of their poverty. When the wages of labour are hardly sufficient to maintain two children, a man marries and has five or six; he of course finds himself miserably distressed. . . . In searching for objects of accusation, he never adverts to the quarter from which his misfortunes originate. The last person that he would think of accusing is himself, on whom in fact the principal blame lies, except so far as he has been deceived by the higher classes of society. . . .

Till these erroneous ideas have been corrected, and the language of reason and nature has been generally heard on the subject of population, instead of the language of error and prejudice, it cannot be said that any fair experiment has been made with the understandings of the common people; and we cannot justly accuse them of improvidence and want of industry till they act as they do now after it has been brought home to their comprehensions that they are themselves the cause of their own poverty; that the means of redress are in their own hands, and in the hands of no other persons whatever; that the society in which they live and the government which presides over it are without any *direct* power in this respect; and that however ardently they may desire to relieve them, and whatever attempts they may make to do so, they are really and truly unable to execute what they benevolently wish, but unjustly promise; that, when the wages of labour will not maintain a family, it is an incontrovertible sign that their king and country do not want more subjects, or at least that they cannot support them; that, if they marry in this case, . . . they are throwing a useless burden on [society], at the same time that they are plunging themselves into distress; and that they are acting directly contrary to the will of God, and bringing down upon themselves various diseases, which might all, or the greater part, have been avoided if they had attended to the repeated admonitions which He gives by the general laws of nature to every being capable of reason." [2]

To foster public awareness of the danger of overpopulation, as well as for reasons more familiar to us today, government undertook the responsibility of providing public education up to some established minimum for those to whom other means were inaccessible; and to bring all this about it

[2] From the book, *An Essay on Population*, by T. R. Malthus, Vol. II, Everymans Library, published by E. P. Dutton & Co., Inc., pp. 170–171.

levied taxes—themselves a form of economic intervention because taxes represent a form of compulsory expenditure rarely corresponding to the pattern of expenditure an individual would adopt for himself.[3]

Public Works

The construction, and sometimes the administration of public works constitutes another responsibility of government which has become continually extended. As industrialism developed, industrial and commercial cities grew; as the market became widened, means of communication and transportation became increasingly important; and as both congestion and movement increased, facilities for living and for traveling became increasingly a matter of public responsibility. In part—for example, the construction and maintenance of streets—society directly assumed the burden because private enterprise could not be expected to assume costs for the construction of facilities which were to be available for free common use. Some of these burdens were assumed by national governments, and others by state, provincial, and even local governments. The point is that they were not left to private enterprise. In part, society assumed the burden because competition, the goad, could not be expected to work where competing units would be uneconomic. In the United States, "natural monopolies" were largely left to private enterprise, but under a stricter degree of state control than other industries; elsewhere the state often owned and operated these outright. In either case, however, state responsibility in some form or other was eventually assumed.

In time, the comparatively small-scale individual enterprise so characteristic of the early days of the Industrial Revolution began to give way to corporate enterprise. Even here, the appearance of the limited liability corporation was itself the result of state action:

. . . the corporation is peculiarly the offspring or creation of the state. It depends for its initial existence on the state, and without the state to recognize and protect it, it could not last for a week. The corporation is, perhaps, the outstanding example of governmental interference with private business. For several centuries governments were exceedingly chary in this grant of power to individuals to create a synthetic personality for the express purpose of conducting a business. By the same token they were slow in accepting the responsibility for protecting the synthetic creation. If there had not been a change in this attitude

---

[3] Notwithstanding the late Justice Holmes' dictum that with taxes we purchase civilization.

of the state on these matters within the last hundred years private business would have remained exceedingly private indeed.[4]

The modern corporation is not, perhaps, quite as slender a reed as the quotation suggests, nor was it created out of nothing.   In legalizing the corporation the state responded to pressure.   Nevertheless, the point is worth emphasizing that the state was the agency which brought the corporation into existence in its present form.   The point is also worth emphasizing that, until the corporation began to replace the simple proprietorship or the partnership as the significant form of manufacturing enterprise, the intrusion of the state into the economic sphere (an intrusion that is still in process) represented, for the most part, only attempts to protect individuals or to free them from unnecessary restraint.   Some restraint, of course, is necessary under any system, but the rationale of capitalism, be it remembered, imposes upon the individual the responsibility to seek his own welfare in fair and free competition with his fellows and to stand on his own merits.   There were exceptions, however, even to that responsibility.

Those exceptions fall into three great groups.   (1) Political democracy, being extended in both England and the United States simultaneously with the development of capitalist industry, fostered governmental intervention to protect the helpless against at least the worst abuses of industrialism.   (2) The development of nationalism outside of England led to governmental intervention, first in the United States and Continental Europe and then throughout most of the world, to develop new industries and to protect weak ones.   (3) The economic instability that manifested itself in the business cycle led to intervention, both to control the cycle itself and to assist ordinary men and women to bear the costs of the cycle.   The American New Deal is an illustration of the latter.

CAPITALISM AND POLITICAL DEMOCRACY

Capitalism developed largely within the nexus of political democracy. That meant that individuals, or groups of individuals acting in concert, were free to seek state assistance in causes in which their independent efforts seemed unavailing, and it also meant that the state was responsive to pres-

---

[4] H. S. Dennison and J. K. Galbraith, *Modern Competition and Business Policy,* Oxford University Press, New York, 1938; p. 65.

sures of this sort, at least when the pressures were sufficiently strong. The liberalization of the corporation laws, the legal recognition of labor unions, and laws for the protection of the consumer can all be partially explained in these terms. More significantly, capitalism from the start has been business oriented, because upon the businessman lay the primary responsibility for organizing the production of the things society needed or thought it needed, and it was, accordingly, business pressures that evoked least resistance and appeared to be most consistent with national prosperity and well-being. In those capitalist states, therefore, in which legislatures have been responsive to public opinion which itself has supported capitalism, governmental intervention has usually followed pressure from business. Thus, in the United States, the agricultural and largely feudal South demanded but did not get free trade, but the manufacturing and capitalistic North demanded, and got, tariff protection; and the decline of competition in the United States began at that point, for a tariff is simply a device for reducing, or even eliminating, one form of competition—competition from abroad.

CAPITALISM AND NATIONALISM

There was yet another reason for the form of state intervention that imposes a tariff: solicitude for "infant" industries that might be blighted by international competition. The mercantilist tradition of national rivalries, and the attendant desirability of an economically strong state, died hard, if it has ever died at all. There was no logical reason why the same arguments for individual and corporate freedom within a state might not have been applied to the economic intercourse among states themselves, or why the harmony of interests might not be interpreted as international as well as intranational. Some people, particularly in England, drew precisely that conclusion, but their disinterestedness was impugned by opponents who asserted that England could afford to argue international *laissez-faire* because England was more highly industrialized than other countries, had a head start over them, was competitively superior to them, and therefore had nothing to gain from national insulation. Our own Alexander Hamilton in his deservedly famous *Report on Manufactures* of 1791 expressed such a reaction to British free trade arguments, and exactly fifty years later Friedrich List, who had been in the young United States and had there been influenced by American protectionist thought, did the same thing with great plausibility for his own countrymen.[5]   In the face of this economic argument, that national prosperity may depend upon active governmental intervention, Adam Smith's celebrated remark that defense is of more importance than opulence seems positively insignificant.   There were still other economic arguments in favor of state intervention for the protection of domestic industry.   Practical politics in terms of national prestige, to say nothing of national interest, seemed to require that a nation develop its own industries even though these required protection (at least in their infancy), and even so doughty a liberal as John Stuart Mill was impressed by that argument.   The argument was effective.   In the United States the clamor of American industry for protection against foreign competition was heeded, although equally valid or invalid pleas by, for example, St. Louis shoe manufacturers for protection against Lynn, would have met *somewhat* greater resistance.   The adverb needs stressing, because competition from any direction is always an irritant, sometimes a threat, and occasionally a menace to established firms.   It just happens that foreign competition is the easiest to choke off, but the United States has its full share of inter-state and even local trade barriers.[6]

The emergence of protection as a matter of national policy in an otherwise *laissez-faire* world is but one aspect of a more fundamental process which has already been suggested: the use of government as one means of fostering private interests.   When private interests can be cloaked in the flag, as they are when foreign economic relationships are under consideration, the protest of adversely affected private interests is heard as no more than a muted lisp if it is heard at all.   But where the issue is of purely domestic import, the halls of government frequently displace the marketplace as the arena of competition, and to such a degree that the harmony of interests becomes a matter for governmental determination and enforcement.   As Clark has observed,

> . . . the distinction between the political character of government and the economic character of business is becoming very much blurred.   Business is becoming distinctly political, what with employees' representation, labor troubles

---

[5] *Cf.* Friedrich List, *Das Nationale System der Politischen Oekonomie,* Stuttgart, 1841.

[6] An amusing example was the addition of red coloring matter to 5,000 quarts of milk brought into Rhode Island from Bellows Falls, Vermont, on August 10, 1937. *Cf.* 76th. Congress, 2d. Session, *Hearings Before the Temporary National Economic Committee,* Washington, 1941; Part 29, p. 16124, and *passim.*

dependent on the verdict of public opinion, and other similar developments. And government is becoming more and more economic.   The political arguments and leverages and the sentimental oratory with which people strive to sway purely economic decisions of government grow more and more anachronistic, even at the same time that business finds more and more use for the arts of propaganda and the spell-binder's gift of arousing emotional fervor.[7]

This blending of the political and the economic is *passively* a response to the push and haul of ever-increasing competing pressures exerted by organized groups within the economy, and *actively* an attempt by government to preserve social peace by balancing one nucleus of economic power against another in order that the energies of society may operate in unison rather than at cross purposes.   The inevitable upshot, however, has been progressive restrictions upon the freedom of action, first of one group, then of another.

CAPITALISM AND ECONOMIC INSTABILITY

The state has also been compelled to intervene for the associated purpose of counteracting the allegedly rhythmical tendency of the economic system to speed up and then to slow down, and of alleviating the distress occasioned by this tendency.   In the United States, for example, no fewer than eleven breaks in prosperity have occurred since the dawn of the nineteenth century—namely, in 1819, 1837, 1857, 1861, 1873, 1884, 1893, 1907, 1914, 1920, and 1929.   At least two of these—1873 and 1929— were followed by particularly long and severe depressions.   Each crisis brought forth shrill cries for relief and sometimes popular movements and demonstrations which a democratic government could ignore only at its peril; and perhaps the surprising thing is that the public response to these pleas and pressures took so long to become systematic and massive.   Relief measures of varying degrees of adequacy were always taken, sometimes by local and state governments, sometimes by private charitable organizations, but as crisis succeeded crisis, as successive depressions bit deeper into public consciousness, and above all as groups and interests became organized, pressure for basic reform rather than mere relief mounted in intensity.   A real difficulty lay in determining precisely how to go about achieving reform,

[7] Cf. J. M. Clark, *Studies in the Economics of Overhead Costs,* University of Chicago Press, Chicago, 1923; p. 458.

for men have never been in agreement concerning the causes of business fluctuations.

An elaboration of this disagreement cannot be undertaken here, but as policy depends upon diagnosis, a simplified description of the more significant diagnosis and of the policies derivable from them must be essayed.

DIAGNOSES OF THE BUSINESS CYCLE

Economic activity has never been perfectly even or steady, but, so far as we know, men in earlier ages simply accepted unsteadiness of prices or business activity without asking technical questions about it.   Not until the seventeenth century did men begin to wonder whether economic activity might not be subject to the precept that whatever goes up must eventually come down.   What made them wonder was the frequently distressing consequence of investment in what our forefathers picturesquely called "bubbles": frenzies of speculation.   A characteristic example of a bubble was the Dutch tulip bubble of 1636 in which speculation in tulips reached such heights that single bulbs sold for hundreds of dollars, until the bubble burst and fortunes were lost.   We need not sneer.   Some of our own fathers invested in a real estate boom in Florida in the 1920's only to find that they had been caught in a snare and a delusion that, sometimes, was also a fraud.

Because bubbles burst, men drew the conclusion that the cause was nothing but whatever it was that made bubbles grow; that it was the financial credit on which speculation feeds that was at fault.   Until the very end of the nineteenth century, indeed, the great economists who wrote great treatises on political economy attributed economic fluctuations (fluctuations not only in financial and commercial activity, but in industrial activity and the volume of employment as well) to the misuse of credit.   Other men, however, began to search for other causes, especially after the development of economic statistics made it possible to search for *regularities* in the fluctuations of economic activity.   Explanations of the regularities that economists thought they had found fell into five distinct categories: (1) that acts of God or nature, acts that contemporary economists more prosaically call "exogenous" to the economic system, explain fluctuations; (2) that the behavior of money is responsible for the upward and downward movements of economic activity; (3) that some maldistribution of income results in the intermittent underconsumption of the products of industry; (4) that investment in capital equipment, the machinery and implements of production, is undertaken in waves that react upon economic activity in general; and, (5), that any condition of economic activity contains forces that eventually will bring that condition to an end, and that the business cycle is accordingly "self-generating."

Acts of God or Nature

A minority of economists has regarded the causes of the business cycle as beyond human control. Agriculture, for example, produces both food and many industrial raw materials, and that makes the economy partially dependent upon agriculture. Agriculture, in turn, depends upon the weather, and toward that the weather man, despite ventures in cloud seeding, can only say *laissez faire*. Rain cycles, or the behavior of sun spots that at least one economist has considered responsible for regular fluctuations in agricultural activity, are among exogenous factors—factors generated outside the economic system.

War is another exogenous factor. It is true that Marxians regard war endogenous (generated within) to the capitalist system, but it is not too difficult for a skeptic to point to at least one war that has been thrust *upon* a capitalist state. Whatever its cause, war does occur and war has economic implications: it distorts the structure of production, it disturbs the monetary system, and it disrupts established economic relationships such as those between buyer and seller. Some economists have suggested that the economic consequences of war follow a course that is repetitive, simply because wars repeat themselves.

We have called weather and war exogenous, and men can be found who classify each as an Act of God. Other men exist who regard a depression as an Act of Nature, in the sense that they consider depression a curative process no more to be interfered with than the bodily processes that counteract the course of disease. Explanations of the business cycle that classify the cycle as resulting from Acts of God or Nature have this in common: they leave the economist neutral. He is neutral because there is nothing he can do about either weather or war. By some, the economist is considered neutral with respect to depression also. The school demanding neutrality of economists is so forthright in its demands that it has been called the "sadistic" school. Consider an example:

. . . just when the disturbing consequences of the cycle descend upon us, all that the economist can in general recommend is patience and confident waiting for the ultimate recovery from the depression, and he must give emphatic warnings against the thousand and one projects for escape which are wont to be conceived in this time in the brains of more or less fanatical reformers. The role into which the economist is thrust is an extremely thankless one. For a generation which has been accustomed to the state's intervening in all cases of economic difficulty or distress does not like to be told that, in face of an economic crisis, we are in no better position than a doctor who, if he does not wish to be a quack, can, in the case of an internal malady, do nothing else than rely on the powers of self-healing of the body, strengthen them, and make their way easier.[8]

According to the "sadistic" school, costs, which largely as the result of misdirected governmental activity have risen so high as to absorb profits, are rigid; they refuse to come down gracefully, so that monopolies, banks, and labor unions—among others—must undergo the purge of depression until the prices of the goods and services they offer are reduced. Quite apart from the economic merits of this analysis,[9] a political dilemma becomes immediately manifest. If sound economics requires that a depression be permitted to work itself out without interference, not only must the clamor for relief be resisted—an increasingly difficult task for a democratic government—but private maneuvers to support wages or to maintain profits must be opposed. That is, the state must enforce freedom by denying individuals the right to protect themselves against freedom's more unpleasant consequences.

We come now to endogenous explanations of the cycle, and there are four categories of these: *first,* that the monetary and credit systems instigate and reinforce upward and downward movements in the economy; *second,* that industry fails to distribute sufficient purchasing power to absorb its aggregate output; *third,* that the investment of savings is uncertain, sometimes distorting the structure of production, sometimes failing to maintain incomes; and *fourth,* that there is an inherent instability in the economic system itself which forces it to oscillate about rather than move toward a position of equilibrium. There is a Marxian variant of these explanations, but its description will be deferred until the discussion of Marxism. It differs from the analyses discussed here in its insistence that this disease of the capitalist system is both progressive and incurable.

[8] *Cf.* Wilhelm Roepke, *Crises and Cycles,* William Hodge & Co., London, 1936; p. 146.
[9] This will be discussed in the Appendix to this chapter.

The Behavior of Money

In its simplest form the monetary explanation of the business cycle identifies the banking mechanism as the villain of the piece.   Optimistic producers borrow funds to increase the scale of their operations, and as they expend these funds other peoples' incomes are increased.   These, in turn, become spent by their recipients so that pressure upon markets becomes cumulative and the prospect of profits rosier.   As industrial and commercial activity increase, demands for loans increase, and the banks continue to acquiesce in these demands.   In the end a point is inevitably reached at which legal or institutional restrictions upon the depletion of banking reserves arrest the process, or at which the continuation of inflation becomes insupportable.   At this point further lending is discouraged by a sudden rise in interest rates; borrowers are then caught short and undergo losses, incomes are reduced, and purchases fall off so that a cumulative downward movement develops.   That movement continues until bank reserves fill up again as loans are gradually, and painfully, repaid, and until competition for business induces banks to pull interest rates down to a level which again offers promise to borrowers.

If this diagnosis is correct, the remedy clearly lies in policing the banks, particularly to curb their easy-money policy in prosperous times.   This can be done; in fact, to curb a boom may be easier technically than to arrest a depression, and for the same reason that it is sometimes easier to stop a man doing something he wants to do than to make him do something he does not want to do.   Unless, however, the physician has the uncanny skill to determine just when the rosy glow of prosperity passes into the fevered flush of inflation, this policy has the drawback that, because prosperity may culminate in depression, prosperity itself may be denied.   Starvation is, indeed, a sure cure for over-eating.   In any event, while most economists would agree that the monetary and credit mechanisms require supervision and some have gone so far as to recommend that commercial banks should be deprived of their right to lend, few would confine public policy to only such policies.

Underconsumption as an Explanation of the Cycle

Underconsumption has often been offered as an explanation of the business cycle, and it is probably the one that has had the greatest public appeal.

Its variants range from the crude assertion that production tends to outrun society's capacity to consume, to highly intricate demonstrations that the output of different kinds of goods and services is out of alignment with the distribution of incomes available for their purchase. But generally this theory has two strands. In the *first* place, if underconsumption is not to occur, the incomes disbursed by society must equal the value of goods and services produced. Business and industry, however, which are responsible for most income disbursements, do not in fact redistribute all the money they receive; some profits are retained, partly for expansion or replacement and partly to meet emergencies, so that unless expenditure elsewhere offsets failure to expend here, the money returned to industry will fall short of the amount required for full consumption. In the *second* place, the very wealthy do not spend their entire incomes, particularly in prosperous times when their incomes are especially high. The unspent portions are saved and these savings tend to be invested in firms which, because of prosperity, wish to expand their operations. Their expansion eventually results in a greater outpouring of goods and services whose prices are thereby depressed. As a result, profits are reduced below expectations, and the consequential decline in business incomes eventually eliminates the over-saving, both because the incomes of the wealthy are reduced and because business firms themselves are no longer under inducement to invest.

In appraisal, underconsumption is very real to the individual who cannot buy all he once was able to, to say nothing of all he would like to buy. To alleviate this distress, government can incontestably arrest depression by sufficient spending as rearmament and then war in 1939–1941 demonstrated. Much public pressure for old age pensions, for public works, for social security generally arises from an almost instinctive recognition of the possibility of supplementing private expenditure by public. But not everyone is really happy over such forms of relief. Rearmament, to say nothing of war, carries too sinister implications, and public spending for other purposes than defense meets formidable resistance. To spend on productive projects involves competition with private industry and just at a time when private industry does not find it easy to continue its own operations. The feeling that public spending is thus at the expense of private becomes formidable, even though productive public spending involves substantial governmental orders for materials and goods which are themselves the products of private industry. Public spending on unproductive projects, like leaf-raking, satisfies no one. Moreover, the sources of funds for governmental expenditure cause anxiety.   If spending is financed out of taxation, we have a process of taking from Peter in order to pay Paul, a process which does not necessarily leave society any better off, even if it were true—which it is not—that taxing the wealthy to subsidize the poor would *significantly* increase consumption.   Underconsumptionists habitually ignore the extremely difficult questions of incentive, of confidence, and of the provision of venture capital, and even were these faced there would still remain the vital question of the consequences of increasing taxation in the midst of depression.   Spending may, alternatively, be financed from loans, which unbalance the budget and, rightly or wrongly, frighten the very kind of people whose confidence largely determines the kind of private economic decisions which count in a capitalist system.   Nevertheless, governments have increased expenditures in depression and most probably will again if the need should arise; this is one aspect of the changed role played by government in modern economic life.

The Role of Investment

Investment—the expenditure of funds to create, develop, expand, or modernize industrial capacity—has most complicated significance in determining the ups and downs of economic activity.   Industrial expansion or development is necessarily dependent upon machinery, steel, concrete and the like, all of them products of the capital-goods industries which are notoriously sensitive to changes in the economic tempo.   When the canning, the appliance, or the automobile industries are preparing to introduce new products, processes, or models, or to increase their production of old types by old processes beyond their existing capacity to produce, they necessarily purchase machine tools and building materials, and the suppliers of these needs may also have to expand.   Even though, as the war has demonstrated, people can, if necessary, make do with old equipment and facilities for a long while, any substantial change in the consumer goods industries tends to be passed on, sometimes in magnified form, to the capital-goods industries.   Furthermore, investment itself carries involvement in long-range commitments and incurrence of long-term debts on the basis of present prospects, and these are not always borne out by events.   This is one cause of instability in a most strategic sector of the economy.   There are a variety of reasons why this uncertainty about investment prospects may assume a cyclical pattern.

First, businessmen, like chameleons, tend to take on the color of their surroundings.   They catch moods from each other, they pass on by a kind of telepathy hopes and fears to which any one of them may have become subject; and, as in whispering games at children's parties, exaggeration and sometimes distortion attend the passage.   When one is optimistic, others are likely to become so, partly because of the sheer contagion of moods, partly because businessmen, like all men of common profession, tend to be alert to the same stimuli and to respond in unison to the same whispers. All do respond, but all do so in varying degrees of ignorance of the extent to which others of their kind are making the same response.   The aggregate result, expressed in investments, is that all of them together sometimes overshoot the mark.   Sooner or later this is bound to be perceived, and then, like the impact of the breath of scandal in a court or congress, there is a general drawing in of skirts and to a degree that impedes motion.   The sensitive ears of business prick up to the whispers of pessimism, and as the ears hear so does the body follow.   In their varying degrees business firms seek shelters where risk may not enter, and because investment is host to risk, investment is eschewed.   When cooks make do with what they have, saucepan makers find it hard to make do at all.

Second, with businessmen as with others, imitation is easier than innovation.   If judgment is not common, if imagination is scarce, and daring unusual, the combination of judgment with imagination and daring is positively rare.   Not everyone innovates, and of those who do few achieve success. When an innovator, like Henry Ford for example, does appear and in time achieves conspicuous success, he disturbs established routine, but eventually he gets others to follow the path he has broken.   A frenzy of imitative investment may follow, but because it is imitative it is all bunched together; but that very process tends to raise costs and prices and thereby eventually to strangle itself.   It is true that a few hardy souls realize what may happen, and they wait until costs come down—the diesel locomotive and the streamliner were introduced during the depression when costs were really down— but most men follow the herd or are carried along by it.

Third, investment for equipment or greater capacity sooner or later results in an outpouring of goods and services in greater volume than before, and this reduces prices and catches people who have made long-term commitments in the expectation of receiving prices higher than those which actually emerge.

And *fourth,* investment necessarily means disbursing incomes to individuals who wish to use those incomes to purchase consumers' goods.   Accordingly, as everybody is buying at once, the time comes when skilled labor, or chromium, or anything else, becomes scarce, with the result that competition for those scarce resources is intensified.   It is intensified both because the consumers'-goods industries compete with capital-goods industries, and because, within each of these industrial categories, individual firms compete with each other.   Bottlenecks raise costs, and the increase in costs, again, catches some people short.   If the victim is sufficiently important, like Baring Brothers or the New Haven Railroad, the collapse, if it takes place, will send expanding deflationary ripples throughout the economy.

The process of investment over the years is a concomitant of industrialization itself, because it is investment that provides the tools, the equipment, and the buildings on which industrialization depends.   As these aids to production are provided in greater and greater volume, society becomes wealthier; but as it becomes so, the economic tasks yet to be completed seem progressively less urgent.   With the inducement to complete those tasks weakened, interest rates—the generalized costs of investment—should decline, partly because the need to conserve rather than to consume resources has diminished—thus making saving less necessary—and partly because a wealthy society is simply one that *should* be able to consume its wealth. Men, however, do not save merely because their savings may earn interest; they also save for emergencies, for old age, even for splurges.   Moreover, the very wealthy are supposed to save almost automatically because they find it too much trouble to find ways to consume *all* their incomes, and corporations occasionally lay aside profit in order to save the interest they would otherwise have to pay for capital they borrow.

Not all income, thus, is consumed, but not all savings are wanted, and the result is underconsumption.   The term is not apt, because the trouble is under-spending rather than only underconsumption.   The symptom of that trouble is a shrinkage of national income, a shrinkage that may even be cumulative.

To the extent that the foregoing analysis is valid—and the discerning reader will have perceived that it is a most foreshortened blend of many divergent and discordant elements—the appropriate prescription seems to lie in so adjusting governmental expenditure as to maintain an even flow of investment.   That task is not as easy as it may sound, because to throttle the spurts of investment *vis-à-vis* consumption entails some risk of also throttling desirable innovations or of strangling continuing economic progress.

Basically, the difficulty has been interpreted as lying (1) in the fact that similar business decisions come all at once, (2) in the periodic decline in the rate of industrial development, and (3) in the obstinate refusal of people to adapt their spending habits, formed during a period of urgent and headlong economic expansion when risk and uncertainty were high, to a condition of moderate development and restrained pace; and the difficulty is, of course, increased by anything like war which expands the capital-goods industries out of all proportion to requirements regarded by most men as normal.   All this underlies the demand for some form of economic planning, both to coordinate and spread out business decisions to invest, and to adjust to each other the withdrawals as savings from the income stream and the opportunities for investment of those savings.   The coordination of savings and investment could be brought about either directly, or by appropriate manipulation of the pressure points of the economy.   More will be said of this in the final chapter; the point to be made here is that yet another form of state intervention in the processes of the free economy has now been suggested.

Self-Generation of the Cycle

Last of all there is a theory that the business cycle is generated, not by particular maladjustments or disproportions which may be singled out for treatment, but by the very nature of the capitalist process itself.   This does not necessarily imply that, for this reason, the cycle is incurable under capitalism—as the Marxians assert—but it does imply a considerable measure of intervention if the cycle is to be brought under control.

Any phase of the cycle is cumulative and self-perpetuating until new and powerful forces are generated which lead the economy into the next phase.   Thus, in prosperity, increased activity raises the demand for labor and augments aggregate disbursements before wage rates begin to rise.   The demand for consumers' goods increases, and is reflected in the form of larger orders for materials, equipment, and the factors of production generally.   The prices of goods and components rise, with the result that higher prices and brighter prospects reinforce each other.   As long as unused capacity exists, fixed costs like insurance, property taxes, upkeep and depreciation are spread more thinly over a larger aggregate output, thereby reducing costs per unit at just the time prices received for the final product may be increasing; profit margins accordingly widen. Eventually, however, the limits of capacity are reached, but they will not be reached simultaneously in all plants or in all industries. The result is an uneven diffusion of opportunities to secure parts and components, because only those plants in which bottlenecks appear are the ones unable to increase production. Moreover, as older and less efficient equipment is brought into use, as overtime has to be paid, as less well-trained or less dependable workers have to be employed, then waste and breakage inevitably begin to mount. At the same time and for the same reasons, the prices of materials and parts continue to rise.

The symptom of all the foregoing difficulties is an increase in costs per unit. Some industries, like the public utilities, find it difficult to raise their selling prices in proportion to the increase in their costs, while some classes of consumers, like those on fixed incomes, are forced to limit their purchases. Prosperity itself, then, develops strains, and sooner or later a break will come, although precisely where or when is unpredictable. Banks may be compelled to raise interest rates abruptly, a railroad may default, the stock market may break, but whatever its locus, the effect of a break is to initiate a cumulative wave of defaults, canceled orders, lay-offs, reduced income disbursements and diminished demand, until inventories have been exhausted and costs reduced to the point where the entire process can begin anew.

Men who hold such an interpretation of the cycle recommend arresting a boom before the strains it engenders compel a more abrupt and dangerous stoppage, mitigating a depression by whatever means are possible and acceptable, and doing whatever can be done to introduce both greater restraint and better coordination into the activities of businessmen.

It should be obvious that these differences in the interpretation of the cycle are partly matters of emphasis rather than of kind, as are the conclusions regarding policy which follow from them. Fundamental disagreements, nevertheless, exist; some urge the stimulation of savings in order that business may draw directly upon these rather than on bank credit as a source of loans, while others would discourage savings for the purpose of checking withdrawals of money from circulation and in order to swell the aggregate volume of consumption. Still others would avoid like the plague any real interference with the course of the cycle, in contrast to others who would go far in the direction of planning economic activities as a whole or of bringing them under the operation as well as the control of government.

The strands draw together, however, when the course actually followed by most modern states is examined. It is prolonged depression that modern practice attempts to avert, even if the costs, in the form of increased government intervention, appear heavy. A fevered boom is regarded with distrust, although it is still treated very gingerly; but a depression, whose most manifest symptom to ordinary men is unemployment, is now generally regarded as politically if not economically intolerable, and every state, democratic or totalitarian, capitalist or socialist, is prepared at least in some measure to experiment with a "full employment" policy. Protection against personal insecurity, at first designed to smooth off the rough edges of an otherwise free and functioning capitalist economy, is now, in all countries, being extended to the very heart of the system itself with an ever-increasing degree of state responsibility for maintaining at least a minimum of economic activity.

NOTE ON CONTEMPORARY ATTITUDES TOWARD BUSINESS FLUCTUATIONS

Most contemporary discussions among economists on the theory of business fluctuations is centered on the analysis of fluctuations that was suggested by Keynes' *General Theory of Employment, Interest, and Money.*[9]

The analysis part arises out of an arithmetical truism, that the size of national income is uniquely correlated with the volume of personal and institutional expediture. That is to say, expenditure for consumption plus expenditure for durable productive equipment (that is, net capital formation) plus whatever may be disbursed by government together make up the fund that is called national money income. In other words, what we have to spend today, for whatever purpose, is at once the result of what was spent yesterday and the source of what may be spent tomorrow. Popular wisdom expresses this by saying that we live by taking in each other's washing. Income is what it is because previous disbursements have made it so.[10]

Changes in income can therefore be regarded as following upon changes

[9] John Maynard Keynes, *General Theory of Employment, Interest, and Money,* London, 1936.

[10] A Payments Table can be contrived to express these relationships in very simplified form. An example will be found on page 463.

in some kind of expenditure, and the question at once arises whether any expenditure can be regarded as more stable than others.   Exactly where, in other words, do changes or fluctuations originate?

Following Keynes, many economists consider personal consumption as the most stable and dependable of all forms of expenditure, largely because habit and custom cause men to attend, first, to whatever they put into their bellies or onto their backs, so that what is left over—their savings—is a residual.   If men habitually hid or buried those savings, they would not be re-spent and the level of income would necessarily fall to whatever basic, minimal amount men insisted on spending for consumption.   Fortunately for the size of aggregate income, most men prefer to put their savings to use, with the result that the really variable component of national income is taken to be the uses that can be found for whatever savings accrue.   The acute reader will notice that this analysis presumes the same stability in governmental expenditure as is assumed for expenditure for personal consumption, a presumption that may be less true today than in the past.

At this point, either of two separate paths may be followed.   One leads to the stagnation in which income permanently remains low because no exhaustive use can ever be found for the savings men wish to make when their incomes are high.   That path we shall explore later.[11]

The second path leads to the roller coaster of the business cycle, on which national income alternately rises and falls because something prevents it from either remaining constant or from rising or falling at a steady rate. What that something may be remains obscure.   Some economists still argue that any upward movement, for example, is bound to come to an end because sooner or later some vital resource is bound to run short, and by its scarcity hold up all further progress, much as a single automobile stopped on an icy hill can block all traffic behind it.   Or else, underconsumptionists can still be found to assert that the failure of consumption to keep pace with income aggregatively earned throws resources out of employment; not all of them, however, bother to suggest convincing reasons why use cannot be found for that part of income kept out of consumption, except for some not entirely persuasive arguments that capital formation is held back because the expectation of profit upon which it depends, becomes increasingly limp the better fed, better clothed, and better housed men become.

An ingenious explanation [12] combines the so-called multiplier with the

---

[11] See below, pp. 94–106.
[12] *Cf.* R. F. Harrod, *The Trade Cycle*, Oxford, 1936.

so-called acceleration principle. If men habitually save any given proportion of their incomes, any given increment in their incomes will be spent and
re-spent as that money is passed from hand to hand, but each time reduced
by the given deduction for savings, until finally the impetus dies out entirely.
If ten per cent of income is habitually saved, only $90 out of an increase of
$100 in income will be spent initially, only $81 in the second round, $72.90
during the third, and so on. If, however, as much as $90 is really to be
spent during the first round, the consumers'-goods industries must equip
themselves to meet that demand. With each successive round, however,
the pressure on the industries that supply the consumers'-goods industries is
eased, so that a decrease in the rate of increase in consumption may be
followed by an absolute decrease in the demand for capital goods and thus
in a corresponding constriction of the opportunity to employ released savings.
Potential offsets, such as the normal increase in population, may not exist,
or they may not operate with sufficient rapidity to be effective. The acceleration principle is like the law against theft. It implies an *if*. *If* you steal
the police will arrest you; *if* consumption slackens, investment may decline.

There are still other explanations, like the one that associates changes in
productive techniques with pressure to overhaul and modernize productive
equipment, and that then goes on to argue that all such changes are bunched
together rather than evenly diffused, because any successful innovator is
immediately imitated, and whenever imitation has been completed nothing
else happens until the next successful innovator appears to crack the complacency of conventional use and wont.

Two or three observations may be pertinent at this point. *First,* the
reader may have noticed that all the illustrations given have tended to explain
why progress stops rather than why depression comes to an end. That is
not due to oversight. Depressions do come to an end, and explanations of
their ending abound, but the more plausible ones owe their plausibility to the
hindsight of the particular past rather than to anything that lends itself to
plausible generalization. On the other hand, no one, today, really expects
economic development to proceed evenly, steadily, smoothly, or without any
hitch, while any interruption—and interruption is bound to throw some
resource out of employment—may have cumulative deflationary impact; and
sooner or later interruption is bound to occur. In other words, at least a
temporary end to progress is predictable. In contrast, the ending of depression seems unpredictable. Past depressions have frequently ended because some great, new industry, like the railroad, has provided a fillip to

investment, or because the outbreak of some war has transformed surplus into scarcity and thereby prompted frenzied attempts at its alleviation, or because some other emergent, arising exogenously from without the economic system and thereby economically unpredictable, has brought change. Because everything that is, seems temporary, economists have been prone to be pessimists. Economically speaking, predictions of an upturn usually amount to no more than assertions that, if enough things wear out at once, the necessity of replacing them will be stimulating. As long as scientists teach us that perpetual motion is an illusion, theologians and biologists will reinforce each other's suggestions that perpetual rest is the ultimate fate of all that is mortal, including economic systems. If economics should ever revert to political economy, the prospect of continuing inflation, subject of course to occasional lapses, might take on greater plausibility. Reasons for that plausibility will be suggested later.[13]

Second, past and present explanations of cyclical economic movement are stimulating, interesting, and usually fun; they are, however, abstractions that frequently imply a determinism in economic history that has yet to be proved. An economic system is more than an economic model; therefore, while the relationships holding within a particular model *may* be relevant to the circumstances of a particular time and place, that in itself constitutes no ground for generalizing the relevance. The merit of a model lies in its revelation of implications, without which the economist is lost. For example, overinvestment to the point where emergent bottlenecks delay or stop further advance has occurred and may well occur again. That likelihood, however, does not preclude other situations in which progress is halted for quite other reasons. The danger of a model lies in the engendering of an infatuation that blinds one to whatever may be outside it, as something always is. Simply because the forces operating upon and within an economy are so diverse and so various, our weakness in regard to theory lies not so much in having too many models as in having too few. If only all possible sets of implications could be arrayed for us in racks, we could, when we wished, pick out whichever set was relevant to attendant circumstance, and we would then know what to do.

We do not know all we should, and yet we need to act. Since the end of the Second World War that need has been reflected, in country after country, in the enactment of legislation to maintain full employment. Our insufficiency of knowledge, in turn, is reflected in our simple reliance upon

---

[13] See below, pp. 473–476.

governmental expenditure to make good any deficiency in private expenditure that may become emergent.   Little, in other words, is proposed by way of assisting private interests or institutions to find their own way out of any future economic slump.   Government spending is the easiest apparent way out, and it is all the easier because big government, today, by reason of its very bigness, contains within itself an automatic stabilizer: governments continue to spend even when tax receipts dwindle following a fall in private incomes, and this continued governmental spending tends to maintain aggregate disbursement.   Less is said about the asymmetry of this role: government expenditure is not resistant to increase, and when tax revenue rises, the expenditures of government are unlikely to fail to absorb them.   It will be suggested later that this fact makes inflation rather than its opposite our most likely long-run prospect.

If government, at any rate, is to live up to its expressed commitment, it must know when to act.   The United States Full Employment Act, passed shortly after the Second World War, created a Council of Economic Advisers to keep a finger on the pulse of economic activity.   The search for that pulse, to say nothing of the interpretation of variations in its rate, accordingly becomes of increasing importance.   That means intensive, empirical, and statistical investigation.

Attempts to undertake exactly that empirical investigation are not quite new, but in the United States at any rate, the most widely known and probably the most successful are those undertaken by the National Bureau of Economic Research, in New York.   The process starts with the attempt to identify so-called "reference cycles," the upward and downward movement of aggregate economic activity.   That attempt has been criticized on the ground that business activity as a whole, unlike, say, steel production or even the magnitude of national income as precisely defined, is not observable and is therefore not susceptible to exact measurement.   The Bureau, nevertheless, makes the plausible point that business fluctuations are nothing other than movements in aggregate economic activity, and that while the entire composite may indeed be beyond reach, a combination of such measurable observations as changes in railroad traffic and investment, security prices and the volume in which securities change hands, steel production, the various interest rates, commodity prices, business failures, foreign trade, and so on, provide a reasonably dependable approximation.[14]   Moreover,

---

[14] *Cf.* Arthur F. Burns and Wesley C. Mitchell, *Measuring Business Cycles,* New York, 1946; p. 96.

our business annals—simple records of what has befallen business activity—run back over a much longer period than that for which we possess precise and detailed statistics of national income. The latter, indeed, run back no further than 1929. We would not know much about the business cycle if our investigation were restricted to the span of only one human generation. Since, then, written history exists where statistics do not, we use history; and if we use it with care and sophistication, as the National Bureau does, the venture is worth trying.

At any rate, the Bureau has hazarded the identification of monthly turning points for business cycles in the United States, and it has also ventured to measure the duration in months of not only each full cycle, but also of the phases of expansion and contraction undergone during each.[15] These are the "reference cycles" against which the "specific cycles," or movements of specific industries or particular aspects of economic activity, can be compared. That comparison is deemed important because the turning points of specific cycles may sometimes precede or sometimes follow the corresponding turning points in the reference cycles, or they may behave quite erratically. The identification of those divergences and the knowledge of the extent to which they may be expected to be recurrent would constitute a most substantial increment to our knowledge of how our economic system really works, and would also suggest the basis for prognostic forecast that would be of considerable value to any government committed to warding off fluctuations in undesired directions, or to business concerned with preparing itself for whatever might come about.

To make this knowledge as accurate and as sensitive as possible, the Bureau breaks down all cycles, both reference and specific, into no fewer than nine stages for each, in order that the dating and duration, together with any observed lag or lead in any one cycle, may be compared with any other, not only in regard to its terminal points but throughout its entire length.

The National Bureau has introduced one other innovation that merits recognition. Other statistical attempts to venture into the bush in the hope of capturing a "business cycle" that could then be brought back for leisurely laboratory examination, have customarily started by eliminating the "secular trend," the long-range direction in which the economy over time is thought to be moving together with the rate of its movement. That means that the cycle was regarded as a fluctuation about the trend, much as the peaks and

15 *Ibid.*, p. 78.

troughs of ocean waves are fluctuations about an abstraction called "sea level." The National Bureau, on the other hand, considers the secular trend as part of the movement of each cycle itself, much as the pools and eddies of a moving stream are part of the downward course of the river. It, accordingly, defines each cycle as the fluctuations about whatever underlying, steady movement may be in process during that cycle, and thereby does not eliminate the intra-cyclical trend. In order to compare one cycle with another it does eliminate the trend *between* cycles.

What, in the last analysis, the Bureau is attempting to do is to find patterns in the cyclical behavior of both the economy as a whole and of its significant component parts, and then by analyzing those patterns over still longer periods of time to determine whether there really are repetitive regularities in the history of our economic experience. The Bureau has been cautious in generalization; so cautious, indeed, that the sheer undigested mass of the statistical information it has provided for us is somewhat terrifying to all men but those with strong digestions. The world still awaits a union between the boldness of clear analytical vision and the carefulness of patient empirical inquiry.

APPENDIX: ECONOMIC STAGNATION

From time to time in the history of economic, to say nothing of philosophical, thought men have pondered the theme that the world may be coming to an end. After that stripling—political economy—left its ancestral home—moral philosophy—the economic pessimists who recurrently appear on the scene, usually in troubled times, have supported their conviction that the known economic system might be approaching its end upon four more or less distinct depressants that are not necessarily combined in any single statement of the "stagnationist" thesis: An economy becomes stagnant (1) because of the progressive exhaustion of the opportunities for development, or (2) because of the depressing effect of the accumulation of capital, or (3) because of the recurrent and cumulative deficiency of effective demand, or (4) because of the increasing rigidity and lack of adaptability of an aging economic system. Put more simply, belief in the inevitability of stagnation arises out of the conviction that the economic machine must eventually wear out, or that it must in time exhaust its fuel, or that it must ultimately reach a dead end in the road. Each condition has been posited.

The younger Mill records in his *Autobiography* an adolescent "torment" lest musical composition come to an end when all possible combinations of notes have been used up. He does not indicate whether he expected the process to terminate abruptly, or whether it would gradually die out as the increasing number of "good" combinations in existence rendered the less pleasing ones yet to be tried progressively less appealing. Applying that metaphor,[16] a stagnant economy is one confined to the playing over of old melodies because there are no new ones to be composed; so resources originally and specifically designed for the invention of new ones remain perforce unemployed. More concretely, the mature economy *has* its basic industries and its communication and transportation systems, so that any undeveloped opportunities that may be discerned appear unimportant, unremunerative, and uninteresting. No stagnationist denies the possibility of new products, processes, or even new industries, but neither has anyone else ever proved *ex ante* that whatever opportunities may be in sight will be adequate to carry the economy forward at the same secular pace displayed in its past. Contemporary stagnationists find something symbolic in their implicit belief that, during industrialization, opportunity seeks the investor, but that after industrialization is completed it is the other way about. Moreover, basic industrialization consumes enormous quantities of capital whereas later developments are designed to conserve it. The industries of greatest significance as absorbents of labor and capital are precisely those that carry the main burden of industrialization, but at a pace that falters when the rate of industrialization slackens. Any diminution in the pressure upon those industries, to say nothing of its complete cessation, will be reflected in an absolute decline in their own demand for resources, therefore in a reduction in their disbursements and subsequently in the disbursements of the industries dependent on them, and finally, therefore, in a shrinkage of the national income.

Still worse, three great propellents of economic development in the nineteenth century—increase in population, a territorial frontier, and open foreign markets—are presumed to have passed their prime. The American population is unlikely to continue growing indefinitely, and an economy adapted toward a given rate of increase will slump when that rate declines. The development of parts of, say, Idaho and Alaska cannot possibly do for

[16] The application was suggested by Alexander Gray, *The Development of Economic Thought,* London, 1931; pp. 284–285.

the swollen United States of today what the westward expansion of the late nineteenth century did for the United States of the Homestead Act era. Finally, prospects for the private and profitable employment abroad of domestically frustrated capital are taken as gloomy.

The disappearance of these three propellents means not only a slackening in the rate of growth, but also a change in the kind of growth if growth is to continue at all.   Meeting the wants of more people means increasing the output of the same kinds of things, and at a reasonably predictable rate, while to satisfy more wants among the same number of people involves greater uncertainty, and may even worsen the relative position of producers of things for which the demand is inelastic; that is, not susceptible of per capita increase.   Likewise, to introduce familiar products and processes into new territory is easy and unlikely to meet fundamental resistance, while the more intensive development of a mature economy is subject also to uncertainty and even to increasing difficulty akin to compressing a spring.

There is this to be said for the thesis: until at least the twentieth century, the American economy has been dynamic, expansive, and vigorous, and its institutions have all been oriented about the necessity for continued growth. It is a commonplace that the capital-goods industries, precisely those that enable growth, are not only the least stable in the economy but are also the primary determinants of the pace of economic activity.   Their prosperity invigorates the entire economy, while their stagnation deadens it.   If it is true, therefore, that the need for those industries beyond mere renewal, replacement, and perhaps moderate improvement in productive facilities, is at an end, and if, moreover, the propellents of economic progress have vanished, a very drastic and difficult structural change is called for.   It is no real answer to invoke the insatiability of human wants which, at least in part, is itself the product of an expanding economy, or to adduce the urgency of raising living standards until sharecroppers, if not Hottentots, have their daily milk.   Of course living standards should be raised, but the stagnation thesis asserts that something has happened within the economy to prevent this. It is entirely and profoundly true that the improvement in living standards that has already taken place has done so largely because the resources to make that improvement possible have been created by the employment of resources on other things.   But to cry *Stagnation!* because those other things have gone is to invoke a *post hoc ergo propter hoc* argument, unless other proof can be given that a direct attempt to raise living standards must be self-defeating.

To put the same argument in another way, neither investment opportunities nor population growth nor territorial expansion are completely exogenous to the process of economic development. It is at least as true to say that a vigorously expanding economy creates its own opportunities, fosters the growth of population, and stimulates the conquest of the frontier, as it is to assert that economic growth depends upon a growing population, a backlog of opportunities for investment, or empty land crying for development. If an economy is not dependent on external propellents, then any inability to exploit opportunities that either are present or that will develop as a by-product of expansion itself must be attributed to something inherent in the economic process itself, something that causes the economy to become so muscle-bound that it cannot reach out to grasp what is at hand.

A constriction of exactly that nature has been suggested, and it takes the form of an eclectic statement that our economic system itself develops the causes of its own stagnation. Disregarding any stagnating forces that may exist external to the system (because these may be considered derivative rather than fundamental and because the point at issue is the adaptability of the system to whatever changes may confront it), that statement may be reduced to three fundamental propositions:

1. The accumulation of capital equipment, which is the very means of economic progress, must eventually throttle itself. That is so both because the mass of existing instruments of production with which a projected new instrument must compete grows continually larger, thereby reducing the prospective profitability of continued accumulation, and because the variety of uses to which capital equipment may be put becomes progressively less important and hence less remunerative as the more urgent tasks are accomplished.

2. As a society develops, its capacity to utilize its growing wealth becomes progressively feebler. This is so both because of its inability to reduce important elements of cost as the necessity to lower costs becomes paramount, and because the scramble for individual security that develops as stagnation impends fosters the simultaneous constriction of consumption and distrust of investment; men hold their money because it seems risky to do anything else. In result, total income is held to whatever level is appropriate to the aggregate willingness and ability to expend funds.

3. The impact of stagnation is made the heavier by the developing inability to make adaptation to change that a maturing economy displays. This inability manifests itself in monopolistic rigidities and restraints: the diffi-

culty in adjusting the structure of industry to a condition of maturity by transferring resources from the capital-goods industries to those manufacturing consumers' goods, the inflexibility and routinization of operations that have become traditional and large-scale, and the devil-take-the-hindmost policy adopted by interests which feel themselves threatened and which themselves are powerful enough to threaten others.

Capital Accumulation

With regard to accumulation, two things should be immediately obvious. First, the acknowledged possibility of saturating an economy with this or that is not the same thing as saturating it with everything imaginable; and, second, the fact that our economy does periodically suffer from apparent general saturation does not necessarily imply the eventual permanence of that unhappy condition.

Adam Smith observed that durable commodities like hardware might "be accumulated for ages together, to the incredible augmentation of the pots and pans of the country." [17]   That sort of particular saturation is entirely possible, partly because wants for particular things can be satiated, and partly because the structure of industry today is the result of yesterday's decisions that may no longer be appropriate for today's needs.   Saturation of this nature, when it occurs, is not the symptom of stagnation but the concomitant of progress, although it may easily have some dragging effect upon further progress.   Again, the industrial legacy of war, for example, or of spectacular technological innovation may comprise some excess industrial capacity.   Also, when adaptation to change is painful or difficult, men sit tight while they decide what they should do or until they acquire the resources needed for change; but by sitting tight they contribute to economic paralysis.

More fundamentally, the accumulation thesis must depend on some or all of three assumptions: (1) the satiability of human wants, (2) the attenuation and ultimate disappearance of technological progress, or (3) some irremediable deficiency in the mechanism by which the fruits of progressive accumulation are passed on and enjoyed.   The first assumption cannot be rebutted by merely asserting the insatiability of wants, for wants are not demand and their insatiability may not be fundamental.   Primitive peoples, indeed, can be found among whom nothing is wanted beyond the satisfaction of some

[17] *Cf.* Adam Smith, *The Wealth of Nations,* Cannan edition, London, 1904; Vol. I, p. 406.

conventional standard of living, but capitalism has had as one of its most significant by-products the awakening of wants; and the size of contemporary advertising budgets does not suggest much pessimism about the possibility of awakening still more.

The assumption of a static technology is not based upon the presumed unlikelihood of innovation, but rather upon the moot difficulty of foreseeing innovations that will press as hard upon capital resources as upon the basic industries and processes already developed.   This assumption loses much of its meaning apart from the first, but the two taken together imply that stagnation is reached when all basic needs have been met and all obvious opportunities exploited so that thereafter all that can be done is to introduce refinements, niceties, and luxuries that cannot muster the driving power exerted in the past by textiles, metals, communications, transportation, power, and the like.   This, however, is simply being wise after the event, and pessimism in that context is possible mainly because the future is inscrutable: great propelling inventions are seldom foreseen much in advance, and since they are not it is probably true that throughout human history the prevailing feeling has been one that regarded most of the economic *agenda* as already accomplished.   The nineteenth century was an exception, but even that century had its moments of despair that were later lifted by some more or less unforeseen technological development.   A "goal which flies before us," in Mill's phrase, however, is something different from an "irresistible necessity that the stream of human industry should finally spread itself out into an apparently stagnant sea." [18]   That necessity can only be based upon something like a Malthusian population principle applied to capital accumulation —a belief, that is, that capital equipment tends to multiply beyond the means of its own support—and that, in turn, can only rest on the law of diminishing returns.   That law, however, is inoperative except upon the assumption of a static technology, so we are back where we started, and the only possible verdict is—Not Proven.   Nevertheless, the prospect of building mills to build more mills forever, as John Bates Clark put it, can be frightening, even if they are not the wrong kind of mills.   Why?

Mills, or at any rate pyramids or public parks, are sometimes constructed simply to provide employment for resources that otherwise would lie idle, and in this context pyramids and parks have the advantage of being themselves unproductive, while mills are not.   Apparently we must sometimes

[18] John Stuart Mill, *Principles of Political Economy,* Ashley edition, London, 1909; p. 746.

build something we don't really want for the sake of getting something we do. That happens in depression, and we all know that depressions happen.   If, however, depression is to slip into stagnation, we are forced back upon the thesis that the accumulation of wealth eventually reaches the point of redundancy symbolized by the necessity of wasting some resources if others are to be utilized at all; but if unsatisfied wants exist and if there is no technological reason for assuming that accumulation must eventually smother itself, the explanation must depend upon some institutional inability to make use of the fruits of accumulation.   That brings us to the second of the three propositions (see page 97) upon which the stagnation thesis rests.

Inadequate Consumption

The supporting arguments for that proposition can be put simply: men enjoying increasing incomes have a "propensity" to increase their consumption more slowly, so that at least part of their higher incomes goes into savings.   Employment for those savings is hard to find, partly because their existence as savings demonstrates that they are not wanted in the consumers'-goods industries, and partly because the interest their employment would earn remains too high to tempt anyone to borrow them.   The last point can be made more specific: if people refuse to spend all their incomes, the prospective profit in making things to sell is going to fall, while if the risk of venturing capital rises, as in such conditions it must, the cost of using capital will exceed the gain from using it, and things will stagnate.

These arguments, in much more complicated and sophisticated form, have been used.   Curiously enough, it is not always realized that their applicability becomes strained if they are stretched to cover any but short periods of time.   To say, for example, that people *permanently* refrain from spending *all* the extra dollars in the pay envelope is equivalent to asserting that twenty years ago people would have consumed proportionately less out of a given income if that income had been as high as it got twenty years later. It also ignores the fact that anticipation of income through buying on installment is not unknown.

It is asserted that the volume of savings is not adjusted to the need for savings, because people save for other reasons than hope of gain from investment: they save to make intermittent pay checks last between pay days instead of "splurging" them all at once; they save to provide for emergencies; and they save in order to be able to seize unexpected opportunities "to make a killing." These are, respectively, Keynes' "transactions," "precautionary," and "speculative" motives. The first is of no great importance; the second would surely tend to be offset by compensatory dissaving if the level of population flattened out and the proportion of old people with nothing to do but spend their capital had increased—and even if reduced numbers of children had not already reduced one of the motives for saving. Finally, if stagnation should really impend, both the opportunity and the incentive to speculative saving would be bound to dwindle. In this most insignificant sense, any trend toward stagnation is self-defeating, because stagnation discourages saving by weakening the incentive to save.

Consider, finally, the level of profit. Prospective profit at any time must be high enough to induce investment, but realized profit cannot remain so high that more is saved from it than can be subsequently invested. If we now beg the question, we may prove a point. Suppose the level of profit necessary to induce people to invest their savings is *above* the level of profit at which savings become excessive: persistence of that condition would pull down national income, because the amount of savings people wished to make would be higher than the quantity of savings people wished to borrow; but why should the condition persist? There is something conventional about the level of profit necessary to induce people to invest their savings, and while a high rate is more glamorous than a low, a low rate is at least higher than zero. It is reminiscent of the student disappointed because he could not get an "A" but who finally reconciled himself because a "D" is at least preferable to an "F."

Many of these inter-relationships that have moment for the short-run receive their significance from the inability of society to adapt itself readily and promptly to change. People refrain from immediately consuming a new increment in income either because they regard the increment as impermanent, or because they require time to alter established habits. Given time, however, for adaptation to be made, frictions and lags of this sort disappear. What we must still look for, then, is some set of permanently stagnating forces that, after a point, compel society to become poorer the wealthier it tries to be. Accumulation *per se* has been disallowed; the savings-investment and interest-profit relationships remain. Here it is possible that we have been asking the wrong question. If there really is no direct mechanism by which plans to save and plans to invest are brought into alignment, and if because of this the only realized alignment we do get is brought about by the frustration of some plans (for example, people planning to save "too much" are frustrated by the fall in their incomes to the point where they can save no more than what can be used), it is worth asking how we have attained the degree of development that we have.   A part of the answer is easy.   The "frustrated" plans of a capital-starved economy with a sense of urgency about the tasks confronting it turn out to be pleasant surprises in the form of higher income, but if the point should be reached where these higher incomes turn out to be drags because their recipients do not know what to do with them, we are again forced back upon some other explanation for stagnation, such as the exhaustion of investment opportunities or the impossibility of further capital accumulation.   It is tempting at this point to describe the whole stagnation hypothesis as a house of cards so put together that its various elements, none of which can stand alone, nevertheless mutually reinforce each other.   This, however, is superficial, and it fails to answer the interesting question, How has our economy, periodically manifesting symptoms of stagnation, come to be as wealthy as it is?   The real answer may be this: Society of itself does somehow manage to apply the very remedies proposed for stagnation, albeit slowly and sometimes even reluctantly.   Consider Boulding's prescription:

 . . . beyond a certain point investment is stupid and . . . the encouragement of investment is no permanent answer to the problem.   Ultimately we cannot avoid the necessity of enjoying the fruits of our labors, if we do not wish merely to destroy them. . . .   A rich society *must* be equalitarian, or it will spill its riches in unemployment.[19]

"Investment is stupid."   But we have just been told that it is the *dearth* of investment opportunities that is the whole trouble.   In other words, if the economy is mature in this sense, the discouragement of investment is, in the long run, simply the means by which society attempts to cure its own disease.   It would indeed be ironic if our recurring success in increasing productivity were to leave the economy with a semi-dormant disease imperfectly cured.

"We must enjoy the fruits of our labors."   But we *do;* we *are* a high consumption economy, although not perhaps as high as we would like to be or could be if our ability to adapt ourselves were a little less clumsy and a little neater.   Our diagnostic errors arise from the fact that the costs of adaptation

---

[19] Reprinted by permission from *The Economics of Peace,* by Kenneth E. Boulding (copyright 1945 by Prentice-Hall, Inc., New York), pp. 175–176, 111.   The italics are in the original.

often loom larger than the gains, especially when its bearers are articulate, and also from the fact that, as we attempt to discern the future, the short-run in which we always know ourselves to be obscures our perception of the long-run to which we may be committed. For example, in the long-run the distinction between investment and consumption, if not completely obliterated, tends to become blurred: for example, a firm like General Electric produces *both* the most massive industrial equipment and the most fragile electric light globes.

"A rich society must be equalitarian." What is a rich society if it is not one in which there is at least a sufficient dispersion of wealth to support a general standard of living higher than in societies regarded as poor. The Arab States contain individuals of great wealth, but no one calls them rich societies, and a more equitable distribution of the wealth they do have would not make them rich.

Nor is the interest-profit relationship necessarily a cause of stagnation. There is no inherent reason for supposing that the rigidity of the interest rate must lead to general and lasting stagnation. Interest as a cost is meaningless in isolation; it must be compared with prospective profits, and it must remain above these if its depressant effect is to endure. Neither accumulation, nor the exhaustion of opportunity nor the failure to expend income in full need press upon profits inexorably or without respite. There is, moreover, an element of conventionality about the rates of both interest and profit that are deemed acceptable. It is entirely possible that the headlong expansion of the nineteenth century has accustomed us to rates of return that cannot be maintained if expansion proceeds more slowly. It is also entirely possible that we may prefer from this point on to progress somewhat more slowly. *Festina lente,* to make haste at leisure, is not stagnation and may have the merit that precipitous impetuosity does not have—that of reducing the amplitude of the fluctuations to which our economy has been exposed in the past, and accordingly of mitigating the uncertainty that at times can paralyze economic activity. If this, however, is to be our choice, we have another problem of adjustment on our hands. If our contemporary industrial structure now reflects an historical allocation of fundamental resources to which we no longer feel committed, that structure will have to be modified. The process will take time, it will involve difficulty, and it will require changes in certain ingrained institutional customs. That does not mean that the task is impossible.

What it does mean is, that whatever rate of interest is regarded as normal depends upon the rate of development regarded as normal, and the latter is more easily derived from the past than scaled to the future. Exactly the same thing can be said about the rate of profit regarded as normal.

In the long-run, the factors impeding a fall in the rate of interest shrink to less alarming proportions. The cost of bringing borrowers and lenders together is not fixed and immutable; even today there are opportunities for investment; and the premium for risk and uncertainty is partly a matter of convention, and therefore subject to change as convention changes, and partly derivative from the risk felt to be present, and that can never be constant. In any case, it is not the rate of interest but the possibility of gain that is fundamental, and some possibility of gain must exist as long as there is anything left to accomplish. If society is so clumsy as to erect impossibly high hurdles between the quest and realization of gain, it may frustrate itself but that frustration is something very different from inherently inevitable stagnation. It is a possibility, and this hypothesis of self-induced stagnation constitutes the last of our three fundamental propositions.

Lack of Adaptability

Rigid prices, monopolistic trade practices, governmental intervention, aggressive labor unions—all symbolize the scramble for position, comparative advantage, and sometimes for security so characteristic of our modern economy. If their combined effect is really to thwart economic activity, it is still difficult to see how it can lead to sustained stagnation; something must give, and usually it does. Things have been "giving" from the very beginning, and much of the tension and friction we see about us is simply the outward manifestation of an evolutionary tendency still in process. Tension and friction of this character will always increase when the direction of change shifts or its pace becomes intensified.

In the long-run, those costs of change, even when they have been incurred, shrink to insignificance, simply because our sights are lifted. We have our railroads today, but their availability today overshadows the sweat, and even the blood and tears expended on their construction in the past. Schumpeter has called the costs of progress the "process of creative destruction"; he might have added that, looking backward, the creativeness is easiest to see, but looking forward, the destruction may sometimes obscure it. Institutions and interests that feel their security threatened even by progress will resist it, and their resistance may take the form either of blocking an emergent competitor or a disfavored innovation, or of simply refusing to forego an apparent opportunity to fortify and strengthen their own position. When behavior of this sort appears intolerable, as it always does appear to someone, a reaction may take the form either of retaliation in kind or of an appeal to the protection of government, which in other respects, is not supposed to intervene in business. Any government at all sensitive to applied pressures or appeals will respond piecemeal, very like an amateur's attempt to equalize the legs of a chair with a saw, and the result looks suspiciously like stagnation.

Practices like monopolistic behavior or piecemeal governmental intervention operate as brakes upon somebody's economic activity, but their aggregate significance is in dispute. Schumpeter has assumed the role of devil's advocate to urge that monopolistic behavior serves as a means of whittling down the destructive impact of innovation and of keeping within salutary limits the process of development itself, that otherwise might be more destructive than creative. If so, this system of checks and balances enables a faster long-run rate of development than would otherwise be possible. As he points out, brakes enable an automobile to speed. The point at issue, however, is whether the brakes may not become locked.

We are back in the short-run, but this short-run is one that may give color and form to the long-run itself. It is true that restraints become less important in an expanding system, simply because the fact of expansion renders threats to particular interests less menacing; but if the protective devices adopted to counteract threats that do menace in hard times become so restrictive that subsequent expansion is thwarted, the long-run itself may become distorted. This need not happen. If there is no fundamental reason why healthy economic growth should come to an end in the foreseeable future, those short-run restrictions may lose significance in the long-run. Yet, it may happen. Like the strength of Antaeus, the tenacity of this instinct for protection waxes with each assault, so that the multiplication of the assaults themselves may really achieve no more than to intensify the resistance to them. If the significance of this condition has increased with the development of our economy, the explanation probably lies in the withering of Adam Smith's invisible hand.

Unlike some of his successors, Smith was under no illusions about the harmony of interests. Dealers and merchants revived his "suspicious attention," [20] and even the diversions of people of the same trade were not pre-

[20] Adam Smith, *op. cit.*, Vol. I, p. 250.

sumed innocent.[21]   Moreover, when anti-social interests constituted an apparent threat, Smith acknowledged the necessity for intervention.[22]   Ordinarily, however, as long as these potentially discordant elements could be kept from collusion and could be kept individually insignificant, the pressure of competition, he believed, would suffice to police the market.   Difficulty arises when special interests acquire sufficient power to coerce others and to manipulate the very forces that should control them.   It does not very much matter whether atomistic competition ever really existed; what does matter is that the trend is away from it.   Understanding of that trend matters still more, for until it and its causes are understood, we cannot intelligently decide whether it should be simply accepted (as some hold) or coercively reversed (as others have proposed), or diverted into controlled channels, or what.   We do not know the answer yet.   That is to say, we do not yet know whether the emergence of imperfect competition is to be explained *generally* by technological conditions, or by economic forces operating, for example, progressively to raise the proportion of overhead to variable costs or by legal institutions that through a combination of patent and corporation law have facilitated the concentration of economic power, or by the alluring financial gain to be derived from organizing large conglomerates, or by what. Until we *do* know this; until, in other words, *political* economy has successfully re-examined the inter-relationships of the economic, political, and social forces that operate upon us in this modern age, the problem of stagnation and much else will not definitively be solved.

[21] Adam Smith, *op. cit.,* Vol. I, p. 130.
[22] *Ibid.,* Vol. I, p. 289.

5

Modern Industrialism

2. THE DECLINING ROLE OF THE INDIVIDUAL

INDUSTRIALISM brought with it an *increase* in the economic responsibilities and importance of government; it also brought about a *decrease* in the responsibilities and importance of the individual man. The pre-industrial craftsman, to be sure, belonged to a guild, but he remained a craftsman; that is to say, he served as designer and executant of the work he was commissioned to perform, and he performed that work at his pleasure.

Craftsmen still exist, but they are no longer characteristic as producers of the goods we all consume. Industrialism means that the individual engaged in production must now conform to the assembly line, and often at the expense of his individual craftsmanship. Industrialism also means that the locus of economic activity and responsibility is becoming increasingly the organization rather than the individual. This has been true of most manufacturing industry for a long time; it is coming to be true of retail trade; it is true on an ever-widening scale for labor; it is coming to be reluctantly accepted by agriculture; in short, it is supremely true throughout the entire system that individuals, in whatever sphere of activity they may be, are increasingly aware that to make their voices heard, they must organize.

THE BUSINESS CORPORATION

The dominant form of organization in the capitalist economy has been the business corporation. This would have surprised Adam Smith who displayed great skepticism about the efficiency of organizations of this kind, but it is nevertheless an entirely natural development. (1) It is natural partly because in industry after industry the march of technology has tipped the scales in favor of mass production impractical for small, impermanent enterprises; (2) partly because capital requirements progressively passed beyond the capacity—and with unlimited liability beyond the willingness—of individuals to provide; (3) partly because the financial and monopolistic opportunities of large-scale organization constituted an almost irresistible temptation; and (4) partly because the right to organize became eventually recognized as one aspect of that individual freedom it was the role of early capitalism to foster. This concept of individual freedom and individual responsibility in time was carried over to apply to the corporation itself. Thus,

The common law is the law of the person. Its actions are between persons; its norms are for personal conduct; the guilt it finds is personal; the penalties it visits are upon persons. . . . And this common law was compelled to find a place for the corporation before its character stood revealed or the significant place it was destined to occupy in the economy could be known. . . . The law resorted to the easy and reasonable short cut of expediency. It called the corporation a "person," thus making the law in respect to the person the law in respect to the collect. So, without fuss or ado, it had a body of law ready made to serve as cases might happen to come along.[1]

Fully developed, the corporation assumed powers and capacities wholly beyond the reach of individuals or partnerships. Again,

The person is a human sort of biological organism, full of the weaknesses to which flesh and blood are heir, and blessed with the capacity to shuffle off the mortal coil. The corporation had no heart to be wrung, no body to be thrown in jail, no soul in mortal peril of being cast into hell. The person corporate draws its legal life from a sheet of paper. At its very birth it is deemed to have reached years of discretion. If in origin "domestic" it starts life as a mature being; if an *immigré*, it has to submit to no probationary period before taking out its second papers. It is endowed with a host of biological traits to which no son of Adam

[1] *Cf.* Walton H. Hamilton, "The Economic Man Affects a National Role," in *American Economic Review, Supplement,* Vol. XXXVI, No. 2; May, 1946; pp. 736–737.

could ever aspire.   Like the amoeba, it can in a twinkling resolve itself into two corporations; like the queen bee's mate it can, living only for one brief moment, exhaust its life in a single creative act; like the phoenix, it can cease to be yet resurrect itself from its own ashes.   It can, like a player on the stage, assume the person of many characters.   It can in fact appear as any number of persons and at will shift from one personality to another.   Nor does it, like you or me or Henry VIII or Banquo's ghost, have to remain itself.   It can, like a celestial host, spiral itself into a hierarchy of corporations; and, like an amorphous spirit, fuse itself with other corporations in such a way as to confuse its own integrity.   It can at any moment be alike one and many, remain itself or give way to a successor, demonstrate the truth of the resurrection, and present to the law which attempted to grapple with it the evasive identity of the angel with whom Jacob wrestled all night yet of whom he could get no hold.[2]

This extraordinary institution is an organized body whose rights and responsibilities are defined in its charter, which it receives from some agency of the state.[3]   It is owned by a changing and amorphous body of stockholders whose shares are transferable, with a life independent of the lives of the individuals comprising it, and whose debts constitute no personal obligation of its owners.   Having collected and mobilized the wealth of countless investing individuals, exactly as the factory system collected and brought under centralized direction the labor of hosts of separate workers, the corporation has come to play an increasingly dominant role in all capitalist economies, and it has even been modified for transplantation into noncapitalist systems.   Before the Second World War Berle and Means reported that over nine per cent of all the transportation facilities of the United States were owned by forty-five corporations, eighty per cent of its public utilities were in the hands of forty corporations, nearly eighty-two per cent of the assets of all life insurance companies were controlled by seventeen companies, twenty banks held twenty-seven per cent of the total loans and investments of all banks, and two hundred large corporations owned over half of all the assets of all the non-financial corporations in the country.   The same concentration of control has been reported with respect to the volume of business performed, the volume of employment offered, and the volume of profits received.   Thirty-three per cent of the total value of all manu-

---

[2] *Ibid.,* p. 737.

[3] Competition among the various states of this union to attract incorporation—for the same reason that the State of Nevada, for example, seeks to attract the unhappily married—has resulted in the bestowal of extremely generous grants of power.   The charter of the United States Steel Corporation, for example, authorizes it to transact any kind of business anywhere.   *Cf.* Harry L. Purdy, Martin L. Lindahl, and William A. Carter, *Corporate Concentration and Public Policy,* New York, 1942; p. 476.

factured products was produced under conditions in which the four largest producers in each case contributed more than three quarters of the entire output, and over fifty-seven per cent under conditions in which the four largest concerns produced over half the output.   One tenth of one per cent of all corporations owned fifty-two per cent of all corporate assets, earned half of all corporate net income, and accounted for forty per cent of all non-agricultural employment in the country.   The same authors even suggest that,

It would take only forty years at the 1902–29 rates [of growth] or only thirty years at the 1924–29 rates for all corporate activity and practically all industrial activity to be absorbed by two hundred giant companies.   If the indicated growth of the large corporations and of the national wealth were to be effective from now until 1950, half of the national wealth would be under the control of the big companies at the end of that period.[4]

It is easy to be wise after the event and perhaps comforting to be able to attribute our present woes to something other than the materialization of this horrendous prospect.   The merger movement has not continued at the rates upon which the perhaps fanciful prospect just quoted was based. That, however, is not the point.   We are concerned with the fact that it is the corporation itself, regardless of size, which is the significant contemporary economic unit.   There are exceptions and interstices.   Corporations have not intruded upon the floor of the Stock Exchange, and corporation lawyers eschew for themselves the form of organization in which they assume professional *expertise;* individuals still sell lawnmowers and remove tonsils, and partnerships are still formed and dissolved.   One can even count up the non-corporate units in the modern economy to reach still impressive totals, provided one does not count the wrong things or draw rash conclusions. All this is true, but it is also and more significantly true that corporate activity dominates the industrial scene particularly, and other scenes importantly, with profound implications for the economic system within which the corporation has appeared.

Manipulation of the Market

In so far as the functioning of the system is concerned, the invisible hand of Adam Smith has been replaced by a rather more visible corporate hand,

---

[4] Adolph A. Berle and Gardiner C. Means, *The Modern Corporation and Private Property,* New York, 1935; pp. 40–41.

despite sporadic attempts to shroud its manipulations behind a curtain. Fewer prices are spontaneously formed in the market and more are fixed by producers themselves; the character and quantity of production are determined less by the sensitive interplay of abstract forces and more by the conscious control of the market process itself; while even competition, still pervasive, intense and usually unpleasant as it is, has changed in character and function by the very course of the corporate attempt to engulf and over-whelm it.   The corporation cannot be and is not controlled by its owners, the stockholders, who, by venturing their capital are theoretically entitled to the fruits of success, but rather by a body of directors serving in principle as trustees for the stockholders but who do not invariably find the interests of these in harmony with their own.   The very facts of size, permanence, and power have resulted in the emergence of an industrial bureaucracy which is comparable in character and function to the civil service of the state and which has served further to diffuse, dilute, and reduce that individual responsibility and initiative upon which the earlier capitalist system was founded.

Price Control

The control of prices has always seemed desirable to those whose incomes depended upon them.   Adam Smith knew this,[5] but he was confident that competition among individuals too insignificant to influence the market would defeat their attempts at control.   The individual competitors today are *not* too insignificant to influence the market.   When an industry is dominated by one or a few large corporations, not only is the old incentive to control prices still present, but to it is added the fact that even the most commonplace act of one of these large concerns cannot but exert an influence, and when that act consists of a decision respecting the quantity in which something or other is to be produced, that decision inevitably influences and sometimes dominates the price-forming process.   An Aluminum Corporation, a General Motors, a United States Steel accounts for so large a proportion of the aluminum, automobiles, and steel produced that the corporation concerned cannot help raising or lowering prices by its decision either to expand or to contract output.   The consequence cannot

[5] Consider one of his most famous sentences: "People of the same trade seldom meet together, even for merriment and diversion, but the conversation ends in a conspiracy against the public, or in some contrivance to raise prices." *Wealth of Nations*, Cannan edition, G. P. Putnam's Sons, New York, 1904; Vol. I, p. 130.

be divorced from the act, yet the act is part of the very function of managerial responsibility which could not possibly be abdicated.   Also, because smaller corporations in the same industries risk everything and may gain nothing by attempts to lower prices, and can only benefit by those price advances which are set by the leader,[6] little opposition to the prices set by dominant firms is made.   This is particularly obvious with commodities so standardized that, like steel rails or packages of sulphur, individual units are indistinguishable from one another, and such commodities tend to have identical prices in the same market.   Generally speaking, the same thing is true for commodities, like automobiles or tooth paste, which are known by the maker's name or the brand: these may be sold at separate prices, but the prices tend to cluster within fairly narrow limits.[7]   Even so, some commodities, like standard cigarettes, are sold at the same prices in the same market even though they are classified by brand names which purport to mark or identify distinct differences in taste, content, effect, or social acceptability.

Price Wars

With respect to retail trade, indeed, the pervasive fear of price wars has led manufacturers to seek and get price laws in most of the states of the Union which compel the adherence of distributors to fixed prices on those branded articles to which their manufacturers wish to accord that protection. As a result there exist markets in which competition does not preclude some control over price by either buyers or sellers, and in those markets the self-regulating processes by which individuals are guided in their economic choices are weakened, and sometimes destroyed.[8]

One consequence of this inflexibility of price is that the modern price system tends to resist rather than facilitate adaptation to changes in demand, technique, or business conditions generally.[9]   Another is that when these changes are sufficiently powerful to *compel* recognition, their impact may be shifted from the controlled price sector to the uncontrolled, or from prices themselves to the volume of employment.   For example, during the depression in the United States from 1929–1934, wholesale prices in the agricul-

[6] *Cf.* George P. Comer, "The Outlook for Effective Competition," *American Economic Review, Supplement,* Vol. XXXVI, No. 2, May, 1946; p. 158.

[7] *Ibid.,* p. 155.

[8] *Cf.* H. S. Dennison and J. K. Galbraith, *Modern Competition and Business Policy,* New York, 1938; p. 31.   One of these authors is an American economist, the other a prominent businessman.

[9] *Ibid.,* p. 31.

tural-implement industry declined fourteen per cent and payrolls eighty-three per cent; for iron and steel, prices went down sixteen per cent and payrolls seventy-five per cent; and in cement, prices declined by thirteen per cent and payrolls seventy-two per cent.[10] Industries which are not subject to the dominance of outstanding firms and in which competition adheres more closely to its classical prototype, absorbed the losses engendered by depression in the form of lower prices and did not shift the burden directly onto the shoulders of other elements of the economy. Agriculture is the most conspicuous example.

Finally, and in the long run possibly most significantly, the contemporary price system does not, as the classicists assumed, automatically insure the production of the kinds and quantities of goods which consumers collectively may wish. As Clark puts it:

> The interest of the community at large calls for the production of the goods which are worth more than the differential cost of producing them. The private interest of industry requires prices to be high enough to cover the residual or constant costs of production. As a result prices are frequently high enough to shut off the production and sale of goods which are economically worth producing for the community. . . . As between present and future, high prices may or may not measure high values in terms of human need. Whether they do or not depends entirely upon whether the high price represents general scarcity or general prosperity. In the case of the business cycle—the most typical cause of large swings of prices—high prices measure prosperity and therefore do not measure high values in terms of human need. Therefore the regulating effect of prices, in putting goods where they will do the most good, is to that extent reversed.[11]

REASONS FOR INDUSTRIAL COMBINATION

The industrial tendency toward coalescence into large units is attributable to far more than the desire merely to reduce or contain competition. It arises partly from the very nature of modern technology, partly from the opportunities offered by the corporate device itself and the legal system which protects it, and partly from the need to make more secure the environment in which business enterprise has to operate.

[10] *Cf.* George P. Comer, *op. cit.,* p. 157.
[11] *Cf.* J. M. Clark, *Studies in the Economics of Overhead Costs,* University of Chicago Press, Chicago, 1923; pp. 448, 460. *Cf.,* also, Dennison and Galbraith, *op. cit.,* p. 37.

Enterprise, like everything else, operates in an uncertain world, and the hazards of uncertainty invite efforts to control them.   Extension of the size and power of an enterprise has the effect both of bringing a greater part of the environment of the controlling enterprise under its control and of increasing the hazards of other enterprises with which the controlling firm has dealings.   The complicated result is to stimulate compensatory coalescence among those other enterprises, and to foster appeals to government for protection against hazards including the hazard of increased power at the disposal of large units.[12]

Technology

It would be extremely uneconomic to build a large number of competing railroads in a region which could not provide sufficient traffic for all.   Clark refers to a remark someone made about railroads—that where there is some competition there is unfair discrimination; where there is great competition there is cutthroat activity; only *no* competition provides security.[13]   It would likewise be the height of inconvenience to have more than one telephone system in a city without at least integration of operations among them. Public utilities, therefore, have been recognized as monopolies, and as such brought under governmental control if not outright ownership and operation.

In other industries, as mass production increases the scale of operations, the number of competing units is inevitably reduced.   A city can support a large number of bakeries when these are small-scale units no one of which can produce more than a score or so of loaves at a time, but can hardly do so when large enterprises capable of producing hundreds, if not thousands, of loaves daily, come into existence.   Moreover, once these begin to appear, the scales are almost invariably tipped in their favor by their superior bargaining power, their financial resources, and their ability to reduce costs.

Furthermore, the complex character of modern industrial processes has introduced a bewildering and multiform array of opportunities for synchronizing operations, for utilizing by-products difficult to store, like blast-furnace gas, for eliminating redundant operations like the re-heating of pig iron ingots for further processing, for simplifying and standardizing parts and compo-

---

[12] *Cf.* W. C. Mitchell, "The Social Sciences and National Planning," in Findlay Mackenzie, *Planned Society, Yesterday, Today, Tomorrow,* New York, 1937; p. 116.
[13] J. M. Clark, *op. cit.,* p. 434.

nents, for specializing the operations of particular plants within a complex of integrated and planned operations—in short, for the planning by individual industries of the entire course of their production.   These most powerful pressures have culminated in a twofold evolution of industrial combination which has contributed, so far as they are concerned, to the reduction of the significance of the individual.   Thus we may note the extension of centralized control over the production of particular items, as, for example, ball-bearing manufacture throughout the world dominated by the Swedish firm known as SKF; and the extension of centralized control over the entire productive process from raw materials to finished product, as illustrated by the Ford Corporation which mines its own iron and supervises the final sale of its cars.

Advantages Inherent in Incorporations

The extension of centralized control has also been facilitated by the outgrowth of the corporation which we have already discussed.   By the issuance of non-voting securities and the development of the proxy system, to say nothing of the lack of interest in and capacity for the responsibility of management on the part of the average stockholder, the formation and execution of policy has been concentrated in relatively few hands.   The holding company device, by which one corporation may control others by the ownership of a block of their voting stock, has enabled the exercise of effective control over vast aggregations of wealth through an astonishingly small initial investment.   The Van Sweringen brothers, for example, secured control of a three billion dollar railroad empire through an initial outlay of scarcely half a million.[14]   Since then, the use of the holding company has been restricted by the *Securities and Exchange Act*.   Interlocking directorates and the emergence of communities of interest which manipulate a hand which it is hoped may be invisible, have still further extended this process.   Finally, the patent system has enabled patent holders in industry after industry to control, first a basic process, and finally a continuing series of extensions, modifications, and improvements upon it, until (as in the case of the glassware or electrical industries) the dominant position of the fortunate few is all but impregnable.   This entire process has gone on regardless of sporadically energetic attempts by the state, at least in this country, to

[14] *Cf.* Harold D. Koontz, *Government Control of Business,* Cambridge, 1941; p. 165.

maintain competition, and has probably reached the point where its arrest or reversal, should that be desired, will require a most sustained, sweeping and comprehensive effort.

Like all causes made their own by propagandists, the danger of bigness has been oversimplified. We need not tremble lest we someday discover that a small group of prehensile industrialists has seized, or even plotted to seize, the economic dominion of the world in the way in which a Hitler or a Stalin have plotted. Giants exist, sometimes in spite of themselves, but giants have their rivals and frequently their internal troubles which themselves can be gigantic. Big firms are frequently more profitable or more efficient than small, but the very big ones do not appear always to have the same advantage over just ordinarily big ones. The big shadows cast by big firms have bemused some of us into shadow boxing.

The danger is not that small business, which exists and frequently thrives, will be driven into abject dependence or penury by today's industrial giants; or that labor, which is itself becoming gigantic, will be forced into an ever-tightening form of modern wage slavery; or even that consumers, upon whom industry is, in its way, still dependent, will be progressively exploited or bamboozled; or, finally, that government itself will be milked of its substance by some malignant financial vampire, or permitted only to pipe to a score composed in Wall Street. The problem is that industry is big, and does not know what to do with its bigness. Competition has not died, but it is no longer the same kind of competition which a century ago was believed capable of exerting a control over the economy which would be both equitable and firm. Individualism, still a social and perhaps an ethical ideal, has lost much of its economic significance and force, and the private collectivism which has displaced it in large segments of the economy has not, at least yet, been able to make itself public so as to provide a new and generally acceptable mode of social and political organization.

Business identity itself tends to lose significance or even to disappear in the maze of interlocked and interdependent corporate relationships.[15] In this maze, the fate of a legally autonomous but practically dependent corporation is frequently determined, not by its efficiency, but by the way it can profitably be used by those who control it. It is not certain that even the profit motive itself redounds to those social ends it purports primarily to serve, in a system in which manipulation and control can be used to promote the financial interests of small groups rather than the social interest in plenti-

---

[15] Cf., Dennison and Galbraith, op. cit., pp. 75–77.

ful and efficient production.[16]   It is not even certain that a corporation will be run in the interests of its owners, the stockholders, who are, in principle, entitled to whatever profits may be earned.   The functions of risk-taking and of management have become separated in direct consequence of the development of the corporation, and of the two, management is in by far the more strategic position.   Design rather than blind competition holds the reins.

Need to Control the Business Environment

The modern corporation has become too large and intricate to permit full freedom of individual responsibility and initiative.   Moreover, submission by smaller concerns to the collective decisions of trade associations, the increasing measure of state control, the development of interest by large labor organizations in prices, production, and profits as well as in wages and conditions of employment, and the growing importance of comprehensive production plans and the systematic mapping out of sales campaigns—all have likewise contributed to the decentralization, diffusion, and delegation of responsibility.   The corporation is becoming a trusteeship and developing into a bureaucracy.   As a government report puts it:

When business is small the problems of control and management are usually simple.   The individual who has the money and the market also runs the business.   Quite a different situation arises, however, when one group of people furnishes the capital and another runs the business for it.   Then, potentially at least, both owners and laborers are dispossessed, as earlier the financier gained control over the craftsman.   Under modern conditions existing in the corporate form of enterprise we have what has come to be appropriately called management control.   The owners own, but they find it difficult to exercise real authority.   The managers do not own, but actually exercise the power which determines the success or failure of the enterprise. . . .

A second consequence of machine technology and corporate finance is the very complexity of giant corporations.   The vaster they become the more difficult are the structural problems of organization, coordination, and control, and the human problems of incentive and leadership.   Large corporations, like other large human enterprises, are bureaucratic.   They tend to live by fixed rules rather than by acumen, by the meshing of many component parts rather than by the quick decision of an entrepreneur.   Organization grows in importance as size increases and trusteeship gains ascendancy.   And like other large organisms, the larger the modern corporation becomes, the more it tends to move slowly,

[16] *Ibid.*, pp. 72–74; 77.

adapt itself with increasing difficulty, and be increasingly concerned with its inner rules and procedures.   Hence it stands in danger of losing that flexibility of price adjustment and resiliency of managerial outlook which is the most valuable social asset of free competition.[17]

More than a decade has passed since the foregoing was written, and it cannot be said that the corporation, even the large corporation, showed lack of adaptability during that very troubled period.   Enterprise, indeed, was conspicuously successful in meeting the very high demands made of it.   The real issue, which is implicit rather than explicit in the *Report* just quoted, has already been suggested: the position of the individual and the locus of authority.

THE IMPACT OF INDUSTRIAL ORGANIZATION UPON THE INDIVIDUAL

The cumulative impact of these forces of modern industrialism upon individual opportunity and security is profound.   Less and less can the individual as producer, laborer, or even as consumer find free vent for his aspirations and capacities.   The fact that there was little vent for them before the era of industrialism is beside the point; the great, massive justification for the economic system in which we have thought we lived has been its acceptance and furtherance of individualism.

The Individual as Producer

Today, individual enterprise, in the strict sense of the term, is generally restricted to the interstices and fringes of the productive system—farming, subcontracting, retailing, repairing, servicing, and selling.   These are still important activities; in the aggregate they are responsible for a large share of all the incomes earned, and some of their individual manifestations are themselves important.   They are not, however, the characteristic form of contemporary enterprise, and where they still exist and are even strong, corporate intrusion has begun.   Individuals seeking to make their own economic way tend to search for employment in an established enterprise, because the founding of a new one is beset with difficulties and fraught with

[17] 76th. Congress, 3d. Session, Temporary National Economic Committee, Monograph Number 11, *Bureaucracy and Trusteeship in Large Corporations,* Washington, 1940; pp. 3–4.

obstacles.   It always has been; but, again, the portentous fact is that modern industrialism has not facilitated the creation of new business.

The Individual as Laborer

As laborer, the individual is puny and insignificant.   His job is often a matter of mechanical routine and its pace set by the impersonal interlocking of a continuously operating productive process which he has little opportunity, or even incentive, to visualize in its entirety.   The growth of combination and the concentration of power within industry has inevitably been matched by organization on the part of labor itself, so that the negotiation of wage rates and working conditions has become the responsibility of paid officials rather than of the workers most directly concerned.   Ironically enough, even labor's own organizations, the unions, do not always serve as agents of the democratically determined wills of their own members.   Some have been virtually captured by their own officials, or even by outside interests, as a result of the collective apathy or impotence of rank and file.[18]

A still more pregnant consequence has been the tendency of labor, first in Europe and today throughout the world, to solicit the aid of the state as freely as capital itself does.   In England, organized labor through its creature, the British Labour Party, has embarked upon and made substantial progress toward the transformation of the economic system itself; in the United States, organized labor has secured the extension over employment of a large governmental mantle of protection against the more egregious hazards and inequities which troubled it.   In short, throughout the entire productive system, technical interconnections, the machine process, the importance of synchronized and closely meshed operations, and the result of all these—the continuing intrusion of governmental control—combine to assign the individual, whether in management or on the working force, his role and to keep him in it if he is to remain in good standing.

The Individual as Consumer

Even the consumer has been led to essay organization in the protection of his interests.   The cooperative movement, in which organized consumers undertake their own retail distribution, and, occasionally, production as well, is the most general and extensive form of this type of protective activity among consumers, but other groups have also been formed to watch prices,

[18] For a detailed account of this process in an important British labor union, *cf.* Joseph Goldstein, *Government of British Trade Unions*, London, 1952; *passim.*

suggest good buys, report on the quality of goods offered for sale, and to represent consumers before government agencies. Exactly as the unorganized worker, acting as an individual, is unable to bargain on equal terms with his employer, in the same way the voice of the independent consumer is inaudible in the organized clamor of the contemporary market.

THE IMPACT OF ORGANIZATION UPON ORGANIZATION

The continuing replacement of the individual by the organization as the focus of economic activity has resulted in the heightened vulnerability of weaker associations, and still more of stubbornly independent individuals, to the hazards of the market. We have already seen how the extension of control over prices and production by organized industry has tended to shift the incidence of loss to less powerful elements in the economic process. These latter, in sheer self-defense, have been compelled to form counter-organizations and, if necessary, even to seek the aid of the state to equalize bargaining power. The crop-restriction program of the New Deal was essentially an attempt to do for agriculture what industry had very largely done for itself, and for the purpose of enabling organized agriculture to stand up to organized industry. Similarly, the labor legislation of the same period was an attempt to enable labor to meet industry on equal terms at the bargaining table. As this march of organization goes on and as the push and haul for position, power, and bargaining advantage becomes more intense and more fraught with portent for the entire society, nodules of private and more or less irresponsible economic power emerge and coalesce. To describe private economic power as irresponsible is not necessarily to impute capriciousness to it. Power is irresponsible when its wielders are essentially answerable to no one but themselves. The possessors of political power in a democracy are answerable to the electorate. To whom, or what, are the possessors of economic power under today's conditions answerable?

THE LOCUS AND RESPONSIBILITY OF ECONOMIC POWER

The pursuit of self-interest, at worst relatively harmless and at best socially advantageous when the contestants are small and many, affects the very life of the community when the contestants become so great that their battlefield is an entire continent.   Any economic activity, whether it is the production of steel, the organization of mine workers, or the distribution of milk, will become implicitly affected with a public interest when it passes into the control of a few men whose decisions can affect the well-being of millions. When business became great, attempts were made, first to place bounds upon accretion in size, then to curb the abuses which size made possible.   When labor became great, the state intervened to moderate some of the extravagancies toward which greatness is tempted.   Society, probably wisely, is sensitive to the possibility that power may be abused even though the possessors of power exercise the most scrupulous self-restraint in its use.   When they do not, they simply provoke retribution.   It is that likelihood of retribution, at least as long as democratic processes survive, that serves as a most potent deterrent to abuse; [19] it is the uncertainty about the means of retribution for or prevention of abuse that constitutes one of the major contemporary problems.

THE ROLE OF THE STATE

So far the state, at least in this country, has made no real effort to reduce private economic power frontally; it has limited its intervention to preventing or punishing abuse.   The Anti-Trust Acts in the United States and the body of judicial interpretation which has been built up about them have resulted in the definition of certain types of business behavior and certain forms of organization deemed to be contrary to the public interest.   Similarly, a

[19] "Observable throughout the world, and in varying degrees of intensity, is the insistence that power in economic organizations shall be subjected to the same tests of public benefit which have been applied in their turn to power otherwise located.   In its most extreme aspect this is exhibited in the communist movement, which in its purest form is an insistence that *all* of the powers and privileges of property shall be used only in the common interest.   In less extreme forms of social dogma, transfer of economic power to the state for public service is demanded.   In the strictly capitalist countries, and particularly in time of depression, demands are constantly put forward that the men controlling the great economic organizations be made to accept responsibility for the well-being of those who are subject to the organizations, whether workers, investors, or consumers.   In a sense the difference in all of these demands lies only in degree.   In proportion as an economic organism grows in strength and its power is concentrated in a few hands, the possessor of power is more easily located, and the demand for responsible power becomes increasingly direct."   Berle and Means, *op. cit.*, pp. 353–354.

beginning has been made to define improper uses of the power inherent in large labor organizations.   Still, the large corporation and the large union exist, still seeking the protection of their own interests as they interpret them, and only a handful deny them their right to exist.   Their existence has consequences, of which not the least is the rigidity of the modern industrial system, particularly in the face of downward movements.   Greater profits, larger wages, even higher prices are accepted in prosperity, but their reduction in depression is bitterly resisted, with the result that unemployment, both of industrial capacity and of men, becomes a characteristic symptom of a slump. The *control over* the market that organization makes possible replaces the *adaptation to* the market that the lone individual perforce must make, with the consequence that the men too weak to exercise control are the men who bear the whole brunt of a slump.

The cumulative impact of all these forces has been to make the modern industrial system far less obvious and simple than had originally been assumed.   It is beset with uncertainty, its course is uneven, it seems to raise up against itself the opposition of even its beneficiaries, and both its friends and its opponents have not hesitated to call upon the state to prop it up or to hold it back.   It has impressed more than one observer with its apparent inability to provide "normal" full employment except under such abnormal conditions as war or inflation.[20]   It has impressed other observers with the extremism of the attitudes toward it which it seems to engender. The late Lord Keynes, for example, commented upon

> . . . the pessimism of the revolutionaries who think that things are so bad that nothing can save us but violent change and the pessimism of the reactionaries who consider the balance of our economic and social life so precarious that we must risk no experiments.[21]

The entire economic system is given an air of mystery by the mass disturbances of the market which have so frequently occurred; to that extent it has lost the semblance of rationality which once characterized it.   This largely explains the emergence of irrational mass movements out of a context which in other respects is marked by the most modern and most rationally developed technological system of production.   Perhaps the most fundamental fact of all is the sense that man has mastered all nature but

---

[20] *Cf.*, for example, Frank D. Graham, *Social Goals and Economic Institutions,* Princeton, 1942; p. 73.

[21] *Cf.* J. M. Keynes, *Essays in Persuasion,* New York, 1932; pp. 359–360.

himself.   When the application of intelligence to physical facts promises fair assurance of success, how can man be expected to remain passive, or worse, defeatist, in the face of economic problems? [22]   Not all men do remain passive.   Some wish to tinker in the direction of reformed capitalism, some to move toward a different organization of economic activity in which the state replaces the market as the great arbiter, and some to freeze the *social* structure of capitalism into a rigid pattern which would inhibit further change.   It is to these ventures that we must now turn our attention.

[22] *Cf.* Gustav Stolper, *This Age of Fable,* New York, 1941; pp. 27–28.

PART THREE

The Socialist and Marxist Dissent

6

The Theory of Socialism

ARLY capitalism rested, at least in principle, upon coordination by the market of the behavior of unorganized,
rational individuals. We have seen how the *facts* of
capitalist industrialism have reduced the individualism and impugned the
complete rationality of the system. We have now to see how the *principle*
of capitalist industrialism came to be challenged.

There has been more than one such challenge, but the earliest—and to
many men still the most persuasive of these challenges—was the socialist
one. The perceptive reader may object, at this point, that there are almost
as many varieties of socialism as there are socialists, and that reference to
a single socialist challenge may, therefore, be misleading. That reader is
right. There are many varieties of socialism, and later in this chapter we
shall pass some of them in review. Nevertheless, all forms of socialism
have certain things in common, and what things they have in common are
all derived from the background out of which all forms of socialism have
come. That background is itself far older than the capitalism with which
contemporary socialism is contrasted.

THE BACKGROUND OF SOCIALISM

From the prophet's denunciation, "He is a merchant, the balances of deceit are in his hand; he loveth to oppress," [1] to the exposures of wartime fraud and profiteering which have been made by Congressional Committees, a vein of moral disapproval toward, sometimes the excesses, and sometimes the very structure of the social order, has appeared red in the warp and woof of human history.   From the kings of the ancient river valley cultures who would have minded neither the epithet *socialist* nor the epithet *monopolist*,[2] to the contemporary totalitarians of the Soviet Union, economic activity has been centrally planned, politically administered, and bureaucratically controlled.   Socialist movements tend to appear when these two strands, of moral judgment and economic planning, are conjoined.

Each strand must be present in a genuine socialist movement.   The mere longing for a better world may lead only to a renunciation of this one, while economic planning by itself may be applied to any sort of purpose.   That is why communal settlements like Brook Farm, the early Oneida Community, or the Mormon colonies were not really socialist in the fullest sense; they were never effective in remaking an entire society.   That is also why fascist economic planning has evoked the abhorrence of most socialists despite the fascists' assumption, in Germany, of the name National Socialist; fascist planning is toward an end which most of the world regards as reactionary and immoral.

Comparison of Early and Modern Socialism

Modern socialism has added another basic element to the moral judgment and the economic planning characteristic of all socialism: the impulse to extend the democratic process from the political to the economic sphere, and with that impulse the conviction that this can be done.   This is perhaps the most complicated and evasive of all the characteristics of an essentially complicated movement.   Until the Industrial Revolution man's economic fortunes were, and were regarded as, beyond the control of ordinary men. The bulk of mankind lived on the margin of subsistence since it was techni-

[1] *Hosea,* 12:7.
[2] *Cf.* Herbert Heaton, *Economic History of Europe,* New York, 1936; p. 22.

cally impossible to afford them any better lot. Famine, misery, and distress existed, and, at least in time of ordinary peace, to a greater degree than is true for capitalistic countries today. Then, however, these were largely accepted as part of the destiny of man born of woman. To early theologians, indeed, private property and its attendant evils were interpreted as consequences of the Fall of Man,[3] with the result that men believed that while poverty could—and should—be mitigated by almsgiving, it could hardly be eradicated. Early socialist movements, therefore, tended to accept production and its technique as given, and to concentrate, instead, on the equitable distribution of its fruits. Modern socialism, on the contrary, emphasizes the collective ownership and use of resources and the socialization of production itself, very largely, although not exclusively, because production too has come to be thought of as amenable to human control.

Socialism and Democracy

Modern socialism, moreover, has been profoundly influenced by the progressive extension of political democracy to include virtually the entire adult population in Western Europe and North America. Democracy is a word which was coined and much used in classical Greece. To these same Greeks, however, democracy and slavery appeared entirely consonant, as they have to many of their successors, and it was not until the nineteenth century that the propertyless and the poor began to be entrusted with the ballot. Once this was accomplished, however, it was almost inevitable that someone would demand for the workers the same rights of self-expression and self-determination with respect to their role in industry that citizens had received with respect to the operations of the state. In a politically liberal environment industrial authoritarianism appears anachronistic. The assertion of this feeling does not necessarily make one a socialist. When, in the spring of 1946, the United Automobile Workers demanded that the General Motors Corporation open its books to the union accountants they were implicitly demanding a voice in the determination of company policy, as, indeed, any union does demand when it seeks to influence the rates at which wages are paid and the conditions under which labor is undertaken. Yet most American unions, the United Automobile Workers among them, are primarily animated by the wholly capitalistic drive to hew out a place for

[3] *Cf.* James Bonar, *Philosophy and Political Economy,* London, 1909; pp. 52–53.

themselves regardless of where or how the chips fall. The distinction is this: while others assert piecemeal the right to participate in control, socialists proclaim it as a general principle.

Socialism and the Use of Wealth

Also, the edge of modern socialism is sharper and its metal more highly tempered than was true of earlier socialist movements, because of the greater ideological contrast modern socialism offers to the social system out of which it springs. Individuals have always sought, prized, clung to, and treasured wealth, but it was left to the apologists of capitalism to proclaim individual wealth as the engine of progress or the yeast of growth. Aristotle was no socialist, but he qualified the right of property with a measure of responsibility, if not trusteeship. The early Christians looked back to the primitive communism of the Essenes who, in the second century B. C., shared housing, clothing, meals, stores, and even the community purse; and they looked back with even greater yearning to the early Church in Jerusalem whose members are reported to have had all things in common:

And all that believed were together, and had all things common; and sold their possessions and goods, and parted them to all men, as every man had need. . . . And the multitude of them that believed were of one heart and of one soul; neither said any of them that ought of the things which he possessed was his own; but they had all things common. . . . Neither was there any among them that lacked: for as many as were possessors of lands or houses sold them, and brought the prices of the things that were sold and laid them down at the apostles' feet: and distribution was made unto every man according as he had need.[4]

Throughout the long history of the Catholic Church private property was made subject in principle to redistribution in case of need, usually through the imposition upon the faithful of the duty of charity. For example, the Papal Encyclical of 1891, *Rerum Novarum,* asserts:

Private ownership is a natural right of man. But if the question be asked: How must one's possessions be used? the church replies without hesitation in the words of St. Thomas: "Man should not consider his material possessions as his own, but as common to all, so as to share them without hesitation when others are in need." . . . When what necessity demands has been supplied, and one's position fairly taken thought for, it becomes a duty to give to the indigent out of what remains over.[5]

---

[4] *Acts,* 2:44–45; 4:32; 4:34–35.
[5] Quoted in E. C. Butler, "The Catholic Church and Modern Civilization," in Edward

Occasionally, indeed, even theft was justified under conditions of extreme urgency:

Since . . . there are many who are in need, while it is impossible for all to be succoured by means of the same thing, each one is entrusted with the stewardship of his own things, so that out of them he may come to the aid of those who are in need.   Nevertheless, if the need be so manifest and urgent, that it is evident that the present need must be remedied by whatever means be at hand (for instance when a person is in some imminent danger, and there is no other possible remedy) then it is lawful for a man to succour his own need by means of another's property, by taking it either openly or secretly; nor is this, properly speaking, theft or robbery.[6]

Throughout the Middle Ages and down to the very modern period the right either to use or to abuse one's own property (*jus utendi et abutendi re sua*) of Roman law was made subject, at least in principle, to the higher urgency of common over individual need, and—again in principle—while the existence of individual wealth was accepted, it was frequently accepted with a certain measure of reluctance and suspicion.[7]   Under capitalism, both early and modern, the attitude toward both property and wealth has been very different.   Pope's advice,

Get place and wealth, if possible, with grace,
If not, by any means get wealth and place,

is peculiarly apt in an economy which regards profit as an incentive, and wealth as both the measure and the accolade of success.

Wealth, to be sure, is subject to interference in the modern capitalist economy; it is taxed, its use is restricted, its very display is often condemned

---

Eyre, editor, *European Civilization, Its Origin and Development,* Oxford, 1937; Vol. VI, p. 1436.   Reprinted by permission of the Catholic Truth Society, London.   Cf. a similar statement from the Encyclical *Quadrigesimo Anno,* quoted *ibid.,* p. 1482. *Cf.,* also, Francesco S. Nitti, *Catholic Socialism,* Allen and Unwin, London, 1895; Chapter IV.

[6] *Cf. The Summa Theologica of St. Thomas Aquinas,* Literally Translated by the Fathers of the English Dominican Province, New York, Cincinnati, and Chicago, 1918; Part II, Second Part, Question 66, Article 7.   Reprinted from the *Summa Theologica* with the permission of Benziger Brothers, Inc., publishers and copyright owners.

The same thing has been defended in more modern times:

"Catholic theologians agree in teaching that the right of property cannot be extended to the point of being invoked against a fellow-creature in danger of starvation. . . ." *Cf.,* Baron William Emmanuel von Ketteler, Bishop of Mainz, *Die Arbeiterfrage,* pp. 77–78, quoted in Nitti, *op. cit.,* p. 126.

[7] *Cf.,* R. H. Tawney, *Religion and the Rise of Capitalism,* London, 1929; pp. 31–32, 34–35, 54–55, 284 and *passim.*

as brash ostentation; but every tax and every restriction is also regarded as drying the springs of enterprise, or, at the very least, as souring its proper reward.   This was perhaps truer in the last century when the world had captains of industry rather than "profiteers," but that is only to say that the wheel of history is bringing the socialist and the capitalist philosophies into sharper contrast.   It is an exaggeration but not a falsification to say that early socialism was directed against the *abuses* and concomitant *injustices* of the prevailing economic system, while modern socialism is an assault upon the heart of the *system itself*.   It is perhaps for that reason that early socialism so frequently appeared implicitly in the form of imaginary Utopias, while modern socialist movements are built upon programs of political action.

Socialism and Maldistribution of Property

Still, modern socialism has inherited much from its forerunners.   Its moral indictment of a social order it deems unjust has its roots in the Hebrew prophets and the classical philosophers, and that indictment, focused upon the maldistribution of property, has crossed ideological frontiers to influence non-socialists as well.   A generally conservative English divine of the late eighteenth century wrote, in a famous parable:

If you should see a flock of pigeons in a field of corn; and if (instead of each picking where and what it liked, taking just as much as it wanted, and no more) you should see ninety-nine of them gathering all they get into a heap; reserving nothing for themselves but the chaff and the refuse; keeping this heap for one, and that the weakest, perhaps worst, pigeon of the flock; sitting round and looking on, all the winter, whilst this one was devouring, throwing about and wasting it; and if a pigeon, more hardy or hungry than the rest, touched a grain of the hoard, all the others instantly flying upon it, and tearing it to pieces;—if you should see this you would see nothing more than what is every day practised and established among men.   Among men, you see the ninety and nine toiling and scraping together a heap of superfluities for one (and this one, too, oftentimes, the feeblest and worst of the whole set—a child, a woman, a madman, or a fool;) getting nothing for themselves all the while, but a little of the coarsest of the provision which their own industry produces; looking quietly on, while they see the fruits of all their labour spent or spoiled; and if one of the number take or touch a particle of the hoard, the others forming against him and hanging him for the theft.[8]

[8] *Cf.* William Paley, *The Principles of Moral and Political Philosophy*, London, 1785; Book III, Part I, Chapter 1.

Socialism and the Dignity of Labor

Again, the contemporary socialist assertion of the essential dignity of labor which the profit system degrades, runs back at least as far as a roseate and fanciful nineteenth-century picture of a harmonious medieval world wherein man gloried in his labor until the industrial system deprived him of the joy of craftsmanship and the instinct of workmanship. William Morris is perhaps the most extreme representative of the viewpoint that only social-ism can restore beauty and culture to men's lives:

. . . you will surely see what a hideous nightmare that profit-market is: it keeps us sweating and terrified for our livelihood, unable to read a book or look at a picture, or have pleasant fields to walk in, or to lie in the sun, or to share in the knowledge of our time—to have in short either animal or intellectual pleasures, and for what? that we may go on living the same slavish life till we die, in order to provide for a rich man what is called a life of ease and luxury: that is to say, a life so empty, unwholesome and degraded, that perhaps, on the whole, he is worse off than we the workers are. . . .

I console myself with visions of the noble communal hall of the future, unspar-ing of materials, generous in worthy ornament, alive with the noblest thoughts of our time, and the past, embodied in the best art which a free and manly people could produce; such an abode of man as no private enterprise could come anywhere near for beauty and fitness, because only collective thought and col-lective life could cherish the aspirations which could give birth to its beauty, or have the skill and leisure to carry them out.[9]

Even today the Guild Socialists and certain variants of Christian Socialism still revert to what they regard as the functional organization of medieval economic life.

It is one of the ironies of history that while modern socialism is gradually abandoning its quondam emphasis upon communal consumption, the mod-ern capitalist world is quite perceptibly approximating it. The kitchenette, that horrid institution, is the apartment house's concession to individualist dining just as the washing machine is to individualist laundering; but the res-taurant and the commercial laundry, at least in metropolitan centers, are forms of common, if not yet communal, consumption of which John Lack-land never dreamed.

[9] *Cf.,* William Morris, "How We Live and How We Might Live," in *Signs of Change,* London, 1888; pp. 11–12, 31. For more specific reference to the pseudo-medievalism of Morris, *cf.,* among others, his *News from Nowhere* and his *A Dream of John Ball.*

THE CONTENT OF MODERN SOCIALISM

Modern socialism embraces a variety of movements which differ widely with respect to the responsibility to be assigned to the state, the technique to be used in attaining power, and the focal points in the economic process upon which social control should be concentrated.   Most socialists today regard the capture and utilization of the machinery of the state as the *sine qua non* for the establishment of a socialist society; but the guild socialists and the syndicalists have preferred to expand and modify labor organizations for the purpose of bringing economic activity under control.   The anarchists propose to do away with the state altogether; and the Marxians— according to what they *say*—regard the existing state as an instrument of class oppression which must be broken and then re-formed before genuine socialism can come into being.   Again, Fabian socialists, the British Labour Party, and the Socialist Party in the United States believe that the transition to socialism can and should be gradual, peaceful, orderly, and democratic; others, such as the syndicalists and the orthodox Marxians, insist that the transition can only be abrupt, deliberately violent but under discipline, and authoritarian.   Finally, the agrarian socialists tend to concentrate upon breaking up and distributing large landed estates, the Marxians rely upon the socialization of production, while most contemporary British and American socialists in general regard public ownership of the means of production as a device by which the economic security of the common man can be assured.   Moreover, if contemporary British practice may be trusted, public ownership is considered a device to be used according to circumstances, rather than right across the industrial board.   Contemporary emphasis, in other words, is directed upon the welfare and economic freedom of the individual rather than upon the economic process as such, as is the case with the Marxian socialists.[10]

All modern socialist movements share, in some degree, the age-old resentment of economic injustice; all, moreover, share the conviction that the capitalist system is inefficient in the sense that its characteristic processes are increasingly divergent from the real needs of society; that it perpetuates and exaggerates a distribution of wealth and income which is not only unjust but economically stultifying as well, and that, in the last analysis, its funda-

[10] *Cf.,* for instance, G. D. H. Cole, *Fabian Socialism,* London, 1943; Chapter IV.

mental instability confronts modern society with two and only two alternatives: fascism or socialism.   The economic part of this analysis was given
its tightest and most systematic expression in the work of Marx and his
direct successors, but, as was also true for Adam Smith, the essential components of the work of Marx were already in existence at the time that he
wrote.

For example, the doctrine of class struggle—the irreconcilable struggle,
in the words of the eighteenth-century French socialist, Babeuf—between
those who starve and those who starve them (*les affamés* and *les affameurs*),
between rich and poor, master and slave, capitalist and proletarian—received
specific expression in France at the time of the Revolution, and in England
during the early part of the nineteenth century, to take account only of the
period which may be called modern.   The labor theory of value—the
theory that labor is the chief, if not only, source of value, and later, that
labor is exploited through contributing more to the productive process than
it draws from it in wages—was expressly formulated in both England and
France a century and a half before Marx wrote.   The idea that economic
progress through the accumulation of capital forces down the rate of profit
was foreshadowed in the writings of the British classical economists upon
whom Marx drew heavily, and, in the same early period, was utilized by pre-
Marxian British socialists to predict steadily increasing poverty in both extent
and degree.

THE SOCIALIST CRITIQUE OF CAPITALISM

Opposition Between Personal and Social Interest

Capitalism, then, is pictured by most socialists as a system in which the
search for profit by private individuals leads them both to hold down the
rate of wages paid to members of the working class and to hold up the prices
of the goods they produce by restricting output.   As both industry and
wealth become concentrated, small business joins labor and consumers as
members of the exploited classes, except as the state is able and willing to
compel observance of some minimum standard of remuneration and competition; and that standard is not presumed to be high, nor the state very
willing.   The first count in the indictment is therefore directed toward the
opposition between personal and social interest which the capitalist system is

presumed to foster.   This opposition is not confined to the world of business, but runs throughout society.   As Fourier put it:

Every person engaged in an industry is at war with the mass, and malevolent toward it from personal interest.   A physician wishes his fellow citizens good, genuine cases of fevers, and an attorney good lawsuits in every family.   An architect has need of a good conflagration which should reduce a quarter of the city to ashes, and a glazier desires a good hailstorm which should break all the panes of glass.   A tailor, a shoemaker, wishes the public to use only poorly-dyed stuffs and shoes made of bad leather, so that a triple amount may be consumed— for the benefit of trade; that is their refrain.   A court of justice regards it as op- portune that France continues to commit a hundred and twenty thousand crimes and actionable offenses, that number being necessary to maintain the criminal courts.   It is thus that in civilized society every individual is in intentional war against the mass.[11]

Exploitation by Monopoly

This condition of affairs, undesirable under all circumstances, is con- sidered particularly undesirable when wealth and monopolistic power are concentrated in so few hands that industry after industry passes beyond com- petition to become administered and operated solely in the interests of the few.   The alleged suppression of patents in order to protect processes threatened by a patented innovation, the manipulation of prices adversely to the interests of consumers, the refusal to produce at capacity, the crush- ing or absorption of competitors, the sweating of labor, and the overcharging and deception of consumers are proclaimed as the first consequences of this condition.   Secondary consequences comprise the attempts at self-protec- tion made by these exploited groups, which lead in turn to the intensification and embittering of the struggle among industries, between industry and labor, and between producers and consumers.

Development of Social Tensions

In the course of this protean, multiform, yet sharply focused antagonism, society itself becomes torn with dissension which increasingly absorbs the minds and energies of its members and deprives it of capacity to function

---

[11] *Selections from the Works of Fourier,* Social Science Series, Vol. VI, pp. 33–34; quoted in Alexander Gray, *The Socialist Tradition, Moses to Lenin,* Allen and Un- win, London, 1946; p. 177.

normally.   The state is then drawn into the arena through the efforts of
sectional interests to assert their rights or to maintain, or extend, their domain, until the situation is such that the state must either become paralyzed
and impotent, or it must become partisan and biased.   The condition of
France just before the German occupation in 1940 is often cited in illustration of the former condition, and such fascist states as Italy and Germany as
examples of the latter.

For example, French measures of economic and social reform, undertaken under the leadership of Léon Blum, were bitterly opposed and ultimately stultified by French conservatives, and their opposition, in turn, led
to a wave of strikes and eventually to a change of government.   Because
the state could find no formula by which dissension could be resolved, and
because neither faction could entirely capture its machinery, it dared attempt
no more than a superficial smoothing over of the lesions of dissension, and
was left powerless and impotent to confront the gravest external danger in
the history of France.   The fascist state, on the other hand, is interpreted as
the creature of capital, the avowed instrument of class oppression, the
created implement of monopoly capital and big business.   This state, organized for repression rather than reconciliation, is free from the restrictions
imposed by bills of rights, parliamentary privileges and powers, and democratic freedoms; it can accordingly act with a decisiveness and singleness of
purpose possible only when public opinion is regarded as something to be
molded and controlled rather than regarded and heeded.

Tendency Toward War

Worst of all, the indictment continues, the deterioration and corruption
which capitalism is believed to entail leads, sooner or later, to war.   If social
dissension leads to governmental paralysis, aggression is invited.   If, on the
other hand, social dissension leads to fascism, as ultimately socialists believe
it must (unless, happily, socialism itself first supervenes!) because governmental paralysis soon becomes insupportable, the glorification of war characteristic of fascist dictatorships eventually brings it on, as must the tensions
and strains which fascism covers over but does not assuage.

Until recently, the inevitability of war under capitalism was pictured somewhat more simply.   International competition for raw materials and markets, accentuated by the dwindling of domestic opportunities for profitable
investment and exacerbated by colonial rivalries, led to imperialist wars of

increasing severity and duration directly instigated by big business and monopoly capital.   This thesis remains part of the orthodox doctrine of many socialist groups.   Nevertheless, there is some indication that moderate socialists are beginning to regard this as too simple.   Big business may like war orders, but it dislikes wartime regimentation and its aftermath; and aggressive nationalism is too complicated to be plausibly explained solely in this fashion, even with the help of the materialist conception of history.[12] Fascism was driven to war by internal as well as external compulsion, and its "have-not" argument was more an excuse than a propellent.   Reduced to its simplest terms, this modern analysis runs: Capitalism leads to fascism, and fascism leads to war to divert attention from internal problems incapable of solution by any methods a capitalist or fascist government is either able or willing to consider.

Tendency to Instability

This indictment of capitalism is still incomplete.   It continues with the assertion that capitalism is inherently, irremediably, and increasingly unstable.   Its vulnerability to the business cycle has become intensified with the development of the system, (1) partly because the monopolistic control of industry has shifted the main burden of instability onto the backs of labor, agriculture, and small business by devices which prolong depression itself; (2) partly because the sweep of industrialization has drawn the world into its orbit and narrowed the opportunities for further territorial expansion which used to serve as a safety valve; [13] (3) partly because the wisdom of the monopolist is presumed to lie not so much in the expansion and development of his own enterprise as in thwarting that of others; and (4) partly because the opportunities for self-support by city-dwellers deprived of employment by depression are considered to be steadily dwindling.   The root of the difficulty, according to many socialists, is under-consumption: the unwillingness or inability of industry to distribute incomes adequate to purchase its output.   Industry, moreover, they say has no interest in full employment.   A pool of unemployment constitutes a reserve from which

---

[12] See below, pp. 151–152.

[13] There remain, of course, large territories which have yet to be industrialized, but the history of the nineteenth century has made the governments of such countries as Iran, for example, wary of foreign penetration, so that foreign investment, if it is accepted at all, is accepted only under precautions and restrictions which frequently render it uninviting to the investor.

workers can be drawn when necessary, and to which they can be returned
when they are no longer wanted; and, in addition to this, the existence of
some unemployment at all times tends to depress wages, and with them industrial costs, and it reduces labor's bargaining power.   Both of these
consequences of just enough unemployment appear desirable to employers
whose interests are regarded as always opposed to those of labor.

Improper Allocation of Costs

Even were this not so, an economic system based upon private enterprise seems to socialists to be unable to take effective account of all the
costs resulting from capitalistic production.   A manufacturer is responsible
for the upkeep of his machinery even when it is idle, for he is the sufferer if
it deteriorates; but he has no corresponding inducement to maintain unemployed labor, since, unlike machinery, the worker is dependent upon himself for his upkeep.   Thus:

The life, security, and health of the workers are sacrificed without being accounted
for as a cost of production.   A socialist economy would be able to put *all* the
alternatives into its economic accounting.   Thus it would evaluate *all* the services
rendered by production and take into the cost accounts *all* the alternatives sacrificed. . . . By so doing it would avoid much of the social waste connected with
private enterprise.[14]

Again, a change in the volume of output by one producer in an industry
affects the efficiency and opportunities of others, yet no single producer is
able to take such factors into account for the purpose of determining where
he stands or what policy he should follow.   This, according to socialist rea-
soning, is another sign of the vulnerability of the capitalist system to the
business cycle.

As a result of the possibility of taking into account *all* the alternatives socialist
economy would not be subject to the fluctuations of the business cycle.   Whatever the theoretical explanation . . . , that cumulative shrinkage of demand and
output caused by a cumulative reduction of purchasing power could be stopped.
. . . In a socialist economy there can be, of course, grave mistakes and misdirec-
tions of investments and production.   But such misdirection need not lead to
shrinkage of output and unemployment of factors of production spreading over
the whole economic system.   A private entrepreneur *has* to close his plant when

[14] *Cf.*, Oskar Lange and Fred M. Taylor, *On the Economic Theory of Socialism,*
edited by B. E. Lippincott, University of Minnesota Press, Minneapolis, 1938; p. 104.
Italics in original.

he incurs grave losses. In a socialist economy a mistake is a mistake, too, and has to be corrected. But in making the correction *all* the alternatives gained and sacrificed can be taken into account, and there is no need to correct losses in one part of the economic system by a procedure which creates still further losses by the secondary effect of a cumulative shrinkage of demand and of unemployment of factors of production. Mistakes can be *localized,* a partial overproduction need not be turned into a general one.[15]

Much of this General Planlessness is attributed to the absence of any central plan for the control of production and distribution. The famous Webbs aver that even in the early phase of capitalism, a hundred shoe makers would respond to the need for one additional pair of shoes, each in the hope of making the sale,[16] with the result that industry, again, was plagued with alternating overproduction and stagnation. In later phases, the development of trusts, monopolies, cartels, and trade associations has not mitigated this essential planlessness which socialists criticize, and cannot until all industry and the entire economy have been cartelized under some form of unified control. For, until that point is reached, the struggle among trusts themselves becomes ever more intense, more cataclysmic and more fraught with consequence to the society within which this struggle occurs; still worse, after that point is reached, society is confronted with the "forced alternative" of socialism or dictatorship:

Thus the modern capitalist profit-makers, by eliminating the simple freedom of competition, have confronted the community with a forced alternative: either passively to submit to the capitalist dictatorship, now recognized and on the point of completion, or else establish without delay whatever social machinery may be required to enable the community to control the industries and services by which it lives. Either the trusts will own the nation or the nation must own the trusts.[17]

Wasteful Use of Resources

Mature capitalism, the indictment goes on, is improvident of resources. The passion for present gain coupled with the struggle for competitive advantage results in the forced dissipation of natural resources which might otherwise be drawn upon more sparingly without any sacrifice of prosperity or general well-being. For, except under abnormal circumstances such as

[15] Lange and Taylor, *op. cit.,* pp. 105–106. Italics in original.

[16] *Cf.,* Sidney and Beatrice Webb, *The Decay of Capitalist Civilization,* Harcourt, Brace & Co., New York, 1923; p. 110.

[17] *Ibid.,* pp. 157–158.

war or the immediate postwar period, this pressure to capture today's profit causes tomorrow's to look small in perspective. Finally, the Gargantuan size of much corporate enterprise leads to a chronic glut of supplies which forces manufacturers to incur wasteful and unnecessary selling costs, so that it becomes a byword among critics of capitalism that it characteristically costs more to sell a commodity than to produce it.

SOCIALIST CONCEPT OF THE CAPITALIST DILEMMA

We have seen that the intervention of the state is invariably besought to eliminate the abuses and reduce the injustices of the system, and that, failing a socialist solution, the state is believed to become either ineffective or dictatorial. Another difficulty now arises, whose resolution places the socialist and the liberal in separate camps. The liberal believes in the possibility of a "mixed economy": a system in which public and private enterprise exist side by side, and he points to contemporary economies such as, for instance, the Swedish, in which precisely that condition prevails. The socialist goes further and asserts that this division of function, while existent, is inherently unstable. Private enterprise cannot operate on any significant scale unless its freedom and its prospects are generally unrestricted. Minimum wage laws, control of the security exchanges, application of the "yardstick" principle to the utilities and, worst of all, the threat that all these controls will be extended if private enterprise fails to observe certain vague, though clamant, standards of public responsibility—all these not only create uncertainty and pessimism in entrepreneurial minds but render private enterprise itself increasingly difficult to plan and operate.

The new order may be socialistic in some things, and not socialistic in others. But it must be either socialist or not socialist in its necessary foundations. It must rest, or not rest, on planning for plenty and social welfare, on collective ownership and control of the key services which determine the general character of the productive system, on collective control of the distribution of the national income, and on an attempt to achieve a social structure which will call for the active participation of as many as possible of the citizens in the work of political and economic government and administration. In these matters, at any rate, it is impossible to "split the difference" between socialism and capitalism without getting the worst of both worlds. For if we are to rely on "private enterprise" to provide the main incentives, we must allow private enterprise a wide range of freedom to do the job in its own way.   If we continually check and hamper it by attempting to control it without superseding it, the result will be that it will work badly—so badly that we may be driven to reinstate unrestricted private monopoly as the lesser evil.   On the other hand, if we decide to invoke the incentives of social service under democratic leadership, we must ensure that the spirit of democratic service is not continually thwarted by capitalist influences.   There is no reason why we should not socialize some services and leave others under capitalist control; but the main driving force of the new society must be one thing or the other, and not a compromise between them.   Compromises may work in secondary matters; when it comes to the really decisive issues there is no evading a real choice.[18]

For socialists, then, capitalism is unjust; and, anyway, it won't work. Like a serpent swallowing its own tail, the farther it gets the greater become its convulsions and the greater the difficulty of further progress.   The tail of this serpent consists of the profit motive and the private ownership of resources whose engulfment, to the serpent, is simply a means of securing food. But the vast and cosmic indigestion which follows seems to call for a radically different diet.   So far, all socialists are agreed, but the selection of the new diet and the treatment of the serpent itself create differences from this point on.   Very moderate reformers propose weaning the serpent, and thereafter letting its tail propel it without choking it.   Others insist on the necessity of an amputation, hoping that the truncated serpent will survive the operation and live to adapt itself to a more innocuous and salubrious diet.   The most extreme, of whom the Marxian socialists are representative, propose throwing out the entire serpent, tail and all, and replacing it with a more domestic and affectionate creature in whose existence they have confidence—although no adult specimen has yet been found.

CONTEMPORARY SOCIALIST MOVEMENTS

The socialist movements which came into the ascendant in Europe at the conclusion of the Second World War rely upon the nationalization of at least key industries and upon the institution of some form of central economic planning to bring about the better economic order they envisage.   In some cases the state simply owns and operates industries, just as the United States government owns and operates the postal system; in others, subsidiary cor-

[18] *Cf.,* G. D. H. Cole, *Fabian Socialism,* Allen and Unwin, London, 1943, p. 167.

porations are established with considerable autonomy and responsibility for
the operation of the enterprises entrusted to them, exactly as the Tennessee
Valley Authority in this country administers its complex of plants and operations within the general framework of policies established by Congress.
Both these expedients involve a degree of centralized control repugnant to
socialists who cherish some vestige of individualism, so that such groups,
seeking to minimize the functions of the state but without abandoning socialism, have variously appeared, and some of them still exist.   The anarchist
joins the exponents of socialism in condemning capitalist society and in
seeking a better and more social, if not socialized, order; but anarchism
receives its primary momentum from its horror of any variety of restraint,
coercion, or authority.   Believing with Rousseau and Godwin that man is
naturally reasonable and good, the anarchist attributes man's corruption to
the mere existence of organization and authority which, logically enough, he
then proposes to do away with entirely.   His disciples, however, are few;
most men, rightly or wrongly, have always agreed with the purport of Gray's
pungent comment,

The fundamental trouble with the anarchist is that, though he may be highly
intelligent, he has no sense. . . . If they [sic] do not realize that they have set
their nest among the stars, no word of man will persuade them that their thoughts
are moving in a world unreal and unrealizable.   Anarchists are a race of highly
intelligent and highly imaginative children, who, nevertheless, can scarcely be
trusted to look after themselves outside the nursery pen.[19]

Syndicalism and Guild socialism, whose respective habitats are primarily
France and Great Britain, share both a distrust of the state and a determination to establish the labor unions as nuclei of the new order, although in
other respects they are hardly upon speaking terms.

Syndicalism

Repudiating parliamentary democracy, scoffing at Fabian-like attempts to
permeate and then win over the middle classes to socialism, scorning compromise and exalting violence, French syndicalism enjoyed a meteoric career
which so terrified others who suspected its fiery hand on every factory wall
and in every labor-union office, that even in the United States the repressive
legislation enacted after the First World War was entitled, in state after

[19] *Cf.*, Alexander Gray, *The Socialist Tradition, Moses to Lenin*, Longmans, Green,
London, 1846; p. 380.

state, "Criminal Syndicalism" or "Anti-Syndicalism" Acts. It was a diffuse and elusive movement, originating spontaneously in the French labor
unions from which it derived its name, and was shored up and rationalized
afterward in the writings of philosophers and intellectuals. For syndicalists, the class struggle is the very heart of socialism. It is a struggle which
cannot and should not be glossed over by parliamentary compromise or
fuzzy middle class squeamishness. The machinery of the democratic state,
animated with a wishy-washy predilection for harmony, agreement, and
compromise, based upon the artificial distinction among political parties
rather than upon the real cleavage between social classes, and decadent with
corruption and mediocrity, is, by them, utterly and completely rejected.
Workers must not plead for what they want; they must take it by direct action,
using for that purpose their own working-class institutions and retaining these
as instruments of working-class will even after syndicalist violence has tasted
success.

Guild Socialism

Guild socialism is a British parallel to French syndicalism, although
purged of excesses, less enamored of violence, and retaining an emasculated
state to moderate somewhat the intransigence of otherwise autonomous
labor unions and to provide at least shadowy representation for that forgotten man, the consumer. But Guild socialism is essentially democratic
in its impulses, and for that reason the state is to be shorn of most of its
functions, which, after all, to this group do not seem really necessary. Men
naturally form themselves into a great variety of organizations and groups
of which the state is but one. As a worker, a man belongs to a union; for
recreation, he may join a bridge club or a mushroom-collecting group; he
may also be a member of the Baptist Church, the Elks, the American Automobile Association, or, like Barnaby's fairy godfather, he may belong to the
Elves', Leprechauns', Gnomes', and Little Men's Chowder and Marching
Society. The point is that these and all other organizations perform some
desired function, or they would not exist. Any great institution like the
state, purporting to be sovereign, general, comprehensive, and universal, cannot really "represent" men, for men differ according to mood or function,
falling into one pattern for recreation, another for worship, yet another for
work, and so on. Guild socialists, accordingly, classify state socialism as
really state capitalism, in the sense that it is unrepresentative, authoritarian,

and bureaucratic, denying the full authority and autonomy which ought to be accorded the recreational, occupational, religious, or other forms of organization which represent other aspects of man's full life. Labor cannot be free until men's functions as workers are entrusted to organizations specifically designed for the purpose and fully responsive to the wills of their members. Labor unions, therefore, are to be re-formed into something of the likeness of the medieval guilds—whence the name, Guild socialism—which shall not only represent workers but also administer and operate the industries for which each guild is custodian, trustee, and governing board.

Gradual or Revolutionary Transition?

Another point of difference among socialists has to do with the question, How shall the transition to socialism be brought about? This is really but one aspect of the older political question, Where does sovereignty reside? In a genuine political democracy socialists have been confident that the exercise of their franchise by a sufficient number of socialists will bring about the transition gradually, peacefully, and democratically. In confirmation of this they point to the continuing seepage of socialist institutions into capitalist economies which has already occurred.[20] As a grand climactic the sweeping victory of the Labour Party in England early in 1946 gives support to the thesis that a gradual and peaceful transition is at least possible.

Elsewhere, however, fear lest entrenched and embittered interests react with violence to counteract emergent socialism has led socialists to assert the inevitability of revolution by violence with ultimate socialist dictatorship. The belief, to be sure, that the propertied class will stick at nothing to perpetuate its control, and that compromise and gradualism are accordingly unrealistic, is to be found even in the Western democracies, and is supported by intemperate assertions and sometimes even actions by some confirmed conservatives. But this belief stems fundamentally from the writings of Karl Marx, although he did not originate it; and Marx, although he wrote in England under the protection of a democracy which permitted the expression of opinions hostile to its existence, was himself a political refugee who had experienced and fled from political and personal persecution and who never

---

[20] For a discussion of this process in the United States, cf. Seba Eldridge and Associates, *The Development of Collective Enterprise, Dynamics of an Emergent Economy*, Lawrence, Kansas, 1943; *passim.*

really understood the democratic process as it can be, and sometimes is, effective.

The important point is that both the revolutionary and the gradualist schools unite to place their reliance upon the state to make socialism work— the revolutionary school, because it can conceive no other instrument after the state has been refashioned according to *its* design; and the gradualist school, because of its confidence that state socialism can be made democratic and genuinely responsive to an enlightened, socialist, public opinion.   For that reason, state socialists today have generally swallowed up and over- ridden the earlier schools in which the state and all its works were somehow the objects of distrust.   Accordingly, the chief responsibility resting upon contemporary socialists is the urgency of insuring that the state upon which they depend shall in fact bring about the better world they all seek.

7

The General Philosophy of Marxism

IN THE SUMMER of 1849 after a troubled, insecure, and frustrated career largely spent in being shifted from one European country to another, a German exile in his thirty-second year settled down in London to spend practically the remaining thirty-four years of his life in the Library of the British Museum. Thwarted in his youthful ambition to become a professor of philosophy in a German university, Karl Marx shifted his interest to the social and economic order in which he lived, a shift which was to exercise a decisive influence upon subsequent history. In continental Europe what Marx wrote, or is believed to have written, became to many a form of Unholy Writ; in the United States and England he attracted fewer disciples, but indirectly at least his influence has been no less great. By his opponents his work has been contradicted, rebutted, ostentatiously ignored, reviled, interred, and even been made subject to autopsy.[1] Yet what he and his collaborator, Friedrich Engels, wrote in 1848 rings with an even more foreboding knell today than it did over a century ago:

A specter is haunting Europe—the specter of Communism. . . . Society as a whole is more and more splitting up into two great hostile camps. . . . All fixed, fast-frozen relations, with their train of ancient and venerable prejudices and opinions are swept away, all new-formed ones become antiquated before they can

[1] *Cf.*, Henry B. Parkes, *Marxism: An Autopsy*, Boston, 1939.

147

ossify. All that is solid melts into air, all that is holy is profaned, and man is at last compelled to face with sober senses his real condition of life and his relations with his kind.[2]

Marx lived and died in poverty, yet the power wielded in his name came to be greater than that at the disposal of the most puissant of princes. This is most assuredly not due to the clarity or charm of his style. Marx was a turgid writer, and even in translation he remains heavy, dogmatic, and all too often incredibly dreary, even though what he wrote is occasionally illuminated by a ringing phrase and is punctuated throughout with strokes of telling irony. The obscurity of his message has troubled some people sufficiently to cause them to rush to his defense in order to explain what he really meant; [3] and one scholar has suggested the need for a definitive work, *What Marx Really Meant, Actually*.[4] Despite this, somehow, Marx' message has seeped down to animate the hopes of multitudes who have never read, and never will read, what he "really" wrote or meant. This was partly because Marx lived and wrote at a time which was especially ripe for his work. Workingmen were already organizing in defense of their own interests, and the suppression of the revolutionary movements of 1848 on the Continent gave both plausibility and emphasis to the communist thesis that the state was an engine created by and in the service of the forces of reaction. In a sense, revolutionary Marxism is a movement of despair. Marx, through his popularizing interpreters, has taken firmest root in precisely those parts of the world where despotism, autocracy, and repression have closed not only the avenues of change but also the parks and rooms where change can be advocated. To be sure Marxism has appeared in countries which enjoy the freedom of genuine democracy, but even there the propagandists of Marxism have been the same kind of people—men and women who, rightly or wrongly, believe that when issues come to a head, the advocacy of change will be subject to police repression. The Marxism which is dangerous is underground Marxism, and, like other denizens of the dark, underground Marxism cannot stand open air or sunlight.

[2] From *The Communist Manifesto*. So many editions of this famous polemic have been issued that it has not seemed worth while to give a more precise reference.

[3] *Cf.*, G. D. H. Cole, *What Marx Really Meant*, London, 1934.

[4] *Cf.*, Alexander Gray, *The Socialist Tradition, Moses to Lenin*, London, 1946; p. 309.

MARXIAN "SCIENTIFIC SOCIALISM"

In the conviction, then, that society is organized against them, the frustrated and discontented turned to Marx because he seemed to offer something more practical than the dream of a better world which could only be attained if the natural goodness of man were given opportunity to realize itself; the very structure and organization of society seemed to block that opportunity. To them, what was needed was a program of action together with the assurance that action was destined for ultimate and inevitable success. The road to Utopia counted more than its description. Marx' unique service was not only to show that Utopia could and would be reached, but also to show that it would be reached by the organized and deliberate action of living men. Marx was a determinist in the sense that he regarded the course of history as foreordained and undeflectable, but he was no fatalist; riding a surfboard on the wave of the future is no passive operation. Because earlier socialists had paid little attention to *how* Utopia was to be achieved but only to *what* Utopia would be like, their socialism was merely Utopian; by contrast, his socialism was "scientific."

The socialism of his predecessors was Utopian because it was beside the point; mere education, exhortation, and even example are futile and often ill-timed. For Marx the forces of resistance to socialism would yield neither to persuasion nor example, and were vulnerable to onslaught only at the proper moment. He saw in the course of history proof that the grasp of vested interests was tight, determined, and tenacious, and capable of being loosened only when muscles were weakened with age and strain. Even then, the act of loosening that grasp must be an act of violence. Thus he described force as "the midwife of every old society pregnant with the new," and revolutions as the "locomotives of history." [5]

This distinction between a determinism which promises success and a fatalism which excuses effort is elusive; sometimes the followers of Marx appear almost to assume that the extension of a hand at the proper moment will *cause* the apple to fall into it, because there is nothing else that can happen. Wilhelm Liebknecht, for example, implies this:

[5] In, respectively, *Capital*, Everyman Library, Vol. II, p. 833, and *The Class Struggles in France, 1848–50*, New York, 1923; pp. 90, 165.

We Social Democrats know that the laws according to which political and social evolution go on can no more be changed or stopped by us than by the authorities of capitalist society.   We know that we can no more introduce at will socialistic production and a socialist form of society than the German Kaiser nine years ago [i.e., in 1890] could carry out his February proclamation against the representatives of the capitalistic class struggle.   Therefore we were able to watch with smiling indifference the attempt of our opponents to crush the labor movement by force.   We were and still are sure of our success, as sure as of the solution of a mathematical problem.   But we know also that the shifting of relations, though it goes on unceasingly, yet goes on gradually because it is an organic movement; and it goes on, too, without destruction of the existing relations (the removal of the dead is not destruction).   The destruction of the existing, of the living, is, in general, impossible.   We saw that plainly in the French Revolution, which was probably the best planned and the most energetically carried out of all political upheavals; but nevertheless, after the "golden period" of ideological groping around and of fantastic and utopian illusions was past, it was compelled to take things as they were and fit the new onto the old.   In the first rush it may be possible occasionally to crowd out the living; but history teaches us that the most revolutionary and despotic governments were finally compelled by the logic of facts to yield and to recognize perhaps in another form, that which was unnaturally and mechanically abolished.   In short, viewed historically, the present is, as a rule, a compromise between the past and the future.[6]

The distinction can be put this way: men make their own history, but they make it because they are driven to.   The engine of propulsion is the class, and the class struggle is its fuel.   No class can evade its destiny, but its destiny is achieved by the collective activity of the individuals comprising the class.   The lone individual is free to act as he wills, but because the individual alone is impotent and insignificant, history can do without him.   Classes do need leaders to undertake the difficult tasks of organization, strategy, guidance, and timing without which no social movement can succeed, but it is the movement which creates or throws up the leaders, rather than the leaders the movement.   Karl Kautsky illustrates this with reference to Cromwell and Napoleon.   The armies which each of these leaders came to command were revolutionary in origin, which meant that they were not ridden with caste and hereditary privilege; ability rather than family or purse was the qualification of the officer, so that it became possible to say, of Napoleon's armies, that every soldier carried a marshal's baton in his knapsack.   Such armies throw up their own leaders, and Kautsky accord-

---

[6] Wilhelm Liebknecht, *No Compromise—No Political Trading*, Charles H. Kerr Co., Chicago, 1919; pp. 35–36.   The tract was written in 1899.

ingly observed that if Cromwell or Napoleon had not appeared, someone else would have.[7]

Marx, therefore, held aloft the beacon of assured success for his followers, because the movement of history could follow no other course. The plausibility of this gesture depended, first, on revealing in broad outline what the forces of history are and how they operate, and then on showing in greater detail how these were undermining the very foundations of capitalism and clearing the path for the emergent communist society.

THE MATERIALISTIC INTERPRETATION OF HISTORY

For Marx and his followers the clue to all history is the fundamental conception of man earning his living. The way this is done differs from age to age and from place to place, partly because of varying technological conditions, but basically because each evolutionary stage of social development except the final, communist, one, generates forces which eventually overthrow it. Thus an agricultural economy is markedly different from an industrial one; or, to put the matter in its proper evolutionary rather than merely comparative form, feudal society becomes obsolescent when conditions become ripe for the emergence of capitalism. What is common, however, to all forms and stages of historical development is the fact that throughout them all the organization and technology of production are paramount in the sense that it is these which give the dominant color, form the characteristic legal institutions, determine the fundamental social relationships between man and man, and shape the political organization of the society which they characterize. Even men's ideas are rooted in the forms and processes of economic life. For Marx the characteristic ideas of any society are the ideas of its ruling class, but it is the material structure of society which determines which class shall rule: "The hand mill gives you society with the feudal lord; the steam mill, society with the industrial capitalist." [8]

Marx and Engels did not deny that religious institutions, scientific beliefs,

[7] Cf., Sidney Hook, *Towards the Understanding of Karl Marx,* New York, 1933; pp. 164 ff.
[8] Cf., Marx, *The Poverty of Philosophy,* New York, n.d.; p. 92. Cf., also, *The Communist Manifesto.*

and inherited traditions are forces which exert their own influences on men's lives.[9]   The fact that ruling classes refuse to give way gracefully to fundamental evolutionary changes which undermine their position (a fact upon which Marx placed very great emphasis) and that therefore history moves by means of revolutions, clearly indicates that man's thinking does not respond simply and directly to changes in the mode of production.   For Marx and Engels, however, man's way of thinking *derives from* the mode of production and sooner or later must conform to it, although delay, resistance, and even intransigeance in making the adaptation commonly and characteristically occur.   Some of their followers go to extremes and attempt to apply this conception wholly mechanically.   For example:

> The pig is an unclean animal even under ideal conditions.   It is a born scavenger, and is believed to be in a state of chronic disease.   Whether it be the case or not, the fact remains that its dead body putrefies more rapidly in hot countries than do other carcases [*sic*].   To eat the flesh of the pig in the torrid East is to court disease of a particularly virulent kind.   Here in Britain a few may eat pork with impunity.   All other things being equal, no ill effects will follow.   Jews as a rule do not eat pork anywhere because of the Arabian or Eastern pork-taboo.   *God prohibited the eating of swine's flesh.*   They may not know it, but the word "God" in this respect is merely a convenient name for a very material set of circumstances.   To eat pig was to court death.   The death of a tribesman weakened the tribe.   To weaken the tribe was to lower its power of resisting hostile tribes.   The greatest "sin" that could be committed was to act contrary to tribal interests.   By the wielders of superstition "tribal interests" became synonymous with "God's interests."   When God told the Jews not to eat pork it was merely tribal law in the struggle for existence speaking in the name of God through the mouths of a priesthood.   It was *necessary* to do this *then,* and because it tended to *preserve the tribe* it was *good.*   But the man today who doesn't eat pork and gives it as his *sole reason* for not eating it that "God forbids it" is a groveling ignoramus.[10]

THE CLASS STRUGGLE

Man earning his living is thus the basic concept.   In the process of earning his living, moreover, man very early discovered and applied the principle

[9] *Cf.,* M. M. Bober, *Karl Marx's Interpretation of History,* 1st. ed., Cambridge, 1927; pp. 267–273.

[10] *Cf.,* John S. Clarke, *Marxism and History,* National Council of Labour Colleges, London, n.d.; pp. 36–37.   Italics in original.

of the division of labor, the principle that productivity is enhanced by dividing up the tasks to be done so that particular individuals can specialize and concentrate upon different elements in a joint productive process.   This principle involves not only the differentiation of function but the differentiation of power as well.   The division of labor implies class distinctions, and class distinctions bring about class exploitation and class war:

The history of all hitherto existing society is the history of class struggles. Freeman and slave, patrician and plebeian, lord and serf, guild-master and journeyman, in a word, oppressor and oppressed, stood in constant opposition to one another, carried on an uninterrupted, now hidden, now open fight, a fight that each time ended, either in a revolutionary reconstitution of society at large, or in the common ruin of the contending classes.[11]

This differentiation of society into opposing classes one of which always exploits the other, does not arise from human wickedness; [12] either Marx or Engels observes, somewhere, that classical Greece was no more to be blamed for having had slavery than for not having had electric lights or steam engines. Without class antagonism, in fact, history would stand still, which is exactly what Marxists expect history to do once the classless society is achieved. It would be tragic, however, for history to stand still before the class struggle has driven society to develop its productive powers to the point where the classless society can be supported in the style worthy of its merits; and that explains why the world has, first, to undergo the travail of all the antecedent forms of social organization.   Marx observed, "No antagonism, no progress." [13]

This "progress" is not slow, gradual, and continuous, although the forces underlying it probably are.   The men who stand, or think they stand, to suffer by progress, resist its advent until the forces of progress, represented in the oppressed classes, become too strong to resist.   Marxian "progress" thus moves by jumps, each jump occurring when an exploited class becomes

11 *The Communist Manifesto.*   It is interesting to notice that Engels added a footnote to the 1888 edition of the *Manifesto* to explain that this differentiation of classes and the concomitant struggle between them applies to *"Written* history" only [italics his]. In the forty years following the first appearance of the *Manifesto* Engels had come to believe that primitive man lived under communism and that society did not come to be "differentiated into separate and finally antagonistic classes" until these "primeval communities" were dissolved.   He attempted to trace how that Fall of Man resulted in expulsion from that Other Eden in his *Origin of the Family* (Chicago, 1902). That book first appeared, in German, in 1884.

12 *Cf.,* Marx's preface to the first edition of *Capital,* reprinted in *Capital,* Everyman edition, Vol. II, p. 864.

13 *Cf.,* Marx, *The Poverty of Philosophy,* as cited, 1910; p. 66.

strong enough to overwhelm the class that exploits it.   Marx asserts that
any society based upon the differentiation of classes, as all societies antecedent to full-blown communism must be, will have within it one class which is
exploited and oppressed.   The emancipation of that class implies the formation of a new society, and emancipation occurs when the cumulative development of *economic* forces has reached the point at which the existent *social*
organization is no longer compatible with them.   Something must give, and
because it is the economic forces which are primal, their development breaks
what Bagehot called the "cake of custom," [14] the structure of established
wont, and a new society based upon a new orientation of social classes conforming to the new structure of production comes into being.[15]

What this means is that each stage of history up to the final, or communistic, one is dominated by the functional (class) interests which originally
brought it into existence.   Being dominant, the ruling class has every interest in keeping things as they are, despite man's ability to learn and to
store his learning.   Eventually, technical possibilities of more efficient production which have arisen both through man's ability to devise and to learn,
and through self-generated causes within the social process, are held back
by the dominant class.   Those very possibilities, however, are created by
and are in the ultimate interest of the exploited class which then gathers its
powers and eventually bursts forth in its might and wrath to forge a new
society in which *it* becomes the dominant class.   So the process goes on and
will continue to go on, until classes themselves become abolished when the
interests of all men have become finally fused and the full release of society's
potential productive power is achieved with the establishment of full and
complete communism.

THE DIALECTIC

Being at heart a German philosopher, Marx had to avoid any simple
description of this recurrent process of social and economic change, superficial quiescence with accumulating tension, and then change again.   He
accordingly subsumed, as the logicians say, the whole process under his
horrendous Dialectic, which he had borrowed and modified from another

---

[14] *Cf.,* Walter Bagehot, *Physics and Politics,* 2d. edition, London, 1873; p. 27.
[15] Marx, *op. cit.,* pp. 146–147.

German philosopher who had an even greater distrust of the simple—Georg Wilhelm Friedrich Hegel. By the Dialectic Marx really meant no more than the law by which all history, indeed all nature, moves. An institution or a given state of society called the *Thesis,* becomes over-developed, unstable, and sooner or later gives way to something opposed and destined to supersede it called the *Antithesis,* exactly as an ocean wave eventually gets too big for itself, disappears in a mass of foam and is replaced by a following wave made up in part of the elements of the older one. This *Antithesis* also expands, becomes top-heavy in its turn, and eventually collapses into the third form, the *Synthesis,* which, like its predecessors, is adequate for a while but not permanently adequate, so the entire process is repeated, again and again. The Dialectic is really a Dialogue in which history, or nature, or whatever the referent may be, is, so to speak, talking to itself, and through this process of dialectical talking back and forth eventually reaches its predestined conclusion. Every undergraduate knows that the ideal debate is a process in which the contestants alternately prove one another wrong until agreement is reached, unless the timekeeper has prematurely brought things to a halt. If Truth is One and the contestants sincere, agreement must ultimately be reached. That may be why Plato expressed his philosophy in the form of dialogues: the belief, in other words, that Truth would be all the stronger for the buffeting it takes in its emergence.

Unlike a college debate, history has no timekeeper and the dialectical process goes on and on, from chattel slavery to empire, empire to feudalism, feudalism to capitalism, and finally capitalism to communism—where the process stops because no further progress is possible. Class antagonism, the propellent of change, vanishes because classes themselves vanish.

We may now paraphrase Marx to show how the characteristic structure of production in any historical epoch creates political and social institutions which eventually become inappropriate and which must therefore eventually give way, through violence, to their "Antithesis" in the form of a new social structure established through the revolutionary activity of a hitherto exploited class.

Organized society is inevitably characterized by a certain structure of industrial production, a structure that is itself formed by the technology, the resources, and the economic relationships existent in the society concerned. That economic pattern, in turn, comprising as it does the ways in which society supports itself, influences, first, the political and legal institutions that come into existence, and then the very ways in which men think—what Marx calls the "forms of social consciousness." Both law and custom, however, tend to be static, while technology, invention, and experiment are subject to constant change, and sometimes to drastic innovation. The result is that, sooner or later, the legal and political "superstructure" of society becomes outworn: it comes to reflect an obsolescent set of economic and technological relationships, and therefore it *hinders* the continued release of man's productive powers.

As Marx viewed history, legal and political institutions are not susceptible to slow, gradual and continuous change; they are seen as shells that serve initially to protect their economic contents, but that end by constricting the further growth of those contents. Like nut meats, therefore, the growth of the seed can occur only by breaking the protective shell when the meat is ripe; "thesis" passes into "antithesis."

At the time Marx was writing, Western Europe was in ferment, and he interpreted that ferment as the breaking of the shell which, originally, had served the purpose of facilitating and protecting the young capitalist society. He thought the capitalist shell outworn, because he saw the capitalism of his day tending to restrict rather than to expand production. Further economic development, then, had to await the "synthesis," the development of full communism whose arrival would end what he called "the preliminary period of prehistory [16] of human society." [17]

It should now be clear why Marx had no use for the "Utopian Socialists." These assumed, in the first place, that social structures and institutions are more or less plastic, capable of being molded and altered by man; that they are in fact the creation of the prevalent idea-systems of the ages and places in which they appear; that they stand in much the same relation to social philosophies as language stands to thought—that is, as their overt, outward expression.[18] To Marx, this was arrant nonsense. For him, politics have their roots in economic relationships, as does morality, and a people's institutions are just the expression of their system of production.

The Utopian Socialists, moreover, relied largely upon exhortation to induce the ruling class to surrender its birthright; what was worse, they all too often addressed their exhortations to the ruling class itself, a procedure which Marxians consider about as effective as importuning a cat to cease sharpening its claws upon the sofa. Their exhortations were futile, and

[16] This most curious expression—*die Vorgeschichte der menschlichen Gesellschaft*—must have been written in haste. The meaning is clear enough: that only with the resolution of class conflict under communism will mankind enter upon its heritage. But then, the historical process, the Dialectic, will have *stopped,* not begun.

[17] Marx, *Contribution to the Critique of Political Economy,* New York, 1904, p. 13.

[18] The French socialist, Saint-Simon, observed, "Politics have their roots in morality, and a people's institutions are just the expression of their thoughts." *Oeuvres,* Vol. III, p. 31, quoted in Gide and Rist, *A History of Economic Doctrines, from the Time of the Physiocrats to the Present Day,* 2d. English edition, New York, 1948; p. 236.

whatever calls to action they did utter were more than likely to be premature, because they had no conception of historical forces and hence no conception of timing action to the appropriate conjuncture of historical forces.   Last of all, the Utopian Socialists blithely assumed that they could utilize the machinery of the state to bring their utopias into being.   To Marx and Engels, on the contrary, "Political power, properly so-called, is merely the organized power of one class for exploiting another." [19]

THE STATE

According to Marx the state arose early in history as the result of class antagonisms which it was, and is, its function to repress rather than to resolve; and these antagonisms will remain until they have worked themselves out through the dialectical process, and as long as they remain the state will persist.   Arising as it did out of strife, the state power is controlled by the dominant class which, as long as it is able, will never consent to let that power be used against itself.   As a sop to the masses in modern times, "The population, every few years, is given an opportunity to decide which member of the ruling classes is to represent them in Parliament." [20]   Being what it is, the bourgeois state cannot be used to bring about the new order of society, and it is destined to "wither away" once that new order has fully emerged. Engels is quite specific about this.   The state did not appear until after the rift between classes made it necessary, for the protection of a ruling class against disorder or revolt by an exploited class.   The rift between classes is itself necessary because of the need to control society for the purpose of exploiting those productive possibilities which can only be exploited by wringing an economic surplus out of the toil of a lower class, and also because new and more productive techniques become developed by a lower class but cannot be applied until that class becomes itself dominant.   When the economy of abundance becomes technically achievable, classes themselves will become unnecessary because there will be no further need to wring a surplus out of anyone; there will be enough for all.   When there is no further need for oppression the state will have lost its function and will

[19] *The Communist Manifesto.*
[20] An otherwise unidentified statement of Marx quoted in E. F. M. Durbin, *The Politics of Democratic Socialism,* London, 1940; p. 198.

accordingly disappear. "A free and equal association of the producers will put the whole state machine where it will then belong: in the museum of antiquities side by side with the spinning wheel and the bronze axe." [21]

This should not be interpreted to mean that communism, like Athena, is to spring full-grown and beautiful from the skull of its parent. A revolution is a messy business, and for a long period after its initial seizure of power the Proletariat is expected to govern and repress. This Dictatorship of the Proletariat is regarded as necessary as long as any vestiges of the old propertied classes remain in existence; as long, that is to say, as any atavistic yearnings for an exploitative world constitute obstacles to the full emergence of that society in which men shall be comrades working together and sharing alike.

THE SOCIAL ROLE OF RELIGION

Marx's conception of the historical process also explains his famous remark that religion is the opiate of the people. Like other social institutions, religion in its form and substance is molded by the mode of production and infused with class interest, although certain psychological propensities of man are conceded to give religion a partially autonomous origin.[22] But established churches, and through these the religious beliefs which are disseminated among the masses of men, reflect the attitudes of the dominant, exploiting class; at best they dull men's minds to the necessity and opportunity for revolutionary action which the pressure of historical, economic forces brings about, and at worst they actively condition men's minds to the maintenance of the *status quo*.

The criticism of religion ends with the doctrine that man is the supreme being for mankind, and therefore with the categorical imperative to overthrow all conditions in which man is a degraded, servile, neglected, and contemptible being, conditions which cannot be better described than by the exclamation of a Frenchman on the occasion of a projected dog tax: "Poor dogs: they want to treat you like men." [23]

[21] Engels, *Origin of the Family,* quoted by Lenin, *The State and Revolution,* New York, 1932; p. 15.

[22] *Cf.,* Bober, *op. cit.,* pp. 160–172.

[23] Marx, *Selected Essays,* New York, 1926; pp. 26–27.

This cursory survey of the Marxian interpretation of history and its inevitable upshot in the emergence of a communist society, can perhaps be made clearer by a summary of the course of actual past history as Friedrich Engels viewed it.[24]

THE COURSE OF PAST HISTORY

Primitive peoples began with common property in land. Even at this stage, however, the economic and material conditions of existence determine the mode of social organization, since the private ownership of land is out of the question when the way of life is nomadic and constant migration is necessary to support herds. The other essential elements for the determination of a particular phase of human history, that is, the mode of exploitation and the organization of production, are not present except in embryo, since the pastoral mode of life produces no appreciable surplus and, without that, exploitation is impossible.

The Division of Labor

Even in this early period, however, the division of labor appears. It appears within the family—with respect to hunting and the rearing of children, for example—and with it appear the seeds of functional antagonism and exploitation.

This differentiation of function paves the way for the introduction of chattel slavery, and with it private property. Both of these develop, first within the tribe, and afterward in the exchange of commodities with peoples outside the tribe. As the production of commodities increases, the original form of distribution within the primitive commune breaks down, and individual shares of material possessions become increasingly unequal. The original commune now becomes a village, each village now tilling its own lands with its own tools. The change in the methods of production and the development of commerce enable the institution of private property really

[24] This summary will be based without further specific reference upon Engels, *Der Ursprung der Familie*, 6th ed., Stuttgart, 1894; *passim*, and also his *Herrn Eugen Duehrings Umwaelzung der Wissenschaft*, 10th. edition, Stuttgart, 1919; *passim*.

to take hold; and the emergence of property, be it noted, is attributed to economic causes. Force plays no role in this particular change, for the simple reason that private property must exist *before* a robber can seize someone else's property.

Chattel Slavery

The development of private property also explains the appearance of chattel slavery. In order to keep a slave, a master must control both the tools of production and the slave's means of subsistence, and this again means that the institution of private property is antecedent. For slavery to exist, a certain development in productivity must have been attained as well as some degree of inequality in distribution. When this point has been reached, the introduction of foreign labor is possible because labor can now create a surplus and labor power has become a "value." Slaves are then recruited through the agency of war: where, earlier, no prisoners had been taken because there was nothing to do with them, prisoners now can be used and they accordingly become sought. Among all peoples, therefore, which have advanced beyond the tribal, communal stage, slavery becomes the dominant mode of production and becomes, in its turn, the primary cause of the further breakup of the communal system.

The introduction of slave labor now makes possible a still higher development of the powers of production, of trade, of wealth, and of accumulation, and this constitutes a great step forward. Slavery, thus, is a necessary phase in the development of human society because, for the first time, it makes fully possible the division of labor between industry and agriculture. Engels, in fact, goes still further to remark that without slavery there would have been no Greece or Rome, without Greece and Rome no modern Europe, and that therefore without slavery modern socialism itself could not have existed.

From this point on slavery has always existed in one form or another, open or concealed, but always expressing itself in the separation of economic and social classes of which one is always dominant and the other exploited. This condition, moreover, must endure as long as the fullest productivity of human labor remains undeveloped. As long, that is, as working people by the very nature of their work are unable to find leisure to devote themselves to science, art, or administration, a specialized class to attend to those affairs will exist, and that class will be unable to resist the temptation to rest more and more heavily upon the backs of ordinary workers. That is why full communism cannot develop until industrial power is sufficiently prodigious to make possible—and necessary—drastic reductions in the length of the working day. When that stage is finally reached, workers will have the leisure hitherto denied them, the upper classes will then become functionally superfluous if not actual obstacles to further progress, and the time will have come to brush them away.

Empire

To return to the course of history as seen through Marxian eyes, chattel slavery, by the mere development of its own potentialities, brings about its own Antithesis—the phase of Empire. Successful tribes continue to wage war, to take prisoners, and to extend their belligerent operations. As conquest progresses, the wherewithal to wage successful war must be derived to an increasing degree from the surplus produced by slaves. As the political unit grows, successful imperialist wars subject additional peoples, and wars come to be waged to increase the possibilities of economic exploitation. You cannot enslave a whole people, however, because you cannot carry them about with you. They have to remain where they have already been, to continue working the lands they have worked, and so chattel slavery gives way to the rule of subject peoples under the suzerainty of empire.

In turn, empire itself contains the seeds of its own dissolution. As its territories become increasingly extensive, the mounting burden of administration necessitates the formation of subordinate administrative units which, with their increasing remoteness from the central imperial authority and eventually with the declining power of that authority, tend to take matters more and more into their own hands. Thus appears the stage of feudalism which, also, in the long run, is no more stable than its predecessors.

Feudalism

The feudal overlord—the descendant of the regional administrator—with his retainers and his serfs attached to the soil, now becomes the center and the representative of the exploiting class until feudalism, in its turn, commences to wane because of the decreasing importance of the individual serf. If one runs away, it becomes too much trouble to catch him. As the developing towns and cities are largely recruited from these runaway serfs, who are more valuable there than they are on the manor, the balance of power begins to shift in favor of the city and against the countryside.   Cities support themselves by industry and commerce until free industrial or commercial cities, or even leagues of free cities such as the Hansa, ultimately destroy the phase of feudalism which, by comparison with the newly arisen order, has become economically inefficient.

Still, however, there remains the exploitation of class by class.   The craftsman owns his own tools, but the exclusiveness of the guilds which control all access to the opportunities for earning an industrial living (by their control of apprenticeship and their regulation of production) is reinforced by the exclusiveness of commercial monopolies which harry the "interloper." The familiar picture of class differentiation persists.

Full-fledged Capitalism

Finally, the growth of the power of capital, largely but not exclusively through the agency of the Industrial Revolution which deprived the worker of his ownership of the means of production, broke down the guild system and ushered in the system of full-fledged capitalism to which Marx paid such attention.   Still, there is one more stage to come.   The accumulation of capital into fewer and fewer hands, the consequent swelling of the proletariat, the increasing concentration of industry which renders inevitable the organization and rise to class consciousness of labor, the increasing poverty of the working classes, the growth in size and desperation of the industrial reserve army of the chronically unemployed, the increasing intensity of industrial depressions and the increasing severity of the dislocation they engender—all these, predicted by Marx, are presumed to act together to bring about the proletarian revolution when, for the first time in history, the majority of the population, by the now sufficiently developed productivity of labor, will be enabled to wrest control from the hitherto dominant minority.   The Dictatorship of the Proletariat will succeed the capitalist state and its institutions which, as the "idealized superstructure" of a collapsed system, will gradually and in good time "wither away" to be eventually replaced by full and complete communism.   The feat which Marx achieved was that he gave full and complete *confidence* to his followers.

8

The Marxian Analysis of Capitalism

TO MOST men living under capitalism and benefiting from it, the capitalistic system of production is the culmination of mankind's successive ventures in utilizing the resources of the earth with equity, economy, and skill. It seems a "natural" system because it does not depend upon deliberate central planning; it is the system which emerges when men are left to themselves to seek their own interests, and as such it is regarded as a permanent system as long as short-sighted and misguided tinkering does not so thwart the natural free play of economic forces as to render them inoperable. Tinkering does exist; and the capitalist apologia has accordingly assumed as one of its major functions the demonstration that the laws of economics are laws of nature, that they can be used exactly as the laws of gases are used in the internal combustion engine, but that they cannot with impunity be ignored, and still less violated. Capitalist economics, therefore, has two characteristics which mark it off from Marxian economics. It is designed, first, to lay bare the structure of a *permanent* system, or at least of a system which ought to be permanent and which will be as long as men do not willfully and blindly seek false gods. Capitalist economics, also, is an *autonomous* system, self-contained and independent, on the whole, of other social disciplines. Men, to be sure, have certain psychological propensities, they live under varying forms of government and they have different social and religious beliefs; but the laws of economics are

163

regarded as consistent with whatever is fundamental in human nature, and reasonably independent of whatever social and political institutions men in their wisdom or their folly bring into existence.

Marxian economics, on the contrary, regards capitalism as but one stage in the long and violent evolutionary development of human society. It is not and cannot be permanent, and its laws, therefore, are peculiar to it and will pass away with the passing of the system. Hence, while capitalist economics is concerned with structure and the tendency toward equilibrium, Marx defined his task as the revelation of "the economic laws of *motion* of modern society." [1] Because capitalism is impermanent and transitory, its laws are subordinate to the fundamental law of social evolution, the Dialectic. Marxism, therefore, is more than a system of economics; it is a whole social philosophy in which the economic element is but one, albeit a most important, strand. Capitalism, then, is viewed in the perspective of history; it emerged from and will merge into other systems.

THE NATURE OF CAPITALIST "EXPLOITATION"

Like all pre-communist systems, capitalism is believed to rest squarely upon exploitation; but unlike its predecessors, capitalist exploitation does not depend immediately upon the whip. The whip exists; its use is symbolic of the function of the state in capitalist society as Marxians interpret it. But the capitalist whip is used, not to drive the worker into mine or factory, but to repress his attempts to rebel against the system. In the labor market, the worker is wholly free to sell or to withhold his labor, and if he sells it the wage he receives is determined by the impersonal forces of the market. Under a system of slavery, workers are not free to withhold their labor; the whip, accordingly, is a means of production as well as of punishment, has an economic as well as a political function; and the slave's sustenance is grudgingly issued by a grasping master. In contrast, the formal freedom of the capitalist worker and the fact that his sustenance is determined by price, exactly as anything else which is bought and sold, indicates that it is not

---

[1] Marx, *Capital*, Preface to the first edition; Everyman Library, Vol. II, p. 864; italics added.

chicanery, greed, or wickedness [2] that characteristically exploit the worker, but the relations of production themselves.

The Labor Theory of Value

The worker is exploited; he is exploited because by his labor he creates a surplus, something which is worth more than the wage he receives. His exploitation is the more pointed, because labor is regarded as the only source of such economic surplus and for just that reason labor is believed to be the only productive element. In making this point Marx was simply following the long-standing precedent of attempting to weed out "unproductive" from "productive" elements. The medieval prohibition of usury stemmed in part from Aristotle's dictum that money was sterile—that is, unproductive. The physiocrats in late eighteenth-century France believed that industrial and commercial operations, in contrast to agricultural, were unproductive in the sense that they only transferred previously embodied values; only on the land did nature cooperate by *creating* hitherto non-existent matter and value, so that only land produced a surplus. Adam Smith himself carried on the tradition and produced a famous and impressive list of "unproductive" classes in which he included kings, menial servants, clowns, opera singers, churchmen, dancers, and physicians.

Labor as the Source of Economic Surplus

Marx reached the conclusion that only labor is productive by the elimination of alternative answers to the question, Where does the economic surplus—that which is worth more than it costs—come from? It obviously arises somewhere within the process of exchange, since, under capitalism, every economic act is an act of exchange. The employer exchanges a sum of money for somebody's daily work, the manufacturer exchanges a sum of

---

[2] The persons of capitalists and landowners are not, in my book, depicted in rose-tinted colours; but if I speak of individuals, it is only in so far as they are personifications of economic categories, representatives of special class relations and class interests. Inasmuch as I conceive the development of the economic structure of society to be a natural process, I should be the last to hold the individual responsible for conditions whose creature he himself is, socially considered, however much he may raise himself above them subjectively. *Ibid.*, p. 864. Except where otherwise indicated, all quotations from *Capital* are drawn from the Everyman's Library edition, translated by Eden and Cedar Paul, by permission of the publishers, E. P. Dutton & Co., Inc.

money for a piece of equipment or a certain quantity of materials, and the middleman exchanges the commodity or service in which he deals for a sum of money.   Each of these exchanges normally gives rise to a larger amount of money than was initially invested in it; otherwise, exchange would not continue to take place.   A sum of money, then, undergoes some mysterious metamorphosis in the act of exchange whereby it is returned with an increment.   Where does the increment come from?   It cannot come from money itself, for, as hard cash, money is simply petrified value not susceptible to changes in magnitude.[3]   It cannot come from the mere act of exchange, for exchange in its essence is a transfer of equivalents which brings its participants increments of convenience but not of value.[4]   Nor can the increment of value derive from a piece of machinery or capital equipment which is but an inanimate, manufactured object, designed for a specific purpose and capable only of transferring, in the course of its working life, the value incorporated in it to the objects upon which it works.[5]   Only man, and particularly man as worker, is creative; only labor can create value and add it to the product of labor.[6]   That is nothing peculiar to capitalism, for this power of creation has always been and always will be inherent in laboring mankind.   Nor does the unique creativeness, or productivity, of labor invalidate the usefulness of contriving, constructing, and then using increasingly intricate and expensive means of production, even though these have no capacity to create the increment Marx was trying to explain.   They themselves are the fruits of labor, and they incorporate in themselves the value of the labor needed to produce them which it is their function to release as they are used.   Obviously, the greater the quantity of stored-up labor they embody, the greater the quantity they can transfer to the things they help produce.   Nevertheless, the sole, ultimate origin of economic surplus is labor, the process of human toil, itself.

Only labor in the course of the normal working period is capable of producing more than labor's own subsistence needs.   Were society so organized that the laborer received for his toil the full fruits of his labor, or their equivalent in value terms, there would still be a surplus and there would still be an increment; but there would be no exploitation because the full increment would accrue to its producer, and no one would be producing

[3] *Capital*, as cited, Vol. I, p. 154.
[4] *Ibid.*, p. 144.
[5] *Ibid.*, p. 199.
[6] *Ibid.*, p. 154.

more than he received in some form or other. Communists, talking about the communist utopia, envisage just such a society: everyone being a laborer, everyone is productive and there is no parasitic class to live upon the surplus produced by others. The peculiarity of capitalism lies in its denial to the worker of the full value of his labor, as, indeed, do all economic systems in which one class of workers performs its toil at the behest and on the terms of another, an exploiting class. Capitalism is able to do this without apparently violating the terms of abstract justice, because the act of being exploited is a free act, with no elements of naked or designed coercion; nevertheless, some stimulant to labor must exist, or the free owners of labor power might exercise their privilege to withhold labor and thereby bring the wheels of production to a stop. That stimulant consists in the denial to workers of everything vendible but their own labor. As long as resources, reserves, particularly the tools and materials of production are in other hands than those of labor, as long as labor has nothing to sell but labor itself, the freedom to withhold labor resolves itself into the freedom to starve.[7] It is that freedom which is the peculiar attribute of capitalism.

Difficulties in the labor theory of value. The worker, of course, must receive at least the means of his and his family's subsistence; otherwise, the only creative element in the entire productive process would be unable to perpetuate itself, and the system would collapse. He may, indeed, receive something over and above a starvation wage; nevertheless, exploitation exists as long as he produces *more* than the value of his wages, no matter how high those wages be. That differential constitutes the increment whose explanation Marx was seeking, and it is both the source of profit and the determinant of values.

The derivation of profit from the difference between wages paid and value received requires no further explanation. But the famous labor theory of value, the assertion that what commodities are "worth" in terms of money or of other commodities for which they may be traded, is simply the labor it has taken to produce them, has occasioned a great deal of trouble. The melody is not Marx's, but the arrangement is, and it is the arrangement with which we are concerned. Certain casual objections can be brushed away forthwith. The fact that not all workers are equally assiduous, intelligent, or skillful can easily be reconciled with the theory that value is just embodied labor by treating skilled, or exceptionally efficient or productive labor as

[7] *Ibid.*, p. 156.

appropriate multiples of unskilled, standard labor—a device which has been utilized down to the present day.[8]   And the fact that money, the measure of prices, may itself change in value, means no more, as Marx himself recognized,[9] than that the medium in which the standard is generally expressed is itself somewhat unreliable.   It does not alter the relative worth of one commodity in terms of another any more than a dishonest butcher's thumb upsets the fact that a pound of bacon weighs as much as a pound weight.

The relation between profit and value.   It would, moreover, be in the highest degree unrealistic to deny the proportionality between the exchange values and the quantity of labor embodied in most commodities in simple economies, and for some things even in our own economy.   A custom-made suit of clothes is still "worth" more than a machine-made one, and the guarantee "hand-made" is today's unconscious tribute to the labor theory of value.

A more serious difficulty emerges in the attempt to fit this explanation of the way exchange value *emerges* into a description of how resources are allocated among different industries; to explain, in other words, how capitalists decide where to place their money and how they get it back.   For if labor is the sole source of new, as against merely transferred, value, it would clearly seem to follow that the larger the wage bill (given the rate of exploitation of labor, or the proportion in which wages paid stands to value received), the greater will be the economic surplus accruing to the employer-capitalist. In other words, the rational employer apparently should keep his expenditure on equipment to a minimum and hire as many workers as possible.   The labor theory of value also appears to suggest that in industries where the ratio of capital to wages, in terms of labor time, is the same, the rate of profit will be the same; and that among industries where this holds, equal quantities of capital will earn equal amounts of profit.   This clearly does not hold.   Industries do not earn profits in proportion to their expenditures on labor; there is no discernible relation between the volume of profit received and the proportion in which capital is divided among labor, and materials, and equipment.   Marx knew this and he acknowledged it: "This law obviously conflicts with all experience based upon the appearances of things." [10]   In the ninth chapter of the third volume of *Capital* he attempted the resolution of this difficulty.   The capitalist employer seeks profit, and profit is derived from the unpaid labor time exacted from the individual worker by the forces

---

[8] *Cf.*, John Maynard Keynes, *The General Theory of Employment, Interest and Money*, New York, 1936; p. 41.

[9] *Cf.*, *Capital*, as cited, Vol. I, p. 72 and Chapter III.

[10] *Ibid.*, p. 317.

of the capitalist market.   Capitalist employers, however, are also in competition with each other, with the result that any industry showing unusual
profits attracts capital from industries which are not so fortunate.   This
"migration of capital," as Marx phrased it, operating through the forces of
supply and demand, brings about divergencies between the "values" of goods
produced, which are based upon incorporated labor, and their prices which
can be realized in the market.

By means of this incessant emigration and immigration, in one word, by [capital's]
distribution among the various spheres in accord with a rise in the rate of profit
here, and its fall there, [capital] brings about such a proportion of supply to demand that the average profit in the various spheres of production becomes the
same. . . .[11]

This distribution of profits among capitalists in capitalist society resembles
the distribution of clams at a clam-bake: the quantities consumed by different
individuals stand in no direct relation to the quantities of clams these same
individuals contributed to the affair.   In the aggregate, the clams dug equal
the clams consumed, but only in the aggregate.   Similarly, in the capitalist
world: in the aggregate, profits generated equal profits received, but profits
are generated in the labor market and realized in the commodity market, and
between the two markets there is a shuffling about among capitalists of the
totality of profits generated, so that for any individual it is only by coincidence that profits generated equal profits realized.

A long and acrimonious controversy has raged about this thesis, that the
profits realized in an industry do not necessarily correspond to the surplus
value generated in the industry, because prices reflect the forces of market
competition in a manner in which values do not.   Many critics of Marx
feel that this concession to the influence of competition and of the forces of
supply and demand really meant the abandonment of the entire theory that
things are worth the labor it has taken to produce them because labor is the
only force capable of creating value.   Marx himself denied this.   He devoted many dreary pages and a good deal of arithmetic to showing that the
labor theory of value is fundamental and ever-present, no matter how different things appear to be on the surface.   The issue really hinges on the question whether or not a commodity has some sort of intrinsic worth independent
of the amount of money needed to purchase it.   In one sense it has: antique
collectors like to dream of the "bargains" to be found in rural attics, and
housewives occasionally refuse to buy steaks they consider over-priced.

[11] Marx, *Capital,* Charles H. Kerr Co., Chicago, 1933; Vol. III, p. 230.

This distinction is more than a matter of individual wealth, for while a professor's wife might consider steak over-priced in the sense that she could not afford it, a successful banker's wife who could easily afford it might still consider the steak over-priced.   Such disparities frequently mean no more than that the market is imperfect: the seller of a Chippendale chair may not know that he could get more for it than is offered by a rapacious tourist, and the banker's wife may know perfectly well that the butcher whom she boycotts is asking more for a steak than his competitors.   That, however, is not the point.   For Marx, there really was such a thing as intrinsic value, and this was both formed and measured by the labor embodied in the commodities involved.   If that is true, if commodities do have some intrinsic worth independent of their prices, there is no logical inconsistency in pointing out the fact.   It is really rather curious that Marx who, as we shall see, was prone to discover "contradictions" in capitalism, should have failed to include among them the inability of the system to price commodities at their "true" values.

Validity of the labor theory of value.   There is still the question whether such values exist, and, if so, whether it is incorporated labor that creates and explains them.   One interpreter of Marx [12] has attempted to cut the Gordian knot by dropping the labor theory of value entirely and reassembling the Marxian analysis about the conception that the economic value of a commodity is determined by its scarcity in relation to the monetary demand for it.   This, however, means abandoning something quite fundamental. Marxism, like some more orthodox economic philosophies, is concerned with the search for economic exploitation—the search for unearned incomes, for payments which are not justified by proportionate services rendered. Marx found this in the wage bargain by which the capitalist employer becomes the legal owner of commodities which are "worth" more than the wages he paid, directly and indirectly, to get them produced.   If this were not the case there would be no exploitation, for in other respects the purchase of labor is like any other purchase.

The owner of money has paid for . . . a whole day's labour.   It is true that the daily maintenance of the labour power costs only half a day's labour . . . with the result that the value which its use creates during a working day is twice the value of a day's labour power.   So much the better for the purchaser, but it is nowise an injustice to the seller.[13]

[12] *Cf.,* G. D. H. Cole, *What Marx Really Meant,* London, 1934; p. 224.
[13] Marx, *Capital,* Everyman edition, Vol. I, p. 188.

It is true that other elements in the Marxian analysis, such as the vulnerability of capitalism to crises, its instability and impermanence, still remain; but the instrument for the overthrow of capitalism is the working class, and to remove the element of exploitation from the analysis is to deprive it of half its strength and of a large part of its appeal to the very agents upon whom it relies.   So most Marxians, even today, still cling to the labor theory of value.

To others—ignoring those to whom the concept is a call to violence rather than reflection—the labor theory of value as something relevant to the twentieth century has a flavor of artificial antiquarianism, like stockbroker's Tudor architecture in the suburbs.   It would not appear if no one wanted it, but it is not what it seems.   Those aware of the intricacies of modern technology realize that, if capital without labor is idle, so labor without capital is impotent.   Recreational fishing is not highly mechanized, but fishermen do cherish their rods and may even impute to them part, at least, of the credit for landing a bass.   To non-Marxians, the factors of production are plural, and if the correct imputation to any one of them of its proper share of the produce it helped bring into being is difficult, that still does not invalidate the fact that production is a cooperative process; and so is life, at least in the modern world.   The fact that not all we earn is disposable income to us means that others share in what we have helped, at least, to produce; it also means that we may share in what others have contributed.   The withdrawals and exactions of the Bureau of Internal Revenue are unpleasant to contemplate, but it may be that the national security, the provision of justice and the education which those exactions make possible would be still more costly if we had to provide them for ourselves, individually.   The labor theory of value, today, rings no more true than stockbroker's Tudor, but just as the latter, today, has at least the merit of perhaps impressing one's relatives and neighbors, so the labor theory of value, today, has the advantage that it may give heart to the comrades; and that is its real function.

THE MARXIAN FORMULATION OF CAPITALISTIC
LAWS OF MOTION

Marx based the search for profit, then, upon the exploitation of labor. But the appetite for profit is so insatiable that no opportunity for capturing

it is likely to be neglected.   The result is that capitalism is dynamic, continually expanding; and as it expands, it continually changes.   This expansion is both extensive and intensive, proceeding both by lengthening the orbit
of the system and by increasing the efficiency of the operations by which
profit is created.   The expansion, however, is not even; it proceeds by jumps
followed by relapses which become increasingly severe as the system develops; and finally the rate of expansion itself slows down as the system
approaches the climax which is to finish it.   The fact that capitalism is
doomed, and that its doom is to be foreshadowed by increasing distress among
its victims, has often obscured the fact that, even to Marxians, capitalism
has had an historical role to play and that its early expansion not only increased production but improved the lot of the workers as well.

The labor market under capitalism produces a surplus which falls into
the hands of the capitalists, and part of that surplus is saved, or "accumulated."   It is not accumulated at an even or steady rate, because the opening
of new markets and the opportunities for new investment which constitute
the occasions for employment of accumulated capital are themselves jumpy;
but capital does accumulate, and as it accumulates it presses for employment
and so makes possible the employment of additional labor as well.   The
accumulation of capital involves, therefore, increase of the proletariat.[14]
That increase is prompted by the rise in wages which the augmented demand
for labor entails, but this does not mean the diminution of exploitation, because without exploitation accumulation itself could not continue.   Marx
puts this, first fancifully, then baldly:

A rise in the price of labour as an outcome of the accumulation of capital, really
means nothing more than that the golden chain which the worker has forged for
himself has become so long and so heavy that it need not be fastened quite so
tightly. . . .
    The law of capitalist accumulation . . . really means nothing more than this,
that its character is such as to forbid any decline in the degree of exploitation of
labour or any increase in the price of labour which might endanger the constant
reproduction of the capital relation and its continual reproduction on an ever-
enlarging scale.[15]

If this expansion, then, of the capitalist system through the continuing
accumulation of capital involves increasing dependence upon industrial
labor, what holds wages in check?   Even though they rise, as Marx says

[14] Cf., Capital, Everyman edition, Vol. II, pp. 676–677.
[15] Ibid., pp. 682, 685.

they do, they cannot rise to the point of seriously cutting into the surplus value for the sake of which all capitalist economic activity is undertaken, or the entire machine would grind to a halt. Marx found the answer in what he called the industrial reserve army. This is made up partly of the "latent" surplus population in rural districts which can always be drawn upon as a source of industrial labor, partly of the "floating" population comprising workers who have been laid off to give place to younger men, and partly of the "stagnant" population, the casuals, who drift from one ill-paid job to another but who reproduce their kind at a faster rate than any other element of the population.[16] This large, "relative surplus population," which includes at the bottom the outright paupers, is continually being swollen by the influx of workers who have been thrown out of employment because of the introduction of machinery.[17]

The result is that this swollen and amorphous mass of potential workers is constantly pressing upon those who are fortunate enough to have employment; it is constantly growing by the addition to it of more and more displaced workers; and its condition continually becomes more wretched and more degraded. In sharp and growing contrast, at the other pole of society is the group of capitalists, constantly becoming smaller in number but greater in wealth and power; for capitalist development expropriates not only the worker, but the good bourgeois and small capitalist as well. The increasing financial strain of keeping pace, the constant elimination of the weak and inefficient, the growing power of concentrated capital and its ruthlessness toward all that stands in its way—all these combine, first to create monopoly, then to fasten the grip of monopoly upon the entire economic system. This grip eventually becomes so tight that production itself is throttled at the very time that workers, massed together in vast enterprises, are learning the techniques and modes of behavior appropriate to a socialized economy simply because they have been living in what are almost socialized communities. Marx's own words are famous and worth quoting:

One capitalist lays a number of his fellow capitalists low. Hand in hand with such centralization, concomitantly with the expropriation of many capitalists by a few, the cooperative form of the labour process develops to an ever-increasing degree; therewith we find a growing tendency towards the purposive application of science to the improvement of technique; the land is more methodically cultivated,

---

[16] *Ibid.*, pp. 708–712.
[17] *Cf.*, Paul M. Sweezy, *The Theory of Capitalist Development,* New York, 1942; pp. 87–92.

the instruments of labour tend to assume forms which are only utilisable by combined effort; the means of production are economized through being turned to account only by joint, by social labour.   All the peoples of the world are enmeshed in the net of the world market, and therefore the capitalist regime tends more and more to assume an international character.   While there is thus a progressive diminution in the number of the capitalist magnates (who usurp and monopolize all the advantages of this transformative process), there occurs a corresponding increase in the mass of poverty, oppression, enslavement, degeneration, and exploitation; but at the same time there is a steady intensification of the wrath of the working class—a class which grows ever more numerous, and is disciplined, unified, and organised by the very mechanism of the capitalist method of production.   Capitalist monopoly becomes a fetter upon the method of production which has flourished with it and under it.   The centralisation of the means of production and the socialisation of labour reach a point where they prove incompatible with their capitalist husk.   The knell of capitalist property sounds. The expropriators are expropriated.[18]

THE NATURE OF CAPITALIST CRISIS

Marx then proceeded to develop a theory of capitalist crisis, or, as we would say today, a theory of the business cycle.   The movement of the capitalist system toward its "inevitable" end is marked by successive crises and depressions which arise out of the very nature of capitalism itself.   Because "crises are the connecting points of the main contradictions of capitalism," [19] they are the means by which capitalist industry temporarily breaks through the bonds which have been increasingly restricting its development, but the release is temporary; the system becomes more tightly bound by the time of the next crisis.   Therefore, crisis does not succeed crisis continually on the same plane.   Crises become worse as capitalism develops, which means that as capitalism itself becomes ripe for supersession, the intensity of crises becomes increasingly severe, and emergence from them increasingly difficult.

The Accumulation of Capital

The matrix in which capitalist crisis inevitably develops is the existence and necessity for the accumulation of capital in a class society, accumulation

18 Marx, *op. cit.*, Vol. II, p. 846.
19 *Economic Crises*, Marxist Study Courses, New York, n.d., Part II, p. 5.

which creates the conditions from which crises emerge and emerge again; for accumulation cannot cease.   This necessity for accumulation, together with its disastrous consequences, is one of the "contradictions" which crises have the function of temporarily resolving.   It is important to understand that it is not accumulation as such that creates crises, but the class structure of the society in which accumulation occurs.   Accumulation, doubtless, will take place in the "classless" society of the future, but because of the absence of class struggle and class contradictions in that society, accumulation will not carry crises in its wake.

Accumulation in capitalist society is made necessary by the pressure of competition which forces entrepreneurs continually to seek means of reducing costs through increasing the productivity of labor.   The unremitting struggle for profit makes industrial survival itself contingent upon keeping abreast of competitors, through the accumulation of more and more and better and better capital equipment.   The intensity of this pressure increases with the development of capitalism; as the final holocaust, the "general crisis of capitalism," approaches, devices to increase the intensity as well as the technical productivity of labor are drawn into more and more common use.

The increase in productivity which accumulation makes possible means that labor is being exploited more effectively: the difference between the costs of employing labor and the returns derived from its employment becomes relatively greater.   At the same time, however, the quantity of ancillary equipment needed by labor has also increased, so that increasingly extensive plant and increasingly expensive equipment are needed to produce the same commodities.   There consequently ensues a sort of race between the mounting costs of making labor more effective and the larger returns which more effective labor can create.

There are certain devices by which these mounting costs can be held in check, at least for a time.   Capital equipment itself becomes cheaper as the result of heightened labor productivity; increases in wages can be restrained by the pressure of the industrial reserve army, and sometimes wages can even be reduced; scientific management—the stretch-out and speed-up systems— can increase the intensity of labor without correspondingly increasing labor costs; the importation of cheap foodstuffs and raw materials together with the export of capital to "backward" areas where profits and interest are high, offset high costs and lower returns at home; and, above all, the increased productivity of labor itself, the incentive behind accumulation, enables a given quantity of labor employed at the same rate of wages to produce a greater quantity of commodities in the same period of time than it previously could.

The Contradictions of Capitalism

Nevertheless, one of the famous "contradictions" of capitalism has become revealed in this process: the tendency for increasing accumulation to reduce the rate of profit can only be offset by raising the productivity of labor through increasing accumulation itself.   This is so because the tendency for the *rate* of profit to fall can be offset only by increasing the aggregate net *mass* of profit through increasing accumulation proportionately.   The relationship is perfectly precise; in order that the mass of profits may remain constant, the multiplier indicating the growth of the total capital (that is, the rate of accumulation) must equal the divisor indicating the fall in the rate of profit.   The total capital must be annually doubled if the rate of profit is being annually halved.   This is not the whole story, however, for since a *larger* net aggregate of profit is the main incentive to accumulation, crises can only be avoided if the multiplier indicating the growth of total capital *exceeds* the divisor indicating the fall in the rate of profit.

The great "contradiction" of capitalist society can now be precisely formulated.   The formulation was suggested by Marx and developed by his successors, of whom Lenin, in this respect, was the most important.   Capitalism, dependent upon profits, is compelled to accumulate increasingly rapidly in order to achieve the necessary increase in the mass of profits, while, at the same time, each increment of new capital causes a fall in the rate of profit by increasing the base against which net profits are calculated; and this forces the addition of still a new increment of capital.   One consequence of all this is a distortion in the structure of industry.   Since accumulation proceeds through the continuous installation of new, and more, plant and equipment, the industries producing capital goods become subject to accelerated development.   As accumulation goes on, however, a critical point is eventually reached at which the final increment added to capital produces no more, or even less, profit than the original amount of capital before the increment was added.   When that point is reached, accumulation comes to an abrupt halt because the incentive to it has disappeared.

Capital accumulation, therefore, carries the primary responsibility for the onset of crises and for the depressions which follow them.   Thus, Marx is essentially no adherent of the under-consumptionist theory of the business cycle as we are sometimes told. He remarks, in fact, that a crisis is usually preceded by a *rise* in real wages because unchecked accumulation tends to get ahead of the natural increase in population, so that prosperity begins to eat even into the industrial reserve army. The consequent relative scarcity of labor forces a rise in wages which reduces the surplus value derived from the employment of labor, and accelerates still further the fall in the rate of profit.[20]

The ensuing crisis is characterized by the simultaneous unemployment of labor and of capital, yet these cannot be brought together again without still further depressing the already unprofitable level to which the rate of profit has sunk. The crisis, however, like capitalism itself, contains the seeds of its own dissolution, for the crisis destroys capital. It destroys it partly through the forced writing-down of capital values, and partly by actual, physical deterioration following its reduced use in production and by the postponement of necessary repairs and replacements. As capitalism nears its end, and its crises become more prolonged and severe, this physical destruction of capital acquires enhanced significance. Deterioration through disuse and failure to repair or replace becomes less significant, while what looms up with mounting portent is the actual, deliberate destruction of capital through the organized policy of capitalist industry itself. The purposive purchase and destruction of "redundant" equipment—such as happened, for example, in British shipyards at the end of the First World War—to say nothing of the control of plant capacity and the restrictions of output which at times are industrial commonplaces, are frequently adduced by Marxians in support of this point.

This diminution in total capital eventually raises the rate of profit again, by reducing the base against which profits are calculated; and the process is helped by the wage reductions and unemployment which accompany depression. Because wage reductions, however, cannot initially keep pace with the fall in prices, this result is not immediately apparent. In the early stages of depression every turnover of capital results in loss, because the market price of commodities is oriented, not to their costs (in terms of labor) of production, but to their costs of *re*-production; when these fall, they bring down with them the values of goods previously produced at higher costs, but not yet sold. Accordingly, the longer the turnover period of capital during a period of falling prices, the greater the loss. This very loss, however, eventually reduces the costs of things industry must purchase and thus cancels

[20] *Cf., Capital,* Chicago, 1933; Vol. II, p. 476; Vol. III, pp. 312–313.

itself through a temporary increase in the rate of profit; but, again, at the cost of a tremendous loss of capital.

Just as accumulation was ultimately responsible for the crisis, so is accumulation the means by which recovery is achieved. The fall in prices and the intensified pressure of competition provide the impetus for increasing aggregate profits by the further concentration of capital and mechanization of processes. A crisis is thus the eventual starting point for a wave of new investment. Accumulation, accordingly, is begun toward the end of depression, expanded in revival, reaches its peak in prosperity, and is abruptly but temporarily checked with the crisis.

The Marxian Doctrine of the Worsening of Crises

It is now possible to see why crises become progressively worse as capitalism develops. The destruction of capital which crises bring about makes further accumulation possible; but, because not *all* capital is destroyed in a crisis, the restoration of capital initiated after a crisis is over commences at a higher absolute level in each successive revival. This means that as time passes the rate of accumulation is accelerated, and thus the continued long-run decline in the rate of profit. The moment will finally come when a small rate of profit on a large total capital will produce an absolutely greater mass of profit than would be produced by a high rate of profit on a small total capital. As it develops, this inevitable concentration of capital forces the small accumulations of small capitalists either to lose their separate identities through merging, or it forces them into speculation or similar uses which do nothing to mitigate the intensity of crises; in the end, these smaller aggregations of capital are either lost or absorbed by the greater. The inescapable emergence of monopoly, or "finance capitalism," means that the concentration of capital becomes so great and the rate of profit so low, that artificial and restrictive measures must be taken to protect even the mass of profit. This is what Marx means by his assertion that capitalism eventually "fetters" the forces of production.

Different enterprises, different industries, and even different nations develop at different rates. The appearance of monopoly in some branches of industry and not in others, aggravates the disparity between industry and industry, between industry and agriculture, between small and big business, and so aggravates the "anarchy" of capitalist production as a whole.[21] Dif-

---

[21] *Cf.*, V. I. Lenin, *Imperialism, the Highest Stage of Capitalism*, New York, 1933; pp. 88, 113, and *passim*.

fering rates of national development sharpen the contradictions of capitalism, intensify the competition to exploit backward regions and countries, foment political and economic tensions, stimulate the concentration of capital, deepen the effects of crises, and prolong the duration of depressions. Monopoly, like other emergents in the development of capitalism, both intensifies existing structural tensions and arises out of them.

Marxian Views on Monopoly

For monopoly does not displace competition; it intensifies and distorts it. Under monopoly, competition does not so much occur among the small, independent capitalists with whom Marx himself, for the most part, was dealing; it occurs among entire industries, among monopolies whose goods may be substituted for each other, and among all monopolies for the largest possible share of the consumer's dollar.[22] It also occurs among imperialist states for markets, colonies, spheres of influence, sources of raw materials, and for the exploitation of backward territories.

Furthermore, under monopoly, or finance capitalism, the export of capital gradually becomes of greater importance than the export of goods, because the pressure of accumulated capital at home drives the rate of profit there considerably below its level in countries where real accumulation has not yet occurred on anything like the same scale. This process accelerates the industrialization of undeveloped regions, fosters the emergence of new or would-be imperialist powers as these regions become themselves industrialized; and by now it has reached the point at which the economic division of the world among these powers has been completed.[23] This means that inter-imperialist competition and rivalry is even more intense than heretofore, since no nation can now extend its sphere of influence or its colonial possessions except by the forcible displacement of some already entrenched power.

Finally, monopoly reduces the consuming power of the society in which it appears. It does so both by depressing the prices of the things it purchases, and hence its disbursements, and by raising the prices of the things it sells thereby leaving consumers fewer funds to expend elsewhere. It can manipulate wages and depress the prices of raw materials, especially those which are agricultural in origin; it expropriates or dominates small producers; and

[22] Cf., E. Varga, *The Great Crisis and Its Political Consequences, Economics and Politics, 1928–1934,* London, 1934; p. 28.
[23] Cf., Lenin, *op. cit.,* p. 70.

by curtailing production through such devices as the quota system within cartels and by valorization schemes, it reduces both employment and the volume of goods available for distribution; and it exacts higher than competitive prices from its purchasers.

As a result of all this there emerges a new "contradiction." In order to maintain selling prices, the expansion of production is curtailed by the restriction of output. But the drive to lower costs of production—a drive which arises from the intensified competition characteristic of monopoly and from the pressure exerted by the still falling rate of profit—forces the erection of technically more perfect plants, equipped to produce on a yet larger scale.

THE END OF CAPITALISM

The period of the "general crisis of capitalism" emerges with the adoption of a permanent policy of restricted output. When monopoly begins to "fetter" production because the development of its productive powers has reached the point at which the minimum rate of profit necessary to uphold the essential class structure of capitalist society can no longer be maintained with full production, then capitalism is being untrue to its historical mission of *releasing* the powers of production; its task is accomplished, its

private business relations and private property relations constitute a shell which is no longer suitable to its contents, a shell which must inevitably begin to decay if its removal is postponed by artificial means; a shell which may continue in a state of decay for a comparatively long period . . . but which will inevitably be removed.[24]

This general crisis is marked (1) by the chronic surplus of labor as manifested in a permanent army of unemployed, no longer reabsorbed in prosperity—except under the impact of war, which recently is capitalism's characteristic way out of its troubles—and hence no longer to be thought of as a "reserve" army; (2) by the chronic surplus of capital, as expressed in unused capacity; (3) by the chronic congestion of trade and the existence of unused bank reserves; (4) by the deliberate physical destruction of goods and equipment for which no *profitable* use or market can be found; (5) by the deep and chronic depression of agriculture and agricultural states—

[24] Cf., *ibid.*, p. 115.

which, again, only war can mitigate; and (6) by the intensification and deepening of colonial struggles and imperialist rivalries which lead inexorably to war.

This general crisis is brought about, very simply, by the fact that the productive capacity of mature capitalist society has become so great that profit, in the capitalistic sense, has become impossible. Society is then ripe for the last, great explosive release of productive powers under communism, an explosion which can be delayed but not averted. Its delay is occasioned by vested interests who can only be injured by the elimination of social classes in the projected new society of the future. Because they resist the emergence of that society, a transitory dictatorship of the proletariat becomes necessary. That dictatorship is necessarily transitory, although the transition may take a long time, because when the task of the dictatorship is accomplished and the classless society has in fact become established, there will be nothing left for the dictator to do; the dictatorship and its machinery will wither away. And then, full communism emerges, with its simple law: From each according to his powers, To each according to his needs.

PART FOUR

Competing Systems as Going Concerns

9

The Structure and Background of Fascism

HE word *fascism* is derived, through Italian, from the Latin *fascis*, or bundle, of which the plural form, *fasces,* signified a symbolic bundle of sticks and axe which was carried in processions in front of high Roman magistrates. The symbolism was baleful: the bundle represented the implements with which criminals were scourged and beheaded. All fascist states scourge, and fascist Germany also beheaded, so the *fasces* were not inappropriate symbols for the more modern societies which adopted fascism as a way of life.

Curiously enough, the *fasces* appear as a symbol on the reverse of the American dimes minted in the twenties, thirties, and early forties, many of which are still in circulation. The symbolism of these, happily, is somewhat different and is expressed in the motto *e pluribus unum,* which appears on the same side of these same coins. The *fasces* were a *bundle,* so they also represented the unity which can be fashioned from diversity. The *fasces* are accordingly a confusing symbol, representing the three elements of unity, diversity, and coercion, but in varying proportions according to the propensities of the interpreter. Americans who use the symbol have not been fearful of diversity; they have observed, In Union There Is Strength, and union implies a union of diversities. Fascists proper have emphasized the unity, primarily because they are fearful of diversity; the suggestion of coercion carried in the *fasces* looms larger.   To the Romans, the *fasces* probably symbolized simply law and order.

The symbol of fascism is somewhat easier to identify than its essence, largely because what fascists say about themselves is inconsistent, opportunist, and expedient.   The Soviet Union shares with avowedly fascist states a totalitarian structure, the denial of freedom to individuals, the oppression of unwanted minorities, and an authoritarian, but erratically veering, party line; yet the term *fascist* is used by the Russians only as an epithet, and a nasty one at that.   The acknowledgedly fascist states have been dictatorships, yet dictatorships existed long before fascism.   Nazi Germany is usually included among the fascist states, yet the anti-Semitism which was so marked a characteristic of Hitler's Germany never really took hold in the state which first called itself fascist.   Was prewar and wartime Japan a fascist society, or simply a tight military dictatorship?   Should Peron's Argentina or Salazar's Portugal properly be called fascist?   The answers differ according to the individuals giving them, and the reason is that the meaning of fascism is essentially elusive.

THE CONTRAST BETWEEN FASCISM AND SOCIALISM

We have seen that communism and socialism are basically attempts to order society in the form of a previously articulated pattern.   So far as the modern world is concerned, the theory of socialism existed long before the large-scale and ultimately successful attempts to establish it which we have been seeing in our own era.   The result is that the basic pattern of socialism is fairly clean-cut; we know that it comprises some form of public ownership and operation of essential industries, the transfer of control of the means of production to labor's collective hands, the bringing to birth of some form of economic franchise of the same extensiveness as the political franchise which became progressively extended during the nineteenth century.   Varieties in both emphasis and accomplishment exist, as well as alternative means of attaining the fundamental ends of socialism; but the basic ideas are always present, and they constitute a standard against which the accomplishments and programs of socialist or putative socialist societies can be measured.   Because there is a standard it is possible to say, for example, that contemporary Great Britain is more socialist than contemporary America.

It is not so easy in the case of fascism.   It is entirely possible to say that one nation is more controlled, more authoritarian, more managed, even more ruthless than another, but it takes thought to assert with conviction and plausibility that one nation is more fascist than another.   One reason is that, in contrast to socialists who try to attain or to live up to a standard, fascists play by ear, by hunch or instinct, and set up their standard, if they bother at all, afterward.   It is not completely false to say that the fascist does not realize what he has been doing until he has seen what he has done, and that *then* he sets about rationalizing it.   Still worse, because fascist programs and policies have frequently been subject to startling reversals in direction and shifts in content, their *ex post* rationalizations, put alongside each other, form a mixture of incompatible and incongruous elements not easy to emulsify.   This is so even in what passes for fascist philosophy:

. . . the fascist parties, whether in Italy or in Germany, have had no coherent political or social philosophy.   What has passed for fascist philosophy is vague, often studiously so; it is a body of ideas taken from various sources and put together to fit the exigencies of circumstances.   It is unrefined by discussion, frequently hysterical in tone and sometimes intentionally so, and largely indifferent to incompatibilities.   Its elements had for the most part been long in existence. These elements have been submitted to new constructions and have been recombined in new and sometimes incongruous ways.[1]

Whatever pattern does emerge is the pattern of opportunism; fascists recoil from binding commitments.[2]

Fascist Nationalism

The distinction between socialism and fascism has another aspect.   The former is avowedly international, not only in the sense that as a standard socialism is internationally accepted by socialists, but also because theoretical socialism looks forward to an increasing amount of international cooperation among socialist states.   Like all standards, except perhaps the double standard of morality, it is somewhat out of reach: socialist Britain, even under the Labour Government that held office between 1945 and 1950, refused to merge its armed forces into a European army, but the standard, nevertheless, is there.

Fascism, on the contrary, is nationalist, and frequently aggressively so.

[1] George H. Sabine, *A History of Political Thought,* New York, 1937; p. 747.
[2] *Cf.,* Herman Finer, *Mussolini's Italy,* Henry Holt, New York, 1935; p. 18.

Negatively, fascists have at least asserted a lack of interest in making converts beyond their national frontiers.   Mussolini remarked that fascism was not for export, and Alfred Rosenberg said the same of German national socialism.[3]

Positively, fascists, like the mercantilists before them, have been obsessed with the conviction that the world's supply of resources is fixed, that the world is a closed system characterized by a frenzied international scramble for something that is scarce, whether it be gold, or prosperity, or power. Just as each ounce of gold brought into seventeenth-century England was welcomed as an ounce of gold denied the Dutch, so every twentieth-century German export to Brazil was acclaimed an export the United States could not make, and every absolute increase in Italian power was interpreted as at least a relative decrease in French might.

Socialism, accordingly, is a philosophy of development in which latencies are thought to be progressively actualized, resources are found as they become needed, and possibilities have the opportunity of becoming quickened into realities.   Fascism, on the contrary, is a movement believing that the more you get the less there is left for me, that it is the division rather than the size of the pie which is meaningful, and that national self-interest requires not only that one's own grasp be both strengthened and extended, but that the grasp of others—who being others are rivals—be loosened and contracted.

All this means that national differences loom very large indeed in fascism; national tradition, frequently in most distorted form, is packaged as a wand or torch to be passed unblemished to the relay of the next generation, and the future is portrayed as a challenge to national achievement.   This makes for a very rigid pattern indeed within any single fascist society, because of the uniqueness of each national tradition; it also suggests a certain formlessness about fascism as a whole, because in the degree in which these national traditions have been captured by fascists they are potentially, and sometimes actually, hostile to each other.   And this reduces generalizations about fascism as a whole to something like Hobbes' war of each against all. More seriously, fascism is difficult to distinguish as a unique entity because everything that a fascist does, considered separately, has also been done by people who were not fascists, and some fascists do things that other fascists

---

[3] Mussolini, "Speech to the Chamber," November 18, 1925, and Pierre Grosclaude, *Alfred Rosenberg et le mythe du xxième siècle,* Paris, 1938; p. 65.

do not.   Secret police, for example, are utilized by fascists, but were not invented by them; anti-Semitism was an integral part of German, but not of Italian, fascism.

Since, therefore, fascists themselves offer little help in defining their movement by what they say, it behooves others to attempt to discern its elements by observing the behavior of societies which have been content to call themselves fascist.   The opportunism of fascist behavior provides the first clue.

Fascist Opportunism

In both Italy and Germany the early fascist movements attempted to be all things to all men.   Shopkeepers and captains of industry, peasants and landed aristocrats, the white-collared salariat together with the horny-handed proletariat, were indiscriminately besought to give their support to a movement which vaguely offered promises of employment, prosperity, security, and fulfillment while conveniently glossing over the hard and stubborn fact that the only means by which some of these ends could be attained must necessarily alienate some of the very elements the nascent movement was seeking to attract.

In its early days the fascist movement in Italy was very close to the socialists, at least in its proclaimed platform.   It supported popular sovereignty based upon universal, equal, and direct suffrage; it advocated a considerable measure of local self-government together with stringent limitations upon central executive authority; it demanded freedom of thought, of association, of religion, and of the press; it recommended the dissolution of joint-stock companies, the nationalization of credit, and the redistribution of wealth in favor of the poor; and, finally, it called for general disarmament, the disappearance of secret diplomacy, the elimination of military conscription, and the general prohibition of the manufacture of armaments.[4]

Similarly, in Germany, the official program of the National Socialist Party as drawn up in 1920, demanded the elimination of unearned income, the confiscation of wartime profits, abolition of the "slavery of interest," the nationalization of trusts, profit-sharing with labor, support of small business, the prohibition of speculation in real estate, the virtual elimination of the system of mortgages, the death penalty for usurers and profiteers, the ex-

[4] Cf., G. D. H. and Margaret Cole, The Intelligent Man's Guide to Europe Today, London, 1933; pp. 619–620.

tension of public education, the abolition of a professional army, and a large measure of religious toleration.[5]

Opportunism, in each of these cases, was used to attain power. But as soon as the fascists in Italy and the National Socialists in Germany became entrenched, the mask came off; blandishment through promises was no longer useful because political weakness could no longer be used as an excuse for not fulfilling them; also, in the last resort, such blandishment was no longer necessary because the castor oil bottle and the rubber truncheon could then openly be employed to elicit—if not support—at least, acquiescence. Blandishment of another variety did develop. Fascist societies are opportunist internally because they are really denied the security of genuine and spontaneous public support. That, at least, is the safest assumption for fascist rulers to make, because they never really know what their subjects are thinking. The closed ranks, the united front, the frowning monolith with which fascist dictators seek to confront a trembling world would crumble were internal challenge tolerated; moreover, the momentum and drive sought to give virility to a thrusting national movement compel the closure of the safety valves of freedom of thought and expression, exactly as the safety valves on Mississippi River steamers used occasionally to be tied down by pilots who wished to increase pressure in the boilers. In each case, that action carried risks: *Naturam expellas furca, tamen usque recurret.*

Because fascist authority dares not give in to public opinion, it must mold it; the Ministries of Propaganda and Enlightenment grow formidable in proportion as the need to divert public attention from what really is being done, or not done, becomes great, or as the need to suggest false justification for genuine sacrifice becomes acute. The possibility of doing either depends upon seizing the vagaries of the public mind, upon the discernment of opportunities emerging in the course of events both internal and external. Events being erratic and opportunity capricious, propaganda must be opportunistic. It was not for nothing that the main character—he can scarcely be called a hero even though he had an urge toward resistance—of George Orwell's *1984* [6] was employed in falsifying the records of the past.

External policy, likewise, is opportunistic. Fascists, like communists, interpret the world as peopled by their opponents; to hesitate is to lose, to

---

[5] *Cf.,* Thomas Reveille, *The Spoil of Europe,* New York, 1941; pp. 319–324.

[6] George Orwell's *1984,* New York, 1949, is, we may hope, a purely fanciful picture of society a generation hence. That society is essentially fascist, and its Leader is known as Big Brother.

be squeamish is to fail; but to seize is to succeed, provided that what is seized is within one's reach; but circumstances, again, determine what can be grasped.   Sometimes opportunism suggests clasping the hand of one who has been, and will yet again be, one's opponent, as in 1938 Hitler and Stalin placed themselves in temporary and tenuous alliance.   Again, it was not for nothing that George Orwell's Big Brother was constantly at war, but a war in which allies and opponents were subject to momentary and capricious interchange.

THE CONTENT OF FASCISM

Repudiation of Democracy

Again, unlike the socialists who are confident of ultimate success because they believe themselves to be waging a campaign to adapt the machinery of the state to the active protection and advancement of the material interests of the common man who, therefore, should be bound in time to fall in with the socialist movement, fascists are never really confident of genuine public support, and are accordingly driven to seek strength in obfuscation, evasion, and, in the last analysis, naked force.   Socialists, at least in Western Europe, Great Britain, and the United States, believe, rightly or wrongly, in the compatibility of socialism with democracy, because they believe, rightly or wrongly, that socialism offers the only contemporaneous hope of assuring that minimum of material welfare without which Bills of Rights become meaningless.   Fascists are driven to repudiate Bills of Rights because their recognition would imperil the only elements in society which have a vested interest in preserving that which fascism really represents.   These elements can be identified by their distrust of democracy; that is, by their fear of labor, their veneration for privilege, and their denial of any inalienable right to life, liberty, or the pursuit of happiness.   As far as fascist behavior is concerned, the repudiation of democracy takes the form of the effective regimentation of labor, the deliberate justification and protection of privilege, the ruthless repudiation of any expression or manifestation of individualism, the express replacement of liberty by authority and discipline, and the unctuous enthronement of duty in place of happiness.   All this becomes evident after a fascist movement has come to power and the need to conceal its real meaning has become obviated by the acquisition of powerful means of propaganda and coercion.

The ballot. Expressed in action, the institutions of democracy are obliterated through distortion when they fall into fascist hands. The ballot, when it is resorted to at all, is an illustration. It is utilized as a device to give a semblance of massive public support, but to a degree inconceivable to those who are really familiar with the raucous push and haul of genuine democratic processes. Few outsiders accept at face value the majorities of ninety-six, ninety-seven, or ninety-eight per cent in support of something proposed by Hitler or Stalin, or of the election of these candidates themselves to offices from which they are unlikely to be ousted by an electorate; what skepticism may exist within fascist states, the world probably will never know.

The party. Not only is the ballot as it exists in democratic societies distorted; political parties themselves are abolished. To be sure, the name is kept for the single permitted organization which is entrusted with political functions, but the Fascist, National Socialist—or, for that matter, Communist—Party is generically different from, say, the Republican or Democratic Party in the United States. For one thing, it is never confronted with organized, but legal, opposition. For another, a fascist party does not simply establish an administration; it captures the state, and intends and is intended to remain permanently in power. It is perfectly true that both the Democratic and Republican parties in the United States have upon occasion remained in office for a generation at a time, but such party dominion is nevertheless quadrennially subject to orderly, legal displacement; and, so far at least, eventual displacement has always occurred. That is a risk which fascist parties are spared. Finally, and perhaps most important of all, the party, in fascist states, is exclusive; continuing, or even initial, membership is not open to everyone, even though non-membership carries hazards. Individuals in democratic societies are wholly free to select and enlist in the party of their choice, to change their party allegiance at will, or even to remain independent. In fascist societies the party *selects* its membership, and membership, accordingly, is a privilege rather than a right. It is a privilege which can be withdrawn and frequently is in order to conserve the distinction which membership carries.[7] In form, the now familiar purges which fascist parties periodically undertake represent simply the

---

[7] "The Party in Italy may be considered as the political elite, drawn from all strata of the Italian people, devoid of sectarian or class interests." *Cf.*, Italian Library of Information, *The Organization of Production and the Syndical Corporative System, an Outline Study,* mimeographed, New York, n.d.; p. 51.

process of searching out and removing those members who have proved themselves unworthy of membership. In fact, the process of purging is frequently something more. The opportunism of fascist policy means that now and then the party line must be changed. Democratic states also change their policies at times, but they do so by turning out the party in power and entrusting the new policy to its successors. A fascist party has no opposition and expects no successor, so that a change-over can only be accomplished by changing the composition of the party itself. Those who are tainted with the earmarks of the now abandoned policy must go, and there is no place for them to go but out.

Education for party membership. Despite the exclusive character of party membership, fascist states do attempt to train as large a proportion of the population for membership as possible. This is particularly true for children. The schools represent only part, although an important part, of the machinery for achieving this. In addition to fascist schooling, however, children at very tender ages indeed are maneuvered into organizations, somewhat resembling the Scouts elsewhere, but with the significant difference that these fascist organizations are most politically oriented, and are also designed to prepare children for the military and labor service they must undergo when they become young men and women. Some erosion, of course, takes place throughout this whole series of educational processes, but their purpose is still to prepare everyone who can qualify for eventual membership in the party and, also, for services to the fascist state. Their intent, also, is to detect potential leaders and to train these for the leadership they must eventually assume.

That is why the erosive process is accepted. Desirable as it may be to have completely unanimous public support, both active and passive, fascists are most sensitive to the inequalities among men. They do not believe the rank and file capable of political judgment; they regard decisions by majority vote as clumsy, capricious, and undependable. The real function of the party, therefore, is to exercise the leadership which the electorate is deemed incapable of exercising, so that the party must comprise only the elite to whom leadership can be entrusted. The erosive process which has been mentioned is designed, therefore, not only to detect dissidents and malcontents, but to identify and expel from the privileged corps of leaders those unhappy individuals who are capable only of being led.

Enthronement of Privilege

The leadership principle. The fascist elite exists to lead; but how is it to do so? Democratic states have leaders, too, but these lead because they command public confidence; in power, they lead because public confidence has entrusted them with political responsibility, and out of power they may lead also because they can make themselves heard. Fascist leaders also seek to lead public opinion, but they are not dependent on it in the same direct and immediate sense. Under fascism, the place of public opinion as the court of last resort is taken by one top, supreme Leader. In place of the chain of responsibility is a chain of command. In place of attempts to guide and convince public opinion is the attempt to condition it. The organization of fascism is the organization of an army, within which the lesser leaders are responsible *to* their superiors, and responsible *for* their subordinates. Power is derived from the dictator and is distributed in unequal doses and with uncertain tenure.

The party, as the creature of the Leader, is in the last analysis outside the law. It exercises the monopoly of political responsibility; it is exclusive and open only to people who have been politically educated for membership by one means or another and who can be certified as worthy to belong; and, in its most developed form—for example, in Nazi Germany—it maintains institutions and exercises responsibilities which elsewhere are reserved for the state itself. It provides the ideological leadership and itself frequently administers the machinery of terror by which the recusant and recalcitrant are kept in line. The state, indeed, may become the appendage of the party under the complete domination of the Leader; in such case, domestically the party becomes the primary agent both of propaganda and of coercion; internationally it frequently becomes the agent of imperialism.[8]

It is in this context in which a completely materialist practice overlies an almost mystical theory, in which authoritarianism walks in the robes of paternalism, that the Germans preached, *Ein Reich, ein Volk, ein Fuehrer;* and the Italians, *Crédere, obbedire, combattere.*

The conditioning of public opinion. One would expect the man in the street, pondering his life and the prospects of himself and his children, to chafe at the compulsions, austerities, and stringencies of fascist society even

---

[8] The Soviet Union which, despite its disavowals, adopts where it did not actually initiate many of the institutions of fascism, illustrates this. The Russian state, formally, minds its own business; the Communist Party minds everyone else's.

if he did not permit his mind to dwell upon its darker aspects. If G. K. Chesterton was right in believing that the ordinary man is more concerned with his beer and his pipe, his Saturday afternoons and his Sunday mornings, than he is with the abstract freedoms, perhaps the fascist man in the street is not unduly distressed over his ability to read only what is printed for him and to hear only what is blared at him. Perhaps for him mild grumbling and the surreptitious whispering of political jokes are adequate substitutes for outright freedom of speech. But what about the disappearance of the church in which he may have been brought up and to which he possibly has been accustomed to resort? What about the moral if not physical seizure of his children, and their training to report to the secret police the political lapses or derelictions of the parents? What about the regimentation of his labor, the compulsion to go where he is ordered, to do what he is told at times determined by others, and for wages and under conditions concerning which he must be mute? There is always the shadow of the concentration camp, but if such questions, even unspoken, were at all general, the concentration camps would have to be numbered among the resources (almost) too scarce to go around. There has been disaffection within fascist societies, as the mere existence of the camps demonstrates, but it was not disaffection which brought Mussolini's Italy or Hitler's Third Reich tumbling into dust. How was the population kept acquiescent?

The obvious but superficial answer lies in the massive and engulfing propaganda so characteristic of all totalitarian states. Propagandists, however, like advertisers and poets, must have something to which they can appeal. Fascist propagandists found exactly that object of appeal in allusions to a glorious national past which could be recaptured in a yet more glorious future, provided sacrifice and discipline were accepted in a meager and taut present. The drabness of the present, moreover, could be laid at the door of enemies, both internal and external, whose existence called forth the need for present sacrifice and national dedication to the task of overwhelming them.

In addition to all this, fascists are well aware that propaganda need not be restricted to the spoken or written word. Programs and festivals, guarantees and accomplishments carry their own message which can be of exceeding great eloquence, and fascists have not been slow to utilize these. Just as the Romans had their "bread and circuses" (*panem et circenses*), so do fascist states in their own measure provide a modicum of economic security and even certain forms of organized fun; and, at intervals, they produce public spectacles which combine flamboyant color with almost religious solemnity.   In the last resort, the state itself, symbolized in the person of the Leader, becomes endowed with a kind of organic personality which engulfs, fuses, and unites the separate individualities of ordinary men and women, and to a degree which makes independent and isolated existence seem barren and empty.

The Emphasis upon Expansion

The glorious future.   In the wonderland of Alice there was provided jam yesterday, jam tomorrow, but no jam today.   In somewhat the same sense Mussolini promised his Italians a renaissance of the Roman Empire, provided they made themselves worthy of the accomplishment; and Hitler, looking back to the great Karl, known to Gallic pilferers as Charlemagne, found inspiration for the creation of a greater Germany in which National Socialism would have room to flex its Nordic muscles and which would endure for a thousand years, provided butter were turned into guns today. It is not certain what Stalin looked back to, but at least his successor may still dream of a greater Russia which can be brought into being provided the faithful eschew, at least for the present, the decadent materialism of the wealthier plutocracies.

The role of war.   Just as the athlete, then, endures the austerities of the training table and the fatigue of track or field for the sake of tomorrow's ribbon, so is the fascist rank and file besought to tighten today's belt for the sake of tomorrow's feast.   More is involved, however, than merely the tightening of belts.   The materials for tomorrow's feast must be seized. Preparation for war, indeed the glorification of war, is characteristic of fully ripened fascist·societies.   This is so because only war can bring the rewards which some, at least, of the fascist leaders have really wanted; it is also so because the atmosphere and institutions of inevitable war are accepted by most men as justifying sacrifices and hardships which otherwise would be scarcely endurable; and it is finally so because the environment and fact of war provide a sort of artificial natural selection which thrusts to the top of the social pot the kind of Leader upon whom fascist society really depends.

Mussolini, in a classic article written for the *Italian Encyclopedia,* observed:

. . . Fascism, the more it considers and observes the future and the development of humanity . . . believes neither in the possibility nor the utility of perpetual peace. It thus repudiates the doctrine of Pacifism—born of a renunciation of the struggle and an act of cowardice in the face of sacrifice. War alone brings up to its highest tension all human energy and puts the stamp of nobility upon the peoples who have the courage to meet it. All other trials are substitutes, which never really put men into the position where they have to make the great decision—the alternative of life or death. Thus a doctrine which is founded upon this harmful postulate of peace is hostile to Fascism. And thus hostile to the spirit of Fascism, though accepted for what use they can be in dealing with particular political situations, are all the international leagues and societies which, as history will show, can be scattered to the winds when once strong national feeling is aroused by any motive—sentimental, ideal, or practical. This anti-pacifist spirit is carried by Fascism even into the life of the individual; the proud motto of the *Squadrista,* "Me ne frego," [Who cares?] written on the bandage of the wound, is an act of philosophy not only stoic, the summary of a doctrine not only political—it is the education to combat, the acceptation of the risks which combat implies, and a new way of life for Italy. Thus the Fascist accepts life and loves it, knowing nothing of and despising suicide: he rather conceives of life as duty and struggle and conquest, life which should be high and full, lived for oneself, but above all for others—those who are at hand and those who are far distant, contemporaries, and those who will come after.[9]

Fascists, thus, have asserted that fascism is in part an attempt to reproduce artificially the selective screening which "Nature" imposes, first upon individuals within a species, and then among species themselves. In practice, this usually means applying the coercive machinery of the state, first, to protect individuals within the nation who can meet fascist canons of superiority against annoyance by the mediocre, and secondly to assure the superior fascist state itself the international hegemony to which its merits presumably entitle it. The former objective is sought through the establishment of an authoritarian, single-party state dominated by its individual Leader and ruled through a combination of cajolery and coercion; the latter, by the espousal, once the state is deemed sufficiently strong, of aggressive imperialism directed both against peoples who are regarded as inferior and toward the acquisition of territories considered strategically or economically desirable to possess.

[9] Benito Mussolini, "The Political and Social Doctrine of Fascism," reprinted from an authorized English translation of the article in the *Enciclopedia Italiana* in 1932, by the Carnegie Endowment for International Peace, *International Conciliation,* January, 1935, No. 306; pp. 7–8. Similar sentiments can be found scattered throughout Hitler's verbose and discursive *Mein Kampf.*

In such an environment it is not too difficult to deflect the attention of the simple but well-intentioned man in the street from the austerity of his own life to the scheming of his enemies; and these may be Jews or capitalists, socialists or Frenchmen, according to the exigencies of the Leader's moment. The point is, that austerity becomes justified by the triumphs it promises ultimately to present.

The Tendency Toward Paternalism

Panem et circenses.   One of the boasts of Italian and German fascism, as well as of Russian communism, was that unemployment had been conquered, that men were at last assured their daily bread.   The boast had its irony; there is no unemployment in a prison camp, and fascism has no dearth of these.   Nevertheless, although Italy, for one, was plagued with mounting unemployment in the late 'twenties, Hitler's emergence in Germany was followed by a general trend toward massive rearmament in which unemployment did cease to be a problem, as it always must when a nation really girds its loins for a fight.   This much can be said: Hitler, who probably represented fascism in its most extreme form, plunged into the boldest economic ventures of any of the fascist dictators.   Seizing Germany at a time when the country was economically almost prostrate, he very soon converted a serious surplus of labor into an equally pressing shortage, and he also succeeded in raising somewhat the living standards of the very poorest strata of the population—at least for those who contrived to keep in good odor politically.   Skillful financial juggling, rearmament, compulsory labor service at rock-bottom wages for young people, and the replacement, for both military and financial reasons, of many imports by substitute domestic products high in labor cost, brought this about.   Bread, if not butter, was at least provided, and the propaganda trumpets were raised to blare forth that accomplishment.

There remain the *circenses*.   Political "circuses" were developed to provide something besides bleakness in the course of ordinary life and to give men something colorful to think about; they were also developed to keep ordinary men and women out of mischief.   Long before fascism appeared, Karl Marx had pointed out that the conditions of modern industrialism foster the development of socialist thought, and in that tradition the fascists were well aware that congregations of workingmen in and out of the fac-

tories, at work or at leisure, were seed-beds of at least potential disaffection.[10]
Not much besides surveillance could be provided for actual working hours,
but something more could be provided to fill in the hours of leisure which,
after all, constituted the greater problem.   Isaac Watts was thinking of
children when he wrote,

> For Satan finds some mischief still
> For idle hands to do,

but the fascists distrusted idleness in adults as well.   Leisure hours were
accordingly filled with organized sports, supervised spectacles, conducted
tours, screened lectures, and other good works.   The Italian *Dopolavoro*
and the German *Kraft durch Freude*—recreational organizations established
for regimented workers—were created to fill in holidays and vacation periods
with cruises and trips, besides the activities just mentioned, usually at very
low rates; and sometimes these included brief trips abroad.   None of this
was formally compulsory; but attendance, so to speak, was taken.   The
fascist shrinks from the dismaying solitude.

On festive occasions and on solemn national holidays this process of pressing in upon the public mind the established fascist dogma, and of pressing
out all alien or even independent thought, culminated in the great spectacles
of military pageantry under the panoply of symbolic banners and emblems,
until the hypnotic tension engendered and sustained by all the arts of bla-
zonry and fanfare broke, in the *Duce, Duce, Duce* directed toward the
balcony of the Piazza Venezia, or burst in the resounding and repeated chorus
of *Heil, Heil, Heil* from the cobblestones of the Nuremburg Square.

The organismic society.   The violence of the fascist opposition to individualism and liberalism can now be understood.   In its simplest form
that opposition is rooted in the conviction that a dictatorship of fascist form
simply cannot tolerate anything which smacks of independent judgment or
which suggests that the fulfillment of individual aspirations or the enrich-
ment of individual personality should be the purpose of social organization
or of political activity; that would imperil the regime.   Yet, that opposition has deeper roots.   From the beginning of civilized society men, building on the belief that man is a social animal, that the division of labor extends and strengthens the arms of labor, that participation in the activities

---

[10] *Cf.*, L. Rosenstock-Franck, *L'économie corporative fasciste en doctrine et en
fait,* Paris, 1934; pp. 50–51.

of groups develops and enriches the capacities with which individuals are endowed, that cooperative behavior brings forth a fullness of satisfaction and a satisfaction of fulfillment of which the puny, isolated, lonely individual is incapable by himself—building upon all this, men have argued that society is more than the sum of its individual components, that it has a purpose and a being of its own, that the state is a great organism for the sake of which individuals really exist rather than the other way about, because only as members and organs of that being can individuals fully live. Accepting this, fascists assert that freedom can be defined as the freedom of participation and that any other concept of freedom is meaningless because it is without context; that welfare is empty except as it is part of the greater welfare of the greater society; that life itself for the great majority is without significance except as it consists in the performance of a function inexorably assigned to each individual according to his capacities and the need society has for these.

In the fascist philosophy . . . man is shifted from his privileged position at the center of the whole universe, and his place is occupied by mankind, or rather, by that collective expression of mankind called Nation. . . . Vainly we offer knowledge, education, wisdom to the common man. . . . To a bastard form of political and social organization which, like all bastard things, cannot last because of its inherent falsehood, fascism substitutes a genuine, life-enhancing organization sprung from the recognition of the fundamental truth of life: the truth that the mass of men is created to be governed and not to govern; is created to be led and not to lead, and is created finally to be slaves and not masters; slaves of their animal instincts, their physiological needs, their emotions and their passions.[11]

The fascist state is, therefore, something unique. It is neither the necessary nuisance of the liberal tradition, nor the engine of class-oppression of the Marxists, nor is it the night watchman against which the German socialist Ferdinand Lassalle protested nearly a hundred years ago:

The bourgeoisie conceives the purpose of the state to consist solely and exclusively in the protection of the personal freedom and property of the individual.
That, gentlemen, is the concept of a night watchman—a night watchman because its whole function is thought to lie in averting robbery and trespass. History, however . . . is a struggle with nature, with poverty, with ignorance, with indigence, with helplessness, and therefore with bondage of all kinds. . . . It is the state which has the responsibility of advancing the march towards freedom, the freedom of humanity. What the state is, is a union of individuals bound into

[11] Mario Palmieri, *The Philosophy of Fascism,* Chicago, pp. 84, 106–107. Hitler's *Mein Kampf* is full of similar outbursts.

a moral whole, a union which multiplies a millionfold the power which would belong to its members merely as individuals.[12]

The mysterious and mystical entity which the fascists make of the state is something still more than this.   Mussolini, almost picking up the argument at the point where Lassalle dropped it, asserts that in the fascist state the individual "is not annulled but rather multiplied, just in the same way that a soldier in a regiment is not diminished but rather increased by the number of his comrades."   But the state is still more than this.   It reaches out and touches every aspect of national life—political, economic, social, even moral.   It represents the embodied will and power to govern and both derives strength from and reciprocally invigorates the capacities of its component members.   It is both the keeper and transmitter of the spirit of the nation, binding the past to the future via the present.   It is an "absolute," in comparison with which all groups and individuals are relative, so much so that apart from the state they are even inconceivable.   "The Fascist State is itself conscious, and has itself a will and a personality." [13]

At the apex of this structure is the mysterious and awesome figure of the Leader.   He is an Individual in the sense in which his subjects are not. He is bound by no law, for law emanates from him; his personality is not "multiplied a millionfold" by the mystical fascist state, for the state is both the expression and arm of his own personality.   To outsiders, this usually appears as naked tyranny, but to confirmed fascists it seems no more than a reasonable and logical amplification of the idea of the family.   This is so even where the corporate state assumes a more benign and certainly less intransigeant form.   For example,

Like a vast family or a great enterprise, the nation, to protect its common interests and to attain its collective end, has need of a coordinating head, of some common center of both life and action.[14]

To understand this, it is important to realize that fascist states have usually arisen out of turmoil in which established use and wont have broken down, in which normal economic life has become or threatens to become paralyzed,

[12] Ferdinand Lassalle, *Arbeiter-Programm: Ueber den besondern Zusammenhang der gegenwaertigen Geschichtsperiode mit der Idee des Arbeiterstandes,* a speech delivered on April 12, 1862; reprinted in *Reden und Schriften,* edited by E. Bernstein, Berlin, 1893; Vol. II, pp. 45–46.

[13] Mussolini, *op. cit.*   The order of Mussolini's thought has been rearranged.   The quotations appear, respectively, on pages 15 and 13.

[14] F. I. Pereira dos Santos, *Un état corporatif; la constitution sociale et politique portugaise,* Paris, 1935; p. 125.   The quotation is from Premier Salazar of Portugal.

in which law and order appear on the verge or even over the verge of collapse; in which, accordingly, frightened men instinctively seek the succor promised them all by the Man on Horseback.

THE MEANING OF FASCISM

We began this chapter with the observation that, while it is not difficult to detect a dictator or an authoritarian, it is somewhat more difficult to identify a fascist. Perhaps, now, we are somewhat better able to distinguish him.

First, fascism is essentially a product of the modern age. This is important because the modern age is the age of industrialism which engenders certain centrifugal forces—forces which push out and away from the standardization and mechanization, the frequent blurring of individual craftsmanship, the shoddiness and at times the squalor which seem to be among its by-products. More immediately, the productivity and therefore the material promise held out by industrialism suggest, to some minds, that poverty and economic insecurity are somehow man-made rather than Acts of God, and that therefore they are correctible by man's conscious action. These centrifugal forces, accordingly, coalesce at two opposite poles, the Left and the Right. They become manifest in movements seeking, on the one hand, to realize through social and economic reorganization the blessing of freedom from want which industrialism potentially holds forth, and on the other hand, to buttress and secure those interests which are vested in resistance to change and which therefore appear threatened by the forces coalescing on the Left. In discussing the stability of an economic system we have already seen [15] how apprehension of an upsurge from below may prompt efforts to thwart and suppress it. Fascism is essentially such a movement.

Second, although fascist movements tend to be led by adventurers, these adventurers are something quite different from the uninhibited freebooters and joyous swashbucklers of earlier ages, although fascism may make place for such forms of self-expression. Marshal Goering was a throwback because he essentially enjoyed life. Genuine fascists, however, have a worm within them which turns to ashes all that otherwise might be enjoyed. The world was Goering's oyster; but real fascists, knowing otherwise, can only

[15] See above, pp. 25–26.

make violent protestation that the world should be such, and in extreme cases violent pretense that the world *is* in fact their oyster. Fascists, essentially, are worried and unhappy men.

The third differentia [16] of fascism is an amalgam of the two preceding. Though fascists repudiate the individualism which threatens the unity and discipline they seek, the standardization brought forth by industrialism thwarts the *superior* individualism which fascist Leaders arrogate to themselves. Earlier adventurers, if they thought about it at all, accepted the principle that might makes right, and let it go at that. Fascists, wearing the mantle of the elite, fear the might which is not right and seek accordingly to forge the might which is their right. They do so within their own societies by asserting and enforcing the principle of leadership; they do so for their own societies by asserting and seeking to realize an international hierarchy of races and nations which can be sorted out as superior or inferior. The shrillness and hysteria of fascism derives from the apprehension that the world is not really with it. How many Italians really believed, with Mussolini, that the twentieth century was destined to be the century of fascism? And how many Germans were really convinced by Hitler's hollow boast that the National Socialist regime would really endure for a thousand years? Because fascists are never secure, fascism, at bottom, is a movement of fear.

---

[16] "The differentia is that part of the essence of anything—or, as we may say, of any species—which distinguishes it from other species in the same genus. . . ." H. W. B. Joseph, *An Introduction to Logic,* 2d. ed., Oxford, 1916; p. 74.

10

The Organization of Fascist Society

ASCISTS have asserted the uniqueness of fascist society, perhaps with more emphasis than assurance. That uniqueness presumably lies in the way fascist society is organized, for it is not easy to discern particular uniqueness in other aspects of fascist society. Fascists, for example, emphasize the importance of the most up-to-date industrial technology, but technology is not unique to fascism. Fascists, again, stress law and order, but few men avowedly repudiate these. Fascists also preach the military virtues, but fascists hardly discovered them. Fascists talk about the fascist state, but the state, too, with both its external trappings and its internal workings was something which the fascists seized, and even partially made over, but which they did not invent.

We must therefore look for fascist uniqueness in the *way* fascists make use of industrial technology, define and enforce law and order, inculcate the military virtues, or organize and utilize the machinery of the state. Superficially the structure of fascist society does not appear markedly different from the structure of any contemporary society. Fascist police may be more numerous and wear gaudier uniforms than police elsewhere, but they remain police; and fascist workers even join unions whose organization has some resemblances to union organization everywhere. For clues to the differentia which do distinguish fascist society, we must examine the internal standards by which organizations and institutions whose *structure* is familiar everywhere, are turned to some unique fascist use.

THE INTERNAL STANDARDS OF FASCISM

Earlier in this book [1] the reader was warned of the danger of attempting to judge one economic system by the standards of another. Failure to heed that principle was responsible for much misunderstanding of fascist economics during the period when fascism was particularly active, thrusting, and clamant. For example, fascism was sometimes described as simply the final and extreme form assumed by reactionary, big-business capitalism. Like many facile judgments this one had an element of truth: both Mussolini and Hitler were helped to power by great industrialists,[2] partly perhaps because these hoped for greater profits from the protection a fascist regime might be expected to accord them, certainly because they saw in fascism an opportunity to avoid harassment by labor unions.[3] Some of these industrialists became disillusioned when they found their own activities constricted by having, for example, to petition for raw materials, or by having the distribution of their earnings taken out of their own control. While fascism inevitably has economic characteristics and implications, fascists never permit purely economic considerations to become dominant. It is what the regime wants that governs, and not what industrialists want, no matter how big, important, or even enthusiastic these may be.

Again, many Americans during the 'thirties confidently predicted that Hitler's Third Reich would collapse from economic exhaustion. They pointed to the developing inflation, concealed though it was by price control and rationing, and by official determination of allocations and priorities. They looked to what appeared to be fascist blind contrariety in buying dear rather than cheap through producing expensively at home what otherwise could be imported economically from abroad. They saw Mussolini, for example, growing his own wheat at fabulous cost, and Hitler insisting upon producing costly and doubtless inferior substitutes for imported rubber and oil. They observed fascist Italy and Germany, like communist Russia, ap-

[1] See p. 14.
[2] *Cf.*, R. D. Charques and A. H. Ewen, *Profits and Politics*, London, 1934; pp. 91, 114–117.
[3] *Cf.*, R. G. Hawtrey, *Economic Destiny*, London, 1944; p. 309.

parently thwarting the economic incentives of their subjects by blocking the "natural" increase in living standards which mounting industrial activity should bring into being; forced saving was politically rather than economically engendered.   They marked what appeared to be a wholly reckless financial policy of irresponsible increase in the public debt—of headlong mortgaging of the future in the apparent interests of an insecure present. They saw all this, and they could not see how it could endure.

What they forgot was the fact that the operations of a fascist economy were not determined by the individual decisions and judgments of individual men and women in a framework of competition—decisions based upon the indicators of the market.   Fascist economics were planned from above and by principles quite alien to liberal economies.

According to traditional financial tropisms, fascist financial policy should have failed because of the lack of confidence it ought to have entailed in the minds of the men upon whom it should have been really dependent.   But it was not so dependent; the forms of the older financial institutions remained, but their function under the fascists became not the doing of what men might wish, but the performance of what they were told to do—and did.

National self-sufficiency, likewise, seemed a short-sighted violation of the liberal principle of extending the international division of labor in order that nations as well as men might buy in the cheapest market.   Self-sufficiency, however, seemed reasonable to fascists, partly because it was a means of providing domestic employment at a time when that was needed,[4] and still more because it was an adjunct to the powerful campaign to build up economic potential for military reasons.   On both counts, the program commanded domestic support.

With respect to living standards, the position was still more forthright. Fascist regimes, as we have seen, do not exist for the sake of their subjects; the mass of men should be led, and should be conditioned to accept leadership.

The heart of the entire issue consists in the orientation of an economic system toward some purpose.   On the whole, in the Western world, the economy is oriented toward welfare.   There do exist ambiguities where different welfares appear to be in conflict; the welfare of manufacturers

---

[4] This justification of national self-sufficiency was not, of course, limited to fascists. It underlies the whole protectionist movement everywhere, and it contemporaneously commanded some support from economists who were brought up in the liberal tradition.   Cf., for example, J. M. Keynes, "National Self-Sufficiency," *Yale Review,* Summer, 1933.

sometimes seems to depend upon rapid obsolescence while that of consumers demands extreme durability, and the welfare of labor and of capital,
of importers and of domestic producers, of fruit growers and of canners do
not inevitably fit into an harmonious whole.   Nevertheless, welfare, however it be defined, is presumed to be the end of economic activity in a liberal
system.

Fascist Orientation Toward Power

In marked contrast, the fascist economy is oriented toward power, the
power of the state or nation.   There are subordinate purposes, and the
assurance of some minimum welfare is necessarily among them, but these
purposes are secondary to the governing drive to develop, maintain, and
increase industrial power for the final purpose of wielding predominant
military power.

The orientation of the economy toward power is not, of course, unique
in fascist society.   It is true of any nation when it is at war, and to a lesser
degree it is true of a nation preparing for war.   This, as we have really seen
already, provides an explanation for the failure of fascist states to collapse
economically.   The glorification of war is based not only upon the hope of
garnering its external fruits in the form of conquest; it is based also upon the
need to reconcile people to the internal discipline and austerity which fascists,
by their inner drive, are compelled to impose, and the justification is effective because men really have been willing to accept sacrifice when war is
thrust upon them or when it appears imminent.

Emphasis on Forced Industrialization

In states which have become fascist, the power orientation has deeper
roots than fascism itself has provided.   In more than one sense the economic
history of the nineteenth century is colored by British industrial predominance, a predominance which arose because both the Industrial Revolution
and the official acceptance of economic liberalism first blossomed in England.   Other nations, in consequence, felt impelled to catch up, if necessary
under forced draught.   As early as 1791 Alexander Hamilton in the young
United States wrote his celebrated *Report on Manufactures* to show the
need of protecting the new nation from the danger of becoming a mere
satellite to the British economy.   Thereafter, Germany, Italy, Japan, and

others fell into the same power nexus, although in varying degrees, of drawing upon the organized and planned activities of the state to reproduce artificially what Great Britain appeared to have achieved naturally under a
laissez faire policy which really worked only because there was nothing to
stop it. An economy which *must* catch up is an economy already partly
oriented toward power, and one in which the instrumentalities and techniques of power may easily become rooted and habitual. These were already in existence, ready for the fascist hand. Realization of the fascist
orientation toward power brings to light certain significant differences, in
both technique and perspective, between fascist and liberal regimes.

CONTRAST BETWEEN LIBERAL AND FASCIST REGIMES

Techniques

Freedom of enterprise is the technique uniquely associated with liberal
economies. Long ago Adam Smith pointed out that it is a reasonable assumption that the individual knows best his own capacities and his needs,
and that he, therefore, is the appropriate agent of choice among alternative
uses of the former and competing satisfactions of the latter. The economy,
oriented in principle toward meeting the needs of its members as they themselves order them and by means which they themselves select, reveals no
incompatibility between technique and philosophy.

A power economy, like a magnifying glass in the sun, is designed to concentrate everything that passes through it upon a single focus; to do so, it
must be manipulated. Cross purposes cannot be tolerated, individual
judgment must be harnessed, individual need must be reduced to insignificance compared to the greater need of the society; above all, the market
whose classic functions have been to serve the needs of individuals and to
offer them guidance in the formation of economic judgments, cannot be
left autonomous; it, also, must be harnessed.

It is true that freedom of enterprise is not the only technique that men
have proposed to attain genuine welfare. Freedom of enterprise involves
wear and tear, particularly upon those who, in Adam Smith's phrase, draw
the blanks in life's lottery. Socialists, to whom that wear and tear looms
larger than it does to orthodox liberals, at this point join fascists in seeking
a controlled economy, although from quite different motives. The fact that

both liberals and socialists,—and perhaps even benevolent despots—seek the general welfare means that welfare may be attained in different ways: complete economic freedom is the traditional liberal way, economic planning for welfare is the socialist way, and regimentation may be the despotic way.

In sharp contrast with welfare as the object of economic activity, national economic power can be had in only one way: through the coercive imposition of an economic plan. When even a welfare economy based upon economic freedom has the attainment of power thrust upon it as an end, that welfare economy must accept some planning, and occasionally even some coercion. During the Second World War the United States, for example, was compelled to seek power, and it did so by planning the use of resources and by compelling individuals to act in conformity with the plan. A welfare economy, in other words, *need* not depend upon the free market; a power economy *cannot*. Power depends upon discipline, authority, and control.

A similar contrast may be made between two subordinate, although associated, techniques. The freedom of international trade is the liberal technique for getting men to be of maximum economic service; the control of international trade is the power technique. Liberal economies accept, at least in principle, the international division of labor, the doctrine that nations like men should not seek to be jacks of all trade, that nations as well as men should specialize instead upon the tasks best suited to their capacities and resources. Like New Year's resolutions, the principle has not been very well observed. Infant industries, including some in their second childhood, have clamored for and secured protection; complicated and sometimes torturing problems of the balance of payments have thrust themselves embarrassingly forward; producers of Swiss-type cheese have insisted that their welfare counts, too; and, above all, specialization, like fun, requires general participation. Unfortunately nations, like children, sometimes will not play.

Power economies, on the other hand, will have no truck with free trade for power requires that everything significant and strategic be kept under one's own thumb. No fascist economy would ever repeat the British decision of 1846 to let North America supply the grain, Argentina the beef, and Denmark the butter and eggs for English mouths, because to do so would entail vulnerability. This is not to say that fascist economists are insensitive to the technical advantages of specialization. Hitler's New Order envisaged the assignment of specific functions to each state or province which came into the fold; but the order, designed in German interests only, was clearly "Made in Germany."

Closely associated is the principle of economy itself which prompts the utilization of the least costly resources which will serve. That is simply part of the obligation to buy cheap and sell dear—an obligation which economic self-interest imposes upon all, at least provided that what is bought cheap is worth its cost. Both Italians and Germans, however, tended to eschew the cheap when it happened to be foreign. Mussolini, unlike the British in espousing agricultural free trade, insisted that Italy grow her own wheat, although at substantial cost. Germany, under pressure, not only bought dear, but sometimes also bought inferior goods. Synthetic rubber was not as good as natural rubber, and *Zellwolle* was shoddy compared with real wool. The reason for producing inferior goods at home instead of buying better goods abroad was made perfectly clear: in place of the welfare principle of utilizing the least costly resources, the fascists held to the power principle of utilizing resources whose sources were under their own control.

Perspectives

The contrast between a welfare and a power system is brought into sharp focus when the perspectives of the two systems are laid side by side.

Generally speaking, in a welfare system it is thought good that an individual should seek and secure his own welfare. There are, of course, restraints. The welfare of pickpockets as pickpockets is not universally supported, a jimmy is doubtless capital to a burglar but its fruits are subject to a substantial and socially approved capital-gains tax, and glaziers would probably not be encouraged to organize dining-room baseball among small boys. The fact that the pursuit of self-interest must be moderated by courtesy, consideration, and forbearance is obvious in cases such as these, but the same thing is true upon a much larger scale. Pure Food and Drug Acts, Security and Exchange Acts, and Antitrust Acts are animated by at least the impulse to provide a social milieu in which individuals may appropriately, safely, and productively seek their own welfare. The motto of the Three Musketeers, *One for all and all for one,* is consistent with the logic of a welfare economy.

In a power economy it is quite otherwise; the individual competes with his society. His competition is bad enough when it seeks resources which could be put to less private use, but it becomes serious when it deflects the individual's mind and conscience from the purposes which the state is determined ought to be his. Power economies try to moderate self-interest, not by courtesy and mutual consideration, but by the demands of sheer political and military strength.

One final contrast can be touched on lightly here; it has already received mention.[5] Welfare is not finite; it is not a fixed quantum subject only to variable division. The grocer is not hurt but rather helped by the opulence of his customers, and nations, likewise, can trade only in proportion as all are prosperous. In David Hume's words,

I shall therefore venture to acknowledge, that, not only as a man, but as a British subject, I pray for the flourishing commerce of Germany, Spain, Italy, and even France itself. I am at least certain that Great Britain, and all those nations, would flourish more, did their sovereigns and ministers adopt such enlarged and benevolent sentiments towards each other.[6]

That the gain of each is the gain of all is true only within a welfare context. Power is threatened by both the wealth and strength of others, and the economic intercourse of power economies is accordingly designed not only to strengthen themselves but to weaken their actual, or even potential, enemies. The ingenious, devious and wholly ruthless international trade policy of National Socialist Germany was oriented toward both those ends.

With the completion of this survey of what the fascist economies really attempt, we can now endeavor to discern the machinery which was devised to achieve fascist economic purposes; its actual working will be discussed in the chapter following.

FASCIST GOVERNMENTAL STRUCTURE

Although the façade presented to the world by a fascist state purportedly refracts its unique national tradition, character, and aspiration, in essence the structure of all fascist states suggests a common blueprint: a strong executive, a docile and pliant legislature, concentration of all real authority

---

[5] See above, p. 188.

[6] These are the concluding words of his essay, "Of the Jealousy of Trade," of which there are many editions. Cf., for example, Hume, *Essays, Moral, Political, and Literary,* World's Classics, Oxford University Press, Oxford, 1903; p. 338.

in a Leader responsible to no one but himself, and a single political party organized in parallel with the government and performing, itself, many of the real functions of government.

ITALY: Political Structure

In Italy, although there was a king, he was tamed exactly as was the legislature; the helm of the ship of state was held firmly by the dictator. That dictator wore two hats, both of them brass. One of them, the executive hat, was labeled Head of the Government, and when he was wearing that hat Mussolini presided over the Council of Ministers, or Cabinet. The other hat was a party hat, labeled *Il Duce,* and this one served to identify the officer presiding over the Grand Council of Fascism, or party cabinet.

On the governmental side, subordinate to the Council of Ministers was a bicameral legislature. The Senate, essentially a carry-over from the pre-fascist era, consisted of about four hundred members appointed by the King for life upon the recommendation of the Head of the Government. The Chamber was somewhat more complicated. The old Chamber of Deputies was continued for some sixteen years after the "March on Rome," although it steadily lost significance and function. Late in 1938 that Chamber took an executive hint and abolished itself, establishing in its stead a Chamber of Fasces and Corporations. This new Chamber consisted entirely of members *ex officio* by virtue of holding some office to which they were appointed by the Head of the Government; their tenure as members of the Chamber was consequently at the pleasure of the *Duce.* Many of these offices whose possession gave their holders seats in Chamber were, as we shall see, Party offices; the Siamese twins who headed Party and Executive, respectively, had their legislative counterparts in the men who held political office *because* they were Party officials even though the Chamber of Fasces and Corporations and the Fascist Party were formally distinct institutions. The Chamber also had economic representatives, in the persons of the members of the National Council of Corporations, shortly to be described. Provincial governments headed by prefects derived their authority directly from Mussolini and the Council of Ministers, and these provincial governments in turn transmitted authority, in conformity with the Leadership Principle, to the various local governments headed in each case by a *Podesta.*

As we have said, the Party was organized in parallel. The Grand Council of Fascism consisted of about twenty-five men who, under the eye of the

Dictator, were responsible for the guidance of the Fascist Party; they were *ex officio* political members of the Chamber of Fasces and Corporations. From this apex the party hierarchy descended to the National Council, presided over by the Secretary of the Party, whose members also held seats in the political Chamber, and thence to the provincial and local party organizations whose leaders, again, were the *Secretaries* of their respective units. Here, also, responsibility was upward, and was symbolized in the words of the Party Oath:

In the name of God and of Italy I swear to obey without question the orders of the Leader, and to serve the Fascist Revolution with all my strength, if need be with my blood.

Economic Structure

Thus far we have seen that fascist Italy developed both a governmental and a party administration, and that these were closely intertwined; it also developed an economic structure, and it was this latter which provided the name Corporate State by which fascism sometimes is known. That economic structure was somewhat complicated because of its mingling of both political and economic elements. The so-called "corporations," as we shall see, were governmental agencies concerned primarily with the performance of Italian industry; because industry was oriented toward political ends, the corporations were political institutions.

On the economic side were the "syndicates," or local associations which could be formed within any industry, or specialized trade or craft; these syndicates were themselves organized, on a national scale, into "confederations."

The main purpose of this political-economic structure of Italian industry was to press the noisy, discordant and sometimes quarrelsome elements of the economy into forced cooperation and unity through a kind of shotgun wedding, intended to be both binding and indissoluble. The syndicates and confederations were designed to impress upon labor its role as bride— namely, to love, honor, and obey. The corporations, concerned with productive efficiency, were intended to assist the industrial groom to serve as breadwinner of the Italian economy. The shotgun was held by the state, embodied in the *Duce*.

The syndical structure. The organizations concerned with the relations between capital and labor operated within the framework of the Labor Charter, an important economic document which was promulgated on April 21, 1927. Its purport was simple: to apply a common, single standard to the entirety of Italian economic life, the standard of service to the state, with responsibility vested in the employer. The first three clauses of that document are worth quoting:

> The Italian nation is an organism, having purposes, life, and capacities superior in both power and duration to the separate individuals or groups of individuals who compose it. It is a moral, political, and economic entity which finds complete realization in the fascist state.

From that same national perspective, independent associations with their own purposes and activities could not be tolerated; their extinction was achieved, but with a fine Italian hand less massive than the mailed fist which accomplished the same task in National Socialist Germany. The Labor Charter provided "complete freedom of professional or syndical [that is, labor union] organization." The catch lay in the necessity for legal recognition by the Ministry of Corporations before any activity could be undertaken.[7]

The place of labor unions was taken by the labor side of the syndical structure; separate syndicates were required for labor and for capital, although artists, professional men, and others who were self-employed could form syndicates of their own. Each syndicate had to be licensed by the Ministry of Corporations before it could function, and licenses were not granted unless (a) a labor syndicate comprised at least ten per cent of the workers in the district engaged in the same type of activity, (b) an employers' syndicate represented sufficient firms in the industry concerned to employ collectively at least ten per cent of the workers of the district, (c) no legally recognized syndicate in the same territory and covering the same type of production was already in existence,[8] and (d) the proposed syndicate undertook to provide for its members vocational training, organized recreation, and other services regarded as welfare work.

Employer and employee syndicates might engage together in something known as collective bargaining, but on the whole the syndicates themselves were more occupied in administering the collective labor contracts drawn up by superior organizations to cover wider stretches of territory. These

---

[7] *Cf.*, Italian Library of Information, *The Organization of Production and the Syndical Corporative System*, mimeographed, New York, n.d.; p. 43.

[8] Formally, other organizations could exist, but legally they could have nothing to do.

contracts, like Fair-Trade Laws in the United States, were enforceable upon everyone, members and non-members alike.

Syndicates for the same industry or occupation were bound together into national or provincial federations, and these in turn reached into nine great Confederations comprising the employers' and employees' associations, respectively, for Industry, Agriculture, Commerce, and Credit-Insurance; the ninth Confederation was built around the self-employed in the professions. As we might expect, the Leadership Principle was discernible in these organizations, as elsewhere; not only did the Confederations supply provincial representatives to exercise surveillance over federations and syndicates, the Ministry of Corporations as well thrust its shadow where it would.   It issued licenses, approved the appointment of officials, examined all collective contracts, and it reserved the right to install a government official in place of association authorities when mismanagement or incompetence was suspected.

The special responsibility of this syndical hierarchy lay in arranging terms and conditions of employment, although they could also be used to execute and administer policies enunciated by government.   Employment was governed by collective labor contracts, reached by negotiation between the respective federations of employers and employees within the industries involved, but always subject to national guidance.   These contracts frequently went into considerable detail about wages, conditions of work, seniority, dismissal, and the like.   One need not feel surprise to learn that the determination of wages was frequently the most difficult of these items.   The only formal guidance the state provided was in the clause in the Labor Charter providing that wages should be determined by the normal needs of the laborer, the productivity of labor, and the productive possibilities of the enterprise; the guidance could not have been very illuminating.

When disputes arose, as they did, official procedures for their resolution had to be provided, since both strikes and lockouts were prohibited.   If the appropriate syndical association failed to secure agreement, a dispute might eventually be taken to the Labor Courts.   These were founded upon the ordinary magistrature supplemented by two experts, in industry and labor respectively, drawn from a panel compiled for each judicial district.   The Labor Courts held jurisdiction only over disputes involving a collective labor contract; individual disputes went to the local magistrate.

The corporative structure.   The Italian Corporations, unlike their nominal counterparts in the West, were not voluntary, fictitious legal persons operating under charter to produce, process, or distribute goods; in other words, they were not private business organizations at all. They were constitutional organs of the state with some control over the productive and distributive activities of industry, but without active participation themselves in those activities. They were essentially regulatory agencies.

Conceptually, the fascist Italian economy was organized into three great "cycles," or stages of production, all the way from the processing of raw materials to the handing over of the finished product to the ultimate consumer. In agriculture, there were eight such corporations, such as those for cereals, edible oils, textiles, and so forth; in industry likewise, there were eight corporations, similarly organized according to function; finally, there were six corporations in the public service cycle, comprising such varied activities as credit and insurance, hotels and tourism, entertainment, and transportation.

Each of these twenty-two corporations contained representatives from the syndicates of labor and capital in the industries or occupations which pertained to the corporation involved; each, also, had whatever technical staff was deemed necessary to enable it to operate.

The duties of these corporations were described as coordinating the materials available with the productive capacity of industry and the requirements of consumers; this, moreover, was to be done through the entire course of the productive cycle. Each corporation, accordingly, had to concern itself with questions of costs, prices, rates of production, and methods of distribution.[9] The onset of the Ethiopian War precipitated an international debate which culminated in a decision of fifty-one nations, acting together in the Assembly of the League of Nations, to impose sanctions upon Italy. Even though those sanctions were enforced only half-heartedly, the embargo upon shipments of arms, credit, and raw materials (except oil) and the curtailment of imports from Italy intensified the nation's economic problems and correspondingly increased the responsibilities of the corporations. They were drawn, for example, into price-fixing, and they had to become active in fostering and planning the campaign to achieve national self-sufficiency.

The governing councils of all the corporations taken together formed the National Council of Corporations. This body concerned itself with the examination and coordination of all the activities of the separate corporations, with particular reference to the impact of any corporate decision upon other cycles of production, and upon the national economy as a whole.

[9] Cf., Italian Library of Information, op. cit., p. 47.

With its 500 members the National Council was too unwieldy a body to exercise much supervision in detail. This work fell into the hands of the Council's executive committee, the Central Corporative Committee, which, accordingly, became a sort of economic general staff for the entire country. The Committee itself was large, having about fifty members representing not only the corporations, but including also the heads of the Confederations of Employers and Employees and high party officials and ministers of the government. It was not, however, so large that it could not serve as a nerve center for the Italian economy.

The Corporative State

The active members of the National Council of Corporations were also *ex officio* members of the political Chamber of Fasces and Corporations. It was the organization of that body which seemed to justify the term *corporative,* or *corporate, state* applied to at least one of the societies otherwise called fascist. The underlying principle is the simple one that the accident of one's place of residence is less significant for both man and society than the fact of his functional place in society. With society viewed somewhat as an organism, it is what the arm or tongue *does* rather than its coordinates of position that counts. Political representation, such as it is in fascist society, is accordingly based upon occupation rather than residence or precinct.

That was the principle; in fact, the representation was nominal. The Chamber of Fasces and Corporations had little autonomy and no independence; its members were appointed, not elected, and they could be summarily removed at the whim of the Dictator; even in office, they could never forget that Mussolini had the power to bind and the power to loose. In essence, the complicated hierarchies of office and function which have been described were designed not so much to provide representation for the cooperating members of a corporate body—although that was the façade—as to create a set of administrative tools which could be taken up or laid down according to the fancy of their proprietor.

GERMANY: Political Structure

The sweep made by the triumphant National Socialists in 1933 was drastic, thorough, and extensive—so much so that one can almost say that, after

1933, Hitler became the German government. Loyalty oaths were no longer directed toward flag or country; men swore allegiance to Adolf Hitler. Almost the first thing the *Fuehrer* did when at last he found himself on the seat of the mighty was to induce the *Reichstag,* or main legislative body, to transfer its legislative authority to the Cabinet [10] whose members were the creatures of the Leader in his role as Chancellor—exactly as Mussolini, as Head of the Italian Government, dominated the Italian legislature. Hitler, too, wore two hats.

Why, after that act of abnegation, it seemed necessary to elect members of the *Reichstag* only from lists prepared by the National Socialist Party, is not entirely clear. The *Reichstag* really had nothing to do but listen to the *Fuehrer's* speeches; between 1933 and 1939, it met eleven times and passed exactly five bills.

The governments of the States (*Laender*), such as Bavaria or Saxony, were swept aside and replaced by administrative units headed by provincial Leaders, and so with local governments; Hitler's personal power reached into the smallest village.

The judiciary, like the army and the housewife, was also *gleichgestaltet,* or "coordinated." Judicial as well as legislative powers were concentrated in the cabinet, and German law became what the Leader willed. Written law was not openly obliterated; indeed, efforts were made to purify it by expunging from it such alien elements as the Roman law which adulterated the Nordic purity of the German system. In 1934 an Academy for German Law appeared in Munich to accomplish exactly that. Written law, however, came to be written as if in water, for the arm of the Cabinet— which was really the arm of Hitler—extended even into the courts.

Formally, the political structure of National Socialist Germany closely resembled that of Fascist Italy. The Cabinet was supreme, and the Cabinet was dominated by the Chancellor. A formerly legislative body was kept in existence, but its membership was controlled and its duties became perfunctory. Provincial and local governments were firmly brought into the hierarchy, with authority downward and responsibility upward. Paralleling the political organization was that of the Party, which also had its cabinet, dominated in this case by the Leader,[11] who, curiously enough, bore the

[10] This was done by the Enabling Act [*Ermaechtigungsgesetz*] of March 24, 1933, which really empowered the Cabinet to do anything it wished except unseat Hitler.

[11] Both the Italian *Duce* and the German *Fuehrer* can be translated by the English *Leader.*

same personal name as the Chancellor. More so than in Italy, the German Party performed governmental functions independently of the government itself. It had its own military formations, the storm troopers, and the dreaded SS, Hitler's bodyguard, and—at least in the early years—it maintained its own Foreign Ministry which concerned itself with the activities of "racial" Germans abroad. Territorially, the Party was organized by *Districts (Gaue)*, rather than by *States (Laender)*, in order to facilitate complete centralization by blurring the distinctiveness which the old provincial frontiers had signified. The name given a District Party Leader, *Gauleiter,* has almost passed into other languages. As in Italy, membership in the party was prerequisite to any kind of political activity, so that a double check, if that were indeed needed, was provided over the reliability of persons in positions of responsibility. The arrangement gave very great political security to the new German Reich, but at the expense of the personal security of both its officials and its citizens. German *subjects,* such as Jews, who were not citizens, had no security whatever.

Economic Structure

The triumph of the National Socialists was accompanied by some pressure from the left wing of the party to bring into being a corporative state more or less along the lines contemporaneously being talked about in Italy. That pressure succeeded only in *naming* one or two of the organizations created to control the economy. The German word *Stand* means *corporation,* in roughly the Italian sense of the term. It is usually translated into English as *estate,* a functioning component of society, as in the expression *third estate* for the French bourgeoisie before the Revolution, or the term *fourth estate* which is sometimes applied to the Press. The Nazis, in this sense, created an Estate of Industry and Trade and a German Food Estate; in spite of this, introduction into Germany of the corporative state got no further than nomenclature. The reason is perfectly clear: although the more radical Nazis wished to see created a group of semi-autonomous bodies which could be combined at the top into some sort of legislative or advisory chamber, the National Socialist State, as it took form, became monolithic, totalitarian, and absolute. It would tolerate no challenge to the principle of leadership, no formation of subordinate groups which might claim even the shadow of autonomy. The blood purge made that quite clear. Accordingly, labor, agriculture, and industry were organized into distinct bodies, to be sure; but the Leader's portrait hung in every office, and his eye and arm penetrated into every nook.

The organization of labor.   On May 2, 1933, Nazi storm troopers occupied the premises and seized the property of the German labor unions and jailed their officials.   Assuagement of the rank and file of German labor took the form of assertions that their quondam leaders had been embezzelers of funds and traitors to the Reich.   Since labor could never be left to its own devices, the place of the old unions was soon taken by the Labor Front, created in 1934 under an Act to Regulate National Labor, characteristically nicknamed the Magna Charta of German Labor.   To emphasize the utterly pervasive character of National Socialist organizations, membership in the Labor Front was not restricted to workers; in the end, the Food Estate, trade associations, employers, business corporations, professional men, even towns and villages became enrolled.   For labor itself, membership was not compulsory, but devices existed to suggest the advisability of membership.

The Labor Front, like other National Socialist organizations, was subdivided both functionally and territorially.   Each factory and plant had a unit, the *Betriebsgemeinschaft* or Factory Community, and all employees of the factory were regarded as members of that.   The "Magna Charta" had proclaimed that the employer was master in his own house, quite in line with the leadership principle.   He accordingly was known as *Betriebsfuehrer,* or factory leader; his labor force was the *Gefolgschaft,* or body of followers.

Significantly enough, the Labor Front was officially considered the link between the Nazi Party and the members of the German working population who did not belong to the party; all Labor Front officials were party members.

The Labor Front came increasingly to dominate all aspects of a workman's life.   Strikes being illegal, the Front undertook to arbitrate disputes; independent activity being suspect, the Front established its own bank, provided vocational guidance, offered welfare services, and, through its affiliate *Kraft durch Freude* (Strength through Joy), organized and supervised recreational and educational activities.   Strength through Joy had its own affiliate, Beauty and Labor, to foster both aesthetic and "eugenic" improvements in places of work.   Even the evening hours were not neglected; a Department of Evening Leisure appeared in February, 1936, to instruct the tired laborer in the attainment of National Socialist contentment.

In every firm with more than twenty employees, a *Vertrauenrat,* or Council of Trust, was established to advise the plant leader on matters of labor discipline and efficiency. After cautious but unsuccessful experimentation with elections of the members of these Councils, membership, after 1935, was made appointive. The selecting officials were the Labor Trustees (*Treuhaender der Arbeit*) who were both government officials and party members, appointed by the Ministry of Labor for each of the Districts (*Gaue*) of the Nazi Party. These Trustees supervised the Councils of Trust, made recommendations to employers concerning plant regulations, issued wage schedules, and passed upon collective dismissals involving more than ten per cent of his working force which an employer might have under contemplation.

Disputes which could not be settled within the plant or by the appropriate Labor Trustee or Council of Trust were taken to special Labor Courts, the Courts of Social Honor (*Soziale Ehrengerichte*). Their name symbolizes the feudal relationship established between the factory leader and his following. Social honor became specifically involved in cases of scurrility, incitement, violations of confidence, frivolous or unwarranted complaints, or, for what it was worth, abuse of power by an employer including the wounding of his workers' "sense of honor."

The organization of agriculture. Agriculture in fascist societies plays a peculiar role because, over and above its economic importance, it is regarded as a way of life which should be fostered for the sake of the social and moral qualities it presumably develops. Its economic significance is sufficiently obvious: foodstuffs and agricultural raw materials are vital national resources whose development at home should be pushed at almost any cost, because dependence upon foreigners for their provision not only drains off precious foreign exchange but threatens national security itself. Over and above this, however, the farmer, in contrast to the city dweller, is physically sturdy, politically reliable, and prolific family-wise; his eugenic vigor should accordingly be carefully guarded. In Germany particularly, the soil was considered in a sense the cradle of the race, and the fostering of agriculture was therefore an end of great urgency. It was fostered in two ways. To develop a peasantry who could be regarded as a "new nobility of blood and soil" the German land, where appropriate, was redivided into hereditary and inalienable farms; to develop and push agriculture itself, the German Food Estate (*Reichsnaehrstand*) was created with power both comprehensive and detailed over all aspects of German agriculture.

On September 29, 1933, the Hereditary Estates Act (*Reichserbhofgesetz*) came into force to free the German peasantry from the "pernicious ascendancy of the worlds of commerce and finance," by arresting the continuing subdivision of agricultural land and by checking the purchase and sale of prized farms as if they were ordinary commodities.   The Act provided that an *Erbhof,* or hereditary farm, could be constituted from agricultural lands constituting at least an *Ackernahrung,* that is, of a size sufficient to support a family of four, and comprising no more than 125 hectares.   An *Erbhof,* that is, should run somewhere between fifteen or twenty to slightly under 309 acres in extent.   In addition, its owner should be able to qualify racially, politically, and technically.   This, in effect, meant that Jews were excluded, that political reliability was an essential, and that the owner knew how to farm.   Mild inefficiency might result in the assignment of an adviser to the farm; correctible incompetence meant displacement in favor of an appointed manager until correction had been accomplished; but complete incapacity involved permanent dispossession.   Dispossession occurred; in Saxony and Mecklenburg, for example, object lessons of this kind were provided for the prompting of the careless.

Since borrowing for any purpose whatever was prohibited, except under license from the Inheritance Court, the single heir to an *Erbhof* received it unencumbered and intact.   The rights of his co-heirs were restricted to the personal property of the original owner, to whatever education or dowry the heir himself, according to the condition and promise of the property, might be able to provide, and to subsistence on the homestead if a co-heir should involuntarily fall into want.

It might be added that, while the *Reichserbhofgesetz* was designed to assure Germany a healthy, dependable, productive *peasantry,* a number of the Junkers, or agricultural aristocrats based largely in eastern Germany, contrived to have their estates classified as *Erbhoefe,* thereby freeing them from danger of foreclosure.

The *Reichsnaehrstand,* or Food Estate, was established on September 13, 1933, with responsibility for the production, marketing, and financing of practically all products of the soil.   Here also the Leadership principle governed, authority descending from the Farm Leader, himself responsible to Hitler, all the way down to the *Ortsbauernfuehrer,* or single peasant leader in each village, designated as local representative of the Food Estate.

The organization was divided into three branches, the Man, the Farm, and the Market.   The first division, the Man, had not only the conventional responsibility for supervising housing, health, and certain types of education; it concerned itself as well with purportedly eugenic functions.   Its Blood

Department was a genealogical agency to assist *Erbhof* peasants to trace their ancestry back at least as far as 1800. Those peasants whom it certified as free from either Jewish blood or hereditary disease received a certificate and a coat of arms. Another department of this first division administered the marriage and the furnishing of loans to approved young rural couples who might be expected properly to replenish the earth. It also provided subsidies and tax relief to approved peasants with at least five children and to agricultural laborers with a minimum of three.

The second division, the Farm, was concerned with productivity. Agricultural technology, land utilization, the improvement of farm equipment, the collection and dissemination of agricultural statistics, and—last but far from least—incessant propaganda through lectures, exhibits, films, and discussion groups, were the most important of its far-flung activities.

Finally, the third, or Market Division, had the basic and difficult responsibility of maintaining good farm prices without enhancing the cost of living. Its procedures will be described in the following chapter; suffice it to say here that this division was empowered to regulate the flow of farm products of all types at every important distributive point, to control the intricate system of food prices, and to apportion supplies to various markets.

The organization of industry. The Nazis inherited a heavily industrialized economy which had already organized itself into a far-reaching and complicated system of trade associations, regional and national chambers of commerce, and cartels. This organization was taken over substantially intact, the only major innovations being the introduction of the Leadership principle and the effective, though diffused, compulsory subservience of industry to the demands of the state. When the dust of reorganization had subsided, the structure of German industry could be discerned as a cross-association of territorial and functional organizations bound together at the top, fused with the Party through the now familiar dual assignments of party members, the whole cumbersome system being supervised and manipulated by a third set of agencies created and maintained by the state. The bold articulation of the system was reasonably simple; its details were appallingly, agonizingly complicated.

The basic law by which the Nazis authorized themselves to do with industry practically what they willed, was the Act of February 27, 1934, to Prepare an Organic Structure for the German Economy. It empowered the Minister of Economic Affairs to create, dissolve, merge or recognize the organizations of industry as sole representatives of industry, to modify, expand or amend their constitutions, to appoint or dismiss their officials, and to make membership in them compulsory.

Local chambers of commerce had long existed in Germany as elsewhere, chiefly to promote local trade. The Nazis took these over and expanded them as Chambers of Industry and Commerce, added to them Chambers of Handicrafts, and made of them statutory organizations with compulsory membership, thus providing a network of local organizations to which every firm or individual employed in any kind of productive activity had to belong, regardless of occupation, industry, or craft. Through these, the control of the Party over the *geographical regions* was assured. Those organs reached up into provincial chambers, and these, in turn, into the Central Association of Chambers of Industry and Commerce in Berlin; this, under the shadow of the Ministry of Economic Affairs, mediated generally between businessmen and government and coordinated the activities of the provincial and local chambers.

Cutting across the lines of this territorial structure were the *Groups,* organized by function. There were seven of these, one each for industry, commerce, banking, insurance, power, tourism, and handicrafts; and each of these, in turn, was subdivided into smaller units. The Commerce Group, for example, comprised sub-groups for foreign and wholesale trade, retail trade, the hotel and restaurant trade, middlemen and agents, and even one for peddlers. These groups, also, extended down from the great national trade associations, through provincial organizations, to local group agencies. Membership in these, also, was compulsory; every firm and every businessman had to belong to his local group as well as to his local chamber. Through the groups, therefore, the control of the party over *occupational activities* was assured.

The purpose of the groups, bound together at the top into the Estate of Industry and Trade which comprised them all and covered all Germany and all industry, was to increase efficiency by disseminating technical information and promoting research, by giving advice on matters within the technical competence of the group concerned, and to provide a medium for the control of the German economy distinct from that provided to control the population.

To keep the territorial and the functional organizations from running afoul of each other, both were merged into the National Economic Chamber, again subject to the Ministry of Economic Affairs under the Leadership principle.

The Political Domination of Economic Activity

The associations just described, dominated though they were by the Party, were *thought of* as agencies of industrial self-government, representing and reflecting the interests of business.   The state, also, had its interests, and it secured these by not only capturing the organizations of industry and commerce, but also by establishing over and superior to these, its own agencies of control.   As in other countries, the onset of war brought a rapid succession of changes in the political organization of the economy.   In the end, however, the important economic Ministries turned out to be those for Forestry, Food (formally superior to the Food Estate), Finance, Labor (formally superior to the Labor Front), and Economic Affairs.   The latter Ministry not only watched over the territorial and functional organizations of industry, but was also responsible for industrial allocations of materials. Over all the these Ministries was the General Commissioner of Economics who was responsible for most normal (i.e., peacetime) economic activities. Over him, in turn, was the Chief of the War Economy, the redoubtable Goering, who also presided over the Office of the Four-Year Plan and administered the system of price controls.

The Nazis plagiarized the Soviet Planning Book, except that they removed one chapter; instead of planning for periods of five years, they planned for four.   The first of the German Four-Year Plans was directed toward reemployment; the second toward rearmament; when rearmament achieved its purpose in the form of overt war, the Office of the Four-Year Plan concerned itself with rationalization, economic development, and autarky.

Among all these organizations and agencies the jurisdictional boundaries were frequently blurred, and hence contested.   There were disputes, jealousies, intrigues, even skirmishes.   A semblance of order was maintained by the pervasive hand of the Party; and over all, was Hitler.

Fascist Systems in Operation

1. AUTARKY AND FOREIGN TRADE

W E are already familiar with the difficulty of defining fascism, because what fascists say is not invariably consistent with what fascists do. Following the proverbial wisdom, that actions speak louder than words, we suggested that fascism is as fascism does. We saw, broadly, that fascism in action involves opportunism, nationalism, and coercion.

We now come to fascist economic behavior and, again, we must ask the question, What is it that fascists do? We shall find that fascists plan, and that the plans fascists make tend to be made on a grandiose scale, with the result that fascist economies are frequently plagued by scarcity and to such a degree that there is mounting resort to economic coercion.

THE GENERAL CHARACTER OF FASCIST PLANNING

Fascist systems are planned, but they are planned in their own peculiar way. Oriented toward power, an undertone of mobilization with its attendant emotionalism and urge toward discipline is ever present; beset by

226

the possibility of domestic disaffection, fascist economies combine strident command and massive coercion with contrived beguilement; dominated by party, calculated opportunism verges at times upon capricious unpredictability; and, suspended between admiration of big business and distrust of its autonomy, fascist economies teeter between industrial self-government and totalitarian *Gleichschaltung*—the compulsory coordination of men and institutions.

Being oriented toward power, fascist economies inevitably become taut and plagued by scarcities which drive the hierarchy of Leaders, Duces, Fuehrers, Chefs d'État, and Caudillos to ration, to allocate, and to control. As we shall see, the first critical sector in which control becomes necessary is that of foreign trade. Imports and the means to purchase them become affected with a public interest.

Disaffection, like a skin disease, is potentially always beneath the surface; that is why such societies need Lipari Islands, Siberias, and concentration camps. Fascist disaffection arises not only as a by-product of coercion itself and of the denial of rights some individuals have regarded as natural; [1] it arises also out of the incessant struggle for individual power and position continually in process beneath the smooth surface. Moreover, irrespective of promise or allegation, the only elements in fascist society to be cosseted or privileged are members of the party, and even their privilege is without tenure. Since the Permit Office takes the place of the impersonal market as the source of orders or resources, the men with "pull," the fixers and five-percenters themselves become resources which business must continually seek; fascist economies, accordingly, become economies of elbowing, jostling, maneuvering, and bribing. [2] Also, since the Leadership principle replaces the balance sheet as the guide to economic activity, the struggle to attain leadership is pervasive and frequently vicious, and involves attendant risk to the loser.

Party dominance resolves itself essentially into the inability of industry to be master in its own house. It involves favoritism which is essentially unpredictable, subservience which is never palatable, and a form of competition which is never challengeable. Janus-like, the party presents two faces to society. One of these smiles upon industry with the promise of relief from unrestricted competition and harassment by labor; the other

---

[1] Mussolini once remarked that the only natural right he could accord the Italian people was the *jus murmurandi*—the right to gripe.

[2] *Cf.*, for example, Guenter Reimann, *The Vampire Economy*, New York, 1939; pp. 22–31, Chapter IV, and *passim*.

lowers with the thrust of its own arrogance, the drive of its own control, and the menace of its own competition.   In Germany, for example, the Labor Front, essentially a party organization, came to control a variety of industrial corporations, largely in banking, insurance, printing and publication; the Gustloff Foundation, party-dominated, was a combination of six corporations including an Austrian munitions concern; above all, the *Hermann Goering Werke,* established initially with a capital of five million reichsmarks to develop deposits of low grade iron ore, had become by 1938 the third largest corporation in the Reich with a capital of 400 million reichsmarks. It was active in exploiting conquered or occupied territories, particularly in Czechoslovakia, Austria, Romania, and Norway, and it never loosened its grip on large iron and steel interests.[3]

The smiling party face turned upon small businessmen suggested curbs upon the power of banks, department and chain stores; the frowning face hinted at the purge.   To the bureaucrat, the pleasant party visage seemed to hold out relief from parliamentary meddling; the other face carried behind it interference by party busybodies.   Even the military were not exempt: wooed on the one hand by rearmament and huge expenditures, they were humiliated on the other by the appearance of political commissars, of paramilitary formations such as the storm troopers which competed with the Army but were not controlled by it, and, worst of all, by the intrusion into the sacred officer corps itself of upstart party generals and colonels.[4]

There is, finally, the ambivalence of the fascist attitude toward industry. Unlike the soviet system there is in fascism no fundamental background of antipathy toward the structure of capitalism, no impulse to expropriate merely for the sake of expropriation.   The Germans, to be sure, did expropriate much property, but this was done generally for racial rather than ideological reasons, and German heavy industry found itself among the beneficiaries of the expropriation of Jewish and conquered foreign property. These properties were to the Nazis what the monasteries were to Henry VIII,[5] but they were special cases.   Far from embarking upon programs of general expropriation, the fascist economies took pains to return, or "reprivatize"

[3] *Cf.,* Franz Neumann, *Behemoth, The Structure and Practice of National Socialism,* New York, 1942; pp. 298–305.

[4] *Cf., ibid.,* p. 397.

[5] When Henry VIII cut England free from *Roman* Catholicism, many of the Roman Catholic monasteries in England—particularly the wealthy ones—were broken up and looted.

much property which, for one reason or another, had earlier been taken over by the state.

During the depression years, for example, Italy had created a sort of public holding company, the *Istituto di Ricostruzione Industriale,* known as IRI, which was organized for much the same basic purpose as the Reconstruction Finance Corporation formed at about the same time in the United States. IRI assumed financial responsibility for, and therefore participated in the management of, a variety of hard-pressed industries threatened with insolvency; later, however, when conditions improved, IRI returned to private ownership its holdings of stock in "industries of no national importance." [6] Much the same thing happened in Germany.   Under the Weimar Republic, a similar holding company, VIAG (*Vereinigte Industrie Aktien-Gesellschaft*) was formed.   It comprised nitrate and aluminum factories, army factories, power plants and other industrial enterprises.   When the Nazis assumed power, VIAG resold to its original owners the shares in the steel trust and the Dresdener Bank which it had earlier taken over; it also passed on to the *Hermann Goering Werke* its entire holdings of stock in the important steel firm, *Rheinmetall Borsig.*[7]

Private industry, then, was in a way encouraged, but it still was not given a free hand.   With the exception of high officials and favored individuals within the party hierarchy, the entrepreneurial sector was the one where the greatest freedom of individual activity and responsibility was to be found. The entrepreneur was not bound to his firm quite as tightly as the peasant was to his farm, his organizations were not suppressed as were those of labor, and, above all, his occupation, interests, and status did not *per se* expose him to the suspicion and mistrust which is the unhappy lot of most others in fascist society.   As far as possible, indeed, the control to which he was subjected took the somewhat Benthamite [8] form of rigging the scene and contriving the incentives so that he would want to do what the state wished him to do. The Germans called this *steering.*

[6] *Cf.,* Italian Library of Information, *Italy Today, Corporative Agriculture and Industry,* New York, 1939, mimeographed; pp. 26–27.

[7] *Cf.,* Franz Neumann, *op. cit.,* pp. 296–297.

[8] Jeremy Bentham was an amiable and eccentric early nineteenth-century reformer, who was interested in all aspects of social organization.   He concerned himself with the penal law, he offered to supply a written constitution to any country that wished to buy one from him; and he even had customers.   In the economic realm, he was convinced that individual self-interest was consistent with social well-being, and he accordingly suggested that the legislator play upon self-interest in order to realize social ends.

This apparent autonomy, nevertheless, had no real substance, even for the cartels and *consorzi* which were the very embodiment of big business. The Nazis made frequent use of their expression, *Gemeinnutz vor Eigennutz* (public interest overrides private) and the Nazi interpretation of that saying reflects the parable the Germans whispered among themselves to illustrate the difference between fascism and communism: While the communists take away a man's cow, the fascists leave him the cow and burden him with its support; but they take the milk.   In both Italy and Germany, small business lived on sufferance, and big business was not accorded full independence. When Mussolini introduced the bill to establish the corporations, he remarked, "When an enterprise appeals to the general public for capital, it loses its private character and becomes a public, or if you prefer, a social factor." [9]

When, therefore, steering (that is, the indirect control of industry through the provision of mechanical rabbits which industrial greyhounds might be induced to pursue) did not serve the purpose, then the harness, the muzzle, and sometimes even the whip were brought into use.   The right to hire and fire was taken over by state and party; freedom to declare dividends was restricted; raw materials were allocated and particular uses to which they might be put were prescribed; compulsory delivery orders were issued; resort to the capital market was constricted; prices were controlled; permits and licenses were required for an increasing variety of industrial activities; and competition from favored party enterprises took the place of nationalization.   In short, the entrepreneur became in essence a civil servant.

STEERING: THE INDIRECT CONTROL OF ECONOMIC ACTIVITY

The most pervasive and insidious of the fascist controls of industry flowed inevitably, and both directly and indirectly, from the massive public spending which is one of the hallmarks of a fascist economy.   This spending had two primary purposes: the need to court public support as an offset to public coercion, and the need to get certain things done.   Propaganda and "enlightenment," the provision of employment, the establishment of organized public recreation, together with the maintenance of expanded police and custodial institutions—all this cost money which flowed into the hands of individuals

[9] Italian Library of Information, *op. cit.,* p. 24.

who pursued the opportunities so created.   On a much larger scale, the rearmament, which has been the main social and industrial objective of fascist societies, stimulated appropriate industries to respond in the way the state wished them to respond; and, up to this point, no further control was necessary.   The trouble was, that point was always overreached.

The entire world now knows that rearmament, or even mere expansion, sets in motion forces hostile to itself.   Aggregate wages rise with increasing employment, and they tend to be spent in ways which add to the pressure upon scarce resources.   When this happens, sooner or later indirect control must be replaced by direct, in order to constrict consumption by rationing and by placing limits upon further increases in wages or salaries.   Even this becomes insufficient; industries which would normally respond to these demands for higher living standards require discouragement; the use, therefore, of resources, including labor, tends to pass under direct control by the state.

In free economies, the intensification of industrial activity which is occasioned by rearmament would be accompanied by an expansion of international trade; resources that are unavailable or expensive at home can be sought abroad, but they must be paid for.   That payment may be made by exporting additional goods and services, or by shipping gold, or by borrowing from abroad.   Loans, however, depend upon a willing lender, unless lenders can be coerced into lending; gold is itself a scarce resource; and unless exports are confined to products deemed non-essential,[10] they represent to that extent a loss to the state.

The danger that scarce resources may be squandered upon unimportant objects looms larger still in fascist economies.   In fascist countries, dependence upon foreign countries for fundamental resources is considered dangerous; the supply may be cut off at any moment, as was natural rubber to the United States after Pearl Harbor.   Fascist economies, therefore, tend to be autarkic; they have sought to exploit exclusively the resources they have, and to develop substitutes (often called synthetics), for those they have not.   Foreign trade also passes under the control of the state, and at this point, too, indirect control of the economy passes into direct.

The financial implications of large-scale rearmament point to another form of control of economic life.   Just as indirect control over resources leads to direct control, so both together involve control over finance.   The inflation-

[10] Even non-essentials, like the harmonicas Germany exported to Eastern Europe before the war, must be produced from steel and by labor which otherwise might be applied to uses considered more important.

ary pressure generated by massive expenditure not only requires damping down, if only for the sake of preserving financial order and stability; it also requires deflection into channels conforming to the main economic purposes of the state.   Price and wage control are utilized to help keep inflationary forces under general control, while the process of investment is guided to the end that the kind of industrial structure the state wishes to develop is actually brought into being.   This is simply one means of saying that *purely* financial considerations are given second place; [11] they are not permitted to distort the economic pattern fascist officials wish to see established, and still less are they permitted to block or even postpone the attainment of fascist objectives.   This is true of all war economies,[12] and it simply underscores the point, that here also indirect control of economic activity eventually must become direct.   Under fascism it did, but it took the form of control which, so far as possible, utilized the existing structure of industry.

All varieties of fascism have accepted the control of industry and have frequently imposed it.   Within the framework of a totalitarian state, however, existing business organizations have been hailed as agencies for the self-government of industry, which to a large extent they have been.   On balance, these organizations have been associations of big business freed from harassment by independent and frequently hostile labor unions, freed also from the threat of competition from abroad, and within certain limits freed from the threat of competition at home.   The important men both in the Italian Corporations and in the German Groups and Chambers were businessmen, and big businessmen at that.   To be sure, the party was also present, and party representation was overriding, but at least business was there and business organization remained intact.   To be sure, also, in order to survive, these men, like all others, had to be politically acceptable to the regime, and in Germany at least, it was better to be "Aryan"; but individual and class security are very different things.

The monolithic appearance of these structures was nevertheless to some degree misleading.   What usually happened was the driving under cover of the unending struggle for competitive advantage and for individual position and power and the transformation of the healthy if sometimes disorderly

---

[11] *Cf.,* M. J. Bonn, *The Crumbling of Empire,* London, 1938, page 191, footnote, for a statement of the political uses of currency manipulation.   For a contravening statement that financial considerations were not secondary in the Third Reich, *cf.,* Burton Klein, "Germany's Preparation for War," *American Economic Review,* March, 1948, pp. 73–76, and *passim.*

[12] *Cf.,* Antonin Basch, *The New Economic Warfare,* New York, 1941; p. 52.

competition of less centralized economies into the covert but none the less bitter and often treacherous maneuvering of cliques, courtiers, and carpet-baggers.

The combination of intensified public control of industry with the entrustment of that control to established organizations of industry meant the reinforcement of monopolistic tendencies, which were already strong, in both the fascist economies with which we are primarily concerned.   The onset of depression in Italy prompted industrialists to form cartels, or *consorzi,* and the establishment of IRI helped along that trend.   We have already seen that "reprivatization" was confined to industries whose ownership the state was content to slough off.   The return of some industries to private hands, however, meant neither a return to competition nor relaxation in the movement to subsume important industries under centralized public control. The Italian government actively facilitated mergers which the Ministry of Finance considered in the public interest, and the government also participated, through IRI, in cartelization of really essential industries.   Italian shipping companies, for example, were organized into four great non-competing groups (each of which monopolized certain routes) in which IRI held the majority of the stock and in which private stockholders shared the directorships with government officials.   In chemicals and synthetics, ANIC (*Azienda Nazionale Idrogenazione Carboni*) was formed as a branch of the great Montecatini combine to hydrogenate heavy oils and lignite—that is, to manufacture synthetic gasoline.   ANIC was a branch, however, in which both public and private capital were involved.   The same thing was true for a specially created division of the Pirelli Company to manufacture synthetic rubber, and for the Burgos Paper Company which was involved in making cellulose from straw.   IRI held more than half the capital of the three greatest shipbuilding companies in Italy, and IRI was responsible for the reorganization of the four leading steel firms according to principles set forth by the Metal and Engineering Corporation.   In all these cases, IRI participated in management in order to assure the safeguarding of national interest within the general framework of the profit system.[13]

As far as private cartels were concerned, the Italian government as early as 1932 stated the conditions under which membership might be made compulsory.   This was required, for example, for firms in the cotton textile industry.[14]   At about the same time the state intervened to control "over-

[13] *Cf.,* Italian Library of Information, *op. cit.,* pp. 25–26.
[14] *Cf.,* William G. Welk, *Fascist Economic Policy,* Cambridge, 1938; p. 170.

production" by requiring licenses for the extension or creation of plant capacity, the licenses themselves being issued by a commission within the Ministry of Corporations upon the advice of the appropriate syndical and corporative organizations of industry.   In 1937 this function was entrusted to the corporations themselves, as were the ancillary responsibilities of price and production control.

The same pattern was followed by the Germans.   The Boards of Directors of many important concerns had both public and private representatives, and this was true for some public institutions as well as private. VIAG, for example, had on its board various private bankers and representatives of Krupp; the *Reichskreditgesellschaft,* a public institution concerned with the supervision over and sometimes the outright granting of industrial credit, was governed by a board containing only two public officials while the rest came from private industries and banks.[15]

National Socialist Germany was equally solicitous about its cartels.   It is true that industrial Germany never displayed the distrust of monopoly characteristic of much American public opinion, but even so the Weimar Republic did exert some effort to squeeze the great German trusts into activities consistent with genuinely public interest; the National Socialists simply utilized them.   In July, 1933, the Reich passed, or rather had passed, two laws to strengthen the authority of the cartels.   The first endorsed any sanctions imposed by a cartel against entrepreneurs showing signs of "unreliability" or against enterprises whose price policies were "unjustified."   The second law, the *Zwangskartellengesetz,* was the famous one on compulsory cartelization.   It gave the government authority to force enterprises to enter a cartel when it wished this to be done; it enabled the government to apply administrative restrictions upon investment in any sector of the economy, cartelized or not, when it felt impelled to do so; and it defined the right of government to supervise the internal activities of cartels.[16]

In a word, what National Socialist cartel policy was directed toward, and what it essentially achieved, was three things.   (1) It sanctioned and extended the authority of the cartels over their members and it denied to independents the right to decide for themselves whether or not to become members of a cartel; (2) it strengthened the influence of government upon the policy of cartels; and (3) it integrated the cartels into the machinery for

---

[15] *Cf.,* Franz Neumann, *op. cit.,* p. 298.
[16] *Cf.,* Samuel Lurie, *Private Investment in a Controlled Economy,* New York, 1947; p. 71.

controlling the German economy.   As we shall see, the cartels were given important responsibilities in the control of prices, and they also were used to help in the assignment of public contracts, the standardization of accounting procedures, the routing of orders, and even in the negotiation of international agreements and the allocation of export markets.   All this did not go unchallenged.   The Groups, particularly—which in many cases were organized alongside the cartels with functions suggesting competing jurisdiction —were not always happy over this form of competition, and the government was occasionally impelled to mediate.[17]   Possibly this confusion arose out of the need for the same hurried improvization into which the United States was thrust between 1941 and 1945; equally possibly, and perhaps more probably, it was due to the Nazi reluctance to entrust any subordinate institution with unchallenged authority even under public delegation.

DIRECT CONTROL OF THE ECONOMY: CONSUMPTION

We have observed how the indirect control of the economy led, by various routes, to direct control.   One of the points at which control had to become direct was consumption, although this did not become necessary until resources became scarce.   In the early years, indeed, the opposite policy of stimulating consumption was cautiously followed.   To provide additional employment the production of new types of consumers' goods, particularly heavy goods, was fostered.   Probably the best known project was the one to manufacture the *Volkswagen,* or peoples' car.   The car was planned to sell for under the equivalent, in German currency, of $250, and was purchasable on weekly installments of about $1.20,[18] but the project was timorously resisted by the German automobile industry.   Although the government pushed the project, notwithstanding industrial resistance, the attempt failed.   It is interesting to notice that the Peoples' Car Works and the associated Peoples' Tractor Works, while they were still viable, were among the corporations controlled by the Labor Front.[19]

It was not long, however, before consumption had to be compressed rather than expanded, and this was done by the familiar devices of strict

17 *Ibid.,* pp. 72–73.
18 *Cf.,* Guenter Reimann, *op. cit.,* pp. 133–136.
19 *Cf.,* Franz Neumann, *op. cit.,* p. 304.

rationing, the control of income, and, in the last resort, by the control of the production of consumers' goods.   Income and consumption became dissociated, except to the extent that black markets and surreptitious under-the-counter deals brought them again into furtive alignment.   Aggregate consumption, particularly after the onset of the Second World War, was adjusted, at least in principle, to the distributable surplus after prior needs, particularly military needs, had been met.   This procedure was given the unctuous justification of being a protective measure for consumers, to prevent them from "rash buying." [20]

DIRECT CONTROL OF INDUSTRY: AUTARKY

Political, social, military, and economic forces combined to force both Italy and Germany, even before the Second World War, to make the most of what they had, to cut themselves off from what they had not but what their citizens might like to have, to seek shelter in something like the ginger-bread house of the fairy stories, except that the gingerbread was made from coal and cellulose.   The full story would make a book in itself, and it would not be a story of utter failure.   If necessity is the mother of invention, invention is the introduction of substitutes.   The safety match was a substitute for flint and steel, and perhaps television will prove a substitute for the motion picture.   Is there any difference between this form of substitution and the substitution of Buna for rubber, Zellwolle for natural fiber, or synthetic oil for natural gasoline?   All substitutes have at least this in common: they appear positively subversive to those interested in the goods threatened with displacement.   Shepherds, whether in Australia or Montana, can scarcely be expected to look with favor upon the Italian Snia Viscosa or the American Dupont.

Perhaps we could say that there is a difference between introducing for economic reasons a substitute which must take its chances in the market, and for *raisons d'état* forcing a substitute upon consumers regardless of market preferences.   That distinction, however, disappears when we recall the German substitution of manufactured rather than mined nitrogen shortly before the First World War, a substitution made quite independently of the market, although the market has subsequently fallen into line.   Simply be-

[20] *Cf., Deutsche Volkswirt,* November 17, 1939.

cause consumers, whether industrial or personal, are compelled to accept a substitute of something they would not initially prefer to the displaced commodity, does not mean that in time they may not for very good reasons come to prefer the substitute.   Buna, Zellwolle, and synthetic oil may eventually come to be so favored.   To illustrate an extreme form of fascist autarky, we need to find a substitute which no consumer, left to himself, would ever be likely voluntarily to substitute for what it was intended to replace.   Italian "substitute" wheat seems as good an example as any.   That substitution may have been politically or ideologically or militarily necessary; it may, under conditions of acute economic distress, even have been economically necessary in order to provide employment, to keep land in use, or to conserve foreign exchange.   Even if that were so, and it is far from certain that it was, the substitution of Italian for imported wheat meant that Italians got less of a more expensive product, and that they also got less of alternative products which were rooted out to make room for substitute wheat.   The Italian "Battle for Wheat" provides a good case study for fascist autarky in its most extreme form.

Italy in the middle 'twenties was importing about thirty-five per cent of the wheat it consumed.   Closure of foreign countries to Italian immigration meant both that more mouths open for wheat remained in Italy, and that the Italian balance of international payments showed signs of strain.   As fascist economic and military objectives took form, alternative uses for Italian foreign exchange loomed larger, and sensitive fascist concepts of national prestige contributed to Mussolini's decision "to free the Italian people from the slavery of foreign bread."   The first step was taken on March 1, 1924, when the *Populo d'Italia* announced a contest for the "Victory of the Grain," the first prize being ten thousand lire.   In the following spring, the tariff on wheat was raised from 50 to 200 lire per quintal.   In the spring of 1926, the Bank of Sicily and the Bank of Naples lost their right to issue bank notes. Since that right is equivalent to the right to make loans to people who do not have checking accounts, as few Sicilians or Neapolitans did, those banks lost that source of earnings; their "compensation" took the form of coercive diversion of their lending activities into the provision of agricultural credit.

There followed a campaign for intensive production, involving such things as research in agricultural chemistry, the establishment of model farms, the distribution of good seed, the provision of new agricultural machinery, all wrapped in incessant propaganda and involving substantial subsidies.   The cost of the campaign between 1925–26 and 1928–29 was reported as being something over two and a quarter billion lire. Formally, the result was success: over 300,000 hectares of land were added to the production of wheat, average productivity per hectare rose from slightly over ten quintals in 1920–25 to something over 14 quintals in 1931–36. That success, however, was had only at a price. In 1932, Italian wheat was selling nearly three times higher than the world price, and the expansion of wheat acreage in Italy had been at the expense of other crops which had comprised part of Italian exports. In the early 'thirties, for example, Italian exports of olive oil fell by nearly fifty per cent, while Spanish exports rose by a like amount. Similarly, Spanish exports of citrus fruits gained at the expense of Italian, although to a lesser degree.[21]

In Germany there were corresponding developments, although they were applied with greater thoroughness and ruthlessness and they led to an even tighter control of foreign trade. We have already seen how the structure of German industry was left largely intact after the assumption of power by the Nazis; let us now see how the Nazis modified to their purposes traditions of economic warfare which stretched back into the German past.

Germany in 1933 had two economic objectives: in the short run, re-employment and recovery from depression; in the long run, rearmament with all that rearmament entails. The two fitted together, as rearmament is one means of reviving a depressed economy that does not run counter to private industry's dislike of governmental intervention to quite the same degree as other policies designed *purely* to provide employment. This conjuncture provided the same *milieu* out of which German mercantilism, or cameralism, had emerged in the seventeenth and eighteenth centuries thereafter to persist into the present century: the concept of an international scramble for something that is scarce and in which the nation had a very vital concern. We already know that this something had been, earlier, gold and national power; under the Nazis it became foreign exchange, raw materials, and national power.

Contemporary relationships between rearmament and re-employment are still more subtle. Unemployment can be reduced only by putting people to work, and that means the placing of orders with the sources of employment. In 1933 orders were rare in both the domestic and export markets, so that only Government was left as a substantial ordering agency. Every-

---

[21] The figures in this section were taken from various issues of the *Annuario Statistico Italiano* and from the London *Economist*.

one knew that the key to real re-employment lay in the capital-goods industries and that there were more direct ways of stimulating these than by subsidizing consumption.   All this fitted beautifully into Hitler's desire to rearm, but neither rearmament nor economic expansion were assured unless access could be had to certain basic raw materials in which Germany was deficient; iron ore, some non-ferrous metals, petroleum, and rubber are examples. To secure these, foreign exchange was necessary, and foreign exchange, also, was scarce; it played the same functional role that gold had played three centuries earlier.   This is not to be taken as implying that gold was unimportant to National Socialist Germany.   Despite the cynical assertion of the *Deutsche Allgemeine Zeitung* in 1940 that American gold would be used after the war only to pave Wall Street, to gild street lights and public buildings, and to decorate the establishments of diplomats,[22] because by then gold would have lost all monetary function, the Nazis sought gold everywhere they went.[23]   But gold was sought precisely because it still was one form of foreign exchange.

Hitler accordingly followed an historically respectable mercantilist policy by which, although some of the techniques were new, the purposes were not. Specifically, he (a) hoarded and rationed what foreign exchange he could get, and that involved controlling internal consumption; (b) he bypassed as far as possible the need to expend foreign exchange by concluding barter agreements with whatever countries he could cajole or coerce into concluding them; and (c) he attempted to build up his resources of foreign exchange by forcing exports and by dumping, both directly and indirectly.[24]

This policy involved risks, but it was consistent with German expansionist ambitions, and it accordingly was deliberately undertaken.   That meant that German policy hinged directly upon power, and—again, like the seventeenth century states—this forced attention upon the sources of power.   Let us now examine, in greater detail, how the fascist states controlled their foreign trade.

[22] *Cf.* Albert T. Lauterbach, *Economics in Uniform,* Princeton, 1943; p. 131.

[23] *Cf.,* Thomas Reveille, *The Spoil of Europe,* New York, 1941; pp. 130–137.

[24] By direct dumping is meant selling German products in other countries for whatever they might bring.   By indirect dumping is meant the resale abroad of foreign goods, usually purchased under barter agreements, thereby confronting the original exporters in their hitherto established markets with the competition of their own products.   Germany did this, for example, with Greek tobacco, Turkish raisins, Jugoslav timber, Colombian coffee, etc.   *Cf.,* Paul Einzig, *Bloodless Invasion,* London, 1938; *passim.*

DIRECT CONTROL OF INDUSTRY: FOREIGN TRADE

In both the two great fascist countries the attempt to control industry indirectly led inevitably to direct squeezing and manipulation of their economies, and in each case the sector first brought under really comprehensive central control was foreign trade.   In Italy, rearmament and autarky both required insulation against the outside world.   Although Italian industry would grind to a halt without the raw materials Italy did not have within her borders, uncontrolled imports would drain the country of precious and scarce domestic resources.   The shortage of foreign exchange compelled its rationing, and as Fascist Italy was also Imperialist Italy, autarky for military reasons became very much the object of national policy.   Italy, therefore, became something more than protectionist.   It limited the amount of money travelers could take out of the country and it controlled the uses to which Italians might put any foreign currencies which came into their possession.   It proceeded to make itself as self-sufficient as possible.

Exactly the same pressures existed within Germany.   Since the German control of these activities was more pervasive, more detailed and was carried further than in Italy, our attention will be concentrated on Germany in order that we may discern, so to speak, where fascist controls really lead and how, in their most extreme form, they really operate.

Just as Roman rulers followed the precept *Divide and Rule,* the Nazi economic hierarchs observed the principle *Divide and Gain.*   In contrast to liberal international trade policy which regarded the world as an economic unit whose specialized subdivisions exchanged their surpluses with one another, the Germans endeavored to balance their commodity trade with each country individually; in contrast to classical monetary policy which accepted gold as a universal medium of exchange into which the several national currencies were freely convertible, the Nazis devised a variety of moneys, each of which was designed for a special, specific function; and in contrast to classical economic policy which permitted and expected individuals to search out their own markets and make their own arrangements, the Nazis bound their foreign traders to particular transactions under controlled conditions.

Bilateral Agreements

Precious foreign exchange could be conserved if German goods and services could be exchanged directly for those foreign commodities for which Germany had need.   This meant arranging the details in advance, and such arrangements were indeed made with whatever countries could be induced to participate.   Foreign exchange then could be reserved for purchase from benighted states which would not play.   The procedure, at least in the beginning, was fairly simple.   The Reichsbank in Germany saw to it that German exporters concerned in these arrangements were paid in German currency, and the participating countries had their central banks compensate exporters in just the same way.   At the end of each accounting period these central bank credits were matched against each other, and any balance due either party could either be carried over into the next accounting period, or it could be settled forthwith on the clearing house principle.   In practice it usually turned out that Germany was the debtor, and that the balance was carried over.   The extraordinary consequence was that the traditional power of a grasping creditor over a helpless debtor gave way to the terrifying bondage of the creditor to a ruthless debtor.   German bilateral debts accumulated so rapidly that their holders were confronted by the hard choice between hanging on while the debt continued to grow, or risking the loss of everything by breaking loose; they generally hung on.

Political considerations as well as economic were involved in this.   Southeastern Europe had long been eyed by German imperialists impelled by the *Drang nach Osten.*   Furthermore, assuming a maritime blockade in the event of war, overseas sources of supply might be imperiled, but the mineral and agricultural resources of Balkan Europe could be secured by the German Army, particularly if those states could be bound commercially to Germany. Moreover, while colonial policy in the nineteenth century had been partially based on the assumption that Trade would follow the Flag, Nazi Germany discovered that the Flag found it just as easy to follow Trade.   If Krupp, for example, should supply armaments, the recipients would be bound to Krupp for service, parts, and replacements; and Krupp, like Germany itself, developed in only one direction.   More generally, German salesmen of all varieties carried samples that really served as traps, and were intended to. Frequently, although not invariably, the samples represented valuable and needed goods, but the German purpose in peddling them was neither pleasing the customer, nor, primarily, finding an outlet for German surpluses. That purpose was the attachment of other economies to the German. The purpose was effective.

Other economies got attached to the German because of German skill in developing the power that a debtor may acquire over his creditor. The unsuspecting debtor who is unwilling to catch the eye of his creditor fails to realize that the creditor, too, may not breathe easily until the debt is repaid. A delinquent debtor may create anxiety lest he default entirely, and an unscrupulous debtor may—quite literally—make capital out of that anxiety.

The Nazis were unscrupulous debtors. They did not hesitate to purchase Roumanian oil, Turkish chrome, Greek currants, Bulgarian tobacco, or Hungarian wheat even if they had to offer something higher than world prices. If more of these products were received than Germany needed for herself, the surpluses could be dumped upon the world markets for whatever foreign exchange they might bring, and that, in turn, could be used to purchase supplies from recalcitrant countries like France, Great Britain, or the United States which were too blind to see the obsolescence of the economic principles to which they insisted upon clinging. When Germany's unhappy foreign creditors were reduced to such straits that they would accept literally anything in partial payment of their claims, the Nazis placated their foreign creditors with exports which constituted no serious drain upon essential German resources. These exports comprised such things as harmonicas in sufficient volume to drown the music of the spheres, and so much aspirin that its only use was to assuage the cosmic headache its mere possession produced.

Special Monetary Forms

The world at large has usually thought of money as something desirable to possess because it can be exchanged at will for things desired by its holder and offered by the market. More constricted experience in wartime has taught the world that subsidiary forms of quasi-money, such as ration cards, coupons, or stamps, could be used under specified conditions in partial exchange for certain indicated, and controlled, types of commodities. Before the last war the Germans discovered that this same principle could be extended and generalized, both to increase the export of German goods and services, visible and invisible, and to concentrate that export upon resources which autarkic Germany could afford to relinquish.   A variety of special currencies, somewhat analogous to ration cards, was accordingly developed, each of which was restricted to a special set of uses and many of which were confined to special categories of holders.   By 1936 there were some twelve special currencies of this kind, as well as the free currency familiar to the rest of the world and recognized by it as just plain money.   Some of these currencies were highly specialized and restricted, but the principle of the system can be sufficiently suggested by a description of one or two varieties.

Registered marks.   Registered marks were offered foreigners who wished to liquidate balances they had held in German banks prior to the financial crisis of 1931 when those balances were frozen.   Those marks were offered foreigners outside of Germany in exchange for the deposits held in Germany, and they were offered at rates of exchange fifty per cent more favorable (to the foreigners) than the official rate of exchange for the reichsmark; but there were strings attached to the offer.

Foreigners could bring registered marks into Germany, but they could not take them out; and, once in Germany, their holder could spend them only for specified purposes: travel and living expenses, the purchase of special types of German property or securities,[25] or to buy whatever goods the Germans were willing to see leave the country.

Travel marks.   Travel marks were a form of tourist currency offered prospective visitors to Germany in their own countries at varying, and frequently substantial, discounts; they could not be purchased inside Germany.   They were valid for travel within Germany, but only up to certain limits, so that many travelers, once safely caught, were compelled to purchase free currency at the official rate of exchange.   Like the Registered marks, these could not be taken out of the country by individuals; only the Government could legally export them.

Aski marks.   The famous Aski marks derived their name as an abbreviation of the horrendous expression, *Auslaender-Sonderkonten fuer Inlands-Zahlungen,* or Foreigners' Special Currencies for Internal Payments.   They were issued in payment for purchases in Germany of certain foreign goods.   Their holders could use them only to buy specified German goods for export

---

[25] The selection of property and securities that might be purchased with registered marks was determined by the balance, in particular cases, between the capital that might be made available to the German economy, on the one hand, and the control by foreigners of portions of German wealth such purchases would involve, on the other.

to their own countries.   The discounts at which these were issued varied both from country to country, according to Germany's individual relations with each, and from time to time, according to the veering and eddying of trade movements generally.   Under certain conditions the holders of Aski marks could sell them to others wishing to import particular German goods in categories approved by the German authorities.

Credit and securities marks.   *Kreditsperrmarken, Notensperrmarken* and *Effektensperrmarken* constituted a category of special currencies derived from the sale by foreigners of securities, mortgages, and property they held in Germany.   These currencies could be used for travel and living expenses in Germany by their owners and their families, they could be used to pay German taxes and to make gifts to Germans, and they could also be used for the purchase of German goods but usually only up to about a quarter of the invoice price; the balance had to be paid in reichsmarks obtained at the established rate of exchange.

Certain observations can be made.   Just as the bilateral barter agreements became devices for the exploitation of foreign governments, many of these special currencies proved admirably designed for mulcting foreign individuals; and the proceeds were frequently used to subsidize German exports. Under the exchange control, foreign owners of income-producing property in Germany could not withdraw their gains.   Gains did accrue, but they accrued only in Germany and they could be used only in Germany, so that only individuals resident in Germany had any incentive to purchase the property from which those gains came, while their foreign owners had some incentive to get rid of German property for whatever they could get.   Much of that property was accordingly "repatriated" by enabling, indeed encouraging, German exporters to exchange the proceeds of their exports into these special currencies, and then to use those to purchase foreign-owned German property at substantial discounts.   That property could then be resold within Germany at its full market value, and the profit devoted to covering any losses which might have been incurred in selling abroad anything which the Reich insisted should be exported.   The same procedure was used to encourage the purchase by Germans of "blocked"—that is, frozen—bank accounts held in Germany by foreigners.   Even this was not quite sufficient.   Germany, as Goering observed, had to export or die, and as early as 1934 domestic business was being taxed in order to make possible the subsidy of exports to the extent of forty per cent, and sometimes even higher, of the export price.   The device was cumbersome and doubt-less unpleasant, but it did produce foreign exchange.

When the Second World War came, still more direct means of fostering the international exchange of goods were developed.   An example was the German-Greek Compensation Company (*Deutsch-Griechische Warenaus-gleichsgesellschaft*), known as DEGRIGES, formed in November, 1942, to facilitate commerce with Greece, to absorb excess profits, and to make Greek goods cheaper in Germany.   It was a private corporation operating under the supervision of the Ministry of Economic Affairs, and it controlled all goods flowing between Greece and Germany.   When the Greek price level became inflated substantially above the German, Greek importers were made to pay substantial compensatory charges to bring the cost of German goods in Greece into conformity with Greek prices; the proceeds were even-tually used to pay part of the expenses of the German Army of Occupation.

Finally, to return to the special currencies, their development enabled the Nazis both to secure more foreign exchange than they otherwise might have done, and to divert foreign purchases of German goods into areas where really scarce German resources were not drained off.   Travel marks, for example, like loss-leaders generally, appeared to be bargains.   They could be had at a discount, but their purchasers could use them only by entering the German shop, in this case the Reich itself, and once in they might be impelled to make other purchases, in this case of reichsmarks at full rates.   Moreover, the consumption by tourists of railway seats, hotel rooms, beer, and porcelain pipes did not imperil the progress of German rearmament.

General Control of Foreign Trade

The devices just described—the conclusion of bilateral barter agreements and the manipulation of the currency system—helped but did not solve the German foreign-trade problem.   In 1933–34 and thereafter, Germany felt driven to export, but to export only those commodities she felt could be spared.   It had to export in order to procure the means of purchasing foreign supplies which could neither be produced nor substituted for at home, at least in sufficient volume.   This meant that individual freedom had to be constricted.   On a larger and more intricate scale, the German problem was that of the price discriminator: the net gains from selling some surplus at less than prevailing prices could be made secure only if the surplus could be kept out of the market where higher prices prevailed.   German exporters, accordingly, had to be directed toward only those markets which authority wished to cultivate, and importers had to be constrained from dealing in either commodities or countries about which authority was unenthusiastic. Here also, consistent with fascist practice, the form of private enterprise was retained, but its conduct entirely redesigned.

Control Boards.   By September, 1934, control over every commodity listed in the Tariff Classification was centered in one or another of twenty-seven Control Boards (*Ueberwachungstellen*) created for various groups of commodities, and this control was both tightened and extended as the National Socialist economy developed.   In the main these Boards had three great functions: (1) to confine aggregate imports to the quantity of foreign exchange available for their purchase; (2) to concentrate purchases in countries which bought equivalent quantities of goods from Germany; and (3) to give priority to specially needed categories of imports, particularly those needed for rearmament.   The essential procedure was simple.   Before a German importer could place an order he had to justify its necessity in an application for an allocation of foreign exchange.   Approval of such an application was usually tied to precise specification of the terms of sale and frequently the selling price of the imported goods, and sometimes approval was made contingent upon purchase from an indicated supplier, or sale to a specified purchaser.   Approval of an application authorized the importer to place his order, but he was not yet finished with the Control Board.   When payment became due he was issued foreign exchange up to the amount requested in his approved application provided he presented evidence, such as a customs house certificate, that the goods had actually been received.   The entire procedure was rounded off by exchange control applied to tourists and to other individuals engaged in the acquisition or sale of foreign exchange.

In summary, then, the system inherited by the Nazis under which most importers were more or less automatically allocated the foreign exchange they required, provided it was available, was replaced by a system of specific permits.   The resulting adjustment of the volume of German imports to the volume of German exports was reinforced by the encroachment of reciprocal barter arrangements upon the old system of multilateral foreign trade, and the upshot was a substantial shift in both the direction and composition of German foreign trade.   Each German export was deliberately directed toward some particular country and resulted in a credit in that country's currency.   It appeared to the Nazis preferable to exhaust that credit in the form of imports from that same country than to shuffle the credit about to secure by its means a different national currency.   In consequence, German trade shifted away from Western Europe where it was difficult to make the kinds of agreements Germany wished, and toward Eastern Europe and Latin America; and the continued rationing of foreign exchange shifted the composition of imports away from consumers' goods and toward more raw materials and capital equipment.

Fascist Systems in Operation

2. DOMESTIC PRICES AND INDUSTRY

FOREIGN trade in all its aspects was, both logically and chronologically, the economic activity first brought under control by the fascist states. We know the reasons: (1) Any economy that is not completely self-sufficient must import whatever it must have, but if its means of payment for imports must be husbanded, only essential imports can be permitted; (2) any economy struggling with domestic shortages, particularly in basic resources, cannot permit those to be squandered—hence only unimportant exports can be permitted; and (3) any economy that wishes to exploit foreign individuals, or even foreign countries, can do so by bringing under control the points at which important foreign economic activities touch upon the domestic. In fascist economies, all three conditions were observed.

DIRECT CONTROL OF INDUSTRY: PRICES

The control of foreign trade undertaken to insulate fascist economies against the intrusion of forces which could not be domestically controlled provided an environment favorable to domestic price control; mounting domestic expenditure made that price control necessary. It, accordingly, was undertaken.

The Act for the Execution of the Four-Year Plan, October 29, 1936, established the Office of the Reich Commissioner for Price Formation. Exactly a month later, on November 29, 1936, came the famous *Preis Stop* by which prices were frozen to their levels of October 18, 1936. There was, of course, provision for exceptions, but the intent of the stop was general: to prohibit all increases in price except those necessary just to compensate sellers for certain permitted rises in their costs. How sincere could that intent have been? Only the very unsophisticated could have believed that a general freeze followed by localized, minor thaws would solve the problem. In the *first* place, the pattern of prices prevailing at any given time is the resultant of the particular forces which *happened* to bear upon particular commodities or the demand for them at that time, and only by the rarest of coincidences would happenstance bring forth the pattern of price relationships which might be *wanted*. In the *second* place, conditions and needs change, and prices immobilized by hard frost need to be thawed before they can jump to an order with the alacrity expected of everything else within a command economy. *Finally,* as the cause of need for immediate modification, there were incongruities between prices frozen to levels set by cartels for the purpose of contrived private advantage and prices left to fend for themselves in what remained of the free market; there were, also, certain prices for which no base date or *Referenz Period* could be found.

Let it be recalled that the responsible official was entitled, not the Commissioner for Price Freeze (*Preis Stop*), but the Commissioner for Price Formation (*Preisbildung*). The freeze could not have been intended as anything but a temporary expedient, but as an expedient it had two clear uses: (1) it provided reassurance to people that inflation would not dissolve their savings; and (2) it provided a breathing spell which could be utilized to take stock and make careful decisions, just as a cautious driver caught in erratic traffic movements will pull over and consider, rather than plunge ahead. At any rate, the subsequent history of German price control is a progressive advance from the freezing (*Preis Stop*) to the formation (*Preisbildung*) of prices.

The first modification was prompted by disparity between "bound" and "free" prices, between "ascertained" and "non-ascertained" prices, and between prices relatively free from distortion by governmental demand and prices modified by substantial market pressure exerted by state purchases. The solution adopted for these difficulties was the segregation of prices into different categories to which different principles of control could be applied.

Bound Prices

Foreshadowing the *Preis Stop* was a decree of November 12, 1934, which required official approval of any contemplated change in cartel price agreements or of any projected conclusion of a new price agreement. Six years later, a decree of November 23, 1940, gave renewed recognition to the price-fixing activities of cartels and trade associations, subject only to intervention in cases of abuse. This was not complete abrogation of public responsibility. It must be remembered that the shell of private enterprise was still cherished, even if the worm of party meddling was permitted to get into the meat. By the time this last decree was promulgated, the government was primarily anxious to assure economically necessary firms an adequate profit and to foster efficiency by permitting particularly good establishments to retain some sort of efficiency premium. The basic principle applied to bound prices was, thus, delegation of primary responsibility to the cartels themselves.

Ascertained Prices

Commodities whose prices were not the subjects of price agreements within cartels but for which the base period price could be ascertained, remained formally under the *Preis Stop,* although the eroding and blurring passage of time caused more and more frozen prices to become subject to modification. The principle remained simple: approved prices should be determined by calculating raw materials at cost, labor at legal wage rates with provision for overhead and—significantly—for contributions to the Party.

Non-Ascertained Prices

Specific prices had to be found and then fixed in the case of commodities for which no base period price existed. These commodities were characteristically new products, or synthetics, which had not been produced at all at the time at which the prices of other things had been frozen. The principle adopted here was the same as that applying to changes in ascertained prices, although sometimes, when uncertainty was particularly acute, maximum and minimum limits were prescribed, with entrepreneurial freedom to set particular prices within the established limits.   The entrepreneur himself could be trusted not to fix a price below the minimum, and a sensitive entrepreneur was deemed responsive to hints that the maximum should not be pushed.

Prices on Government Orders

There were many commodities—such as food for the armed forces— for which the government was a heavy although not the only buyer.   The prices of those commodities were subject to the *Preis Stop* and to the modifying principles just described.   There were other goods, however, such as munitions or mail sacks, the demand for which was monopolized by the government.   On these, prices were generally fixed at such a point as would assure to the manufacturer the recapture of approved costs plus some controlled profit; but the costs approved were not those experienced by each separate firm involved.   In this preliminary period prices on these goods were fixed on the bulk-line principle; that is, they were set high enough to bring forth the "bulk" of the supply needed so that high-cost producers were excluded while the very low-cost producers received an efficiency, or luck bonus.   The Price Commissioner, of course, passed upon permissible cost.

As the war developed and the economy became progressively stretched, the classification of prices into different categories for the purpose of control underwent a change: *Preisbildung* came increasingly to the fore.   Three broad categories of prices ultimately emerged.

Individual and group prices.   What the Germans called *Einheits- und Gruppenpreise* were imposed upon commodities intended for general sale. The underlying principle was the desirability of establishing uniform prices for the products of uniform work, but to do so by grouping different plants according to their costs of production.   The basis for this particular type of price-formation was the average cost, not of all plants in an industry, not even of representative firms, but the costs of moderately good firms of something better than average efficiency.   The costs of "artificial green-house firms" [1] were specifically excluded from the calculation of that average. Under this system the costs of war risks, even war losses themselves, could not be reflected in legal prices, although there was provision for subsidy from

---

[1] *Cf., Vierjahresplan,* September 29, 1939.

a Price Equalization Fund in the case of favored firms which were under-going real hardship.   The authorities were anxious not only to encourage but to compel the development of efficiency, which a simple cost-plus system will not do; that is why firms of high rather than average efficiency were taken as the standard.   Slight deviations from that standard were, however, permitted in approving the costs of *groups* of plants, following a principle which had first been developed by the General Staff in fixing the prices of supplies pur-chased for the armed forces.   By essentially the same principle, the holders of inventories which had been purchased at different times for different per-mitted costs were not permitted to average the prices of these, because of the risk that such a procedure would amount to concealed increases in price. The Heaven to which all good Price Commissioners go is an orderly realm in which there are firm, fixed, and uniform prices upon every class of com-modity which enters the market.

Like other attempts to regulate, the German effort to move toward that ideal condition forced the authorities to essay other kinds of intervention. They were compelled, for example, to prescribe detailed accounting pro-cedures in order that the calculations of cost presented by different firms should be both understandable and comparable.   One of these procedures, bearing the formidable name *Hintenanhaengekalkulation* (calculation of cumulatively stuck-on costs), was designed to prevent an authorized increase in price at some early stage of production from growing like a rolling snow-ball as the product neared its destined consumer.   Understandably enough, that kind of prescription sometimes brought difficulty to smaller establish-ments, which had not hitherto paid much attention to cost accounting.

These various techniques applied on the whole to goods already produced, or being concurrently produced under known and more or less standard con-ditions.   The procedures about to be described applied to cases involving new contracts or when contracts were about to be let under conditions of some uncertainty.

Quasi-fixed cost prices.   Selbstkostenfestpreise were prices fixed some-what before firm contracts were placed, and when the order was to be split among different firms with varying costs.   Here, also, an efficient firm was selected as the norm, and it received cost plus a guaranteed profit; the price fixed for it then was applied to all similar products.   That was the principle, but like some other principles, this one frequently underwent some modifica-tion in its application.   In the manufacture of soap, for example, when com-pulsory standardization of the product and prohibition of the future use of trade marks were imposed, new costs and conditions of production had to be estimated ahead of time.   What was done was to determine some standard cost of production which then was regarded as the maximum legal cost for all firms.   The more efficient plants which were able to produce at still lower costs were permitted to retain, as an efficiency premium, one tenth of the surplus so gained; the balance was skimmed off by the government which used it to subsidize raw materials as a means of preventing increases in their market prices.

Actual cost compensation prices.   Prices based upon actual costs (*Selbst-kostenerstattungspreise*) were prices intended to assure each manufacturer his actual costs.   These prices were sparingly established, but they, or something like them, seemed necessary when completely new products like synthetics or substitutes were about to be produced before anything like standard costs or conditions of production could be determined.   In other words, these prices were based upon straight "cost-plus" for each producer.   After experience brought less uncertainty, uniform prices were generally fixed according to one or another of the techniques already described.

General Purposes and Procedures of Price Control

The Germans were determined to emphasize efficiency, but they were unwilling to become involved in unnecessary administrative work.   Their control of prices, accordingly, rested upon the principle of identical prices for identical products, or, when that was clearly unwise, upon group prices for broad categories of products.   When reductions in price were ordered, as sometimes they were, the reduction was forced all the way through to subcontractors as well as prime contractors.   A minor problem arose concerning special levies and taxes; the authorities had to secure revenue, they wished to discourage unnecessary consumption, but they also were concerned to keep prices from getting out of hand.   What they finally did was to permit dealers to charge prices which included genuine indirect taxes, such as the fifty per cent excise on beer.   "Contributions" (which were formally voluntary, although their timing and their volume combined to suggest thousands of Nazi hearts beating as one) might not be incorporated in prices charged, although they might be indicated separately (as hints to buyers) on invoices or in advertisements.

Within this system the individual enterprise was lost.   It was dangerous to attempt to go out of business, it was dangerous to show a lack of alacrity in accepting a government order, and it was positively perilous to attempt to evade the price controls. An enterprise which could not attain the degree of efficiency the established norm imposed, simply had to accept losses. The larger and more powerful enterprises managed to survive, but many smaller ones went under and many were forced into absorption by larger firms. It was partly the shoulders of small businessmen on which fascism rode to power; but once on those shoulders, fascism, like the Old Man of the Sea, kept on riding.

THE DIRECT CONTROL OF INDUSTRY: RESOURCES

Let us pause, briefly, to take stock. We have examined fascist control of foreign trade undertaken to make fascist economies airtight—that is, to insulate them against counteracting forces which, unchecked, would have imperiled the economic policies the fascist states sought to pursue. The intervening hand of government, accordingly, intruded further and further into economic activity. We have observed the attempt to guard the domestic price system against both the erosion which exposure to world markets might have entailed and the instability which inflationary pressure at home carried with it. Governmental intervention in both those areas could not, however, be confined to those areas; it inevitably had to be extended.

Even if fascist states had not been concerned to direct resources into rearmament and therefore to control their use, it would not have been easy to confine the control of resources to the rationing of foreign exchange. Controls tend to spread. Conclusion of a bilateral barter agreement with Romania meant both that a use for imports from Romania be found and that guaranteed exports to Romania really be produced and exported; that, in turn, involved the control of at least part of the *domestic* economy. If Romanian oil were imported under such an agreement, the domestic industry producing the synthetic oil in which Germany had so great an interest could scarcely be left completely alone. Just as the development of a superior motor fuel may prompt the adaptation of engines to it and that, in turn, stimulate experimentation with larger and heavier trucks which then compel the strengthening and straightening of roads which, thereafter, carry so much more and so much faster traffic that highway police forces must be expanded; all the more, then, do more general changes in a great sector of the economy tend to ramify outward.

The development of special currencies deflected foreign demand away from certain sectors of the economy and into others.   (See pages 242–245.) It was intended to do so, but the intention would have been aborted unless the structure of the economy had been adapted to the intention.   The control of prices was pregnant with still more intervention.   One of the functions of price is to ration, and the scarcer a good becomes the higher its price must be for the rationing function to be effective.   If price is prevented from rising, rationing still is necessary, simply because the supply of the scarce good will not go around.   An insistent buyer can bribe the seller; by doing so, he is paying a surreptitiously high price instead of a natural high price.   An early buyer can get at the head of a queue, and substitute loss of sleep for loss of money.   In either case, unscrupulousness or insomnia replaces the market function by which price adjusts available supply to effective demand.

If neither unscrupulousness nor insomnia is regarded as desirable as means of rationing something that is scarce, price control involves the deliberate rationing of the final products whose prices are held down, and the allocation of the materials whose prices are likewise fixed.   Costs had to be controlled, and so did wages as a component of costs.   Plant capacity had to be regulated, and to do so private investment needed to be brought within the range of governmental intervention.   Let us see how all this was managed.

Investment and Finance

The first problem confronting the fascist economies was that of industrial depression, but the techniques developed to solve that problem proved equally adaptable to the very different economic problem posed by rearmament and war.   Each of these situations required the control of industrial capacity— depression, because much capacity seemed redundant; and war because unnecessary or non-essential capacity seemed intolerable.   Italy, accordingly, in 1933, required approval by the Ministry of Corporations before new plants could be constructed or old ones enlarged.   In 1937 this responsibility was transferred to the Corporations themselves, and by March, 1938, the Corporations had considered some 971 applications for the creation or expansion of capacity, and of these they had approved 649, denied 161, deferred 132, and had 29 still under consideration.[2]

Germany did likewise, but it reinforced this procedure by even tighter con-

---

[2] *Cf.*, Italian Library of Information, *Italy Today, Corporative Agriculture and Industry*, New York, 1939, mimeographed; p. 28.

trol over financial operations, so that, here also, the German procedure will be used as a case study.   In the very beginning of the regime, the state empowered itself to prevent the expansion of existing industrial capacity, or the creation of new capacity if it regarded this as contrary to the interests of the Reich.   In the fall of 1934 even retailing was constricted; no new store might be opened without a license.[3]

To assure observance of that prohibition, as well as for other reasons, financial resources for the creation or expansion of capacity were brought under control.   In mid-1934 the Dividend Limitation Act (*Anleihestockgesetz*) was passed to provide that profits in excess of six per cent, or sometimes eight, could neither be distributed as dividends to stockholders, nor retained by the enterprise without official approval.   The restriction upon the declaration of dividends had behind it a growing official feeling that stockholders, except in their role as purely passive contributors of industrial capital, were simply nuisances.   This attitude was ultimately given legal recognition in the draft of a Company Act which asserted that "the interests of the enterprise as such are as worthy of protection as the individual interests of the stockholders."[4]   In the end, management was made largely independent of the stockholders whose rights even to information became legally restricted.[5]

The restriction upon the retention of profits by the enterprise which had earned them was justified by the simple theory that the Reich had better uses for them.   Profits that were excessive in the sense that enterprise could not retain them, had, therefore, to be deposited in the Golddiskont Bank, which thereupon invested them, formally on behalf of the stockholders, in governmental securities.   These securities were to be made redeemable much later, but only under restriction concerning use of the proceeds.   In 1941 and following years, for example, they were to be used only in payment of taxes.

The real purpose of this was to control investment, and the effect was eventually to close the capital market to private industry.   Because German heavy industry, like the American, had become increasingly able to finance itself out of earnings, the closure of the capital market could be made

[3] The reasons for this and more of the details of the prohibition will be discussed later.   See, below, pp. 267–268.

[4] *Cf.*, Franz Neumann, *Behemoth, The Structure and Practise of National Socialism*, New York, 1942; pp. 286–287.

[5] *Cf.*, Samuel Lurie, *Private Investment in a Controlled Economy, Germany 1933–1939*, New York, 1947; pp. 143–145.

effective only by tapping the means of self-finance.   That is one reason why excess profits were drained off.

The determination of the government to pre-empt capital to itself compelled it also to bridle the banks.   By the Law of December 5, 1934, a Credit Supervision Board and a Reichs Commissioner for Credit, appointed by Hitler, were brought into being.   Thereafter this Board issued revocable licenses to all banks and their branches, and concerned itself as well with the prevention of banking abuses by such measures as those controlling reserves and the extension of credit to employees of banks.   Again, the real purpose was to prevent competition between public and private demands for credit. Having brought the institutions themselves under control, another crumb could be held out to private enterprise through "reprivatizing" stock in several of the *Grossbanken* hitherto held by the government.

This was not entirely unpopular.   To common folk the world over, bankers, as moneylenders, do not always appear to be flowing with the milk of human kindness, and what milk they do have usually seems sour to defaulting debtors.   Depression in Germany as elsewhere brought many defaults, so that the "slavery of interest," condemned in the original National Socialist Program, appeared bondage indeed to a great many Germans in 1933 and 1934.   The Nazis, accordingly, drew a famous distinction between *schaffendes* and *raffendes Kapital,* or creative and predatory capital. The former was honest, productive, industrial capital; the latter was the rapacious capital of the financier which was supposed to have captured all power in modern society and subjected the world to the slavery of interest. It was also suspected of being either Jewish or international capital, and was thus particularly appropriate for seizure by nationalist Nordics; that, at any rate, was one of the reasons given for the expropriation of Jewish property in Germany before the Second World War, and of foreign property in occupied countries after the war had started.

Even the Reichsbank, the great central bank of the Reich, did not escape unscathed.   It, like the Bank of England later, was taken over by the State, but this act of nationalization did not arise out of the particularly *raffendes* character of the finance capital it controlled; it arose for a technical reason— the governmental need for almost unlimited credit and on terms to be determined only by the government.   The Nazi economic program was both expansive and expensive, but it nevertheless seemed so important that financial reasons alone could not be permitted to imperil it.   That program could have been financed by the printing press, but public memories of the inflation

of the early 'twenties were too sharp and too bitter for such a recourse to
have been safe, even if it had been wise.   Accordingly, on June 15, 1939,
the Reichsbank was changed from an independent bank of issue to a governmental institution responsible only to Hitler, who alone was to determine the
amount of credit the bank was to extend the government.   Thereafter all
formal restrictions on the amount of credit the bank could extend were removed, and all restrictions on governmental borrowing were revoked.   Gold,
which was then in short supply, was declared merely a subsidiary cover for
the German currency which now became based on *Arbeitswaehrung,* a sort
of labor backing.   The principle behind this must have been easier to invoke than to apply: it was simply the maintenance of a "reasonable" proportionality between the volume of currency in circulation and the output
of goods by German labor.

In summary, the German financial problem was twofold: to secure financial resources for expansion, rearmament, and then war; and to prevent their
being used to destroy the stability of the currency.   The former was achieved
by a combination of spontaneous and contrived increases in the flow of funds
to the Treasury; the latter by a combination of increased taxes and contributions with the imposition of comprehensive and strict control over the movement of prices.

Tax revenues were automatically increased by the rise in national income,
and this same rise brought about increases in the flow of public savings to
insurance companies and savings banks, which, in turn, were induced to invest these in governmental securities.   Industrial expansion raised profits
which, under the mandatory restriction upon the distribution of dividends,
could either be reinvested provided the government approved the purpose
and procedure of reinvestment, or, otherwise, diverted also into governmental
securities.   Increased employment both reduced public disbursements under
the system of unemployment insurance, and increased the volume of contributions toward unemployment insurance which, since 1930, had been paid
at the rate of six and one half per cent.   The Reich Unemployment Office
used the surplus so built up for public investment.   By banning or restricting private capital issues, the government was able to monopolize the savings
and capital resources of the country; between 1933 and 1936 public borrowing amounted to about ninety per cent of the net accumulation of German
capital.   By the sale of a variety of short-term treasury bills the government was able to secure the use of a very substantial part of German bank
credit.   Finally, there was sheer confiscation.   A tremendous quantity, first

of Jewish property and later of foreign property under conquest, was seized and expropriated.   Even when this passed directly into private hands, as much of it did, taxation and compulsory investment insured its use for public purposes.

The Control of Labor

An account has already been given of the fascist abolition of labor unions and of the organizations designed to take their place, and we have already described the devices introduced under fascism to resolve or prevent labor disputes and to determine wage rates and conditions of employment.   We are concerned, here, with labor as a resource, a factor of production which had increasingly to be conserved, parceled out, and rationed.   The most extreme form according to which labor is allocated is, of course, slavery, known euphemistically to this tender age as forced labor.   That, fascist societies have.   Germany, during the Second World War, imported hordes of foreign workers, sometimes under contract, sometimes under sheer duress, who were housed in labor camps akin to concentration camps, assigned their tasks, and kept under restraint when they were not actively engaged in work. The Soviet Union, also, has vast labor camps populated, in this case, by her own citizens who have had the misfortune to displease the rulers of the workers' paradise.

Military conscription is another form of compulsory allocation of labor which is not limited to fascist society.   Fascist states do conscript, but they also extend the principle of conscription.   Young men and women are expected as part of their duty to the state to put in a period of labor service, usually on the land.   The American philosopher William James once suggested something very similar as a "moral equivalent of war," [6] but fascist labor service is usually, among other things, part of the moral and physical preparation *for* war.

These, however, are special forms of the allocation of labor, concerned with particular forms and categories of labor.   As a basic, fundamental resource, labor *per se* comes under control exactly as do other resources. Italy, as in so many other cases, started down this road but did not follow it as far as did the National Socialists in Germany.   Section Two of the Labor Charter announced that "All forms of labor, intellectual, technical, and

[6] *Cf.,* William James, "Moral Equivalent of War," in *Memories and Studies,* New York, 1912.

manual, are a social duty.   As that, and only as that, is labor protected by
the state."   That statement reflects the official attitude; its main implementation took the form of a Royal Decree of March 29, 1928, providing that
employers seeking labor could secure it only through a public labor exchange.[7]

Germany, likewise, since June 28, 1935, had given the labor exchanges a
monopoly over employment, but when the Reich began to confront a shortage of labor in 1937, more drastic measures to allocate a tight resource were
taken.   The number of apprentices, particularly in the metal-working and
construction industries, was increased by governmental assignment; and employment priorities favoring, first, rearmament and then food, domestic raw
materials, the export industries, and construction, were invoked.   Agricultural labor was tied to the land and workers were forbidden to seek employment in the cities.   In 1936, metal workers and, in 1937, carpenters
were enjoined from changing either their jobs or their places of residence
without official sanction.   Even this, however, did not solve the problem,
and the final step of establishing industrial conscription was taken in the
year following.

On June 22, 1938, the Office of the Four Year Plan issued a decree to
authorize the compulsory assignment of every German citizen either to
specific employment at fixed wages, or to some form of vocational training
at the discretion of the authorities.   Even this was not enough.   The following year, on February 13, 1939, a supplemental decree extended that
obligation to all *inhabitants* of the Reich and made the period of compulsory
labor of indefinite length.   Thereafter it was presumed that assignment of
an individual to specific employment automatically implied the existence of
a labor contract which could not be abrogated without the permission of the
authorities.   That meant that employers were no longer able either to hire
or fire at will, and it also meant that labor was forbidden to change or to
quit jobs without permission.   These provisions were made most difficult to
evade by requiring every worker to carry a Work Book (*Arbeitsbuch*), which
identified him, described his skills, his training, and gave the record of his
past employment.   Without a Work Book no one could secure employment, and since the Work Book was frequently held by the employer during
the tenure of employment, unsanctioned changes of employment became
practically impossible.   Indirectly, the system was just as binding upon employers, since no employment could be given without proper endorsement

[7] *Cf.*, William G. Welk, *Fascist Economic Policy,* Cambridge, 1938; p. 294.

of the Work Book, and a written record of illegal employment was something few men dared to provide.

The procedures just described had to do with the employment of labor. There remained the question of raising the *efficiency* of labor, and this was managed by a combination of exhortation and of wage-fixing similar in intent and function to the control of prices to assure industrial efficiency. (See page 252.)

By a Law of January 25, 1938, the Labor Trustees were empowered to fix maximum as well as minimum wages. The basic wage came to be considered that paid to an average, normal worker under the average conditions applying to the branch of industry which employed him, but the particular wage of a particular workman depended upon flexible elements more or less controlled by his employer.

Wages were considered compensation for the amount of effort expended. As a result, a system of effort wages (*Leistungsloehne*) became established under which the wage paid fluctuated not only with the hours of work but with the effort expended as well. Thereafter, deviations from official minima and maxima were permitted. Almost every collective contract came to have a clause authorizing deviations from the minimum wage in the case of less efficient workmen, when the reasons for the deviation lay "in the person of the follower." [8] It was the responsibility of the Work Leader in consultation with the Council of Trust to determine when such conditions prevailed. Deviations from maximum wages were correspondingly adjusted to reward superior degrees of efficiency or effort. It is interesting to notice that the Stakhanovite system in Soviet Russia is a similar effort to give efficiency premia to superior efficiency.

The Control of Industrial Processes

The theme of this account has been the tendency for any attempted control of a fascist economy to ramify and grow. To some extent, that is always true; governmental control of the American economy has also grown. Except in wartime, however, when conditions somewhat similar to those prevalent in fascist societies appear, governmental control of the American economy has been at least *intended* to achieve for individuals or groups what

[8] It will be recalled that the Nazis came to call the employer the Plant Leader, and his working force his Following, or *Gefolgschaft*.

they would like, but apparently cannot, achieve for themselves.   Farmers have had the prices of their products supported, labor has had its right to organize assured, industry has been sheltered against the seemingly cold winds of foreign competition, and consumers have been safeguarded against extreme adulteration of what they buy or exaggerated misrepresentation of what they are besought to buy.   The extension of American controls has arisen because each separate act of control has consequences which then must be attended to, and also because, with growth, the American economy has become more complicated.   But there has been no *intention* to control everything, and the principle still accepted is that the individual should be free to try anything he can safely be left to try.

Fascist control is very different because its *purpose* is the attainment of ends separate and different from the ends individuals set for themselves. That is why the wartime organization and management of the German economy has been selected as, so to speak, the epitome of fascist systems.   The wartime organization of the American economy was, and was taken to be, exceptional, forced by circumstances, to be abandoned as soon as happier circumstances permitted.   The wartime organization of the German economy was simply an extension and development of the principles and purposes of fascist society even in peacetime.

The very heart of the system of fascist control was directed upon the flow of materials into and through industrial firms.   As we are now in a position to suspect, the formal structure and the organized institutions of private enterprise were left intact, but their operations, their performance, and their purposes were completely transformed.

In the early, depression-plagued years, the problem was one of sheer industrial survival, and the solution adopted was simply the sharing, through something like industrial blood transfusion, of whatever nutriment was at hand.   Firms, accordingly, were limited to whatever proportion of their capacity or turnover they had utilized in some base period.   This allocation was determined, whenever possible, on the basis of quota assignments within cartels.   Nevertheless, that device had little more than transitional significance.   The limitation of output to the rate typical of some base period was inconsistent with the expansion generally sought, and the *accidents,* or unnecessary and casual characteristics,[9] of the structure of production in a base period could hardly be generalized into a system of total control.   Very soon, then, emphasis came to be directed upon economic products them-

[9] *Cf.,* H. W. B. Joseph, *Introduction to Logic,* Oxford, 1916; p. 75.

selves.   When, first expansion, then rearmament and war, transformed surpluses into scarcities, the state resorted to licenses, priorities, and eventually
to compulsory orders.   Purchasing licenses were required fairly early of
the first processors of scarce raw materials; when the number of producers
was smaller than the number of industrial consumers, purchasing licenses
were replaced by sales licenses.   Processing licenses soon were required in
order to control the use of stocks already on hand and to regulate the inter-
relationships of plants at various stages of production of some end-product.
When scarcity became acute processing for purposes deemed non-essential
was prohibited.   Finally, while the control of raw materials was never relinquished their control *as* raw materials came to be recognized as inadequate:
the alternative uses to which raw materials might be put became increasingly
matters of public concern, so that control at the point of consumption came
to be of greater and greater importance.   This happened, first, in the case of
iron and steel; by 1937 the finished product was, generally speaking, the
focus of control.   Let us now see how this form of control developed.

Control of Industrial Processes Through Allocation

As we have seen, allocation was first centered upon raw or semi-finished
materials, and was first based upon a firm's past consumption.   Such allocations were usually made quarterly, and they came eventually to be tied to
production orders.   The exact procedure depended in each case on the importance and potential uses of the material concerned.

As pressure increased, the Germans found that what they called the "steering of production," through tying allocations to a firm's share in the manufacture of the end-product, would eliminate much unnecessary production.
That is, the state first decided what end-products were needed and who was
to manufacture them—then raw materials could be distributed accordingly.
If shortages were severe, efforts were made to find substitutes, or, at least,
to alter the composition of the product.   Each month producers were required to submit to the Economic Group to which their industry belonged
a complete report of outstanding orders arranged according to the ultimate
use of the end-product.

"Quota-claimants," the recipients of allocations, were divided into three
great groups: (1) Chief Claimants (*Hauptbedarfstraeger*), comprising the
armed forces, the railroads, the party, and similar great and important consumers; (2) groups of industrial firms that, as large consumers, were en-

titled to global quotas; and (3) those agencies of government that were responsible for less essential industrial needs and for consumption by civilians.

Indirect Allocation: Types of Orders

The consumer's certificate. The consumer's certificate (*Verbrauch-ererklaerung*) was the least rigorous, the least bureaucratic and the least used of all allocating devices. It was simply a form on which a manufacturer stated that he was aware of his responsibility to conserve resources and of the penalty for violation. Its most frequent use concerned specific commodities, such as certain technical rubber goods, which, being used only by certain industries for very special purposes, were easy to watch.

The trader's certificate. The Trader's Certificate (*Haendlererkaerung*) was issued in certain branches of wholesale trade in which the material could easily be traced all the way from producer to consumer. Rubber, paper, and leather are examples. These basic products were allocated in global quantities from central points to processing firms, to government agencies, and to other large consumers. The certificate authorized its holder to purchase from any supplier who was willing and able to sell to him. In tight cases, this quota system was easily adapted to rationing.

Direct Allocation: Types of Orders

General orders. Little more than mention need be made of the sheaf of direct orders of various sorts designed to squeeze the German economy into the desired shape; their names indicate the functions they served. There were orders to requisition, prohibitions of sale, and prohibitions of production. There were many consumption licenses, particularly for such things as chemicals, and there were standardization orders which laid down specific instructions concerning the kinds and quantities of materials to be used in manufacturing certain goods. Frequently the technique or process of production was also prescribed. All these led, eventually, to the use of production orders (*Herstellungsanweisungen*) which compelled their recipients to manufacture prescribed quantities of specified products from assigned materials, and these frequently were combined with prohibitions or restrictions upon the non-essential use of the materials to be conserved.

Special techniques: The cemented allocation. The cemented allocation was a tight device by which the allocating office assigned the manufacturer his quota of materials and the particular supplier from whom he had to procure it.   Paper and chemicals were allocated in this way.   The procedure was usually for the allocating office to instruct each supplier to deliver a prescribed quantity of indicated materials to a particular recipient within a designated period of time.   By "cementing" buyer and seller together the channel of trade was determined with sufficient precision to assure the purchaser the right to buy and process the materials to be used.

The general issue of allocation rights.   This was a somewhat looser form which preserved a vestige of competition.   A manufacturer was issued a purchase permit and was then free to choose his source of supply.   It put the burden of *finding* supplies on the recipient, but by adjusting approved total demand to known total supply, it was taken for granted that competition among would-be buyers would result both in steering supplies to the most eager and efficient demanders and in guaranteeing each efficient demander the supplies he needed.   This device, of course, was not used in cases where supplies were really scarce.

The check, mark, and stamp system.   Check, mark, and stamp all refer to forms of means of payment.   A check, as we all know, is simply a means of payment created by the issuer against a fund held for him by an agent known as a bank; the mark is the unit of German currency; a stamp is the means of payment used for sending a letter or parcel through the mail.

The Germans adapted these common means of paying for things in general to the special purposes of controlling the uses to which things in particular were put.   Approved processors of materials were assigned quotas of materials that they needed.   Against those quotas they were issued a "check," the *Warenscheck* or *Warenschein,* which they then could use to draw upon their quotas almost as if these had been deposited in a bank account.   Those quotas of materials were then treated as if they were bank deposits, subject to withdrawal by check.   Such a check, properly endorsed, was transferable to other approved processors, or it could be used to secure stamps or marks in smaller denominations which then could be issued to subcontractors or smaller processors by the prime contractor who had been issued the original check.   A central accounting service debited claimants' commodity accounts for all withdrawals by *Warenscheck.*

This procedure was first used to control iron and steel, whose processors received "steel rights" according to their outstanding contracts and the priorities assigned them.   These rights were embodied in steel checks which were issued against applications for them, endorsed with (1) the contract "steering number" assigned the particular contract for which steel was needed, (2) a statement of the specific purpose for which the steel was to be used, and (3) evidence that sufficient steel was still credited to the account against which application for a "check book" was being made. Receipt of his checks empowered the manufacturer to issue his own steel transfer checks to subcontractors who could exchange them at the proper Economic Chamber for smaller denomination steel coinage or stamps. No steel could be shipped except against checks or stamps.

The universal check system. This system, established November 20, 1943, was clearly an extension of the one just described, and was designed to tie the allocation of materials more closely to production orders. The procedure was the very simple one of attaching to each order for compulsory delivery the commodity checks necessary to assure the manufacturer the materials he would need to fill the order. In essence, this meant that entrepreneurs became industrial civil servants: they were told what to produce, and what price to charge for it; they were issued their materials; they were assigned the necessary labor; the accounting procedures by which they kept track of what they did were prescribed for them; and they frequently were provided technical assistance. Sometimes that assistance was heavy-handed, for many standardization committees insisted upon the erasure of entrepreneurial individuality. Procedures deemed wasteful were prohibited, the retention of trade secrets was forbidden, the exchange of technical experience and knowledge was mandatory, and certain *Wettbetriebe* (plants to emulate) were designated as models to which others were strongly invited to pay heed. To offset this loss of entrepreneurial freedom, firms were assured a market and, provided they could maintain prescribed standards of efficiency, they could count upon a steady income.

Both the functional and territorial agencies already described [10] participated in this system. The assignment of global allocations and their supervision was made the responsibility of the functional Groups, while the territorial Chambers kept themselves informed of the capacity of plants in their territory, the rate at which capacity was being used, and the availability of various types of labor and equipment.

[10] See above, page 224.

CONTROL OF MARKETING

Marketing was made subject to very similar forms of control.   These will be briefly described, even at the risk of some repetition, because they emphasize, again, the principle by which the National Socialists controlled the German economy.

From the very outset, marketing was important.   The Nazis were assisted to power by the Fighting Alliance of the Industrial Middle Class (*Kampf-buende des gewerblichen Mittelstandes*), a depression-born organization which took up the sword of small business against consumer cooperatives and chain and department stores.   The triumphant Nazis "Aryanized," that is, they liquidated, many of these large firms on the formal ground that they were of Jewish or communist complexion, and for a time the small merchant was extended hope.   The opening of new stores was forbidden unless it was clear that the interests of established retailers would not be imperiled, and local authorities were permitted to screen the qualifications and aptitudes of applicants for a retailing license.   Later, this severity was softened; new entry was discouraged only if it threatened to bring about general over-crowding.   Still later, under the banner of efficiency, a "combing out" of handicraftsmen and retailers took place; the victims became laborers.   They became so when rearmament made labor scarce.

When the system finally took form, Marketing Associations (*Marktver-baende*), dominated as usual by party and state, came to rule the channels of distribution.   First, imports, then domestic supplies competitive with imports, became subject to purchase and sale only through license.   As markets tightened the state began to hunt for or to develop critical distributive points through which the entire supply of goods flowed or could be made to flow and at which the flow could be controlled.   Dairies, local markets, and packing houses are illustrations.   In the end, the middlemen, like other entrepreneurs, became essentially salaried public servants.   Even their name changed; they became Distributors (*Verteiler*) instead of Traders (*Haend-ler*).   Agricultural products, such as milk, no longer were permitted to appear in the free market.   Dairies were compelled to deliver assigned quotas to specified buyers at fixed prices, and free sales were prohibited.   The state assumed the responsibility of distributing rural surpluses over metropolitan deficit areas; it monopolized such imports as were permitted, and it prescribed the milk or butterfat content of milk products.   In place of being allowed initiative, distributors, both wholesale and retail, were restricted to passing along assigned quotas at prescribed margins.

13

The Russian Governmental and Social System

I N April, 1917, a sealed railway car rumbling northward across Imperial Germany bore a man whose arrival in Russia gave coherence and focus to a series of events of profound significance to the contemporary world.   Lenin did not make the Russian revolution, but to both Russians and outsiders he symbolizes it, and it is right that he should: without Lenin, the course of that revolution might have been very different.   That fact in itself is important, but it is not as important as another fact that is not always so well remembered: that the Soviet revolution was a Russian as well as a communist phenomenon, and, strictly speaking, it was not even communist.   It certainly was carried through by people who described themselves as communist, it was directed toward the formation of a communist society, but—as we shall see —even the Russians acknowledge that the attainment of full communism lies in the future.

Superficially, the coexistence of collectivism in Russia and of capitalism in the United States might appear to offer an unparalleled opportunity to compare two competing economic systems, but since the communists are *Russians,* and the capitalists *Americans,* national as well as ideological characteristics intrude to complicate the comparison. The fact that Russia as a nation was technologically backward and economically underdeveloped when the Revolution occurred complicates even the economic comparison. This is forcibly brought out in the anonymous remark which one writer quoted on the title page of his book on Russia: [1] "I think that it is a disaster for the idea of planning that Russia should have been the country where it has first been tried out."

Sometimes the difficulty in the comparison is neatly evaded by discussing only principles, that is, the way the Russian and the American economies *ought* to work regardless of the devotion or efficiency with which the people of each country attempt to apply the principles to which they pay at least lip service. Sometimes, also, the principles are entirely ignored in descriptions of, for example, Russian procedure, even though exactly the same principles might be applied very differently indeed if the communist operators happened to be Germans, Englishmen, or Americans.

THE UNIQUE CHARACTER OF THE RUSSIAN EXPERIMENT

The disentanglement, then, of the various elements which in combination give the Russian experiment its unique character is extraordinarily difficult. The issue is not merely academic. At a time when the United States is almost the only great power which is not deliberately experimenting with some form of collectivism, men must inevitably speculate upon the possibility that even Americans may some day essay a designed venture into other ways. If that possibility really exists, it is extremely important that we endeavor to distinguish the features of contemporary collectivist systems which derive from the systems themselves from those features which stem from the peculiar national traditions, histories, and psychologies of other peoples. To what extent, for example, is the lower *per capita* productivity of the Soviet Union, or its totalitarian character, due to Russian rather than to purely communist characteristics? A precise answer, if it is possible at all, can come only from extended and specialized study of the past and present of the Russian system, and that is beyond our purview. A hint, however, is provided in the suggestion by an historian that the Soviets inherited from the Czarist regime the emphasis upon force wielded by a secret police, reliance upon a swollen

---

[1] *Cf.,* Colin Clark, *A Critique of Russian Statistics,* London, 1939.

bureaucracy backed by the army, acceptance of great centralized power at the disposal of the state without any attempt to distinguish, as Bentham did, between the proper *agenda* and *non-agenda* for the state, and the curious tendency almost to deify the sovereign or leader.[2]   A counter-suggestion, far stronger than a hint, is contained in Hayek's argument that collectivism in and of itself necessarily entails centralization, extension of state power, increasing reliance upon coercion, and progressive extension of the area in which coercion becomes necessary.[3]

It is true that centrally controlled economies have generally been totalitarian; it is also true that no contemporary state with an established, well-rooted democratic tradition has yet gone totalitarian.   It remains true that no state flirting with collectivism can afford to ignore the political and social implications of an extension of centralized control in any direction.   It is nevertheless true that governmental control of any variety of activity need not lead to totalitarianism as long as government itself is not responsible only to itself. The strength of democracy lies in the possibility at any time and the certainty at some time that one government will be replaced by another, by *orderly and constitutional means.*   Replacement alone is not enough.   Someone once described the Byzantine Empire as a despotism tempered by the likelihood of revolution, but when revolution occurred, the replacement was, all too often, simply a substitution of King Stork for King Log.   The balance between freedom and control in this troubled age becomes of increasing moment, and that balance ultimately rests upon the wisdom, the restraint, the imagination and the forbearance, the vision and the tolerance—in short, upon the intelligence and moral strength of the people contained within an economic and social system.   For that reason, the observer attempting to appraise Soviet accomplishment and failure should constantly keep at the back of his mind the question—Would Frenchmen, or Danes, or Americans do this the same way?

THE SOVIET GOVERNMENT

Structurally, the Soviet Union is a federation of sixteen constituent republics, each with a certain measure of cultural autonomy, but with economic

[2] *Cf.,* B. H. Sumner, *A Short History of Russia,* New York, 1943; p. 48.
[3] *Cf.,* Friedrich A. Hayek, *The Road to Serfdom,* Chicago, 1944; *passim.*

policy certainly and political policy generally, firmly in the grasp of the central government. It is true that in February, 1946, the constituent republics were permitted to establish their own Ministries of Foreign Affairs and arrange their own diplomatic representation, but the unkind explanation has been offered that this was a splitting off of identical cells designed to assure the communist bloc in international organizations a multiple rather than a single vote. No one has ever suggested that the central government and the Communist Party do not continue to rule.

The Central, or as the Russians call it, the All-Union Government, rests formally upon the Supreme Soviet, a bicameral legislative body which meets semi-annually and whose members are elected by the Russian populace. That electoral procedure, however, is something quite different from the one to which Americans are accustomed, although there are certain formal similarities. Before an election an Electoral Commission for the entire country is created and other, subordinate Commissions for the various political subdivisions of the country are simultaneously established.[4] It is the responsibility of these Commissions to insure that elections conform to the principles set forth in the Constitution of 1936—an appealing document purporting to be the fundamental law of the land but interpreted, apparently, in a most obscure manner. Specifically, the local Commissions, as the first of their duties, prepare lists of qualified voters. These lists are posted well before an election so they can be scrutinized; anyone believing himself improperly omitted may appeal to a court. The press, public bodies, organizations of labor, and similar associations are entitled to appoint representatives to observe the counting of ballots.

The Soviets have introduced one novelty into their electoral procedure. Americans are sometimes surprised to learn that candidates for election to the British House of Commons need not run in the districts where they live, but may seek the approval of electors in any district in the country. The Russians have turned that procedure upside-down by permitting a Russian voter to cast his ballot wherever he may happen to find himself on election day. Thus, passengers on through trains are considered electors for the district in which the train has the longest run during voting hours, and electors on ships may vote for candidates running in the vessel's port of registry.[5] This might be regarded as an extension of the procedure of democracy, were

---

[4] This statement is based upon the procedure prescribed for the Russian election of 1946, described in the *Information Bulletin of the Embassy of the U.S.S.R.,* Washington, November 25, 1945.

[5] *Cf.,* Drew Middleton in the *New York Times,* February 10, 1947.

it not that voters in the Soviet Union have no function beyond signifying approval or disapproval of the single candidate whose name appears on the ballot for each office to be filled. Essentially, they vote Yes or No, and their choice is limited to these alternatives. The real fight occurs earlier, in the selection of the candidate.

Any organized association, such as the members of a unit of the armed forces, a labor union, a youth group, or an organization of peasants, is privileged to nominate its candidate for an open office, and to campaign for its nominee—who need not necessarily be a member of the Communist Party. Elected representatives of the various nominating organizations then meet for the purpose of selecting the candidate, who must eventually be certified by the appropriate Electoral Commission as the successful nominee. The official "campaign" which follows consists of exhortations to vote—rather than suggestions that the rascals be turned out, or that it might be time for a change! The resulting near unanimity of the votes [6] cast then become the subject of general official rejoicing over the widespread public support enjoyed by the regime.

The Supreme Soviet

The legislative body whose members are so elected is organized to give representation to different nationalities as well as to geographical areas. One of the Chambers, the Union Soviet, represents the Russian population on a geographical basis; the other, the Council of Nationalities, represents the constituent republics, which themselves are based, roughly, upon the more important ethnic groups which comprise the Russian population. The two chambers have equal legislative powers, and their joint acts, expressed as Acts of the Supreme Soviet, have priority over any acts or regulations of any of the constituent republics. Disagreements between the two chambers which cannot be reconciled by a conciliation committee eventually may result in the dissolution of the Supreme Soviet and a new election. To insure continuity of legislative responsibility, a Presidium of about forty members, elected by the two chambers of the Supreme Soviet meeting in joint session, has authority to issue edicts when the latter body is not sitting, although its actions are subject to later ratification.

[6] Cf. In the election of 1946, for example, only eight tenths of one per cent of the votes cast registered opposition to the approved official slate. Cf., *Information Bulletin of the Embassy of the U.S.S.R.*, Washington, March 12, 1946.

The "highest executive and administrative organ of state power in the U.S.S.R." [7] is the Council of Ministers, which corresponds in general to the cabinet elsewhere. Its decrees have the force of law, although they, too, are subject to ratification, in this case by both the Presidium and the Supreme Soviet. The ratification is usually assured. Like the members of the Presidium, the Ministers who head the various executive departments of the Soviet Union are appointed by the two chambers of the Supreme Soviet sitting in joint session.

Except for the Presidium—an institution intermediate between parliament and cabinet—none of this is markedly different in structure from the governmental institutions of other countries. There remain, however, three characteristics of the Russian government which stand out in sharp contrast to governmental institutions and responsibilities in, for example, the United States: (1) its "soviet" character; (2) the peculiar role played by the Communist Party, which corresponds closely in organization and function to the fascist parties we have already examined; and (3) the completely totalitarian character of its activities.

Subordinate Soviets

The second and third articles of the 1936 Soviet Constitution provide that "The political foundation of the U.S.S.R. is formed by the Soviets of toilers' deputies, which have grown and become strong as a result of the overthrow of the power of the landlords and capitalists and the conquest of the dictatorship of the proletariat," and that "All power in the U.S.S.R. belongs to the toilers of the town and village in the form of soviets of toilers' deputies."

The uprising of 1905 in St. Petersburg threw up local, spontaneously organized, committees of workers, very much in the tradition of the local democracy which underlies much of Russian history even in its most autocratic periods. These committees became known by the Russian name, *soviets*. The institution was revived by Lenin when he returned to Russia in 1917. His purpose, apparently, was to provide a link between Party and People through which he hoped the dictatorship of the proletariat might operate without losing contact with the grass roots. Until 1936 those revived soviets quite explicitly played that role. Elections were indirect and were based on occupational representation. Members of the old ruling classes together with others presumed to be sympathetic with them were

---

[7] *Constitution of the U.S.S.R.*, 1936; article 64.

denied the franchise; city-dwellers were given an electoral advantage over peasants; and elections to the local soviets consisted, quite simply, of a show of hands in the factories and other places of work. Since 1936, the electoral functions of the local soviets have been lost, and the franchise has been broadened. Articles 134 and 135 of the Constitution provide that "Deputies to all Soviets of toilers' deputies; the Supreme Council [now the Supreme Soviet] of the U.S.S.R.; Supreme Councils of the Union Republics; territorial and provincial Soviets of toilers' deputies; Supreme Councils of autonomous republics; [8] Soviets of toilers' deputies of autonomous provinces; regional, district, city and village soviets of toilers' deputies . . . are elected by the electors on the basis of universal, equal, and direct suffrage by secret ballot," and that "Elections of deputies are universal; all citizens of the U.S.S.R. who have reached the age of eighteen, irrespective of race and nationality, religion, educational qualifications, residential qualifications, social origin, property status, or past activity, have the right to participate in elections of deputies and to be elected, with the exception of the insane and persons deprived of electoral rights by court sentence."

This suggests sweeping electoral freedom and confronts us with a puzzling incongruity—the great gulf between the clear liberalism of the Constitution itself and the combination of harshness and capriciousness with which the Soviet Union is actually governed. The obvious and simple explanation is that the Constitution with all its guarantees is a façade intended to fool the gullible. That explanation, however, may be too simple, even though it is entirely true that all totalitarian regimes have a propensity to erect façades, to dress things up. The real question is whether the Russians themselves are aware of the incongruity between their avowed principle and their apparent practice. All societies abrogate civil rights in time of crisis, and Soviet history has been a succession of crises. It is, also, doubtful whether Russia has ever really participated in Western European civilization with its tenderness toward the individual. Russian generals have had the reputation of being prodigal of manpower, and it may be that this callous attitude reflects a national sense that human life does not really matter very much. It

---

[8] The existence in the U.S.S.R. of nearly two hundred different nationalities speaking approximately one hundred and fifty different languages, has resulted in the development of a complicated hierarchy of governmental bodies. The soviet policy of granting cultural and linguistic autonomy within a federal system, provided expediency or over-riding policy does not dictate otherwise, explains the fact that the more important national groups form Constituent Republics, and that within these are found subsidiary groups with a modicum of autonomy, such as Autonomous Republics, Autonomous Provinces, National Districts, and so on.

is also true that the Soviets are obsessed with the urgency of getting things done, of getting industry established; for that reason, economic carelessness or inefficiency is considered a *crime.*

All this, however, is still superficial.   The Russians use the word "democracy" a great deal, although they use it in a sense strange to Western ears. No one, however, who has ever talked to a confirmed Russian communist can fail to have been impressed with two things: (1) the Russian's utter inability to grasp Western individualism or to understand Western acceptance of individual judgment with all that that entails; and (2) his complete conviction that Russian society really does offer its adherents a fullness of free dom not to be found elsewhere.   Reduced to its simplest terms, this attitud reflects the common feeling that there is something the matter with an, who does not accept one's own way of life, that he is missing an opportunity, that he ought to be made to see reason, and that when he does see it he will realize what he has hitherto missed.   It is the attitude of a parent toward a child reluctant to practise his music lesson: the child's recalcitrance not only jeopardizes his own development, but it may also contaminate other children, so he must be made to practise.   In more extreme form, it is the attitude of the inquisitor who insists that the recusant must be coerced into salvation even at the expense of his life, and for essentially the same reasons: to safeguard the security of society and to repress the appearance of disquieting unbelief.[9]   ●

For what it is worth, then, the Soviet Union has a constitutional system which accords the citizenry in general the electoral functions which previously had been entrusted to the soviets.   Those soviets still remain the fundamental units of local government, ranging in size from approximately twenty deputies in the villages to over two thousand in the Moscow soviet. The legislative bodies of the Autonomous and Constituent Republics are called soviets, just as the organ of the Union Government is called the Supreme Soviet.   The subordinate soviets, again in the same way as the central legislature, have thrust up executive committees under various names to assert legislative authority when the soviets themselves are not in session, and to mitigate the numerical unwieldiness of the larger soviets.

The Russian Legal System

Soviet laws are enforced by the courts and by the procurators, who correspond, very roughly, to the district attorneys associated with the American

[9] *Cf.,* J. L. Talman, *The Origins of Totalitarian Democracy,* London, 1952; *passim.*

legal system.   The highest court of the land is the Supreme Court whose members are elected for five-year terms by the Supreme Soviet.   It is a large court, consisting of some thirty judges headed by a President and, under him, a Deputy President.   It concerns itself with cases involving high governmental officials, with cases involving disputes among the Constituent Republics, and it is a court of appeal from decisions rendered by the Supreme Courts of the Republics.

At the base of the judicial structure are the so-called Peoples' Courts which concern themselves with criminal and civil cases involving individuals; they also pass upon allegations that the electoral lists improperly omit certain names, and they enforce the labor laws and labor contracts.

In both their organization and their performance the Peoples' Courts differ from lower courts elsewhere.   Each court comprises a presiding judge with legal training and experience, and two people's justices, who are not lawyers, but ordinary citizens from almost any walk of life.   Judge and justices alike are elected directly by the citizens of the proper judicial district, and they can also be popularly recalled before the expiration of the three-year term for which they are purportedly elected.   The people's justices are unpaid for their judicial work, but the wages or salaries due them for their regular work—whether as workers, farmers, officials, or teachers—continue to be paid them while they attend sessions of the court.

Decisions of the Peoples' Courts are reached by a simple majority vote, so that the legal experience of the presiding judge avails him nothing unless he has also the gift of tongues.   If a decision is appealed, any minority opinion which may have been rendered is attached to the disputed decision being sent up for consideration by a higher court.

This curious institution of people's justices runs all the way to the very top of the judicial hierarchy, including the Supreme Court itself.   The orthodox explanation is rooted in the Soviet concept of a workers' state in which all citizens are under obligation to participate in all varieties of collective activity, including the judicial, and in which all institutions are presumed to be close to the people and charged with safeguarding both the interests and the responsibilities of the "toiling masses."   An unvoiced explanation of the system may possibly lie in the mistrust felt by the ruling elements of a totalitarian society toward the autonomy of any profession which has its own standards and its own loyalties.   The appointment of lay justices prevents the professional lawyers from becoming laws unto themselves, exactly as the assignment of political commissars to units of the Soviet Army was designed as a device for keeping watch and ward over professional soldiers.   Like the military profession, the legal profession, everywhere, tends to develop an *esprit de corps* which, in a sense, sets it apart from lay society; the dilution of legal responsibility, therefore, may be regarded as one means of keeping lawyers within the fold.

The procurators, from the State Procurator General (appointed for seven years by the Supreme Soviet), down to the local procurators for each district and city (selected by procurators of higher rank) operate under the aegis of the Ministry of Justice. These officials receive from aggrieved citizens or officials complaints which, if approved, they pass on to the courts; they have also the right to initiate complaints on their own responsibility. The procurator, unlike the American prosecutor, is not supposed to take sides in a judicial proceeding. He and his staff investigate complaints brought to their attention, but even if as the result of a procurator's investigation the case seems to him to warrant prosecution, he is still expected to keep an open mind—and to such an extent that it remains his duty to move the dismissal of any case which appears to him not to be substantiated as the judicial process develops it. Beyond this, an element of unpredictability in judicial procedures arises from the right of anyone associated with a case to question any of the witnesses. Even a judicial decision does not terminate the responsibility of the procurator, who is finally responsible for reviewing all the evidence together with the decision of the court, and to move an appeal when he finds anything with which he is dissatisfied. Such is the system that is reported; how exactly it works is known by few men this side of the Iron Curtain.

It is a peculiar system. Superficially, the rights of defendants appear to be safeguarded even beyond the degree characteristic of our own judicial procedures. The 1936 Constitution, for what it is worth, assures the same civil liberties that are embodied in our own Bill of Rights, and the informal legal procedure combined with the theoretical impartiality of both court and procurator seem to go about as far as one could hope to get. Unfortunately, the reality is not so simple. That very homely quality in the judiciary may imperil rather than protect a defendant charged with an emotion-ridden offense. In the United States, judicial aloofness—that cherished regard toward a professional attitude—is justified precisely because it remains unmoved by the hysteria of excited public opinion. In a totalitarian society public opinion is not independent; it is conditioned. A court which reflects that kind of public opinion is a court upon which the regime may depend. When the jury is safe, the prosecutor may be forgotten.

THE ROLE OF THE COMMUNIST PARTY

In communist theory, the gradual attainment of full communism is accompanied by the "withering away" of the state. As we have seen, the Marxians regard the state as primarily an engine by which a dominant, exploiting class maintains its prerogatives and represses the attempts of a subordinate, exploited class to assert its own interests. In a really classless society the state would atrophy through loss of function. Between the overthrow of the old system, however, and the attainment of the new there is an interim period in which the proletariat must protect itself against both the assertion of counter-revolutionary tendencies at home and the threat of hostile intervention from abroad. During this period of the dictatorship of the proletariat, the state still exists because both its protective and its coercive functions remain necessary, but the form of that state is presumed to be something different from that characterizing other societies. Just as, economically, the Soviet Union has not yet reached full communism, so, politically, dictatorship is still maintained, and the Communist Party is its agent. Since, however, there is formally only one class in the U.S.S.R., there is no need for more than one party. Shortly before the adoption of the new constitution, Stalin is reported to have observed,

In the Soviet Union there is no basis for the existence of several parties, or, consequently, for the freedom of parties. In the Soviet Union there is a basis only for the Communist Party.[10]

Moreover, this political monopoly enjoyed by the Communist Party is not the only distinction which sets it off, together with the various fascist parties, from the parties more familiar in the democratic states. The Party, in Russia, is an elite comprising only a fraction of the Russian population, whose members bear heavy responsibilities as well as privileges, and feel a sense of dedication about their task. Lenin observed to the Eleventh Party Congress in 1922,

Communist principles, excellent ideals, are written large on you, you are holy men, fit to go alive to paradise, but do you know your business? . . . We must learn to begin anew again and again. . . . In the masses of the people we are

[10] *Pravda,* November 26, 1936, as quoted in *Communism in Action,* 79th. Congress, 2d. Session, House Document No. 754, Washington, 1946; p. 97.

as a drop in the sea and we can govern only if we adequately express what the people feel. . . . We shall not fail because we are not afraid to speak of our weaknesses and will learn to overcome our weaknesses.[11]

Membership is strictly limited to exceptionally qualified and attested individuals who have passed through a period of probation and who, today, have largely been prepared and screened by prior membership in the organizations of children and youths which are attached to the party.   Out of a population of nearly 200 million, party membership rose from 40,000 in April, 1917, to approximately five million, including candidates, in 1946.[12]   Even party membership, despite the care with which it is bestowed, does not carry complete security.   In the mid-thirties a series of drastic purges removed from the roles members who were deemed undependable or untrustworthy, and some of these were imprisoned, or even executed; since party members are held to higher standards of personal and professional behavior than ordinary folk, the irresolute, incompetent, or faint-hearted can be removed at any time.

Party members are thus a disciplined group, expected to be first in the performance of arduous, dangerous, or unpleasant tasks, to educate those about them by both precept and example, and to carry through established policy without cavil or question.   It was Lenin who established the principle of "democratic centralism," that is, some individual freedom of debate on undecided issues, but complete and whole-hearted adherence to decisions once reached.   As a result, first, of the purges, and then of the war, the democratic part of this principle seems to have been weakened in favor of the centralizing part, so that at present the Party Line appears to be set pretty decisively by those vested with real authority.

The mere existence of a compact, devoted, and able body of men and women of this sort, clothed with immense prestige and enjoying a complete monopoly of political power, would probably be sufficient in itself to control the state without much regard to the structure of party organization.   As a matter of fact, the organization of the party, as in fascist societies, corresponds almost exactly with that of the government, from the party cells at the lower levels through the various regional and intermediate organizations, all the way up to the Party Congress which matches the Supreme Soviet.

[11] Quoted by Frederick L. Schumann, "Government and Politics," in *U.S.S.R., A Concise Handbook,* edited by Ernest J. Simmons, Ithaca, 1947; p. 156.
[12] *Ibid.,* p. 156.

The Central Committee corresponds to the Presidium, and the various committees of the Central Committee—in particular, the powerful Political Bureau—correspond to the Council of Ministers. This means that, like fascism again, almost every governmental agency has a counterpart or twin in the form of some party organization, and that the party twin is the dominant one. They look alike, they think alike, and they act alike, but initiative is unequally divided between them. More than this: at the top of the two parallel hierarchies, the agencies of government come to resemble not so much the twins as the shadows of their party counterparts, because they move with the movements of the party body.

This raises the question of the reason for the existence of such a bifurcated system. One reason is doubtless sheer expediency; it is convenient at times that the voice should be the voice of Jacob, but the hands those of Esau. One very important illustration is the control of Communist parties outside of Russia.[13] Those parties, at their weakest, are thorns in the flesh of other nations, and at their strongest are aggressively subversive elements, and it might be embarrassing, even hazardous, for the Soviet government to have to acknowledge that *it* was guiding and supporting them. No one is fooled; it does guide and support them. Neither the proselytizing zeal of the Russians nor their sense of insecurity in a world they deem inevitably hostile will permit them to abandon these far-flung eyes and hands of Mother Russia. They can disclaim, however, and frequently have disclaimed, responsibility for the activities of their foreign missionaries.

Perhaps another reason for the parallelism between party and state is suggested in the curious Russian insistence on the democratic character of their institutions. That insistence seems peculiar and even hypocritical to foreigners to whom the Russian connotation of "democracy" appears distorted. Paradoxically, however, the Soviets have attempted to foster among their citizens a measure of controlled individualism, both responsibility and initiative, perhaps to provide a forcing ground for new communists. A curious and isolated illustration is reported by Maurice Dobb:

You teach your men that they are facing formations. Against formations a man expects explicit orders. We teach our men that they are fighting individual

---

[13] Although the Communist International, the Comintern, was "dissolved" during the Second World War, it is perhaps unnecessary to argue that the separation of those parties from the Russian amounted to little more than a *divorce de convenance*. The behavior of the Cominform created after the war suggests that new Cominform is but the old Comintern written large.

enemies. . . . The Commander instructs them to the best of his ability. But if his way does not succeed, we expect our men to find their own way.[14]

That concession to individualism, which we shall shortly examine and which in later chapters we shall find cropping up in all sorts of places, may justify in Russian eyes their formal disinclination to let the party monopolize *everything*. Candidates for public office need not be party members, the economic organs of Soviet society are governmental or cooperative institutions rather than purely party agencies, and governmental agencies themselves are structurally distinct and separate from the corresponding party institutions. The numerically large non-party sector of Russian society is, in one sense, the training and testing ground from which the party elite are recruited. In another sense, that sector justifies the party. An avowedly classless society could hardly select an elite which openly and unbashedly dominates. The elite is recruited *from* the mass, but must not cut itself off entirely from it; that elite, accordingly, has its shadow institutions.

The Role of the Individual

A population whose only function is to obey orders is likely to become, at best, ineffective and apathetic, and, at worst, dissatisfied and mutinous. Negatively, that risk can be countered through propaganda and coercion, both of which the Russians assuredly employ. A great deal more can be done positively, however, by giving the individual some sense of participation, particularly in the formation of decisions which affect him. Non-party members, accordingly, are permitted and perhaps even encouraged to seek elective office, to share in local discussions, and occasionally to criticize the execution of policies whose basic purport they may not question. From time to time the Russian press is reported to print complaints about slackness, inefficiency, and suspected graft, and there are presumably other, less public channels through which complaints may be conveyed. That safety valve has a governor: the press is a state press and prints only material the state wishes to have appear, and it is to be hoped that individual critics can sense the division between the licit and the illicit.

All this is a sort of extension to the citizenry of the principle of democratic centralism which we have already seen operating within the party itself. It

---

[14] George Stevens, citing a Russian officer, in the *Manchester Evening News*, June 22, 1942, quoted by Maurice Dobb, *Soviet Planning and Labor in Peace and War*, New York, 1943; p. 66.

is extraordinarily difficult for a foreigner to assess that principle.   At one extreme it may merely be a means of fostering the illusion of democracy; the exclusion of alternative choices from the ballot and the rule of unanimity which characterizes deliberative decisions together with the overwhelming affirmative majorities which emerge in Soviet elections appear to warrant that interpretation.   At the other extreme, the Russian system may simply be a means of assuring what, after all, is essential to the maintenance of political stability: the acceptance, in good grace, of any important decision which has been reached.   From that viewpoint, the eventual withdrawal of all but one candidate before ballots are cast may simply reflect the fact that a Russian election ratifies decisions reached in preliminary discussion rather than decides the result, as is the case with us,[15] and that the unanimity rule emphasizes the fact that even a democracy finds it difficult to function without near unanimity on very fundamental issues.   Whatever the interpretation, however, Russian elections must occasionally be the subject of yearning by political bosses elsewhere.

Moreover, it should not be forgotten that the Russians regard their entire experiment as a campaign, a campaign to achieve security, to overtake and eventually outpace the rest of the world.   This military analogy is carried down even to the details of organization and the terminology which is employed.   Technicians of different grades, for example, are organized into *cadres; flying squads* of doctors and nurses are kept in readiness for special tasks; *shock brigades* of specially efficient and productive workers are maintained; tractors and gangs of workers are *mobilized* for employment; distinguished service in all walks of life is rewarded with *decorations;* the achievement of the famous economic plans is sometimes referred to as the *Bolshevik offensive;* and, even in diplomacy, the Russians before 1939 attempted to organize a *united front* against fascism.[16]   In such an emotional environment it is far easier to insist upon, and to secure, national unity than under more placid circumstances, if for no other reason than that the paramount objectives which are placed before the nation, such as security, prosperity, education, are those to which no one could reasonably take exception.

---

[15] Sometimes that same process is suspected elsewhere.   For example, "I am sure that most of us who have attended these meetings [of American legislatures] have the feeling that we are listening to speeches 'for the record' and not to change votes, and that when the roll is called we are witnessing the formal recording of a decision taken elsewhere." Lane W. Lancaster, "The Ivory Tower—No Vacancies," *Bulletin of the American Association of University Professors,* Summer, 1947; p. 282.

[16] *Cf.,* Sidney and Beatrice Webb, *Soviet Communism: A New Civilization?,* 2d. edition, New York, 1938; Vol. II, pp. 773–779, 1027.

In that environment, also, the contribution of each individual *counts,* and must be "mobilized." The precept, From each according to his powers, has a certain individual significance.

Finally, while the Soviet Union is a tight and ruthless dictatorship, some of its rulers have at least placed themselves on record as looking forward to the day when authoritarianism can be relaxed with the "withering away" of the state. The adoption of the 1936 Constitution, which extended the franchise and, at least apparently, guaranteed such individual rights as the right to work and to leisure, to education and social security, and to freedom of speech and assembly, was widely hailed as the beginning of this process; and while the existence of an irresponsible secret police is hard indeed to reconcile with civil rights as we know them, those rights exist at least on paper. Unhappily, they appear to exist only on paper, but the paper, for what it is worth, is consistent with the formal promise of some Soviet leaders that the future will bring the extension rather than the restriction of democracy.

If those promises should be genuine, and particularly if a real program for the relaxation of the dictatorship should ever come into being, then an additional theoretical reason appears for keeping party institutions in parallel with those of the government. The withering of the state does not mean political anarchy. In a famous phrase Engels observed that, under full communism, "The government of persons is replaced by the administration of things . . . ," [17] and Lenin spelled out the details:

> For when *all* have learned to manage, and independently are actually managing by themselves social production, keeping accounts, controlling the idlers, the gentlefolk, the swindlers and similar "guardians of capitalist traditions," then the escape from this national accounting and control will inevitably become so increasingly difficult, such a rare exception, and will probably be accompanied by such swift and severe punishment (for the armed workers are men of practical life, not sentimental intellectuals, and they will scarcely allow anyone to trifle with them); that very soon the *necessity* of observing the simple, fundamental rules of everyday social life in common will have become a *habit.*
>
> The door will then be wide open for the transition from the first phase of Communist society to the higher phase, and along with it to the complete withering away of the State.[18]

Although Lenin conceded that attainment of that ideal was not assured, it still had to be striven for. That striving is essentially a process of educa-

[17] *Cf.,* Friedrich Engels, *Socialism, Utopian and Scientific,* translated by Edward Aveling, New York, 1892; p. 77.

[18] V. I. Lenin, *State and Revolution,* revised edition, New York, 1932; pp. 84–85. Italics in the original.

tion. One function of the dictatorship of the proletariat may thus be, in theory, the education of others to assume in increasing measure the responsibility for organizing and administering the "higher" communism of the future.

This vast country, then, is a dictatorship, but not one in which *all* responsibility is concentrated at the center. During the thirty odd years of its existence, the Soviet Union has followed a frankly experimental policy, creating first one set of institutions and then another, redefining and adjusting their several functions over and over again. But throughout these opportunistic and pragmatic shifts in policy, one basic line of contact has been held constant: national and local associations, both regional and occupational, have, since the first settling of the revolutionary dust, been created to undertake duties too *un*important to concern the central authorities, to mitigate the inefficiency resulting from over-centralization of administration, and to give flexibility to the system and some scope to individual initiative.

THE GOVERNMENTAL ROLE OF LABOR UNIONS

The role played by labor is an illustration of the way responsibility is assigned organizations subordinate to the state. Exactly as the political structure involves delegation, economically a great deal of subordinate responsibility is delegated to such institutions as the trusts, the cooperatives, and the labor unions. While the two former perform duties very similar to those undertaken by analogous institutions elsewhere, the Soviet labor unions which Stalin once described as "a school for communism," [19] are in a somewhat different category. Like all Soviet institutions, their role has shifted with the veering eddies of Soviet policy. In the early months of the Revolution, workmen assumed that they themselves were to operate industrial enterprises through their own factory committees. Thus, for example, masters of Russian ships took their orders from committees of sailors, and the schedules of trains on the Moscow-Petrograd railroad were determined by the station staffs.[20] Following the Civil War the government instituted its so-called New Economic Policy (NEP) by which it temporarily permitted a certain amount of private industry and trade—particularly in agriculture

[19] Stalin, *Leninism*, New York, 1928; Vol. I, p. 29.
[20] Sidney and Beatrice Webb, *op. cit.*, Vol. I, p. 167.

in order to build up food supplies—while the state concentrated its own energies on the development of heavy industry. During this period the unions assumed the role, familiar to us, of protecting the interests of their members against private employers, as well as the more unusual role of "rectifying the faults and exaggerations of economic bodies so far as they proceed from a bureaucratic perversion of the machinery of the State." [21] For the duration of the NEP, indeed, each separate union, exactly as in other countries, pushed for higher wages and shorter hours for its own members without much consideration of the impact of its activities upon workers in other industries or upon the national interest as a whole. Their relations with the government as employer were ambiguous.

This ambiguity came to a head with the abandonment of the New Economic Policy and the great diminution in the opportunity to earn private profit which that step entailed. The unions, still formally distinct from the government, were instructed to concentrate upon increasing productivity, not only in each particular enterprise or industry in which they were represented, but for the economy as a whole. The Secretary of the All-Union Central Committee of the Trade Unions declared, in 1932,

> The primary task of the trade unions in the Soviet Union is to make workers realize that, as the sole owners of the means of production, they must learn to take responsibility for the maintenance of these means. . . . [Hence] the Soviet trade union is not an isolated body, but an integral part of the entire Soviet system, assisting in the fulfillment of production programmes by organizing socialist competition and shock brigades, and attending to the cultural and economic requirements of the workers.[22]

That meant, essentially, that labor was expected to divert its concern from its share in the gross "profits" of the industry which employed it toward the productivity of the entire economy and the conditions of life of Soviet workers as a whole. It is exactly here that the major difference between Russian and other unions lies.

There is a partial resemblance between Russian unions and the unions of governmental employees in the United States. Such unions do exist here, and some of them are affiliated with the great national federations; but since strikes against the government are not permitted,[23] the role of these unions

---

[21] *Report of Commission of 1921,* of which Lenin was a member, cited in Robert W. Dunn, *Soviet Trade Unions,* New York, 1927; p. 26.

[22] Quoted, *ibid.,* p. 172.

[23] Sometimes school teachers and certain municipal employees, like the operators of the city-owned transit system in New York, do strike. It is still true, however, that, in principle, strikes against the government are not permitted.

differs from that of the militant unions of industrial workers. The unions of employees of government, apart from recreational and welfare activities, limit their activities to keeping a sort of watching brief over the interests of their members and to undertaking a degree of collective bargaining with the appropriate governmental agencies. Exactly the same thing is done by Russian unions in industry generally. Collective agreements within the framework of the prevailing economic plan are reached with respect to working conditions and the disposal of the aggregate sums earmarked, under the plan, for wage payments. This activity is purely negotiatory; there are no strikes. The scope of the negotiations themselves cannot be very great. As far as wages are concerned, Russian industry operates under conditions similar to those assumed by the classical economists for industry generally: the size of the fund from which wages are paid is determined in advance, and the only undetermined element is the division of that fund among its recipients. The classical economists, to be sure, derived that fund from previous accumulations of capital, and the Russians determine it by governmental decision, but in each case a *wages fund* is the datum from which analysis starts.

Russian unions, accordingly, may argue and recommend concerning the determination of time- or piece-rates, or the remuneration paid for overtime, but they may not press for a larger aggregate share in the national income. There is one area, however, in which they do have more responsibility. A considerable proportion of labor's real income in Russia is made up of "socialized" wages, such as the provision and maintenance of sanatoria, rest houses, sponsored vacations, medical services, and the like, and part of this is financed from the earnings that enterprise is permitted to retain. The unions administer many of these funds. One American writer has gone so far as to suggest that this is one of the ways in which the state, in the Soviet Union, is tending already to wither away:

. . . control of the many-billion-ruble social-insurance fund, the sanatoria, rest homes, all workers' medical services and the protection of labor passes from the hands of the government to the trade unions. Thus, formally at least, the process by which, under socialism, the state dies a slow death through attrition has advanced another step.[24]

In this respect, the Russian unions appear to be organizations of consumers rather than workers. But the distinction is not sharp; unions are also used

[24] Louis Fischer, in *The Nation,* New York, July 10, 1933, quoted by the Webbs, *op. cit.,* Vol. I, p. 204.

to handle grievances which workers, either individually or in groups, have against management.

A major function of Soviet unions consists in cooperating with management to attain, or exceed, the degree of productivity necessary to fulfill its assignment under the economic plan. From the very beginning the Soviets have been obsessed with productivity—as well they should be if they are ever to overtake the rest of the industrialized world—and they have done everything possible to elicit the assistance of labor in this effort. Thus, the unions have sponsored "socialist competition," under which plant competes with plant and group against group, with rewards and decorations going to the outstandingly successful. The fancy of the outside world has been caught by the Stakhanovite movement, named after a coal miner who, in 1935, re-discovered some of the principles of scientific management which the Russian authorities have encouraged, sometimes in exaggerated form. Piece rates, also, are employed, but cautiously; they are made high enough to encourage individual effort, but not so high as to increase costs more than productivity. In all such attempts to increase production the unions are expected to help.

Since the inauguration of the first Five-Year Plan, Russia has suffered from a labor shortage, and this has occasioned great concern. This shortage has been partly met by putting political prisoners to work under the terrible forced labor system which has absorbed, perhaps, some seven million workers.[25] While, however, the Russians impose the obligation to work upon all their citizens,[26] they have not, except under extraordinary circumstances, assigned to forced labor ordinary individuals who have not come under the disfavor of the regime—if for no other reason than that they are aware of the inefficiency of involuntary work. Without general coercion no amount of mere exhortation has eliminated considerable labor turnover and absenteeism on the part of workers who are formally free to choose their occupations. Here, also, the unions have been besought to assist in reducing that turnover and in discouraging the tendency of "aviators," as they are called,[27] to flit from job to job following rumors of better working conditions, higher wages, or a better chance to secure scarce consumers' goods for those working in industries having preferential access to these.

[25] Cf., Vera Micheles Dean, *Russia, Menace or Promise?*, New York, 1947, p. 39.
[26] "Work in the U.S.S.R. is an obligation and a matter of honor for each citizen capable of working, according to the principle: 'He who does not work does not eat.' In the U.S.S.R. the principle of Socialism is being realized: 'From each according to his ability, to each according to his work.'" *Constitution*, Article 12.
[27] Cf., Barbara Wootton, *Plan or No Plan*, New York, 1935; p. 76.

THE TOTALITARIAN CHARACTER OF THE SOVIET REGIME

The fact that the Soviet Union is ruled by a dictator hardly needs belaboring, even if the dictator occasionally feels frustrated when his tools buckle in his hands.   To be sure, Russia has a written constitution, but the writ is not dependable; it has labor unions, but these do not labor with independence; it permits internal critcism, but the critics who survive are the critics who sense the line they may not overstep; and it has elections, but the electors all have minds with but a single thought.

The Russian government is despotic, but despotism is nothing new in Russia; the Russian government has always been despotic.   Czar and dictator, alike, have held the reins of personal power in their hands, power that seems ultimate, beyond appeal, and subject to no principle but whim or caprice.   No human power, however, is really ultimate; the power of Czar or dictator is no greater than the devotion and competence of the human instruments upon which rulers must depend will permit.   Stalin is reported to have once observed to President Franklin Roosevelt, that he, the Dictator, had no power to make commitments that his subordinates might covertly resist.   Dictator though Stalin was, his generals, his commissars, to say nothing of his wartime allies, were groups upon which he was dependent and to whose judgment, feelings, and even prejudices, he had to give heed.   Even a dictator must command confidence.

The Soviet Union, however, is more than just another dictatorship; it is a *totalitarian* dictatorship.   A simple dictatorship is one governed arbitrarily or according to the caprice of the dictator, but it is primarily concerned with the perpetuation of dictatorial prestige and power.   A totalitarian dictatorship seeks, not just conformers, but believers.   A simple dictatorship represses opposition, and it may do so with savagery; a totalitarian dictatorship represses, but it also seeks to convert.   A simple dictatorship will treat dissidence as wicked, but a totalitarian dictatorship regards it as immoral.

These differentia of a totalitarian dictatorship exist in contemporary Russia.   Repression exists, but beside it flourish all the arts of sustained and systematic persuasion.   The care lavished on the education of children, the missionary zealotry displayed toward potential believers, the incessant propaganda directed at the soul as well as at the mind of the recipient—these are more than devices to elicit mechanical conformity.   They are expressions of a genuine conviction that a new way of life has in fact been found, a way of life so superior to any known alternative that men *must* be thrust into conformity with it.

The distinction between simple dictatorship and a totalitarian dictatorship like the Russian, is thus a distinction between mere, naked rule, and rule justified by something taken as a moral sanction. It is that sanction that demands total devotion in a totalitarian system. It is also that sanction that makes the mere existence of Russia so utterly disruptive in the modern world. Communism is feared because even its enemies sense that it can command devotion.

Totalitarianism, then, is a most powerful force, because the support it elicits rests as much upon appeal as upon fear. Nevertheless, it has its dangers, and those dangers can be discerned in the Soviet Union.

Internal Dangers of the Regime

There clearly exist two dangers, at least from the perspective of those who dislike dictatorship: (1) the danger that as long as a vestige of capitalism, or even of other variants of socialism, exist elsewhere, the Russians will not deem it safe to relinquish their dictatorship; and (2) the danger that prolonged personal rule, together with the popular adulation and even semi-deification of the Leader will render the voluntary relinquishment of personal power even more difficult. The Russians have been used to that kind of power for far longer than the duration of the Soviet regime, and perhaps they do not recognize these as dangers.

There are, however, two dangers which they should recognize: (1) factionalism, and (2) intellectual sterility. The great dispute between Stalin and Trotsky over whether the Soviet Union should attempt to establish socialism in Russia alone or whether it should give precedence to bringing about World Revolution is a famous example of the first danger; the recurring purges represent the emergence of the second danger out of attempts to ward off the first.

Following the Second World War there was speculation, at least outside Russia, whether the Red Army might not seek to challenge the political supremacy of the party, and the relegation of the Field Marshals to comparatively obscure positions suggests some awareness of that risk inside Russia. The fact that all the factional strands were united in the person of Stalin, who was Marshal of the Red Army as well as Secretary of the Party and Leader of the Nation, offered but tenuous security against the peril of some future struggle for power within Russia. This may constitute an additional reason for decentralization, for bringing into existence established institutions and procedures which are not too intimately associated with the structure of either government or party and which, therefore, offer some hope of continuity and order.

The danger of intellectual sterility is at once more subtle and more ominous. The Red Terror had as one consequence the elimination of many of the freest and boldest, who could not bring themselves to hew exactly to the party line. Exactly the same thing happened after the French Revolution,[28] and it was not until order had finally supervened that French intellectual life revived. In that sense, order has not yet supervened in Russia, for intellectual life, there, is still in bondage.

The insistence upon orthodoxy, not only in politics, sociology, and economics, but in such things as science and music as well, is partly due to the sense of insecurity already mentioned, and may in that degree be relaxed as the Soviet regime comes to feel itself more firmly established. Imposed orthodoxy, however, is also due to that conviction of being right, of holding the only truth, which animates most communists. In such a context, intellectual heterodoxy is not something which can be tolerantly discounted by those who "know" it to be wrong; it is something which appears immoral, subversive, and vicious, and therefore to be repressed. In the Soviet Union today, even the principles of genetics must conform to party doctrine. In an environment of that kind, intellectual activity runs the heavy risk of becoming sterile through its constriction to the mouthing of scholastic platitudes. Intellectual unanimity of this sort, which the Russians apparently regard as strength, is in reality one of the most insidious weaknesses of the Soviet regime because it debars the regime from further progress.

[28] Cf., Henry M. Leclercq, "A Chronicle of Social and Political Events from 1640 to 1914," in Edward Eyre, editor, *European Civilization, Its Origin and Development,* Oxford, 1937; Vol. VI, p. 337.

─────────────────────14

The Structure of the Russian Economy

IT IS COMMON knowledge outside of Russia that the Soviet economy is dominated by the state, that most industry is owned and operated by the state, and that agriculture, while perhaps not quite as thoroughly nationalized as industry, is also pretty much a public institution. All this is true, yet, as with the fascist states, the monolithic front that the Soviet state presents to the outside world conceals variation and exceptions to trumpeted principle; these, however, can be discerned if one peers through the cracks. Thus, while private ownership of the means of production appears anathema to a proper communist, Russian peasants still have something pretty similar to full rights over the plots of land they occupy. Private property, except for such minor items as toothbrushes whose nationalization could scarcely appeal to even the most doctrinaire communist, is supposed to be prized in only backward and reactionary social systems, yet Russians may own and build their own houses. Private investment for the sake of private return, apparently the exploitative privilege of case-hardened capitalists, exists in Russia in the form of state bonds which Russians are permitted, even encouraged, to purchase. Something approximating economic equality is presumed to mark a genuinely socialist state, yet marked disparities in not only economic status but also in perquisite and privilege have tended to grow rather than dwindle within the Soviet system. Even piece rates, so disliked as a principle of wage-determination by organized labor in most other countries, are by now an accepted part of Soviet wage policy.

None of this necessarily invalidates the old communist slogan, "From each according to his power, to each according to his need," but much suggests a re-interpretation. The first part of the slogan most definitely holds: the differential wage system was deliberately contrived to stimulate application and exertion in order that the output of each really would be in accordance with his powers. Distribution according to need, however, has been stored away in the attic. The Russian Constitution of 1936, indeed, rephrases it, "To each according to his work." [1] One can only observe that distribution accords with need only if whatever is, is right. At any rate the economics of reward are easier to discuss than its ethics.

The Soviet Union—just as the Italy and Germany we have described— has pursued an economic policy which has been experimental and opportunistic. The structure of the Soviet economy, accordingly, is, so to speak, stratified, with the lower strata containing the fossils of earlier experiments. For example, the wooing of the peasants in the 1920's for the sake of assured agricultural production is reflected, according to this economic stratification, in the fact that one and one half per cent of total agricultural output in 1938 still came from individual peasant farms. [2]

The Soviet economy, in short, has not been cast from the same, simple mold. State enterprise exists and is most important, but there also exist certain forms of cooperative enterprises and even some individual enterprise.

INDUSTRY

In the discussion of fascist economies we have occasionally made cross references to the Soviet Union. It is appropriate to speak of a communist and fascist dictatorship in the same breath, for they all share totalitarian organization, they all accept the principle of terror, and they all simultaneously display almost contemptuous indifference toward men as indi-

[1] *Constitution,* Article 12.
[2] *Cf.,* Alexander Baykov, *The Development of the Soviet Economic System,* New York, 1947; p. 327.

viduals but sedulous attention toward men in the mass.   There are, however, differences, and these must now be considered.

In contrast with the willingness of fascists to utilize the institutions created by large-scale industry, communists display rooted hostility toward the institution of private capitalism.   Sometimes the assertion is made [3] that the headlong and precipitous transformation of industry in the first years of the Bolshevik regime arose partly out of the absence in Russia of any monopolistic organization which the state could simply take over.   That is true, but it is not the entire story.   The Russian communists had preconceived ideas in a sense that the fascists did not have, and among these were ideas about the public ownership and operation of industry.   From late 1917 through 1920 there was a wave of nationalization; a decree of December 29, 1920, provided for the seizure by the state of all enterprises using mechanical power and employing more than five workers, and for the seizure as well of establishments which did not use mechanical power but which employed a minimum of ten workers.[4]   Provincial and local governments joined the race to socialize, without paying much heed to how the requisitioned enterprises were to be run.   The old managers and owners were completely hostile, and when they were not evicted forthwith, they frequently attempted to close or to abandon the plants which hitherto had been theirs to operate. Workers, on the other hand, were untrained and inexperienced in the responsibilities of management.   The authorities attempted the complete centralization of control, but the loss or absence of necessary records, the lack of technical knowledge, and the early inability to command a competent and dependable administrative organization meant that centralized control was exiguous.   Plans, factories, and enterprises went their own way, "scrounging" what supplies they could get and frequently bartering their products among themselves heedless of what Moscow thought they were doing or wanted them to do.   The result was sheer economic chaos.

In the fall of 1921 came the famous New Economic Policy, the backward step to make more secure the next forward leap, the pause to enable the nation to catch its breath and tighten its shoe laces.   For the time being at least, only the basic and essential heavy industries were to remain nationalized, and control over that nationalized sector was to be tightened.   The only nationalized plants to be operated were those possessing the necessary equipment and capital and with assured sources of raw materials.   Indus-

---

[3] E.g., by Baykov, *op. cit.*, p. 5.
[4] *Ibid.*, pp. 6–7.

tries and plants not affected with a public interest in this sense were to be leased to cooperative associations or even to private operators. Smaller concerns, and enterprises which the state either could not or would not handle, were to be thus "reprivatized." Redundant plants were to be closed and their workers reassigned. By 1923 nearly ninety per cent of the firms registered in the Census were again in private hands, although most of these were extremely small establishments; in the aggregate, they employed only slightly over twelve per cent of the total Russian labor force.[5]

This period was the real beginning of the careful control of the Soviet economy. The characteristic industrial structure, shortly to be described, began to take form, the famous Five-Year Plans for the expansion and development of the economy were introduced, and the more serious economic problems of the regime began to be solved. Troubles, of course, were not over. Lags, break-downs, defective equipment and shoddy workmanship kept appearing, and industrial managers, as everywhere, bore the responsibility. That responsibility was grievously heavy; the consequences of mismanagement, or even of sheer bad luck, were realized not in the bankruptcy court, but in the police court. The ancient custom of executing defeated generals appeared to the Russian communists admirably suited to unsuccessful captains of industry. The industrial purges of 1929, for example, were aimed, first, at technicians who had been carried over from the pre-revolutionary era, and then extended to include specialists in general— and to such a degree that an hysteria of "spetz-baiting" swept over Russia.[6] Throughout their history, indeed, the Soviets have tended to suspect sabotage whenever anything has gone wrong, and at periodic intervals these suspicions have exploded into purgings and the trials of "wreckers."

Apart, however, from these industrial misfortunes which caused heads to roll, order has on the whole been brought out of the economic chaos of the early years of the regime. The older generation of technicians who never were trusted because they were products of the Czarist era have now been superseded by younger men, plucked out of the ranks or selected from the graduates of the newer technical schools, who have experienced nothing outside of Communist Russia and who, therefore, are free from at least the *prima facie* suspicion associated with the wrong class background. The government, likewise, has worked out its administrative procedures and has acquired experience in applying them. The earlier, naive fascination with

[5] *Ibid.*, p. 107.
[6] *Ibid.*, p. 174.

sheer size has abated, and the great industrial super-giants, if an astronomical term may be borrowed,[7] which were created in the 'twenties, have begun to be whittled down to more manageable proportions. Attention has now begun to be given to developing medium- and even small-scale enterprise in order to increase flexibility, to get production started more quickly after construction of new units has been undertaken, and to reduce the heavy burden on the transportation system when production of an item is geographically concentrated rather than diffused. Moscow no longer insists on supervising everything itself, although major decisions and the direction and structure of the economic plan are still determined there.[8] Particularly in recent years, there has been a tendency to decentralize, both functionally and territorially. Industry since the war has been partially relocated, and efforts have been made to develop the hitherto backward regions of the Soviet Union, especially east of the Ural Mountains.

General Structure of Industry

The governmental structure for the administration of Russian state-owned industry is both more detailed and more intricate than, perhaps, anywhere else. The Council of Ministers, responsible to the Supreme Soviet, or to the Presidium when the Soviet is not in session, comprises the officials in charge of the major governmental departments. Generally speaking, each economic Ministry has jurisdiction over a single, great industry, although there are variations. There are Ministries, for example, for Iron and Steel, for Rubber, for Chemicals, and for Labor Reserves. There are two Ministries concerned with Coal—one for the west and one for the east—and there are likewise two for Oil. There are separate Ministries for Marine and for River Transport and for Railroads, for Agricultural Stocks and for Industrial Crops. All the foregoing, and others, are the so-called All-Union Ministries, responsible for jurisdictional areas in which national policy is intended to be centralized and uniform. In other cases, such as Food, Light Industry, Finance, State Farms or Agriculture, provincial and regional differences are permitted, and in these cases the Constituent Republics have their own Ministries, cooperating with but subordinate to the so-called Union-Republic Ministries in Moscow. In still other cases, Welfare and Education, for

---

[7] *Cf.*, Fred Hoyle, *The Nature of the Universe,* Oxford, 1950, p. 93.
[8] *Cf.*, Baykov, *op. cit.*, pp. 305–307.

example, the Republics have their own Ministries although the Central Government does not. That does not mean that control is not exercised.

This is the superstructure. Within each Ministry are subordinate divisions charged with the general supervision and coordination of the various Trusts which comprise the industries in that part of the Russian economy which is centrally organized, owned, and operated. These subdivisions, corresponding somewhat to the Bureaus within the Departments of our own federal government, appoint or dismiss the managing boards of the Trusts, audit their accounts, approve or disapprove their reports, arrange research and training programs, and impose penalties—frequently fines—in cases where contracts have been breached.

The Trusts

The Trusts are the great operating units of state-owned, large-scale industry. Production is their business; they, accordingly, are responsible for the detailed organization and management of the operating plants. Trusts are administered by Boards of Managers appointed by the appropriate Bureaus or Ministries, and their Boards, in turn, appoint the responsible managers of the Trusts. Control of the Trusts' equipment and physical assets is vested in the Boards, although ownership, of course, is that of the state. As in other totalitarian societies, all these officials are either members of the party, or, at the very least, not known to be out of step with the party.

There is the widest variation in the way the Trusts are organized. Their legal status was first set forth in a decree of April 10, 1923, which asserted:

By State Trusts are meant State industrial enterprises to whom the State has accorded independence in the carrying out of their operations in accordance with the statutes approved for each of them, acting on the principle of commercial calculation with the aim of deriving profit.[9]

It should be observed that the Trusts are expected to earn a profit. Despite the loose assertions sometimes heard, that socialist and communist economies are hostile to profit, it is the disposition rather than the earning of profit that really concerns them. The *name* can go; but if enterprise does not collectively earn a return over cost, the solvency of even a communist regime is jeopardized. The Russian Trusts, accordingly, are ex-

[9] Quoted, *ibid.*, p. 110.

pected to show profit, and when they do, most of the profit is turned over to the Treasury, although approximately twenty per cent may usually be retained as a source of operating capital, as a source of bonuses for both management and labor, and, when this seems possible and desirable, as a source of increments to the workers' welfare fund accruing to the enterprise.

Trusts have a fair amount of operating autonomy, subject to conformity with planning decisions by government, but they remain state enterprises. They do not own or really control their capital. Higher authority may merge, dismember, or liquidate them. Their fixed capital they hold "in trust" and may dispose of only by permission; their working capital on the other hand, the source from which their creditors must be paid, is freely disposable by the Trusts themselves. Baykov [10] mentions an interesting distinction embodied in Russian law between fixed and working capital. Fixed capital, such as tools or equipment, is used up gradually over the course of time; working capital, like coal, can be used only once. This is reminiscent of a distinction made during the formative period of the classical political economy in England.[11] Apart from their ideas about how an economy should be organized, there is here and there a curious parallelism between *contemporary* Russian and *early* Western economists.

Certain Trusts are geographically concentrated while others are responsible for enterprises scattered throughout the Union. Some, just as holding companies do elsewhere, control a number of establishments, while others are coterminous with one single vast operating enterprise. Some are organized horizontally with control over all enterprises of the same type and function, while others are vertical organizations controlling all stages of production of a given product. However variously they are organized, they all have in common their subordination to the Ministries and their responsibility to agencies above them for the details of their own operations. They make contracts with each other for the interchange of products and materials, they arrange the sale of final products to state or cooperative purchasing agencies, they are responsible for maintaining efficiency, for applying approved technological developments, and for keeping track of their own operations through proper accounting and full reporting.

[10] *Ibid.*, p. 110.

[11] "Capital which . . . fulfills the whole of its office in the production in which it is engaged by a single use is called circulating [i.e., working] capital." John Stuart Mill, *Principles of Political Economy,* Ashley edition, London, 1923; p. 91. *Cf.,* also, David Ricardo, *On the Principles of Political Economy and Taxation,* Sraffa edition, Cambridge, England, 1951; p. 31.

Industrial Management under the Trusts

Subordinate to the Trusts, except in those cases where Trust and enterprise are identical, are the enterprises, the actual plants and factories, managed by directors appointed by the Trusts.   An enterprise is subdivided further into shops, with managers appointed by the Director of the enterprise, and the shops themselves are composed of sections, controlled by foremen, and sometimes even the sections are made up of brigades headed by brigade leaders.

There is thus a chain of command, a managerial hierarchy which has been tightened rather than loosened with the passage of time.   Before the Second World War, the Russians experimented somewhat with having both party and Labor associate themselves with the management of industry, but divided authority seems to have been no more workable in the society freed from the contradictions of capitalism than elsewhere.   The hand of the party is still present; it undertakes a great part of the welfare and recreational activities carried on in the country, and it is expected to "assist" directors in maintaining efficiency and a good *esprit de corps*.   Occasionally a local party organization will nominate a director, and, ominously, the party may not only make suggestions to a director, it may also make complaints about him.

Labor, which in the early years sometimes took over enterprises, has by now been pretty generally squeezed out of management.   Russia may still be under the dictatorship of the proletariat, but it has become dictatorship *over* rather than *by* the proletariat.   The director is now responsible for his enterprise.   To be sure, what he produces is determined by higher authority. As in National Socialist Germany, he is essentially a civil servant.   The fixed capital he employs is provided for him, he is allotted his materials, told what prices to charge, and more or less told how to produce.   Within these limits, however, he is responsible.   He arranges his production schedule and sees that it is observed; he is expected to hold down costs and hold up quality. To do so he appoints and dismisses his foremen, and, in accordance with legal procedure, he hires, transfers, and disciplines his labor force.

Producers' Cooperatives

Not all industry is directly undertaken by the state.   Since the New Economic Policy was instituted, the interstices of the Soviet economic structure have been occupied by various forms of quasi-private enterprise.   To this day, such consumers' goods as musical instruments, furniture, toys, some prepared foodstuffs, certain office supplies, etc., which need little heavy or complicated equipment to produce and which are made and sold locally from materials locally available, are produced and sold by cooperative associations of more or less independent artisans.   Like the collective farms shortly to be described, these producers' cooperatives operate under a model charter drawn up by the state.   The members of each cooperative, who may number from about twenty to several hundred, elect a Board entrusted with the details of its administration.   Usually the membership retains for itself the determination of conditions under which members may be admitted or should be expelled, and it also, subject to the model charter, determines general policy.   An initiation fee, payable either in cash or in tools and equipment and payable, if necessary, in installments, is charged each new member.

Members receive wages at time or piece rates determined by the membership, and, financial conditions permitting, they may also receive occasional bonuses based upon the quality and quantity of their work.   The finished products of the cooperatives are usually sold at state-approved prices calculated to return a surplus of ten to twenty per cent over cost, and that surplus, after taxes, is usually retained by the cooperative to be used for expansion, for welfare or recreational activities, or as the fund from which bonuses are paid.

Being local organizations, the producers' cooperatives are controlled by the appropriate Ministries of the several Republics rather than by the central, All-Union Government.   The prices at which their products are sold must conform to public requirements and their productive activities must fit into the national economic plan; but as long as these conditions are observed, the cooperatives receive considerable public assistance.   New associations are exempted from taxes for the first year or so of their existence, and they are eligible for grants-in-aid.   All approved cooperatives are assigned their premises, allotted their equipment and materials—for which they pay, of course, at officially fixed prices—are extended credit, and are provided with outlets for their products.

AGRICULTURE

Agriculture presented the Bolsheviks with some of their most grievous problems, occasioned some of the most bitter ideological disputes, and was responsible, possibly, for some of the greatest ruthlessness displayed by the regime and its supporters.   Russia was overwhelmingly agrarian prior to the Revolution and the agricultural problem was among the very first to be tackled.   On the second day of the October Revolution,[12] November 8, 1917, a decree was issued safeguarding peasants in their ownership of land, but nationalizing other land and providing for its transfer to rural committees or local soviets.   The peasants themselves did not wait; they seized what they wanted and they were not gentle in the manner of their seizure.   As a result, the new government more or less lost control over what was happening in the countryside, and a further result was the disappearance of food from the cities.   Rural uncertainty verging on chaos was the first cause, but this was supplemented by the confusion which revolution and civil war injected into the normal channels of distribution and by the nearly complete breakdown of the transportation system.   The state, attempting to avert profiteering in the urban sale of increasingly scarce foodstuffs, set fixed prices on these but so low that the peasantry were disinclined to accept them, and consequently the food shortage grew steadily worse.   The first reaction was an attempt at systematization; on May 13, 1918,[13] a State Grain Monopoly was created to which all grain, except that legally retained by peasants for seed and subsistence, had to be sold at fixed prices.   This step elicited little agrarian enthusiasm, and the next reaction was a venture into naked force. Three months later, in August, the state sent into the countryside armed bands of industrial workers and some poorer peasants, to seize what grain supplies they could find.   Still later, regular troops were used, but peasants everywhere are adept at concealment, and what the Russian peasantry feared it could not conceal, it destroyed; the cities continued to starve and the regime faced a mutinous countryside.

The New Economic Policy of 1921 both introduced concessions and sought rural allies.   The principle of land nationalization was upheld and

[12] At the time of the Revolution the Russians still held to an old-style calendar slightly behind that in use by the rest of the Western world.   It was this fact that gave the name October Revolution to an event now dated in November, 1917.

[13] This date, as all others given later will be, is that of the new calendar.

the prohibition against the purchase or sale of land was reaffirmed, but the actual occupant of farming land was now assured protection of his investment in buildings, equipment, and livestock. He was permitted to lease these, he was cautiously given some approval even to hire labor—that most capitalistic of processes—and, above all, he was given a free hand to organize his own production and to sell his products where he could. At the same time, pointed hostility began to be specifically directed toward the wealthy peasant, or *kulak*. The poor peasantry were wooed as members and supporters of the working class, the peasantry of middle station were accepted as friendly toward the regime and were given kindly nods and, at times, a helping hand; but the kulak was branded a class enemy, and from then on his existence was intended to be solitary, poor, nasty, brutish and short.

In 1927 another crisis set in. At the Communist Party Congress of that year, the left wing demanded a return to complete socialization, while the right wing insisted that such a policy was still utterly premature. Eventually the moderates emerged the victor, with a policy of increasing financial and technical aid to the poorer peasantry, of accelerating the merging of individual peasant homesteads into collective farms, and of developing new State Farms, on almost the factory principle, in areas where these would not encroach upon land held by the peasantry—especially in Old Russia and the Ukraine. The first Five-Year Plan, introduced in 1928–29, gave additional impetus to the organization of collective farms, and both the number of these and the number of individual peasant farms incorporated in them, increased rapidly. In the summer of 1929 the fateful decision was taken to eliminate the kulaks entirely as a class; and, once again, the situation got out of hand. The poorer peasants, in whose eyes the kulaks had by now replaced the aristocracy as exploiters and oppressors, rose once more to seize, burn, and slaughter. Collectivization, also, proceeded at a headlong pace, and the upshot of the whole venture was another famine. This one was the result, partly, of the prodigious destruction of livestock which could neither be fed nor cared for in the ensuing disorder, and which also were deliberately slaughtered by the kulaks on the principle that what they could not keep, no one else should enjoy.

It was not long before the state, again, was compelled to apply the brakes. After Stalin made a famous speech—"Dizzy with Success"—the pace of collectivization was slowed, withdrawal from hastily or coercively organized collective farms was permitted, and toleration of agrarian individualism—provided this did not reach into the upper income brackets—was once again promised. In time, slow agricultural recovery made a second start within a generation, and the now established structure of soviet agriculture began to take form.

The Collective Farm

Collective farms in agriculture, like producers' cooperatives in industry, are cooperative associations of more or less independent individuals operating under public guidance and distributing among themselves a considerable share of the fruits of their joint labor. Like the producers' cooperatives again, they are organized under a model charter drawn up by the state. Each farm has a manager and an executive board elected by the membership for terms of, usually, two years. The members themselves are organized into brigades of two- or three-score members, led by brigade leaders who, coincidentally, are frequently members of the party. Basic directives are issued by the appropriate Ministries.

Although title to all land in Russia is vested in the Government, the collective farms are assured "perpetual" use of the land allotted them. In amount, this works out at an average of roughly fifty acres for each of the peasant families belonging to a farm; some of the collective farms themselves run up to an aggregate of several thousand acres, although they are generally not nearly as large as the state farms. Their lighter equipment is cooperatively owned, but the heavier and more massive mobile equipment is leased from the machine tractor stations shortly to be described. There is no common pattern for the activities of the collective farms; some engage in general farming, some in livestock farming, others specialize intensively in a few, or even in only one, product.

Unlike the producers' cooperatives, members of the collective farms do not receive set wages; they are paid in *pro rata* shares of the total return as computed at the end of an accounting period. On each farm, different tasks are assigned different weights or "norms" based upon the estimated "value" of these tasks in "working day units." These units are so calculated that each normal day's work should entitle the worker to a credit ranging from one half to two working day units. The completion of an assigned task entitles the performer to the proper credit entry in his Work Book (which corresponds to the German *Arbeitsbuch*) regardless of the time it has taken him to carry out his assignment.   Presumably tasks are rotated to avoid egregious discrimination in the earning of credits.

At the end of each accounting period the total credits awarded are summed; simultaneously the amount of each crop or product available for distribution as earnings is divided by the total number of credits earned, and so each member's wage in kind is determined.   Money wages are similarly calculated: the "wages fund" for each collective farm is divided by the total number of credits awarded, and the quotient is multiplied by the number of credits assigned each individual, and so his wage is determined.   Bonuses are sometimes given for exceptional productivity, and various non-monetary awards such as medals or honors can also be earned.

The incomes of the members of collective farms are thus paid both in cash or kind, according to the policy approved by the membership of each farm but subject to higher approval.   However wages are paid, their source, obviously enough, is the gross produce of the farm, but certain deductions at the source must be made before the net produce becomes available for distribution to members.   There is, first, the compulsory delivery to the government of a part of the produce, at very low prices.   This tax, for that is what it amounts to, is adjusted roughly in proportion to the natural advantages—such as fertility of the soil—enjoyed by each farm, so that in a sense it serves the purpose of a single tax, the absorption by the state of differential rents.[14]   There are deductions, also, for the administrative expenses of the farm, for seed reserves, for payment of interest and principle upon borrowed funds, for payment of services rendered by the machine tractor stations, for contributions toward the farm's welfare and recreational fund, and occasionally for payments into a fund for improvements.

Manifestly, the cash received by a collective farm must be derived from the sale of its produce.   There are, generally, three markets in which this sale can be made.   Over and above its compulsory exactions, the government will purchase, and at prices higher than those paid for compulsory deliveries, supplies from collective farms; buyers' cooperatives will purchase produce for eventual re-sale, and industrial enterprises will sometimes buy supplies for factory stores and canteens; and, finally, there is the free market in cities and villages in which produce not taken by the other markets (which have a measure of priority) can be sold for what more or less the traffic

[14] This was suggested by Maurice Dobb, *Soviet Economy and the War,* New York, 1943; p. 69.

will bear.   These buying institutions will be described later in this chapter.

Since the members of collective farms, like other Soviet citizens, pay income taxes on their earnings, the Soviet Union has a system of double taxation akin to that in other countries where taxes are levied both on the profits earned by corporations and on the dividends received by stockholders. Whether or not there is in Russia the same protesting chorus at the government's double-take is not clear; if there is any at all, it is doubtless muted.

Perhaps as a sop to the individualism which seems to be characteristic of countrymen everywhere, the Russian government in 1935 permitted members of collective farms to mark out for themselves—under control, of course —individual homesteads on collective farm property, homesteads with a bit of land attached which the occupants could use as they chose.   There the members might live, and there they might also raise garden produce, keep bees or chickens or rabbits, either for their own use or for sale.   These homesteads generally varied in size from about half an acre to not quite three acres, depending on the quality of the land.   The system proved disconcertingly popular.   So much work was performed so enthusiastically on private plots that collective work tended to be skimped.   Yet again, this time in 1939, the government had to intervene to undo some of the consequences of its agricultural policy.   Thereafter, members of collective farms were held to a minimum of sixty to one hundred days' collective labor in a year; violators were liable to expulsion from membership in the farm and confiscation of their property, and collective farms themselves which tolerated violations rendered themselves subject to penalty.

Machine tractor stations.   Almost from the beginning the Russians have driven hard to mechanize their agriculture.   In so doing, they have had to face the problem of the most efficient use of large-scale equipment.   The state farms were large enough to own and operate their own equipment, but it would have been uneconomical to attempt to equip each collective farm with a full set of equipment which it could only partially employ; there was also another reason (to be mentioned in a moment) for not providing collective farms individually with everything they needed if they were to continue to function.   The solution which the Russians found is somewhat reminiscent of the "threshing bees" on the frontier lands of the expanding United States, described, for example, in the novels of Hamlin Garland.

The machine tractor stations are simply equipment pools, financed by the Treasury, manned by mechanics and agricultural experts, and designed to service collective farms in rotation in order to plough, harvest, or thresh according to season and crop.   In 1938 each Machine Tractor Station provided these services for an average of slightly more than thirty collective farms, but there is nothing necessarily final about that ratio.   Baykov records lively discussions in the Soviet press about what the optimum size of these stations should be.[15]   Since collective farms are entirely dependent upon these stations, and since the stations are state rather than cooperative enterprises, the control over cooperatives and the concession to individualism embodied in these institutions, are perhaps not as great as they superficially seem.

State Farms

State farms are vast establishments, frequently described as agricultural factories.   They are organized along the same general lines as other industrial enterprises in the Soviet Union that are owned, financed, and operated by the state.   Labor is hired as in other factories, managers are appointed, and the output belongs to the appropriate Trust, such as the Sugar or the Cotton Trust, under the supervision of the proper Ministry.   The history of the state farms parallels, in a sense, the history of other industrial undertakings.   The first state farms were created in 1918 upon estates which had hitherto belonged to the great landowners, the Church, or to the state itself. The propensity for giganticism which misled industrial management in the early years extended, also, to the agricultural authorities.   By 1931 mounting complaints of inefficiency, even of dishonesty, culminated in public investigations which were followed by tightening the administration and reducing the pressure to establish these institutions.   Between 1932 and 1935 some state farms were abandoned and their equipment and property sold to collective farms, and many others were reduced in size.   Their average size still remained impressive.   In 1938, the usual state farm devoted to the raising of grain crops was nearly 58,000 acres; dairy farms averaged nearly 71,000 acres, and sheep ranches ran slightly over 268,000 acres.[16]

Individual Farms

Between them, collective and state farms comprise most soviet agriculture. In terms of sown area, collective farms in 1938 made up eighty-five per cent

[15] Cf., Baykov, op. cit., p. 330.
[16] Cf., Baykov, op. cit., p. 333.

and state farms nine per cent of the Russian land; in terms of total agricultural production, collective farms were responsible for nearly seventy per
cent and state farms just over nine per cent.   The members of collective
farms occupied individual homesteads aggregating four per cent of the
sown area, but those homesteads produced over twenty-one per cent of the
total agricultural production.   The figures are suggestive, for it will be remembered that in only the following year, 1939, the state intervened to
discourage what it considered disproportionate time devoted to individual
plots.

Some purely individual, peasant farming still remains.   Six tenths of one
per cent of the sown area in 1938 was individually farmed, and one and one
half per cent of the total crop came from those farms.[17]   These figures are
not startling, and certainly cannot be alarming to communists, except, perhaps, as reflections of the persistence of individualism in the countryside.
These lone peasants remain, so far, unmolested, except for the higher rates
of taxation to which they are subject and for the various subtle inducements
to collectivize themselves which must continue to be offered them.

MARKETING AND TRADING INSTITUTIONS

The system by which goods are placed in the possession of their destined
consumers has had the same vicissitudes as the system by which the goods
are brought into being.   The lack of discipline and control in the early
years, which we have already seen manifested in other sectors of the economy, is evidence that local authorities had taken the same free hand concerning trade as they had with industry and agriculture.   In many parts
of the country merchants were exposed to monetary exactions under threat
of confiscation of their entire property; sometimes, when they themselves
either would not or could not pay they were seized as hostages to induce
others to come to their financial assistance.[18]   Shops and stores were engulfed in the same tidal wave of nationalization that swept over other, in
fact all, sectors of the economy, and when this wave receded the same retrenchment became necessary here.   The New Economic Policy involved
a fairly substantial restoration of various forms of private enterprise in

[17] All the foregoing figures come from Baykov, *op. cit.,* p. 327.
[18] *Ibid.,* p. 24.

internal marketing, and still later these private enterprises in their own turn became subject to the now familiar encroachment of state and cooperative enterprise. The proportions and the geographical distribution of the two latter forms of enterprise have continued to shift. For a time, as we shall see, consumers' cooperatives were encouraged throughout the extent of the Soviet Union; later they were somewhat discouraged, and still later they were again brought back.

Late in 1935 the consumers' cooperatives in the larger cities were ordered to transfer their facilities to state stores; eleven years later, they were encouraged to re-establish themselves in the cities and in workers' settlements. These shifts constitute one more illustration of the tension that has existed throughout Soviet history, the tension between the temptation to nationalize everything, to subsume all forms of economic activity within state-owned-and-operated enterprise, and the hard fact that it has been impossible to do so all at once or more rapidly than custom, the use and wont of the Russian people, can be brought into conformity with that simple, but extreme, principle.

Cooperative enterprise, whether in industry, agriculture, or distribution, represents a sort of compromise between complete individualism and absolute collectivism; it is clearly preferable, in collectivist eyes, to the first, but probably inferior to the second. Between 1935 and 1946, at any rate, consumers' cooperatives, discouraged in the cities, were kept going in the countryside. It is tempting to suggest that their retention there was due to the hope that they might serve as an easy and gentle means of accustoming the peasantry to cooperative activity as a first step toward real communal association. Perhaps the return of the cooperatives to the cities in 1946 appeared a comparable means of providing city dwellers with appropriate incentives. Perhaps, also, cooperation by consumers as well as by farmers and industrial producers is now considered a satisfactory combination of decentralized responsibility and centralized control, embodying just the right mixture of local initiative and flexibility with conformity to the purposes and objectives of the prevailing national economic plan. The Russians have changed their minds more than once upon this issue of the locus of detailed responsibility, and there is no certainty that they will not do so again.

Whatever the explanation may be, the Russians for a generation have simultaneously maintained a variety of marketing institutions and procedures which, taken together, have served to do more than simply provide consumers with the physical means of subsistence. They have also most effectively drained off surplus purchasing power through skillful use of a device developed in capitalist countries for the purpose, simply, of maximizing profit: price discrimination. When customers, that is to say, can be divided into separate groups, or markets, sellers are under great temptation to set different prices for each such market. A *de luxe* edition of a book, for example, contains exactly the same words, arranged in the same order, as the ordinary trade edition; yet the former is more expensive. The profitability of price discrimination is apparently known by communists as well as by capitalists.

Consumers' Cooperatives

An important part of the marketing structure of the Soviet Union is the consumers' cooperative. Allusion has already been made to these; it is now time to examine them systematically.

Consumers' cooperatives in Russia are organized on pretty much the same principles that prevail elsewhere and that descend from the rules worked out in England by the Rochdale Pioneers in 1844. These cooperatives are voluntary associations of individuals who buy their way into membership for the sake of some form of preferential treatment accorded members. As do other Russian institutions, they undertake a variety of cultural, educational, recreational or welfare activities which are available only to their members. Sometimes goods of particularly high quality are reserved for members of the cooperative which has made a fortunate purchase. Rebates or dividends, on the principle well known elsewhere, are distributed to members in proportion to the volume of their purchases whenever a surplus for that purpose exists at the end of an accounting period.

The membership is collectively responsible for the determination of policy, subject to the law and custom of the land. Detailed operations are administered by a Manager directly responsible to an elected Management Board. Buying and selling prices are, of course, set by the central price-fixing authority under the Council of Ministers, and the direction of cooperative activity is made to conform to the prevailing economic plan. Cooperatives, as we should now expect, operate under a model charter interpreted and administered by the Ministries of Trade of the several Republics.

The cooperatives have organized a central purchasing agency which operates warehouses filled with inventories in accordance with contracts the agency makes with the Trusts and with collective farms. Individual cooperatives also purchase locally from producers' cooperatives, and some of them, like many cooperative associations elsewhere in Europe, produce for themselves such things as soap, rope, and certain foodstuffs.   Here and there the consumers' cooperatives operate their own auxiliary farms, and some of them, in season, make organized forays into the countryside to collect mushrooms, nuts, berries, herbs, and game.   Some cooperatives also operate tearooms and restaurants, and the rural cooperatives frequently send traveling shops from village to village, much as peddlers or traveling salesmen move about in the United States.   Consumers' cooperatives at present receive special tax concessions and, like the collective farms, their facilities are "protected" against encroachment by state enterprises.

State Stores

Like the Trusts and the state farms, state stores are fully socialized institutions, operated by the government, usually under the Ministries of Trade of the several Republics.   Sometimes Trusts or other public agencies will operate state stores as outlets for their own products.   The prices paid and charged are, of course, fixed for them, and their turnover is planned in advance by the state planning authorities.   Just as the cooperatives have their own purchasing organization, the state stores, when they do not purchase directly from the Trusts, have recourse to state operated wholesale organizations.   Some of the latter have been known to display initiative—studying, and occasionally even developing, regional consumers' tastes and building up inventories with which these can be satisfied.   Chain stores commonly are operated as state stores, and, in the larger cities, the state maintains department stores.

Being completely public institutions, the state stores can be, and frequently have been, used for special purposes, or to meet the requirements of special categories of buyers.   During the 'thirties, for example, TORGSIN was developed as a chain of stores stocking attractive goods for sale exclusively to foreigners, and exclusively for gold or for acceptable foreign exchange.

Factory Stores

Factory stores correspond somewhat to the Post Exchanges familiar by now to so many young Americans, except that they are attached to industrial enterprises rather than to military units. They are operated by separate enterprises exclusively for employees of the enterprise, and they are usually financially independent ventures. They are administered by full-time Managers appointed by the directors of the enterprises to which they pertain, and they are financed separately by the State Bank and are under the jurisdiction of the Ministries of Trade of the several Republics.

Like other marketing institutions they both purchase from producing agencies, like Trusts, collective farms, and producers' cooperatives, and maintain auxiliary farms and workshops of their own to supply part of their inventory. They also garner the fruits of the countryside when that is possible, and many of them maintain service establishments such as laundries, barber shops, restaurants, shoe-repair shops, and dry cleaners. The prices they charge are fixed by the state to allow a small profit, part of which may be retained for their own development.

Peasant Markets

Peasant markets, resembling somewhat the roadside stands on American highways, constitute outlets for the surplus produce grown by peasants either on their own farms or on the homesteads allotted them as members of collective farms, which remains to them after obligations to the state have been met. Interestingly enough, these markets are almost wholly uncontrolled. Generally they are open booths in villages and towns, at which various foodstuffs are sold to all comers for whatever prices they will bring. Sellers are liable to income tax on their gains, but it is reported that no attempt is made to collect the turnover tax [19] on products sold in these markets. That is doubtless a concession to reality.

Price Discrimination

One special reason exists for the variety of marketing institutions within the Soviet Union. As we shall see in following chapters, inflation has constantly dogged the steps of Soviet planners. Intense governmental activity involved massive governmental expenditure. That expenditure took two forms: (1) investment in heavy industry caused by the driving pressure to industrialize, and (2) heavy military outlay caused by concern over national defense. While government spending was high, financial stability could be

[19] See below, pp. 340–342.

assured only by re-absorbing part of the purchasing power that governmental expenditure necessarily distributed among the Russian people.　Re-
absorption was particularly necessary because production of the kinds of
goods for which ordinary people spend their money was held down, in order
to release resources for industrialization and defense.　A problem thus was
created by having more money in circulation than goods for which it could
be spent, at least at stable prices.

The government wished people to spend their money, because expenditure
in stores owned by government provides government with revenue.　The
government, however, did not wish to see a wild and uncontrolled scramble
for scarce goods that might leave the timid, the weak, or the busy without
any goods at all.　A simple solution to the problem was found.

Limited quantities of consumers' goods could be bought by approved
purchasers at fairly low prices, usually in closed establishments like factory stores to which only certain categories of buyers had entry.　Additional
supplies could be bought, when they were available, in state stores at substantially higher prices.　If, after paying for these purchases, there still
existed any consumers with money, recourse could always be had to the
peasants' market, where prices have generally been uncontrolled and were
accordingly high enough to blot up practically any floating currency still
about; these markets, in fact, are sometimes described as legalized black
markets.

The principle of all this is extremely simple.　Russian citizens are sup-
posedly assured a ration of subsistence goods at prices within their means,
although, unfortunately, they have not always been able to find even their
ration.　Subsistence being assured, no real harm can come from letting
them pay what they like for any surplus they can find.　The range of price
discrimination which has been reported is extremely wide.　In 1932, for
example, wheat was delivered to most stores at between seven and eight
kopecs per kilogram; rationed wheat flour was sold at 19 kopecs, unrationed
flour in state stores sold at 450 kopecs, and peasants were reported to be
selling flour at between 580 and 650 kopecs.　The variation in the prices
of a quasi-luxury were still more spectacular.　Butter, for example, sold
on the ration at 466 kopecs per kilogram; it reached 4,820 on the peasant
market.[20]

The combination of open and closed markets had a psychological as well
as an economic advantage; it enabled people to enjoy an occasional splurge.

[20] Cf., Baykov, op. cit., p. 244.

In the years immediately following the Second World War, for example, both the Russian and the English diets were drab and monotonous. An Englishman who wanted a beefsteak could get one only by resorting to the black market, or by leaving the country. The Russian who wanted a beefsteak could save up for one and eventually buy one at home, and with perfect legality. The Russian's steak was fantastically expensive; but it could be had.[21]

MONETARY AND CREDIT INSTITUTIONS

We shall have more to say about monetary and credit institutions when we come to survey the manner in which the Soviet economy operates, because much of the control exerted by the government over its own economic creatures is both suggested and achieved through monetary phenomena. At this point we shall only lay the groundwork for that discussion by providing brief descriptions of the institutions themselves.

Money

Russian money consists of inconvertible paper issued by the State Bank (*Gosbank*). It is intended solely for internal circulation; both the export and import of Russian rubles, consistently with the exchange control so characteristic of managed economies, is forbidden. The State Bank, accordingly, monopolizes foreign exchange as well, and for the same reason it serves as the only dealer in the monetary metals.

Long-Term Credit

Strictly speaking, credit is perhaps not the best term to apply to the financial resources made available to new or expanding enterprises. Long-term loans are indeed made, but non-repayable grants-in-aid are also not uncommon, and occasionally a loan is canceled when the government wishes to subsidize one part of the economy out of the gains of another. Whatever the form, all investment capital comes from one of four specialized banks, all of which operate under the general supervision of the Ministry of Finance.

[21] I am indebted to Professor Edward Ames for this comparison.

The Trade Bank.   The Trade Bank is responsible for the capital outlay by the various marketing institutions already described.   The building of new shops and stores, grain elevators and warehouses, as well as the expansion of old ones, is financed by this bank, and, curiously enough (for they are not primarily trading bodies), the producers' cooperatives also are tied to it as far as their capital resources are concerned.   Unlike many of the collective farms, as we shall shortly see, most of the cooperative associations which borrow from the Trade Bank are expected to pay interest on their loans and eventually to repay the principal.

Communal Banks.   Communal Banks exist to serve cities themselves and the institutions—sometimes even individuals—in the cities.   Local soviets wishing to undertake a housing project are eligible for either grants or long-term loans, according to the will or whim of the government, from the Communal Bank.   So, also, are hospitals, schools, theaters and clubs for their own construction or expansion.   Municipalities may borrow from it to provide or develop such local utilities as street car or bus systems, water works, or electric power plants.   Even individuals who wish to construct a house may borrow from this bank provided their applications are approved.

The Industrial Bank.   Like the State Bank (see page 316) the Industrial Bank is a large institution with branches throughout the country.   It performs exactly the same service for Russian industry that the State Bank does for commerce: it provides long-term credit for expansion and development. It is a rather exacting creditor.   The Industrial Bank does not blithely make a loan and then expectantly await repayment; it supervises the manner in which loans are used, and it does so in two ways.

First, it makes its loans in driblets rather than in lump sums.   It does so, moreover, not by entrusting its debtors with credits upon which they may draw at will, but by paying the bills incurred by its debtors as they fall due —and then, only after the Bank has satisfied itself that the bills are for goods or services consonant with the approved purpose of the loan.   Suppose, for example, that a tractor factory has borrowed in order to construct a new wing on an old building.   As payrolls for construction workers and vouchers for construction materials fall due, they are presented to the Industrial Bank for payment.

Second, the Bank makes certain that the funds it expends are properly used, and it does so by keeping inspectors on the very scene of construction.

Those inspectors presumably keep the Bank informed of both the progress and the quality of the work for which the Bank has extended credit.

The power over its debtors that the Industrial Bank has is, therefore, substantial. If it considers any bill presented to it for payment excessive or improper, it can disallow that bill; if it considers progress on the job slow, or inefficient, it can refuse to make any more payments.

The Industrial Bank originally received its own capital funds from the state. With the passage of time, however, its capital has been replenished by the repayment of loans made by the Bank, and augmented by the receipt of a portion of the profits earned by those enterprises whose activities were made possible by the credit extended them by the Industrial Bank. Russian industrial development is in a sense, therefore, self-financing: the capital for future development is derived from the fruits of past development.

The Agricultural Bank. The Agricultural Bank finances the expansion and development of state and collective farms, and of machine tractor stations. It supervises the expenditure of its funds in exactly the same way that the Industrial Bank does. In one sense, however, the Agricultural Bank is something more than just a bank: it is a kind of bureaucratic Santa Claus. It provides subsidies. In 1934, for example, the entire capital indebtedness that had been incurred by collective farms before 1933, was simply wiped out with the stroke of a pen. Subsequent cancellations of long-term debt have also been reported.

Short-Term Credit

The traditional distinction between long-term and short-term credit is based upon the distinction between the construction or expansion of facilities and the performance of the functions for which the facilities were designed. The line drawn between the two kinds of credit, in other words, represents a division of function, not just the difference between two periods of time. The time element is derivative from the functional, simply because it takes longer to repay a loan for construction than one for routine operation. It may take years, for example, before the cost of erecting a sugar refinery is paid off; it may be only weeks before the cost of a carload of sugar beets is met by the sale of the sugar made from them.

In the Soviet Union, as in other countries, financial institutions specializing in one or the other of the two kinds of credit have been developed. In the

Soviet Union, however, in contrast with practice in such countries as the United States, the provision of short-term credit is wholly monopolized.

The State Bank.   The State Bank possesses that monopoly of short-term credit.   That is to say, no selling agency is permitted to extend credit, and all buying agencies must pay for their purchases at least upon delivery, and frequently even before.   Payment in these cases is made against bills of lading or invoices while goods are in transit, and they usually take the form of a check, or order on the Bank, to debit and credit the appropriate accounts.

All economic units in the country—trusts, enterprises, state and collective farms, marketing agencies, and so on—maintain deposits in the State Bank, which is a vast institution with branches all through the country.   It is, indeed, the equivalent of a Ministry inasmuch as the Chairman of its Board has a seat on the Council of Ministers.

The purpose of this monopoly of credit is simple: (1) to enable the Bank, by watching the accounts of its depositors, to keep track of how well the current economic plan is being fulfilled, and of how efficiently various enterprises are carrying out their responsibilities; and (2) to direct credit, the life blood of the economy, into channels where it appears most needed. New enterprises, accordingly, are provided by the agencies to which they are responsible with revolving funds deposited in the Bank.   Thereafter the receipts these enterprises subsequently earn must be paid into their accounts in the State Bank.   This necessity clinches the control which the state has over enterprise.   An establishment with impending obligations which it cannot meet may apply to the State Bank for a loan to tide it over. If approved, the credit is usually extended for no longer than three months and it carries interest ranging generally between two and four per cent.

In addition to the activities just described, the State Bank handles the current accounts of the four investment banks already described, all financial transactions between foreigners and governmental agencies, and it is the depository for tax receipts.

Savings banks.   Savings banks fill a peculiar niche in the structure of the Soviet economy.   They exist primarily to absorb surplus cash in the possession of individuals or organizations.   That cash is surplus either in the sense that its holders do not wish to spend it at once, or in the sense that (because of the shortage of consumers' goods) they could not spend it without raising prices.   The Russian savings banks, in other words, are like our own savings banks insofar as they receive deposits; they are unlike our banks because they also exist to discourage the withdrawal of deposits.[22]

As credit institutions, therefore, Russian savings banks are hard—perhaps impossible—to classify. They are required by law to invest their reserves in government bonds, reportedly to assure the state a market for its own securities. That requirement makes them purveyors of long-term credit to the state. The savings banks, however, also issue letters of credit cashable throughout the Soviet Union; and that function brings them closer to the status of short-term credit institutions.

Perhaps they can best be called service institutions. They are of service to individuals by offering checking accounts to those who wish them, by handling payments on social-security account, and by serving as agents through whom individuals or institutions purchase state bonds. They are of service to government by absorbing deposits from individuals and such organizations as labor unions or collective farms.

The system is convenient, as branches are maintained in factories and in libraries, in post offices and in railroad stations. Deposits are attracted by the association of the savings banks with the state lottery system. Those deposits that are repayable on demand receive no interest, but they do entitle their holders to participation in lotteries in which the winning tickets carry cash prizes amounting to specified proportions of the deposits against which the tickets are issued. The lottery is apparently the Russian counterpart of our own give-away radio programs.

Depositors are encouraged to keep withdrawals to a minimum by the promise that interest will be paid on deposits frozen for six months or longer.

All the operations that have been described—industrial, agricultural, commercial and financial—depend upon each other. In Russia that dependence is worked out and controlled by the officials who prepare the economic plan, to which we must now turn.

---

[22] It is true that American savings banks may discourage the withdrawal of deposits by requiring advance notice before a withdrawal may be made; that is why deposits in savings banks are known technically as "time," in contrast to "demand" deposits. Savings banks, however, seldom exercise their right to request advance notice.

15

The Soviet System of Planning

To UNDERSTAND an economic system, we must understand not only how it is put together, but also how it works. We saw in the last chapter how the Soviet system is put together, and we shall see in the next how it works. We cannot proceed immediately to that task, however, because—unlike our own economic system—the Soviet economy is not, even in principle, supposed to work by itself. Its working is arranged for it, and the arrangement is called a plan. We must, accordingly, understand the plan before we can understand how the plan works out.

THE GENERAL PROBLEM OF PLANNING

It is both true and misleading to describe the Soviet system as a planned economy. It is true because for twenty-five years the Russian economic plan has been crucial for the determination of how and to what end the Russian economy should be operated.[1] It is misleading, because it is not

[1] The Russians talked about planning from the very beginning of the Soviet regime, and certain experiments in planning were essayed at the start. As we shall see, however, it was not until 1928 that anything like a firm plan was introduced.

planning, nor even control of the economy, that sets the Russian system off from others. There are elements of planning in every contemporary economy, and every contemporary economy is in some measure controlled. The fascist economies we have studied were both planned and tightly controlled; we have, indeed, already noticed many similarities between the fascist and the soviet systems. There are, nevertheless, differences, and the differentia [2] of the Russian system consists in the *operation by the state* of almost all industry and a substantial part of agriculture and commerce. The description of the Russian economy as planned is true, but its description as administered is distinctive: In the Russian economy the state is entrusted with the ownership and operation of substantially all enterprise.

This, however, makes planning all the more essential, so that while planning may not be a differentia of the Soviet system it is a most important element in it. An introductory word about the nature and implications of economic planning, accordingly, seems called for.

In the Western World, at least, the appeal of planning has probably been greatest during periods of depression. These are just the times when resources, set against the opportunities for their employment, appear most abundant; in other words when the costs of error appear least, because any waste in the use of resources appears positively desirable. When manpower is employed in "boondoggling" and when other resources are underutilized, the most urgent economic and social need appears to be the taking up of slack, and if the market does not promise to do so other means must be planned. Under those circumstances, the host of statisticians and accountants required to prepare the details of the plan and to keep track of its progress are easily regarded less as manpower diverted from physical production than as labor for which employment has been found.

Although the popular *appeal* of planning is high when resources appear abundant, that appeal nevertheless rests, not upon abundance, but upon scarcity—in this case, the scarcity of employment. Planning appears to be the offspring of necessity. The *need* to plan emerges when physical resources themselves come into acute shortage.

It thus may appear reasonable to plan the employment of resources for which spontaneous employment is apparently not to be had, but it is imperative to plan when resources are in such short supply that their utilization

---

[2] "The *differentia* is that part of the essence of anything—or, as we may say, of any species—which distinguishes it from other species in the same genus . . ." H. W. B. Joseph, *An Introduction to Logic*, 2d. edition, Oxford, 1916; p. 74.

cannot be left unplanned.   Wartime provides a conspicuous illustration, because war, economically, is simply a condition in which everything but problems becomes scarce.   During the Second World War even the individualistic United States was driven to ration, to allocate, to hunt for substitutes, to control prices—in short, to plan.

To this powerful incentive to planning must be added its aesthetic appeal to those seeking a kind of visible order in economic activity which, to them, the market is incapable of imposing, and its moral appeal to those seeking a distribution of income which, again, the market does not appear to provide.

In consequence, the running controversy over planning which is still in process has, at least in its popular manifestations, taken the form of assertion and counter-assertion regarding its necessity or desirability with little attention given to its *difficulty*.   That difficulty is not insurmountable, but it is great and warrants a quick glance at its elements.   The concept of an economic plan has become so popular that its content no longer arouses wonder; yet it should.

Disregarding temporarily the important problem of what to plan for, let us assume that a planner knows precisely what economic structure he wishes to bring to birth, what the composition of gross output should be, what total volume of production so composed he wishes to see attained, and how rapidly he desires—or hopes—to achieve those ends.   It is true that the determination of those ends is in itself a prodigious problem, but we have provisionally put it aside.

The planner, if he is to be at all effective, must know in considerable detail the resources, equipment, tools, and materials at his disposal; otherwise, his plan is no more than a daydream.   He must know how to make use of what he has; otherwise, his plan may produce something as unsatisfactory as the proverbial bride's cookies.   Moreover, if planning is technically to justify itself, the planner must provide for improvement in the effectiveness and economy with which his resources are used.   The conscientious planner, indeed, must frequently be haunted by the tension between the security of staying with proved procedures at the risk of failing to keep abreast, and the lure of experimentation which carries the risk of failure. Having no competitor, moreover, he has available no market standard by which he can determine at least whether he is as efficient as he should be; but that, perhaps, is not invariably taken as a disadvantage.

Like a navigator, the planner must keep his bearings.   If he gets off course, he must realize it before he gets hopelessly lost.   That means three things: (1) he must have at his disposal a constant flow of information of how his plan is progressing, of the points at which it may be ahead of schedule and of the channels in which it may be lagging; (2) he must be capable of grasping, classifying, and absorbing this information without becoming hopelessly entangled in streams of paper festooning themselves about his desk faster than he can clear them away; and (3) his reaction time must be quicker than the onset of surplus or shortage in order that he may make adjustments in both his plan and its operations as they become necessary and before they become unmanageable.

If we now relinquish our initial assumption and add to these problems that of determining what to plan for—that is, the degree of emphasis to be placed upon national economic power as against individual material welfare, or standardization compared with variation in the goods produced, and so on—we can see that the effective planner must combine qualities verging upon both omniscience and omnicompetence. But even that is not all. In contrast to *laissez-faire* systems in which responsibility is diffused, in which the compromise between following proved rules of thumb and venturing upon alluring but hazardous innovation is reached according to the boldness or conservatism of separate entrepreneurial personalities and the opportunities they believe to confront them, in *planned and administered systems* all responsibility is ultimately borne by the planner. The failure of an individual entrepreneur is indeed a tragedy for him and those dependent upon him, but society generally can absorb the shock of his failure. The wrong decision made by a national planner, however, may have repercussions extending far beyond a single enterprise and may even entail a political as well as an economic penalty. The unsuccessful private entrepreneur is seldom suspected of having committed deliberate sabotage against himself, but the unsuccessful state planner, particularly in a suspicion-ridden society like the Russian, may find himself indicted for guilt as well as for incompetence.

THE DEVELOPMENT OF RUSSIAN PLANNING

The Russians themselves appear to have under-estimated the difficulty involved in first contriving and then administering a comprehensive economic plan. One of their first acts after their seizure of power late in 1917 was to establish a Supreme Economic Council intended to assume responsibility for planning and regulating Russian economic activity.   The assignment was too vast, however, particularly under the confused and disordered conditions characteristic of the early years of the Soviet experiment, and the most that the Supreme Economic Council could accomplish was the administration of certain separate industries—something very different from administering an entire economy.

Another venture was essayed in 1920.   A general plan, known rather horribly as *Goelro,* was devised for the development of electric power as the basis for further industrialization.   This too, however, remained only a plan on paper for some time to come, primarily because neither the *expertise* nor the institutions for putting a comprehensive plan into effect had yet been created.   These slowly came into existence during and after the period of the New Economic Policy.   As we have already observed, in that period the state took over the "commanding heights" of the economy, a position of strength it was subsequently to extend rather than constrict, and that fact alone thrust upon it both the necessity and the opportunity for comprehensive economic planning.

In 1921 the State Planning Commission (*Gosplan*) came into being. At first this institution limited its activity to examining and passing upon the plans and programs devised for individual industries and activities, but as time passed this inevitably led toward their coordination in the form of a general plan for the economy as a whole.   The first attempt to provide exactly that came in 1925 when *Gosplan* experimented with assembling and comparing the various production schedules submitted to it, projecting these into the future and labeling the result a "plan."   It really was not; it was no more than a forecast, but it was a forecast which a little later was to culminate in real planning.   Before that could happen, however, certain additional steps involving primarily *changes in attitude* needed to be taken.

The 1925 "control figures"—the estimates, production schedules, and forecasts for the ensuing year—together with *Gosplan's* suggestions for solving the most urgent problems it expected to appear, were rejected by the Soviet Government, and they were rejected on the interesting ground that they were too "capitalistic." [3]   At this point a speculative digression may perhaps be permitted.

After the Bolsheviks had assumed power in Russia and had achieved a

[3] *Cf.,* Alexander Baykov, *The Development of the Soviet Economic System,* Cambridge, England, 1947; pp. 431–432.

measure of domestic order, they drew a sharp distinction between the technological knowledge of the West and its "bourgeois" social and economic institutions.   The former they admired and sought to imitate, but the latter they disavowed as representing the dead hand of a reactionary and obsolescent social system.   Two interesting consequences followed from this distinction.   First, foreign engineers and technicians who could be induced to accept employment in Russia were welcomed for their knowledge of how to make things work; at the same time, however, they remained suspect with respect to their ideas about how to organize institutions.   Accordingly, techniques of economic management perfectly familiar outside Russia and entirely capable of adaptation to Russian administrative needs were disdainfully rejected at first, only to be introduced in the end after a long period of improvisation and experiment.   We have already noticed how the Soviet economic structure, oriented throughout to the two fundamental objectives of industrialization and defense, has nevertheless undergone a series of reorganizations and mutations which may not yet have terminated.   For an understanding of the Russian system, therefore, the bare bones of its administrative structure are more important than its habiliments, and the pattern of its articulation is of greater moment than the details, or the names, of its forms of expression.

We must also remember that by 1925 the Russians had not yet had time to develop a new generation of their own technicians who would be without personal memories of their capitalist past.   They were still dependent, in other words, upon experts whose modes of thinking had been formed before or apart from the newer and presumably superior Soviet institutions then coming into being.   Under these conditions it is perhaps not surprising that the 1925 control figures seemed "capitalistic," nor that they were rejected. But precisely how were they "capitalistic"?

Primarily because they were derived from essentially the same kind of analysis developed and used by contemporary Institutes for Business Cycle Research in capitalist countries; [4] they were extrapolations of observed trends rather than plans for reaching a desired end; they were passive rather than active.   The essence of economic planning is the attempt to bring into existence conditions which would never appear by themselves, and that is just what the economists and statisticians who had prepared the 1925 control figures had not even attempted to do.   As a result they lost their jobs and party control over planning agencies was strengthened.

[4] *Ibid.*, pp. 432–434.

In the following year, therefore, the control figures for 1926–1927 were drawn up in the light of the kind of economic structure which it seemed desirable to develop.   Real attention, in other words, was paid to the classes and forces which seemed to be developing socialist institutions and to the dangers which might beset these.[5]   In this perspective, it soon became clear that a single year was too short a period in which to bring about significant changes in national economic development.   Five-year periods were accordingly substituted, and thenceforward—except for the war years in which the Soviet Union, like other belligerents, lived economically from hand to mouth—a succession of Five-Year Plans has governed the economic life of the country.   This emergence into a system of genuine planning is symbolized in the contemporaneous change which took place in the concept of the Industrial Trust.   Prior to 1927 this was a socialized institution, to be sure, but one of its primary purposes was the capitalistic one of earning profits for the state.   In 1927, however, the Model Charter drawn up for the Trusts dropped that requirement and replaced it by a clause requiring the Trusts to devote themselves to the fulfillment of planned assignments on terms approved by the appropriate planning agencies.[6]

THE AGENCIES OF PLANNING

GOSPLAN

The State Planning Commission (*Gosplan*) is at the apex of the economic hierarchy, and is, indeed, the center of the nervous system of the entire economy.   It is an advisory body without executive authority, although it is a subsidiary of the Council of Ministers which, as we have already seen, corresponds to the executive cabinet elsewhere.   It is organized functionally, with divisions corresponding to the major economic, social, and even cultural activities of the country; it has, for example, departments for mining, foreign trade, art, education, and many others.   It has close affiliations with Soviet research, technological and scientific institutes, and it operates an academy for training its own personnel.   Subordinate to it is a complicated system of subsidiary planning agencies which, as in fascist societies, are organized both territorially and functionally.

[5] *Ibid.*, p. 437.
[6] *Ibid.*, p. 426.

The Ministries

Each of the Constituent Republics has its own Planning Commission, as do the various provincial and local territorial units. It is the same with the functional governmental agencies. Each Ministry has a planning unit which, in turn, supervises the planning sections attached to the Trusts, Combines, or Collectives over which the Ministry has general jurisdiction. The system ramifies down to the planning groups belonging to all enterprises, factories, mines, farms, schools, hospitals and so on, to be found in the country.

The reason for this bifurcated system is the simple and obvious one that any effective plan has implications both for the activity which is subject to plan and for the place where the activity goes on. Accordingly, any plan submitted to the State Planning Commission by any territorial division, for example, must comprehend the plans of all enterprises to be found within the territory. One of *Gosplan*'s most important responsibilities is the reconciliation and coordination of the territorial and functional implications of approved plans.

THE PROCESS OF PLANNING

Character of the Plans

We have already intimated that Russian planning did not really come into existence until the Soviets had hit upon the device they call control figures, or constantly revised estimates of available resources and practicable output, and that after this point had been reached economic planning proceeded in five-year jumps.

It is important at this point to grasp precisely what these plans are. They are, *first,* political decisions as to how resources should be allocated, and *second,* economic decisions about how to make that allocation effective. The planners must decide upon what they are to concentrate: the development of heavy industry, for example, or the manufacture of consumers' goods; the provision of armaments or of agricultural equipment; or the production of goods for domestic consumption or for export. Planners must determine the location of new industries, right down to the decisions where particular new plants should be established and what each plant in the economy should produce.

These decisions determine the *direction* of economic activity. The *rate* of activity is determined by the resources at hand and the means for processing, transporting, and distributing them, all of which must be known to the planners, and in detail. Moreover, these two essential factors are mutually dependent: political decisions determine the way resources shall be used, but the availability of resources (and in the broadest sense) determines which political decisions are practicable.

So far, the Russians have found the basic political decisions, what to do, easier than the economic, how to do it. From the very beginning they have sought to industrialize, to develop heavy industry, and they have been willing to depress the standard of living in order to do this. In consequence, approximately one quarter of the national income has been applied to economic development from the very beginning.[7]

The Collection of Information

The starting point of each plan, therefore, is the collection of essential information as to resources. An estimate is made of the working population, excluding children, old folk, invalids, students, governmental employees, soldiers, and the like, for labor constitutes the basic resource. Questionnaires are then sent to every productive enterprise in the economy, covering its operations in the recent past, its current activities and its expectations for the immediate future. These statements must include figures concerning the numbers of workers of different grades and categories, the amounts and kinds of materials and components which have been or will be required, and the corresponding demands upon financial and transportation services. At the same time, retailing and marketing institutions of all kinds must report on the number of customers they have been supplying and expect to supply, with what kinds of goods and services and in what amounts, and they must state which of these they expect to procure from domestic sources and which must be imported from abroad. The state itself must estimate, largely on the basis of past records, what demands and output can be expected from individual peasants and nomads. Finally, similar information is sought from transportation, communication, and even cultural institutions. To secure all this, *Gosplan* maintains a corps of inspectors who are sent into the field to give assistance and to prod laggards.

[7] *Cf.*, A. R. Yugow, "The Economy of the Soviet Union," in R. J. Kerner, editor, *U.S.S.R. Economy and the War*, Russian Economic Institute, New York, 1943; p. 17.

Analysis of Information

Analysis of all this material enables *Gosplan* to derive, for each line of
production, figures showing the quantities of labor, fuel, materials, and so
on, that are needed to achieve a given output program.   The next step is to
examine these figures to see whether resources are, in fact, available to meet
this complex of output programs, both nationally and regionally.   The
whole calculation is complicated still further by the Russian desire, not
only for national self-sufficiency *vis-à-vis* the outside world, but also for a
measure of regional self-sufficiency in order to ease the strain upon the
transportation system.

Correlation of Information

In the meantime, the economic ministries, under guidance from the Party,
have been reaching decisions as to the direction and rate of further development and expansion, and these decisions from above have to be correlated
with the estimates of future activity which have come up from below.   *Gosplan* eventually emerges with a master plan for the allocation of all resources, and this is then passed down the line finally to reach every individual plant and enterprise for comment, for suggestions and for criticism, and
in the end for a breakdown into detailed, subordinate plans.   When these
have at last been returned, *Gosplan* is in a position to prepare the final,
definitive plan for the approval of the Government.   The Plan is thus an
estimate, made in advance, of what ought to be achieved; but not every
element in the complicated series of balances which comprise the plan is
susceptible of control, so that constant revision of the estimates is necessary.
The weather, for example, to say nothing of the carelessness or even interference of man, may prevent the delivery of the agricultural quota imposed
upon some collective farm.   As time passes, therefore, the annual and
quarterly plans take on the character of revisions of the basic Five-Year
Plan.   In the end, it is the quarterly plans which are the really operative
ones.

As far as physical resources are concerned, the plan is no more than a
procedure for shuffling things about and a technique for keeping track of the
results.   However, human resources are required as well as physical, and
this introduces two complications.   Human beings are not quite so easy to
manipulate, and they demand remuneration.   With the exception of in-

dividuals who can be assigned specific tasks, like members of the party or the unhappy victims of the forced labor system, the allocation of labor is on the whole determined in the long run by adjusting training opportunities open to young workers, and in the short run by campaigns to recruit labor for plants and industries in need of it and by setting differential wage rates in accordance with the "social value" of any kind of labor in scarce supply. The continual complaints about the high rate of labor turnover attest the resort to these devices in addition to the forced labor imposed upon those who incur the disfavor of the authorities.

The Effects of Planning on Prices

In contrast to free economies in which private expenditure is permitted to determine the direction of production, in Russia consumers' sovereignty neither exists nor is it wanted.[8] In Russia, accordingly, planners have the additional problem of preventing the price system from significantly influencing the allocation of resources; priorities take the place of prices. It is true that, even in Russia, excessive demand may be followed by higher prices, as happened between 1928–1935 and again during the Second World War. This happens because the Government permits it; it might just as easily impose rationing and hold prices as constant as it is able to. People obviously cannot purchase *more* than the total output of consumers' goods, and the volume of that output is determined by what resources are left over after the needs of heavy industry have been met. At the same time, however, Russians are unlikely to buy *less* than the total output of consumers' goods, for Russian living standards are still low and there is less incentive for personal saving (which reduces consumption) than elsewhere. Subsidies for children, the provision of free education, and the comprehensive social-security system shift to the state those financial responsibilities which in many other countries are borne by individuals out of their personal savings. Russian consumers, accordingly, are left free to spend their incomes on the goods and services permitted them under the plan; they are not free to change either the volume or the composition of what they are permitted to buy.

----

[8] We shall see in the following chapter that the state does take some pains to ascertain, and in some cases even to adapt its policy to, the character of consumers' demand.

The Effects of Planning on Savings

The volume of saving on a national scale, therefore, is largely determined by the planners, from above, rather than from below by the aggregate decisions of independent individuals; and its determination consists, quite simply, in deciding by how much the income distributed to consumers shall fall short of the national income. If prices are not to change, and they sometimes do, this decision must be consistent with the decision determining the allocation of resources between the heavy and consumers' goods industries. If the government fails to hold aggregate consumers' incomes to an amount which will clear the market at current prices, national saving still can be brought about by curtailing consumption either through inflation, or through rationing, or through a combination of both.

Thus savings, in the large, represent deferred or unsatisfied individual consumption. They may appear in some forms familiar to us, such as deposits in savings banks or purchases of state bonds. They may also, however, appear in less familiar guise: as planned or realized profits accruing to particular enterprises.

The Effects of Planning on Profits

Profits are planned by adding to the price of output a permitted margin over average, planned costs of production, allowing for regional and other peculiarities. Such planned profits represent savings rather than industrial success (to which *we* attribute profits), because they are calculated not by any standard of efficiency to which an enterprise presumably should be held, but by the prices deemed necessary to adjust aggregate demand to planned supply. The function of planned profits, therefore, is to reduce consumption. Sometimes, to be sure, planned profits may be negative; the firm is expected to incur a loss. The planning of loss, in this sense, occurs when the price a firm would have to charge in order to make a profit is too high to be consistent with the plan under which the firm, and its customers, operate. The firm is then subsidized.

Sometimes, also, the profits actually realized by a firm fail to correspond with the profits planned for it. In such cases the planned savings (corresponding to the planned profits of industry) are either greater or less than the realized savings (corresponding to realized profit). Discrepancies between planned and realized savings (or profits) are not necessarily un-desirable; they may even be useful.　If an excess of realized over planned profits in one firm, for example, is greater than in another firm, there is some reason to believe that the first firm is more efficient than the second. That information is useful to have.　Or, if an excess of realized over planned profits rises as time goes on, the conclusion might be drawn that efficiency was increasing.　That, too, is useful knowledge.　Both those kinds of knowledge are matters of concern to planning officials.

TYPES OF PLANS

The Production Plan

The core of the plan, then, is the program for capital construction which determines the relationships between different branches of industry which are to prevail within the planning period.　From these are derived, by the method of balancing resources against needs, the entire system of output programs for all the products of the economic system.

Planning of this sort may sound easy in principle, but has turned out to be highly complicated in detail.　In both preparation and implementation, a wealth of statistical information must be at hand, and it must be accurate, pertinent, and up-to-date.　That has not been easy to insure.　It is re-ported, in fact, that the Russians have had greater difficulty in checking the progress of their plans than in preparing the plans themselves.[9]　The sta-tistical procedure involved in both preparation and checking consists in striking certain significant balances.　The method was worked out simul-taneously with the development of the control figures to which, indeed, they are necessary.

Initially, balances were struck separately for important groups of com-modities—grains, metals, and so forth—as a necessary but still imperfect device for ascertaining whether the various sectors of the economy were developing in proper alignment with each other.　As facility increased, these balances came to be more purposefully compared with one another so that, when the 1928–1929 control figures were drawn up the balances themselves constituted the core of the plan for the ensuing year.[10]　This was possible

---

[9] Cf., Baykov, op. cit., pp. 452–453.
[10] For a fuller description, cf., ibid., pp. 437 ff.

because, with the balances brought into a system and properly coordinated, impending bottlenecks were immediately revealed, the kinds and volume of production needed to fulfill the assignments set forth in the plan became immediately evident, and, in result, the responsibilities assigned particular industries together with the capital expansion to be planned for each, and the composition and volume of imports and exports, could be more or less precisely determined. With this information at hand, GOSPLAN is in a position to coordinate separate balances into an integrated system, and this done, it can then very easily determine whether the program submitted to it by its subsidiary agencies and departments are mutually consistent and compatible with the approved plan.

All this, complicated as it is, constitutes only a production plan. Provision has still to be made for pricing the various products and for determining the incomes of the various workers engaged in these processes. Specifically, the production plan serves as a basis for formulating a credit, or financial, plan, a cash plan, and a system of prices. To these we must now turn.

The Financial Plan

The credit, or financial, plan is designed not only to facilitate the execution of the production plan, but also to enable its fulfillment to be watched and to insure against the improper use of resources.

Let us recall how both current operations and programs of capital development in both industry and agriculture are financed by a series of specialized banking institutions. (See page 314.) At the center is the State Bank of the U.S.S.R. (*Gosbank*), which operates as a central bank and as a source of short-term credit. The provision of long-term credit is the responsibility, according to the sector concerned, of the *Prombank* for industrial development, the *Selkhozbank* for agricultural expansion, the *Tsekombank* for municipal construction, and the *Vsekobank* for financing cooperative societies. There is also a savings bank which can be used as a source of short-term loans, but which usually invests its deposits in Soviet Government bonds.

Under a centrally planned economy, financial considerations tend to be subordinated to economic. Central banking consists primarily in facilitating the execution of the economic plan, and credit is extended to particular enterprises *not* according to their financial prospects, but only in amounts and for purposes consistent with the plan. Thus, the central bank and the central offices of the other banks exercise very little initiative, but they still exercise more than their various branches throughout the country. These are autonomous only for accounting purposes; they are expected to cover their expenses out of the interest and commissions they are permitted to charge, but in other respects these branches do little more than to keep accounts, make payments, and check applications for loans for compatibility with the plan.[11]

Procedure. The process of financial planning starts with the submission to the appropriate bank of applications for credit. These come from enterprises, farms, in fact from all the great variety of institutions which are preparing their programs for the impending planning period. Those applications are compared with the corresponding production plans and, when approved, are passed downward through the planning hierarchy until each operating unit knows its exact assignment and the financial resources to be made available for its fulfillment. At the beginning of each accounting period, therefore, every enterprise in the economy is provided with an amount of working capital theoretically just sufficient to enable it to carry out its expected minimum program. This fund is supposed to be divided into separate accounts for such things as fuel, wages, raw materials, and so forth; but beyond this, the firm has general control over its capital.

If, in the course of its activity, the enterprise finds it needs additional capital, it may apply to the appropriate bank, but any such application is subject to minute scrutiny. Banks grant credit only when they are satisfied that the loan is for purposes already approved under the plan, and they may recall loans which have been put to uses they consider improper.

Control by the ruble. Banks, moreover, must investigate the causes of any losses which appear, and they must examine invoices to assure themselves that price regulations are being observed. In addition to all this, the power of the banks extends still further to affect suppliers of raw materials and component parts. They may extend "transit credit" to finance the purchase of materials, but they may also, if they choose, withhold payment until the finished product has been sold.[12]

Planned loans, as the name indicates, are granted for approved purposes for which a firm's working capital is inadequate, and are automatically self-

[11] *Cf.,* W. B. Reddaway, *The Russian Financial System,* London, 1935; p. 18.
[12] *Cf.,* Leonard E. Hubbard, *Soviet Trade and Distribution,* London, 1938; p. 135.

liquidating as finished products are sold and the proceeds credited to the firm's account. By watching the rate at which these credits are liquidated, the banks are able to keep track of the progress of the production plan and to spot delays, hitches, and bottlenecks, with respect both to day-by-day operations and to each major accounting period.

Unplanned loans are also made to tide an enterprise over an emergency, such as the tying up of inventories as a result of congestion in the transportation system. These loans are made for very short periods, and, being indicative of difficulties, they occasion some sensitiveness.[13] Unplanned loans may also have to be made when the plan is revised; a firm having to adapt its activity to the revision of the plan may need supplemental credit.[14]

This system of financial control, or "control of the ruble" as it is sometimes called, serves as an effective checkrein upon the proclivity of industrial managers to hedge against potential trouble by accumulating and hoarding unnecessarily large inventories. It operates in three ways: (1) By rationing capital and controlling credit the authorities can keep inventories under firm control. (2) By making each enterprise an individual accounting unit and by planning its costs and prices so that the "normally" efficient firm will just pay its way, the income statements of other firms will either reveal inefficiency, or, in the case of exceptionally efficient firms, will enable the accumulation of a surplus which can be partly used for reinvestment within the firm, partly paid into the State Budget, and partly used as "socialized" wages—organized cultural or recreational activities—for the firm's employees. (3) By pooling the other portions of these surpluses, the government can keep capital development itself under control.[15]

Planned and unplanned profits. It is important to distinguish between the "planned" and "unplanned" profits of a Soviet enterprise. The former is the sum for which the plan provides and which ought to emerge if prices, costs, and volume actually do correspond to their planned quantities. Part of this planned profit, when realized, goes directly into the State Budget through taxation, part of it is paid into the fund held by the Prombank for financing capital development generally, and part is retained by the enterprise to be used for improving the working and living conditions of the labor

---

[13] "It does not do to press Soviet officials too much on the subject . . ." Reddaway, *op. cit.,* p. 34.
[14] *Cf.,* Maurice Dobb, *Soviet Planning and Labor in Peace and War,* New York, 1943; p. 38.
[15] *Cf.,* Reddaway, *op. cit.,* p. 27.

force. "Unplanned" profit comprises whatever may be earned in excess
of the planned figure; up to half of this is retained by the enterprise, and
may be used at the discretion of the management. Bonuses and premiums
are frequently paid from this sum to the laborers and staff members of the
fortunate enterprise.[16]

Taxation. About three quarters of the country's capital expenditure is
normally financed through the budget, supplemented by the reserves of the
Prombank. The government's income is largely derived from taxes, the
most important being the "turnover tax" which bears most heavily upon the
output of the consumers' goods industries. This tax is similar to a sales tax,
except that, formally, it is levied upon the industry rather than upon the
consumer; but it is passed on in the form of higher prices just the same. It
is extraordinarily high by Western standards, ranging from thirty per cent
to almost one hundred per cent *ad valorem*. The tax is concentrated upon
retail prices for two reasons: (1) it is useful to have that method of adjusting
prices paid by consumers to the amount of purchasing power possessed by
consumers, and (2), it is pointless to levy such a tax upon goods purchased
by industry, for to do that would mean, simply, that the government was
taxing itself. This is so because, since the state is the only consumer of
such products, the only effect of such a tax would be to increase the amount
of capital necessary to carry out the objectives of the Plan.[17] Government
funds are supplemented by the private savings deposited in the savings banks
or invested in Soviet bonds, and by the collective savings accumulated by the
methods already described. Through the budgets of the various banking
institutions, financial resources are concentrated in the hands of the state.
This results in their being used to foster the harmonious and even development of the national economy. Reddaway makes the observation that this
system gives to capital, as a factor of production, the full mobility taken for
granted by Western economic theorists, sometimes without empirical warrant.[18]

The financial plan consists, as we would expect, in a program of planned
receipts and expenditures. These, balanced against each other, indicate the
necessity for expanding or contracting the currency, and thus lead directly
to the formulation of the cash plan.

[16] *Cf.*, Hubbard, *op. cit.*, p. 199.

[17] *Cf.*, Reddaway, *op. cit.*, p. 20; Dobb, *op. cit.*, pp. 35–36; and Yugow, *op. cit.*,
p. 42. A more extended discussion of the State Budget and of the taxation system
will be found in the following chapter. (See pages 338, 340.)

[18] *Cf.*, Reddaway, *op. cit.*, p. 40.

The Cash Plan

In the Soviet Union, just as in other countries, the amount of currency that will be needed in any given period of time is a function (1) of the aggregate disbursements to be made, and (2) of the average time period elapsing between disbursement and the return of the cash to the issuing authority. The first of these, aggregate disbursements based upon the estimated number of transactions, is easily determined in the Soviet Union, at least as far as advance planning is concerned. For industry, the cash plan depends simply upon the total planned wages and salaries bill; for agriculture, it depends upon the planned payments to members of collective farms for compulsory deliveries of agricultural produce to the State, plus the estimated amount of currency needed for sales of agricultural produce on the free market. Revision of the production and financial plans bring corresponding adjustments in the cash plan.

The second factor significant for the cash plan, the velocity, or rapidity of turnover, of the currency is calculated regionally as well as nationally, and is based upon the return of currency to the state in the form of taxes, savings, or expenditures in the state stores. From these calculations each regional bank determines whether its holdings of cash seem to be adequate to meet expected withdrawals, whether it can retire part of its holdings, or whether it must draw upon the central bank for additional amounts.

More than this, the cash plan plays its part in facilitating the regional and local distribution of supplies. Each financial institution analyzes anticipated conditions in its territory for the purpose of determining the total value of the consumers' goods that will be needed in the coming planning period, and thereby is aided in its determination of the total amount of credit to be granted the various retail establishments.[19]

Under the Soviet system it is, in principle, not too difficult to plan the whole currency issue within fairly precise limits. The production plan fixes the output and the distribution of commodities, and the financial plan determines disbursements. Prices in the very substantial, socialized sector of the economy are planned, and so are incomes. Hoarding is no problem since most personal incomes are too low to provide much surplus, and savings pass through the channels previously described right back to the state. With most incomes disbursed by the state and the greater part of

[19] *Cf.*, Dobb, *op. cit.*, p. 39.

most incomes returning to the state, there is not much of anything left that is beyond the reach of state control.

THE PRICING SYSTEM UNDER PLANNING

The smooth operation of this system of inter-related plans for production and finance clearly depends on the consistency of those plans with the plans concerning prices and costs.   Prices are cumulatively built up by adding a planned profit to the planned costs (including provision for depreciation, overhead, and so on) of each enterprise.   That profit is usually calculated at rates varying according to the importance accorded the product; it is figured as a percentage upon turnover, and the aggregated total of all costs plus profit becomes the planned price at which the finished product will be credited to the producer when final delivery is made.

We have observed that unplanned, or efficiency, profits may also arise; in fact, they are encouraged as a sort of socialized incentive to economy and efficiency.   Since, however, these unplanned profits arise through success in reducing costs below their planned level, they do not constitute an ingredient of price in the way that planned profits do.

As we also have seen, efficiency can be tested by fixing planned prices on the basis of planned costs at each stage of the operations, and by then examining income statements to see how *realized* costs and prices correspond to their planned levels.   Here, however, one difficulty arises which has plagued other governments than the Russian in their experiments with price control.   When many plants of varying sizes and different degrees of efficiency all produce the same article, the costs of production in the several plants will not necessarily be the same, and this complicates the determination of a single price for their collective output.   The Russians have occasionally made allowance for this by permitting different prices to prevail in different regions, but more generally the Trusts have been utilized as economic shock absorbers to equalize these differences.

The Trusts, be it remembered, are organizations of all plants producing the same product.   These institutions serve as agents for assessing the planned cost of each enterprise, for comparing those costs, and for determining the average cost of production of the product for the economy as a whole.   Being an average, that cost is higher than the actual cost of the efficient plants, and less than the average cost of the inefficient; consequently, the Trust concerned must re-allocate planned costs and planned profits among its constituent members.   This the Trust does by purchasing, at different prices (based upon the particular costs of each enterprise), the entire output of the product.   That product is then re-sold at a single price determined by the Price Fixing Commission.   If the Trusts have normal skill in negotiating with their constituent plants the particular price to be paid each, on the basis of its own cost, the emergent single price for the product as a whole will bring about equality between the Trust's total receipts and its total expenses, including the cost of the Trust's own operations and its own profit.   A Trust which is more than normally efficient, in this sense, will reap an unplanned profit, which is treated exactly as unplanned profits arising elsewhere; and, contrariwise, a less than normally efficient trust will incur unplanned losses.

The sale price of any commodity is, therefore, essentially an accounting price at which transactions among various state enterprises take place. Since, until the final consumer is reached, the finished output of one industry is the raw material of the next, the price-forming process is cumulative until the final emergence of the market prices at which consumers' goods are bought.   At this final stage, the accounting price, which includes the costs and planned profits of manufacturers, of wholesale and retail distributors, and of transportation agencies, is transformed into market price by adding certain supplementary charges designed to equalize the demand and supply of particular goods.   The first of these charges is the turnover tax, already mentioned.   The second is a high supplemental tax paid by establishments which, for one reason or another, sell at higher prices than prevail elsewhere although the cost of their supplies is the same.   Throughout the entire Soviet system, the basic pricing principle is the simple one that the normally efficient enterprise should just pay its way.[20]

[20] For an elaboration of this discussion of pricing in the Soviet Union, *cf.*, Dobb, *op. cit.*, pp. 34–36; Reddaway, *op. cit.*, pp. 28–30; and Hubbard, *op. cit.*, *passim*.

16

The Soviet System in Operation

EVENTS and developments in Western countries have recently thrust upon economists cognizance of the importance of government as a factor in economic life. Quite apart from its deliberate control of much economic activity, government absorbs money through loans and taxation and that absorption influences both the willingness and ability of individuals to commit themselves to economic decisions. Government also spends, and its expenditure, likewise, has become increasingly significant and sometimes determinant as a force shaping economic ends, rough-hew them how men will. If this is true in capitalistic countries where economic decisions are, in principle, left to individual determination, how much more true it must be in Russia where government is both planner and entrepreneur!

THE STATE BUDGET

In Russia all the manifold activities we have been considering lead into, are reflected in, and are governed by the State Budget. The Budget is the means by which both the receipts and the expenditures of the state are classified and compared. Receipts comprise (1) the taxes levied upon individuals and institutions, (2) the profits accruing to state enterprises, and (3) even the savings accumulated by individuals.   Savings get into the Budget because the deposits in savings banks and the proceeds from the sale of Soviet bonds come under the disposal of the state.   Through the Budget, then, the financial resources of the nation are pooled.   The state's expenditures consist (1) of the disbursements normal everywhere for such things as administration, national defense, public health and education, but also (2) of most substantial advances for the development and maintenance of the fixed capital of the country.   Those expenditures represent the definitive formulation of the economic structure of the country.   National income is accumulated in the Budget and redistributed through it.   This being so, the Budget is necessarily correlated with the Economic Plan; the two, in fact, are usually approved together.   The Budget is essentially an index of the direction and rate at which the economy is developing, for the expenditures it authorizes constitute the financing of approved projects while the revenues it records represent the returns derived from projects under way.

The State Budget of the U.S.S.R. is a consolidated and most bulky document.   It is prepared by the All-Union Minister of Finance in collaboration with the Finance Ministers of the Constituent Republics.   These latter, in turn, do their part in conjunction with the finance officers of the territories and regions subordinate to them, and so on down to the separate communes and municipalities whose individual budgets are, so to speak, blended into the budgets of the administrative units immediately superior to them.   It is said that the final, comprehensive Budget, when approved by the Supreme Soviet, incorporates over 70,000 subordinate budgets.   All the multifarious financial transactions of all these units are handled by the State Bank (*Gosbank*).

Taken together, then, State Budget and Economic Plan constitute the system by which the Soviet economy is developed, oriented to its approved ends, and controlled.   The joint process of planning and budgeting commences with the analysis of the reports and figures which indicate the degree to which the Plan and Budget for the previous year have been fulfilled in actuality; these are then put together with the corresponding proposals for the following year.   Just as the really operative plan is the quarterly plan, so is the significant budget the quarterly one.   Also, just as the planning agencies employ field inspectors to assist them in their advisory and regulatory duties, so budgetary inspectors are employed to investigate and report upon budgetary difficulties and blockages wherever they may appear.

TAXATION

The Turnover Tax

The Turnover Tax, bringing in about fifty-five per cent of all state receipts, is the largest single source of revenue. This tax, however, is important for other reasons as well. It is a method for observing and controlling the financial behavior of enterprise, and, above all, it is a means of regulating prices.

Marketing institutions, like all others, are required to submit periodical financial statements. These are audited to determine the turnover of goods in the period concerned and the amount of the tax due at the established rates. This audit, by revealing the financial position of enterprises, also offers clues as to the adequacy of planned prices. That check upon how the financial plan is progressing is supplemented by an inquiry into the rate at which the production plan is being fulfilled. The turnover tax, there-fore, provides an opportunity for collecting, summarizing, and drawing oper-ative conclusions from information it compels enterprises to provide.

We know that prices are planned, and we also know that they are planned to bring the effective demand for a commodity into alignment with its planned supply as fixed in advance. The activities and needs of particular enter-prises are irrelevant to that purpose.

Reminiscent of the classical economists in nineteenth-century England, Soviet economists regard the *actual cost* of goods as equal to the aggregate wages expended on their production and distribution.[1] Marx himself was a classical economist in a sense, and the labor theory of value (see pages 165–171) which loomed so large in classical analysis lives on today primarily in its Marxian habitat.

In contrast with actual cost the *social cost* of the totality of goods produced includes the wages and salaries paid to everyone, regardless of whether or not they are engaged in physical production. Here, also, the analysis is reminiscent of the classical distinction between "productive" labor, engaged in the production of material, storable, valuable goods, and "unproductive" labor, otherwise, although not necessarily, uselessly employed. Within such an analytical context, the income-price relationship which is planned must

[1] *Cf.*, Alexander Baykov, *The Development of the Soviet Economic System,* Cambridge, England, 1947; p. 368.

insure that the output of "productive" labor is shared with "unproductive" workers; prices, thus, must be high enough to prevent "productive" labor from consuming all its own output.

The difference between actual and social cost, then, depends upon the proportion of the population engaged in the production of consumers' goods (upon which the great part of all personal income is expended) to the population otherwise occupied. Suppose some laborers are diverted from the production of consumers' goods by being drafted into the army. The *actual* total cost of all goods produced will then fall, because fewer goods are produced, but their *social* cost will not fall (at least in proportion), because the drafted soldiers continue to receive incomes although they are no longer producers. Assume, for simplicity, that total expenditure remains unchanged: a smaller proportion of that expenditure is devoted to productive activity, but a larger one to unproductive. *One of the purposes of the turnover tax is to absorb the difference between actual and social cost.*

All the foregoing is simply another way of saying something that has already been said—that the Soviet Union has always been under some degree of inflation because the Soviet Government has been unwilling to produce the quantity of consumers' goods that the Russian people would like to purchase and, at stable prices, could afford to purchase. The turnover tax is designed to relieve people of whatever portion of their incomes is "surplus" —surplus in the sense that there are no goods which that surplus could buy at prevailing prices.

In other words still, the planned cost plus planned profit on an item of consumption is an accounting concept calculated according to the financial plan for *industry;* to make the planned price consistent with the financial plan for *consumers,* the turnover tax is added to the planned price, and at a level that will bring the effective demand for the item of consumption into alignment with its planned supply. The tax is added to price instead of simply raising the price itself, because the state sees no reason why industry rather than the Treasury should receive the yield, particularly since the planned price incorporates an allowance for normal profit.

On most industrial goods the tax is fixed at a given percentage of the planned price (that is, planned cost plus planned profit). On agricultural goods which, be it remembered, are not always sold at fixed prices, the tax is usually a fixed sum per unit of quantity.

Turnover tax rates vary from commodity to commodity and sometimes from region to region. They also vary according to the proportion in which any class of goods is expected to be consumed by individuals or by industry. There is little pyramiding of the tax; once a tax is levied, the taxed commodity passes into consumption without further imposition, except that in cases in which a commodity is made from a previously taxed material, a second, much lighter tax is sometimes added. Like a sales tax, the Russian turnover tax brings a continuous flow rather than a bunched access of revenue to the Treasury.

Personal Income Taxation

Like most other countries today, Soviet Russia imposes a graduated personal income tax upon its citizens. In three respects, however, the Russian system differs from systems prevailing elsewhere. *First,* it is aggregatively rather unimportant, bringing in only about nine per cent of public revenue. *Secondly,* because a substantial part of rural incomes are paid in kind, income taxation in the countryside takes the form, to a considerable degree, of payment in produce rather than in money. *Thirdly,* and most important of all, is the fact that the Russian income tax is graduated according to the relative social desirability of different occupations. Here, also, the tax is as much a method of social control as a source of revenue. Some illustrations will make this clear.[2]

Wage earners receive comparatively high exemptions and pay taxes at relatively low rates. In 1940, a laborer with a 12,000 ruble income paid 42 rubles plus seven per cent on that portion of his income exceeding 12,000 rubles. Professional men were less fortunate; they paid eight per cent on the first 1,800 rubles, then a fixed tax ranging up to a maximum of 86,364 rubles on incomes exceeding 300,000 rubles plus fifty per cent upon that part of their incomes above 300,000 rubles. Craftsmen, artisans and other self-employed workers fared still worse. They paid a fixed tax of forty-eight rubles on the first 1,800 rubles of income, plus six per cent on the excess over 1,200 rubles. In the higher brackets, the fixed tax was 8,952 rubles plus sixty per cent on incomes above 24,000 rubles. Worst of all were the unhappy recipients of incomes classified as unearned. They paid slightly over thirty-eight per cent on incomes up to 5,000 rubles, and at steeper rates thereafter culminating at eighty-seven per cent on incomes

[2] Like so much in this section, most of this material is taken from Baykov, *op. cit.,* pp. 381–384.

above 24,000 rubles. Servicemen, however, and the holders of certain medals and decorations were exempted from income tax.

Corresponding discrimination existed in agriculture. Collective farmers fared best, individual peasant farmers next, and those receiving unearned incomes paid the steepest taxes.

Subsidiary Taxes

Brief mention may be given four other taxes which were, essentially, forms either of the turnover tax or of the profits tax about to be described. Enterprises which manufactured or processed goods made from materials supplied by their customers paid a revenue tax, as did enterprises performing various kinds of services. Movie theaters paid a tax on their box office receipts. Cooperative associations were among a group of public institutions subject to income tax. Finally, and more as a method of financial control than as a source of revenue, collective farms were obliged to pay a monetary income tax.

The Profits Tax

For the sake of symmetry, the contribution to the State Budget paid by enterprises within the socialized sector of the economy have been classified as taxes, although some may prefer to call these dividends paid by enterprise to its only stockholder. It is, at any rate, the government and not the management that determines the rates and conditions of payment. Whatever the nomenclature, the tapping of profits yields revenue which has characteristically been used for new capital investment.[3]

Part of its earned profit is, of course, retained by enterprise to swell its working capital, its resources for its own development subject to plan, and the Director's Fund.[4] The balance is paid into the State Budget. This withdrawal from earned profit comes, of course, out of realized rather than planned profit; the *rate* of deduction, however, is set in the financial plan. For this purpose, enterprises have been classified into three groups.

In the *first* group are enterprises whose revenues either fall short of, or

[3] It has not been a substantial source of revenue. In 1949, for example, the profits tax was estimated to yield only eight hundredths of one per cent of total revenue. *Cf., The Economist,* London, March 26, 1949; pp. 564–565.

[4] *Cf.,* Baykov, *op. cit.,* p. 374.

at best do no more than equal, the expenditures planned for them.   In these cases, even if developmental expenditure has to be supplemented by grants from the State Budget, some profit is withdrawn by the state, but at the minimum rate of ten per cent.[5]   The purpose is not revenue but the checking of the success with which the enterprise is fulfilling its planned assignment.

In the *second* group are the enterprises whose incomes exceed planned normal expenditure but which are earmarked for expansion beyond their own immediate financial reach.   In these cases, deductions from profit range between ten and eighty-one per cent, depending upon the particular proportion prevailing in each case between income and planned developmental expenditure.

The *third* group includes those enterprises whose incomes, again, exceed planned expenditure but for which no expansion is projected.   Since the sole use of retained profit in these cases is to augment the Director's Fund, these deductions from earned profit are exacted at the maximum rate of eighty-one per cent.

All these payments are assessed quarterly, but within each quarter they are paid into the State Budget monthly.   Here also, then, is a source of continuous revenue to the Treasury.   But like so many of the forms of payment we have been describing, provision of revenue is not the only purpose of Russian taxation of profits.   The system is used also to control the uses to which enterprises put their assets and to make possible a continuing check upon the correspondence between planned and realized accumulations of capital.   For purposes of control, the profits tax and the turnover tax complement each other.   The former is adjusted to the *financial* activities of enterprise, while the latter is oriented toward the supply and demand of *commodities*.

CONTROL BY THE STATE BANK

All payments into and expenditures from the Budget pass through the State Bank (*Gosbank*), possibly the largest and almost certainly the most secretive financial institution in the world.   With its four thousand branches extending into the satellite countries and its monopoly of short-term credit,

[5] Baykov, *op. cit.*, p. 375.

note issue, and foreign exchange, its services as financial agent of the government and as tax collector and its responsibility for auditing the operations of the economy of the entire Soviet empire, *Gosbank* has indeed the power to bind and the power to loose.

We have seen (see page 316) that the primary function of the Bank is the provision of credit to Russian enterprise for purposes approved in the Plan. Since *Gosbank* also assists in the determination of those purposes and oversees their realization, it serves as both legislator and executive. With the passage of time its executive function has become steadily more important, and appears now to be directed to fostering the profitability of enterprise. It is reported, in fact, that *Gosbank* will no longer extend credit to an enterprise which cannot show a profit.[6]

A turning point in Russian financial history was the reform of 1930. Till then, there had been a general tendency to expand credit, partly because grants of credit were made automatically according to approved plans which were sometimes over optimistic, partly because the managers of enterprise tended to play safe by overstating their need for credit. The reform introduced in that year consisted generally in tightening what has come to be known as "control by the ruble." A system of so-called "loan accounts" was introduced to distinguish between current and credit transactions, and attention came increasingly to be directed to the *particular* operations of enterprise. Buying and selling transactions between enterprises had to be expressed in individual and most detailed contracts, with penalties for default. The Second World War loosened this system somewhat, but a 1949 decree reimposed financial penalties for breach of contract and reemphasized the maintenance of quality.

Types of Deposits

All Russian enterprises keep their funds as deposits in *Gosbank,* but these deposits are of two kinds: (1) "clearing" accounts that correspond to ordinary bank deposits in this country, and (2) "loan" accounts that represent indebtedness to the bank. In the United States the same bank account serves both purposes; it is made up both of the cash paid in by the depositor and of whatever credit the bank extends him when he borrows from the bank. In Russia, credits are segregated.

[6] *Cf., The Banker,* London, June, 1952; pp. 327–330.

Concept of Working Capital

A Russian firm ordinarily borrows when its working capital is insufficient for the expenditures approved for the firm under the Plan. Essentially, it is the definition of approved expenditures that underlies the distinction between the two kinds of deposit. "Clearing" accounts are adjusted to norms established for each enterprise. Those norms represent the working capital calculated as necessary to maintain minimum stocks of materials over a stipulated period of time. If the minimum stock, however, is underestimated, or if the prices at which that stock can be bought should rise, the "clearing" account will no longer suffice to maintain the norm, and a "loan" account becomes necessary. Solvent enterprises control their own "clearing" accounts; the Bank may debit them on its own initiative only when a firm falls into arrears.[7]

Working capital, then, is used for normal, current expenditure at some constant rate. Expenditure exceeding that "normal" rate is sometimes necessary for seasonal or other reasons, and the "loan" account is drawn upon for these. Before authorizing loans of this character, it is customary for the Bank to verify the "clearing" account to ascertain whether this could be used instead. At each stage of production or distribution, therefore, some form of credit is brought into being which is liquidated when the transaction is completed. Assignment and supervision of those credits gives *Gosbank* its control over enterprise.

The contracts made between enterprises must, of course, conform to the planned programs for the production and financing of goods; they must be consistent, in other words, with the production plan, the financial plan, and the cash plan. The total of all these programs is nothing other than the current Economic Plan, promulgated by the Government with the force of law. As we have previously stated, the primary agencies for planning are the State Planning Commission (*Gosplan*), the State Bank (*Gosbank*) and the appropriate Ministries. It is the responsibility of *Gosbank* to audit each transaction initiated according to plan.

At this point, a second general principle is brought into play to reinforce the first, "control by the ruble." It is nothing else than strict business accounting (*Khozrashot*), designed to check the economy and profitability of each separate transaction. To *foster* these, a third general principle, "socialist emulation," is resorted to. This is simply the encouragement of

[7] *Cf.*, Baykov, *op. cit.*, p. 403.

competition among enterprises to reduce costs, increase efficiency, and expand profits. The encouragement consists both in the possibility of retaining a part of the unplanned profits which may accrue, and in the likelihood that sooner or later failure will recoil unpleasantly upon unsuccessful management.

The relationship between enterprise and the State Bank has thus come to be based upon the behavior of profits which appear as deposits in *Gosbank*. An unplanned increase in these deposits represents an expansion of profits signifying, usually, an unexpected increase in efficiency. We have already discussed the disposition of these windfalls. An unplanned reduction in these deposits is followed by an investigation by the Bank, and sometimes also by inquiry on the part of the planning agencies concerned with the plant and industry affected. Profits, therefore, play a real role in the Soviet economy. As in the West, the behavior of profit is presumed to be correlated with a firm's efficiency; unlike the West, however, profit, though important, is subordinate to the general Plan as the determinant of whether a firm should expand, contract, remain as it is, or even close. As in the West, however, the management of a firm which fails to earn at least planned profit has occasion for apprehension.

THE CHRONIC PROBLEM OF INFLATION

The Russian system is essentially a means of allocating resources among competing uses. Apart from technical difficulties, this process is generally simple and straightforward as far as inert and inanimate resources are concerned. The matter is not quite so simple with respect to the allocation of labor resources, partly because, for the nation as a whole, inducement rather than naked coercion is involved (although coercion is not unknown), and partly because the inducements offered have consequential economic significance; for labor, unlike other resources, has income to spend. Since, in Russia, nearly all *personal* income consists of wages,[8] the basic decisions on

---

[8] The state being the only landowner, rent is paid to it and not to persons. There being no private enterprise to speak of, there is no private profit. The supplementary incomes received by members of collective farms through selling their own produce do contain elements of profit, but these are quantitatively small and functionally insignificant. While interest is paid on Soviet bonds, it is not unreasonable to classify this, together with pensions and social insurance payments either as deferred wages

wage policy represent simply the obverse of the basic decisions respecting
the allocation of resources to the consumers'-goods industries.   At least,
it should be that; but even if it is, it clearly does not do to push the point
further by attempting to correlate wage policy in *particular* industries with
the allocation of resources *among the different* consumers'-goods industries.

In a scarcity-ridden economy like the Russian, any discrepancy between
these two basic decisions can only appear in the form of an excess of purchasing power over the quantity of consumers' goods available at current
prices.   This excess may be reduced by drawing off part of it into deposits
in savings banks or by stimulating purchases of government bonds, both of
which the Russians have done; it may be counteracted by adjustments in the
turnover tax to relieve pressure on scarce commodities, which also have been
made.   Unless, however, these mitigants are applied promptly and dras-
tically, the danger of an inflationary rise in prices is present as long as the
casual discrepancy persists.

Some have argued that cumulative general inflation is impossible under
the Soviet system:

> It may be said, indeed, that the Soviet ruble notes operate over the whole
> range of buyers' transactions almost precisely as postage stamps everywhere oper-
> ate in the single commodity of postal service.   An unnecessarily large supply of
> postage stamps in the pockets of the people does not raise the postage rates, nor
> cause any greater number of letters to be sent to certain places rather than
> others.   A scarcity of postage stamps has equally no effect in lowering postage
> rates and none whatever in our choice of persons to whom we choose to write.[9]

That is perfectly true, but it is scarcely relevant.   The same thing could
be said of any currency restricted to a single type of purchase—in this case
mail service—for which the demand is generally independent of price.
Russian rubles are money, usable to purchase anything available in the
market, and the Russian problem has been one of too much money chasing
too few goods.   At times the problem has been so acute that drastic action
has had to be taken: rationing is one example; the compulsory exchange
of bank notes and the writing down of bank deposits shortly after the Second
World War is another.[10]

The danger of inflation has existed throughout Soviet history, and largely

---

or as the redistribution of incomes originally paid as wages.   *Cf.,* W. B. Reddaway,
The Russian Financial System, London, 1935; p. 53.

[9] Sidney and Beatrice Webb, *Soviet Communism: A New Civilisation?* 2d. edition,
Charles Scribner's Sons, New York, 1938; Vol. II, p. 1195.

[10] See below, pp. 356–357.

for the same reasons that have caused reductions in the value of the American dollar during and after every one of the major wars in which the United States has participated.[11] This being so, the significant question, perhaps, is not why the Russians have been exposed to inflation, but why they have not had more of it.

Control of Inflation

Sheer authoritarianism is doubtless part of the answer; the state has been both willing and able to take very severe measures indeed to counteract inflationary pressures. Certain aspects of the Russian system facilitate both the willingness and the ability to do so.

Except perhaps for the peasantry (who, like independent farmers, presumably wish for high prices), there are no classes in Russia with a vested interest in inflation, and in any case an authoritarian society has recourses for control that are intolerable in democracies. There are, moreover, no inter-personal creditor-debtor relationships to complicate the issue, and in particular, there is no *rentier* class which a serious rise in prices would threaten with extinction.

Moreover, the Soviet State has a nearly complete monopoly over sales of all kinds, so that in Russia any inflationary fever to get rid of money before prices rise still further has the effect of increasing governmental rather than private income. Under other systems, inflation tends to be cumulative because the mounting difficulty of meeting public expenses forces governments to borrow in increasing volume. In Russia, higher prices on sales to consumers benefit the Treasury, so that unless state expenditures increase in proportion, enough revenue should eventually flow in to finance the investment in heavy industry which being at the expense of consumption may have started the trouble in the first place; and at this point the inflation should be arrested. To put the matter another way: when the state pays people to produce things which are not to be offered for public sale, the expenditure of those incomes will increase the potential effective demand for things which are *not* being produced in sufficient quantity because resources are being used to produce other things. The scramble to procure what little

[11] We have already suggested that the Soviet economy is essentially a *Wehrwirtschaft*, an economy oriented toward military power. That is to say, the major economic effort of the U.S.S.R. has always consisted in the manufacture of things which never enter the consumers'-goods market although the wages expended in their manufacture constantly seek that market.

there is will force prices up, and this process will continue until prices are high enough to absorb all the purchasing power of all workers, regardless of how they are employed.   As long as the total amount of purchasing power is not increased still faster, particularly as long as wages are not so increased, inflation is simply one means by which government can get what it wants in a world in which resources are insufficient to meet all needs.   Unless governmental needs continually rise, inflation will have served its purpose when the government has got what it wants.

In spite of these factors, inflation in Russia is not essentially different from inflation anywhere else.   The most capitalistic of governments can also meet its needs by keeping its expenditures one jump ahead of inflationary price increases, provided it can stand the political consequences; and periods of war have been those in which just that has characteristically happened.

When inflation does occur, the ones who suffer are those whose incomes remain relatively fixed, no matter what the economic system under which they happen to live.   In a capitalistic system, however, one can predict which classes or groups will fall behind in this sense, but under communism one can only say that inflation bears most heavily upon whatever classes remain financially neglected, whether by accident or design.   On the other hand, under capitalism one can predict which classes will be able to compete with the government for resources that are scarce because their incomes have kept pace with inflation; under communism, it is unlikely that any such competition will appear at all.

The Goods Famine: Causes

At any rate, Soviet Russia has undergone a "goods famine" throughout most of its history, a famine which expressed itself in the much publicized bare shelves and long queues which every retail shopper experienced.   It should now be clear that the rationing system which prevailed until 1935 and which was reintroduced during the Second World War, was not an attempt to mitigate a condition which the state was powerless to remove entirely; it was a compromise, to make as palatable as possible a condition which the state had deliberately fostered.   The goods famine was the result of three factors, each of which the Soviet Government considered it essential to retain.

First, such economic incentives as differential wage rates and preferential access to housing and other scarce supplies were utilized to attract labor into

favored occupations.[12]   This resort to incentives necessarily had the result
of increasing the demand for scarce consumers' goods.

Second, the increased individual employment consequent upon the program of economic development resulted in raising aggregate payrolls, and
this reinforced consumers' pressure upon supplies.   Some idea of the magnitude of these two factors, taken together, may be gleaned from the report
that during the period of the first Five-Year Plan, the number of workers
in industry approximately doubled, while the total wages and salaries bill
about quadrupled.[13]

Third, the primary emphasis in the employment of these workers was on
increasing industrial capacity and providing for national defense, rather
than on manufacturing consumers' goods.[14]   The result had to be the sterili-
zation, somehow, of workers' incomes, or else an increase in prices.   As a
matter of fact, both happened, but in ways that seem strange to dwellers
under other systems.

This strangeness arose because the existence of the three factors which
explain the goods famine involved the Russians in certain inconsistencies.
Thus, reliance upon economic incentives is inconsistent with the discouragement of consumption; the rationing of consumers' goods tends to deprive
a monetary system of meaning because money cannot be freely spent; price
inflation renders the maintenance of constant wage rates increasingly difficult, while to increase wages both accelerates the inflationary forces and
deprives them of their serviceability to a socialist state bent upon capital
development.

THE WAGE SYSTEM

The incentive wage system has had at various times three main forms in
the Soviet Union.   (1) Piece rates are depended upon to increase productivity; (2) differential wages are among the devices used to attract labor to

---

[12] As Dobb has pointed out, this did not mean the reintroduction of the profit
motive.   It is the Soviet State rather than the self-interest of individual entrepreneurs
which determines what shall be done.   In other words, economic incentives represent
a subordinate device at the disposal of a socialized economy but not the principle by
which such an economy functions.   *Cf.,* Maurice Dobb, *Soviet Planning and Labor
in Peace and War,* New York, 1943; pp. 7 *et seq.*

[13] *Ibid.,* p. 49.

[14] *Cf.,* Leonard E. Hubbard, *Soviet Trade and Distribution,* London, 1938; p. 264.

the more essential industries; and (3) supplemental or cheaper rations are used to entice labor into industries where labor is badly wanted.

Piece rates, particularly after the emergence of the Stakhanovite movement (see page 288), did become correlated with increased output per man. But two difficulties also appeared. (1) An increase in output may also arise from more or better capital equipment, or from improved techniques of management, and in such cases increased wages would not represent increased effort or skill on the part of labor. (2) Even if piece rates do stimulate labor to greater effort or to greater economy of effort, if these improvements become imitated and then diffused throughout the industry and the workers employed in it, the gains resulting from increased productivity may be swallowed up in increased wage costs. Moreover, the Soviet system, like any other, must continually keep deciding whether to pass the fruits of increased productivity on to labor or to retain them in the hand of government, and if the former, it must decide whether to pass them on in the form of increased wages to the labor directly concerned or to diffuse them generally in the form of lower prices. The Russians have done a little of each. The wage system is still based upon piece rates, but at the same time the unions are constantly reminded that the welfare of their members should be gauged more by the productivity of the economy as a whole than by the financial position of the firm or industry in which workers happen to be employed. And labor costs [15] have been restrained from mounting by either raising wages in somewhat less proportion than the increase in output, or by periodically revising upwards the estimates of normal output per man upon which piece rates are based, as improved techniques become diffused among the mass of workers.[16]

The chronic shortage of consumers' goods—which is at once a cause and a result of the industrialization program—has also complicated the reliance upon incentives to attract labor to the heavy industries. For the sake of political stability, if for no other reason, any severe shortage of basic necessities makes imperative the control of supply, but at the same time the control of supply makes it difficult for laborers to spend the larger incomes and hence deprives the larger incomes themselves of part of their allure. The problem is to assure some minimum standard of living for all without destroying incentives by reducing everyone to the same low level. The Russians have

[15] Labor costs per unit of output must of course be distinguished from wage rates per man. If output per man increases faster than wages per man, wage rates may rise while labor costs fall.

[16] Cf., Dobb, op. cit., pp. 80–89.

met the difficulty by a series of compromises which underlie their bewildering and ever-changing marketing system. But the fundamental principle throughout has been that of preferential allocation; it is a principle embodied in the Soviet Constitution.[17]

We shall consider later the workings of that marketing system, but let us first look at the organization and operation of the Russian unions whose members are the recipients of the wages we have been describing.

THE ORGANIZATION OF LABOR

Russian labor unions are organized industrially rather than by craft; that is, all workers employed in the same industry, regardless of their individual trades, belong to the same union. There are nearly two hundred national unions which merge, upward, into the All-Union Congress of Trade Unions, and extend downward to incorporate the local unions comprising members employed in the same plant. Although membership is voluntary, something like four fifths of the Russian labor force belong to one union or another. This may be so because union members have preferential rights to such things as the allocation of houses and in the selection of groups to visit vacation resorts. It probably is also true because what is "voluntary" in totalitarian systems frequently has suggestive overtones not to be found in more casual civilizations. One such suggestive element is the fact that the leadership of Russian unions comes from the Communist Party.

Most of the activities of Soviet unions are carried through by elected committees on which roughly one fifth of the total membership is active. These activities fall into five main groups. *First,* the social insurance system, to which both enterprise and government contribute, is administered by the unions. *Second,* much recreational, cultural, and general service activity is undertaken by the unions. Nursery schools are maintained for the children of working mothers, rest homes in the countryside are constructed by the national unions, concerts are sponsored, workers' education is encouraged, and so on. *Third,* criticism of management is a responsibility entrusted to unions at all levels. Local unions, for example, may pry into all

[17] Article 12: In the U.S.S.R. work is a duty and a matter of honor for every able-bodied citizen, in accordance with the principle: "He who does not work, neither shall he eat." The principle applied in the U.S.S.R. is that of socialism: "From each according to his ability, to each according to his work."

phases of the operations of a plant and may suggest sweeping reforms.   At
the other extreme, Ministers of State are frequently invited to union meetings at which they are exposed to questioning and sometimes to quite sharp
criticism.   *Fourth,* grievances are sent initially to joint standing committees
on which both labor and management are represented.   In case of dead-
lock, the matter is referred to the courts, which have final jurisdiction.
Grievances frequently arise because the managers of enterprise, who are
personally responsible for reducing costs and maintaining efficiency, are
under constant temptation to interpret the labor laws in their own way.
The unions, however, have a powerful voice in drafting those laws and have
an interest in defending their own interpretation of them.   *Fifth,* and finally,
unions concern themselves with industrial efficiency and are frequently assigned the responsibility for tackling special problems, such as absenteeism.
There is one thing that Russian unions do *not* do: they do not call strikes.

THE MARKETING SYSTEM

The now familiar shortage of consumers' goods which has been chronic
in the U.S.S.R. has meant that a rationing system has been necessary during
most of Soviet history.   To be sure, rationing was abolished in 1935 when
basic necessities became somewhat more abundant, but it had to be temporarily re-established during the Second World War.   Under this system
workers were graded both according to occupation (workers in essential
industry, for example, being given preference) and according to physical
need (special favors being given children, expectant and nursing mothers,
etc.).   Rationing, moreover, was peculiar in that (1) rations were not
maxima but purported to be guaranteed minima; and (2) alongside the
rationing system was the complicated marketing system which enabled individuals with spare cash to supplement their basic rations, although at higher
prices.   The system, however, had its imperfections.

During the period of wartime rationing, for example, Russians were supposed to be able to buy up to the limit of the coupons assigned them and at
prices intended to assure a minimum standard of living to all.   This was
the purpose of the state-operated coupon stores, open only to coupon-
holders.   Alongside these stores, however, were government-operated
"commercial" stores in which "surpluses" were freely sold at substantially

higher prices. Unfortunately, all too often these "surpluses" represented supplies diverted from the coupon stores to stock what amounted to an official black market. A Gilbertian touch, to bring that market within the pale of respectability, took the form of giving cards authorizing substantial discounts from "commercial" store prices to such favored citizens as soldiers and artists.[18]

Foreshadowing the second abolition of rationing in December, 1947, was a decree of November, 1946, requiring the cooperative stores to reintroduce the sale of foodstuffs and certain manufactured goods in cities and in workers' settlements. They were required, specifically, to be more active in purchasing from collective farms; those purchases were to be at free prices, but the sales price to consumers, while intended to be profitable to the cooperatives, could not exceed the prices at which "commercial" stores were selling the same supplies without coupons. This appears to be the imposition of a measure of competition.

The free, peasant market continues to exist, and it remains relatively uncontrolled. State stores, however, and factory canteens, and cooperatives are required to post the prices they charge, the weights and measures they use are supervised, and their giving of full measure is checked by a corps of public inspectors. Consumer credit does not exist, but a substitute for it has been found in the form of a kind of installment buying in reverse; the delivery of anything that is ordered and on which a down payment has been made is withheld until the final payment is made.

One result of the Soviet rationing system—indeed, to some extent, its purpose—was to reduce the connection between income and consumption. The purchasing power of an individual depended not only upon his income, but also upon his ration category, upon his membership or otherwise in a closed cooperative or factory store, and upon the particular priority of the cooperative to which he belonged, if any, and of the factory by which he was employed.[19] Moreover, where larger money incomes were paid, their price impact was concentrated upon the peasant markets and the "commercial" stores.

---

[18] Cf., Irving B. Kravis and Joseph Mintzes, "Soviet Union: Trends in Prices, Rations, and Wages," *Monthly Labor Review*, July, 1947.

[19] Cf., Dobb, *op. cit.*, pp. 54–56.

THE PRICE SYSTEM

It was no easy administrative task to assign to different stores and factories priorities which would be consistent with differential money wage rates.   The Soviets have always looked forward to the day when a single price system, under which everyone could buy the same item for the same price, could be established.   Accordingly, two separate attempts to achieve such a system have been made: one in 1935, before the Second World War; the second in 1946–1947 after that war came to an end.

The *first* of those attempts involved the abolition of rationing, resort to the turnover tax, and use of the savings and state loan systems for the purpose of insuring that the *real* differences between different-sized incomes would not be as great as the *money* differences.   The tax was adjusted so that price increases tended to be concentrated upon non-essentials and luxuries,[20] and some inducement was offered to postpone consumption through making savings more remunerative.

The *second* of those attempts merits more attention, because the financial consequences of the war made the task more difficult.

Currency Reform and the Second Abolition of Rationing

After the end of the Second World War, the Soviet Government again wished to establish a single price system, but the task was complicated by the existence of a great deal of liquid purchasing power whose expenditure on derationed commodities threatened to jeopardize any reform.   Peasants, no less in Russia than elsewhere, had profited from the free market (which in other countries was called "black") and other citizens had substantial savings in the form of savings-bank deposits, government bonds, and plain cash.   There was also the problem of the great disparity between the prices charged in "coupon" and "commercial" stores.

The first step toward reform was taken in 1946 when "commercial" prices were reduced simultaneously with substantial increases in the prices of rationed goods.[21]   At the same time, the wages of low-bracket workers were raised to enable them to meet the higher cost of rationed goods.   The pur-

[20] *Ibid.,* p. 58.
[21] *Cf.,* Kravis and Mintzes, *op. cit.*

pose of these moves was, purportedly, to wipe out a considerable part of the personal savings accumulated during the Second World War, partly to reduce the effective demand for food to the point at which scarce supplies would go around, and partly to reduce still further consumption by "non-productive" citizens.[22]

The second move came on December 14, 1947, when rationing was abandoned and a new currency introduced. Between December 16 and 22, all outstanding currency was called in for exchange at the rate of one new ruble for ten old ones, and thereafter the old currency was declared invalid.[23]

Bank deposits, also, were revalued according to a scale sliding with the size of the deposit. The exchange was one ruble for one upon the first 3,000 rubles; then two new for three old rubles were given upon that portion of deposits between 3,000 and 10,000 rubles; thereafter, one new ruble was given for two old. Deposits of cooperative societies and collective farms were exchanged at the flat rate of four new for five old rubles. Interest on government bonds was reduced from four per cent in most cases, to two per cent, and the bonds themselves were revalued at the rate of one new ruble for three old ones. Most contractual payments, such as interest on the indebtedness of enterprises, taxes, wages, and so on, were paid in new rubles at the old rate.

With the abolition of rationing, a complicated repricing of different commodities took place, of which only one or two illustrations will be given. Textiles, shoes, and clothing were reduced in price to about thirty-five per cent of their old "commercial" prices, while the prices for tobacco and matches were kept unchanged. Milk, tea, and eggs were revalued at prices somewhere between their old coupon and "commercial" rates. Meat, vegetables, sugar and candy were kept at their old coupon prices. Cereals were reduced ten per cent, and bread and flour twelve per cent below their old coupon prices.

There was a reason besides the sheer simplicity of a single-price system for the desire to achieve it. In Russian eyes the marketing structure of capitalist society reveals a bias in favor of the wealthy: the Russian says that since retailers seek profits, it is the demand from the wealthier elements, rather than the standard demand of the masses, that plays an inordinately preponderant role in determining the character of production.

In socialist society, on the other hand, production is for "use" rather than

---

[22] Cf., The Washington Post, June 30, 1947; p. 9.
[23] For the text of the decree, cf., the New York Times, December 15, 1947.

for "profit"; there is no private enterprise, hence no exploitation; and since a consumer's money income is supposed to represent his value to society, all elements in society should be satisfied in proportion to their worth to the community.[24]   This simple relationship between wage rates as a measure of worth and consumption in proportion to worth was obscured, somewhat, by the rationing and differential marketing system.

This raises another interesting point.   If consumption is really to be the reward of merit in the sense just indicated, at least the consumers of most value from the social point of view should be permitted to influence the direction of production.   Under a single-price system without rationing this could be done, even in a society in which the state decides what is to be produced, by directing the appropriate officials to give ear to the kinds of things consumers were demanding in the stores.   The Russians, to some extent at least, have been doing precisely that,[25] subject to the important qualification that political considerations rather than differential demand determine the fundamental allocation of resources, and that within the field of consumers' goods themselves, prices reflect administrative decisions rather than inter-relationships between supply and demand.   But these decisions are not reached in a vacuum.   The planned supplies of given commodities are data, and the prices placed upon them are dependent variables ad-

[24] See Article 12 of the Constitution, quoted above, p. 353.   *Cf.,* also, Hubbard, *op. cit.,* p. 103.

Even so, the inequality of incomes which assuredly exists in Russia constitutes a mildly complicating factor.   Under the Russian incentive system, the well-paid manager, official, or expert is stimulated to efficiency and economy by catering somewhat to his demand.   But to prevent his demand for high-quality goods and luxuries to prejudice the production of basic necessities for the masses, the turnover tax is kept high on that type of product.   *Ibid.,* pp. 213–214.

[25] So far this problem has not been acute, simply because of the general scarcity of most consumers' goods.   Preferred customers have been permitted to consume larger shares, under the rationing system, and certain specially fortunate groups like officials, favored artists, or writers or valuable research workers, have simply been allotted automobiles, better housing, and so on.   The issue under consideration will not become acute until supplies of food, clothing, and shelter become so abundant that the planning authorities must turn their attention to the question whether to produce cameras or fishing rods, cook books or fantastic hats.   When that problem does become acute, however, it will be less necessary to husband resources for the very reason that acute scarcity has been alleviated, and then a larger margin of waste will be tolerable.

It ought to be added that, even under acute scarcity, there may be a measure of concealed waste.   When supplies are generally inadequate in both quantity and quality, consumers are glad to get anything they can.   The state can therefore get rid of any "surplus" by depressing its price, or including it in rations, or both.   There is no self-acting monetary check upon that kind of waste.

justed to clear the market according to the estimated demand.[26]   Thus, relatively scarce goods have to be priced higher, and, *ceteris paribus,* relative demand will influence although not necessarily determine, decisions to expand the facilities for producing one type of consumers' goods rather than another.

The authorities have adequate means for estimating the relative demands for different types of goods and services.   They have statistical records of the rate of turnover of stocks of various commodities at prevailing prices.   They have reports from all kinds of stores indicating what lines and varieties of goods have been popular and which have not.   Most important are the turnover tax returns which reveal something of the relative pressures of demand for different kinds of things.

The abandonment of rationing between 1935 and 1941 brought some of the issues just mentioned to the fore.   Customers for the first time had some freedom to shop around.   There was still no such thing as a buyers' market, but some attention had yet to be paid to buyers' wants, and the result was that retail establishments were given a greater degree of autonomy.[27]   The territorial allocation of planned and controlled goods was made according to estimates of effective demand, while local allocation, particularly of different types and qualities of goods, was largely controlled through preliminary orders placed with manufacturers by the retail stores themselves.

The Russians have made another approximation to institutions with which we are more familiar.   They have attempted to influence, and even to stimulate, demand, through exhibitions of new products and designs with sample ballots taken on the exhibits.   This process extended even to certain types of capital goods.[28]   Even advertising exists in Russia, although, as we might expect, it is informative rather than competitive in character: "insults" to other products are frowned upon.

The fundamental problem in all this is the maintenance of efficiency. There is no significant price competition to keep enterprises on their toes, and as long as scarcity persists there is no sales resistance and therefore no real need to please the customer.   Even the attempt to impose efficiency

[26] *Cf.* E. M. Chossudowski, "Derationing in the U.S.S.R.," *Review of Economic Studies,* November, 1941; Dobb, *op. cit.,* pp. 40–42; Hubbard, *op. cit.,* Part V; and Reddaway, *op. cit.,* pp. 63–66.
[27] *Cf.* Hubbard, *op. cit.,* pp. 211–212.
[28] When the Stalin Tractor Works came into operation, there was almost no demand for tractors.   By collectivising the peasantry, that demand was created.   *Cf. ibid.,* p. 314.

from above through punishing mistakes is partially self-defeating, since officials tend to play for safety by avoiding experiment and eschewing initiative.

AN APPRAISAL

Whatever else it may have done, the Russian experiment has demonstrated that a centrally controlled and planned economy can persist, and not only persist but expand. Since the inauguration of their first Five-Year Plan, the Russians have steadily built up their economic strength until, in the last three years before the Second World War, the average annual rate of increase in Russian industrial output as a whole was thirteen per cent.[29]   To be sure, this development was at the expense of any solid development of living standards, but this was the result of deliberate political action; only the Russians can tell how long and how severely the Russian consumer can be squeezed before the system is exposed to social and political instability. And there is nothing inherent in the system to preclude the possibility, if the authorities so choose, of suddenly changing sights and diverting resources to the production of consumers' goods.

Till now, at any rate, the Russians have concentrated on pushing the development of heavy industry, and by and large they have achieved the targets they have set for themselves.   Consumption remains low.   In 1951 the *Economist* calculated that a family of four whose breadwinner was a semi-skilled laborer would have just about enough to live on: sufficient for housing, a minimum of clothing, and an adequate but austere diet, but almost no margin for anything else.[30]   After Stalin's death in March, 1953, his successor, Malenkov, made a bid for popularity by halving the price of fruit, vegetables, and potatoes, and by reducing other food prices by ten to twenty per cent.[31]   Only time will test the permanence of that improvement.

The planners remain optimistic.   The fifth Five-Year Plan, announced to run through the years 1951–1955, projected a sixty per cent increase in the national income and an increase of seventy per cent in aggregate industrial output.[32]   Those estimates are high, but they are not out of line

[29] *Cf. The Economist,* London, March 2, 1946; p. 326.
[30] *Ibid.,* November 17, 1951; pp. 1197–1198, 1201.
[31] *Ibid.,* April 18, 1953; pp. 160–161.
[32] *Ibid.,* August 30, 1952; pp. 505–506.

with projections in previous plans, and projections which, in many instances, have been justified. Soviet industrial development, be it remembered, started almost from scratch and a low base makes a rapid initial rate of progress plausible. The Russians, also, have been moving under forced draft and have not permitted themselves the slackness in the intensity of labor sometimes to be seen elsewhere.

In all this, the efficiency of neither management nor labor has been up to Western standards, and at times the resultant wastage has been appalling. This inefficiency has sometimes been ascribed to the Russian economic system, and we have already suggested some elements of danger inherent in their system. It must not be forgotten, however, that at the time of the Revolution, Russia was technically very backward; that the pace of development since then has been headlong, and that all of it has been under the direction of engineers, managers, and experts who were assigned responsibilities for which they had seldom been fully trained. The Russian obsession with speed at the expense of finish appears to be characteristic of the reconstruction program planned for the postwar period.[33] The chronic shortage of skilled labor and the inability to keep labor on the job are other indications of this same frenetic restlessness which makes the accomplishment of tomorrow's task seem more important than full preparation for it.

The Russians are fully aware of their relative inefficiency, and it is far too early to conclude that they will not ultimately overcome it. Here and there, indeed, they have appeared able to match the precision and productivity of Western producers.[34]

Russia's economic future will be materially affected by the extent and character of her intercourse with the outside world. To continue the present struggle for self-sufficiency will involve heavy costs: insulation from the immense technical resources of the West; continued disproportionality between the output of producers' and consumers' goods; prolonged underconsumption; and little or no respite from the mutual suspicion and distrust which continues to becloud the relations between these two parts of the modern world. That suspicion both creates and is fed by the quest for self-

[33] A Soviet engineer in Stalingrad remarked in the summer of 1946, "Over there are thousands and thousands of kilometers (*sic*) of land crying for tractors. The important task is to get tractors onto the land. Later we can worry about more stylish tractors." *New York Herald Tribune,* July 22, 1946.

[34] Wendell Willkie reported, after visiting a war plant on the Volga, "If I had not known I was in Russia, I should have thought I was in Detroit or Hartford. I have been greatly struck by the high degree of skill and organization, and I speak as an American used to high standards of efficiency." *New York Times,* September 21, 1942.

sufficiency.   The Russians, no more than ourselves, are entirely sure that the two economic systems can co-exist harmoniously.

And yet, it is not so much the economic systems as the social and political systems of the two parts of the world that are divergent.   The similarity of the economic forces working upon all contemporary systems will be suggested in the concluding chapter, but it may be pointed out here that industrialism, mass production, ever closer integration of industrial operations, and even an increasing measure of economic control and planning, are characteristic of both systems.   The Russians, to be sure, have so far freed themselves of the scourge of the business cycle, but they have exposed themselves to the inflexibilities of planning which may produce its own maladjustments.   The responsibility of Russian business management to the state has certain similarities to the responsibility of the American corporate director to the stockholders: both serve as agents.   Even the financial conditions under which enterprise operates in the two systems are not as dissimilar as might at first appear:

It might be said—and this is not merely a joke—that the difference between a capitalist country and Russia is the following.   In a capitalist country, where a company has ten millions profit, this profit belongs to it, but it must pay something like seven millions to the government as a *tax*.   In Russia, if a trust has ten millions profit, this profit belongs to the state; but the government "donates" three millions to the Trust to stimulate it!   In both cases, the government has seven millions and the Trust three.[35]

[35] Robert Mossé, "How Far Has Communism Been Reached in Soviet Russia?" in Robert J. Kerner, editor, *U.S.S.R. Economy and the War,* New York, 1943; p. 51.

————————17

British Socialism: The Background

and the Problem

POSSIBLY no recent political event has been so disturbing to political complacency as the British General Election of 1945. That England, the royal throne of kings, the sceptered isle, at once the cradle and citadel of capitalism should turn from the path which had taken her to demonstrable greatness, seemed more than pity; it seemed betrayal. For when the dust and smoke of electioneering had settled and the rumble of Churchillian oratory had died away, the realization dawned that capitulation rather than conquest had been the fate of British capitalism. That march of subsequent events made this yet clearer. The electoral victory gave the Labour Party a majority of over sixty per cent [1] of the membership of the House of Commons; surely the minority members could at least fight a Thermopylae. They did not. Until the steel industry was brought before the bar, the principle of nationalization was scarcely challenged. Even in the campaign of 1950, when Conservatism appeared to have a second chance, debate on basic principles gave way to controversy over details. While Labour candidates promised the extension of social services and emphasized full employment, the Conserva-

[1] 393 out of 640 seats.

tives did little more than grumble at economic controls, complain about high taxes, and point derisively at the continuing housing shortage.[2]

Even after the General Election of October, 1951, which returned the Conservatives to power by the slenderest of margins,[3] no attempt was made to reverse the postwar direction of events. The steel industry, to be sure, was formally and perhaps temporarily returned to private hands, and private truckers were again given access to the highways. Apart from this, there was no interference with the sector of industry which the Labour Government had nationalized. In fact, the guiding industrial principle which the Conservatives set for themselves was one to which no one could take exception:

[The Government] will seek to promote flexibility in those industries which have been brought under public management and to stimulate free enterprise by giving it a fuller share in our economic activity. They will be mindful of the great demands on our productive capacity, and will consider all methods for creating that spirit of partnership between management and workers on which industrial harmony and a higher level of productivity must depend.[4]

Conservatives' Acceptance of Nationalization

This Conservative silence about fundamentals does not appear to be explained by socialist moderation in limiting the ultimate grasp of nationalization to no more than twenty per cent of British industry,[5] for that twenty per cent, comprising coal, transport, electricity, gas, steel, and finance, represents the heart and blood of any developed industrial system. Nor does Conservative acquiescence appear to be due to the shock induced by the repudiation of its way of life by the British electorate in 1945. Shock there was indeed, but the wearing off of that shock did not leave in Conservative breasts the dedicated sense of mission that animates so many of their socialist opponents. The truth is that, for those who had eyes to see, the writing had appeared upon the wall decades before the wall collapsed. Conservatives themselves had recommended nationalization in more than one instance, and Britain's economic predicament in 1945 implied to many the necessity

---

[2] Cf. The Political Quarterly, London, April–June, 1950; p. 109.

[3] In Parliament, they received 321 out of a total of 625 seats; representing 48 per cent of the total vote, slightly under the 48.8 per cent received by Labour. Cf. Labor and Industry in Britain, British Information Services, New York, December, 1951; p. 145.

[4] Ibid., p. 146.

[5] Labor and Industry in Britain, as cited, September–October, 1947; p. 162.

for national action.   For half a century certain traditional foundations of British national prosperity had been crumbling, and to the evident need of somehow shoring these up was added the grim necessity of somehow recovering from the devastation wrought by war.   In result, to all but doctrinaires, the fundamental pattern of postwar economic policy was predetermined by both circumstances and public opinion, so that party differences necessarily turned themselves primarily into differences of emphasis and tempo. It is true that if the Conservatives had remained in power there would have been far less nationalization, but that does not mean that really free enterprise would have remained sovereign.   National control over industrial policy and economic life would have remained so tight that freedom of enterprise would have remained but a name, reminiscent of a vigorous past, a mockery of the drab present, although perhaps a hope for a more tranquil future.

The Character of British Economic Planning

Postwar Britain, then, has resorted to planning, but to planning of a peculiarly British kind.   We noticed earlier [6] how economic institutions in being tend to take coloring from the national character and traditions of the people who adopt and administer them.   While Russian planning, then, is authoritarian and doctrinaire, English planning is flexible and democratic.   The Russians, seeking to develop their economy and to do so with self-sufficiency, do their planning in a succession of five-year stretches; the British, seeking better adaptation of an already developed economy to the outside world upon which it is dependent, plan only from year to year, and sometimes for even shorter periods.   The Russians, conscious of public opinion but only as something to be formed and controlled, impose their plan from above and shroud many of its details in secrecy; the British planners, creatures of the electorate, plan only as they are permitted to, and whatever they do plan is exposed to pitiless publicity from press, Parliament, and public.

Most significant of all, while the Russians profess "democracy," that institution, like some Italian wine, has not traveled well; the vintage in Russia is tainted with vinegar.   In England, on the other hand, democracy with its connotation of individual freedom is established, sturdy, and instinct with life.   In the Western democracies, and notably in England, something has taken place which is unthinkable in Russia: a reassuringly vigorous, impas-

[6] *Cf. supra,* pp. 8–9, 270.

sionate, but still courteous controversy over the compatibility of planning with freedom.[7]   Still more reassuring is the story of British planning itself. The electorate retains its sovereignty; the change of steersman in the general election of 1951 did not rock the boat; and no matter who the steersman has been, planning has not yet been made an end in itself.   It is, first, a necessity forced by the exigencies of England's immediate postwar plight; in the longer run, it is a means of assuring the kind of economic and social structure many Englishmen seek, but only as long as traditional British freedoms are not really imperiled.

POSTWAR ECONOMIC RECONSTRUCTION

The furling of the battle flags in 1945 revealed an England only two thirds as wealthy as it had been before the outbreak of the Second World War. Unfortunately, this did not mean that by taking in the national belt to a corresponding extent, a leaner and hungrier England could start anew the re-creation of John Bull's familiar profile.   The wealth destroyed meant the loss of precisely the means by which wealth is formed, so that England's most pressing economic problem lay in finding means to survive at all in a world increasingly independent of the services England had equipped herself to provide and by which she had lived.

Great Britain is an intensely industrialized country, but one whose factories subsist on huge quantities of raw materials drawn from abroad and whose workers have depended for half their food upon imported supplies. Except for coal, Britain is relatively poor in basic raw materials.   She must import all her non-ferrous metals, rubber, petroleum, cotton, and tobacco; nine tenths of her wool, more than four fifths of her timber, and about half of the iron ore which feeds her great steel industry.   Of her foodstuffs, over half, in the aggregate, are imported.   By categories, all coffee, tea and cocoa, all citrus fruits, nine tenths of all edible fats, six sevenths of the cheese, four fifths of the sugar, more than three quarters of the wheat and flour, and half of all the meats come into England from the outside.

These imports had been purchased not only from the proceeds of British exports, but also out of the yield of British overseas investments.   In 1938, for example, England imported goods and services valued at 835 million

---

[7] This issue will be discussed in the final chapter.

pounds and the government expended an additional 16 million pounds abroad, making a total of 851 million.   Offsetting this, British exports amounted to 533 million, income from foreign investment to 175 million, and returns from shipping and other services to 73 million.   This still left a deficit of 70 million pounds in the balance of payments on current account, but it was a deficit which was manageable.

By 1946 the picture had changed very much for the worse.   Prices abroad had risen, so that even with compulsory exclusion of imports deemed unimportant, the bill for imported goods and services amounted to 1,092 million pounds.   Income from shipping and other items had dwindled to 39 million and from foreign investments to 75 million; and while the value of British exports had increased to 888 million pounds, government expenditures abroad had likewise risen to the huge total of 290 million pounds.   In result, the adverse trade balance had increased to 380 million pounds.[8] How had all this come about, and to what extent did it represent a structural rather than temporary adverse change in the British position?

Causes of Economic Distress

First, over a billion pounds worth of British foreign investments had been sold during the war and the proceeds long since transformed into smoke and scrap.   This entailed a permanent reduction in income, and unfortunately the rise in foreign prices meant that the income which remained would not stretch as far.   To make matters worse, the war-induced shortage of foodstuffs and industrial raw materials brought about a greater increase in their prices than in the prices of British manufactured goods, so that to purchase the same quantity of imports in 1948 as in 1938, England would have had to export one fifth more goods by volume.

In the *second* place, both outbound and inbound goods had to be shipped, and unless they could be shipped in British bottoms, freight charges for the use of foreign carriers would cut still deeper into England's dwindling means of payment.   Here, also, the British position had worsened.   In 1914 Great Britain, with 18 million gross tons of shipping, had owned approximately forty-five per cent of the world's ocean ships.   By 1939, the British share had fallen to something over a quarter, partly because of an absolute reduction in British tonnage to 17 million gross tons, and partly because of sub-

[8] *Cf.* The White Paper, *United Kingdom Balance of Payments, 1946 and 1947,* His Majesty's Stationary Office, London; Cmd. 7324.

stantial increases in the ships flying other flags.   The Second World War accelerated this relative decline, so that by 1945, in spite of wartime accretions, England had only 13 million gross tons, representing about one sixth of the world's shipping.   Even this does not tell the entire story, for the kinds of shipping constructed during the war were not entirely adapted to normal peacetime trade routes or to normal peacetime traffic.[9]

In the *third* place, and most fundamental, albeit obvious, was the necessity of producing goods if foreign trade was to continue at all; financial difficulties and shipping shortages, bad as they may be, dwindle to nothing if there is nothing to purchase or ship.   Moreover, the need for industrial production was intensified by the reduction of income from other sources, with the result that England faced a predicament something like that of the White Queen: she had to produce more than ever in order to eat the same.   The target figure set is now famous—three quarters more exports than the 1938 volume were predicated for the balancing of British payments in the postwar world. Balance, however, was like the carrot tied in front of the donkey's nose: that target was almost reached in 1951, but British payments were still very far from balance.   Three years later the target was still out of reach.   Unhappily, even the maintenance, let alone the increase, of the prewar volume of production was difficult, as three examples should indicate.

(1) Coal is Great Britain's great natural resource, and coal has underlain all British industrial strength; yet the output of coal in 1945 was only 182 million tons compared with 227 million in 1938.   (2) Modern industry cannot operate without electric power, but insufficient generating capacity in 1946 was responsible for an estimated shortage of over 1,260,000 million kilowatt hours.   (3) Industry, always and everywhere, depends upon labor. British labor after the Second World War was restive, weary, and seeking the brave new world it believed to be in sight, yet it could be neither fed nor housed adequately.   The roast beef of Merrie England was only a memory, and if every Englishman's house was his castle, it was now one which had to be shared.[10]   The result was an "austerity regime" in which

[9] Most wartime construction in both Great Britain and the United States was of the large, bulk cargo carrier type, unsuited for the specialized purposes for which a considerable part of the pre-war British merchant fleet had been designed.

[10] Nearly four and one half million houses had been damaged or destroyed during the war, and since then only the most urgently needed construction had been permitted.

The foregoing summary of Britain's postwar condition has been taken from *Labor and Industry in Britain,* as cited, February, 1947, p. 28; March, 1947, p. 71; September–October, 1947, p. 175; March, 1950, p. 25; and from *Britain, 1950–51,* A Reference Handbook, Central Office of Information, London, 1951; pp. 61–62, 191–192.

the accepted economic incentive of more of the good things of life had to be foregone because, *first,* the means of producing good things were inadequate, and because, *second,* of those good things which could be produced the greater part had to be sold to foreigners to provide sufficient drab things to keep Englishmen alive to produce good things for foreigners.

Distrust of the Market Mechanism

The apparent viciousness of this circle created a general distrust of the market mechanism as either an appropriate or a desirable means of escaping from its constriction.   It was imperative, for example, to produce more coal, and to do this the recruitment of additional miners was essential.   The orthodox procedure would have been to offer miners higher wages, but to increase wages which could not be spent because the objects of expenditure were unavailable did not seem workable, particularly in the case of an industry which had been becoming repellent rather than attractive to labor. There were still other difficulties.   To raise wages for new workers only would have been inequitable and hardly practicable, while to raise wages all around would increase expense unnecessarily and would endow employed workers with the surplus known as economic rent at just the time when the Government, because of inflation, was attempting to hold incomes down, and also at a time and in a milieu in which unearned incomes or increments were deemed unmeet and impolitic.   Suppose, however, that the wage incentive had been successfully tried in the form of a wage high enough to attract labor from other industries; when recruitment was completed, should further influx be arrested by lowering coal wages or raising other wages?   Still more difficult was the problem of whence to draw additional miners.   Despite the fact that in the first twelve months after the Second World War the number of men and women employed in war industry and the armed services fell from nine million to slightly over two million,[11] a critical shortage of manpower still persisted, and the problem of directing labor was one of finding a Peter to rob in order that Paul might be paid.

Necessity for Governmental Intervention

As J. E. Meade points out,[12] private industry itself could not rationally plan its own operations under postwar British conditions.   He adduces

[11] *Labor and Industry in Britain,* September–October, 1947; p. 166.
[12] *Cf.* his *Planning and the Price Mechanism,* London, 1948; pp. 2–4.

producers of brick whose operations become almost unpredictable when the volume of construction is subject to large and erratic fluctuations depending, for example, on the volume of lumber imports which are themselves dependent upon the quantity of foreign exchange earned by British exports and on how that foreign exchange is allocated by the Government.

HISTORICAL TRENDS TOWARD SOCIALIZATION

All this means that no British Government, whatever its political complexion, could have kept the finger of the state off the economic throttle in 1945, and in the years immediately following. In principle, a variety of techniques ranging from the maximum permissible degree of *laissez-faire* to complete nationalization of production, distribution, and exchange were at hand. In fact, neither extreme was attempted, but, instead, a complex policy compounded of the nationalization of certain industries, direct controls (such as licensing and rationing) over other aspects of economic life, voluntary agreements with labor and industry over still other activities, and attempts to rig the market through taxation, subsidy, and price control so as to induce still other desired responses. The specific decisions as to where to nationalize, where to leave alone, where to control, where to seek agreement, and where to rig the market, were made against the background of British conditions and traditions. The policy of the Labour Government was not created all at once out of a desire to fashion a land fit for heroes. Even the socialist elements in that policy represented the culmination of a trend toward socialization that had begun decades before the nationalization of British industry began to take place. Really to understand contemporary British socialism, then, requires some familiarity with the more important of those trends. The significant areas are social security and welfare, the role and responsibility of labor, and the peculiar problems emerging with time within some of the traditionally important British industries.

Social Security and Welfare

At almost the beginning of the modern industrial age the British State commenced a process of increasing interference in economic processes for the protection of the more helpless victims of the Industrial Revolution.

The basis for this interference was a sense that it was not inappropriate for the state to cast a mantle of protection over those who were clearly incapable of protecting themselves, thin though that mantle all too frequently was.

The Factory Acts.   That mantle of protection took the form of the so-called Factory Acts that were passed by Parliament early in the nineteenth century.   The first of these to be passed, the Health and Morals of Apprentices Act of 1802, was intended to correct the sometimes appalling abuses undergone by pauper children employed in cotton mills to which they were farmed out as apprentices by the poor-relief authorities.   That particular Act was never enforced, but it was followed by a succession of legislative enactments setting minimum ages and maximum hours of work for children in industrial employment.   The Act of 1833, for example, provided for three hours of daily schooling for wage-earning children between the ages of nine and thirteen.   In 1844, children and women were limited to a maximum of sixty-nine hours of work in a week, and during the course of the next thirty years the ten-hour day became effective for women and children in textile mills.   Generally speaking, until 1900, this type of protection was formally restricted to women and children, although in the many cases in which the work of men depended upon juvenile or female assistants the ten-hour limit applied perforce to them as well, so that pressure for general factory legislation inevitably developed.   That pressure, of course, did not arise solely from the fact that women and children were protected *de jure* and some men *de facto*.   To go back no further than the Chartist era beginning in the late 1830's, there had existed clamor for

> Eight hours work, eight hours play
> Eight hours sleep and eight shillings a day.

Social insurance.   The early years of the twentieth century brought the unavoidable response, to both the strongest and the weakest laboring groups in the realm.   In 1908, on the one hand, the well-organized coal miners secured the eight-hour day and, in 1912, a legal minimum wage; and in 1909, on the other hand, the British Government created Trade Boards to set minimum wages in sweated industries.   In the same period England began to follow the example set by Bismarckian Germany a generation earlier in applying the principle of insurance to some of the hazards of industrial life. In 1911, National Health Insurance was introduced, and by 1928 approximately one third of the British population was protected in some measure against financial inability to secure medical attention. Simultaneously, unemployment also became the object of public concern.[13] In 1909, the Government established labor exchanges, and, in 1911, compulsory unemployment insurance came into existence.

This development of factory legislation and social insurance has been adduced by a distinguished legal scholar as opening the door to what he called the "Period of Collectivism," foreshadowed in the 1830's and 1840's, and definitely introduced in the 1870's:

> The factory movement introduced socialist enactments into the law of England and gave prestige and authority to the ideas of collectivism.[14]

Developing that statement, we can perhaps conclude that the protection of the helpless led to the protection of all; that public safeguards against exploitation ripened into guarantees of a minimum degree of security; [15] that the compulsory shielding of workers against industrial accidents prepared the way for the screening of the entire population against impure foods or noxious drugs; and that the first cautious resort to the machinery of the state to sustain the well-being of the most helpless and least fortunate was the precursor of the contemporary British attempt to assure security to everyone from womb to tomb.

The Role and Responsibility of Labor: The Labour Party

The vehicle of contemporary British socialism is the British Labour Party, a party unlike anything existing in the United States. It was formed in 1906 primarily as a federation of labor unions, although certain avowedly socialist organizations were also affiliated with it. Though called a "party," individuals were not admitted to membership until 1918, and to this day the Labour Party is mainly the political representative of *organized* labor. Its platform, therefore, and its objectives are bound in a peculiarly intimate sense to the aspirations, attitudes, and judgments of the British labor movement which have themselves developed out of the background of British labor experience.

---

[13] It is both interesting and significant that the terms *unemployment* and *unemployed* did not come into use until the 1880's. *Cf.* J. H. Clapham, *An Economic History of Modern Britain,* New York, 1938; Vol. III, p. 419.

[14] *Cf.* A. V. Dicey, *Lectures on the Relation Between Law and Public Opinion in England during the Nineteenth Century,* London, 2d. edition, 1914; p. 238.

[15] Old age pensions were provided in 1908.

This is a source of strength in so far as it keeps the Party in touch with the "grass roots," but it can also be the source of embarrassment. For example, in the summer of 1950 the Premier of France proposed to the world the "Schuman Plan" for the pooling of European steel facilities. The British Labour *Government* prepared a White Paper expressing cautious sympathy for the plan, but, unfortunately, the day before its release, the British Labour *Party* almost completely nullified the effect of the White Paper by releasing a statement expressing far more distrust of European economic integration.[16]

As in the United States, the British labor movement developed first along craft lines. The cotton industry was the first to adopt the factory system, and in the 1820's and 1830's cotton spinners constituted the spearhead of the union movement. By 1870, labor had pushed itself to a position of national significance, both politically and industrially.

Politically, the unity and cohesion which the Chartist Movement [17] had given labor resulted in the first important legislative recognition of unionism in modern English history. In 1800 "combinations" had been prohibited during the apprehension and hysteria engendered in England by the excesses of the French Revolution. In 1824 that prohibition was abrogated, although labor organizations were not yet accorded protection against prosecution under the common law of conspiracy. In 1871 and 1875, however, labor unions were recognized as "voluntary societies," [18] and specific protection against common-law prosecution was provided. That is to say, an act which was not criminal when committed by one person alone was now declared not indictable when performed by two or more persons acting in connection with a labor dispute.

---

[16] *Cf. The Economist,* London, June 17, 1950; pp. 1313–1315.

[17] Chartism, which flourished in two phases between 1836 and 1848, derived its name from the Great Charter which it unsuccessfully attempted to push through Parliament. That Charter took the form of a model Act of Parliament to provide universal, adult, male suffrage, the secret ballot, annually elected Parliaments, salaries to be paid members of Parliament (so that representatives of labor, particularly, could afford to serve), equal electoral districts, and the abolition of property qualifications to determine eligibility for membership in Parliament.

Labor had already learned something of political *expertise* from its earlier association with upper and middle class supporters of its campaigns for factory legislation and agricultural free trade. What the Chartist Movement did for labor was to alienate middle class sympathy so that labor became unified through having to stand alone.

Cf. C. R. Fay, *Great Britain from Adam Smith to the Present Day,* London, 1932; p. 388.

[18] That is, as unincorporated bodies. It was assumed, at the time, that unions could not be sued.

"New Model Unionism"

Industrially, the establishment of the Amalgamated Society of Engineers [19] in 1851 introduced the so-called "New Model Unionism," the organization of centrally administered unions working toward greater cooperation with employers, disavowing rash militancy, and employing substantial financial resources for such beneficial purposes as pensions, sick pay, and unemployment relief. Thereafter unions rapidly became forces to be reckoned with. Occasional resort to arbitration in place of strikes led to the introduction of machinery for arbitration, and finally, in the 1890's, to the creation of permanent Conciliation and Arbitration Boards, or Wages Boards, which become particularly significant in the steel and mining industries. These Boards comprised equal numbers of employers and employees, and their primary purpose was to provide recourse to an umpire when amicable resolution of a dispute could not otherwise be achieved. Resort to either strikes or lockouts during negotiations was debarred. The procedure so adopted was so successful that the state adopted the same basic principle in the Conciliation Act of 1896 which empowered the Board of Trade [20] to investigate disputes generally, to attempt to bring disputants together, and to appoint a conciliator at the request of one party to a dispute, or an arbitrator on request of both.

The "New Unionism"

Unfortunately, by the turn of the century new notes of militancy could be heard. Unskilled labor had been largely left out of the foregoing developments, and not all skilled labor was entirely satisfied with them. The malcontents, accordingly, began to experiment for themselves during the 1880's and ultimately brought forth something called the "New Unionism," or large industrial unions which soon became especially prominent among longshoremen, miners, gas workers, and general laborers. A successful strike of London "match girls" in 1888, the victory of the London dockers in the following year, and the peaceful attainment of the eight-hour day in the gas industry represented the first substantial successes of this new type of union.

---

[19] In England the "engineering" industry comprises a large and important group of metal-using industries, including the manufacture of machinery and equipment, ordnance and small arms, radio and electrical goods. For a description, see *Britain, 1950–51,* as cited, pp. 120–121.

[20] The Board of Trade later became the Ministry of Labour.

The Beginnings of Socialism

The same period also marked the beginning of the coming of age of British socialism, although for a time this was apparent only as a cloud scarcely bigger than a man's hand. On the whole, Britain was complacent during the 1890's. Real wages were rising, arbitration and conciliation of labor disputes were increasingly being resorted to, the Marxist theory of increasing misery appeared demonstrably false, and, until 1899, even the labor unions tended to confine their political activities to attempts to elect their own candidates to Parliament. The cloud, however, was there.

The Fabian Society. In 1883 the Fabian Society had been founded, and four years later the enunciation of its "Basis," or "Statement of Principles," committed it definitely to socialism. Its socialism, however, was not Marxian. Denying the class struggle, the Fabians asserted that no precise line between socialists and others could be drawn; they were, in fact, able to secure the support of many non-socialists for some of their specific proposals for reform. Repudiating the necessity for violence, the Fabians predicted, and thought they already discerned, the gradual and ineluctable transformation of capitalism into socialism. It was, indeed, the avoidance of crisis or pitched battle which gave the society its name. During the Second Punic War when Hannibal was invading Italy, the Roman General Quintus Fabius Maximus, nicknamed *Cunctator,* or Delayer, hardened his troops without jeopardizing them by harassing but not engaging the Carthaginian invader.[21] The tactics of Fabius were taken over by the Fabian Society, which emphasized them by the adoption of his name.

In action, Fabian tactics took the form of "permeation," that is, the penetration by Fabians of the Civil Service, the professions, local governments, and even business administration. In thought, these tactics were based upon the conviction that the State, through factory and social-security legislation and through progressive taxation, had already placed its foot across the threshold to socialism, and accordingly the Society need only do what it could to maintain momentum.

The Independent Labour Party. To convert the labor unions to socialism and to provide a means for getting the representatives of labor into Parliament, Keir Hardie, in 1893, organized the Independent Labour Party. This party should not be confused with the Labour Party itself, although its existence and its activities prepared ground for the seed which later was

---

[21] *Cf.* Tenney Frank, *A History of Rome,* New York, 1923; pp. 118–120.

to germinate into the Labour Party which eventually pushed Great Britain into partial socialism.   The Independent Labour Party, however, was a small, almost splinter party; it was infused with missionary zeal which did not appeal to the rank and file, but which nevertheless produced its own contagion.   Its existence as a political party in the closing years of the nineteenth century was resented by some because it threatened to split the progressive vote, but it did succeed in electing its founder to Parliament.   Representing as it did the left wing of the politically active part of the British labor movement, its influence lives on today among the followers of Aneurin Bevan, the leader of the radical wing of the Labour Party.

Just before the dawn of the twentieth century, therefore, socialists had equipped themselves with a brain in the form of the Fabian Society, and an arm represented by the Independent Labour Party.   The unionization of unskilled labor, moreover, had been largely prompted by socialists, and although these were socialists of the gradualist rather than the revolutionary variety, they were nevertheless instrumental in breathing into the new industrial unions a greater measure of militancy and class consciousness than could be found among the older, craft unionists.

Labor Unrest

The clouds gathered rapidly.   In 1901 the House of Lords affirmed a judgment of 23,000 pounds damages against a union which had struck against the small Taff Vale Railway Company in the Welsh coal fields, and thereby undermined the comforting security against law suits which the British unions had thought they possessed since the legislation of the 1870's. One of the Lords Justices, indeed, observed,

If the Legislature has created a thing which can own property, which can employ servants, and which can inflict injury, it must be taken to have impliedly given the power to make it liable in a court.[22]

One consequence was the cessation of union growth.   Labor union membership, which had risen to just over two million in 1900, remained stationary until 1906.   In the same period employment fell off, and a decline in miners' wages was reflected in a fall in the national wage index.

The victory of the Liberal Party in 1906 inaugurated a wave of strikes which persisted up to the eve of the First World War, but was also instrumental in obliterating the implication of the Taff Vale judgment.   The

[22] Quoted in Clapham, *op. cit.,* p. 491.

Trade Disputes Act of 1906 gave immunity to union funds from liability for torts (private or civil wrongs). It also extended immunity from civil liability to the same acts which the legislation of the 1870's had protected against criminal liability, and it provided that certain acts, such as breach of contract or interference with another's business, were not actionable if they were committed in the course of a labor dispute.

Still another issue was faced in these last few years of international peace. In 1900, to get more dependable labor representation in Parliament, the Labour Representation Committee was founded; in 1906 this was transformed into the Labour Party, and two years after that the Party had nearly fifty of its members in Parliament. Since, however, members of Parliament received no salary until 1911, those labor members had to be paid out of union funds. In 1907, following protests from a member of the Amalgamated Society of Railway Servants that he, although a Liberal, was being assessed to support a Labour member of Parliament, this use of funds was challenged as illegal. In 1909 the House of Lords upheld the challenge on the ground that the laws under which unions were organized did not specifically authorize participation in political activities. This hint that the legal definition of a union was a complete and exhaustive statement of the scope of its legitimate activities raised disquieting questions about the legality of the educational and beneficial activities in which many unions were engaged. The result was a redefinition of the scope of unionism in an Act passed in 1913 which permitted the expenditure of funds for any purpose otherwise legal, provided that financial support of candidates for, or members of, Parliament had to be specifically authorized by a majority ballot of the members of each contributing union. Thereafter, any member who so chose could "contract out"—that is, he could give written notice that he would not contribute to funds to be used for political purposes—without impairing his good standing in the union of which he was a member.

The Responsibility of Labor

Thus, by the outbreak of the First World War, British unions had secured both legal and social acceptance as significant elements in the national life. Even unskilled labor had commenced successful intervention in the determination of wages and conditions of work which, subject to the law, had hitherto been the exclusive prerogative of management. Unions were secure in the use of their funds, and their normal activities in the course of a labor dispute were protected. They were becoming politically active and, in contrast to Continental European happenings, the formation of the British Labour Party enabled the unions to capture the socialists rather than to be captured by them.

During the years of war, the Labour Party suspended its campaign to increase the social and political influence of organized labor; instead, it supported the Government in order that the war might be won. In one respect, cooperation between labor and management was indeed fostered during the war, but at the instigation of the Government rather than of labor. In the last years of the war and in the first postwar years, the so-called Whitley Councils, somewhat analogous to the Wages Boards of the 1890's, were created to give labor a partial voice in management. There existed seventy-three of these in 1921, chiefly in industries where labor was imperfectly organized and in which improved methods and greater reliance upon collective bargaining were deemed desirable. On the whole, these Councils were not of great moment in the inter-war period. Only fifty were still in existence by June, 1925, and while a few of these had been active in fostering education and industrial research as well as settling difficulties within the more conventional realm of collective bargaining, most of these were simply paper organizations.[23] During the Second World War similar councils were organized under other names, and after 1945 the Labour Government attempted to use them to maintain industrial peace, reduce costs, and raise productivity.

The General Strike and Its Consequences

The two outstanding developments in the period between the two World Wars were (1) the renewal of industrial strife during the 1920's followed by a loss in union membership which temporarily weakened labor's industrial power, and (2) the coming of age of the Labour Party.

Industrial unrest culminated in the general strike of 1926, and the failure of that strike underscored the general weakening of British unionism which had been in process since the end of the war. Depression in the heavy industries, the migration of industry from the North, where unions had always been strong, to the South, the Midlands, and Greater London, where they had been generally weaker, and the relative growth of service industries and light manufacturing employing a larger proportion of women who were somewhat less amenable than men to the blandishments of the organizer—

[23] *Cf.* Clapham, *op. cit.,* p. 541.

these factors had already cut into union membership.[24]   The general strike added public irritation to hostility of capital, and by 1928 union membership had declined to 4,800,000.   Another consequence of the strike was the Trade Disputes and Trade Unions Act of 1927 which reintroduced legal uncertainty about what unions might safely do.

The Trade Disputes and Trade Unions Act declared illegal any strike against the Government which either directly or indirectly caused public hardship, and it also proscribed any strike which had any purpose beyond the promotion of the striking union's objectives in the industry in which the strikers were employed.   The Act protected persons refusing to participate in an illegal strike, defined and prohibited intimidation, restricted the right of public employees to join unions with political affiliations, prohibited the union shop in public undertakings, and empowered the Attorney General as well as interested private persons to seek to enjoin the use of union funds for the furtherance of an illegal strike.   Finally, the 1927 legislation replaced the "contracting out" provision of the Trade Union Act of 1913 with a "contracting in" clause: thereafter, union members were exempted from political contributions unless they individually served written notice of their willingness to contribute.   The natural result of the "contracting in" provision was a fall in the trade union membership of the Labour Party from 3,239,000 in 1927 to 2,025,000 in 1928.

Nevertheless, despite these reverses, the growth of the Labour Party and its replacement of the Liberal Party as one of the two major political parties in England, gave British unions an unprecedented degree of political prestige and power.   The tighter organization of unions and the federation movement among unions contributed to the centralization of control and fostered cohesiveness of policy.   In 1900 there had been 1,323 registered unions; [25]

---

[24] In 1920, unions had 8,346,000 members; in 1925, 5,500,000.

[25] A registered union is one which has voluntarily registered with the Registrar of Friendly Societies.   Registration for unions is, in a sense, what incorporation is for a business enterprise.   A permanent Board of Trustees carries the right to hold property and to sue and be sued.   The Trustees are responsible for the property of registered unions, and officials are subject to punishment for misuse of property on the complaint of any member.   A registered union may engage in certain types of insurance with greater freedom than is accorded regular insurance companies, and its benefit funds are partially exempt from income tax.

On the other hand, every registered union must file its rules and its list of officers with the Registrar, must make provision for periodical audits, must open its books and its membership list to anyone with an interest in union funds, and it must submit an annual report of its financial condition and the use made of each category of its funds.   In 1947 about 85 per cent of total union membership belonged to registered by 1944 the number had fallen to 962, and, by 1945, to 780, although the total membership of British unions was contemporaneously rising to a new peak of 8,714,000 in 1946.[26]   This change reflects chiefly the merging or federation of unions.   These federations themselves have tended increasingly to serve as collective bargaining units.

The Trades Union Congress

Most British unions are affiliated with the important Trades Union Congress,[27] a body created in the 1860's as a sort of debating society designed to bring pressure to bear upon Parliament.   It was reorganized after the First World War to give greater coherence to British unionism and to provide closer liaison between unions and the Labour Party.   Its General Council, a permanent body with an able Secretariat, exercises wide though undefined powers over the constituent unions, but has used these chiefly to reduce jurisdictional disputes rather than to impose any sort of common pattern upon its members.   Another cementing agency is the National Joint Council on which are represented the Trades Union Congress itself, the Labour Party, and the Labour Members of Parliament.   It concerns itself primarily with the determination of questions of general policy in between meetings of the Congress of the Party, but its decisions were subject to ratification, or rejection by, the annual or special meetings of the Congress.

What all this means is that, particularly after the First World War, British labor developed two strings to its bow—one industrial string and one political string—and tended to use each alternately.   The slump of 1921 tended to weaken the industrial string, and so labor turned to the political action which brought to power the first Labour Government of 1924.   Within a year of the fall of that Government resort was again had to the industrial string until the failure of the general strike of 1926.   A second Labour Government came into rather precarious office in 1929 and lasted, this time, for two years.   The depression of the 'thirties weakened labor, both politically and industrially until the Second World War set in motion the march of events

---

unions.   *Cf. Trade Unions in Britain,* Supplement to *Labor and Industry in Britain,* December, 1949; pp. 4–5.

[26] *Cf. Labor and Industry in Britain,* March, 1948; p. 22.   The total working population was 20,414,000 at the end of 1946, of whom 1,440,000 were in some form or other of military service.

[27] At present more than 80 per cent of the entire membership of British labor unions is concentrated in unions affiliated with the Trades Union Congress.   *Cf. Trade Unions in Britain,* as cited, p. 7.

leading up to the decisive Labour victory of 1945. It was that third Labour Government which sponsored and achieved the nationalization of a substantial sector of the British economy.

THE IMMEDIATE BACKGROUND OF NATIONALIZATION

To observers in other countries, and particularly in the United States, the Labour Party's program of nationalization seemed the most firm, the most decisive, and the most important of the economic changes introduced in 1945. Perhaps they were, but Englishmen themselves, even those inside the Labour Party, are not in firm agreement with one another about why to nationalize, what to nationalize, or whether, indeed, nationalization should be regarded as the Thruway to the prosperous and secure future which all seek.

Defense of Nationalization

Various and not necessarily mutually consistent arguments in favor of nationalization have been suggested.[28] These can, with some overlapping, be grouped into three great divisions, each centering upon an issue of accepted and substantial importance.

First, nationalization has been defended as a means of diffusing and democratizing economic power. Hitherto, a few men in control of basic industries upon whose activity and behavior the well-being of the entire economy depends, have been responsible not to society, but to private groups of stockholders. When an industry is of national significance it is argued that its management should be responsible to the nation. It is also argued that labor is entitled to a voice in management and that managerial positions should not be reserved as a safe haven for sons, nephews or Old School friends, but should be more generally opened through promotion to qualified members of the labor rank and file.

Second, nationalization has appeared to some as a powerful tool for the redistribution of wealth and the furtherance of social security. Nationalized enterprise cannot be regarded as a milch cow to be exploited for the

[28] *Cf.* Ben W. Lewis, *British Planning and Nationalization,* New York, 1952; pp. 43–45.

benefit of the few but instead as a public institution to be used in the public interest.   As such, nationalized industries are means of transferring wealth from stockholders to labor and to consumers.   They are also, as recipients of public investment, direct means of providing public employment in periods of depression.   They are sources of employment for another reason as well.   Being publicly controlled, these industries can be relocated in more or less permanently depressed areas, while private industry is not quite so easy to push about.   English socialists also assert that the public domain can be safeguarded more fully under a regime of nationalized industry.

Third, and finally, nationalization is supported as a means of furthering industrial efficiency in both the private and public sectors of the economy. Under the yardstick principle, a nationalized firm operating alongside and in competition with private industry serves both as a standard and as a prod to performance; sometimes, indeed, the same effect can be achieved by the mere threat to nationalize.   On occasion, for example, in the case of coal, nationalization seems necessary to avert the sheer breakdown or collapse of an industry.   Also, for such natural monopolies as the public utilities, direct public operation is deemed simpler, cheaper, and more efficient than mere regulation, which tends to be cumbersome, slow, and clumsy.   In the end, public ownership and operation of all essential industry receives support because this presumably makes possible better coordination, superior organization, the economy of operation on a larger scale, and substantial improvement in labor relations.

The astute reader will have noticed the possibility of disharmony amongst these several reasons for nationalizing industry.   The furtherance of industrial efficiency, for example, does not automatically follow from the relocation of a nationalized plant in a depressed area, and the yardstick principle that the competition from public industry gives an edge to the performance of private firms may also cut the other way: some private competition may be salutary for the alertness, flexibility, and competent performance of nationalized industry itself.

That, however, is not really the point.   Socialism with its presumed connotation of greater social justice than capitalism purportedly can produce, has an appeal to its devotees which transcends the logic of argument; for them, socialism is a cause as well as a principle.   The interesting thing is that, although socialism is a cause, the British socialists have not been doctrinaire in their experiment in partial socialism.   They have gone part way, then paused to take breath; and more recently, as we shall see, members and supporters of the Labour Party have among themselves begun to question whether further nationalization is the only, or even the most important, road to the welfare state.

18

The Program and Character of
British Socialism

THE EMERGENCE of socialism in England was sudden, but not unexpected. It was sudden in the same way that the bubbling of water that has just reached the boiling point is sudden: it happened quickly, but its happening was predictable. The assertion, however, that the emergence of British socialism was predictable requires understanding of what it does not imply as well as of what it does.

For a long time both socialists and communists have been predicting the demise of capitalism, and their prediction has even been reluctantly accepted as valid by some men who have little sympathy with either socialism or communism. That prediction, however, was not necessarily validated by the accomplishment of the Labour Government between 1946 and 1951, because what was defeated was not abstract capitalism, but British capitalism. British history specifically, not economic history generally, explains the predictability of British socialism. A determined campaign to nationalize a substantial part of American industry might eventually succeed, but it would have to overcome substantial opposition. The campaign to nationalize a substantial part of British industry met hardly any opposition at all.

THE INITIAL ACCEPTANCE OF NATIONALIZATION

In 1946 and 1947 the Labour Government succeeded in nationalizing the Bank of England, the coal industry, civil aviation, telecommunications, electricity and gas, and inland transport; iron and steel were taken over in 1950–1951.   With the exception of inland transport, particularly trucking, and iron and steel, all this was accomplished without serious opposition.   On the whole, Parliamentary criticism in the course of debate was directed, not against the principle of nationalization, but against the specific procedures proposed: vagueness in the definition of the powers of the Ministries concerned with the administration or supervision of socialized industries, lack of clarity in the organization recommended for those industries, whether or not the compensation proposed for dispossessed owners was adequate, the absence of exact provision for full publicity, and failure to suggest standards of efficiency against which the performance of nationalized industry could be measured.   It is true that expression was given to obvious fears—the danger of making decisions on political rather than economic grounds, the risk of stagnation arising from dependence upon the heavy and listless hand of bureaucracy, the absence of incentive or spurs to efficiency—but only in the cases of inland transport, to some extent in the distribution of electric power, and particularly in the very controversial bill for the nationalization of the steel industry was anything like organized opposition discernible.

The reason for this was not Conservative disorganization arising from political defeat.   From the very beginning such spokesmen as Winston Churchill were doughty in opposition, while acute, persistent and formidable criticism of governmental policy has animated the pages of the independently critical but not intransigeantly hostile, pages of the London *Economist.* Conservatives to be sure were hostile, and their hostility became crystallized in a manifesto issued by the Conservative Party in 1947.[1]   Industry, however, again with the exception of the railroads and the steel industry, accepted and in some cases welcomed nationalization.   The conclusion seems inescapable that, just as the climate of American opinion in 1933 made effective opposition to the New Deal extremely difficult, so British opinion in 1945

---

[1] *Cf. The Industrial Charter: A Statement of Conservative Industrial Policy,* published by the Conservative and Unionist Central Office, London, May, 1947.

generally accepted at least the first part of the Labour Party program as the consummation of a long and inexorable historical process. The platform upon which the 1945 English election was won distinguished between *agenda* and *non-agenda* in a manner entirely consistent with this interpretation:

There are basic industries ripe and over-ripe for public ownership and management in the direct service of the nation. There are many smaller businesses rendering good service which can be left to go on with their useful work.

There are big industries not yet ripe for public ownership which must nevertheless be required by constructive supervision to further the nation's needs and not to prejudice national interests by restrictive anti-social monopoly or cartel agreements, caring for their own capital structures and profits at the cost of a lower standard of living for all.[2]

THE PROGRAM OF NATIONALIZATION

How that *agenda* came to be selected is one of the most interesting and significant aspects of British socialist policy.

The Bank of England

The Bank of England has always stood in a peculiarly intimate relationship with the Government. Although for 252 years it existed as a private, joint-stock bank, it had originally been created out of political need. It was established in 1694 to give financial relief to the hard-pressed Whig Government of William and Mary. In return for its charter it loaned its entire initial capital of 1,200,000 pounds to the state at eight per cent, and successive renewals of its charter by Parliament confirmed its original monopolistic position as a joint-stock bank. In its early years, the Bank was the favored child of the state, and in its later ones it came to play the role of an essential, albeit unofficial, part of Government itself.

Its notes supplemented by the sound currency established by the recoinage of silver in 1696–1699, largely under the guidance of no less a person than Sir Isaac Newton who served first as Warden, then as Master, of the Mint, made the Bank partner of the state as joint guardian of the British monetary system. Its notes replaced gold as legal tender during the Napo-

---

[2] Quoted in *Labor and Industry in Britain,* British Information Services, New York, December, 1949; p. 177.

leonic period, and after 1844 it, together with the Treasury, was given the monopoly over note issue.

Originally a Whig institution, the Bank was founded amidst the welter of party politics. Tory financial policy, indeed, was so distrusted by the Whig "City" [3] of which the Bank was very much a part, that in 1710 the Governor and Court of the Bank unsuccessfully petitioned Queen Anne not to dismiss her Whig ministers.[4] Furthermore, for a long time the Bank was not always free from the suspicion that it was placing the interests of its stockholders above the interest of the nation. For that, among other reasons, David Ricardo himself proposed in 1824 that the Bank be nationalized.[5] Its national importance and its responsibility, however, soon caused the Bank to rise, first above Party, and in the course of the nineteenth century, to acceptance of the principle that the first charge upon it was the maintenance of financial stability rather than the earning of dividends. Dividends, and good ones, were nevertheless paid. Since 1923, for example, stockholders received twelve per cent annually.[6]

This institution, organized as Walter Bagehot suggested almost as a government in itself,[7] monopolizing the note issue, serving as banker for the state, managing the national debt and conducting a large part of the monetary business of the colonial governments, was, by 1946, so pre-eminently a national institution that its nationalization really made no difference:

It does not seem to me to make a ha'p'orth of difference one way or another whether it is nationalized or not.[8]

The Bank was nationalized partly because it seemed appropriate that an institution that was national *de facto* should be made one *de jure*. More significantly, however, the Bank was nationalized to bring under firm public control the credit machinery of the nation. The British Government, like others, had controlled capital investment and commercial credit during the

---

[3] The "City" is an English expression carrying, roughly, the same connotation that "Wall Street" does in the United States.

[4] *Cf.* Esme Wingfield-Stratford, *History of British Civilization*, London, 1930; p. 651.

[5] *Cf.* Ricardo, "Plan for the Establishment of a National Bank," in *Works and Correspondence*, edited by Piero Sraffa with the collaboration of M. H. Dobb, Cambridge, England, 1951; Vol. IV, pp. 271 ff.

[6] *Cf. Labor and Industry in Britain*, December, 1946, p. 214; and December, 1949, p. 189.

[7] Its Governor "is the Prime Minister of the Bank Cabinet," Bagehot, *Lombard Street*, New York, 1874; p. 185.

[8] Geoffrey Crowther, editor of the *Economist*, in a speech at Cambridge University. *Cf. The Times*, London, August 3, 1946; p. 3.

Second World War, and that experience made it clear that, if the British economy were to be transformed into a planned one, this vital sector of the economy must also come under planning:

> In day-to-day affairs, the nationalization of the Bank may at present make little difference. But it is profoundly significant in the power it gives the Government, in any emergency, to control credit and investment policy. In the words of the Chancellor of the Exchequer: "It brings into the safekeeping of the nation an indispensable keypoint for all future financial planning." [9]

Coal

The Industrial Revolution in England rested squarely upon the coal industry. It was this industry that made first use of the steam engine (for pumping water) and which, quite literally, developed the first railroads. Mined coal was originally carried from seam to pit head in baskets or on sleds. Later, wooden boards and then iron plates were laid down, and sleds or carts were pushed along these. Finally, toward the end of the eighteenth century, these plates were replaced by rails and flanged wheels were put on the carts.[10]

Coal was pre-eminently both the fuel and the power of the early industrial age and the industry expanded at a headlong pace. Output, estimated at three million tons in 1700 and ten million in 1800, rose to 35 million in 1841, to 117 million in 1871, to 225 million in 1900, and reached an all-time high of 287 million tons in 1914. By the outbreak of the First World War coal constituted more than one tenth of all British exports by volume, was producing profits of $65 million annually and an additional $30 million as royalties [11] and was directly supporting about one twelfth of the British population.

Despite this apparently healthy condition, signs of danger were perceived even before the First World War. The distinguished nineteenth-century economist Stanley Jevons, whose popular reputation still rests on his suggestion that the movements of the business cycle are correlated with sun spot activity, wrote a still readable book [12] in which he predicted trouble in the

[9] Cf. *Labor and Industry in Britain,* December, 1946; p. 183.
[10] Cf. Herbert Heaton, *Economic History of Europe,* New York, 1936; pp. 526–527.
[11] Under British law ownership of coal went with ownership of the land's surface. Landowners typically leased mining rights to entrepreneurs and drew royalties on the coal produced on their property.
[12] W. S. Jevons, *The Coal Question,* London, 1865.

early twentieth century from the exhaustion of the more accessible coal seams, the increased cost of mining coal at greater depth, and from intensified competition from the coal industries of other countries which would still be able to draw upon vast reserves of cheap coal.

The slump in productivity which has so plagued contemporary England set in early. Between 1901 and 1911 employment in the mines increased by thirty-six per cent, but output rose by only nineteen per cent.[13] The British coal industry was not keeping pace technologically. In 1901 fifteen per cent of British coal was being cut mechanically, and nineteen per cent by 1924. In contrast, twenty-five per cent of American coal was mechanically cut in 1900 and about sixty-six per cent in 1924.[14] Geological conditions such as narrow, tortured seams which only hand labor could get at were partly responsible for this relative technological backwardness, but much of the explanation lies in sheer apathy on the part of the industry. Intensely individualistic and comfortable in the steady flow of apparently assured profit, the mine owners exerted themselves only to counteract the rise of unionism and to curb social legislation. The result was militant unionism in the industry which received the distinction of being the first for which its employees demanded nationalization. It is no accident that the first representatives of labor to be elected to Parliament were drawn from the miners.

Real trouble, however, was held off until after the First World War when the industry was caught between rising costs and falling demand. Costs rose because of increased wage rates, the necessity of resorting to poorer and deeper seams of coal, and the failure to increase productivity. Demand fell because of marked economies in the use of coal,[15] the increase in foreign output[16] which intensified international competition in the export of coal, and finally because of depression in the heavy industries and stagnation in

---

[13] Cf. J. H. Clapham, An Economic History of Modern Britain, Vol. III, Machines and National Rivalries, New York, 1938; p. 63.

[14] Cf. C. R. Fay, Great Britain from Adam Smith to the Present Day, London, 1932; p. 264.

[15] For example, gasoline and diesel oil were developed as motor fuels, ocean shipping was increasingly converted to oil [in 1913, 1,500,000 tons of merchant shipping burned oil, but by 1925 the oil-burning tonnage had increased to over 20 million tons], and the development of hydroelectric power went ahead by leaps and bounds in the inter-war period.

[16] For example, between 1913 and 1929 Holland increased its production of coal from less than two million tons annually to almost 13 million. France, Spain, and Russia also increased production. The development of autarky in country after country stimulated this process.

international trade.   These forces were world-wide; before 1914 the world's consumption of coal had been increasing by about four per cent annually, but between 1914 and 1929 the *total* increase in world consumption is reported at only nine per cent.[17]   Their impact, however, was particularly serious for a country peculiarly dependent upon exports, and one, moreover, whose exports were directly or indirectly dependent upon coal.   The French occupation of the Ruhr in 1923, by severely interrupting German production, temporarily offset these forces so that their full pressure was not felt in England until after the General Strike of 1926.   By 1933, however, production had fallen to 208 million tons; it rose to 227 million in 1938, but by then technical and labor problems were so serious that, even during the Second World War when need was paramount, it was not possible to increase production.   Only 189 million tons were mined in 1946.[18]

The writing on the wall was already distinctly apparent in 1919 when the Chairman of a Royal Commission appointed to report upon the industry recommended that coal be nationalized.   In 1924 miners benefited by a national subsidy that augmented their wages, but the subsequent withdrawal of the subsidy prompted a disastrous and protracted strike.   In 1930 Parliament passed a Coal Act to promote compulsory mergers and to create Executive Boards of owners to administer "selling schemes" based on the control of output and price.

Eight years later (in 1938) Parliament took a more drastic step.   The Coal Reorganization Committee established by the 1930 Act was given additional power.   Still more significantly, the new Act nationalized Britain's coal reserves.   This meant that, although the industry was left in private hands, underground coal seams were taken over by the state and landowners thenceforth ceased to receive royalties.   Their compensation took the form of government securities to the value of fifteen times the royalty annually received.[19]

During the Second World War the problems of productivity and serious labor unrest brought the industry under tight national control.   Following the war, the coal industry became the subject of a series of investigations of which the most important was probably that made by the Reid Committee

---

[17] *Cf.* A. C. Pigou, *Aspects of English Economic History, 1919–1925,* London, 1947; p. 48.

[18] *Cf. Labor and Industry in Britain,* September–October, 1947; p. 185.

[19] The cost to the Government was 70,500,000 pounds.   *Cf. Labor and Industry in Britain,* February, 1946; p. 23.

which reported in March, 1945.[20]   That Committee recommended the thorough overhauling of the system of mining and of the underground transportation of coal, the comprehensive training and education of workers, and a greater degree of mechanization.   It stressed the necessity of sinking new shafts and the closure of uneconomic mines, and it urged a degree of concentration of control and even of management that was beyond anything yet attained.   It concluded thus,

It is evident to us, as mining engineers, that [these necessary changes] cannot be satisfactorily carried through if the industry is organized as it is today. . . . An authority must be established which would have the duty of ensuring that the industry is merged into units of such sizes as would furnish the maximum advantages of planned production.[21]

When the issue finally came to a head in 1945 the industry made a last minute attempt to stave off nationalization by proposing a Central Board to enforce technical and financial decisions.   But the miners were more insistent than ever that the mines be nationalized, and public opinion now supported them.   The plight of the industry was too acute and the degree of governmental control already so great that nothing could stop nationalization.

Civil Aviation

The nationalization of civil aviation, particularly overseas aviation, was fostered by considerations of imperial communications and national defense. For a quarter of a century the Government had been subsidizing and controlling the industry, and to such a degree that the process of nationalization had really commenced before the Labour Government took office.

Civil aviation developed after the First World War.   For two or three years private, unsubsidized firms, operating with war surplus equipment in many cases, struggled fiercely for survival.   The inability of all to succeed, together with the need, for reasons of security, of keeping skilled men and specialized equipment in being, impelled the Government in 1921 to begin

---

[20] The Committee consisted of seven prominent mining engineers; its Chairman was Charles [afterwards Sir Charles] Reid who later became a member of the National Coal Board appointed to administer the nationalized industry.

[21] Cf. *Coal Mining: Report of the Technical Advisory Committee*, H. M. Stationary Office, Cmd. 6610, London, 1945; p. 150.   Reprinted by permission of the Controller of Her Britannic Majesty's Stationary Office.

subsidizing various companies operating between London and the Continent.   In April, 1924, Imperial Airways came into existence with financial aid from the state,[22] a device possibly adopted in imitation of the fostering in European countries of one large, national company, favored with a subsidy and accorded the privilege of monopoly.   Germany had been setting the pace.   Her central position and her inability, under the terms of the Versailles Treaty, to develop military aviation, left her free to concentrate on civil aviation.   She did so by fostering and subsidizing successive amalgamations, culminating in the establishment of *Luft Hansa* in 1926.

In 1926 the British Air Ministry published a report [23] stating its plans for linking the Empire together through a system of airlines, and imperial airlines soon were developed.   In 1929 flights to India were inaugurated, and lines to South Africa, Singapore, and Australia soon followed.

Even so, dissatisfaction with service was continually expressed and official investigations of the industry followed one another in fairly rapid succession. On the eve of the Second World War the Government took the decisive step of nationalizing a part of the industry.   In 1939 the services to Europe operated by British Airways, Ltd., and those throughout the Empire which Imperial Airways controlled, were merged into the British Overseas Airways Corporation (BOAC), wholly owned by the Government.[24]

During the Second World War the Ministry of Civil Aviation prepared a plan for the postwar reorganization of the industry under which imperial communications were to be operated by BOAC, domestic and European services of all kinds were to be entrusted to private companies (travel, air, railroad, and steamship), and South American airlines were to be turned over to British steamship companies.   The Labour Party, however, was committed to the nationalization of key industries, among which it included civil aviation.   Since, in any case, a Conservative Government in this instance had set a precedent six years earlier, nationalization of civil aviation was not difficult to push all the way through.

---

[22] In 1929 the Government reported that in the preceding six years it had paid 1,613,380 pounds in direct subsidies to airlines.

[23] *The Approach Toward a System of Imperial Air Communications,* H. M. Stationary Office, London, 1926.

[24] British Airways received compensation of 573,500 pounds and Imperial Airways of 2,659,085 pounds.   The liabilities of the two companies were assumed by the state, and all employees were retained on terms at least as good as those prevailing under private ownership of the industry.   *Cf. Labor and Industry in Britain,* December, 1949; pp. 179, 188.

Communications

Over a century ago country after country established publicly owned and operated postal services.   That precedent made it easy for many countries, including Great Britain, to nationalize the telephone and telegraph.   That same precedent, of sufficient maturity in our own age to have acquired the respectability of familiarity, was now reinforced by the same considerations of imperial integration which we have seen operative for civil aviation, and the upshot was the nationalization of overseas telecommunications in 1947.

Private industry had operated the first British telegraph companies, but a rate war in the early 1860's followed by collusive rates and mounting demands from the public for integrated and uniform service, caused Parliament to nationalize the telegraph in 1868 [25] and to entrust its operation to the Post Office.   The cost of acquisition was eleven million pounds.

Essentially the same thing happened to the telephone, but by a more roundabout process.   In December, 1880, the courts had ruled that a telephone was legally a telegraph, but the Post Office was reluctant to operate the new instrument itself,[26] and for some time private telephone companies continued to serve under Post Office license.

A series of amalgamations ended in 1888 with the absorption by the National Telephone Company of its two principal competitors.   Existing patents were to expire in 1891, and when that happened many people expected the Post Office to acquire the entire telephone system.   The Associated Chambers of Commerce had voted in 1888 for a national system, and the influential *Economist* was expressing decided preference for public rather than private monopoly.   The merger of 1888 was apparently prompted by the anxiety of private telephone interests to strengthen their bargaining and financial power in the face of that threat to their independent existence.[27] The National Telephone Company, however, never succeeded in acquiring a complete monopoly.

By 1881 the Post Office, then under the administration of the blind economist Henry Fawcett (who was also the first paid Professor of Political

---

[25] Two years earlier the Associated Chambers of Commerce had petitioned Parliament for governmental ownership of the telegraph. *Cf.* C. R. Fay, *Great Britain from Adam Smith to the Present Day,* London, 1932; p. 213.

[26] Alexander Graham Bell had visited London in 1877 to demonstrate the telephone, but the Post Office was not yet convinced that it would work. *Cf. ibid.,* p. 215.

[27] *Cf.* Clapham, *op. cit.,* pp. 390–392.

Economy at Cambridge University), had established a number of municipal telephone systems (not too successful in operation), and these were still under Post Office control when the private merger came about.   In 1892 the Post Office acquired the trunk lines, leaving most of the local services to the National Telephone Company, but the situation was still unstable.   Between 1900 and 1912 certain English cities operated their own telephone systems, but these also were not entirely successful.   London was a special case; it was divided into three zones, one reserved for the Company, one for the Post Office, and one in which the two systems competed.[28]   Finally, in February, 1905, the National Telephone Company succumbed and agreed to wind up its business in favor of the state.   Parliament ratified the agreement in August, and on December 31, 1911, the Post Office took over the facilities and franchise of the company at a cost of 12,500,000 pounds.

Only cables were now left.   These were particularly important as links of Empire and they received attention on that ground.   During the First World War a Dominion Royal Commission had recommended the nationalization of private cable lines within the Empire.   By 1923 the Government had purchased an Atlantic cable from an American company and had taken over another which had been German.   In 1928, Cable and Wireless, Ltd., was formed by merging nine private companies, and to an increasing extent thereafter the Government participated in its ownership and management.   From the beginning of its existence two of its directors had been appointed by the Government, an Imperial Communications Advisory Committee had to be consulted on questions of policy, and a portion of the company's earnings had to be applied toward rate reductions or to any other purpose set by the Committee.

In 1938 the Government acquired over one eleventh of the company's capital stock in exchange for radio facilities transferred to the company by the Post Office, but even this arrangement became increasingly unsatisfactory as sentiment developed that so critical a service as imperial telecommunications should not be left in private hands.   During the Second World War discussions were held between the Home and Dominion Governments which culminated in a Commonwealth Telecommunications Conference.

That Conference unanimously recommended the establishment of a Commonwealth Communications Board to determine the rates [29] and policies

[28] Cf. Fay, op. cit., p. 216.
[29] Considerable concern was expressed at the prospect of cutthroat international competition which appeared imminent as a result of the great expansion of radio facilities during the Second World War.

of various overseas cable and radio services to be acquired, respectively, by the British, Indian, and Dominion Governments. The Board would be charged with the integration of the services so acquired, with their coordination with imperial defense, with the sponsoring of research, with the solicitation and conclusion of agreements with foreign interests, and with arrangements for pooling the revenues of the various nationalized services. The nationalization by Great Britain of Cable and Wireless, Limited, on January 1, 1947, accorded with these recommendations.

Power and Gas

Electric power and gas, as public utilities, have in England as elsewhere been subject to public ownership and operation, or, if provided by private enterprise, to considerable public regulation. In England until the 1840's it required a Special Act of Parliament to incorporate any public utility firm; then came special enabling Acts [30] for the incorporation of various types of firms. This special treatment was deemed necessary because utilities sometimes had to do things, such as condemning private property, which it would be dangerous to leave without restriction in private hands. The privilege of incorporation, therefore, was extended subject to carefully defined control over the power which incorporation bestows.[31]

After 1875, when municipalities were granted general powers to erect water and gas works, English cities began experimenting with municipally owned and operated utilities. Since private gas companies had already become established in many cities and since cities were not given power of compulsory purchase of private plants, emphasis was placed first upon municipal acquisition of water works, urban transportation systems, and, for a time, local telephone services. By the late 1920's municipal enterprise was providing two thirds of the electricity, two fifths of the gas, and four fifths of the urban transportation consumed in England.[32]

Even this was not entirely satisfactory. As "municipal socialism" developed it became increasingly clear that local operation, particularly in the case of electricity, precluded the realization of certain types of economies. When municipal law prevented, as it sometimes did, a city from selling

[30] *E.g.,* The Railway Clauses Act, 1845; the Gas Works Clauses Act, 1847, etc. *Cf.* Fay, *op. cit.,* p. 316.

[31] *E.g.,* corporate funds could be used for no other purpose than those specifically authorized in the charter.

[32] *Cf.* Clapham, *op. cit.,* p. 442.

electric power outside its corporate limits or restricted cities from pooling their several facilities, costs were bound to be higher than they otherwise would have been, and certain rural areas were denied adequate service. Parliament recognized this in 1919 when it created a national Board of Electricity Commissioners to encourage mergers, to create electricity districts, to suggest schemes for the integration of facilities within each district and to provide, when necessary, for governmental distribution of power.

A still stronger measure was taken in the Electricity Act of 1926 which created the Central Electricity Board to operate the "National Grid," an interconnected, nation-wide system of high tension lines. The generation of power was then centralized in a number of plants, some privately and some municipally owned, whose output was purchased by the Board and sold to distributors throughout the country.

Still, the industry was not adequately integrated. In 1936 the McGowan Committee conducted an official investigation which revealed complete lack of standardization of voltages or of rate schedules, a sore lack of services in the countryside, and an unnecessary multiplicity of small generating plants. That Committee recommended that any plan for the reorganization of the industry should consider the possibility of ultimate nationalization. By 1945 the balance was so weighted in favor of the municipally owned plants [33] and there was such clear necessity for governmental provision of a substantial part of the capital required for postwar reorganization and reconstruction, that nationalization seemed a foregone conclusion.

Inland Transport

The possibility that British railroads might someday be publicly owned has existed for a century. The first English railroads were private, small-scale, and intensely competitive enterprises. In the 1840's they began merging, thereby bringing to public attention the possible dangers lurking in monopolistic operation, and at the very time that national railway systems were beginning to appear on the Continent. The Railway Act of 1844 accordingly provided that the state might purchase British railroads, and it gave the state twenty-one years to exercise that option. The option, however, was not unencumbered with restrictions and qualifications, and it was never taken up. Since public ownership of railroads was postponed until

---

[33] 149 generating plants were privately and 197 publicly owned. *Cf. Business Week,* December 14, 1946.

after the Second World War, some other means had to be found of bringing order and responsibility into an industry that was both fiercely competitive internally and potentially exploitative with respect to its patrons. Parliamentary intervention, accordingly, continued.

Control of rates was inaugurated in 1844 when the "Parliamentary fare" of a penny a mile became the base against which other passenger fares were computed. Control of freight rates became national policy in 1888, and thereafter railroads were generally free to reduce rates but not to raise them,[34] and this provision applied at a time when costs were rising. The ratio of operating expenses to receipts rose steadily throughout this period in which railroad policy was being formed:

RAILROAD OPERATING EXPENSES AS A PROPORTION OF RECEIPTS [35]

1860	47%	1913	63%
1880	52%	1920	97%
1900	62%	1927	81%

Parliament was simultaneously scrutinizing amalgamations. It worked out a general rule that end-to-end mergers were to be permitted but that amalgamations of competing lines would not be. At the outbreak of the First World War over 120 separate lines still existed. Railroads were put under obligations to provide reasonable service, to accept and forward through traffic and goods from other lines, and to avoid undue discrimination.

During the First World War the state supervised the railroads as an integrated national system. Operations were left to the companies, but the Government met expenses and took the receipts, paying each road annually the net revenue it had received in 1913. At the end of the war, unscrambling was difficult and in many eyes inadvisable, while labor, as in so many other areas, was demanding nationalization. Parliament then was not prepared to go as far as that, but it did move toward nationalization in the Act of 1921 which merged British railroads into four great regional systems.

In the interval between the wars, railroad traffic was reduced both by depression and by intensified competition from motor transport. The Rail-

---

[34] Interestingly enough, the Railway and Canal Act of 1913 authorized the railroads to increase rates and fares when they could satisfy the Railway Commissioners that higher costs were caused by improvements in the conditions of labor. *Cf.* Clapham, *op. cit.,* p. 355.

[35] *Cf.* Clapham, *op. cit.,* p. 350, and Herbert Heaton, *op. cit.,* p. 548.

way Road Transportation Act of 1928 empowered the railroads to operate trucks and buses, but while they proceeded to do so, their purpose was their own protection rather than the integration of the two forms of transport. Moreover, the railroads continued to suffer under the handicaps of greater fixed costs—for rights of way, termini, and so forth—and far less flexible rate schedules. In 1938 and again in 1946, the railroads made suggestions for equalizing those burdens and for closer meshing of rail and road transportation facilities. The Labour Government's solution, however, was the nationalization of each.

Iron and Steel

The most serious of the controversies over the nationalization of an industry turned upon labor's plans for the steel industry. Here as elsewhere there is a record of governmental intervention and a history of accusations that the industry was slothful, backward, and monopolistic; but unlike the other cases we have surveyed, there was and is here no general acquiescence that nationalization is the only workable solution.

Great Britain led the world in the early development of the industry which is *par excellence* the capital-goods industry. By 1870 England was producing nearly half the world's iron and steel, but this was the high point. The industrialization of Germany and the United States, together with the erection of tariff barriers abroad, cost Britain her predominance, and by 1913 she was responsible for no more than one tenth the world's output.

The distress undergone by the British steel industry after 1918 was attributed by many to overcapacity, to cosseting of inefficiency, to obsolescence of plant and equipment, and to antiquity of organization. In 1932 Britain accorded tariff protection to the steel industry on condition that it modernize, and in the same year the British Iron and Steel Federation was organized with the blessing of the Government to coordinate the policies of the various trade associations in the industry. The Bank of England simultaneously gave financial assistance to a number of firms which undertook substantial reorganization. Output, which had fallen to 5.2 million tons in 1932 from 9.6 million in 1929, rose to almost 10 million in 1935 and to nearly 13 million in 1937. But prices also rose. With 1930 as the base, the index price was only 98.7 in 1934, but by 1938 it had risen to just over 139,[36] and this prompted accusations that nationalization was lagging and

[36] Cf. *Labor and Industry in Britain,* December, 1948; p. 159.

that the industry was setting monopolistic prices.   It is perfectly true and not astonishing that control of price and output by the industry itself have as long a history in the case of steel as in any other except, perhaps, coal and salt.   For example, an official investigation of trusts undertaken in 1919 revealed considerable sheltering of inefficient steel plants [37] by means of price supports operated by the steel industry.

Output was high during the Second World War, reaching 13 million tons in 1943, and 12 million in 1944 and 1945, but this was achieved only at considerable cost in deferred maintenance and replacement, to say nothing of outright damage or destruction by enemy action.   In May, 1945, the Churchill Government requested the Iron and Steel Federation to submit a four-year plan for reconstruction and development.   This was duly made and published as a White Paper [38] not long after the Labour Government came into power.

The Federation estimated that domestic demand for steel would aggregate about 13 million tons *per annum* between 1950 and 1955, and export demand at 3 million tons.   It accordingly proposed that capacity be increased to 16 million tons, which meant adding about 5 million tons to the capacity of blast furnaces and the construction of 6 million tons of capacity for turning out steel ingots.   Construction was to commence forthwith, would be in full swing by 1950, and would be completed by the middle of 1953.   Considerable scrapping of old plant was recommended, and that, in turn, meant that a strong central authority able to carry through its decisions would have to exist.   The Federation appeared unabashed at the implication that it would itself be that authority, but that same implication was too strong for socialist stomachs and was also misliked by others who distrusted the use a private organization might make of massive monopolistic power.

Another subject of criticism was the Federation's proposal for the relocation of certain plants.   Domestic British iron ore is of lower grade than much ore that can be imported, so that possible savings accruing through the use of domestic ore in plants located in the Midlands near the mines had to be weighed against the possible technical advantages of using imported ore in plants on the coast accessible to the great seaports.   The Federation recommended that no more than one million tons of the projected new capacity should be based on domestic ore.   This met immediate opposition, on the grounds that the coastal sites would prove to be uneconomic if the subsidy

[37] *Cf.* Clapham, *op. cit.,* pp. 303, 305–306.
[38] *The Iron and Steel Industry,* H. M. Stationary Office, Cmd. 6811, London, 1946.

on imported ore were ever to be dropped, and that the newer, interior sites would be unprofitable if Treasury aid for industrial development were ever ended.

The Federation's estimates of the future demand for steel were also assailed as being restrictive, and counter-suggestions were made that the industry should set its sights upon a figure somewhere between 17 and 25 million tons of additional capacity.

Two points about all this are of interest. *First,* it is clear that there was no general consensus that the British steel industry was "ripe and over-ripe for public ownership and management in the direct service of the nation." Apart from the broad issue of nationalization itself, most of the organized and effective opposition, in both England and elsewhere,[39] to the Labour Government's program was directed against the Steel Bill.

Second, this long-drawn-out episode constitutes the only instance in which the proposals of an affected industry really formed the basis of discussions for that industry's reconstitution. It is true that a committee of mining engineers diagnosed the sickness of the coal industry and proposed remedies for its cure of which many were accepted, but the substance of the Coal Industry Nationalization Act was supplied by the Government. The railway *industry* was the only one besides steel to propose a plan, but its plan was a counter-proposal to nationalization and received little support from labor or from socialists. In the case of steel, however, the Government accepted the Federation Report as a basis for planning, although it made substantial changes in emphasis and in many of the details; essentially, it superimposed nationalization upon the structure already suggested by the industry.[40]

SPECIAL AREAS OF SOCIALIST CONCERN

Agriculture

Intervention of the British Labour Government in the development and use of agricultural resources was comprehensive and exacting, yet the entire

[39] In opposing the Steel Bill the *Economist* specifically mentioned American dislike of the proposal to nationalize steel, and urged the Government not to push it lest aid under the Marshall Plan be jeopardized. *Cf., The Economist,* London, November 6, 1948; pp. 729–731.

[40] *Cf. Labor and Industry in Britain,* December, 1949; p. 187.

program contained little with which English farmers have not been familiar for a generation.

In 1846 Great Britain lifted its agricultural tariff (the famous "Corn Laws") and thereafter imported the bulk of its food for which it paid with industrial exports. With the development of grain lands on the American prairies, and later with the appearance of large-scale beef raising in the Argentine, British agriculture became specialized, concentrating on filling only certain shelves in British pantries. The problem of adjustment, particularly after the onset of the great depression of the 1870's, was acute, but the British Governments of that era, unlike their successors, acknowledged no temptation to provide relief. One explanation, of course, is the strength with which the philosophy of *laissez-faire* was then held; another may lie in the peculiar organization of British agriculture under which working farmers were characteristically tenants who could look to their landlords for a certain measure of relief. In 1873, for example, over half of England was reported owned by 2,250 persons possessing estates averaging 7,300 acres each.[41] After the First World War, on the other hand, more than one third instead of the earlier one ninth of British working farmers were independent, so that these could turn only to the state when they were in trouble.[42]

Until the First World War, at any rate, governmental interest in agriculture was largely confined to the protection of farm tenancy and the encouragement of "small holdings," or family-sized farms. A series of Agricultural Holdings Acts between 1875 and 1908 codified the standard British custom under which landlords provided land, buildings, and permanent improvements, but left tenants generally free to farm what and how they pleased. The chief result of these Acts was that tenants were given legal assurance of compensation, not only for improvements they themselves had made upon the farms they worked, but also for any unusual setbacks they might have suffered. Another form of relief to agriculture appeared in the Agricultural Rates Act of 1896 which exempted agricultural land from one half of the burden of local taxation—a principle which was extended in the early 1920's.[43]

For a long time Englishmen interested in agriculture had debated the relative merits of large-scale and small-scale farming. In 1848 John Stuart Mill

[41] *Cf.* Heaton, *op. cit.,* p. 433.
[42] *Cf.* Clapham, *op. cit.,* p. 535.
[43] *Cf. ibid.,* pp. 332, 525.

gave an eloquent defense of the latter, largely on social grounds, and a Select Committee appointed by the House of Commons in 1888 supported this position. An Act passed in 1892 to authorize County Councils to purchase land for re-sale or lease in relatively small holdings proved abortive, but in 1907 the Councils were given powers of compulsory purchase and the Board of Agriculture was instructed to prod the Councils into exercising those powers. Under this Act, 14,000 small holdings averaging fourteen acres each had come into existence by the end of 1914.[44]

It was the First World War which again made British agriculture the subject of national concern. To stimulate vitally needed production, farmers were given guaranteed minimum prices, while consumers were protected by the imposition of maximum prices, and incompatibility between those sets of prices was alleviated by subsidy. In the same manner agricultural labor was assured a minimum wage while landowners were restrained from increasing rents. Thereafter, England never really broke away from the agricultural pattern forced upon her during those years of war even though, for a brief time, there were signs that the pre-war structure of British agriculture was re-emerging.

By 1925 Britain again was dependent upon other countries for more than four fifths of its grain and over half its meat. In that year the state began to pay a subsidy upon the domestic production of sugar beets, and by the early 1930's English agriculture had again become a public charge. Guaranteed prices, publicly sponsored marketing and quota systems, and the reappearance of tariffs upon agricultural imports from foreign, although not from imperial, areas became probably permanent components of British agricultural policy. The Second World War, the postwar dollar shortage, and the consequential scarcity of food heavily underscored a problem which, to discerning eyes, had become visible even before 1914.

In this context the contemporary scarcity of British resources makes understandable the tight control over the use of land exercised today by the Government. It should be emphasized that it is not only the agricultural use of land that is kept under surveillance. The need to diversify and even to disperse the industries in the old "depressed areas" that were so hard hit during the depression has brought the industrial use of land under public control. Moreover, the wartime destruction of houses and factories gave opportunities, acknowledged by both conservatives and socialists, for the planning of cities as well as of the countryside.

[44] Cf. *Labor and Industry in Britain*, September–October, 1947, pp. 108–109.

Housing and Land Planning

Public interest in housing has been increasing in England since the middle of the nineteenth century.   As early as 1855, for example, the Corporation of Liverpool owned over four hundred tenements, and by 1909 the number had increased to more than seven thousand.[45]   The mere provision of public housing eventually developed into an interest in the planning of public housing, and that interest, in turn, led logically to interest in the planning of entire cities.   In February, 1943—two years before an avowedly Labour Government came into power—responsibility for suggesting and coordinating plans for the English land was vested in a new governmental agency, the national Ministry of Town and Country Planning.

Beginning in 1868 a series of Housing Acts gave local authorities general powers to clear slums and demolish unsanitary buildings.   The Housing and Town Planning Act of 1909 authorized municipalities to undertake a measure of city planning, although nothing much came of the authorization. Perhaps more significant for the future was the clause in Lloyd George's famous Budget of that same year that taxed away the "unearned increment" on land values.[46]

It was the First World War, again, which gave a note of urgency to the need for housing.   In 1919 the Government began to subsidize builders, but the subsidy was short-lived for the economy drive following the postwar slump stopped the whole program.   In 1923 an Act sponsored by Neville Chamberlain offered subsidies, again, to anyone who would build a house.[47] The Labour Government of 1924 tied the subsidization of houses to the control of rents, and made an unsuccessful effort to control the prices of building materials as well.   All of this did result in new construction: between 1919 and 1929, approximately 600,000 houses each were constructed by private industry and public authorities, and 400,000 houses were built by private builders under subsidy.[48]

Between the two World Wars housing came increasingly to be considered in relation to land planning and the location of industry.   In 1932 Parliament passed two measures, the Town and Country Planning Act and the

[45] Cf. Clapham, op. cit., p. 440.

[46] That tax produced more controversy than revenue and it was abolished in 1919, but the British Government of 1947 returned to and extended the principle which Lloyd George had introduced.   Cf. infra, pp. 439–441.

[47] Cf. G. D. H. Cole, The Intelligent Man's Guide to the Postwar World, London, 1947; p. 621.

[48] Cf. Heaton, op. cit., p. 723.

Prevention of Ribbon Development Act (to control houses built in rows)—
both designed to extend a minimum degree of planning over the whole country. Planning Committees were put to work in specific areas, and those
Committees were encouraged to work in cooperation with each other and,
when necessary, to prepare joint plans for contiguous or overlapping districts. The results were not spectacular, as there was considerable apathy
and occasional downright opposition to be overcome, but the principle then
established was one which the Socialist Government was to follow.

The problem of industrial location was more troublesome. The South
of England, particularly London, had been attracting industry at the expense
of the older industrial areas in the North and in South Wales. The result
was stagnation in the stranded regions and appalling congestion in the newer
ones. The social and economic problems which sprang from this migration had become so serious by the late 1930's that the Barlow Royal Commission was established to investigate and report, which it finally did in 1940.[49]
The Commission recommended that an Authority be appointed to disperse
industry and population from congested centers, to plan for the industrial
diversification of each region of Great Britain, and to give attention to the
development of small towns capable of industrial development, of suburban
"garden cities," and of "Trading Estates" which were an outgrowth of an
experiment conducted by the Board of Trade during the depression. That
Board had reached the conclusion that the development and diversification
of industry in the depressed areas was being restrained by the absence of
proper facilities to tempt the establishment of new enterprise. It accordingly initiated and encouraged the formation of Trading Estates, or companies which borrowed money from the Treasury and used the capital so
secured to purchase and develop land that had been zoned and planned for
industrial use, to erect buildings, and to install utilities. These buildings
were then available for lease to enterprising industrialists.[50]

The Barlow Report went on to recommend that municipalities be empowered to deal jointly with planning and development and that their dealings be subsidized. The wartime Government accepted the principle of
the Report by promising "that the principle of planning will be accepted, and
that some central planning authority will be required," [51] and it proceeded

[49] *Distribution of Industrial Population,* H. M. Stationary Office, Cmd. 6153, London, 1940.
[50] *Cf. Labor and Industry in Britain,* April, 1946; pp. 63–65.
[51] Quoted in Cole, *op. cit.,* p. 626.

to explore some of the implications by appointing two other Committees. The Scott Committee was charged with surveying,

. . . the conditions which should govern building and other constructional development in country areas, consistently with the maintenance of agriculture, and in particular the factors affecting the location of industry, having regard to . . . the well-being of rural communities and the preservation of rural amenities.[52]

Its Report [53] was issued in 1942.

The Uthwatt Committee, directed to prepare the legal basis for acquiring land and using it in the national interest on terms that would still be fair to owners, precipitated much controversy when its report appeared.[54] That Committee deemed the nationalization of land to be "politically impracticable," but it nevertheless made proposals which, if accepted, would deny landowners the right to use their land as they chose and would deprive them of ownership of any increment in the value of their land which might be a by-product of the land's development under public auspices. Since land so developed would in many cases have to be condemned, much of the issue turned upon the valuation of condemned land.

These reports, in the words of an agency of the British Government,

. . . were followed, during the war itself, by a spate of government measures, all designed to make certain that, during reconstruction, Britain would shake itself free, in town and country planning, from the grim legacy of the *laissez faire* industrial age, and put no private interest or dead wood traditionalism before a truly modern approach to decent living.[55]

The last venture of the wartime coalition government in this area is represented in the Distribution of Industry Act which became law in 1945, shortly before the Labour Government came into power. By this Act the Board of Trade was given general authority over industrial development in the "development areas." The Board may, subject to Treasury consent, purchase land and erect buildings, or it may loan funds to Trading Estates operating in those areas. Outside the Development Areas, the Board was to be given certain powers to inhibit industrial construction where "the provision

---

[52] Quoted, *ibid.,* p. 626. Reprinted by permission of the Controller of Her Britannic Majesty's Stationary Office.

[53] *Land Utilization in Rural Areas,* H. M. Stationary Office, Cmd. 6378, London, 1942.

[54] *Compensation and Betterment,* H. M. Stationary Office, Cmd. 6386, London, 1942.

[55] *Cf. Labor and Industry in Britain,* September–October, 1947; p. 160.

of further industrial premises would be seriously detrimental to the proper distribution of industry." [56]   That quoted clause finally had to be dropped in order to get the Bill passed before Parliament adjourned.[57]

None of these various measures in aid of housing, town and country planning, or the optimum utilization of land went as far as socialists demanded. They were, however, all taken before Britain had a socialist government, they were taken as the result of pressure which had been accumulating for years, and, in the aggregate, they provided a very solid floor upon which the Labour Government was to build.

[56] *Ibid.*, April, 1945, p. 54.
[57] *Ibid.*, July, 1945, p. 101.

19

British Socialism in Operation

1. CONTROL OF THE ECONOMY

T HE THEME common to the two preceding chapters is the essential continuity of recent British economic and social history. To many outsiders, and possibly even to some Englishmen, the performance of the third Labour Government of Great Britain appeared as a startlingly abrupt and portentous break with the past. The transition from capitalism to socialism seemed as abrupt as the succession of day by night in those tropics in which there is no twilight. We, however, have seen that the series of apparent plunges taken by the Labour Government was no consequence of any capricious, spur-of-the-moment decision. The socialists came to power at a time when Britain's economic plight, which was partly but not wholly the result of participation in two devastating wars, combined with and reinforced the historical momentum which for decades had been edging the nation toward the socialist threshold. It was as if those entrusted for a time with the administration of British destinies had been caught in a slowly moving, tightly packed throng. They were entirely willing to move with the throng; which was just as well for them because they had no alternative choice. While their destination, however, may have been clear in their own minds, the veering and eddying of the throng by which they were propelled had in it something of the erratic:

there were brief spurts followed by pauses, and the emergence and duration of each were not possible to predict.

Declining Emphasis on Nationalization

England, then, is really shuffling rather than plunging into socialism. What seemed in 1945 to be a plunge was only the lurch which finally carried Britain over the threshold.   Movement beyond that threshold has not proceeded very far, and some steps, indeed, have been retraced—the denationalization, for example, of steel and long-distance trucking.   That movement backward, although resisted, did not call forth shrieks of socialist anguish, and one reason it did not is the realization by many socialists that what they really want is the Welfare State, and that the Welfare State is not necessarily or solely to be attained through the channels of doctrinaire socialism.   Specifically, even among socialists, questions have been raised whether nationalization is the only answer.   Those questions came to be raised because of the dawning realization that nationalization is a means rather than an end, and that some of the ends which the public ownership of industry had hitherto been presumed to secure have already been substantially attained by other means.

"Exploitation," in the sense of returns to the owners of capital deemed disproportionate, has been reduced through both heavy taxation and the redistribution of income expected by expanding the scope and magnitude of social legislation.   Full employment has been no problem since the Second World War, and its continuance in the longer run of the future is regarded as something to which further nationalization is irrevelant.   Internally, with one fifth—albeit a most important fifth—of British industry already in public hands, the direction and tempo of economic activity is considered as being under firm control.   Externally, with Britain's heavy dependence upon her foreign trade, the volume of domestic employment is governed by forces beyond British control and to which nationalization, again, is irrelevant. The question of industrial efficiency remains moot.   Socialists assert that the record of the industries already nationalized is at least no worse than the record of those same industries before nationalization.   In any event, to safeguard and extend industrial efficiency in any industry, public or private, calls for attention and care to which, once again, nationalization is not directly relevant.   Finally, nationalization itself cannot alone assure to labor the sense of participation and functional responsibility which it admittedly has not had under any system since the development of large-scale industry. Nationalization, in fact, can complicate the attainment of that objective by replacing the identifiable, human, personal "boss" by the massive, impersonal and aloof state against which strikes may be prohibited.[1]

While, therefore, English socialists still flirt with the possibility of taking additional industries into public ownership—chemicals, sugar, and machine tools, among others, have been variously mentioned—and while a future Labour Government, for reasons of pride if nothing else, may well renationalize steel and long-distance trucking, the formation of a monolithic industrial state is something no one contemplates and few really want.   For some time to come, the structure of the British economy will remain "mixed."

In 1947 the Labour Government observed that its complete program involved the nationalization of no more than about twenty per cent of British industry.[2]   That proportion, indeed, requires interpretation.   One of the Labour members of Parliament estimated that, if governmental employees and members of the cooperative movement (which is closely associated with the Labour Party) were to be added to the employees of the industries either already nationalized or slated for future nationalization, something over six million workers out of a labor force of twenty million would be working in the public sector of the economy.[3]

Objectives of British Socialism

Nationalization, therefore, seems to be regarded even by its advocates as no more than one component among the means by which a larger end is to be attained.   In the large, that end is the maximization of output, the attainment and maintenance of full employment by controlling economic fluctuations, the equitable distribution of the national income, and the coordination of the use of resources with physical, social, and strategic requirements.[4]

[1] For a more leisurely account of this withdrawal from nationalization as the only, or even most important, element in the program of the Labour Party, cf. Austen Albu, "The Organization of Industry," in R. H. S. Crossman (editor), New Fabian Essays, London, 1952, particularly pp. 126 ff.

[2] Cf. British Information Services, Labor and Industry in Britain, New York, September–October, 1947; p. 162.

[3] Cf. John Parker, Labour Marches On, Penguin, London, 1947; p. 60.

[4] Cf. Central Office of Information, Post-War Britain, 1948–49, London, 1948; p. 53.

Economic Planning

The means by which this larger end is to be achieved reduce themselves, simply, to prolonged economic planning. By now it is reasonably clear that, whatever the political complexion of future British Governments, economic planning in some form is unlikely to be jettisoned, although its direction, details, and procedures will, of course, be subject to change.

In the 1945 election, for example, *both* major political parties were committed to the same policy of national social insurance, to the development of the National Health Service, to compulsory purchase if need be of land for housing and town planning, and to a policy of full employment.   The Conservative victory of 1951 left intact the far greater part of the enactments of the preceding Government.   Observe, finally, the caution with which one of the rising, younger Conservatives has summarized Conservative policy for the future:

(1) A halt to further schemes of nationalization until some ground exists for claiming success for some of the more controversial of these;

(2) The loyal operation of nationalization already in effect; and

(3) An industrial policy of our own which will render the case for further nationalization unplausible or unattractive.[5]

This seems almost Bismarckian, but that, too, is in the tradition of British Conservatism.[6]

THE MACHINERY OF ECONOMIC PLANNING: GOVERNMENT AGENCIES

Contemporary economic planning in Britain is necessarily a continuation of the procedures and techniques developed since 1919.   Concern for the British balance of payments goes back to the period following the First World War and involved, initially, various attempts to nationalize industry. In some cases industry itself tightened the powers of its various trade associations; in others, the state intervened to impose some sort of control over

[5] *Cf*. Quintin Hogg, *The Case for Conservatism*, Penguin Books, Inc., 3300 Clipper Mill Rd., Baltimore, Maryland, 1947, p. 295.

[6] *Cf*. Élie Halévy, *History of the English People, Epilogue, 1895–1905*, Book 2, Penguin, London, 1939; pp. 155–172.

both production and distribution.[7]   In the decade before the Second World War Britain abandoned complete free trade, established "imperial preference" and began experimenting with bilateral trade agreements.   Between 1939 and 1945 the nation acquired—the hard way—intimate experience with economic problems as problems which had to be approached from a national rather than a sectional, or even an ideological, perspective.   It is the continuation, if not even the exacerbation, of these same problems, reflecting themselves in severe shortages, which goes far to explain the common ground shared by both the Labour and the Conservative Parties.

As early as 1929 the Treasury issued a memorandum, *The Course of Prices in a Great War,* which forecast with considerable accuracy what another war would entail in such matters as the control of prices, profits and wages, taxation, output, imports and rationing.[8]

Centralized responsibility became necessary early in the course of the Second World War when its absence manifested itself in jurisdictional disputes among governmental departments and in a tendency to pass embarrassing problems on from agency to agency.   Centralization took two forms: *first,* resort to joint agreement rather than imposition of agreement from above so that Cabinet Committees settled among themselves such issues as joint priorities; and *second,* the balance sheet method by which estimates of total production and total requirements were set alongside each other for the purpose of revealing any discrepancies.   That latter procedure was worked out by a distinguished French official, Jean Monnet, in an abortive attempt to integrate the French and British economies in the first nine months of the war.[9]   A great part of British economic planning still consists in estimating and attempting to resolve such discrepancies.

The Cabinet

The ultimate planning authority is, of course, the Cabinet.   It assumed direct responsibility for this during the war when the Cabinet Secretariat was expanded to become virtually an Economic General Staff; a measure

---

[7] *E.g.,* the Coal Mines Acts of 1930 and 1938, the Agricultural Marketing Acts of 1931 and 1933, the Sugar Industry (Reorganization) Act, the Cotton Spinning Act of 1936, and the Cotton Industry (Reorganization) Act of 1939.

[8] For comment, *cf.* W. K. Hancock and M. M. Gowing, *British War Economy,* His Majesty's Stationary Office, London, 1949; pp. 47–58.

[9] *Cf. ibid.,* pp. 185–186, 384 ff.

of specialization was achieved when the Ministers Without Portfolio were charged with the coordination of economic policy.

This general procedure was carried on during the first year of the Labour Government when the responsibility for supervising domestic economic policy was assigned to the Lord President of the Council, Mr. Herbert Morrison. By 1947 the deepening economic crisis and the necessity to reconcile the sometimes conflicting requirements of short- and long-run economic policy brought about the concentration of responsibility for economic affairs in the hands of the Chancellor of the Exchequer,[10] and the creation of two new planning agencies.

The *first* of these agencies, the Central Economic Planning Staff, is a body of permanent government officials and of economists and statisticians from the Universities. It is purely an advisory body with no executive responsibilities whatever. It was established to coordinate the use of economic resources, to stimulate thought, and to propose action upon important economic issues. It emits, in March of each year, a new publication, the *Economic Survey* which is at once a report upon the economic state of the nation and a suggested program for the ensuing year.[11]

The *second* of the new agencies, the Economic Planning Board, was established "to advise His Majesty's Government on the best use of our economic resources, both for the realization of a long-term plan and for remedial measures against our immediate difficulties." [12] This Board has two major functions: to accord men of practical experience an opportunity to review proposed economic projects, and to keep both industry and labor initially and continuously in touch with governmental plans. To achieve this dual purpose, representatives of organized labor and of industry sit on the Board alongside senior officials of the Treasury, of the Central Economic Planning Staff, and of other important economic departments.

The departments themselves are the primary executive agencies for realizing approved plans. This does not mean that they are nothing more than passive executants. Their permanent officials have an *expertise* which it would be sheer folly not to consult. Accordingly, in addition to departmental representation on the Planning Staff and the Planning Board, there

[10] In September, 1947, Sir Stafford Cripps was made Minister of Economic Affairs. When he went to the Treasury, two months later, that office was abolished, but he carried its functions with him.

[11] The *Economic Survey* is thus similar to the *Reports* of the Council of Economic Advisers in the United States.

[12] *Cf.* Central Office of Information, *Britain, 1950–51, A Reference Handbook,* London, 1951; p. 8.

exist a variety of inter-departmental committees concerned primarily with breaking down the various departmental projects into such major categories of economic planning as—the program for capital investment, the balance of payments, and problems of manpower.   Representatives from the Economic Secretariat of the Cabinet, the Central Economic Planning Staff, and the Central Statistical Board serve on these committees together with members of the interested departments.

The Ministries

The more important of these departments are the Treasury, the Ministries of Supply, Food, Agriculture, Works, Civil Aviation, Transport, Fuel and Power, and the Board of Trade.   A "sponsoring" system, which developed during the Second World War, has been continued since then, so that each broad sector of the economy has a sponsoring department to which it can refer its problems.   In broad outline, these sponsoring departments stand as follows:

The Ministry of Supply: capital-goods industries

The Board of Trade: consumers'-goods industries

The Ministry of Fuel and Power: electricity, gas, and coal

The Ministry of Transport: railroads, roads, and (together with the Admiralty) shipbuilding

The Ministry of Works: industrial and public construction and civil engineering

The Ministry of Health: water supply and some responsibility for housing

The Ministry of Agriculture: forests and fisheries, agricultural production, imports of animal feeds

The Ministry of Food: processing, importation, purchase and distribution of food.

METHODS OF PLANNING

The longer-run objective of planning an economy for both stability and expansion has been overshadowed by more immediate urgencies attributable largely, but not wholly, to the war.   In consequence, the English people still live, to a perceptible degree, in an economy distinguished from a war economy only by the absence of a *single* economic objective commanding general support.

During the Second World War the need to win was paramount in all minds, and that need justified to almost everyone the necessity for economic controls toward which not everyone has subsequently been so acquiescent. The reluctance of some manufacturers to produce for export and the appearance of "spivs" and "drones" who evade labor regulations constitute some indication that there has not been complete unanimity about Britain's postwar program. The increasing ground swell of criticism of that program by men who are perfectly sympathetic with its basic purposes is another indication.

The struggle to make ends meet has been forced upon the nation by circumstances and—some would say—by policy. One consequence of that struggle is a seeming incongruity between the ultimate objective of British planning, the attainment of tranquil and assured general well-being, and the more immediate necessity of imposed austerity and tightened belts.

The Immediate Predicament

We are already familiar with the British predicament. During the Second World War, heavy sales of British investments in other countries reduced the income thence derived to less than 100 million pounds, while at the same time Great Britain incurred foreign debts amounting to 2,795 million pounds.[13] This wartime destruction of the resources upon which Britain's postwar livelihood would depend was described by Keynes as a story

of financial imprudence which has no parallel in history. Nevertheless that financial imprudence may have been a facet of that single-minded devotion without which the world would have been lost. So we beg leave to think that it was worth while—for us, and also for you.[14]

To complicate matters still further, one quarter of British merchant shipping was destroyed during the war, and that meant a substantial reduction in a very important earning asset. To this must be added the damage, destruction, or conversion of manufacturing facilities which whittled down the volume of exports immediately available. Moreover, increasing difficulties

[13] For a simple account of those happenings, *cf.* G. D. H. Cole, *World in Transition,* New York, 1949; pp. 322 ff.

[14] Quoted in *Labor and Industry in Britain,* as cited, September, 1949; p. 136.

in the coal industry meant not only that a traditionally important export item was jeopardized, but that a vital raw material for the domestic economy could not be had in adequate volume. Finally, British gold and silver reserves had been reduced by about one half. All this amounted to a really serious curtailment of the means of payment for the nation's very sustenance.

At the same time the need for that sustenance had increased. Population had risen [15] and employment was higher, which meant either that the volume of imports had to rise or that the standard of living had to be driven down. This is one instance of the incompatibility between short- and long-range policy alluded to earlier. The British standard of living has been held down; how to get it up again is a problem to plague any government.

Britain did find it possible to shift somewhat from foreign to domestic sources of supply, but at considerable cost. During the Second World War the acute scarcity of shipping meant that space rather than cost had to be economized. Therefore, bulky products like grain tended to be produced at home, at the expense of pasture land and therefore of meat production. The cost, in real terms, amounted to a dietary shift away from meat, eggs, sugar, fruits, and fats in favor of potatoes, cereals, and fish. The following figures are illustrative:

FOOD CONSUMPTION IN BRITAIN, POUNDS PER HEAD PER YEAR [16]

	Prewar	1948	1949	1950 (Provisional)
Meat (edible weight)	109.6	73.8	74.6	94.1
Dairy products (milk solids)	38.3	49.1	52.4	54.2
Sugar and syrup (sugar content)	109.9	85.3	91.1	82.6
Oils and fats (fat content)	45.3	38.1	44.3	45.0
Potatoes	176.0	237.2	255.5	252.8
Cereals	210.1	249.4	238.0	221.6
Fish, game, poultry	32.8	37.2	35.2	28.4

In economic terms, the cost was twofold. War-induced changes in the world production of food forced Britain, even as late as 1947, to purchase 47 per cent of her food from the hard currency area of the Western Hemisphere, in contrast with only 27 per cent before the war.[17] This, in turn, reinforced the pressure to raise food uneconomically at home, so that, in 1947 for example, the volume of foods and feeds imported was only 75 per

[15] It was 47 million in 1937, and 48.2 million two years later. *Cf. Labor and Industry in Britain,* June, 1950; p. 75.
[16] Source: *Labor and Industry in Britain,* December, 1951, p. 169.
[17] *Ibid.,* June, 1948, p. 69.

cent of the 1938 volume.[18]   The saving in foreign exchange so brought about, and particularly the saving in dollars, was at the expense of high domestic costs of production in a country where a large industrial population simply cannot be supported from indigenous agricultural resources. To producers, although not to the economy, those high costs were partially offset by food subsidies aggregating 400 million pounds in 1947–1948; 485 million in 1948–49; and 410 million in each of the two following years. Those figures represent slightly more than ten per cent of governmental revenue derived from taxation.[19]

Expenditure for imports of industrial raw materials was still more difficult to reduce, particularly in the face of rising foreign prices.   Britain must import all her rubber, cotton, silk, jute, hemp, copper, and many other nonferrous metals; most of her flax, oil, lumber and wood pulp, wool, lead, paper, hides and leather; and a large fraction of her iron ore.   It could produce domestic substitutes for some of these, but again, in many cases, the raw material for the substitutes would have to be imported.   This dependence is permanent, but its significance since the war had been aggravated by the necessity of importing much machinery as well, in order to make up for wartime losses.

Between 1939 and 1945, for example, disinvestment resulting from physical destruction and deferred maintenance and repairs amounted to about three billion pounds.   An example of the importation of industrial equipment was the purchase from the United States of a 30,000 ton steel rolling mill at a cost of $36 million.[20]

The British Government has summarized its basic problem in one paragraph:

> The severity of this country's balance of payments difficulty dates from the war, and the devastation left behind by the war which threw out of gear the mechanism by which the United Kingdom used to pay its way in the world. During the war itself, in a ruthless effort to divert men and materials to the Forces and to production for the common cause, the volume of United Kingdom exports was cut to less than one third of the 1938 volume.   A large part of our foreign investments accumulated over generations were sold; heavy debts to allied and other countries were incurred; a big proportion of our merchant fleet was lost; and great physical damage was suffered.[21]

[18] *Ibid.,* p. 69.
[19] *Ibid.,* June, 1948, p. 61; June, 1949, p. 60; June, 1950, pp. 62–63; and December, 1951, p. 168.
[20] *Cf. ibid.,* June, 1950, p. 70, and December, 1948, p. 161.
[21] *Cf.*   Reprinted by permission of the Controller of Her Britannic Majesty's Stationary Office, *Economic Survey for 1948,* Cmd. 7344, London, March, 1948; p. 5.

An additional complication developed with the war-induced dependence of Western Europe generally, and including Britain, upon the so-called "dollar area" in the Western Hemisphere. The European countries which also had been ravaged by the war not only ceased supplying Britain with essential supplies, but turned themselves to North America for the same kinds of supplies which Britain was simultaneously seeking in the same market. In 1938, 31 per cent of British imports came from the Western Hemisphere, and in 1947 44 per cent; in the same period, the proportion of British *exports* to the Western Hemisphere dropped from 17½ per cent to 15 per cent.[22]

Short-run Planning

So far, Britain has met the problem just described by the ruthless curtailment of all but essential imports, by the continual drain of gold and dollar reserves, by further foreign borrowing, by aid extended her from the United States and the Dominions, and by a strenuous effort to increase the volume of exports at least 75 per cent above their prewar volume. The reduction of imports and the diversion of domestic production to foreign, especially dollar, markets [23] has meant, quite explicitly, a denial of supplies for British mouths and backs, and that, in its turn, has forced the continuation of economic controls and a large degree of economic planning. In so far as that planning is directed to the solution of the balance-of-payments problem, it takes the following forms:

1. The *reduction of excessive dependence* upon the Western Hemisphere as a source of supply. The Government hopes to pare down that dependence to no more than 17 per cent of total imports, in contrast to the 44 per cent figure which held in 1947.[24]

2. The *reduction of the total volume of imports* by stimulating domestic production and developing substitutes, and, in particular, by increasing agricultural production by 50 per cent over the prewar level.[25]

[22] Cf. *Postwar Britain, 1948–49,* as cited, p. 44.

[23] As an example of what this means, many British households since the war have boasted about their acquisition and ownership of chinaware, for example, classified as "export rejects." Many store windows have had displays marked—"For Export Only."

[24] Cf. His Majesty's Stationary Office, *European Cooperation: Memorandum Submitted to the Organization for European Economic Cooperation Relating to Economic Affairs in the Period 1950–51–52,* Cmd. 7862, London, 1950; p. 16.

[25] Cf. *Postwar Britain, 1948–49,* as cited; p. 41.

3. The *expansion of the volume of exports,* particularly to the dollar area, by at least 75 per cent of the prewar level.

The British themselves have described the task which confronted them at the end of the Second World War:

> . . . industries all require increased *manpower,* which must be found by drawing off labour from less vitally important industries. *Productivity* can be increased by re-equipment, re-deployment of manpower, improved management technique, and by giving full play to inventive genius. Increased *capital investment* will require national savings. Restraint will be necessary both in *consumption* to reduce imports to a minimum and increase exports to a maximum and also in *wage demands* and the *distribution of profits* in order to avoid inflation and rising prices.[26]

Types of Control

To bring all the above into effect, the following types of controls have variously been imposed:

1. *Imports have been controlled* either through direct purchase or through a licensing system administered by the Board of Trade. The stringency of control has varied with economic need. In November, 1948, and again in March, 1949, the Labour Government lit two "bonfires of controls" in which the licensing of imports was greatly eased, and the Conservative Government has not hidden its dislike of economic control. The machinery for it has nevertheless not been dismantled.

2. *Raw materials have been allocated* to industry in accordance with prevailing priorities by a variety of governmental agencies of which the Board of Trade, the Ministry of Supply, and the Ministry of Works have been among the most active.

3. *Industrial goods in short supply*—of which certain types of machinery and machine tools are typical—have had their acquisition or disposal controlled under a similar licensing system.

4. *Manpower* has been subjected to an ebb and flow of controls according to need. At the end of the Second World War, military conscription was the only important control which remained, and it still remains. Subsequent crises forced the temporary restoration of manpower controls which had played important roles during the war. The *Registration of Employment Order* required all employable persons [27] who were either engaged in

---

[26] *Postwar Britain, 1948–49,* p. 50. Italics are in the original.

[27] *I.e.,* men aged 18 to 50 inclusive, and women 18 to 40 inclusive, except for women having in their households children under 18.

some unimportant activity (for example, peddling) or who were not gainfully employed at all, to register with an employment exchange. The *Control of Engagement Order* required employers seeking labor, or workers seeking jobs, to have recourse either to a local office of the Ministry of Labour or to an approved employment exchange, in order to channel labor to the industries deemed most essential. Few specific directives were made under this Order, however, and all controls over manpower, except for military conscription, were ended in 1950.[28]

5. *Production* has been controlled, *negatively,* by denying raw materials or labor to non-essential projects, and *positively,* by compelling the production of certain "utility goods," that is, "goods designed to meet essential needs in a sensible manner, produced in the most economical manner possible and sufficiently clearly defined for their prices to be fixed." [29] The production of "utility goods" was initiated during the war in order to assure the civilian economy adequate supplies of standardized, dependable, necessary, and cheap goods. Their specifications were drawn up by the British Standards Institution (corresponding in general to the Bureau of Standards in the United States Department of Commerce) and their production was supervised by the Board of Trade.

One of the most difficult and important of the decisions that had to be made pertained to the division between the production of producers' goods and consumers' goods. Production of the former was urgent, partly to re-equip British industry and partly because capital goods constitute an important part of British exports, which, also, had to be expanded. At the same time, in a "pressure economy," the production of anything is necessarily at the expense of something else foregone, and postwar Britain was also semi-starved for consumers' goods. The Government nevertheless insisted on according high priority to gross capital formation which, despite cuts made in the fall of 1947 and again in 1949, has averaged over twenty per cent of the gross national product since the war, in contrast to fifteen per cent in 1938.[30] To support investment at this rate has required careful budgeting coupled with effective control over the use of resources, high taxation, and, for a time, stringent rationing of consumers' goods. Rationing of such things as meat, fat, cheese, and coal continued for years.[31] In July, 1954, all rationing came to an end.

[28] *Cf. Labor and Industry in Britain,* as cited, March, 1953; p. 38.
[29] This official definition of "utility goods" is quoted, *ibid.,* June, 1946; p. 97.
[30] *Ibid.,* June, 1950; p. 95.
[31] *Cf.* British Information Services, *Britain in Brief,* New York, Revised edition, June, 1953; p. 5.

6. The *distribution of consumers' goods,* particularly food, fuel, and clothing, has been controlled primarily through rationing, although other devices have been found for influencing the volume and the kinds of goods available for consumption.   One of these was the system of "utility goods" already described, although the Conservative Government has thrust that system largely into abeyance.   Other devices have been the control of exports through priorities and licensing, and trade agreements with other countries and even industries.   For example, an agreement was made with American oil companies for their payment in sterling rather than in dollars, and that made it possible to relinquish the rationing of gasoline.[32]

Taxation and its opposite, subsidization, are extremely important methods of controlling expenditure, and hence consumption.   Within the domestic economy, personal incomes are taxed at a standard rate of 45 per cent subject to exemptions for small incomes and for dependents, and incomes above 2,000 pounds are subject to steeply progressive surtaxes culminating in a tax and surtax of 95 per cent upon incomes exceeding 15,000 pounds. Customs duties and "purchase" (that is, sales) taxes contribute to directing consumer expenditure into channels deemed necessary and away from those the Government wishes to block.   For example, essential domestic and industrial articles, surgical equipment, and such "utility" goods as are still extant are exempt from the purchase tax; so are purchases by tourists who are willing to undertake the sometimes long-drawn-out procedure necessary to exempt them.   Rates are high and schedules complicated.   Jewelry, for example, pays a 75 per cent tax, cars and radios pay 50 per cent.   Many household appliances are subject to a 25 per cent levy, and that last rate holds even for so necessary and familiar a British possession as the common umbrella.[33]

7. *Financial controls* are largely exerted through the Budget, although the powers held by the Treasury and the nationalized Bank of England [34] over commerical banks are also important.   There are, moreover, certain statutory and institutional procedures designed to make financial control effective.

The important *Borrowing (Control and Guarantees) Act* of 1946 made permanent that control by the Treasury of the capital market which had been

[32] *Cf. Labor and Industry in Britain,* as cited, June, 1950; p. 49.

[33] *Cf. Labor and Industry in Britain,* as cited, June, 1953; pp. 55–56.

[34] The *Bank of England Act* (1946) gave the Bank new powers over commercial banking.   It may request information from, or give directions to, commercial banks, and without Treasury approval.   The Treasury, on the other hand, needs the sanction of the Bank in order to give directions to commercial banks. *Cf. Postwar Britain, 1948–49,* as cited; p. 63.

introduced as a wartime measure. A Capital Issues Committee controls the raising by any one concern of capital sums exceeding 10,000 pounds, in any given year, except that borrowing working capital from a bank in the normal course of business remains uncontrolled. That control includes the very important right to prohibit fund-raising *at all* by any concern in an industry not deemed to be sufficiently in the public interest. The *Exchange Control Act* of 1947 consolidated and adapted the various wartime *Defence (Finance) Regulations* concerning dealings in foreign currencies.

Two financial corporations were established in 1945, shortly before the Labour Government assumed responsibility for British affairs, and they may yet come to play an important part in supplementing the regular institutions of the British counterpart of Wall Street. One of these, the *Industrial and Commercial Finance Corporation,* was established to provide capital for small borrowers whose enterprise might be wanted, but whose needs might be too insignificant to appeal to the dignity of the traditional and conservative City, yet too large for commercial banks to meet easily. It is empowered to make loans ranging between 5,000 and 200,000 pounds, and it does so in two ways: (1) It makes advances repayable in regular installments for periods up to twenty years at four to four and one half per cent; or (2) it may purchase stock or options to purchase stock in order "to participate both in the risk and the profit, to insist that part of the latter be ploughed back into the business, and to maintain regular contact with the borrower, in whose hands alone, however, the business of management remains." [35]

The second of these institutions, the *Finance Corporation for Industry,* operates on a more grandiose scale, assisting firms or industries which are essential to the national interest, but which, for one reason or another, are unable to raise capital by the normal procedure. It may make loans in amounts upwards of 200,000 pounds, and in form it is a private, limited company owned jointly by a large group of insurance companies (40 per cent), trust companies (30 per cent) and the Bank of England (30 per cent).

8. *All* these *planning* and *control mechanisms,* some of which are adaptable to long- as well as short-run planning, reach upward to and *are centralized* in the *annual National Budget.*[36] That fact is both obvious and revolu-

---

[35] *Ibid.,* p. 67.

[36] Sir Stafford Cripps remarked, as Chancellor of the Exchequer, in his Budget Speech of April 18, 1950: "The Budget can be described as the most important control—the most powerful instrument for influencing economic policy—which is available to the Government." Quoted in *Labor and Industry in Britain,* as cited, June, 1950; p. 58.

tionary. Fiscal policy is no longer oriented primarily toward keeping the Budget in balance whenever it is possible to do so. The Budget, instead, is contrived to so direct total national expenditure as to guard against either inflation or deflation, whichever seems the greater danger. Since the Second World War, the pressure has been mainly inflationary, and the purpose of budgetary manipulation has accordingly been to hold expenditure to a minimum—or, more accurately, to eliminate "unnecessary" forms of expenditure. When we come to discuss the Welfare State we shall see that certain forms of expenditure take precedence over even budgetary considerations, and are expected to do so even in the long-run. There are, however, still other considerations.

Control of Inflation

Financial counteraction to inflation may take either or both of two forms: a reduction in governmental expenditure or the discouragement of personal expenditure. Postwar Britain has not been alone in finding the latter easier than the former, and postwar Britain, rightly or wrongly, has shown greater determination in pursuing that latter course than any other country west of the Iron Curtain. The inflexibility of governmental expenditure has been defended by allusion to international and defense commitments that cannot be reduced, the substantial outlays the Government has had to assume for the re-equipment and development of British industry, and the costly popular "mandate" to expand social services. At any rate, the British Government, like others, has found it difficult to reduce its own disbursements, and even the Conservatives have been unable to do more than re-arrange the direction of expenditure, as the following table indicates:

ESTIMATES OF EXPENDITURE AT BEGINNING OF EACH FISCAL YEAR
(In millions of pounds) [37]

	1950–51	1951–52	1952–53	1953–54
Interest on debt, etc.	517	564	590	638
Sinking Fund	20	20	35	35
Defense	824	1,342	1,549	1,636
Education	243	252	259	286
Housing	61	60	61	70
Food subsidies	402	410	250	222
Social services	797	815	746	832
Other ordinary expenditure	658	757	660	540
TOTALS	3,522	4,220	4,160	4,259

[37] Source, *Labor and Industry in Britain,* as cited, June, 1953; p. 56.

Explanatory argument for inability to reduce governmental expenditure frequently rings familiar to American ears,[38] and that is not mere coincidence. We shall see later that contemporary governments become bound in the same inflexibilities.

Since public expenditure was difficult to reduce, private expenditure had to be if inflation were to be held under control. Private expenditure, accordingly, was reduced, and by means of taxing personal incomes at very high rates. The *purpose* of high taxation of personal incomes was not only to control inflation, but also to release goods for export through rendering Englishmen unable to afford them, and to provide a margin for capital formation by the Government, again by constricting the pull of private expenditure upon the use of resources.

The *effect* of this taxation, however, has been the subject of controversy. Following a suggestion by the economist Colin Clark, there has been considerable and interesting speculation whether income taxation at rates exceeding, perhaps, twenty-five per cent of income, may not really be inflationary rather than deflationary. High taxes, in short, may discourage the assumption of the risks of production simply because the fruits of production do not accrue to the producer; yet increased production is one of the means of counteracting an inflation in process.

Whether or not taxation may become inflationary because it discourages production remains controversial. There really is one way, however, in which taxation may contribute to inflation: that is when it provokes successful demands for compensatory increases in wages and salaries. In England those demands did mount, and to such a degree that, early in 1948, the Government was compelled to take a public stand in the form of a statement by the Prime Minister to the House of Commons, suggesting:

. . . the following general considerations as a guide to all those whose deliberations and actions contribute to the settlement of the amount of personal incomes, from whatever source,

(A) It is not desirable for the Government to intervene directly with the income of individuals otherwise than by taxation. To go further would mean that the Government would be forced itself to assess and regulate all personal incomes according to some scale which would have to be determined.[39] This would be an

[38] For example, Sir Stafford Cripps defending his 1950 Budget in a radio speech remarked, ". . . the next time anyone talks to you about cuts in Government expenditure, ask him to tell you what he'd cut and how much it would save and who'd pay for it afterwards." Quoted in *ibid.*, June, 1950; p. 65.

[39] This statement cannot have been pondered for long. The British system of steeply progressive personal income taxation has exactly the effect of assessing and regulating all personal incomes according to a scale which *is* determined—by the tax.

incursion by the Government into what has hitherto been regarded as a field of free contract between individuals and organizations.

(B) In the view of the Government it is essential that there should be the strictest adherence to the terms of collective agreements.   One of the main advantages of a system of collective bargaining is that it tends to ensure that wage and salary movements take place in an orderly manner and with due regard to the general as distinct from the individual interest.   Departure from the agreed conditions by individual employers, whether public authorities or private concerns, will inevitably constitute a grave danger to the stability of the system of collective bargaining, and may well lead to competitive bargaining, and thus to general but unjustifiable increases in wages and salaries and to serious inflation. . . .

(C) In present conditions, and until more goods and services are available for the home market there is no justification for any *general* increase of individual money incomes.   Such an increase will merely raise costs of production, without making more goods available, and so can only have an inflationary effect.   Unless accompanied by a substantial increase in production, it would drive up prices and charges, adversely affect pensioners, children, and other recipients of social services benefits, increase the money costs of our exports and so reduce their salability, and by black market pressure make it almost impossible to operate the controls necessary in view of the continuing scarcity of supplies and manpower.

(D) It does not follow that it would be right to stabilize all incomes as they stand today.   There may well be cases in which increases in wages or salaries would be justified from a national point of view, for example where it is essential in the national interest to man up a particular undermanned industry and it is clear that only an increase in wages will attract the necessary labour.   It does not, however, follow that each claim for an increase in wages or salaries must be considered on its national merits and not on the basis of maintaining a former relativity between different occupations and industries.[40]

In the spirit of that basic policy, the Government attempted to induce labor unions, through the powerful Trades Union Congress, to exercise restraint in seeking higher wages, and to discourage corporations from declaring higher dividends.   For example, following the balance-of-payments crisis of 1947, the Chancellor of the Exchequer introduced an interim Budget to adjust purchasing power to the fact that more goods than ever had to be exported and fewer imported.   In his Budget Speech the Chancellor remarked upon the "continued persistence of many corporations to declare increased dividends"—and the profits tax was forthwith doubled.[41]   The unions, likewise,

---

[40] *Statement on Personal Incomes, Costs and Prices,* February 4, 1948, Cmd. 7321. Reprinted in full in *Labor and Industry in Britain,* as cited, March, 1948; pp. 25–27.
[41] Cf. *ibid.,* November–December, 1947; p. 237.

have at times kicked over the traces,[42] although they have not done so to the extent that one might have expected.

Both unions and Government, however, face a dilemma. The unions, traditionally concerned with protecting and advancing the interests of their members, are driven by considerations of circumstances and politics to give weight to the national interest as well. Many of their leaders have sufficient political and economic sophistication to realize this, as the series of statements and even exhortations repeatedly issued by the Trades Union Congress demonstrates; but it can be no easy task to convince the average workman of the validity of the reasons for eschewing at least in part the old policy of seeking increases in wages when conditions for success appear propitious. It is both a tribute to his essential reasonableness, and perhaps also to the traditional British penchant for feeling one's way rather than going by the book, that the newer policy has met the success it has had. There has been no coercive wage freeze. The Government has relied upon collective bargaining, and has exerted persuasive rather than regulatory pressure.

The Government also faces a problem. Whatever its political complexion, it must reckon with labor, but a Labor Government must reckon with it in a peculiar way. The record of the first postwar British Government exposes the issue with some distinctness. Dependent upon the Labour Party, committed to a long-run policy of raising living standards and economic well-being, that Government nevertheless was under the embarrassing necessity of curtailing disposable income, restricting consumption, and prolonging—even extending—wartime "austerity." It met the issue, *first,* by an extended campaign of public information designed to disseminate as widely as possible understanding of the nature of, and reasons for, the economic problems which confronted the nation. The keynote, for whatever its persuasive effect may have been, was struck by Prime Minister Attlee in an address to the nation on March 3, 1946: "You are not just working for wages or profit. You are working for the Nation." [43] *Second,* the Government inaugurated a variety of projects, such as the guarantee of full employment and the expansion of social services, and while it did so out of genuine conviction that they could and should be attempted, that program had the additional merit of placating those supporters of the Government

[42] In 1951 pressure from the rank and file forced the Trades Union Congress to insist that "there must be greater flexibility of wage movements in the future." *Cf. ibid.,* March, 1951; p. 13.

[43] *Ibid.,* April, 1946; p. 53.

whose hopes for the more abundant life had, in other respects, been frustrated.

The specific problem of wages was faced, *first,* by the guarantee, implemented through collective bargaining, of a minimum realized wage in a substantial number of industries. That guarantee, which was reassuring to labor, took the form either of an assured number of hours of work each week to be paid for at standard wage rates, or of an assured minimum percentage of the normal weekly wage. Some examples follow:

GUARANTEED MINIMUM WEEKLY EARNINGS OR EMPLOYMENT [44]

Industry	Normal Work Week	Guarantee
Coal mining	5 shifts of 7½ hours plus one "winding time"	Full time
Heavy chemicals	44 hours	Full time
Cement	48 hours	34 hours
Pottery	47 hours	34 hours
Brick	48 hours on kilns and boiler, 56 hours for firemen	Two thirds
Engineering	44 hours	34 hours
Cotton	45 hours	About 80%
Wool	45 hours	75%
Shoes	45 hours	75%
Laundering	45 hours	40 hours
Flour	44 hours	Full time
Baking	48 hours	Full time
Construction	44 hours (winter) 46½ hours (summer)	32 hours
Industrial canteens	47 hours	44 hours
Motor buses	44 hours	Full time
Docks	44 hours	Set payment

The Government also attempted, not entirely successfully, to approve wage increases only when they were associated with increases in productivity. The Chancellor of the Exchequer himself remarked, on October 4, 1949,

On piece rates or incentive rates, based on production, we want people to earn all they can—the more the better. It is basic rates that we cannot afford to see increased.[45]

[44] Source: *Labor and Industry in Britain,* as cited, June, 1948, p. 84. Columns 2 and 3 have been interchanged.

[45] Quoted in British Information Services, *British Economic Record,* May 15, 1950; p. 1.

Long-run Planning

We have devoted considerable space to a discussion of the machinery for short-run planning in Great Britain. Paradoxically, perhaps, much less space will be needed to account for the long-run. The reason is neither ennui nor exhaustion, but the simple fact that the British, like most others, are always caught up in the moment at the moment. Lord Keynes once observed that in the long-run we are all dead, and what he meant was, not that the future is not worth bothering about, but that it can only be reached through a succession of presents, and the present together with the immediate tomorrow is nothing but the short-run. Even the Russians whose planning is structurally more doctrinaire, and hence more rigid, than that of the British, do not really plan for more than five years ahead, and we have seen that their operative plans are quarterly plans. There is no short-cut to the future.

Nevertheless, there are two senses in which it is possible to talk about long-run planning in England. *First,* there are the aspirations which men hope to quicken into living reality and which therefore color, however subtly, what they do today. British aspirations encompass the realization of the Welfare State. The road thereto is devious and frequently rough, but whatever turnings or detours are made necessary by the immediate terrain, the engineers are determined that the road, despite its twisting, shall be bent toward that bourn. That bourn is to be the subject of the following chapter.

Second, the more distant purpose toward which the British strain comprises the extension of public responsibility in the arena where economic decisions are made and the deflection of economic activity itself toward the satisfaction of public and national, rather than private and personal, needs. All the machinery of planning which the British have devised, used as it is to meet the exigencies of the present, can be turned toward that end, and this is particularly true of the program of nationalization. Indeed, the essential explanation of why nationalization has occurred at all lies in the presentiment that public ownership is the passkey to diffused prosperity. Public control through governmental intervention, if sufficiently firm and prescient, would suffice to overcome the crises of the present, but public control alone carries the implication that interference with private responsibility is at most a necessary evil and that there is something worth saving in private industrial property and responsibility. It is exactly that something that socialists recoil from. Contemporary qualms about the extent to which nationalization should be carried, to which we have alluded at the beginning of this chapter, arise not out of any return of belief in the merit of rugged economic individualism, but out of a sense that all-out nationalization would defeat its purpose by concentrating rather than diffusing power. The British do not wish King Stork to succeed King Log. Just enough nationalization, then, to provide a governor, or a balance wheel, for the British economy is what appears to be sought, and in that sense nationalization represents a tool of long-run planning.

Economic Control through Nationalization

The nationalization of British industry has been undertaken in those cases "where, in the view of the Government, supported by a majority in the House of Commons, common ownership is urgently needed for high production and efficiency, or generally for the economic welfare of the nation." [46] We have already observed that in most of these cases there is a long history of antecedent pressure, either for outright public ownership or for a degree of public control that would amount almost to public operation. The Labour Party clarified its policy in a public statement issued in April, 1949, proposing that the Government start new public enterprises when these were clearly needed to "take over inefficient concerns which are woefully failing the nation," and to purchase any existing businesses which might be offered for sale and operate these "fairly and squarely" in competition with private industry. [47]

Still further clarification came during the General Election of 1950 in which little public enthusiasm, or even interest, in further nationalization is reported to have been manifest. Both the Labour Party and the Trades Union Congress then proposed that subsequent extension of the public sector of industry take place, not by outright nationalization, but by developing government "yardstick firms" to compete with private industry and thereby to set standards for it to follow, or by taking over the delinquent firms of an industry not considered to be pulling their weight. [48]

Although for a long time socialists in Britain, as elsewhere, thought of public enterprise in terms of a sort of Post-Office nationalization, the indus-

[46] Cf. *Labor and Industry in Britain,* as cited, December, 1949; p. 177.
[47] British Labour Party, *Labour Believes in Britain,* quoted *ibid.,* p. 177.
[48] Public policy statements issued in August, 1950. *Cf.* the *New York Herald Tribune,* August 27, 1950.

tries taken over in Great Britain since the Second World War are not operated by a government department like the Post Office.   When the comparative rigidity and the lack of full autonomy characteristic of government departments came to be recognized as handicaps to the effective operation of
industry, British socialism turned to "municipalization," or operation by
local governments.   That also proved unsatisfactory in the case of industries which ought to be operated on a regional, or even national, scale, so
that in the 1920's the public corporation [49] was introduced as a device for
the operation of services nation wide in scope.   This was the procedure followed by the Labour Government from 1945–1951.

Public corporations correspond in form and power to the private corporations of industry.   They have separate legal existence with clearly defined
statutory powers and duties; they can sue and be sued, and are subject to
taxation; they have as much autonomy in decision and freedom in operation
as is deemed compatible with public accountability; and they are administered by Governing Boards corresponding to the Directors of a private corporation, except that these are responsible, not to a constantly changing body
of stockholders, but to one or another of the Governmental Ministries.

The responsibility of the Governing Board of one of these public corporations is potentially very great; in practice, it depends upon the extent to
which it is left alone by the Ministry to which it is responsible.   In principle
it is charged with appointing the chief officers of the Corporation, determining output, planning development, fixing prices—although in accordance
with general principles laid down by Parliament—[50] dealing with labor, considering criticism, handling jurisdictional and other disputes with other public
corporations, fixing policy on research and technological progress, and so on.
Parliament sometimes gives general directions,[51] and the ultimate authority

[49] *E.g.,* the Central Electricity Board, 1926; the British Broadcasting Corporation,
1927.

[50] For example, the *Coal Industry Nationalization Act* provides that, "The policy
of the Board must be directed to securing, consistently with the proper discharge of
their duties, that the revenues of the Board shall not be less than sufficient for meeting
all their outgoings properly chargeable to revenue account (including interest and contributions to reserve fund) on an average of good and bad years." Quoted in *Labor and
Industry in Britain,* as cited, December, 1949; p. 183.   Reprinted by permission of the
Controller of Her Britannic Majesty's Stationary Office.

[51] For example, the *Iron and Steel Act* required the Iron and Steel Corporation to
operate so as "to secure the largest measure of decentralisation consistent with the
proper discharge by the Corporation of their duties." . . . Quoted by D. N. Chester,
"Organisation of the Nationalised Industries," *Political Quarterly,* London, April–June,
1950; p. 127.

of the responsible Ministry is real indeed,[52] but the real division of responsibility remains moot.   With the exception of the Court of Directors of the Bank of England, members of the Governing Boards have no tenure.   They are appointed by the Minister, and may be dismissed by him;[53] moreover, in most cases, the size of the Board is legally indeterminate so that a Minister, if he so chose, could pack the Board of a recalcitrant corporation.[54] On the other hand, Ministers have been able to evade questions in Parliament by denying responsibility.[55]   What apparently has been happening is that Ministers exert influence in private, to which Boards perforce give great heed, but are cautious about asserting overt responsibility.[56]

This seems confusing, but the confusion arises out of the fact that neither the locus of responsibility for the operation of nationalized industry nor the precise criteria for determining how to operate them have yet been worked out.   In principle, the public operation of industry reflects the belief that economic responsibility should be vested in the Nation, exactly as political democracy is presumed to reflect national responsibility for political decisions; but in both cases, the size of the electorate and the need for specialized technical competence have compelled the delegation of authority.   Politically, it has taken centuries to grow into an established system of use and wont, and problems still arise; economically, the venture has only just begun.

The determination of appropriate criteria by which to guide nationalized industry is still more difficult and new.   Should their primary function be the earning of profit, the provision of employment, the purveyance of cheap supply—if need be, under subsidy—the redistribution of income, the determination of a yardstick standard to be emulated by whatever private enterprise may be tolerated, the conservation, through wisely controlled utilization, of scarce natural resources which should be regarded as part of the

[52] Sometimes it is spelled out: for example, the *Coal Act* provides "that the Minister of Fuel and Power may give 'directions of a general character' to the Board on matters affecting 'the national interest,' and that they must reach agreement with him on all large-scale planning activities."   *Cf. Labor and Industry in Britain*, as cited, December, 1949; p. 183.

[53] This has happened.   When the African ground-nuts (*i.e.*, peanuts) project proved far less successful and far more expensive than had been planned, the then Minister of Food, John Strachey, dismissed two members of the Overseas Food Corporation Board.   *Cf.* W. A. Robson, "The Governing Board of the Public Corporation," *Political Quarterly*, as cited, p. 148.

[54] *Ibid.*, p. 137.

[55] By Parliamentary convention, Ministers need not answer a question transcending the limits of their responsibility.   *Cf.* Ernest Davies, "Ministerial Control and Parliamentary Responsibility," *ibid.*, p. 154.

[56] *Ibid.*, pp. 154–156.

public domain, or as the forcing ground for the development and nurture of incentive deemed superior to the lust for private profit?

These are questions for the future. The plan for the Welfare State has only just begun to be subjected to the test of hard reality and no one can yet discern the properties of the state that will emerge. So far, however, nationalization as the key to the future has not really unlocked many doors.

The industries that have been nationalized in Great Britain have shown neither startling success nor hideous failure, but this lack of failure may be largely attributable to their momentum. In most cases they are operated by the same men who managed them as private corporations, and their day-by-day operations have been conducted in the same manner, by the same principles, and toward the same ends as hitherto.

It is curious to reflect how predominantly ritualistic is the difference that nationalization has made. The same people do the same things; the original stockholders continue to receive incomes (although as interest on government bonds rather than as dividends on stock); the nationalized railroads continue to run on nationalized coal; but individual Englishmen continue to choose between first- and third-class compartments as if the egalitarian society of the socialist dream were nothing but a dream. Like the word *Rumplesnitz* in Heywood Broun's fable, *The Fifty-first Dragon,* nationalization so far has served largely as a word by which self-confidence, perhaps even self-satisfaction, is whipped up.

─────────────────────20

British Socialism in Operation

2. THE WELFARE STATE

IN THE United States the expression "welfare state" is frequently used in derision to connote a kind of social para-
sitism, the desire to get something for nothing. That connotation is so common that even those Americans who would like to see the
Government guarantee full employment, or assure adequate medical care
to everyone, eschew the expression.

It is quite otherwise in England. Attainment of the welfare state is quite
generally acknowledged to be an appropriate objective of public policy.
Even British conservatives concede the necessity, if not the desirability, of
providing the British people with a good part of the substance of the welfare
state; conservative opposition is directed toward the *extent,* but not the *fact*
of governmental responsibility for welfare.

In England, accordingly, the obstacles to the attainment of the welfare
state have arisen more from the economic predicament in which England
has been placed than from opposition to the program itself. Despite those
obstacles, however, very substantial progress has been made toward the
realization of the ultimate socialist end—provision of a guaranteed minimum
for everyone.

THE MAJOR GOALS OF BRITISH POLICY

The major components of the policy of the Labour Party since the Second World War appear to be (1) the maintenance of employment as high, and of unemployment as low, as it is possible for them to be maintained, (2) the completion of the structure of the Welfare State the foundations for which began to be laid over a century ago, and (3) the preservation and continuation of the shift in the distribution of the national income in the direction of greater equality.[1]

These objectives are clearly interdependent, and the means for the attainment of one contribute as well to the achievement of the others.   Perhaps it is worth remarking, again, that the policy of striving toward these ends does not carry exclusively the hallmark of socialism; other political parties than the Labour Party give lip service to, if they do not actively seek, the realization of at least part of the same goals, although they are in frequent disagreement with the Socialists upon the timing, the scope, and the ability to meet the costs.

Underlying Emphasis on Full Employment

The British are now confident that it is within their powers to maintain full employment, at least so far as internal economic forces are concerned. The resort to fiscal policy for non-fiscal reasons, the readiness to pour substantial public investment into a halting industry in time of slackness, the redistribution of income in favor of the poorer classes whose sustained consumption is thereby supported, together with the nationalization of important sectors of industry—all these combine to keep the domestic economy under control; and control is the clue.   Unemployment, in a word, is presumed to appear when things get out of hand, and control is needed to keep them from doing so.

The haunting fear of unemployment which does still persist arises from the number and strength of the economic forces which are beyond the reach of British control.   Of these, the most important is felt to be British economic dependence upon foreign trade, particularly with the dollar area which is regarded by the British as still vulnerable to depression and in which a

[1] *Cf. The Economist,* London, June 3, 1950; pp. 1201–1202.

slump would reduce British income, deprive Great Britain of part of her market, and make it correspondingly more difficult for her to provide herself with needed foodstuffs and industrial raw materials. If that, however, should be the area in which things get out of hand, there is little that any British Government could do about it.

Domestically, however, the implications of the organized stretching toward welfare are, and remain, inflationary rather than the other way about. Since the war, Britain, like other countries, has persistently generated income faster than goods have been produced. Sir William Beveridge, indeed, whose hand shaped a substantial part of the edifice of living British socialism, was so concerned with the moral and social degradation which is the bitter fruit of massive and prolonged unemployment, that he proposed a continuing policy of artificially holding the number of jobs slightly in *excess* of the number of men and women available to fill them.[2] The inflationary consequences of so doing were regarded as less undesirable than the consequences of workmen competing with other workmen for jobs too few to go around.

The British, in fact, have not gone as far as to create more jobs than jobholders. On the contrary, when the Economic and Social Council of the United Nations sought governmental suggestions for a full employment "standard," the British Government replied, in 1951, that it considered the employment of 97 per cent of the domestic labor force at the seasonal peak the equivalent of full employment.[3] One of its reasons for selecting that figure was the somewhat doubtful one that it did not carry inflationary implications. This is a technical issue to which we shall recur.

The completion of the transformation of the British economy into a Welfare State, including public measures to redistribute the national income in favor of the otherwise poorer classes, represents the justification of other forms of governmental intervention than nationalization. To these we must now turn.

THE BALANCED ECONOMY

The Distribution of Industry

Coal mining, the manufacture of iron, steel, and tin plate, ship-building, and heavy engineering are industries which were particularly hard hit by

[2] *Cf.* Sir William Beveridge, *Full Employment in a Free Society,* New York, 1945; pp. 125–129.
[3] *Cf. The Economist,* London, March 31, 1951; p. 731.

the depression of the 1930's. They also happen to be industries which are heavily concentrated in Northern England, Southwest Scotland, and South Wales. That geographical concentration of industry involved a like concentration of human unemployment when depression struck: in the areas named, more than half the insured labor force were out of work throughout the black depression years.

In other parts of Great Britain conditions were not quite so bad. Metropolitan London and Birmingham, for example, contained a greater proportion of light industry whose products enjoyed a somewhat more sustained demand than did those of the capital-goods industries in the older industrial regions. The obvious but superficial remedy for the geographical concentration of unemployment was the migration of labor from the less prosperous areas to the more prosperous. Some migration did occur; between 1921 and 1937, for example, more than half a million people moved into London,[4] but that migration was no real remedy. It increased congestion in the centers of immigration, without really relieving unemployment in the cities the migrants left behind them.

Englishmen at last reached the conclusion that the solution for unemployment in the blighted areas was to move industry *to* them rather than men *out* of them. An effort to accomplish exactly that was made during the 1930's, but without conspicuous success. In 1945 the Coalition Government made a fresh start with the *Distribution of Industry Act*. Under that, the regions of Great Britain to be pushed into an industrial renaissance were defined by statute and re-named Development Areas. In those, the Board of Trade was empowered to purchase land, under compulsion if need be, construct factories upon it, and provide these with necessary utilities and services. With Treasury approval, the Board of Trade could also lend funds to Industrial Estates [5] when these were prepared and willing to assume responsibility for developing industrial premises. The Treasury was also empowered to offer financial assistance to manufacturing enterprises in actual or prospective operation in the Development Areas.

All this was helpful, but it did not meet socialist wishes to plan the regionally balanced distribution of industry. That defect, if such it was, was given at least statutory attention in 1947, after the Labour Government had come into power.

[4] *Cf*. His Majesty's Stationary Office, *The Distribution of Industry*, Cmd. 7540, London, 1948; p. 8.

[5] Industrial Estates succeeded the older Trading Estates which began to appear in 1936. They are private, non-profit companies formed with the blessing of local government authorities to buy, develop, and then lease land to industry.

The *Town and Country Planning Act,* among other provisions,[6] enjoined local planning authorities from approving any application for the construction of any factory to have more than 5,000 square feet of floor space without certification from the Board of Trade that the proposed construction conformed to the "proper" distribution of industry.[7] Thereafter, the Government could inhibit unwanted industrial development. It could not, however, compel private industry to extend itself in regions which private industry would not select of its own accord, although presumably nationalized industry could be thrust anywhere. What the Government did try was the enticement of the cat with cream.

The function performed in the United States by chambers of commerce, some railroads, and some municipal and state governments of wooing coy entrepreneurs, has been assumed in England, and on a national rather than a local scale, by the Board of Trade. That agency, which keeps itself in touch with other interested Departments such as the Ministry of Town and Country Planning, the Ministries of Labour and Works and the Treasury, boasts a "Planning Room," an institution long known to General Staffs but in this case dedicated to Vulcan rather than to Mars. It is equipped with all the paraphernalia of planning such as maps, descriptions of various industrial areas, and the records of every factory in England which employs more than a hundred hands. All this material is placed at the disposal of anyone seeking to build a factory, and it can be supplemented by even more detailed information in the possession of the Board's regional offices.

These services can be, and are, used to manipulate the extension of industrial development into favored, and away from undesired, regions. There is nothing rigid about the procedure; negotiation with a would-be entrepreneur is informal, casual, and courteous; many industrialists are reported to have been convinced that their original plans were not completely in their own interests, but in other cases the Board of Trade has itself given way.[8]

Information is reinforced by other inducements. Physical facilities equipped with necessary utilities can be leased, either from the Board of Trade or from Industrial Estates, and financial assistance also can be offered to enterprises which give promise of being going concerns. The Board of Trade, with Treasury consent, may make grants or loans out of its own

[6] The Act as a whole will be discussed later. *Cf., infra,* pp. 438–441.
[7] *Cf.* Ben W. Lewis, *British Planning and Nationalization,* New York, 1952; p. 178.
[8] *Ibid.,* p. 180.

resources, and the Treasury itself, with approval of the Board, may extend aid.   In terms of results, somewhat more than half of the factories constructed in Britain since the end of the Second World War have been concentrated in the Development Areas.

Town and Country Planning

Closely associated with the distribution of industry is the planned use of the land that supports not only industry, but the whole population and all its activities.   During the past half century British society has moved progressively from sporadic interference to correct or prevent abuses, to deliberate public control in order to relieve congestion, protect the countryside, secure access to open land in even crowded areas, and to maintain a proper balance between the agricultural, industrial, residential, and recreational use of land.   The framework of recent ventures in these directions consists of three basic Acts: the *New Towns Act* of 1946, the *Town and Country Planning Act* of 1947,[9] and the *National Parks and Access to the Countryside Act* of 1949.[10]

Planning of new towns.   The *New Towns Act*, as its title indicates, was designed to safeguard the citizenry of new or growing towns against the congestion, confusion, and sometimes bleakness that helter-skelter development too frequently entails.   The Act empowers the Minister of Town and Country Planning [11] to designate any area, including if necessary the site of an existing town, as the setting for a proposed new town, provided he can persuade local authorities that planned development of their territory is in the national interest.   The Minister may then establish corporations to acquire, hold, develop, or dispose of land in any manner consistent with the development plan proposed by the corporations and approved by the Ministry.[12]

In areas without existing utilities, the corporation concerned may develop and thereafter provide these.   All development plans must be submitted to

[9] There were really two *Town and Country Planning Acts,* one for England and Wales and one for Scotland.   They will, however, be treated as one, since the major differences between them pertain to the locus of administrative authority.

[10] For a more extended account of these Acts, *cf.,* Central Office of Information, *Britain, 1950–51, A Reference Handbook,* London, 1950; pp. 240–244.

[11] In January, 1951, his title was changed to Minister of Local Government and Planning.

[12] The only statutory limitation of this power is the restriction, in all but exceptional cases, of all leases to a maximum period of 99 years.

the Minister, and each corporation must submit an annual report to Parliament.   After a new town has come into being and has established itself, the Minister is expected to dissolve the founding corporations and transfer their powers to local governments of the conventional type.   The capital cost of development is advanced to a corporation out of the Consolidated Fund, and is ultimately to be repaid.

The corporations are permitted considerable freedom to experiment in order not to jeopardize variety and flexibility among the different development plans.   In general, the optimum population of a new town is regarded as about 50,000, although development plans approved up to 1951 provide for populations that range between 10,000 and more than 60,000.[13]

A balanced social composition is sought, and particular care is given to proper zoning.   The purposes that zoning may achieve have been examined somewhat more thoroughly than in the United States.   Americans have generally used zoning laws to protect areas against undesirable kinds of encroachment; to keep slaughter houses out of residential areas, for example. In England, zoning has been used not only for the negative purpose of providing protection against unwanted intrusion, but also for the positive purpose of assuring convenient and ready access to centers of resort.   Homes, for example, are grouped so that stores, public buildings, playgrounds and parks, centers of employment, schools and churches, and last, but to Englishmen far from least, the open country, are all within close and easy propinquity.

A substantial number of these new towns are to be developed near London; others will be in or near to existing or prospective industrial areas, and they will be designed to relieve congestion without jeopardizing the labor supply needed by manufacturing or mining establishments.   Some have already come into existence, frequently in the form of older towns that have been absorbed into the new.   Perhaps for that reason, but perhaps also because they were conceived in the halls of government, they are not conspicuous for variety in design or for flexibility in execution.   Perhaps in time age will provide the patina that conveys charm.

Planning of towns and country.   The desired balanced national distribution of industry, agriculture, and residence could scarcely be had by giving thought only to the development of new towns.   The purpose of the *Town and Country Planning Acts* of 1947 was to bring the use of land, *for all purposes,* under a system of national control.   The control authorized in those

[13] *Ibid.,* pp. 242–243.

Acts was stringent indeed: no development of any kind could be undertaken without prior approval from the appropriate authority, and no owner of land might benefit from any enhancement in its value which development might bring about. We shall shortly see that there has subsequently been partial relaxation of those controls.

The Acts imposed upon County Councils and County Borough Councils [14] the *duty* of submitting development plans for the areas under their jurisdictions to the Ministry. That means that planning for this purpose is to be concentrated in the hands of men with intimate knowledge of the areas for which they are planning, but who are not themselves primarily planners or necessarily sympathetic with the idea of planning, and whose tenure of office is beyond the reach of the Ministry.

The Act provides that the preparation of a plan must be preceded by a survey of the physical, economic, sociological, and other conditions and resources in the area of each planning authority's responsibility. The plan itself is expected to embrace the course and content of future development, and should explicitly indicate any proposed improvements in transportation or road facilities, the land to be reserved for agricultural use, and the direction in which towns may expand, and all this is to be indicated in stages specifying the rate at which planned development is to occur. Provision is made for publicity before submission of a plan so that affected interests will not be taken unawares by what is planned for them, and provision is also made for review and possible revision of plans at five yearly intervals.

The impact of this upon the owners of land is potentially severe. Part of the severity was mitigated by the *General Development Order* of 1950 by which public control over most buildings on farms, most ordinary additions to dwelling houses, and certain small additions to factories was relinquished. Financial implications, however, remain.

The Act permits local authorities to purchase land under compulsion when it needs that land for development either by themselves or by private developers approved by them. Any such purchase was intended to be made at a price based upon the *existing* use and value of the land. It was, indeed, the intention of Parliament that any future sale of land with the buildings erected upon it should be priced at its existing, and not its potential,

[14] County Councils are the local governments of smaller districts; County Borough Councils are the corresponding authorities for larger units. Normally, County Boroughs contain at least 50,000 people, and recent legislation provides that no new County Boroughs may be established for areas with populations below 100,000. *Cf., ibid.,* p. 11.

value; in other words to eliminate, not only speculation in land values, but the accrual in private pockets of any future increments in the value of privately-owned land.[*]

This, like so much else accomplished by the Labour Government, was no fledgling panacea whipped together on short order by contemporary socialist druggists. John Stuart Mill himself had proposed nationalizing any future "unearned increase in the value of land" by taking the present market values of all lands as normal and appropriating to the state any future increases in those values.[15]

To make this effective the Act provided that a landowner wishing to develop his land in a manner approved by the local planning authority, should pay to the Central Land Board a "Development Charge," presumed to be equal to the difference between the existing value of his undeveloped land and its anticipated value when later developed. To alleviate hardships and to provide compensation to the owners of any land whose value might depreciate because of developmental activities about it, the Government allotted 300 million pounds which the Control Board might use at its discretion to settle claims.

This, also, has been modified. Late in 1952 the Government, then Conservative in political complexion, announced that both the "Development Charge" and the obligation to settle claims out of the 300 million pounds set aside for that purpose, had been abolished. The slate, however, was not wiped completely clean; the Government also announced its intention to require that permission still must be sought before most forms of development could be undertaken, and that *denial* of a developmental request would, under certain conditions, entitle the proposer to compensation.[16]

At this point much speculation could follow without enduring enlightenment. The Labour Government's original system of freezing land values was understandably unpopular with landowners. They could never be certain that compensation in amounts reasonable to *them* would be paid, and the Act must have enhanced the difficulty of finding a purchaser for land which had to be sold. At the same time, the replacing principle of paying compensation for the *denial* of an application to develop has allurements that may yet plague the civil servants in the Ministry, even if irresponsible or purely speculative applications are declared ineligible. Also, although Americans, too, have acquired familiarity with the practice of payment for

---

[15] *Cf.* John Stuart Mill, *Principles of Political Economy*, Ashley edition, London, 1909; pp. 818–821.
[16] *Cf. The Statist*, London, November 22, 1952; pp. 638–639.

not doing something, that practice has implications whose full import has yet to be grasped. All that can be said at this point, however, is that the development of British land, like the future of British steel, remains controversial and uncertain, and much time will elapse before the dust settles sufficiently for a stable solution of the issue to be discerned.

Planning of National Parks. The *New Towns Act* and the *Town and Country Planning Act* constitute two legs of the tripodal structure of British land planning; the third is the *National Parks and Access to the Countryside Act* of 1949, designed to conserve as an inviolate national resource the areas of relatively wild or particularly beautiful countryside. The *Town and Country Planning Act* had already placed restrictions upon outdoor advertising, especially on highways, had provided for the protection not only of woods but also of individual trees,[17] and had secured the preservation of buildings of special architectural or historical interest: now the British landscape itself was safeguarded. Buildings, wildlife, in fact whole areas of historical, esthetic, or naturalistic interest were turned into National Parks to which the public were given access even though established agricultural operations continued to go on.

A National Parks Commission was created, and subsequently three out of a possible total of twelve National Parks were set aside. The Act also established the Nature Conservancy to delineate regions as reserves for wildlife, both fauna and flora. The Act also instructed County Councils to make, within their several territories, complete surveys of all footpaths and bridle paths in order to provide—and for the first time—a complete national map of all public rights of way. Local authorities were instructed to maintain and preserve existing pathways, and when necessary to develop new ones; and where long-distance trails were involved, the National Parks Commission was assigned the responsibility for keeping trails open. Particular attention was directed toward certain historical trails like the old Coastguard Path along the entire coastline of England and Wales. Finally, the Act safeguarded public access without trespass to beaches, mountains, moors, cliffs, and heath.

Agriculture

Control of the uses to which land may be put manifestly entails control of agricultural operations, although we now know that this is far from being

---

[17] A British landowner must secure official permission before he may cut down a tree, even on his own property.

the only reason for the interest taken by the British people in their agriculture. Both world wars heavily underscored the importance of agriculture as a national resource, and one to be conserved, and the socialist venture toward the welfare state re-emphasized interest in both the abundance and the cheapness of food as an element in the standard of living. The *Agriculture Act* of 1947, accordingly, building to be sure upon foundations laid before and during the Second World War, had as its primary purpose the securing of "a stable and efficient agriculture capable of producing such part of the nation's food as in the national interest it is desirable to produce in the United Kingdom, and of producing it at minimum prices consistently with proper remuneration and living conditions for farmers and workers in agriculture, and an adequate return on capital invested." [18]

That Act assured the British farmer a minimum price and guaranteed market for about three quarters of all domestically raised agricultural products. The procedure is for representatives of farmers together, with representatives of the Minister of Agriculture and Fisheries, the Secretary of State for Scotland and the Home Secretary, to review the economic conditions and prospects of each covered type of agriculture. Those Ministers then set prices intended to be consistent with the desired volume and composition of production. That done, farmers know the actual prices and volume of sales upon which they can count for at least eighteen months ahead of the harvest of the covered crops, and twelve months ahead for livestick products. In addition, they know at least the *minimum* prices and the sales of livestock products for from two to four years ahead. [19]

The form of price-fixing varies with circumstances—consisting either of flat subsidies or acreage payments, or, sometimes, of prices calculated according to an approved cost formula. Most prices are fixed annually, but they can be changed in case of emergency. [20]

Payment of the piper carries the privilege of calling the tune, and the tune in this case is called on the theme of agricultural efficiency. Almost all contemporary governments attempt to provide various aids to good farming. The British Government does likewise, but it goes further; under the Act just cited, it has equipped itself with sanctions by which efficiency can be enforced. County Agricultural Executive Committees comprising representatives of landowners, farmers, and farm labor, appointed by the Minister

[18] Quoted from the Act, in *Britain, 1950–51,* as cited, p. 141.
[19] *Cf. ibid.,* p. 143.
[20] *Cf.* Ben W. Lewis, *op. cit.,* p. 262.

of Agriculture and Fisheries, execute agricultural policy throughout the land. Farmers, whether owners or tenants, are expected to observe the principles of good husbandry, and the owners of agricultural land must likewise conform to canons of good estate management. Failure to do so exposes the delinquent initially to official supervision; he may be directed to mend his ways and instructed how to do so. Failure to observe a directive order, or failure after a year of supervision to demonstrate acceptable improvement in the practice of management or husbandry, may entail dispossession, although provision exists for appeal to appropriate tribunals. A dispossessed tenant is simply evicted from the land he has unsuccessfully worked, while a dispossessed owner loses his land through compulsory sale to the state. This powerful sanction has so far been used sparingly; between 1947 and 1949, 40 cases of dispossession bringing 62,286 acres of agricultural land under governmental control, had taken place.[21]

Those deterrents to *bad* farming are supplemented by more conventional aids to *good* farming. Agricultural research is actively fostered in a variety of research institutions, both publicly and privately sponsored, but in all of which the Ministry of Agriculture and Fisheries takes an intimate and continuing interest. Agricultural education, ranging from the minimum of technical training provided by local educational authorities to full courses in agricultural and other institutes or Universities and culminating in the award of agricultural diplomas, is made available to qualified and interested students. Lastly, the mechanization of agriculture has been pushed and given governmental assistance; the provision of housing for agricultural labor has been given priority; and, in proper centers, pools of agricultural labor and equipment have been maintained.

What all this means is that British farmers are guaranteed assured markets and minimum prices, but must justify that guarantee by a demonstration of professional competence which they are assisted to attain. During and after the Second World War the burden upon consumers which this program would otherwise have entailed was eased by massive subsidies of consumption. Just as the Government bought necessary foreign food stuffs in bulk and then re-sold them—at a loss if necessary—so did the Ministry of Food purchase domestically produced foods at prices fixed according to the procedure prescribed in the 1947 *Agriculture Act,* and then re-sold these to consumers at a loss amounting, at its peak, to over 400 million pounds per year. In 1952 the Conservatives sharply cut the food subsidy to 250 million pounds,

[21] *Ibid.,* p. 263.

but made simultaneous adjustments in old-age pensions and other welfare payments together with increases in the exemptions from income tax, in order to insure that the very poor did not suffer from higher food prices.[22]

Controls still exist. While the flour subsidy has been abandoned and white bread may once again be produced, the so-called "national loaf" baked from flour of 80 per cent extraction still continues to be sold at a subsidized price. The guarantee of markets and assured prices for agricultural products remain as accepted parts of national policy,[23] and there is no indication that they will not long remain so.

Housing

Reference has been made to the priority accorded the provision of housing for agricultural workers. That priority is but one facet of a nationally organized program to provide subsidized housing for all the inhabitants of the Welfare State who are in need of it. The components and emphasis of the program may shift with changes in government, but the program itself goes on.

The recent increase in the population, the shift in the geographical distribution of the population together with the destruction of housing during the Second World War have combined to enhance the urgency of solving a problem whose roots extend back to the period of the First World War. Between 1919 and 1939 housing subsidies on both national and local scales were offered to enable local authorities to maintain low rentals for the houses they controlled, and in 1945 the new Labour Government accepted, not without glee, the challenge of housing as one object of national planning.[24] Shortages of both labor and materials sharpened the problem, and interdepartmental cooperation was invoked to meet it. Responsibility was centered in the Ministry of Local Government and Planning; the Ministry of Supply concerned itself with building materials, except for timber which was controlled by the Board of Trade; the Ministry of Works dealt with construction; the Labour Ministry was involved in whatever labor problems might arise; and the Ministry of Agriculture and Fisheries was drawn into consultation whenever possible agricultural land was eyed as a promising site for housing.

[22] Cf. *Labor and Industry in Britain,* as cited, March, 1952, pp. 8–10, and March, 1953, pp. 43–44.
[23] *Ibid.,* March, 1953, p. 42.
[24] Cf. Ben W. Lewis, *op. cit.,* pp. 226–230.

In the years immediately following the Second World War, when well over a million new houses were badly needed,[25] private construction was very tightly controlled in order that the national effort might be concentrated on constructing houses for rental.   All expenditure for construction above a stipulated minimum was made subject to license by local authorities under general guidance and supervision by the Ministry.   Licenses were granted according to the size and type of house for which application was made, with priority given smaller dwellings designed to conserve materials; all licenses, naturally, were subject to global allocations of materials made by the Cabinet.   Until late in 1952, only one fifth of the licenses granted were given to private contractors; all others were reserved for rental houses to be constructed by or on behalf of local governments.   Since then, the corresponding ratios have been half and half.   On January 1, 1953, another relaxation of control was made: except for local zoning provisions and continuing restrictions upon the use of timber, building licenses were no longer required for houses with less than 1,000 square feet of floor space.[26]

Construction under this entire program has been substantial, amounting to more than 1,250,000 new houses since 1946.   The annual rate of increase in dwelling construction reveals the emphasis placed upon provision for housing:

PERMANENT HOUSES AND APARTMENTS CONSTRUCTED [27]

Year	Number
1946	55,400
1947	139,690
1948	227,616
1949	197,627
1950	198,171
1951	194,831
1952	239,922

Since the end of the First World War, rentals have been tightly controlled and have been placed under the jurisdiction of local rental tribunals.   The practice generally followed is to fix maximum rents on old houses at the rate paid on August 3, 1914; on new houses at the rate in effect September 1, 1939.   The tribunals fix the rents for houses constructed since the latter

[25] Cf. Britain, 1950–51, as cited, p. 244.
[26] Cf. Labor and Industry in Britain, as cited, March, 1953, p. 44.
[27] Source: Labor and Industry in Britain, March, 1953, p. 39.

base date, and they have authority to lower rents in particular instances. Landlords are given some protection in the form of assurance against increases in the interest they pay on mortgages, and are protected against foreclosure as long as legal interest payments continue to be made.[28]

There has been much complaint against the British system of rent control —complaint taking the form one might expect: that the system is costly, that its impact upon different individuals is fortuitous and inequitable, that it has discouraged private landlords, at any rate, from properly maintaining the houses they own, and so on.   Much of this criticism is justified, yet British rent control has been in existence for a generation, which is simply to say that, if it be an evil, it is one that has acquired the comfort of familiarity.[29]   One of its longer-run implications appears to be the thrusting of rental housing more and more into the public domain.   The construction of new houses and apartments for rent seems increasingly to be the responsibility of municipalities, while private building is normally undertaken only for occupancy by the owner, or—to the extent that speculative building is permitted—for sale rather than for lease.

THE "GUARANTEED MINIMUM"

Health Services

The assurance of good health, in so far as mere man can proffer it, and the treatment of ill health when that occurs, regardless of the financial status of the sufferer, are among the components of the Welfare State.   This, also, is not new, but like other things whose growth seems almost organic, its infancy in contrast to its maturity appears small and innocent of controversy. The English local health Authorities who, today, carry much responsibility for the administration of the British system of socialized medicine, were themselves established in the nineteenth century to supervise such things as the disposal of sewage, the provision of pure and drinkable water, the development and enforcement of public sanitation, and the control of epidemics.   Compulsory health insurance for workers in the lower income brackets, although not for their dependents, came in 1911.   It involved

---

[28] *Cf. Britain, 1950–51,* as cited, p. 247.
[29] "The oldest and best known evil was ever more supportable than one that was new and untried"—Montaigne, *Of Vanity.*

compulsory contributions from workers, employers, and government, and carried guaranteed medical care and sick pay for those who were covered. From that day on there followed Act upon Act concerned with the control of such plagues as tuberculosis and venereal disease, and with the development of child and maternity welfare.[30]

The Second World War accelerated this movement and directed it toward the expansion of industrial health services, increased attention to the rehabilitation of the disabled, and greater care to proper diet, particularly through the provision of meals for school children, the Welfare Foods Service for expectant mothers, and the development of industrial canteens.[31]

Medical care. The special interest of the Labour Party in health services was made known to the world early in the present century in a series of Resolutions emanating from the Annual Conferences of the Party, advocating the nationalization of hospitals, the provision of adequate medical, surgical, and hospital services for all, free treatment for school children, and the organization of health services upon a national scale.[32] All these services ultimately converged. The establishment, therefore, of a National Health Service, on July 5, 1948, was a culmination and not an abrupt innovation. Being a culmination, it was generally accepted. Parliamentary debate upon the *National Health Service Act* of 1946 was benign, and what opposition to the bill did appear took the form of criticism of detail but not of principle.[33] Since the inauguration of the health system itself there has indeed been criticism, and criticism that has been followed by amendment. Again, however, the object of criticism has been detail—the cost of the service, its involvement in red tape, or the waste which followed inordinate haste. Costs did exceed all original expectations and have made necessary some retrenchment, and there is also considerable evidence that the first bite was of indigestible magnitude. Doctors have been overworked—partly because of demands upon their time by malingering patients that waxed because malingering now is free—and consequently some serious needs have not been promptly met. Still, however—except for the few outraged voices bound to make themselves heard in a society which retains respect for individuality sometimes verging upon affection for idiosyncrasy—the principle of what Americans call socialized medicine has not been really challenged, even by doctors themselves.

[30] *Cf. Britain, 1950–51,* as cited, p. 222.
[31] *Ibid.,* p. 222.
[32] *Cf.* Lewis, *op. cit.,* p. 191.
[33] *Ibid.,* p. 192.

The system is based upon a division of responsibility between the national government and local authorities. The Minister of Health [34] is charged with (1) the provision throughout the nation of hospital and specialist services; (2) the care and treatment (subject to quasi-judicial safeguards for individual liberty) of the feeble-minded and those suffering from mental disease; (3) the conduct of organized medical research including help, largely through grants-in-aid, for privately undertaken research; (4) the administration of Public Health Laboratories; and (5) the operation of a blood-transfusion service.[35]

Local authorities are responsible for the provision of ordinary medical care. That provision is administered by Executive Councils, usually one for each County or County Borough, composed of representatives of the Ministry of Health, local health authorities, and of local organizations of physicians, dentists, and druggists. - Nearly all hospitals, both public and private, have been nationalized [36] and organized into a single system. Almost from the inauguration of the system 95 per cent of the British population has been covered and, although participation by professional men was and remains voluntary, 88 per cent of all doctors, 95 per cent of the dentists and practically every druggist joined at once.[37]

Medical participants in the Health Service are free to quit it, free to retain private practice if they wish it, free to refuse to accept individual patients even within the service if they do not want them, and free to remove from their lists the names of individual patients whom they no longer wish to serve. Individuals seeking treatment must register with a physician whom they choose for themselves, subject to his consent; they likewise may change from one physician to another.

These are the freedoms of the system; there are also restrictions. Patients who require hospitalization are not free to select the hospital of their preference, and when the service of a specialist is necessary, neither the patient nor his ordinary medical adviser may choose which specialist to consult.[38] The reasons are (1) the great shortage of hospital beds and (2) the equally great shortage of specialists. The latter shortage is the more serious of the two, because specialists tend to seek the great cities and to avoid rural

[34] In Scotland, the Secretary of State for Scotland is responsible.

[35] Cf. Britain, 1950–51, as cited, p. 223.

[36] The few exceptions comprise hospitals which, for one reason or another, the Minister of Health did not want.

[37] Cf. Lewis, op. cit., p. 218.

[38] Ibid., p. 217.

areas. The two shortages taken together have forced the husbandry of both beds and specialists; husbandry has taken the form of assignment of patients to particular facilities or men.

There was also inherited a geographical maldistribution of general physicians, but this difficulty has been met by other methods. The country is divided into areas classified as "open" or "closed." The former are those underserved by doctors, while the latter are adequately staffed. No physician may undertake to practise in any area without permission from the local Medical Practices Committee, composed of seven local doctors and two laymen appointed by the Minister of Health. Except when the number of applications to practice is greater than the number of vacancies, permission to practice in an open area is freely granted, but it is difficult to enter an area in the closed category. Appeal may be made to the Ministry of Health which has final jurisdiction, and which also has power, subject to some safeguards, to disapprove a name accepted by a Medical Practices Committee and replace it by another.[39]

Dental care. Dental services are provided under a slightly different system. In place of registering with a single practitioner to whom he is thereafter bound until he goes through the rigmarole of re-registering, the distressed possessor of a toothache may seek relief from the first dentist who will take him; even so, he may have difficulty. Dentists, too, are in scarce supply, a condition which makes it necessary to put children and expectant mothers at the head of the line. Before the dental program was started, the authorities estimated that there might be perhaps four million cases requiring dental treatment each year; in point of fact, by the end of March, 1949, cases were averaging seven million annually.[40]

That underestimation of the magnitude of the task to be done was characteristic of the planning of the entire health service. Pressure upon physicians, dentists, hospitals, and specialists; the quantity of prescriptions sought and received; the number of people seeking relief for ailments serious or slight, real or fancied—all, almost from the start, went beyond all anticipation. Part of this, undoubtedly, was response to the opportunity to get attention, to secure something for nothing, or to get sympathy at least from oneself if not from others; however, another part of it unquestionably sprang from the chance to get skilled treatment for aches and pains which, hitherto, had simply not been treated at all. The consequence, whatever the reason,

[39] *Ibid.,* p. 198.
[40] *Ibid.,* p. 204.

was staggering cost and dreadful pressure upon both personnel and facilities, and to such an extent that some modification in the system has had to be made.

The cost was originally estimated at about 200 million pounds annually; strenuous efforts have had to be made to keep them under 400 million, and these efforts have taken the form of imposing certain charges upon beneficiaries of the system even though treatment, drugs, and appliances were initially provided gratis. The imposition of those charges, indeed, has been one of the irritants that has split the Labour Party, more notably than before, into a Right and a Left wing.

Recipients of eyeglasses and dentures, for example, now pay half their cost, except that the maximum charge for dentures is four pounds, five shillings—roughly, not quite thirteen dollars. All prescriptions provided under the Health Service now cost a standard fee of one shilling (fourteen cents), except that patients in hospitals continue to receive free drugs, and war pensioners and people on public relief are entitled to refunds. The purpose of any charge at all is not only to reduce costs, but to reduce also unnecessary or frivolous demands upon doctors' time. Dental examinations continue to be free, but dental treatment now costs one pound, or full cost if that is less than a pound, except that children under twenty-one, expectant mothers, and women who have borne a child within the proceeding twelve months continue to receive free dental care. Certain appliances, such as abdominal belts or the controversial wig, are billed at amounts running up to one-half their cost. Local authorities are now permitted to charge for the care of children in day nurseries.[41]

Remuneration of doctors and dentists. A sore spot that appeared very early concerned the remuneration of doctors in the system. Criticism *expressed itself* simply as complaints at the income received for the amount of work that had to be done, but it probably arose in part out of dissatisfaction with the abrupt change thrust upon what had been established use and want. Physicians no longer could practice where they chose, the burden of record-keeping and report-making was substantially increased, and the traditional right to buy and sell medical practices much as business firms buy and sell good will, was now abolished. While financial compensation for many of these deprivations was offered and paid, physicians remained unsatisfied. The issue was finally submitted to adjudication and some changes were made, effective on April 1, 1953.

[41] *Cf. Labor and Industry in Britain,* as cited, June, 1952; pp. 81–82.

As things now stand, medical practitioners receive a base payment of seventeen shillings per patient *per annum*. The maximum number of patients a physician may accept under the system was reduced from 4,000 to 3,500 if he practices alone; the number any member of a partnership may accept is set at a maximum of 4,500, provided that the average number of patients per partner does not exceed 3,500. An additional 2,000 patients may be taken in cases where a permanent assistant is employed.

To this base remuneration a "loading" of ten shillings is added for each patient within the range 501 to 1,500 on a doctor's list. In addition to this, newly licensed doctors entering the system receive, under certain safeguards, an Initial Practice Allowance of 600 pounds in the first year, 450 in the second, and 200 in the third. Besides the fees for whatever private practice a physician may undertake, there remain various additional sources of revenue. Elderly physicians who might suffer a loss of income under the new scheme are entitled to compensation. Inducement payments are offered doctors to practice in unpopular areas. Grants are made for supervising the training of assistants, and a system of special fees has been continued from the original remuneration schedule. Drugs and dressings which a doctor supplies in emergency cases entitle him to minimum payment of two shillings six pence (thirty-five cents) for every hundred persons on his list of patients except those to whom he regularly dispenses drugs. Regular dispensing entitles a physician either to reimbursement for cost incurred, or to nine shillings nine pence ($1.37) per year for each such person on his regular list, with additional payment for unusually expensive drugs. Hospital Management Committees provide remuneration to physicians serving on hospital staffs, and fees are paid for providing anaesthetics or treating hemorrhages in dental cases. Obstetric and ophthalmic services rendered by general practitioners are likewise remunerated.

Doctors who joined the Health Service by or shortly after July, 1948, received compensation for loss of their chance to sell their practices upon retirement. Full compensation is not paid until they do retire, but in the meantime they receive interest at $2\frac{3}{4}$ per cent on unpaid compensation money. All doctors in the system are entitled to retirement benefits. Those who participate contribute to the retirement fund six per cent of their net annual receipts, and the Treasury contributes eight per cent. After a five or ten year qualifying period a variety of benefits comprising, according to circumstances, a pension, widow's annuity, death benefits, or compensation for disability may be paid.

Income derived *only* from the base payment of 17 shillings per patient per year plus the ten shillings "loading" for patients numbered in the 501 to 1,500 bracket works out thus:

COMPENSATION FOR PHYSICIANS IN THE HEALTH SERVICE [42]

Number of Patients	Remuneration in pounds	Dollar income [43]
500	425	$1,190
750	763	2,136
1,000	1,100	3,080
1,250	1,438	4,026
1,500	1,775	4,200
2,000	2,200	6,160
2,500	2,625	7,350
3,000	3,050	8,540
3,500	3,475	9,730
4,000	3,475	9,730

Compensation for dentists is simpler. For ordinary treatment, a dentist sends his bill to the Dental Estimates Board which thereupon pays him at officially approved rates. Except in emergencies, dentists must secure approval of the Board before proceeding with any special or unusual treatment not already on the standard list.[44]

Druggists present monthly bills for prescriptions filled under the system and are paid by local Executive Councils. For this purpose, thirteen pricing regions have been delineated for England and one for Wales, and each of these has a Pricing Bureau which sets prices upon prescriptions and certifies to the proper Executive Council the amount due each claimant druggist.[45]

Despite the general concern over the cost of the Health Service and the steady stream of complaints about such things as the heavy burden of paper work imposed upon practitioners, or delay in securing medical attention, or sometimes its perfunctory character when it is secured, there exists no indication of any serious intention to revert to the old system. The provision of free, or very cheap, medical, surgical and hospital care for all is

---

[42] Source: British Information Services, Reference Division, *Payment of Doctors in the National Health Service,* Mimeographed Information Paper Number ID 1138 (Revised), New York, April, 1953.

[43] Sterling income has been converted to dollars, in round numbers, at the official exchange rate of $2.80 to the pound. No allowance has been made for differences in the purchasing power of the two currencies.

[44] *Cf.* Lewis, *op. cit.,* p. 204.

[45] *Ibid.,* p. 208.

now firmly embedded in the structure of the contemporary British Welfare State.

Social Security

What is known in the United States as Social Security, the assurance of the means of subsistence in the face of the occupational and other hazards to which mortal man living in organized and specialized society is vulnerable, is familiar even in contemporary capitalist society.   While its principles ramify further into the British system than into the American, they still appear less strange to outsiders than do tight control over the use of land, public manipulation of the distribution of industry, or the provision of health services; they can accordingly be given more cursory treatment.

There exists in Britain national insurance against unemployment, illness or industrial injury, with provision for maternity, retirement, widowhood or death grants.   Except for such categories of the population as children, married women and old people, contributions toward this insurance are compulsory for all individuals and are supplemented by contributions from the state as well as from employers, at least for individuals who are not self-employed or independent.   Cases in which insurance benefits are either not available or are inadequate to sustain the accepted minimum standard of decency are either replaced, or supplemented, by public relief, known in Britain as National Assistance.   Outside the insurance system is the program of Family Allowances, financed out of taxes, under which parents receive a cash benefit of eight shillings ($1.12) a week for each of their children except the first.[46]

The provision of social security has gone so far in Britain that an interesting issue, only latent elsewhere, has there been brought to the surface. Should the Welfare State set its sights toward the extension of its benefits to everyone, or should it concentrate upon the protection of the under-privileged only?   The British have been ambitious.   Members of the dwindling and increasingly lonely company of English millionaires are entitled, if they so wish, to free hospitalization in a ward and to free drugs while they are there; more pointedly, perhaps, millionaire and vagrant together have had their consumption of food subsidized by the state.

A plausible case can be made for extending some social services to every-

[46] *Cf.* British Information Services, *Britain in Brief,* New York, Revised, June, 1953; p. 6.

one, whatever his financial resources may be.   The provision of good roads is a public service everywhere, and a public road is open on equal terms to limousine or jalopy.   Immunization against epidemics is not only available, but sometimes imposed upon, all, because bacilli are blind to class distinctions.   Likewise, many people today argue that the consumption of education should be adapted to the receptive capacity of the child and not to the pocketbook of his parents.

Nevertheless, as the British are coming to realize,[47] one of the drags upon the extension of the kind of welfare socialists seek is its cost.   In this sense, the indiscriminate subsidization of all impedes raising standards for those in greatest need.   A significant part of the unfinished business of British planners lies, or should lie, in thinking through such issues as this.

[47] Cf. "Crisis in the Welfare State," *The Times,* London, February 25, 1952, p. 7, and February 26, 1952, p. 5.

PART FIVE

Conclusion

21

The Competition of Systems

FOUR social-economic systems have now been examined in regard both to their internal logic—by which they seem justified, at least to their supporters—and to their performance as going concerns. That examination being behind us, it is now possible, so to speak, to place these systems side by side before us so that we may essay a synopsis. Such a venture as this is, today, more than an academic exercise undertaken purely for the intellectual pleasure it may produce. Capitalism, fascism, socialism and communism are not fossilized deposits to be disinterred from a hillside only to be re-interred in a geological museum for the edification of the passing tourist. Nor are these systems fanciful Utopias constructed as exercises in escape, although there are utopian elements in the rationale of each. It is precisely these elements that give each system whatever appeal it may command. These four systems, however, are going concerns, competing with each other for allegiance and support, and competing with a stridency that needs no loud speaker to impress upon those with ears to hear the magnitude of the prize that is at stake.

Capitalism, to be sure, is hard to define because it is dynamic and evolving. Whatever its essence may be, it evokes allegiance. Fascism as an operating system underwent a setback with the collapse of Mussolini's Italy and the smashing of Hitler's Third Reich, but there are still forces in contemporary America that may be called fascist and there are overt yearnings toward it elsewhere.   Communism in any sort of definitional purity is unlikely to be reached even by societies which call themselves Communist, but at least the name has been adopted by a contemporary society which is disciplined, vigorous and prepared, if opportunity offers, for conquest.   Socialism, too, has its supporters with their own creed.   It has had its victories abroad, and even in the United States it is believed to have enjoyed some creeping success.

The differences among these systems are conspicuous and significant, but since the preceding chapters have been largely devoted to their exposition, these need no longer be belabored.   There are also, however, similarities among these systems that are important enough to merit some attention.

ELEMENTS COMMON TO CONTEMPORARY SYSTEMS

Viability

First, and perhaps most important, each system has demonstrated that it can work—at least as an economic system.   While the collapse of capitalism has been foretold again and again and while its demise has more than once actually been announced, the reports have, so far at least, been premature.   Fascism, at least in its self-styled manifestations, did go under, but by military assault and not by internal economic collapse.   While fascism, indeed, was bitten, only a bold prophet would assert that some future fascist historian may not record the event in the form of Goldsmith's epitaph:

> The dog, to gain his private ends
> Went mad, and bit the man.
> The man recovered of the bite,
> The dog it was that died.

Communism in its Russian form has also shown viability.   It has undergone vicissitudes but, like Antaeus, it has emerged from each with renewed —and over time, with increased—vigor.   Lastly, there is socialism.   Much has been made of the eventual failure of the various socialist or communist communities that proliferated in the nineteenth century, many of them in the United States.   These were small-scale ventures comprising, usually, a single community, founded by some strong-minded and strong-willed reformer who was able to impress upon his followers the urgency of withdrawing from the sinful world and to animate them with the momentum and drive to carry on.   Some of these settlements, like Economy, Pennsylvania, or Zoar, Ohio, or Bethel, Missouri, or Oneonta, New York, were largely religious in inspiration.   Robert Owen's New Harmony and the various Fourierist settlements in the Middle West and Middle Atlantic, organized as the result of the preaching of Horace Greeley and Arthur Brisbane, illustrate other, non-religious, variants upon the same theme.   Whatever their origins, all were organized on a self-contained socialist or communist basis, but none left more than a slight mark upon the fabric of the larger society from which they had withdrawn but within which they had established themselves.[1]   The significance of their failure, however, should not be exaggerated, for they were artificial communities, withdrawn from but still surrounded by and engulfed in a larger, alien culture they could not influence and that ultimately engulfed them.   Their survival, while it persisted, resembled the survival of the beating hearts biologists are reported to keep on occasion in laboratory bottles: dependent upon some form of artificial feeding, provided, in the case of the communities, by their founders and usually ceasing with their death.

Socialism writ large is the socialism of an *entire* society.   Skepticism about the capacity of such a society to sustain life is frequently expressed as an assertion that such a way of life is contrary to human nature, despite the fact that it takes all kinds of men to make a world.   British socialism, the example of this larger society that we have selected, is still too young for its survival to be predicated upon its history.   It would, however, be rash to leap to the conclusion that large-scale socialism is incapable of survival. Judgments of that kind reduce themselves to judgments about the organization of industry that, as we shall see, presuppose differences that are no longer valid.

Socialism—or for that matter any system competitive with capitalism —might, *as a set of economic institutions,* validly be contrasted with capitalism of a century ago.   Today, the differences among systems are not so much economic as they are social, political, and, in the last analysis, moral. The truth is that the *economic* similarities among competing systems are rapidly overtaking the differences, and primarily because the facts of industrialism, of money, of the economic role of government, and of the extension of the division of labor expose all to essentially the same stimuli and therefore provoke essentially the same responses.

[1] For a fuller account, see the article "Communistic Settlements," *Encyclopedia of the Social Sciences,* New York, 1930; Vol. IV, pp. 95–102.

Collective Organization

In all contemporary systems the collective element looms large, and with the passage of time is likely to loom still larger.   Manufacturing industry in all systems is responsible to some collectivity and is administered by bodies of quasi-trustees in whom that responsibility is vested.   Stockholders, Ministers, or Governmental Departments *employ* the officials who immediately direct the great industries of the world, and although there are substantial differences in the principles and objectives imposed upon management, and in the tightness with which the reins harnessing these officials are held, the reins are always there.   Moreover, no great industry anywhere is any longer a law unto itself.   That is clearest in the case of the Russian Trusts whose managers dare not assume too great initiative.   We have seen how the managers and directors of fascist enterprises tend increasingly to become paid servants of the state, while, likewise, the men responsible for the operation of nationalized industry in Great Britain know pretty much what is expected of them.   The same thing is true, although in a somewhat more diffused sense, of the management of the great corporations in the United States.   *Positively,* their labor relations, their ability to combine among themselves, and in certain cases even their pricing policies have been removed by statute from their private domain.   More *subtly,* the responsibility of American enterprise has become collective in another sense.   There are today no great tycoons who would dare say with Vanderbilt, "The public be damned!"   Contemporary American industrialists have vested themselves with a public interest even in those cases where statute has not done that for them.   That is crudely expressed in the observation made by the Secretary of Defense in the first Republican Administration the United States has had since 1933:—that what is good for General Motors is good for America. Strictly, and in some of its details, that remark is not invariably true, but symbolically it has a truth that is profound.   *Formally,* the great American corporation remains an institution created to produce profits for its owners, but *socially* and *fundamentally* it is a device for generating part of the income, providing part of the goods and services, and offering part of the employment on which the economic survival of American society depends.

Internal Interdependence

All contemporary economic systems have an internal interdependence that pushes them further and further toward internal integration.   That inter-

dependence is technological, economic, and social.   Technologically, industry in all systems is bound together by the ordered flow of materials, parts,
and components from one to another, by an almost paradoxical union of
increased specialization with a tropism toward enhanced self-containment,
and by the economizing incentive to find by-productive use for otherwise
waste products.   This theme, both large enough and important enough to
merit a book to itself, can here be given only sketchy illustration.

The high-school chemist knows the magic pregnancy of a piece of common coal.   The object of an industry of its own, coal is also the subject
of mysterious transformations into countless forms and essences impreg-
nating the very fabric of contemporary civilization—so much so, indeed,
that its most familiar and obvious use may well be its most wasteful.   The
grubbiest of chimney sweeps and the most exquisite of fine ladies have in
common their dependence upon coal, the one for his livelihood and his
grime, the other for her nylons and perhaps her perfume.   The warmth of
an apartment house, the thrust of a steam locomotive, the color of a neck-
tie, the magic of a drug, the temper of a razor, the wage of a miner, the
prosperity of a laundry, and the glow of electric light—all these and many
others are among the gifts locked into the blackness of ordinary coal.   What
happens to coal happens also to the economy.

Let us consider one other illustration of technological interdependence.
Most men today, no matter what the particular economic system to which
they belong, live in dwellings to which a thousand specialized arts have cooperatively contributed.   The carpenter with his tools and his materials,
the plumber and the electrician, the painter and the plasterer, the shingler
and the paper-hanger, the building inspector and the trucker, to say nothing
of the architect and the surveyor, are but first instances.   Our dwellings
also draw upon the skills by which utilities are provided, sewage, trash, and
waste removed, and the roads and channels which carry all this traffic maintained.   Just as the manufacturer must know that his subcontractors will
supply him at the rate, in the volume, and of the kind to which his operations are oriented, so must the building contractor be assured of the arrival
of the electrician when he wants him, and the house-holder know that he
can get the plumber when he needs him.

All this, as readers of Adam Smith know, is nothing new, nor is it specially
profound.   It is, however, significant, because it is something that is growing.   Today, many men repair and some men construct their own houses,
but if that practice were as common as it was in the backwoods of the early

American frontier we would not today have the houses we do. With industrial development, personal self-sufficiency becomes anachronistic, and that is coming to be true even nationally. Increasing dependence upon others stimulates, as a natural consequence, the desire to overcome it through bringing under one's control as many ancillary and contributory operations as possible. That type of industrial imperialism is not peculiar to capitalism, and it has not really worked anywhere. It leads to giganticism that becomes too unwieldy for its own survival. Neither captains of industry nor Caesars, any more than the dinosaurs, have proved able to carry their own weight when that has passed some critical point.

Technologically, then, the fact of industrial interdependence in all contemporary societies, based upon the necessity to find dependable suppliers for the countless materials and components any great enterprise requires, and also upon the need for assured outlets for the equally countless products and by-products of industry, imposes conditions that coerce, bind, impel all varieties of industrial management.

There are likewise *economic* reasons for interdependence. Long ago Adam Smith taught his generation that the division of labor is limited by the extent of the market. The division of labor, in one of its aspects, is nothing other than a device for reducing waste, whether it be waste of resources, of money, of time or of motion. What the great political economist was really saying in that statement—which, today, seems almost a cliché—is that the distinction between the waste that is a necessary cost and the waste that is avoidable is drawn by the extent to which an economy, an industry, or even an enterprise has developed. That is true under any system. Consider an illustration upon a small scale.

In the kitchen of a great restaurant the division of labor has separated the services of the pastry cook from those of the salad maker, to say nothing of the still more marked differentiation among cooks as a group, waiters, and dishwashers. That differentiation of function is possible because such a restaurant has enough business, its market is sufficiently extensive, to keep all those various specialists fully occupied, and because that is so the economies Adam Smith saw in the division of labor are really operative. On the other hand, to attempt to introduce that specialization of function in a domestic household would entail, not economies, but waste of another kind. Because the household "market" is much more limited, Mom is perforce a Jane of all trades.

On a larger scale, irrespective of the will to reduce costs which the competent manager of enterprise has under any system, his ability to do so depends as much upon the economic as upon the ideological environment within which he operates.   For years, in the United States, natural gas was "wasted" through being burned off in the field because neither facilities for its transportation nor markets for its use had been developed.   Even now, slabs of firewood ideal for domestic hearths are burning day and night on the scene of lumbering operations, simply because it would be "wasteful," at least for the enterprise, to attempt to garner and transport them.   Economic history, in perhaps all but Toynbee's "fossilized" civilizations, is the record of adaptation to both opportunity and circumstance.   Another fundamental element common to all systems is the similarity of the adaptive alternatives that confront them at corresponding stages of economic development.

Sensitivity to Changes in the Flow of Money

Yet another element that penetrates iron, bamboo, and all other curtains, is the possibility of repercussion from changes in the rate of disbursement by spenders important enough to have economic impact.   Consider in illustration a grossly oversimplified picture of an economic system that comprises only a farmer, a builder, a tool-maker, and a weaver.   These specialists would earn their several livings from the interchange of each others' products and services, facilitated, we may assume, by some sort of monetary system.   Let us, at random, contrive a set of payments and receipts from one to another, and examine their implications:

PAYMENTS AND RECEIPTS [2]

Year 1

		Payments →		
		Farmer	Builder	Tool-maker	Weaver
Receipts ↑	Farmer	x	$110	$65	$90
	Builder	78	x	28	97
	Tool-maker	35	84	x	40
	Weaver	52	27	100	x

[2] This is an adaptation of the Payments Table to be found in Kenneth E. Boulding, *Economic Analysis,* Revised edition, New York, 1948; p. 303.

Omitting the "imputed" payments which pass from one pocket to another in the same person's coat (indicated by "x" in the table above), we see, for example, that the farmer has paid $110 to the builder, and that the weaver has received $40 from the tool-maker. Collecting all the payments and receipts, we find this result:

	Payments	Receipts	Balance
Farmer	$265	$165	$—100
Builder	203	221	+18
Tool-maker	159	193	+34
Weaver	179	227	+48
TOTAL	806	806	0

Aggregate payments and receipts are truistically equal, and their magnitude, $806, is nothing other than the national income in its monetary form. Individual payments and receipts, however, need not and in most cases would not balance, although the algebraic sum of the individual balances is—again truistically—zero. The interesting questions that emerge from a hypothetical situation like the one portrayed above are, how individuals respond to whatever their balances may be and what the consequences of their response amount to.

If laying up riches on earth jeopardizes the accumulation of treasure in Heaven, or if our mortal men are obsessed by the fact that their worldly wealth is negotiable only on earth, we might conclude that our builder, tool-maker and weaver are in a predicament from which they can extricate themselves only by increasing their worldly disbursements. In our kind of world, however, it is the farmer whom we should expect to be least happy, partly because he has violated the precept of Dickens' Mr. Micawber—that happiness depends on keeping in the black—and partly because, unless the well of his resources is bottomless, the time will come when he will be compelled to retrench unless he mends his financial ways earlier. Let us make him retrench by postponing $100 worth of repairs to his house. We then have this situation:

PAYMENTS AND RECEIPTS

Year 2

		→ Payments →		
	Farmer	Builder	Tool-maker	Weaver
Farmer	x	$10	$65	$90
Builder	78	x	28	97
Tool-maker	35	84	x	40
Weaver	52	27	100	x

(↑ Receipts ↑)

Or, in sum,

	Payments	Receipts	Balance
Farmer	$165	$165	$0
Builder	203	121	−82
Tool-maker	159	193	+34
Weaver	179	227	+48
TOTAL	706	706	0

The farmer has now reached that financially neutral condition that is neither black nor red, and aggregate payments and receipts still balance, but at a figure $100 less than in the preceding year; but the builder now has the deficit which he in turn may attempt to pass on, perhaps to the weaver by making last year's suit do. We need not follow this bit of conjectural history further, since it is already clear that the farmer's success in pulling himself out of a hole resulted in putting the builder into one, and also in reducing the national income by more than twelve per cent.

In the real world, reductions in individual disbursements are continually in process, but fortunately these are either too insignificant individually to be perceptible or bothersome in the aggregate, or they are offset by increased expenditure elsewhere, or both. Sometimes, however, the impact of reduced expenditure is both perceptible and serious. In 1890, for example, the South American Republics defaulted upon their obligations to the great British banking house of Baring Brothers thereby reducing the bank's receipts. The hole into which that institution was thus thrust was too deep to permit unaided egress. The hole, in turn, into which the British economy would have fallen if Baring Brothers had closed was too deep to be contemplated with any equanimity, so that a consortium of other banks, including the great Bank of England itself, was formed to guarantee Baring's liabilities. The same problem would arise in any system confronting the same kind of crisis, although response or adaptation to the problem would be formed according to the institutional and customary peculiarities—frequently more than merely economic in character—that give different systems their individual color and structure.

Contemporary Americans know how apprehension lest capitalistic disbursements be cut, with unhappy consequences to their expectant recipients, has underlain much of the endeavor to impart to government a gyroscopic function—that of keeping the economy on an even keel. In extreme form that endeavor tends to push society into some form of socialism. We shall very soon have occasion to see that the increasingly important, and sometimes dominant, economic role of government is another factor common to contemporary systems. Generalizing the foregoing discussion, we can see that the deficit financing long advocated for and recently practiced during periods of depression in those economies in which the play of the market is accorded a measure of freedom, here joins the massive public expenditure of totalitarian systems to prove the rule that not only the direction but the sheer volume of expenditure, in any system, have causes and consequences that acknowledge no ideological frontiers.

The simplified illustration we have given of the importance of disbursement happens to have been pointed downwards, but of course it need not have been. Since 1945, the circulatory blood pressure of all systems has been high and national money income almost everywhere has mounted. There is indeed reason to suspect that, despite expectable lags and relaxations, the long-run prospects in all systems are inflationary. One reason is nothing other than the progressive abandonment, everywhere, of the old principle that government should remain economically neutral.

The immediately preceding analysis has skirted about an interesting, pregnant, but sometimes mysteriously neglected point: that there are such things as monetary principles inherent in money wherever and however money exists, which now is everywhere. Just as glut or famine can affect health irrespective of its object's creed or complexion, so can inflation or deflation infect an economy no matter what its political or social texture. During and immediately after the Second World War the monetary diet of all regimes, capitalist or fascist, socialist or communist, was rich. All, therefore, were forced at one time or another either to adopt some form of commodity rationing or to permit monetary depreciation to reduce the value of money. Just as technological exigencies produce, everywhere, opportunities and problems common to all systems, so does the behavior of money constrict the complete freedom of action of both reactionary and radical.

The Dominant Role of Government

In all systems there are social forces that make men increasingly members one of another, with the result that no system anywhere can afford to ignore the ricochet or the echo of many individual actions. In the United States the national memory recalls with a degree of wistfulness the day when only Mother Nature, and not her children, set limits to the material security of the individual. Like most memory, that one recalls much that never existed and imparts to the recalled past a soft color that its indwellers would not have recognized, or perhaps even have wanted. It is true, however, that the frontiersman certainly, and even the townsman to some extent, could once secede from the market place, draw upon his own resources, and, after a fashion, subsist. The family farm, or even the back lot with its corner of pasture, were there to serve when need arose as mitigants against the more serious vicissitudes of commerce. Even in the market place, the rationale of early capitalism placed upon the individual and largely upon him alone the responsibility for his own economic fate, and hence, in the aggregate, for the fate of society itself. There was acknowledgment that the infirm and the incapable could not bear that responsibility, and some generally unofficial provision for their assistance was made. These unfortunates, however, were deemed the exceptions; so much so that even well into the present century poverty and indigence were believed by many to be the fruits of improvidence or individual incapacity and that these could only be worsened by attempts at organized alleviation.

The climate of opinion today has changed because the winds of fortune have blown men together; and, like technology and money, those winds acknowledge no man-made frontiers. In our own age common hazards and common wants, made more recognizable by both metropolitan and occupational propinquities, have driven men to organize, to combine, to seek by collective means collective ends and thereby to attempt to manipulate destiny rather than merely to accept it. Today, only insurance companies really acquiesce in Acts of God.

All the forces and tensions just described meet somewhere in the center of the Government, and there combine to make Government not only the arbiter but sometimes the regulator and even the molder of the economic system. For the contemporary world in the large the result has been substantially the same, although, like the construction of a tunnel, it has been brought about by movements in opposite directions starting from opposite poles. In the totalitarian world, the movement started from the authoritarian pole, the acceptance of a strong executive responsible to no electorate as something proper and right, in and of itself. In fascist Italy and Germany and in communist Russia, society has been conceived as something to be led and the economy as something to be centrally planned and administered. In the political democracies, on the other hand, government is still regarded as the agent or delegate of a more fundamental authority vested, somehow, in a sovereign people. Nevertheless, the power and responsibility, and hence the economic impact, of that agent have steadily increased, sometimes with reluctant acquiescence on the part of the sovereign people, sometimes by design, sometimes suddenly and all at once as in wartime, sometimes by fits and starts as sporadically revealed abuses become recognized as intolerable. Occasionally those abuses appear to be borne uniquely by one segment of society, as when farmers complain that the free-price system discriminates against them so that they feel impelled to seek publicly enforced price parity. Occasionally, abuses seem to bear upon society as a whole, as when irresponsible swashbuckling, first by big business and later by big labor, results in the imposition of publicly enforced moderation upon offenders.

These are designed intrusions of government into the market place. A less designed but more pervasive and implacable intrusion is a by-product of sheer size. A long developing conjuncture of circumstances, social, political, military, and economic, has brought it about that the first, and very substantial, lien upon individual incomes is held by the tax collector; that the first professional call upon the energies and talents of young men is made by the armed services; that the greatest single pressure upon much industrial capacity is exerted by governmental purchasing agents; and that a very palpable reduction in the value of money is the consequence of governmental fiscal policy which, at times, appears to be subject to no law but that of its own development. The great, and in some ways frightening consequence is assumption by the state of more and more responsibility for economic affairs, partly because the state is the most obvious agency to which men turn when they seek alleviation or improvement in their own circumstances, and partly because of the dominance of sheer size.

The result is that regardless of the direction from which the impetus comes, the state, today, is everywhere the most important organized force operating upon economic systems. Everywhere, its absorption and later release of a most substantial share of the national money income imposes a man-made pattern upon economic activities, which hitherto have been considered ruled only by the autonomous laws of the market. Its entrepreneurial activities range from the casual sale of razor blades in a Post Exchange to the massive generation of electric power by a Tennessee Valley Authority. Through a combination of social insurance and public subsidy the state is becoming increasingly the means of support of the aged, the indigent, and the chronically ill. It dominates the price system in markets as competitive as agriculture and as monopolistic as the railroads. It eyes, and sometimes attempts to restrain the impulsive behavior of a captain of industry, and it minds and sometimes tries to contain the exuberance of a labor union boss. While it may not seek to plan the economy, today's economy, nevertheless, is largely what government makes it. It does all this, and it cannot abdicate.

It cannot abdicate, even in systems in which abdication may be sought, because government remains the agency to which men turn when they seek relief, protection, or other intervention on their behalf. As they succeed, whether their success takes the form of a tariff, a minimum wage, a protected price, the restoration of something hopefully called competition, the abolition of something despairingly called unfair trade practices, the construction of a new Post Office, the breaking of a strike, the employment of a wife, or the payment of a veteran's hospital bill, implications follow, and in general they follow only one road. The intervention secured by any group of men prompts further intervention on behalf of others, simply because the economy is interdependent. This can be illustrated in a form whose over-simplification reveals the principle.

The support of an agricultural price in an interdependent economy may be reflected in a cost-of-living index. Wages that may have been tied to the cost of living will be correspondingly adjusted with consequential impact upon industrial costs. That impact, in turn, can be followed by revision of commodity prices causing farmers to seek higher support prices for what they sell in order that they may be compensated for the higher prices they are forced to pay—and so on.

All this causes government to grow, and its sheer size is an additional reason why it is difficult for government to abdicate. When government becomes great, even its involuntary movements may dislodge or crush those who are in its way. For many, abdication by government would be a worse form of dislodgment, a dislodgment from the source of their livelihood. That in itself would be interpreted as one of the misfortunes for whose alleviation men have become accustomed to turn to government. The wheel has come full circle, and Economics is again Political Economy.

Industrialism

In discussing the collective elements common to contemporary systems we have obliquely touched upon the role of the corporation, the great industry, the trust, the collective enterprise. These are the forms of Proteus, and the common substance underlying them all, regardless of their particular locus, is the fact of modern industrialism—the joint association of masses of men and equipment in order to exploit the great opportunity that modern technology and techniques of administration offer. Both directly and indirectly that fact, as we know, has prompted parallel and partly compensatory concentration of labor into unions, and even of consumers into cooperatives or purchasing unions. Industrialism with the concomitant legal, social and political adaptation to it that its growth has fostered, has brought it to pass that, in the contemporary United States, roughly sixty per cent of all economic activity and over ninety per cent of manufacturing activity is organized in corporate form. From system to system both the details and the magnitudes differ, but the underlying structure is recognizably the same everywhere. Contemporary economies are all either industrialized or actively seeking to become so, and industrialism imposes its own pattern because it has its own laws. That is why all systems confront the same problems. When industry is great, should its administration be centralized or decentralized? The responses may differ, but the problem is one. When industry is great and therefore immune to the goad of many almost identical competitors, how shall its efficiency be safeguarded? When industry is great, how shall the timidities and conventionalities of its necessarily bureaucratic administration be overcome? When industry is both great and so interdependent that it is almost interlocked, how shall the adaptability that is the breath of life be assured without risk that adaptation in one sector will not cause disaster in others? That last question merits elaboration.

Vulnerability to Adaptation

The heading of this section is the obverse of a characteristic of the American economy that has received much attention: its rigidity. We can derive what comfort we may from the fact that all systems are prone to certain rigidities, and for essentially the same reasons. In good times, men everywhere are tempted into comfortable human complacency and disinclined to heave themselves out of its comforts, while in bad times the terrifying unpredictability of consequences may cause them, like frightened rabbits, to stand, stare, and perhaps tremble. There is, of course, more to it than that. Sometimes consequences are perfectly predictable, but still unpalatable. We have heard much in recent years of the menace of economic stagnation, but if any stagnation is at all imminent, it is not because opportunity has vanished but because men do not dare seize it. A mature economy is not one whose agenda is completed, but one become so interdependent that the margin of tolerable individual movement within it has been cut below the safety point. Like an army, it must move all at once or it cannot move at all, and just as armies exist under all flags, so do rigidities appear in all systems.

The implication of adaptation is some change in the established allocation of resources. When the American economy changed from a peacetime to a wartime orientation, the consumers'-goods industries were perforce throttled down, just as the Soviet capital-goods industries may be cut back in the hypothetical future when some more benign dictator decides to cosset the consumer. Those are, or could be, spectacular instances of a more pervasive and insidious tension—prevalent wherever there is economic movement at all—between change and stability. Much has been written about the processes of change in a *capitalist* economy without explicit recognition that the principles of economics, which exist, carry similar implications for *all* systems.

Any innovation is charged with insecurity, partly because of the risk to the innovator of his own failure, but more importantly, perhaps, because of the risk his success may carry to others. Where there is change there is economic history, and economic history is not only the record of thrusting advance, of pulsing innovation, of response to glowing opportunity; it is also the record of the displacement of the somnolent, the complacent, and the obsolescent. We, today, see romance in the relegation to the Smithsonian Institution of the stage coach, the water mill, and the kerosene lamp, but to their makers and dependents that relegation frequently meant tragedy. In the American past, the margin of tolerable individual movement to which we have alluded was sufficiently wide to permit both adaptation and compensation for it, partly because such resources as family farms and western lands served as reserves upon which the displaced could ultimately draw; but more importantly because the pace of American economic development was so headlong that mere development drew into itself those who were capable of adaptation to it. If our, or any other rate of development should slacken, adaptation would have to take the form of finding sustaining rather than developmental uses for the released resources. That adaptation is not impossible, but it is difficult and it takes time.

Fundamental economics—the study of adaptation to changes in the competitive pull upon resources that are scarce—should enable us to understand that adaptation of this kind becomes manifest in a *structure* of industry appropriate to the particular adaptation that has been made. The form and character of that adaptation may be left for the market to determine, as happened in our own economy when oil and gas began to displace coal as a source of heat for American homes; it may be imposed coercively from on high, as when Marshal Goering paid for his guns with the butter taken from German mouths; or it may pleadingly be referred to an electorate or legislature for deliberate political decision, as when the British Labour Party recommended the diversion of resources to permit provision of free medical services for the bulk of the British people. The basic, allocative decision in favor of using resources one way or another, of responding to this felt need or that discerned opportunity, may be made on any grounds whatever, depending on where the center of decision lies and what the principles of decision may happen to be. They need not be economic, and frequently are not. Once the decision is made, however, economic consequences inevitably follow.

An economy, whatever its political complexion or organization, may have adapted itself to a particular rate of development, or it may have deliberately set its sights upon some consciously selected rate. Given time for adaptation to be made, resources sort themselves out into piles earmarked, respectively, for subsistence or for expansion. The process of sorting may or may not be left to the market, but the relative size of the two piles always has economic implications. If, now, the size of one pile relative to the other should be changed for any reason whatever, the *processes* that ensue are known to all systems. Price systems are exposed to the same pulls and the same pressures, disguised though these may be, and the same need exists, however it may be met, to find something to do with the resources released because of their removal from the pile whose size has been reduced.

In the Appendix to Chapter 4 (see page 94) we have examined the so-called Stagnation Thesis, that there exist forces that operate to reduce the size of the pile of resources oriented toward expansion and that also prevent, somehow, compensatory increase in the pile upon which subsistence depends. It is really remarkable that this predicament should have been associated so peculiarly with capitalism. If men and women should indeed become less fruitful, so that the earth were replenished less rapidly, if the empty spaces of the earth should anywhere become harder to reach and to develop, or if the fertility of man's inventiveness should atrophy anywhere because invention had exhausted itself, the economic system to which all this befell, whatever its character, would confront the same necessity of adaptation to a slackened pull upon its resources. Differences among systems appear, not in differential vulnerability to change in the pull upon resources that may occur, but in the kind of adaptation to such a change that differing social, political or strategic structures will permit or encourage.

Susceptibility to Inflation

Today, nearly everywhere, the pull upon resources appears on long balance to be increasing, and thus is exposing all systems to the common pressure of inflation. The rising trend of prices will not everywhere follow the same course, and in the less authoritarian regimes it may even be subject to temporary reversals. Contemporary wars, for example, may become colder and thus release rather than absorb resources, and the well-rooted oscillatory tendencies in the freer economies may not yet have been completely eradicated, despite the continuing intrusion of government into the market place. Nevertheless, all contemporary economies have developed antibodies against serious or protracted deflation that were either embryonic or not yet even conceived in the last century.

The organization of labor—both motivated by, and resulting in, the protection of wages—has brought it about that wages are increasingly tied to the cost of living and this at a time when prices are rising. Moreover, anxiety to assure full employment has by now become strong enough and organized enough to render unlikely any public tolerance of substantial or prolonged unemployment. The implications of each of these two developments are inflationary, the former because wages tied to a rising cost of living will almost always outrun any offsetting increases in productivity; the latter because the means of insuring full employment—depreciation, low money rates, deficit financing—are themselves inflationary, because they all mean, or result in, a lowered value of money.

Social security in its various forms, realized and pending, joins organized labor and claimants to employment in opening the public purse strings. Potentially, indeed, the drain of the social services on the public purse is almost without limit, and for three reasons. (1) As more sectors of the population are brought within a social-security system, the pressure to include those who remain excluded inevitably mounts; (2) as more services are brought within a social-security system, pressure to round out the system by providing still other services also mounts; and (3) as additional people are brought within a system and as additional services are provided, the possibility of calculating and exacting contributions upon an actuarial basis becomes increasingly remote.   The result is a net increase in expenditure not offset by any corresponding increase in individual contributions for the insurance or security they receive; the doors of the Treasury tend to open wider and wider.   This arises not out of perversity, or greed, or even despair; nor does it merit blind condemnation.   The constriction of the margin of individual maneuverability within an increasingly interdependent economic system both explains and justifies much of this pressure.   The fact, however, must be faced that the pressures are inflationary.

The pressures are inflationary, not only because they keep the stream of public expenditure flowing strongly and steadily, but because they also accelerate, both directly and indirectly, the flow of private spending.   The direct effect is quite obvious: people have more money.   The indirect effect of supported wages, full employment and of expanded social services is that their beneficiaries, who characteristically are people who would like to buy more than they can afford, now are able to afford a little more.   In other words, the redistribution of income brought about by the combination of progressive income taxation with increasing Treasury disbursements involves the transfer of purchasing power from groups accustomed to make substantial savings to groups that prefer to spend.   The result is upward pressure upon the cost of living.

The same inflationary pressures exist, although for other reasons, in authoritarian systems.   In the degree that these are militaristic, expenditure on armaments undertaken with something less than the reluctance shown elsewhere, and undertaken largely for its own sake rather than because the condition of the world compels it, exerts unremitting pressure upon the price system.   Moreover, totalitarian systems like the Russian, or even lagging economies like the British, that are being steered by deliberate design toward industrialization or modernization, are ridden by scarcities that themselves are at once the cause and the consequence of inflationary pressure. Finally, the provision of *panem et circenses* characteristic of fascism, and not unknown in the Soviet Union, is symbolic of the great and continuing public expenditure habitually undertaken by totalitarian systems, and with inflationary impact.

In the international economy, also, the resultant of the prevailing economic forces appears to be inflationary.   *First,* undeveloped areas falling within the orbit of one or the other of the two great power centers of the contemporary world, the United States and the Soviet Union, are seeking and securing technical, financial, and economic help in making increasingly skillful and effective use of the resources they possess.   Turkey and China, respectively, are illustrations.   *Second,* even the more developed economies have, in their several ways, been drawn within this system.   The United States has in essence underwritten the economic viability of Western Europe, and presumably the mercantilist exploitation of Eastern Europe by the Soviet Union entails at least the obligation, out of sheer self-interest, to maintain these economies as going concerns.   In each of these cases, resources become subject to increased drain.

Third, and reinforcing the pressures already suggested, is the concern of the politically independent states of the world to maintain themselves. The abandonment of the international gold standard, together with the development of increasingly tight and effective exchange controls, has meant that an internal price level anywhere, one that happens to be higher than the price levels without, is not automatically and with reasonable promptness pulled down to the common level by the flight of gold or the loss of foreign exchange reserves.   Even when gold or its substitutes eventually do seep out, as ultimately they do, their loss can be offset by devaluation, which is itself inflationary.   These same politically independent states, for similar reasons, control the movement of goods as well as the entry and exit of money in its several forms.   The contemporary world is very largely protectionist.   The postwar movement to clear away the man-made obstructions in the channels of international free trade has been little more than a tinkling cymbal within the sounding brass of the clamor to maintain them.   This, also, is inflationary for the essentially simple reason that protection isolates the consumer from access to cheaper markets and diverts his expenditure to domestic, and more costly sources.   The flow of money is maintained, but the output of goods is reduced.   There is, however, more to it than that.

It might seem that the increased price of imports which usually follows upon a tariff and the increased cost of domestic substitutes for imports no longer welcomed, would be offset by proportionate loss in the capacity to export.   There is, however, a time lag that effectively prevents the deflation associated with a decline in exports from ever really overtaking its opposite. A tariff affects imports at once and enables interests quickly to become vested, while its impact upon exports is both diffused and delayed with the result that, here, adaptation can always keep ahead of its consequences. Professor Dobb's analogy from another context is applicable here: the tendency for reduced exports to cancel the effect of reduced imports is like the recurring frustration of a tottering old lady seeking exit from a subway whose door she can never quite reach before the train moves on.

The theme running through the foregoing account is the exposure of all economic systems to certain common forces, both internal and external. Exposure is a challenge to which response is invited, and when exposure is of the same character the responses are likely to resemble each other. That explains the great number of elements that appear to be common to contemporary systems, at least in their economic aspects.

DIFFERENCES AMONG SYSTEMS

Nevertheless, there are very important differences among the systems with which we have been concerned. That is why, and how, they can be in mutual competition. These differences among systems appear clearly enough when we compare the ways in which different systems respond to economic stimuli and blockages that are common to them all. Those differences loom particularly large, however, when we compare systems in their entirety, as *wholes*—wholes that are social, political, and moral as well as economic. When we make that comparison, we cannot help seeing that each different system has its own individual past and tradition and that those different traditions sometimes involve clashes among systems. We see, also, that each different system has its hopes and aspirations and that those hopes and aspirations may lead to conflict because they are not mutually consistent. It is the trends, the purposes, and the standards of systems that essentially distinguish them one from another.

Capitalists who object to socialism may think their opposition rests upon socialist inefficiency and socialist frustration of instincts that to them are both natural and good; they forget, however, or they do not realize that a socialist industry and a capitalist corporation are organized on essentially the same principle, operated by essentially the same rules, and seek, generally with similar success, to control their markets in essentially the same way. What capitalists really dislike about socialism is socialist refusal to accept *private* profit as a *public* standard; the ends of the two systems are not in harmony.

Likewise, liberals object to regimented systems, not because their purely economic contours are particularly strange, but because they find the values of those systems repugnant. That is why different national systems, competing with others as they do, are so difficult to compare. The standards of one are not accepted by supporters of another. Criticism of one system by advocates of another is frequently directed toward the existence of problems, or troubles, that appear unique to the system under deprecation. Individual systems do have problems peculiar to themselves, but those problems arise within the conjuncture of purpose and organization, of tradition and aspiration, of political and social structure, and of economic organization; and in the end they emerge out of the set of standards that make these systems what they individually are. The competition or comparison of systems resolves itself ultimately into the competition and comparison of standards.

The Competition of Standards

The essential point has just been made; it can be illustrated by looking at other contemporary systems from the perspective that may be taken to be American.

The totalitarian systems—the societies that are fascist or communist—make no pretense of tolerating individual advocacy of anything deemed nonconformist, or of permitting the association of individuals under uncontrolled conditions, or of allowing individual behavior that is incompatible with standards set from above. Within these systems there is frequently much mouthing of the word "freedom," but the connotation of the word as it emanates from an authoritarian context rings upon Western ears with a note both alien and abhorrent. Those who accept the premises and implications of Western democratic society, as exemplified perhaps in Bills of Rights, will never be tempted by the blandishments of regimenting disciplinarians.

When we turn, however, to the various forms of planned economic systems or to the variants of socialism, we confront an issue that is not nearly as clean-cut and that may, indeed, have components that are heart-rending in their implications. Most socialists in the contemporary Western world profess democracy, and they appear to profess it with whole minds. Indeed, a substantial part of the case they make rests upon the thesis that only under planning, and planning that leads logically into socialism, can the mass of mankind be freed from the economic insecurity and the material anxiety that constrict their opportunity to develop their own capacities for both creation and enjoyment—in short, to realize the freedom that formally they are supposed to have.

Against this, a powerful case has been made that planning, and still more, socialism, are themselves incompatible with genuine freedom, and increasingly so. The case is both empirical and analytic. Empirically, fingers are pointed at those authoritarian states in which the extension of control has been accompanied by the progressive, and ultimately by the utter, loss of freedom, an accompaniment that has been enforced by all the apparatus of coercion and of terror at the command of those societies. That apparatus is the more dreadful because it is habitually wielded by the worst elements of society, and seemingly plausible reasons have been given for believing that the extension of authority goes hand in hand with the release of tolerated brutality, and that therefore as society becomes more controlled its worst elements rise, like scum, to the top. That very fate has been predicted for both England and the United States if those countries persist in extending the reach of government.[3]

Analytically, the argument consists of a demonstration that control cannot be contained. A price cannot be effectively fixed without controlling the production, not only of the commodity immediately affected, but also of the others that may be substituted for it. That, in turn, entails fixing the prices of those substitutes as well. The control of production and of prices implies not only limitation of the freedom of an individual to produce what and how he chooses, but also the full freedom to consume and eventually the freedom to seek or leave employment.

That leads to control of industry and this, in its turn, ramifies out into control of the whole economy, and when that has been accomplished men are assigned their employment and may even be bound to it; they are issued their wages and salaries which they are not permitted significantly to influence, because the articulation of the Plan and the financial and productive balance of the economy would be disrupted were unpredictable or uncontrolled pressures permitted free scope. Furthermore, men consume whatever planners decide shall be produced and not what they themselves might

[3] *Cf.* Friedrich A. Hayek, *The Road to Serfdom*, Chicago, 1944; chapter 10, "Why the Worst Get on Top."

prefer to have, because, again, capricious preferences, like those resulting in a stampede of passengers on an excursion steamer, might upset the boat.

This loss of freedom does not stop there. The mere fact that newsprint is one of the controlled commodities serves as a constraint upon the freedom of the press, and the fact that radio is monopolized implies the power to withhold as well as to extend its facilities. Moreover, in the interlocked and interdependent industrialized economy of the modern world, criticism of the way a controlled industry is operated can be disruptive, while criticism of the principle or—still worse—objection to the fact, of control, might be seriously disruptive. Worst of all is the impossibility of exerting control without acquiring power, and at this point of the argument there is introduced the remark attributed to Lord Acton, that "power corrupts and absolute power corrupts absolutely." In other words, economic planning and the socialism that tries to be democratic are simply way stations along the road to the totalitarian state, and the farther that road has been traversed the more difficult it is to turn back. What are we to make of that argument?

Its empirical component depends, for its validity, upon the analytical. To say simply that we should eschew planning because we abhor the form planning has taken in, let us say the Soviet Union, is to put ourselves in the position of Mark Twain's cat that refused to go near a cold stove after having sat on a hot one. Even that is misleading, because the cat's precautionary behavior may have rested on the correct inference that it is the function of a stove to become hot, and that turns the issue into one of properly identifying a stove. That is a question of properties, and our question is the analytical one, whether it is one of the properties of planning, or of socialism, to be unable to avoid plunging, or slipping, into some totalitarian form. That question is really fundamental, because there is today no economy that is not subject to some form of deliberately imposed control. Moreover, it is difficult to deny with conviction that control does entail power and that power does carry temptations to its abuse—as its victims, if not its possessors, have always known.

The great appeal of classical political economy lies in its lesson that an economic system can be both organized and policed without any concentration of power, that competition among individuals so numerous as to be individually anonymous replaces the very personal rule of a monarch by the impersonal control of the market. Unfortunately, history has not conformed to precept, and power has never been expunged. It has, however, been contained, except in the totalitarian states where the failure to contain it can be attributed to the absence of any challenge to it.   In our own past, the containment of power has been possible because the nuclei of power have been plural.   Organized capital has been offset by organized labor, organized private interests have been curbed by organized government, and organized government itself has been compelled, on more than one occasion, to bow to the behest of an organized electorate.

That is where the ultimate decision rests, at least in the political democracies, and the form of its ultimate determination will depend upon the wisdom, the restraint, the sophistication and the balance of that electorate. That is why it is so salutary and healthy that any extension of control should have to confront suspicion and even hostility.   It is encouraging that in countries like Great Britain the development of curbs should accompany the extension of controls, and that even socialists show awareness of the safety residing in political pluralism.   In a society like our own, the danger lies not so much in supine or unconscious acceptance of governmental encroachment upon our freedoms, as in public intolerance of attitudes and activities that stubbornly, even unreasonably, are non-conformist.   Our hope lies in the determination with which we refuse to permit the bandwagon ever to become a juggernaut.

Bibliography

NATURE, COMPARISON, AND APPRAISAL OF ECONOMIC SYSTEMS

BURKE, EDMUND, *Speech on Conciliation with America,* and *Reflections on the Revolution in France.*

Among other writings (there are various editions; a convenient one is his *Works,* World's Classics, Oxford University Press) these spell out a philosophy of reasoned conservatism—reasoned because he wished to conserve. For Burke, the state was something almost organic, resting upon a religious foundation, and its viability depended upon controlled adaptation to circumstance. He wrote, "The question with me is not whether you have a right to render your people miserable, but whether it is not your interest to make them happy."

BURY, J. B., *The Idea of Progress,* The Macmillan Company, New York, revised edition, 1932.

A classic account of man's recurring (and lapsing) belief that the movement of human history is, on the whole, all for the best.

HERTZLER, J. O., *The History of Utopian Thought,* The Macmillan Company, New York, 1923.

A standard account of the great Utopias; the Utopias themselves are much more fun to read, but this book tells you at least what to look for.

MUSTAFA KEMAL, *Speech Delivered from October 15 to 20, 1927,* Koehler, Leipzig, 1929.

A translation of an extraordinary non-stop speech by a revolutionary whose "treason" did "prosper" and who, within a generation, transformed a corrupt, artificial, decadent state into a young, increasingly democratic nation with a future.   The speech tells how it was done.

SCHUMPETER, J. A., *Capitalism, Socialism and Democracy,* Harper, New York, 3d. edition, 1950.

A lively, readable book.   The account of capitalism as a dynamic, changing institution rests upon the same author's more technical treatment in *The Theory of Economic Development,* Harvard University Press, Cambridge, 1936.

TOCQUEVILLE, ALEXIS CHARLES HENRI MAURICE CLÉREL DE, *The Old Regime and the Revolution,* translated by John Bonner, Harper, New York, 1856.

A classic and readable account of one set of "haves" who blinded themselves to the writing on the wall and who finally took the consequences.

TOYNBEE, A. J., *A Study of History,* Oxford University Press, London, 9 volumes, 1934–1954 (the final three have yet to appear).   The study has been abridged into one volume under the same title, by D. C. Somervell, Oxford University Press, London, 1946.

An erudite, fascinating, and terrifyingly documented speculation concerning the forces that cause societies of men and women to develop, to perish, or to stagnate.

CAPITALISM

ARNOLD, THURMAN, *The Folklore of Capitalism,* Yale University Press, New Haven, 1937.

A sprightly account of the stereotyped beliefs, rationalizations, wishful thinkings, and "myths" about itself that the indwellers of capitalism have developed.

COMMONS, JOHN R., *The Legal Foundations of Capitalism,* The Macmillan Company, New York, 1924.

A solid, well-known and meritorious description of the legal principles that have colored and shaped the economic system that became dominant in Europe and America in the course of the nineteenth century.

DOUGLAS, PAUL, PAUL HOFFMAN, and NEIL JACOBY, *What is Capitalism?* University of Chicago Round Table, Chicago, September 1, 1946.   Reprinted in Hess, Gallman, Rice and Stern, *Outside Readings in Economics,* Thomas Y. Crowell Company, New York, 1951, pp. 794–804.

Two distinguished American economists, and a well-known businessman who has a record of governmental service, discuss with insight, judgment, and balance an economic system that is no more controversial than any other.

DRUCKER, PETER, "The Function of Profits," *Fortune,* March, 1949.   Reprinted, *ibid.,* pp. 319–329.

Paradoxically, profits seem to be the least understood aspect of the profit system.   Traditionally they have been described as the earnings of business management which turns them into a kind of wage, plus the rewards of ownership which reduces them to something like interest, plus a premium for the successful assumption of risk which either turns them into a bribe or ignores the gains to be had from either refusing to assume risk or transferring risk to someone else; and when these are all added up, there seems nothing left for profit by itself.   Or, profit has been considered a measure of deviation from competitive equilibrium—e.g., the reward of monopoly, or the temporary gain from successfully trying something new before imitators catch up with you—which means that, even in a profit system, profits disappear when things become normal; and some economists have argued exactly that.   Or, profits have been regarded as the undeserved reward of applying economic thumbscrews to an exploited class, which is something that no self-respecting capitalist would ever dream of doing.   The man in the street along with the accountant has the common-sense definition of profit as that which is left over after costs have been met, but that does not really tell you what profit is paid *for*.

Wages, interest, even rent, have a conceptual clarity about them that is denied profit.   The difficulty lies in determining the uniqueness of the service for which profit is paid.   The reference, above, is one attempt among a great many to grapple with just that problem.   It has at least the merit of brevity.

SMITH, ADAM, *An Inquiry into the Nature and Causes of the Wealth of Nations.* There are various and many editions; the best-edited one, and in convenient form, is the Cannan edition, Modern Library, New York, 1937.

The *Wealth of Nations* is, of course, the *locus classicus* for an eloquent justification of the system of natural liberty, and one that was made before the emergence of such a system seemed even remotely possible.   That is what gives it part of its charm; like other men seeking a change that has yet to come about, Adam Smith was not troubled with the litter that accomplished change leaves behind it.

He should be read.   Far from being the encrusted Tory that some yearning but unlettered students consider him, Smith embodied "common humanity" (his own phrase).   He also had practical insight, shrewd common sense, a wise and mature tolerance, and the gift of tongues—for example, "the insolent outrage of furious and disappointed monopolists," the "sneaking arts of underling tradesmen," "by sending his son abroad a father delivers himself . . . from so disagreeable an object as that of a son unemployed, neglected, and going to ruin before his eyes," "with the greater part of rich people, the chief enjoyment of riches consists in the parade of riches."   There are many more.

SNYDER, CARL, *Capitalism the Creator,* The Macmillan Company, New York, 1940.

An impassioned and impressive defense of the thesis that it is capitalism par excellence that originally developed, now sustains and will continue to foster man's effective control over the resources on which he depends for sustenance.

WEBB, SIDNEY and BEATRICE, *The Decay of Capitalist Civilization,* Harcourt Brace, New York, 1923.

An impassioned assertion of the thesis that it is capitalism that thwarts not only man's continuing control over material resources, but also the application of those resources to the sustenance of all rather than just a few, together with observations on the social and moral implications of that thwarting.

INDUSTRIALISM

ALLEN, F. L., *The Big Change*, Harper, New York, 1952.

A graphic account of the change from an agricultural to an industrial economy in the United States, the implications of that change, and the prospects that perhaps confront our economy.

AMERICAN ECONOMIC ASSOCIATION (through an official committee), "Problems of Economic Instability," *American Economic Review*, September, 1950. Reprinted in Hess, Gallman, Rice and Stern, *Outside Readings in Economics*, Thomas Y. Crowell Company, New York, 1951, pp. 593–628.

An analysis by a selected group of professional economists of the major unsettling forces in contemporary American capitalism, with suggestions for dealing with them.

BERLE, A. A., and G. C. MEANS, *The Modern Corporation and Private Property*, The Macmillan Company, New York, 1935.

This interesting but unabashed speculation about what the hand of the business corporation has been writing on the wall was avidly read in the late 1930's. It is still worth reading, partly to point the moral that extrapolative prediction carries hazards, but partly also because it raises some issues that still have pertinence.

BURNS, A. B., *The Decline of Competition*, McGraw-Hill, New York, 1936.

A carefully documented although somewhat "dated" account of the economic implications of the rise of big business.

COLM, GERHARD, "The Nation's Economic Budget and the Government," *Annals of the American Academy of Political and Social Science*, November, 1949. Reprinted in Hess, Gallman, Rice, and Stern, *op. cit.*, pp. 651–652.

A clear and brief statement of how the private and governmental sectors of our economy are tied together and how that interdependence can be utilized to foster full employment. The implicit theme of the paper is the growing impossibility of keeping government aloof.

COUNCIL OF ECONOMIC ADVISERS, *Reports*, Government Printing Office, Washington, various dates.

The Employment Act of 1946 created a Council of Economic Advisers to give economic advice and assistance to the President. Until 1953, it reported semi-annually, and its *Reports* were made the subject of comment by the Joint-Congressional Committee on the Economic Report. The Council's *Reports* did not invariably carry the stamp of scientific disdain of political partisanship, but they do illustrate the economic thinking of an influential group of men.

After the election of 1952, changes were made in the organization and functioning of the Council, but the new fruit of the new Council has not—at the time of writing—been garnered.

DENNISON, H. S., and J. K. GALBRAITH, *Modern Competition and Business Policy*, Oxford University Press, New York, 1938.

A prominent businessman and a well-known economist pool their views about the organization and performance of the contemporary American economy.

DEWEY, JOHN, *Individualism, Old and New,* Minton Balch, New York, 1930.

A readable account of the contemporary twilight of individualism in all its aspects, by one of the great writers among American philosophers.

DIMOCK, MARSHALL, "These Government Corporations," *Harper's Magazine,* May, 1945. Reprinted in Hess, Gallman, Rice, and Stern, *op. cit.,* pp. 255–266.

Governments tax and governments spend, and by so doing they influence economic activity. Governments also enjoin and prohibit, and thereby they control economic activity. In our own age, governments frequently undertake economic activity themselves, and they do so by taking a leaf out of the book of private industry. They establish corporations to do for them what private corporations do for stockholders. In this country the Tennessee Valley Authority is a conspicuous example.

This article attempts to portray the reasons and the consequences of such governmental activity, and to suggest principles for both the creation and the performance of government corporations.

ELDRIDGE, SEBA, *et al., The Development of Collective Enterprise,* The University of Kansas Press, Lawrence, 1943.

A survey of the extent to which collective institutions and ideas have so far developed within the American economy. In general the thesis is the same as that suggested, for nineteenth-century England, in A. V. Dicey, *Lectures on the Relation between Law and Public Opinion in England during the Nineteenth Century,* Macmillan Ltd., London, second edition, 1914, except that Dicey is incisive, analytical and profound while Eldridge is discursive and primarily descriptive.

GALBRAITH, J. K., *American Capitalism, the Doctrine of Countervailing Power,* Houghton Mifflin, Boston, 1952.

An interesting application to the economic world of, almost, the Newtonian doctrine of action and reaction, with the added suggestion that, in the end, the two offset each other. This book admirably supplements Eldridge and Dicey (see above). We live in a world that is called dynamic because it is continually changing. To the complacent, change sometimes seems superficial movement about something regarded as fundamental and therefore called "normal," much as feminine legs are "normally" encased in skirts even though the demarcation between skirt and leg is subject to fashionable change. To the determined optimist, change is progress piped to the theme of *Excelsior.* To the unreflective Tory, change is deterioration wrought by a frivolous and carefree younger generation. To the reflective, however, change is neither superficial nor ineluctably upward or downward; it is something that itself must be explained, and perhaps guided.

For the past century and a half capitalism has been changing, and one of the commonest interpretations of its change has been the developing pressure upon government to moderate the growing power of capitalist industry. Galbraith now suggests that the process is more complicated because, apart from, but not excluding, government, the development of industrial organization provokes "countervailing" developments all through society. He thus goes even further than Sumner Slichter who (in *The American Economy*, Knopf, New York, 1949) seems to expect our capitalistic economy to transform itself simply into a "laboristic" economy.

LYNCH, DAVID, *The Concentration of Economic Power*, Columbia University Press, New York, 1946.

A workmanlike, competent, but on the whole unevaluating summary of the T.N.E.C. *Hearings* (see the following item). Except for sheer browsing, this book is easier to use than the *Hearings* themselves, because it is properly organized.

TEMPORARY NATIONAL ECONOMIC COMMITTEE (T.N.E.C.), *Hearings and Monographs*, Government Printing Office, Washington, 1939 and following years.

A mine of fascinating but unedited and uncritically reported information about the performance and behavior of the American economy up to the outbreak of the Second World War. It consists of statements and testimony offered the Committee by economists, businessmen, and others on all aspects of economic life.

THE BUSINESS CYCLE

ACHENSTEIN, ASHER, *Introduction to Business Cycles*, Thomas Y. Crowell Company, New York, 1950.

A competent and interesting description of both the facts of the cycle, to the extent that these are known, and of the explanations of those facts that have been hazarded. The book is written from the perspective of the National Bureau of Economic Research. See Gordon, below.

BURNS, A. F., and W. C. MITCHELL, *Measuring Business Cycles*, National Bureau of Economic Research, New York, 1946.

A formidable but indispensable selection from the still more formidable collection of facts about the cycle that the National Bureau has assembled, together with some attempt to put those facts in order. The book is not designed for the tyro, but the interested tyro could well look at it just to see how really difficult the task of the conscientious economist can be.

GORDON, R. A., *Business Fluctuations*, Harper, New York, 1952. An excellent contemporary text covering description and analysis of the cycle.

MITCHELL, W. C., *Business Cycles, The Problem and Its Setting*, National Bureau of Economic Research, New York, 1927.

An old book, but still something of a classic for its insight, its balance, and its clarity.

SCHUMPETER, J. A., *Business Cycles*, 2 vols., McGraw-Hill, New York, 1939.

Hard reading, but solid description and equally solid analysis of industrial fluctuations.

STAGNATION

HANSEN, ALVIN H., *Full Recovery or Stagnation,* Norton, New York, 1938.
Almost any other book by Hansen would do, but this one is the first he published after Keynes (see below) upset his generation of economists, and it is in many ways the freshest exposition of the theme with which Hansen's name is associated: that, unless society exerts itself deliberately to find things for it to do, the wealthier it is the less it will be able to do.

KEYNES, J. M., *The General Theory of Employment, Interest and Money,* Harcourt Brace, New York, 1936.
For better or for worse, this is the book that has dominated economic thought for nearly a generation.   Keynes thought his orthodox predecessors had erred in assuming that economic equilibrium entailed full employment.   He thought, on the contrary, that a full-employment equilibrium was just one special case of equilibrium, and not a very likely one for a really developed economy, which is why he thought *he* had worked out a general, rather than a special, theory.

The trouble, as he saw it, is that our incomes arise out of the disbursements of others, because what we receive somebody else pays, and what we pay someone else receives, so that if anyone holds on to what he has received others perforce go short.   That is nothing new, but Keynes went on to add this: The likelihood that people will hold on to what they have increases as society develops economically—partly, but only partly, because increasing abundance of material things reduces their value and hence the prospective profit in producing still more of them; partly because the cost of producing them will not fall as rapidly as their values, so that people will not spend to produce; and primarily, because, when the future is dark or uncertain, men prefer to keep their wealth in the most exchangeable, liquid form, and money is the most liquid form wealth can take.   So men hold on to money.

The main reason why costs refuse to fall is that interest, the cost of using liquid capital, refuses to adjust itself to the volume of savings men in the aggregate wish to make, primarily because savings arise only incidentally out of the hope men have that they may earn interest; they also arise because men like something to fall back upon in case of either emergency or opportunity.   In the end, because savings are unemployed, men become unemployed, but while savings may disappear with the disappearance of the incomes their expenditure would have generated, it is not so easy to make men disappear; they just go on the dole.

Keynes wished to save capitalism, and that makes much loose contemporary talk about the "Keynes-Marxian" heresy simply wrong.   Keynes and Marx would never have been able to stand one another.   Keynes, however, thought capitalism could be saved only by radically transforming it, and at the expense of the taker of interest, the *rentier*.   That puts him into the long tradition of men who have sought either the elimination or reduction of one or another of the standard distributive shares.   Some mercantilists considered high wages drains upon the economy; socialists have much the same attitude toward profits, although Keynes did not share that opinion; single-taxers and Ricardians have long defined rent as a surplus; and now the Keynesians anticipate the "euthanasia of the rentier."

Unhappily, the *General Theory* is not for novices.   Keynes could turn a phrase as well as Smith, but his phrases are oases in some pretty barren land whose passage calls for great endurance and even greater skill.   Simpler versions of his argument will be found in Dudley Dillard, *The Economics of John Maynard Keynes,* Prentice Hall, New York, 1948, and in parts of S. E. Harris (ed.), *The New Economics,* Knopf, New York, 1947.

SWANSON, E. W., and E. P. SCHMIDT, *Economic Stagnation or Progress,* McGraw-Hill, New York, 1946.

A careful but somewhat arid attack upon the thesis that a mature capitalist economy necessarily becomes stagnant.

TERBORG, GEORGE, *The Bogey of Economic Maturity,* The Machinery and Allied Products Institute, Chicago, 1945.

A challenging and vigorous assault upon the stagnation thesis.

WRIGHT, CARROLL A., *First Annual Report of the Commissioner of Labor: Industrial Depressions,* Government Printing Office, Washington, March, 1886.

There is nothing new under the sun.   Nearly 70 years ago someone thought the economic *agenda* had been completed and that the American economy faced stagnation.

SOCIALISM

BECKWITH, B. P., *The Economic Theory of a Socialist Community,* Stanford University Press, Stanford, 1948.

An elaborate blueprint of *how* a socialist economy will work.   The issues raised by this and the Hayek and Mises books may seem today pale shadows of past controversy, because we can point to socialist institutions, even socialist economies, as going contemporary concerns.   The issue itself is interesting, however. Hayek and Mises represent a group that believes it impossible for members of a socialist community ever to know whether or not they are using their resources efficiently, because the only real test of efficiency is provided by the autonomous market which does not exist under socialism.   In competitive capitalism, the individual (a) competes with his kind and must meet their minimum standards, and (b) serves his consumers whose satisfaction he must meet. No one rigs that market, so no one can do anything but adapt himself to it, or go under.

Under socialism, the market *is* rigged.   There is no competition and therefore no spur to efficiency; even worse, there is not even any test of efficiency, for industrial bureaucrats set for themselves the conditions by which they judge themselves, and there are no other judges.   There being no competition, dissatisfied consumers have no alternative market to which they can turn; like occupants of a boarding house, they can eat only what is put before them for they have no other source of food.

The opposition asserts that this is an imaginary nightmare—that socialist industry can take its goods to market exactly as capitalist industry does, and, by a process of trial and error, find both the product and the price that, given consumers' incomes and tastes, will work.   Two observations may be made.   *First,* the critics of socialism are comparing socialism with the competitive capitalism of the textbooks and not with existing markets which, in a variety of ways, are rigged, so that perhaps even we do not know whether or not *we* are really efficient.   Are resources that go into featherbedding, or corporation expense accounts being used efficiently?   (See Thorstein Veblen, *The Theory of Business Enterprise,* Huebsch, New York, 1904.)   *Second,* socialist industry, at least as we know it today, operates pretty much the way capitalist industry does, and frequently by exactly the same people.   The nationalized British industries continue to be operated by their old managers, and the only difference is that these make their reports and are responsible to a different set of persons from the old stockholders. The principles of administration remain pretty much the same.   People used to think of socialism as a sort of gigantic, all-embracing monopoly, making and doing everything all at once.   Suspicions that that sort of socialism would not be very efficient are not implausible.

BEER, MAX, *A History of British Socialism,* Harcourt Brace, New York, 1921.

A clear and interesting account of the development of British socialist thought. It is most useful for its account of the pre-Marxian and non-Fabian writers, primarily because these have been neglected.   The Fabians saw to their own publicity, while the Marxians have not been reluctant to have publicity thrust upon them.   Socialist individualists, however, have not had the same fortune, and early nineteenth-century England was rich in solitary writers who worked out some form of socialist analysis for themselves and then spilled their ideas upon a world that was largely unresponsive.   They are an interesting lot, springing from all kinds of backgrounds—a retired naval officer, a physician, a job printer, and so on.   They anticipated many Marxian ideas, as Marx himself knew and acknowledged.   The world first learned of them from H. S. Foxwell's introduction to the English translation (by M. E. Tanner) of Anton Menger, *The Right to the Whole Produce of Labour,* London, 1899.

GRAY, ALEXANDER, *The Socialist Tradition, Moses to Lenin,* Longmans, Green, London, 1947.

There are many histories of socialist thought, but astonishingly few really good ones.   Some are slipshod, some shallow, some biased one way or the other, while of those whose content is dependable altogether too many are preternaturally dreary.   Here, however, is one that is both scholarly and ironic, learned but not ponderous, substantial and also difficult to lay down.   It is not only witty—it is gay.

HAYEK, F. A. VON (ed.), *Collectivist Economic Planning,* Routledge, London, 1935.

Contains a classic demonstration that socialism will not work.

LANGE, OSCAR, and FRED M. TAYLOR, *On the Economic Theory of Socialism,* University of Minnesota Press, Minneapolis, 1938.

Contains a classic demonstration that socialism will work.

MISES, L. VON, *Socialism, An Economic and Sociological Analysis,* Yale University Press, New Haven, new edition, 1951.

A critical account by a formidably rugged individualist.

PEASE, EDWARD, *History of the Fabian Society,* Fabian Society, London, second edition.

Indispensable for an understanding of how the British Labour Party came to be the way it is.

STRACHEY, JOHN, *The Theory and Practice of Socialism,* Gollancz, London, 1936.

A well-known defense of socialism by one of its foremost British supporters.

SWEEZY, PAUL M., *Socialism,* McGraw-Hill, New York, 1949.

An interesting and sympathetic account by a scholarly American supporter.

MARXISM

BOBER, M. M., *Karl Marx's Interpretation of History,* Harvard University Press, Cambridge, second edition, 1948.

A clear account of the Marxian philosophy of history.

BURNS, EMILE (compiler), *A Handbook of Marxism,* Random House, New York, 1935.

A very useful selection of writings by such prominent Marxians as Marx himself, Engels, and Lenin.

COLE, G. D. H., *What Marx Really Meant,* Knopf, New York, 1934.

A distinguished academic socialist's version of what Marx *ought* to have meant. Marx himself could not be consulted, which is perhaps just as well. Cole thinks the labor theory of value should be added to other relics in the Marxian Museum of Antiquities. Perhaps he should have inscribed his book with the remark attributed to Marx in another context: "I am not a Marxist."

————, *The Communist Manifesto.* Reprinted in Burns (see above), and there are many other editions.

This may yet turn out to be the most seminal pronunciamento of the modern age.

DOBB, MAURICE, *Political Economy and Capitalism,* Routledge, London, 1937.

A very interesting account of Marx against the background of classical political economy in England, and of more or less modern (pre-"Keynesian") economic thought against the background of Marx.

ENGELS, FRIEDRICH, *Socialism, Utopian and Scientific,* International Publishers, New York, 1925.

This is one of the minor Marxian classics in which a line is drawn between orthodoxy and heresy.   The heresy consists in the dreaming of dreams in which a socialist world is wishfully thought up; orthodoxy consists in a "scientific" demonstration of the inevitability of socialism.

Every now and then someone speculates upon communism as a "religion."   It unquestionably has its prophets, and perhaps it also has its deities, at least in the sense in which Hellenistic kingdoms deified their rulers (see W. W. Tarn, *Hellenistic Civilisation,* Edward Arnold, London, 1927; pp. 45 ff.) and in which German National Socialism attributed "charismatic" properties to Hitler (see Franz Neumann, *Behemoth, The Structure and Practice of National Socialism,* Oxford University Press, New York, 1942; Ch. III).   Many of its followers have, also, a genuine sense of dedication that sometimes leads them to court martyrdom, and an impulse to propagate the faith is not unknown among them. Engels' book, above, and much in Marx, to say nothing of the later Russian converts, suggest the greater intolerance of heresy than of unbelief that marks the zealot.

HOOK, SIDNEY, *Towards an Understanding of Karl Marx,* John Day, New York, 1933.

A well-known interpretation which is interesting but not always plausible. Marx was deterministic but he was not mechanically deterministic.

LENIN, V. I., *Imperialism, the Highest Stage of Capitalism,* International Publishers, New York, 1933.

This begins where Marx left off, because Marx concerned himself with the inner dynamics of a closed capitalist system more than with the push of an internally frustrated capitalist economy to secure for itself breathing space, or *Lebensraum.*   Lenin, as he himself acknowledged, picked up a hint from John A. Hobson's *Imperialism* (London and New York, 1902, and many subsequent editions), and gave a Marxian twist to the older suggestion that capitalism must expand outwards, come what may.   This is it.

――――, *State and Revolution,* International Publishers, New York, 1932.

This, also, begins where Marx left off.   Marx said a good deal about the state as an organ of class oppression, and with that perspective both he and Engels ventured into an analysis of the European uprisings in 1848.   He also suggested the "withering away" of the state when there was no longer any class either to oppress or to be oppressed.   Lenin, here, attempts to analyze the whole transition from capitalism to communism, *via* the "dictatorship of the proletariat."   This is perhaps the best single source of information on neo-Marxian political science.

MARX, KARL, *Capital.*

The first volume, in translation, can be had in a Modern Library edition, and the Everyman Library has a better translation.   The second and third volumes, in translation, can be had only in the edition published by Kerr (Chicago, 1906–1909).   The origins of it all.   All kinds of selections exist.   Burns (see above) has a judicious lot.   They are essential if Marx is really to be understood, but they are hard to get through.

ROBINSON, JOAN, *On Re-reading Marx,* Students' Bookshop, Cambridge (England), 1953.

A distinguished English economist lets herself go.   This is English wit at its best, but the novice may find it bewilderingly allusive.

STRACHEY, JOHN, *The Nature of Capitalist Crisis,* Covici Friede, New York, 1935.

The economic "contradictions" of capitalism viewed through a Marxian glass. Emphasis is on the downturns of economic activity and some attention is given to the "final crisis of capitalism" when the whole system pulls into a siding and the fires are extinguished, because the end of the line has been reached.   Strachey is one of the rarer writers who understand that Marx was not an under-consumptionist.

SWEEZY, PAUL M., *The Theory of Capitalist Development,* Oxford University Press, New York, 1942.

A lucid contemporary re-working of Marxian economic analysis.   Its luminosity is at the expense of neither accuracy nor depth.

FASCIST ECONOMIES

Italy

EBENSTEIN, WILLIAM, *Fascist Italy,* American Book Company, New York, 1939.

A text-bookish account of the structure and something of the meaning of fascist Italian society.

EINZIG, PAUL, *The Economic Foundations of Fascism,* Macmillan Ltd., London, 1933.

Although thin and somewhat incomplete, this account of the conditions out of which Italian fascism arose is still worth reading.

FIELD, G. LOWELL, *The Syndical and Corporative Institutions of Fascism,* Columbia University Press, New York, 1938.

A dependable survey of the way the fascists tried to organize the Italian economy.   Fascists being play actors, the sound effects and the stage sets were given loving care; the shoddiness was kept to the dressing rooms.   The fascists never really established the corporative state which has its appeal for those who would like to make believe in the harmony of interests.   In this book is the appearance, and behind it something of the reality of the institutions Field describes.

MILLER, HENRY S., *Price Control in Fascist Italy,* Columbia University Press, New York, 1938.

More appearance and reality.   This book is brief, interesting, and clear. The control of prices throughout an economy is an appallingly difficult technical task, and would be so even in a world peopled only by the disciplined and the docile.   The Italians were intelligent about the manner in which they would like prices to behave, but, as Adam Smith could have told them, they were to be frustrated by the "sneaking arts of underling tradesmen" and the "insolent outrage of furious and disappointed monopolists."

SALVEMINI, GAETANO, *Under the Axe of Fascism*, Viking Press, New York, 1936.

An impassioned, descriptive denunciation written in exile by an author who knew what he was talking about.

WELK, WILLIAM G., *Fascist Economic Policy*, Harvard University Press, Cambridge, 1938.

Probably the best account, in English, of the organization and operation of the fascist Italian economy.

Germany

BRADY, R. A., *The Spirit and Structure of German Fascism*, Viking Press, New York, 1937.

A good, clear description of the organization of the National Socialist economy, at least before war-induced changes set in. It also has a powerful and provocative, albeit controversial, hypothesis in regard to the sponsorship and significance of National Socialism.

BRUCK, W. F., *The Social and Economic History of Germany from William II to Hitler, 1888–1938,* Oxford University Press, London, 1938.

A perceptive, penetrating, analytical, and lucid book that does exactly what its title promises. It should be better known.

BUTLER, ROHAN D'O., *The Roots of National Socialism,* E. P. Dutton, New York, 1942.

Someone once observed that while German metaphysicians may dig deeper, they come up muddier than other mortals. We may be more modest and leave the appraisal of the *genus* to the licentiate, but members of the *species* upon which the National Socialists drew, directly or indirectly, were incontestably muddy. Even popular accounts of blood-thinking, "spirit," the Aryan myth (were not the Japanese once declared "honorary Aryans"?) or the German "soul" leave something less than enduring understanding.

Butler's book draws a sophisticated line between making what sense there is and making what there is sensible, of the tortured philosophical antecedents of National Socialism. We may scoff; Hitler was defeated; but let us look about to ascertain our right to cast even a little stone.

LURIE, SAMUEL, *Private Investment in a Controlled Economy, Germany 1935–1939,* Columbia University Press, New York, 1947.

A technical, compact, but lucid analysis of how National Socialist Germany financed—and forced—its industrial growth.

NEUMANN, FRANZ, *Behemoth, The Structure and Practice of National Socialism,* Oxford University Press, New York, 1942.

A learned, forthright and interesting account of the organization, performance, and significance of the Third Reich.

STOLPER, GUSTAV, *German Economy, 1870–1940,* Reynal and Hitchcock, New York, 1940.

A readable account of the progress of error in a great nation from the perspective of an old-fashioned (nineteenth-century) liberal.

THE SOVIET UNION

ARNOLD, A. Z., *Banks, Credit and Money in the Soviet Union,* Columbia University Press, New York, 1937.

This book is what its title indicates.   It is a descriptive account; for an analysis of what it is all about, see Reddaway, below.

BAYKOV, ALEXANDER, *The Development of the Soviet Economic System,* The Macmillan Company, New York, 1947.

Probably the best single source of information on how the Soviet system is organized and how it really operates.   The organization of the book is somewhat clumsy, and it is packed with facts—so much so that, in places, it is only slightly more readable than a statistical abstract.   It is, however, a decidedly useful book.

BERGSON, ABRAM, *The Structure of Soviet Wages,* Harvard University Press, Cambridge, 1944.

A slim but illuminating account of the processes of Russian wage determination.

BIENSTOCK, GREGORY, and SOLOMON M. SCHWARTZ, *Management in Russian Industry and Agriculture,* Oxford University Press, New York, 1944.

A fascinating account of managerial responsibility and performance.

CARR, E. H., *The Soviet Impact on the Western World,* The Macmillan Company, New York, 1947.

A provocative, balanced, literate analysis of the shadow cast by the Soviet Union.

DOBB, MAURICE, *Soviet Economy and the War,* International Publishers, New York, 1943.

———, *Soviet Planning and Labor in Peace and War,* International Publishers, New York, 1943.

These two books, written by a sympathetic observer, are luminous accounts of how the Soviet economy operates, at least in some of its aspects.   They are solid, but they are also easy to read.

HUBBARD, L. E., *The Economics of Soviet Agriculture,* Macmillan Ltd., London, 1939.

———, *Soviet Labor and Industry,* Macmillan Ltd., London, 1942.

———, *Soviet Money and Finance,* Macmillan Ltd., London, 1936.

———, *Soviet Trade and Distribution,* Macmillan Ltd., London, 1938.

Mr. Hubbard's four books are mines of information.

PARES, SIR BERNARD, *Russia,* Penguin Books, London, 1941.

Brief, but informative and illuminating.   This book fully conforms to the high Penguin standard.

REDDAWAY, W. B., *The Russian Financial System,* The Macmillan Company, New York, 1935.

A superior piece of analysis.

SCHWARTZ, HARRY, *Russia's Postwar Economy,* University of Syracuse Press, Syracuse, 1947.

A convenient and useful source of information on how the Russians attempted the re-organization of their economy after the Second World War. It is descriptive rather than reflective.

SUMNER, B. H., *A Short History of Russia,* Reynal and Hitchcock, New York, 1943.

A compact, well-written and well-organized book, particularly useful for bringing out the continuity in Russian history even after the great break in 1917.

VARGA, E., *Two Systems: Socialist Economy and Capitalist Economy,* International Publishers, New York, 1939.

An interesting and uninhibited comparison of capitalism and communism as going concerns, written from a perspective that will strike Americans, according to their individual temperaments, as either unbelievable or irritating. Varga has another book (*The Great Crisis and Its Political Consequences, Economics and Politics 1928–1934,* International Publishers, New York, n.d.), in which he attempts to place the great depression then under way in capitalist countries into the framework of the Marxian theory of crises. The exercise is an interesting one. Much of the Marxian literature that gets written in, or translated into, English consists of the re-formulation or re-exposition of formal, abstract Marxian economic theory, with illustrations—and *only* illustrations, picked out pretty much the way little Jack Horner pulled out a plum—drawn from the presumable degeneration of some capitalist economy.

Here are two attempts to demonstrate the actual working out, and before our very eyes, of the decline of capitalism which Marxians have so long predicted.

WEBB, SIDNEY and BEATRICE, *Soviet Communism, A New Civilisation?* 2 volumes, Scribner, New York, second edition, 1938.

A voluminous, comprehensive and laborious account of all aspects of Russian society and life as the authors thought they saw them. It is interesting, and—used with care—useful; it is also extraordinarily naive.

BRITISH SOCIALISM

BEVERIDGE, SIR WILLIAM, *Full Employment in a Free Society,* Norton, New York, 1945.

A much-read, influential book, by one of England's best known economists, which helped determine the structure and orientation of the British welfare state. England suffered not only from the great depression of the 1930's; it went through bad times even in the decade before, with the result that some sort of guarantee of full employment was a political "must," accepted by all political parties, when the Second World War came to an end. Sir William Beveridge had almost specialized, professionally, in the problem of unemployment, and he was entrusted with the chairmanship of a Royal Commission to make recommendations on just that subject. This is not the official report, but it is based upon it. The book attempts to define full employment—and that is not as easy as it may appear—and it proceeds to work out a program for ensuring satisfactorily full employment. Great Britain adopted the program without substantial modification.

BRITISH LIBRARY OF INFORMATION, New York, *Labor and Industry in Britain.*

This is an attractively printed information bulletin. In its various issues may be found brief descriptions of the organization and performance of the postwar British economy in almost all its aspects.

Britain, An Official Handbook, Central Office of Information, Her Majesty's Stationary Office, London, 1954.

A convenient reference book and source of information about the structure and life of modern England.

BRADY, R. A., *Crisis in Britain, Plans and Achievements of the Labour Government,* University of California Press, Berkeley, 1950.

An account of the British movement toward socialism, written at a time when the British economic future seemed particularly dark. Implicit in the book is a sense of regret that Britain appeared to be only dawdling into socialism.

COLE, G. D. H., *A Short History of the British Working-Class Movement, 1789–1937,* Allen and Unwin, London, 1938.

The prolific Professor Cole recounts the history of the movement that sought, in 1945, to transform the British economy. The book is more up to date, and a little more readable than the classic survey by the Webbs (see below); but it is less solid.

CROSSMAN, R. H. S. (ed.), *New Fabian Essays,* Turnstile Press, London, 1952.

The logic, the purpose, and, to some extent, the performance of the British welfare state by contemporary representatives of a most influential society.

HOGG, QUINTIN, *The Case for Conservatism,* Penguin Books, London, 1947.

A brief and intelligent statement of the Conservative Party position, interpreted by one of its younger parliamentary representatives. Contrast Parker, below.

LEWIS, BEN W., *British Planning and Nationalization,* Twentieth Century Fund, New York, 1952.

Commissioned by a competent and well-known research organization, this book is a sympathetic and reasonably optimistic but balanced account of the achievement of the Labour Government that came into power in 1945.

PARKER, JOHN, *Labour Marches On,* Penguin Books, London, 1947.

A brief and temperate statement of what British labor hopes to accomplish, and why.

WEBB, SIDNEY and BEATRICE, *The History of Trade Unionism,* Longmans, Green, New York, 1920.

One of the best books the Webbs ever wrote.   It is a classic account of the difficulties, the aspirations, and the policy of the British labor movement.

WILLIAMS, FRANCIS, *Socialist Britain, Its Background, Its Present, and an Estimate of Its Future,* Viking Press, New York, 1949.

A good-humored, popular, but competently written statement of British labor's accomplishment since the Second World War and labor's hope for the future.

THE COMPETITION OF SYSTEMS

CLARK, J. M., *Alternatives to Serfdom,* Knopf, New York, 1948.

An eloquent but temperate answer to Hayek (see below).

AMERINGER, OSCAR, *If You Don't Weaken,* Henry Holt, New York, 1940.

A lively, pungent autobiography by a heterodox Mid-western American journalist.   Indirectly, it provides understanding of why and how capitalism provokes opposition.   Ameringer, nevertheless, is no doctrinaire; he has too good a sense of humor.

HAYEK, F. A. VON, *The Road to Serfdom,* University of Chicago Press, Chicago, 1945.

One of the most controversial of contemporary books.   It is a pleading, at times passionate, argument that even the mildest flirtation with collectivism threatens society with relapse into a new dark age.

MISES, LUDWIG VON, *Omnipotent Government,* Yale University Press, New Haven, 1944.

An even more forthright assertion of Hayek's theme.

SCHUMPETER, J. A., *Capitalism, Socialism, and Democracy,* Harper, New York, third edition, 1950.

A provocative and beautifully written analysis of the contemporary competition of systems.   It leads, reluctantly, to the conclusion that capitalism will not survive, but for reasons that are anything but Marxian.   Capitalism will fail because it has been too successful, pretty much as Aristides was "ostracized" (the Greek word means blackballed, and that is exactly what happened to Aristides), because he was too good to be tolerable.   Just because they are successful, the carriers of capitalism lose their function; and people get tired of the system anyway.

TALMAN, J. A., *The Origins of Totalitarian Democracy,* Seeker and Warburg, London, 1952.

The title of this book is the product of neither carelessness nor propaganda. Totalitarians believe themselves to be democratic, and this book attempts to explain why.   The "democracy," particularly of the communists, is based on the conviction that what people *ought* to want, they should have, especially because that is what they really do want whether they realize it or not.   The origins of

that idea are traced back to the eighteenth century, and with great skill.   The
book requires close and careful reading, but it merits it.

WOOTTON, BARBARA, *Plan or No Plan,* Farrar and Rinehart, New York, 1935.

———, *Freedom under Planning,* University of North Carolina Press, Chapel
Hill, 1945.

Two statements, each complementing the other, that contemporary capitalist
society needs to be planned, and that it has nothing to lose by planning.

Index

Index